Microsoft Azure Security Technologies Certification and Beyond

Gain practical skills to secure your Azure environment and pass the AZ-500 exam

David Okeyode

BIRMINGHAM—MUMBAI

Microsoft Azure Security Technologies Certification and Beyond

Group Product Manager: Wilson Dsouza
Publishing Product Manager: Vijin Boricha
Senior Editor: Athikho Sapuni Rishana
Content Development Editor: Sayali Pingale
Technical Editor: Shruthi Shetty
Copy Editor: Safis Editing
Project Coordinator: Neil Dmello
Proofreader: Safis Editing
Indexer: Tejal Daruwale Soni
Production Designer: Nilesh Mohite

First published: September 2021
Production reference: 1070921

Published by Packt Publishing Ltd.
Livery Place
35 Livery Street
Birmingham
B3 2PB, UK.

978-1-80056-265-3

`www.packt.com`

I am grateful to many people who have helped and supported me through the process of writing this book. To my wife and best friend, Brenda Tao. To my parents, who taught me everything I know (Jacob and Hope Okeyode). And to the three best sisters and encouragers in the world (Pemi, Elizabeth, and Esther). I love you all.

– David Okeyode

Contributors

About the author

David Okeyode is a cloud security architect at the Prisma cloud speedboat at Palo Alto Networks. Before that, he was an independent consultant helping companies secure their cloud environments through private expert-level training and assessments. He holds 15 professional certifications across the Azure and AWS platforms, including the Azure Security Engineer, Azure DevOps, and AWS Security Specialist certifications. He has also authored two cloud computing courses for the popular cybersecurity training platform Cybrary.

David has over a decade of experience in cybersecurity (consultancy, design, and implementation) and over 6 years of experience as a trainer. He has worked with organizations of different sizes, from start-ups to major enterprises to government organizations.

David has developed multiple vulnerable-by-design automation templates that can be used to practice cloud penetration testing techniques. He regularly speaks about cloud security at major industry events, such as Microsoft Future Decoded and the European Information Security Summit.

David is married to a lovely girl who makes the best banana cake in the world. They love traveling the world together and intend to do missions in Asia very soon!

About the reviewers

Dharam Chhatbar is a seasoned information security professional who has more than 11 years of experience in various verticals of InfoSec, delivering impactful and high-quality risk-reduction work. He has helped secure many banks and retail firms and is currently working at a top Fortune 500 company. He holds a master's degree, is a fervent learner, and has earned several global certifications, such as CISSP, GSLC (GIAC), CCSP, CSSLP, GMOB, and some related to the cloud, such as Azure (AZ500), GCP (PCSE), and AWS (SAA). His key competencies include vulnerability management, application security, cloud security, VA/PT, and managing teams/vendors. He has also reviewed the book *CISSP (ISC)² Certification Practice Exams and Tests* by Ted Jordan.

I would like to thank my parents, Bina and Jagdish; my wife, Chaital; and my sister, Hina, for their continued support and encouragement with everything that I do and for motivating me to always achieve my ambitions.

Rod Trent is a security CSA for Microsoft and an Azure Sentinel global SME helping customers migrate from existing SIEMs to Azure Sentinel to achieve the promise of better security through improved efficiency without compromise.

Rod is a husband, dad, and recently a first-time grandfather. He spends his spare time (if such a thing does truly exist) simultaneously watching episodes of *The Six Million Dollar Man* and writing KQL queries.

Table of Contents

3
Azure AD Hybrid Identity

4
Azure AD Identity Security

5

Azure AD Identity Governance

Section 2: Implement Azure Platform Protection

6

Implementing Perimeter Security

7

Implementing Network Security

8

Implementing Host Security

9
Implementing Container Security

Section 3: Secure Storage, Applications, and Data

10
Implementing Storage Security

11

Implementing Database Security

12
Implementing Secrets, Keys, and Certificate Management with Key Vault

13
Azure Cloud Governance and Security Operations

Assessments

Other Books You May Enjoy

Index

Preface

Security is a key part of any well-architected design. In this book, you will gain both the knowledge and the practical skills to significantly reduce the attack surface of your Azure workloads and protect your organization from constantly evolving threats to public cloud environments such as Azure.

Beyond preparing you for the Azure Security Engineer certification exam (AZ-500), this book will help you gain a clear understanding of how to secure your Azure environments and workloads using native Azure security capabilities.

This book is a comprehensive security guide for those who are looking to take the AZ-500 exam and for those who are interested in securing their Azure infrastructure. Complete with hands-on tutorials, projects, and self-assessment questions, this easy-to-follow guide will take you beyond the foundations of Azure security. You will not only learn about security technologies in Azure but also how to configure and manage them.

By the end of this book, you will be well-versed in different Azure security technologies/services and will also have learned how to protect your Azure infrastructure from modern threats.

Who this book is for

This book is for new and experienced security professionals, cloud administrators, architects, and developers with an interest in understanding Azure platform security and how to implement workload security in Azure.

Technical professionals who are preparing to take the Azure Security Engineer certification exam (AZ-500) will also benefit tremendously from reading this book.

What this book covers

Chapter 1, Introduction to Azure Security, helps you to understand how security works in Azure and set up a practice environment.

Chapter 2, Understanding Azure AD, helps you to understand what Azure **Active Directory** (**AD**) is and how to implement identity management.

Chapter 3, Azure AD Hybrid Identity, covers how to implement Azure AD hybrid identity and configure its status.

Chapter 4, Azure AD Identity Security, covers how to protect Azure AD identities with advanced identity security best practices.

Chapter 5, Azure AD Identity Governance, covers how to protect privileged access using Azure AD Privileged Identity Management.

Chapter 6, Implementing Perimeter Security, covers how to implement platform perimeter protection to secure Azure workloads.

Chapter 7, Implementing Network Security, covers how to configure network security best practices for IaaS and PaaS.

Chapter 8, Implementing Host Security, covers how to implement host security best practices in Azure.

Chapter 9, Implementing Container Security, covers how to implement container security best practices in Azure.

Chapter 10, Implementing Storage Security, covers how to protect data in Azure Storage using multilayered security.

Chapter 11, Implementing Database Security, covers how to protect Azure SQL databases against unauthorized access, data theft, and vulnerabilities.

Chapter 12, Implementing Secrets, Keys, and Certificates Management with Key Vault, covers how to secure privileged application configuration and credentials using Key Vault.

Chapter 13, Azure Cloud Governance and Security Operations, covers how to implement Azure cloud governance, address cloud security challenges with Security Center, and manage security operations with Azure Sentinel.

To get the most out of this book

Foundational-level knowledge of the Azure cloud platform, as well as a general knowledge of technical concepts such as AD, networking, and encryption, is required.

Software/hardware covered in the book	OS requirements
Angular 9	Windows, Mac OS X, or Linux (any)
TypeScript 3.7	
ECMAScript 11	

Download the color images

We also provide a PDF file that has color images of the screenshots/diagrams used in this book. You can download it here: `http://www.packtpub.com/sites/default/files/downloads/9781800562653_ColorImages.pdf`.

Download the example code files

You can download the example code files for this book from GitHub at `https://github.com/PacktPublishing/Microsoft-Azure-Security-Technologies-Certification-and-Beyond`. In case there's an update to the code, it will be updated on the existing GitHub repository.

We also have other code bundles from our rich catalog of books and videos available at `https://github.com/PacktPublishing/`. Check them out!

Conventions used

There are a number of text conventions used throughout this book.

`Code in text`: Indicates code words in text, database table names, folder names, filenames, file extensions, pathnames, dummy URLs, user input, and Twitter handles. Here is an example: "The UPN format for external user accounts is `<alias>_<HomeTenant>#EXT#@domain.suffix`."

A block of code is set as follows:

```
CREATE USER "<EMMY_UPN>"
FROM EXTERNAL PROVIDER
WITH DEFAULT_SCHEMA = dbo;
```

Any command-line input or output is written as follows:

```
New-Item -Path "c:\" -Name "packtaz500" -ItemType "directory"
Set-Location -Path "c:\packtaz500"
```

Bold: Indicates a new term, an important word, or words that you see onscreen. For example, words in menus or dialog boxes appear in the text like this. Here is an example: "Click **Exit** to close the **Microsoft Azure Active Directory Connect** window once the configuration is complete."

> **Tips or important notes**
> Appear like this.

Get in touch

Feedback from our readers is always welcome.

General feedback: If you have questions about any aspect of this book, mention the book title in the subject of your message and email us at `customercare@packtpub.com`.

Errata: Although we have taken every care to ensure the accuracy of our content, mistakes do happen. If you have found a mistake in this book, we would be grateful if you would report this to us. Please visit `www.packtpub.com/support/errata`, selecting your book, clicking on the Errata Submission Form link, and entering the details.

Piracy: If you come across any illegal copies of our works in any form on the Internet, we would be grateful if you would provide us with the location address or website name. Please contact us at `copyright@packt.com` with a link to the material.

If you are interested in becoming an author: If there is a topic that you have expertise in and you are interested in either writing or contributing to a book, please visit `authors.packtpub.com`.

Share Your Thoughts

Once you've read *Microsoft Azure Security Technologies Certification and Beyond*, we'd love to hear your thoughts! Scan the QR code below to go straight to the Amazon review page for this book and share your feedback.

https://packt.link/r/1-800-56265-9

Your review is important to us and the tech community and will help us make sure we're delivering excellent quality content.

Section 1: Implement Identity and Access Security for Azure

A common attack entry point for Azure environments is identity compromise. This is why mitigating identity security risks and configuring secure access is a key component of a comprehensive Azure security strategy. In this section, you will gain a clear understanding of **Azure Active Directory** (**Azure AD**), Microsoft's cloud-based identity and access management service, and how to secure your cloud identities using features such as multi-factor authentication, password protection, conditional access, identity protection, and privileged identity management. Not only will just the concepts and theory be made clear; we will also walk through many exercises as well!

This part of the book comprises the following chapters:

- *Chapter 1, Introduction to Azure Security*
- *Chapter 2, Understanding Azure AD*
- *Chapter 3, Azure AD Hybrid Identity*
- *Chapter 4, Azure AD Identity Security*
- *Chapter 5, Azure AD Identity Governance*

1
Introduction to Azure Security

Security is a core component of any well-architected environment, and this is no different for Azure. Every workload that your organization implements in Azure needs to be implemented with security in mind. The risk associated with not doing this could range from an attacker being able to use your Azure resources to mine cryptocurrency at your expense to an attacker being able to gain access to sensitive customer data that could result in massive fines or sanctions against your company. It could also lead to reputation damage that may lead to customers moving to a competitor.

But how does cloud security work? Is it different from traditional security? Do you have to unlearn everything that you know about managing on-premises security and start from the beginning? You'll be glad that the answer to that latter question is "*No.*" The principles of digital security are the same whether your workload sits in a traditional on-premises data center or in a cloud environment such as Microsoft Azure. The way you apply those principles, however, is quite different. Some of those differences are due to the dynamic and elastic nature of cloud environments. The ability to rapidly provision and release resources introduces new challenges that traditional security models struggle to address effectively, but we'll be covering how to solve this in this book – that is, we'll focus on how we apply security principles to secure dynamic Azure environments.

In any discussion on Azure security, it is critical to understand the "shared responsibility model," that is, which security tasks are handled by the cloud provider (Microsoft in this case) and which tasks are handled by the cloud consumers (us). In this chapter, I will introduce this concept and show how cloud security responsibilities vary depending on the type of service that you are using in Azure – **Software as a Service** (**SaaS**), **Platform as a Service** (**PaaS**), or **Infrastructure as a Service** (**IaaS**). I will also walk you through how to set up an Azure subscription that you can use to follow along with the hands-on sections of this book.

In this chapter, we're going to cover the following topics; however, feel free to skip to the next chapter if the information covered is already familiar to you:

- Shared responsibility model
- Setting up a practice environment

Technical requirements

To follow along with the instructions in this chapter, you'll need the following:

- An `outlook.com` account that you will use to sign up for your Azure subscription. Make sure that this is an account that you have not previously used to sign up for a free trial Azure subscription. This is because every Microsoft account is entitled to only one free trial signup. You can sign up for a new outlook.com account by going to `https://outlook.live.com/owa/` and clicking **Create free account**.
- **A PC with a web browser**: The PC can run Windows, macOS, or GUI-based Linux, as long as it has a web browser installed and it has internet connectivity.
- **A credit card**: This will be needed during the sign-up process to validate your identity. The credit card will not be charged during the trial. You have to explicitly convert a free trial subscription to a pay-as-you-go subscription for it to be charged.
- **A valid phone number**: This will also be needed to validate your identity.

Shared responsibility model

As organizations transition their workloads from their on-premises data centers to the Azure cloud platform, the responsibility of security also shifts. One of these shifts is that you are no longer solely responsible (as an organization) for all aspects of security as you may be used to in a traditional environment. Security is now a concern that both the cloud provider (Microsoft) and the cloud customers (us) share. This is called the **shared responsibility model** and all cloud providers, including Microsoft's competitors such as **AWS** and **GCP**, follow this model as well.

The diagram in *Figure 1.1* clearly highlights this. It is from a whitepaper on the shared security model that was published by Microsoft. You can download the whitepaper from this URL: `https://azure.microsoft.com/en-gb/resources/shared-responsibility-for-cloud-computing/`. In the diagram, the gray represents the security responsibilities that are transferred to Microsoft when we adopt Azure, while the blue represents security responsibilities that we still have to take care of as Azure customers:

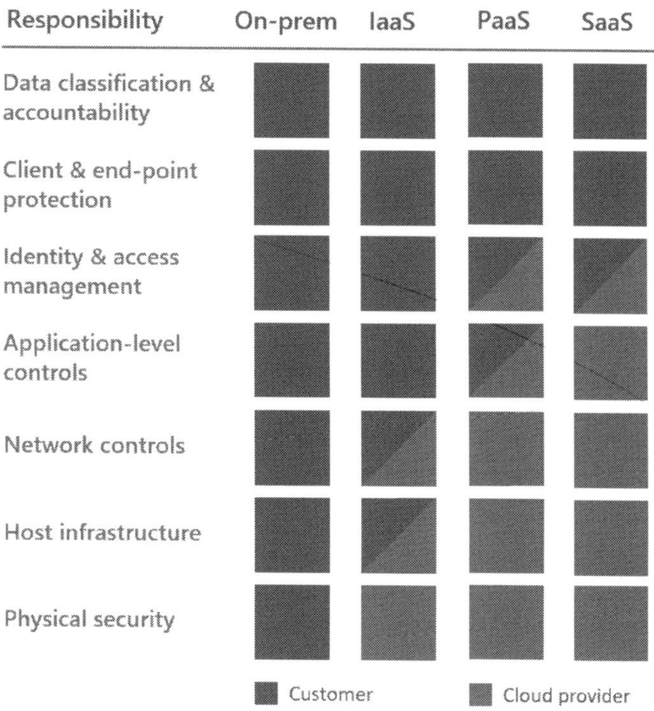

Figure 1.1 – Shared responsibilities for different cloud service models

One of the things that I would like to highlight in the diagram is that regardless of the cloud service model that we are using in Azure – IaaS, PaaS, or SaaS – *we are never without security responsibility*. Here are some other lessons that I want you to take from this section:

- *Your security responsibility varies depending on the model of service that you are using in Azure.*

  If you are using an IaaS service such as a virtual machine, you have more security responsibilities to take care of. For example, you are responsible for patching the operating system of your Azure-hosted virtual machines.

If you are using a PaaS service such as Azure App Service, you have fewer security responsibilities to take care of. For example, you are not responsible for patching the operating system used by the service, but you are still responsible for how you configure the service and also for controlling access to it.

If you are using a SaaS service such as Azure Search, you have even fewer security responsibilities, but you are still responsible for controlling access to your data.

- *Not fulfilling your security responsibilities leaves you exposed to threats and attacks in those areas.*

  Have a good look at the diagram again. Wherever you see blue in the diagram, if you do not have a strategy to address those responsibilities, you are leaving yourself exposed to threats! Don't worry too much about this right now – by the end of this book, you'll be equipped with the knowledge and skills that you need to effectively take care of these security responsibilities.

In this section, we established the foundational concept of shared security responsibilities in Azure. This clarified for us what we are responsible for depending on the service model that we are using. In the next section, we will set up a test environment that we can use to practice the implementation of security controls in Azure.

Setting up a practice environment

One of the best ways to learn a new concept is through hands-on practice. This book includes walk-throughs that allow you to gain a practical experience of the concepts being discussed:

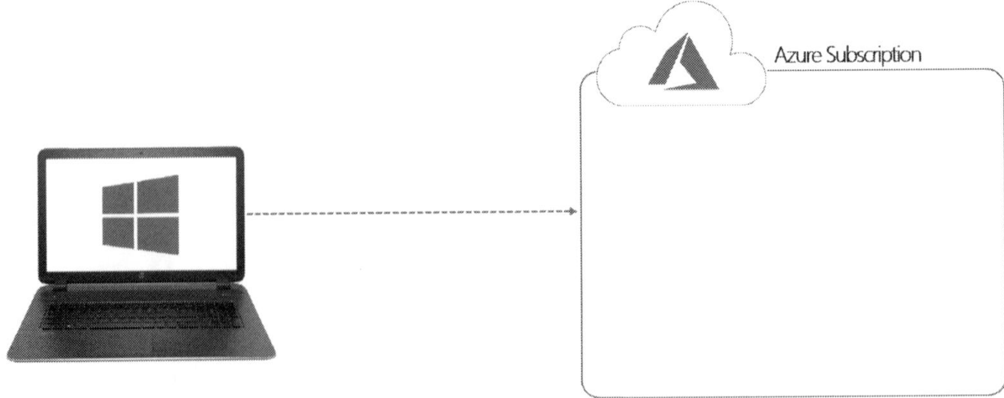

Figure 1.2 – Practice environment

To follow along with these walk-throughs, you will need access to an Azure subscription, and I will be walking you through how to sign up for one if you do not have an existing subscription now. If you have an existing subscription that you can use, feel free to skip the next section.

Create a free trial Azure subscription

To set up a free trial subscription, follow these steps:

1. Open a browser window and browse to `https://signup.azure.com/`.
2. In the **Sign in** window, enter your Outlook.com account and click **Next**:

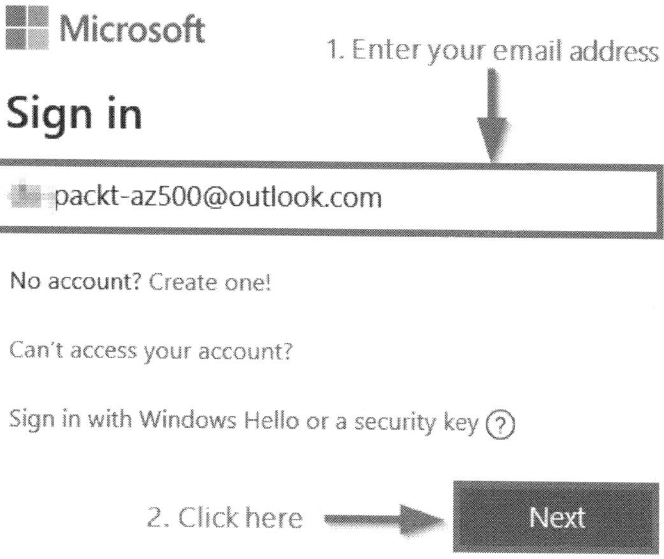

Figure 1.3 – Enter your email address

3. In the **Your profile** window that opens, the **Country/Region**, **First name**, **Last name**, and **Email address** fields should already be completed using information from your email profile. Enter the right values if the auto-completed values are not correct.
4. Enter your phone number (without the country code).

5. Skip **Company VatID**. Leave it empty and click **Next**. Depending on your **Country/Region** setting, this field may not be displayed, or you may be presented with a different option:

Figure 1.4 – Enter your profile information

6. In the **Identity verification by phone** section, ensure your country code and phone number are correct, then click on **Text me**:

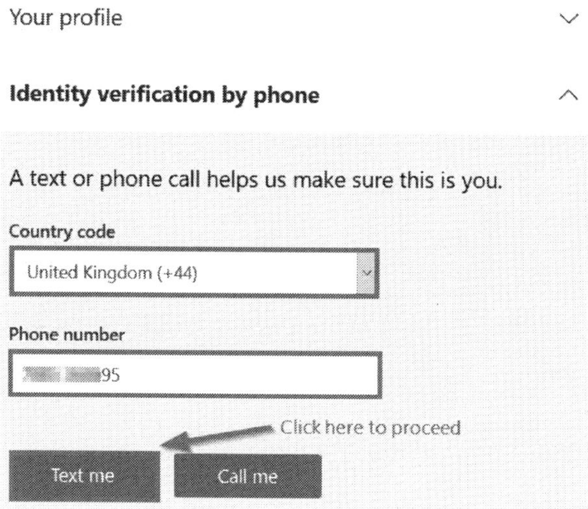

Figure 1.5 – Enter your phone number for identity verification

7. A verification code will be sent to your phone number. Enter the *verification code* and click **Verify code**.
8. In the **Identity verification by card** section, fill in **Cardholder Name** (as it appears on your credit card), **Card number**, **Expires**, and **CVV**:

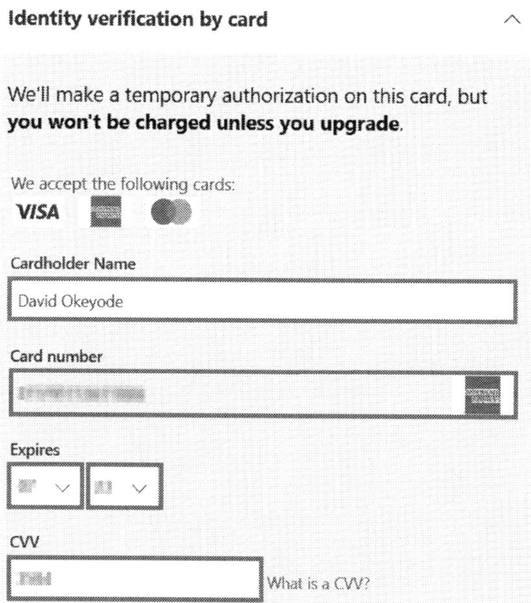

Figure 1.6 – Enter your credit card information

9. Enter your address information and click **Next**.
10. In the **Agreement** section, select only **I agree to the subscription agreement, offer details, and privacy statement** and click on **Sign up**:

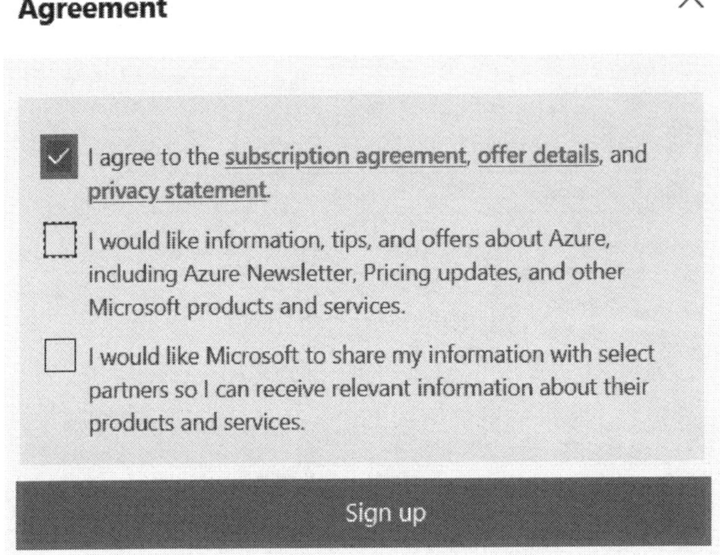

Figure 1.7 – Conclude the sign-up process

> **Important note**
>
> Clicking on **subscription agreement**, **offer details**, and **privacy statement** will take you to the respective documentation, where you can read the details to stay informed of what you are agreeing to when signing up.

The signup process will begin. It should only take a few minutes, after which you will be redirected to the Azure portal.

11. To verify your subscription, in the Azure portal, click on **Microsoft Azure** in the top-left corner and click on **Subscriptions** under **Navigate**:

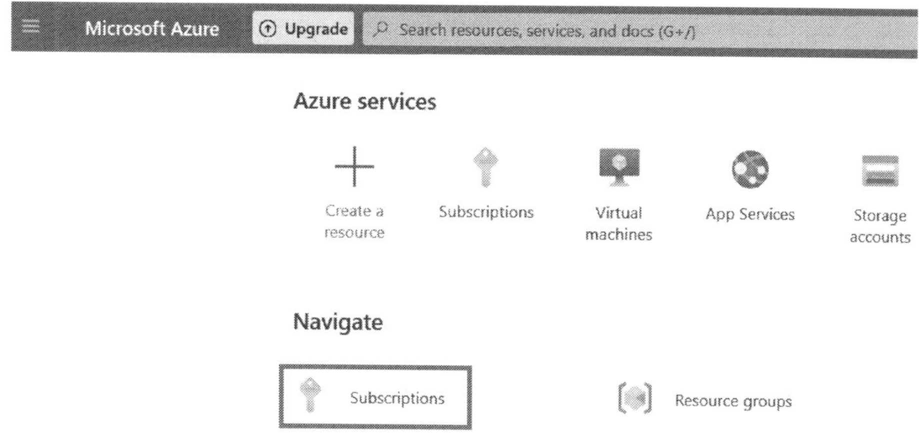

Figure 1.8 – Verify your new subscription

12. In the **Subscriptions** window, you should see a subscription named **Free Trial**:

Subscriptions
Default Directory
Add
View list of subscriptions for which you have role-based access control (RBAC) permissions to manage Azure resources. To view subscriptions for which you
Showing subscriptions in Default Directory directory. Don't see a subscription? Switch directories
My role
8 selected
Status
3 selected
Apply
Showing 1 of 1 subscriptions
Show only subscriptions selected in the global subscriptions filter
Search

Subscription name	Subscription ID	My role
Free Trial	5d5	Account admin

Figure 1.9 – Your new trial subscription

Congratulations! You now have an Azure subscription that you can use to follow along with the rest of the book.

Summary

In this chapter, we saw how cloud security is similar to yet different from traditional security. We also discussed the shared security model concept and highlighted how we have fewer security responsibilities when we adopt a cloud platform such as Microsoft Azure, but we are never without security responsibilities! And finally, I walked you through the process of setting up an Azure subscription, which puts you in a great place to follow along with the hands-on sections in the rest of this book.

Azure security is a deep and complex topic and we're only just getting started. In the next chapter, we'll start discussing one of the most important aspects of implementing security for your Azure environments – securing identity and access using Azure Active Directory.

Questions

As we conclude, here is a list of questions for you to test your knowledge regarding this chapter's material. You will find the answers in the *Assessments* section of the *Appendix*:

1. True or false: When a workload is migrated from on-premises to Azure, you offload all security responsibilities to Microsoft.

   a. True

   b. False

2. Which cloud service model requires the greatest security effort on the part of the customer?

   a. Infrastructure as a Service (IaaS)

   b. Platform as a Service (PaaS)

   c. Software as a Service (SaaS)

3. True or false: The principles of digital security are the same whether your workload sits in a traditional on-premises data center or in a cloud environment such as Microsoft Azure.

   a. True

   b. False

4. Which security responsibility is solely that of the cloud provider when we move to Azure?

   a. Network controls

   b. Client and endpoint protection

   c. Physical security

   d. Identity and access management

Further reading

To learn more on the topics covered in this chapter, you can refer to the following links:

- Azure shared security responsibility documentation: `https://docs.microsoft.com/en-us/azure/security/fundamentals/shared-responsibility`

2
Understanding Azure AD

Many cloud-related security breaches start with a compromised user identity. Once an attacker gets a foot in the door using the compromised credential, they can escalate privileges or gather intelligence to move further in the attack chain. This is why securing identity is important in any discussion on cloud security. This chapter will equip you with a thorough understanding of **Azure Active Directory** (**Azure AD**) – Microsoft's cloud-based identity and access management service, which functions as the identity provider for Azure and other cloud services. The foundational concepts discussed in this chapter are needed to fully grasp the identity security topics covered in the third and fourth chapters. Here are the topics that we will cover in this chapter with accompanying hands-on exercises:

- What Azure AD is not (what is Azure AD?)
- Modern authentication protocols
- Azure AD editions
- Azure AD object management

What Azure AD is not (what is Azure AD?)

From my experience, knowing what Azure AD is not is as important as knowing what Azure AD is. Understanding what Azure AD is not will help you avoid some of the common confusion out there about this service, so let's start out with this statement: *Azure AD is NOT on-premises Active Directory in Azure!* As a matter of fact, it has a different use case and structure from on-premises Active Directory (AD). I personally would have called it *Azure Identity Service* or some other name to avoid confusion with on-premises Active Directory, but it seems that Microsoft wanted to keep the Active Directory brand name going.

So, if Azure AD is not on-premises AD in Azure, what is it then? I will give you *two descriptions* to help you understand what it is. Here is the first one: *Azure AD is the identity provider for Microsoft cloud services.* You may be thinking to yourself, what does that even mean? Let's check it out.

Azure AD versus on-premises AD

Let's have a quick look at the differences between Azure AD and on-premises AD.

Azure AD is queried using the REST API over HTTP (`80`) and HTTPS (`443`) instead of LDAP, which is used to query on-premises AD over TCP ports `389` (LDAP) or `686` (LDAPS).

Azure AD uses modern authentication protocols that use web transport such as SAML, WS-Federation, and OpenID Connect for authentication (and OAuth for authorization) instead of Kerberos, which is used by on-premises AD.

Azure AD users and groups are created in a flat structure, and there are no **Organizational Units** (**OUs**) or **Group Policy Objects** (**GPOs**). On-premises AD has a hierarchical structure with OUs and containers.

Azure AD includes native federation services (for example, it has native federation built in with other Azure AD tenants). It does not rely on (ADFS).

Azure AD – an identity provider for Microsoft cloud services

When a customer signs up for any Microsoft cloud service (an Azure subscription, an Office 365 subscription, or a Dynamics365 subscription), as you did in the first chapter, an Azure AD tenant is transparently created in the background. This is where the identities (users, groups, and service principals) that are allowed to access those services are stored and managed (*Figure 2.1*):

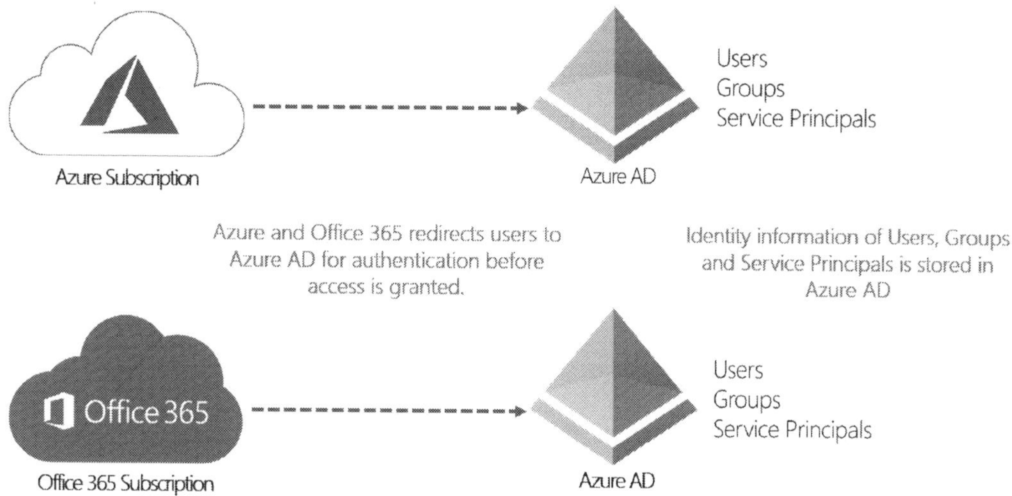

Figure 2.1 – Azure AD as identity provider for Microsoft Cloud Services

In order to access Microsoft cloud services such as Azure, users are redirected to Azure AD to authenticate. Only when authentication is successfully completed in Azure AD can access be granted.

So, does this mean that for every Microsoft cloud service that you sign up for, you always have to have a brand new separate Azure AD tenant? (By the way, *Azure AD tenant* refers to a single instance of Azure AD):

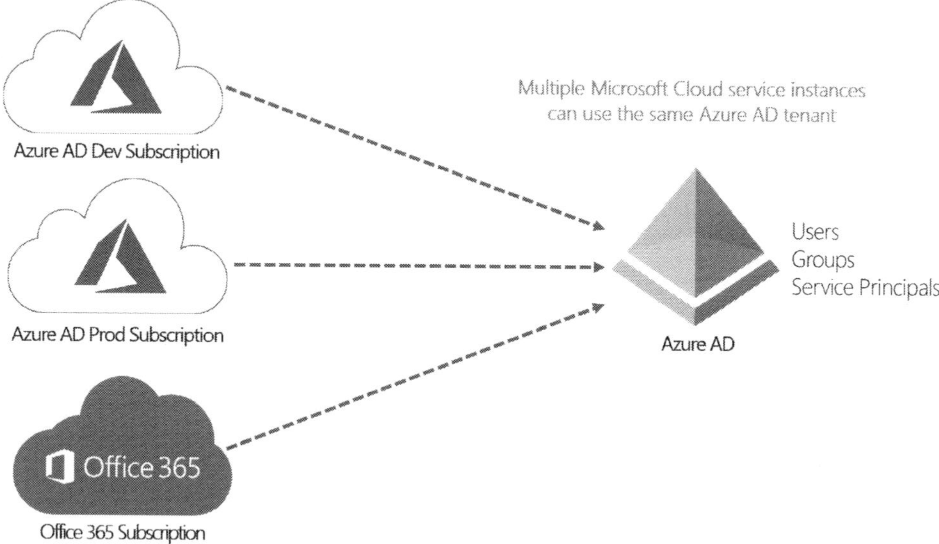

Figure 2.2 – A single Azure AD tenant linked with multiple Microsoft cloud services

The answer to that question is *NO!* Organizations do not have to have different Azure AD tenants for multiple Microsoft cloud services. Multiple cloud service instances can be linked with the same Azure AD tenant. For example, it is common for organizations to implement separate Azure AD subscriptions for development and production workloads. These subscriptions can both be linked with the same Azure AD tenant (*Figure 2.2*).

Azure AD – an identity provider for modern applications

My second description of Azure AD is related to its use case – *the PRIMARY use case of Azure AD is to securely authenticate access to applications that support modern authentication protocols regardless of where they are hosted!*

That statement sounds profound but what does it mean? It means that beyond support for Microsoft cloud services, Azure AD can actually provide authentication for any **software as a service** (**SaaS**) or hosted application that supports modern authentication protocols (*Figure 2.3*)! This is powerful as it means that we can centrally manage authentication and access for all our cloud and supported on-premises applications with Azure AD. This includes thousands of SaaS applications, including popular ones such as Salesforce, Box, AWS, and Dropbox. It also includes custom applications that may be hosted on-premises or in the cloud:

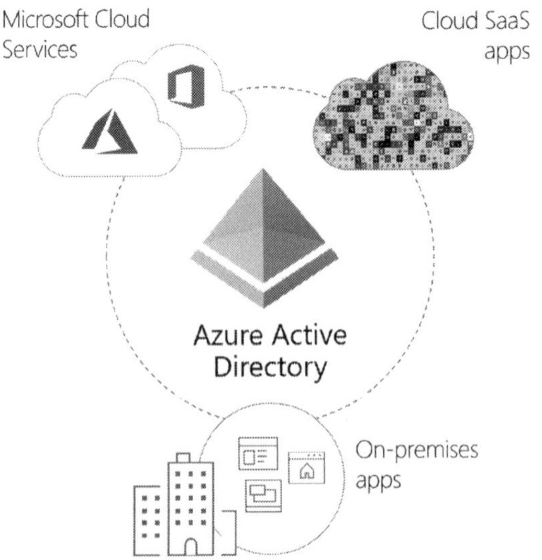

Figure 2.3 – Centralized identity management using Azure AD

But what do modern authentication protocols mean? Why do we need them? What was wrong with the authentication protocols that we had?

Modern authentication protocols

To understand why we need modern authentication protocols, let's go back in time to see how things were. Years ago, a typical organization needed only on-premises domain controllers (running Active Directory) to provide authentication for their business applications. This was a time when the users, the servers running the business applications, and the domain controllers lived happily within the same network perimeter. Authentication occurred using either Kerberos or NTLM, which are both protocols designed to authenticate scenarios where both the application and the identity provider lived on the same network. You could tell this from the number of network ports that needed to be opened for Kerberos to work (*Figure 2.4*).

Times have changed since then! The majority of business applications that organizations use are now cloud-hosted (living in someone else's data centers). It is not practical to expose all the ports that Kerberos alone needs to work to the internet! This was why we needed modern authentication protocols! The most common modern authentication/authorization protocols are **OpenID Connect 1.0**, **SAML 2.0**, and **OAuth 2.0** (authorization framework):

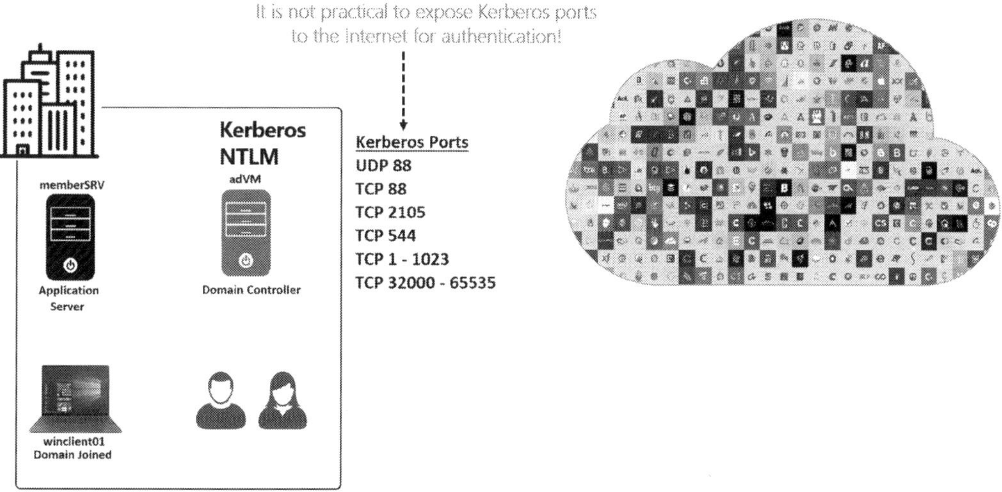

Figure 2.4 – Legacy authentication protocols

All modern authentication protocols have one thing in common (regardless of the differences in their specific implementations) – they operate using web transport. This means that they can pass authentication and authorization tokens over HTTP and HTTPS, making it easy to deliver authentication and authorization across different environments.

Hands-on exercise – review your Azure AD tenant

Now that you have some understanding of what Azure AD is, let's go to the Azure portal to review the Azure AD tenant that was created for us when we signed up for our Azure subscription in *Chapter 1, Introduction to Azure Security*. You will need to do this from your Windows or macOS machine with an internet connection:

1. Open a web browser and browse to the Azure portal URL: `https://portal.azure.com`.
2. Sign in to the portal using the account that you used to sign up in the previous chapter.
3. Click the portal menu icon in the top-left corner and select **Azure Active Directory**:

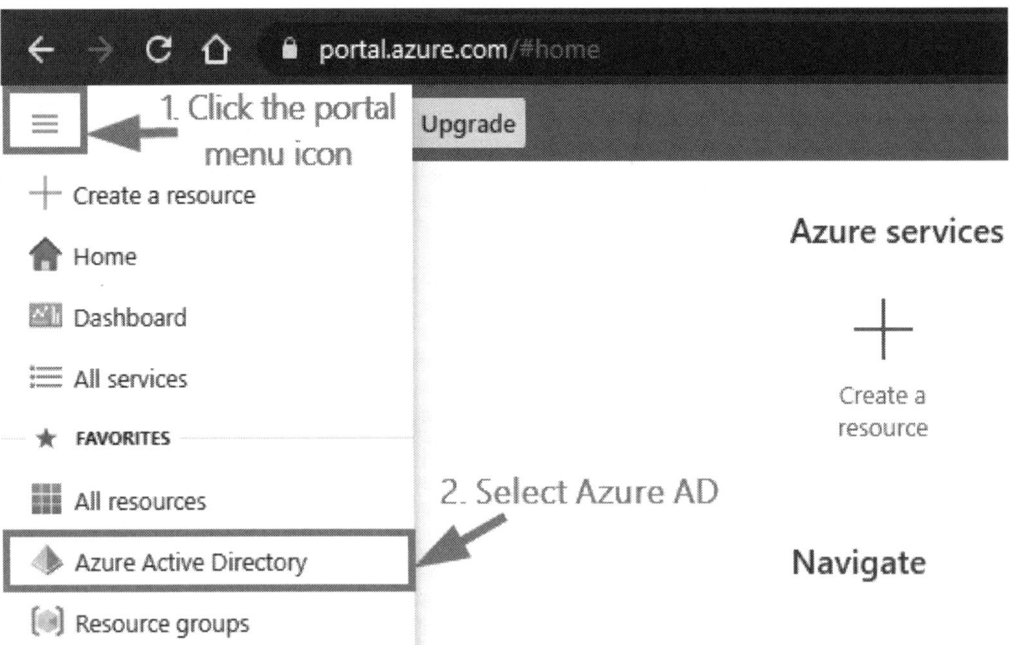

Figure 2.5 – Select Azure AD

4. In the **Default Directory | Overview** blade, review the information contained in the **Tenant information** section:

   Your role shows the role that the signed-in account has in Azure AD. The **Global administrator** role gives full control to perform all operations on the tenant. We will be covering Azure AD roles in a later discussion.

License shows the current edition of our Azure AD license. Our current license edition is **Azure AD Free** (license options and differences will be covered later in this chapter).

Tenant ID shows the unique tenant ID of our Azure AD tenant.

Primary domain shows the default domain name that was created for our Azure AD tenant when we signed up for our Azure subscription. This initial domain name is made up of information from the email that we used to sign up with a suffix of `onmicrosoft.com`. This domain name will be used as the **User Principal Name** (**UPN**) suffix of our users. For example, if I create a user called `david` in my Azure AD tenant, the UPN for my user will be `david@davidpacktaz500outlook.onmicrosoft.com`. Obviously, this is not ideal for an organization. We can add a custom domain name to replace the default one as the primary and we will be doing this in an optional exercise shortly:

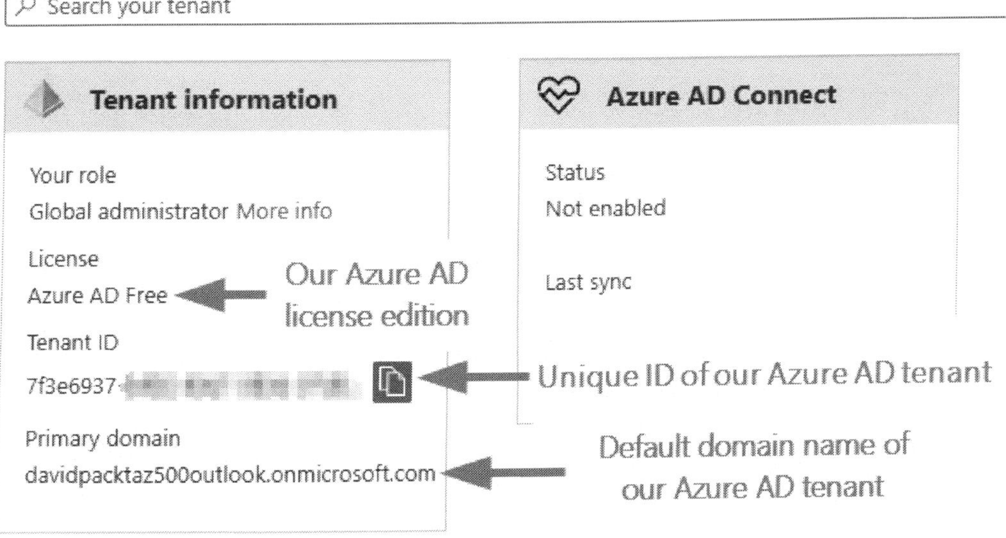

Figure 2.6 – Azure AD tenant information

5. Still in the **Default Directory | Overview** blade, click on **Users** (in the section labeled **Manage**):

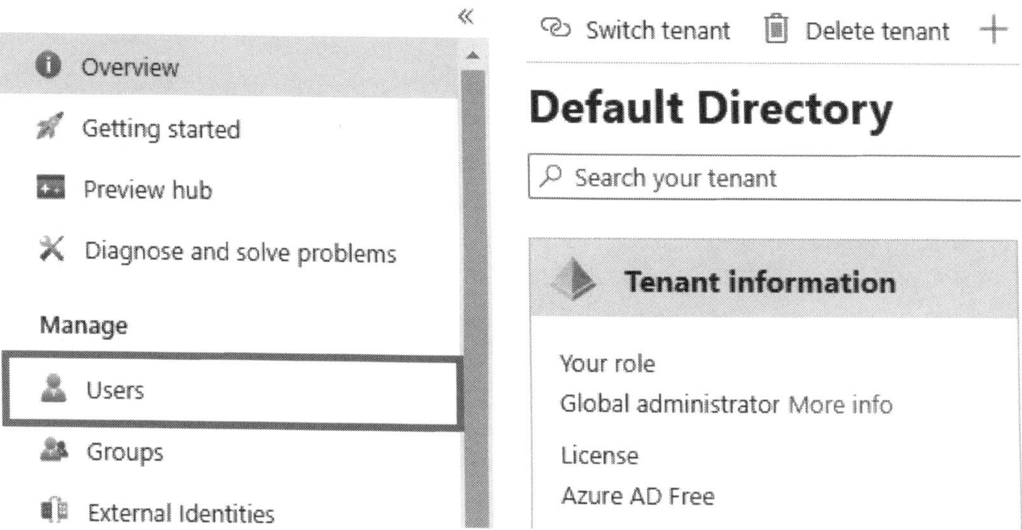

Figure 2.7 – Azure AD Users option

6. You will see a list of users in your Azure AD tenant:

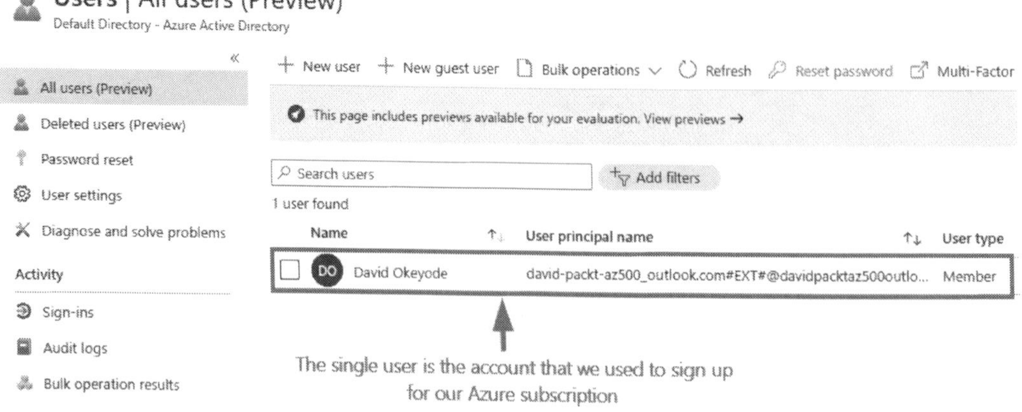

Figure 2.8 – Azure AD Users blade

At the moment, we have a single user, but we will be adding more users in later exercises in this book. Leave the browser open for the next exercise.

Hands-on exercise – add a custom domain to Azure AD (optional)

In this exercise, we will be adding a custom domain name to Azure AD. This domain name will be used to replace the `onmicrosoft.com` default name. This exercise requires you to have a public DNS name that you have purchased from a DNS provider. You must also have the permissions to manage that DNS zone as you will need to create new records as part of this process. In my case, I have purchased `azureblueteam.io` from GoDaddy (`https://godaddy.com`) and I will be using this for the instructions:

1. We will stay in the **Users | All Users** blade, click on **Custom domain names** (in the section labeled **Manage**), then click on **Add custom domain**:

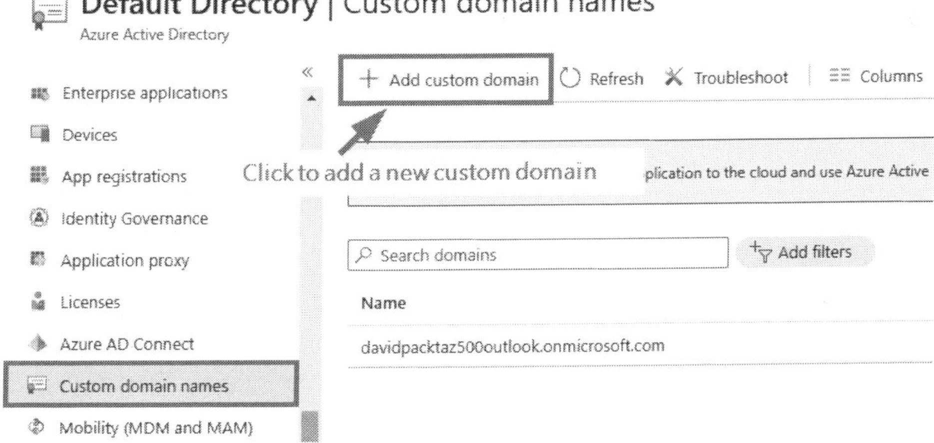

Figure 2.9 – Click to add a custom domain

2. In the **Custom domain name** box, enter the public DNS name that you want to add to Azure AD, then click **Add domain**:

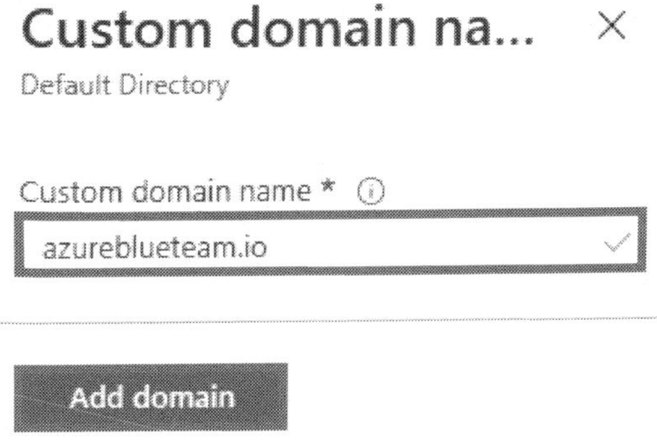

Figure 2.10 – Add a custom domain

3. In the window that opens, make a note of the information displayed as you will need to add the record to your DNS zone for verification. You can choose to use either a **TXT** record or an **MX** record. I will be using the **TXT** record for my verification:

azureblueteam.io

Custom domain name

Delete | Got feedback?

To use azureblueteam.io with your Azure AD, create a new TXT record with your domain name registrar using the info below.

Record type	TXT / MX
Alias or host name	@
Destination or points to address	MS=ms98302515
TTL	3600

Share these settings via email

Verification will not succeed until you have configured your domain with your registrar as described above.

Make a note of this information as it will be needed for verification

Verify

Figure 2.11 – Domain name verification record

4. Head over to your DNS zone and add the required record using the information from *Step 3*. My DNS provider is `GoDaddy` and my DNS zone is hosted with them. Make sure to allow some time for the DNS record to replicate:

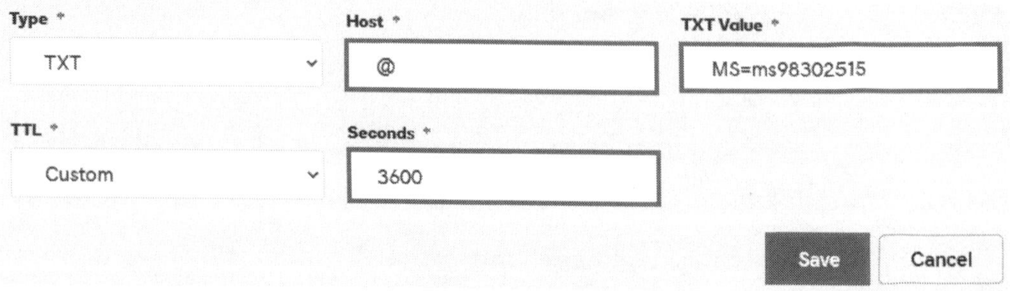

Figure 2.12 – Add a verification record

5. Back in the Azure portal, click on **Verify**.
6. After the record is verified successfully, click on the **Make primary** option to configure the newly verified domain name as the primary domain name of your Azure AD tenant. Click on **Yes** to confirm:

azureblueteam.io

Custom domain name

✓ Make primary | Delete

Verification succeeded!

Type	Custom
Status	Verified
Federated	No
	To configure azureblueteam.io for federated sign-on to your Azure Active Directory, run Azure AD Connect on your local network.
	Download Azure AD Connect
Primary domain	No
In use	No

Figure 2.13 – Configure the primary domain name

If you head back to the **Default Directory | Custom domain names** blade, you should see that your new custom domain is verified and that it is configured as the primary domain name:

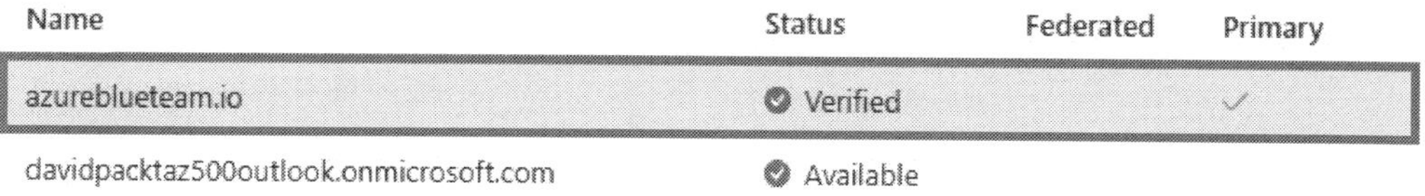

Name	Status	Federated	Primary
azureblueteam.io	Verified		✓
davidpacktaz500outlook.onmicrosoft.com	Available		

Figure 2.14 – Verified primary custom domain name

Now that you have a clearer understanding of what Azure AD is, its use cases, and how to work with it, let's shift our focus to talk about Azure AD editions. The significance of this will become clearer as we get deeper into Azure AD features in later chapters.

Azure AD editions

The features of Azure AD that you can use depends on the edition of Azure AD that you have, and your licensing based on pricing. For example, if you want to implement advanced identity security capabilities of Azure AD such as Identity Protection and Privileged Identity Management, you need to have the right Azure AD edition that enables these capabilities. We will cover both Identity Protection and Privileged Identity Management in *Chapter 4, Azure AD Identity Security*.

Before July 2019, we had five editions of Azure AD (Free, Basic, Office 365 Apps, Premium P1, and Premium P2) but after July 2019, we only have four editions (Free, Office 365 Apps, Premium P1, and Premium P2). The reason for bringing this up is to give you a clearer context in case you come across an older blog or document that still references the *Basic* edition of Azure AD. Just be aware that the *"Basic"* edition has now gone away!

Alex Simons (`https://twitter.com/Alex_A_Simons`), the Corporate Vice President of Product Management at the Microsoft Identity division, took to Twitter to announce the end of the Azure AD Basic edition: `https://twitter.com/Alex_A_Simons/status/1159556024207962112`. I recommend following Alex if you are interested in getting the latest updates on Azure AD.

Here is a short description of the Azure AD editions that we have:

- **Azure AD Free**: This is the edition of Azure AD that is included with new Azure subscriptions. It includes enough features to get us introduced to the capabilities of Azure AD, but it lacks advanced management and security features. It also does not have any **Service-Level Agreement** (**SLA**) guarantee!
- **Azure AD Office 365 Apps**: This is the edition of Azure AD that is included with new Office 365 subscriptions. It has a few more capabilities than the free edition (capabilities such as Self-Service Password Reset, which allows users to reset their own passwords without the need to contact an administrator) and has an SLA.

- **Azure AD Premium P1**: This edition can be purchased as a standalone offering or as part of the **Enterprise Mobility Suite** (**EMS**) or Microsoft 365 bundles. It has important security capabilities such as conditional access, Self-Service Password Reset, and so on. If you are interested in implementing identity and access in the best possible secure way, at a minimum, you need to be on the Premium P1 edition.
- **Azure AD Premium P2**: This edition includes every feature of all other Azure Active Directory editions enhanced with advanced security capabilities such as Identity Protection and Identity Governance (Privileged Identity Management, access reviews) capabilities. We'll cover what these are in later chapters.

For a full comparison of the features of the various Azure AD editions, please refer to this link: `https://azure.microsoft.com/en-gb/pricing/details/active-directory/`.

Hands-on exercise – sign up for an Azure AD Premium P2 trial

For us to implement the full feature set of Azure AD and gain the experience that we need to not only pass the AZ-500 exam but also to be successful on the job, we need to have the Azure AD Premium P2 license. In this exercise, we will be signing up for the Azure AD Premium P2 trial for our tenant:

1. In the Azure AD blade in the Azure portal, click on **Licenses**:

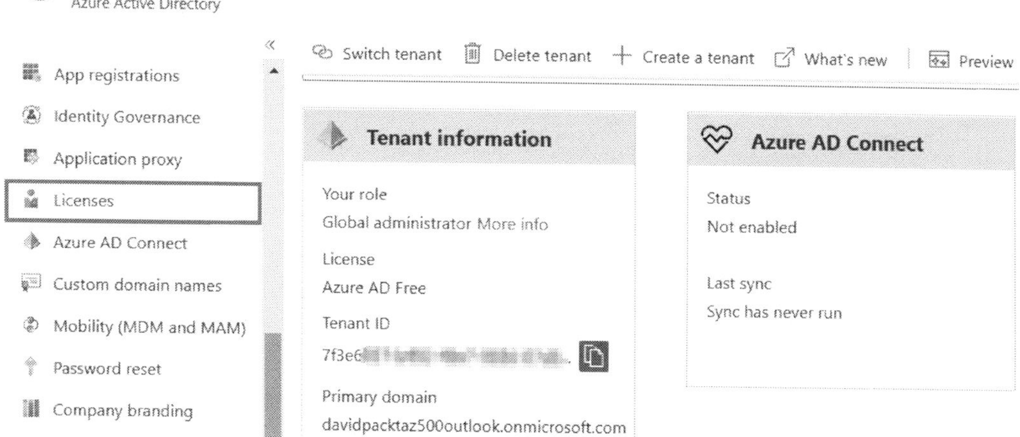

Figure 2.15 – Azure AD Licenses

2. In the **Licenses | Overview** blade, click on **All products**, then click on **+ Try / Buy**:

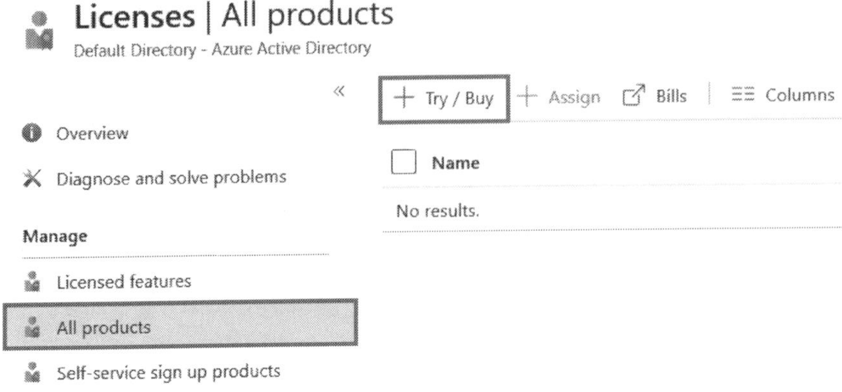

Figure 2.16 – Try the Azure AD Premium P2 license

3. In the **Activate** blade, click to expand **Free trial** (under **AZURE AD PREMIUM P2**), then click on **Activate**:

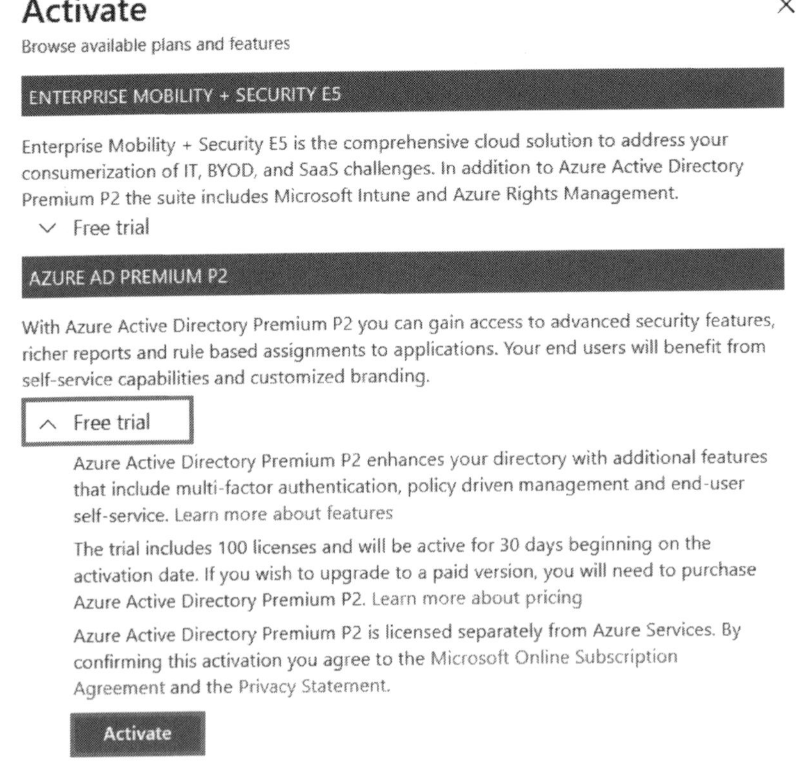

Figure 2.17 – Activate Azure AD Premium P2 trial license

4. It could take a few minutes for the license to be activated even after you get a **Successful** message. You may also need to refresh the browser for the activated trial to be visible. Once this is completed, you should have 100 Azure AD Premium P2 licenses, which we will be assigning to new users in future exercises:

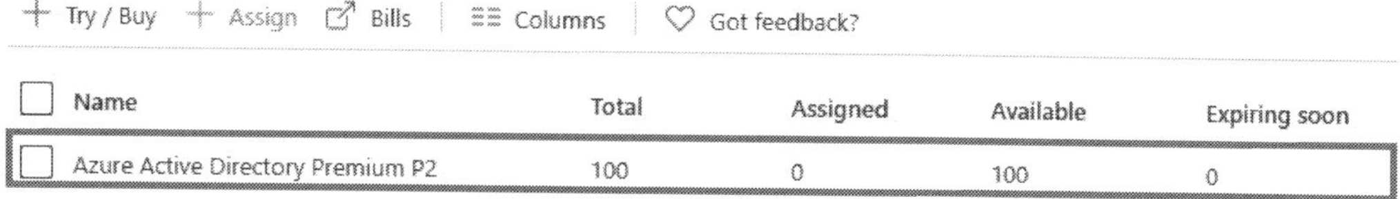

Figure 2.18 – Azure AD Premium P2 licenses

5. In the left-hand menu, click on **Overview**. The **Tenant information** section should now display your license as **Azure AD Premium P2**:

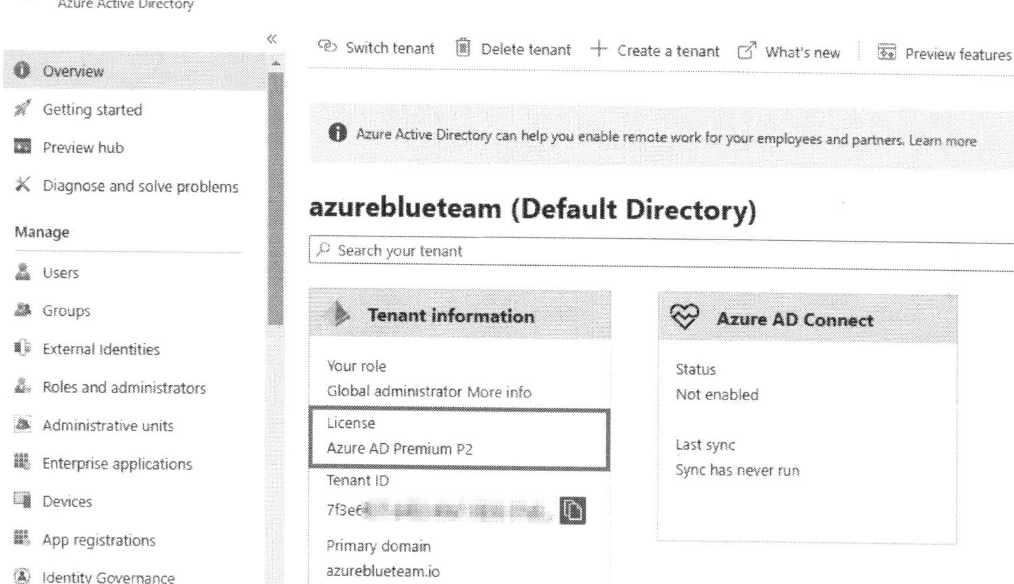

Figure 2.19 – Validating tenant license information

Leave the portal open for the upcoming exercises.

Now that you understand the different editions of Azure AD, let's look at how to manage the different objects that Azure AD supports in the next section.

Azure AD object management

There are different types of objects stored in Azure AD, with each object fulfilling a specific role regarding identity and access. The main objects that we will be covering are the following:

- Users
- Groups
- Roles
- Service principals

At the end of this section, we will be completing some hands-on exercises to create and manage the different object types that we have discussed.

Azure AD users

We mentioned in previous sections of this chapter that the primary use case for Azure AD is to manage secure authenticated access to an organization's Microsoft cloud services and applications that support modern authentication protocols regardless of where they are hosted. For users to be able to access these services that are protected by Azure AD, they need a user account. There are two main types of user accounts in Azure AD – internal and external.

Internal user accounts are user identities created in the Azure AD tenant by an administrator or user identities that are synchronized from a connected on-premises Active Directory environment to Azure AD (we will cover on-premises synchronization in *Chapter 3, Azure AD Hybrid Identity*). The UPN format of an internal user is `<alias>@domain.suffix`. For example, if I create a user called `david` in my Azure AD tenant that has a custom primary domain name of `azureblueteam.io`, the user will have a UPN of `david@azureblueteam.io`.

External user accounts are user identities from other Azure AD tenants or Microsoft accounts (`outlook.com`, `hotmail.com`, and so on) that are invited as guest users to an Azure AD tenant. The UPN format for external user accounts is `<alias>_<HomeTenant>#EXT#@domain.suffix`. For example, if a user called `brenda` who belongs to the `cloudsecnews.com` Azure AD tenant is invited as a guest user of my tenant, Brenda's UPN in my tenant will be `brenda_cloudsecnews.com#EXT#@davidpacktaz500outlook.onmicrosoft.com`:

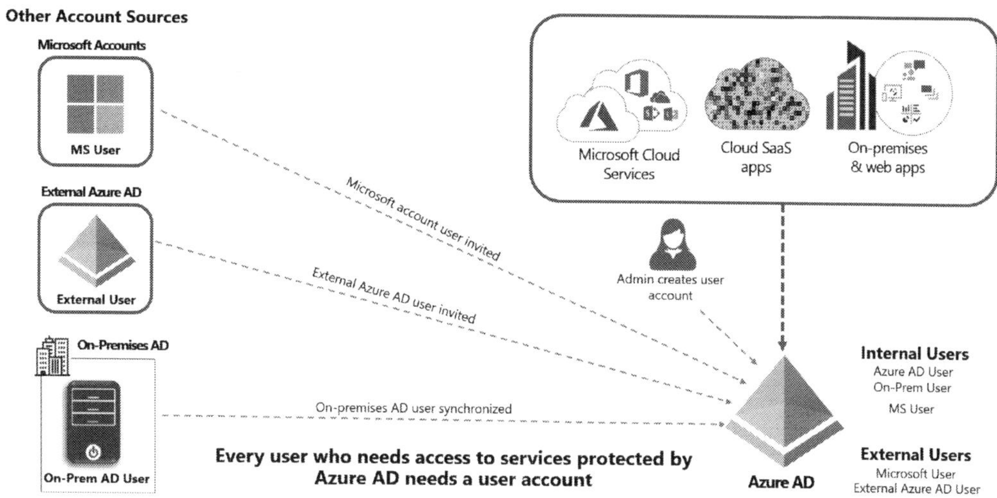

Figure 2.20 – Azure AD user account sources

Now that you understand the user object in Azure AD, in the next section, we will cover the group object in Azure AD.

Azure AD groups

Groups in Azure AD serve the same function as groups in any other identity system, they are used to organize users and they make it easier to assign and manage permissions. For example, it is more effective to assign permissions to a group than to individual users. Once access is granted to a group, future access can then be granted or revoked through group membership going forward. Like user accounts, groups can either be created by administrators in Azure AD or synchronized from a connected on-premises Active Directory environment.

Azure AD supports two types of groups: security groups, which are primarily used to manage access to shared resources, and Microsoft 365 groups, which serve a similar function to distribution groups, which you may be familiar with in Active Directory (but it can also be used to assign access to resources).

When we create groups in Azure AD, we need to specify how members will be assigned to the group. This can either be by direct assignment, where we manually add or remove users from the group (this is called **assigned** membership) or by **dynamic** assignment, where we define membership rules based on user or device attributes and the group membership is automatically derived as a result (this is called **dynamic** membership). Dynamic assignment requires a minimum of an Azure AD Premium P1 license. A dynamic group assignment can be either for devices or users, but not for both. (To make your life easier, consider assignment and membership to be synonymous terms for this paragraph.)

It is also important to note that groups can have owners and the owners do not have to be a member of the group. Group owners are able to manage the group and its membership.

Azure AD and Azure RBAC roles

The term **role** describes *a collection of permissions*. **Permission** describes an action that can be performed on a resource such as read, write, and delete. We can examine the permissions under a role to see what it allows us to do.

A key point to note is that Azure resources (deployed in our Azure subscriptions) and Azure AD have separate permission systems. This means that the roles used to grant access to Azure AD are different from the roles used to grant access to Azure resources (*Figure 2.21*):

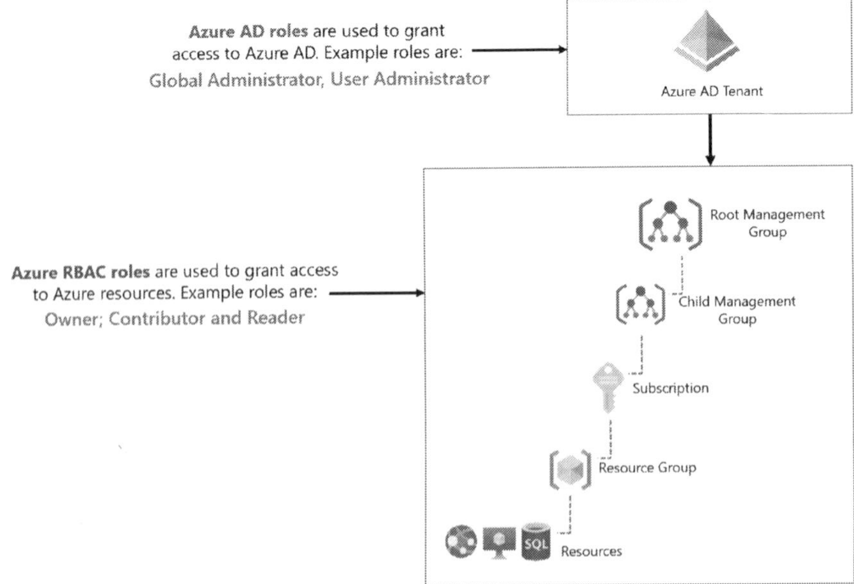

Figure 2.21 – Azure AD roles versus Azure RBAC roles

Azure AD roles are used to manage access to Azure AD while Azure **Role-Based Access Control** (**RBAC**) roles are used to manage access to Azure resources such as storage accounts, SQL databases, and so on. Both Azure AD and Azure resources have multiple built-in roles with predefined permissions that organizations may use to grant access to users and applications. Both support custom roles that are created by administrators. At the time of writing, there are currently 60 built-in Azure AD roles and over 220 Azure RBAC built-in roles. We will cover RBAC in greater detail in *Chapter 13, Azure Cloud Governance and Security Operations*, later in this book.

Service principals

It is not only users that need to authenticate to Azure AD to access resources. Applications may also need to authenticate to Azure AD! But how does Azure AD identify an application that cannot perform an interactive sign-in? It does this using a special identity called a service principal. A **service principal** is an application identity in Azure AD. You can think of it as an Azure AD object representing an application that needs access to Azure resources.

The object has a `client ID` (which you can think of as the application username) and it can either use a generated secret or an uploaded certificate as the `password`. Both the `client ID` and the `certificate` or `secret` can then be used from within an application code to authenticate to Azure AD. This is the preferred way to grant access to an application instead of creating a *dummy user account*. The process of creating a service principal for an application is called **application registration**.

Hands-on exercise – Azure AD user creation and group management

In this hands-on exercise, we will work with the two most common object types in Azure AD – users and groups. Here are the tasks that we will be completing in this exercise:

- Create three Azure AD users (Brenda Tao, Emmy Crown, and John Lakeside).
- Create a static Azure AD group called `cloud-architects` with Brenda and Emmy as members.
- Create a dynamic Azure AD group called `hr-team` that automatically adds any user whose department attribute is set to `HR` as a member.

Figure 2.22 illustrates where we will be at the end of this exercise.

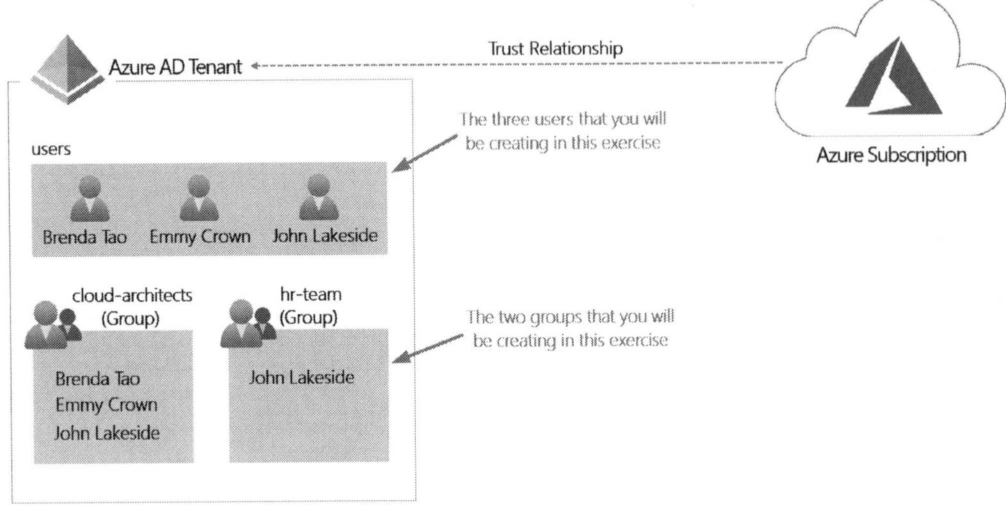

Figure 2.22 – Creating Azure AD users and groups

Let's complete the tasks with the following steps:

1. Still in the Azure AD console (within the Azure portal), under the **Manage** section, click on **Users**, then click on **New user** to create a new user:

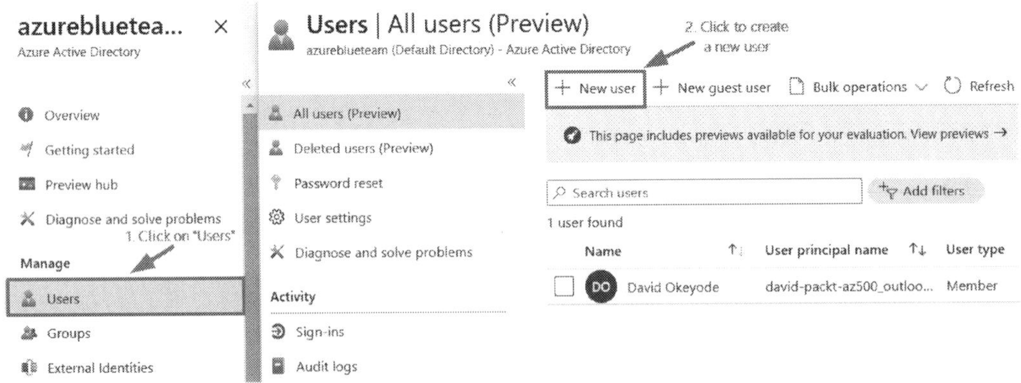

Figure 2.23 – Create a new Azure AD user

2. In the **New user** window, configure the following:

   Create User: `Selected`

   Add the following under **Identity**:

   User name: `brenda`

   Name: `Brenda Tao`

   First name: `Brenda`

   Last name: `Tao`

   Add the following under **Password**:

   Select **Let me create the password.**

   Initial Password: `QqLXXma6hAfs` (You can enter any complex password. I recommend using the same password for all the exercises to keep things simple.)

   Add the following under **Groups and roles**:

   Groups: Leave default setting:

   Roles: Leave default setting.

New user
azureblueteam (Default Directory)
Got feedback?

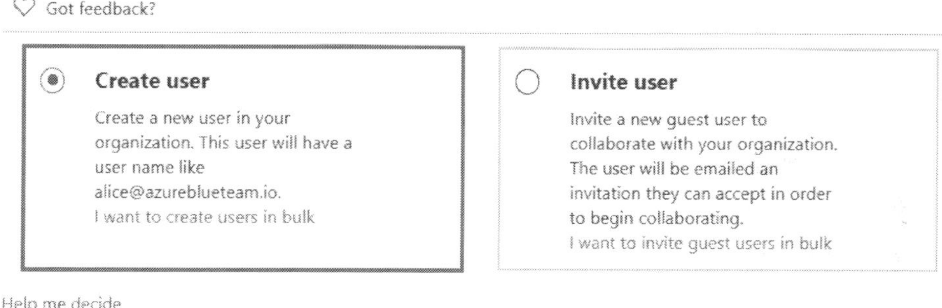
Create user
Create a new user in your organization. This user will have a user name like alice@azureblueteam.io.
I want to create users in bulk
Invite user
Invite a new guest user to collaborate with your organization. The user will be emailed an invitation they can accept in order to begin collaborating.
I want to invite guest users in bulk

Help me decide

Identity

User name * brenda @ azureblueteam.io
The domain name I need isn't shown here
Name * Brenda Tao
First name Brenda
Last name Tao

Figure 2.24 – Configure new Azure AD user

Add the following under **Settings**:

Block sign in: No (This configuration is useful if you want to create an account before a user needs it. If it is set to Yes, the account will be created but sign-in will not be allowed.)

Usage Location: Select a location close to you. I will be using **United Kingdom**.

Add the following under **Job Info**:

Job title: `Cloud Solutions Architect`

Department: `IT`

Company name: Enter the name of a fictional company. I am using `Azure Blue Team`.

Manager: Leave default setting:

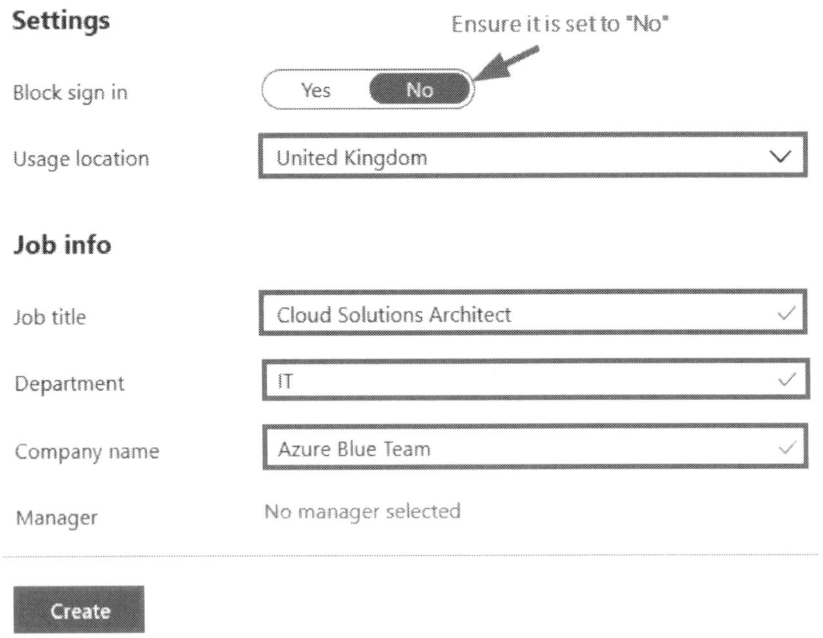

Figure 2.25 – Configure new Azure AD user

3. Repeat *Steps 1* and *2* to create the following users:

   Emmy Crown:

   User name: `emmy`

   Name: `Emmy Crown`

   Job title: `Cloud Solutions Architect`

   Department: `IT`

   John Lakeside:

   User name: `john`

   Name: `John Lakeside`

   Job title: `HR Manager`

   Department: `HR`

4. We should now have four users in Azure AD, including the three new users (*Figure 2.26*). Notice that the **Directory synced** column displays **No** for all the users. This is because they were all created directly in the cloud and not synchronized from an on-premises Active Directory server. We will cover this in a later chapter:

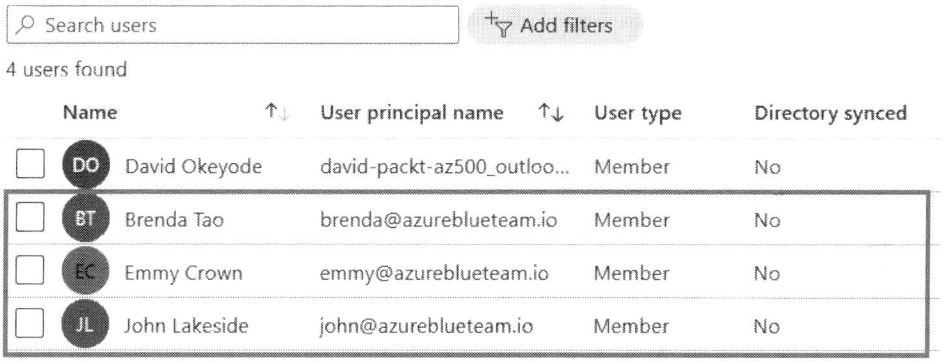

Search users | Add filters

4 users found

Name	User principal name	User type	Directory synced
DO David Okeyode	david-packt-az500_outloo...	Member	No
BT Brenda Tao	brenda@azureblueteam.io	Member	No
EC Emmy Crown	emmy@azureblueteam.io	Member	No
JL John Lakeside	john@azureblueteam.io	Member	No

Figure 2.26 – New Azure AD users

5. In the Azure AD console, under the **Manage** section, click on **Groups**, then click on **New Group** to create a new group (*Figure 2.27*):

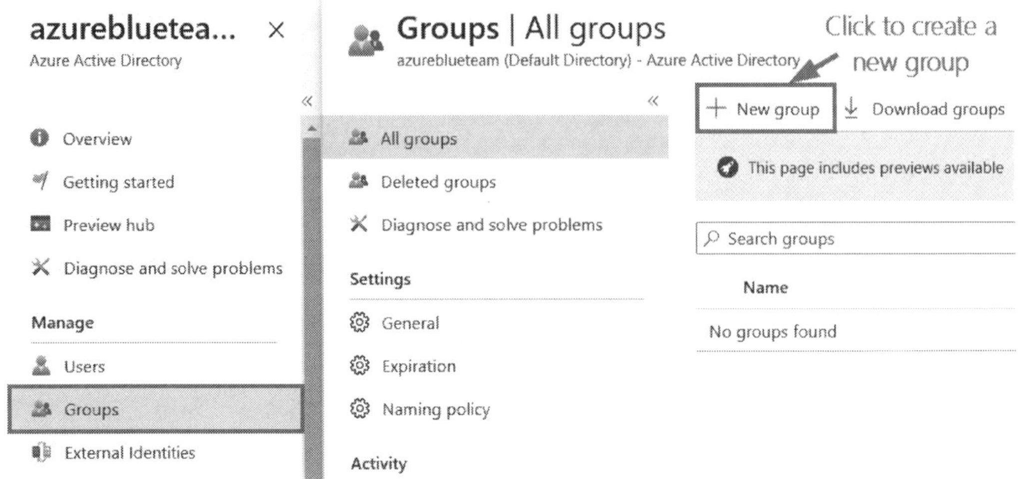

Figure 2.27 – Create a new Azure AD group

6. In the **New Group** window, configure the following:

   Group type: Security

   Group name: `cloud-architects`

   Group description: `A Group for Cloud Architects`

   Azure AD roles can be assigned to the group: **No**

   Membership type: **Assigned**

   Owners: Click on **No owners selected** → select **Brenda Tao** → click **Select**.

   Members: Click on **No members selected** → search for and select **Brenda Tao** and **Emmy Crown** → click **Select**.

   Click on **Create**.

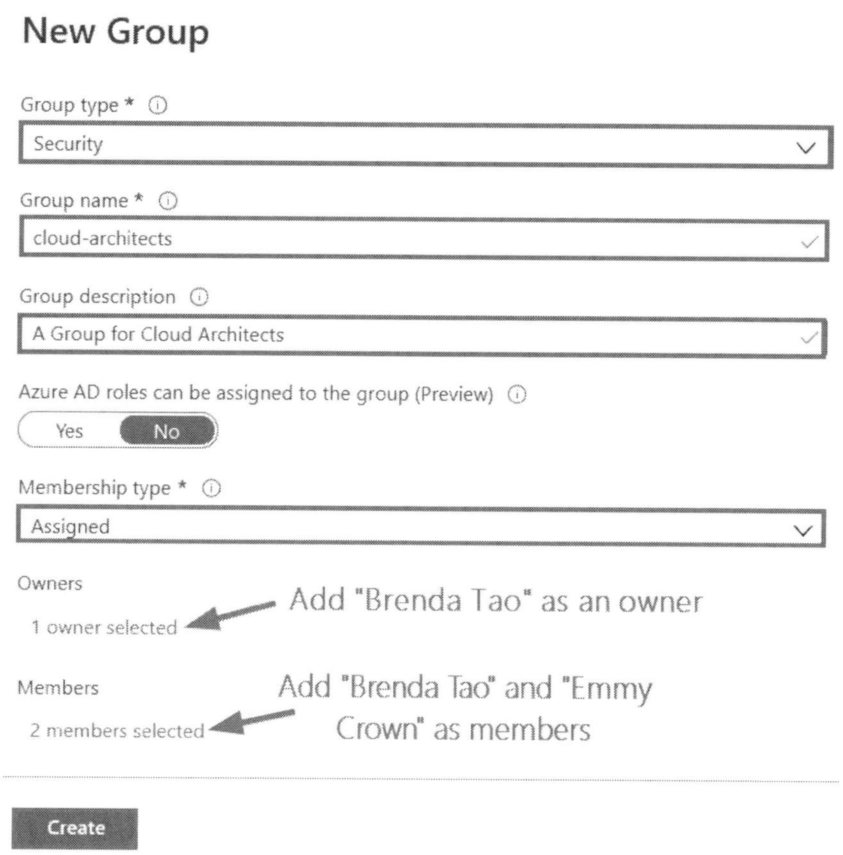

New Group

Group type *

Security

Group name *

cloud-architects

Group description

A Group for Cloud Architects

Azure AD roles can be assigned to the group (Preview)

Yes No

Membership type *

Assigned

Owners

1 owner selected

Add "Brenda Tao" as an owner

Members

2 members selected

Add "Brenda Tao" and "Emmy Crown" as members

Create

Figure 2.28 – Configure a new Azure AD group

7. In the **Groups | All Groups** window, click on **New Group** to create a second group.
8. In the **New Group** window, configure the following:

   Group type: Security

   Group name: `hr-team`

   Group description: `A Group for HR Department Members`

   Azure AD roles can be assigned to the group: **No**

   Membership type: **Dynamic User** (Notice how you can either select **Dynamic User** or **Dynamic Device** but not a mixture of both!)

   Owners: Leave default setting.

Dynamic User Members: Click on **Add dynamic query** → in the **Dynamic membership rules** window, in the **Configure Rules** section, configure the following:

Property: **department**

Operator: **equals**

Value: **HR**

Click on **Save:**

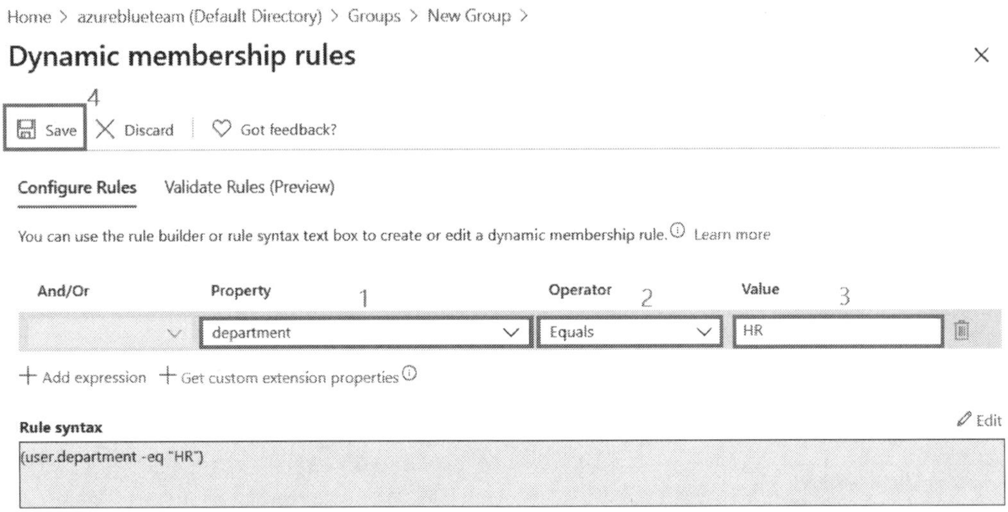

Figure 2.29 – Add a dynamic group membership rule

9. Click on **Create**.
10. We should now have two groups in Azure AD: one static group and another dynamic user group (*Figure 2.30*). Notice that the **Source** column displays **Cloud** for both groups. This is because they were all created directly in the cloud and not synchronized from an on-premises Active Directory server. Leave the window open for the next exercise:

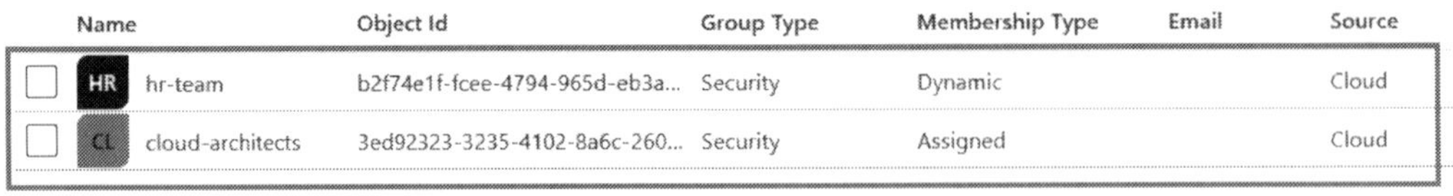

Name	Object Id	Group Type	Membership Type	Email	Source
HR hr-team	b2f74e1f-fcee-4794-965d-eb3a...	Security	Dynamic		Cloud
CL cloud-architects	3ed92323-3235-4102-8a6c-260...	Security	Assigned		Cloud

Figure 2.30 – New Azure AD groups

In this exercise, we created three Azure AD users, a static Azure AD group, and another Azure AD dynamic user group. In the next exercise, we will assign roles to these objects to grant them permissions in Azure AD and to our Azure subscription.

Hands-on exercise – Azure AD role assignment

In this hands-on exercise, we will assign permissions to users and groups using role assignments. Azure AD has a separate permission system from Azure resources. Users having permissions in Azure AD does not mean that they also have access to Azure resources. Here are the tasks that we will be completing in this exercise:

- Assign the **Global Administrator** role to `Brenda Tao` in Azure AD.
- Assign the **Owner** role to the `cloud-architects` group in our Azure subscription.

Figure 2.31 illustrates where we will be at the end of this exercise:

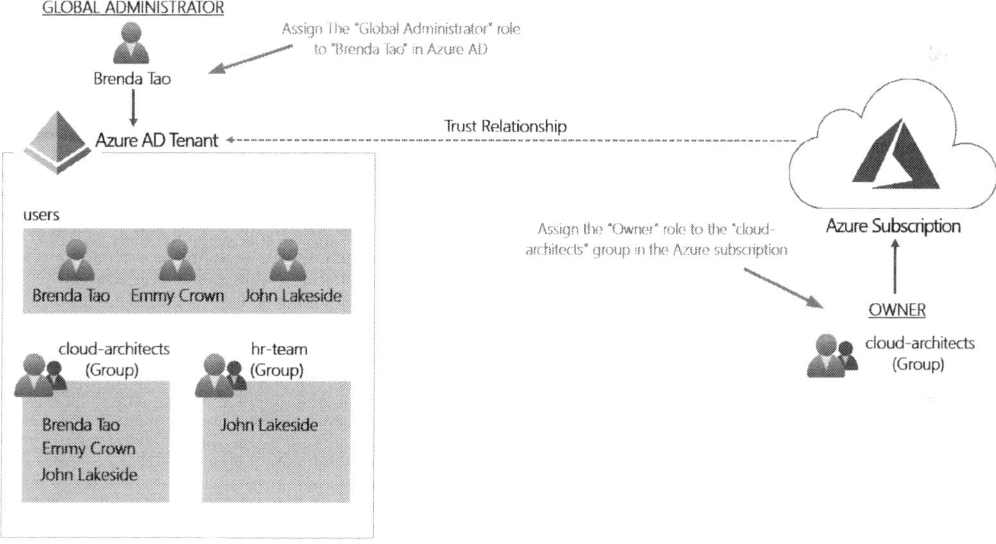

Figure 2.31 – Configuring Azure AD and Azure subscription role assignments

Let's complete these tasks with the following steps:

1. In the Azure AD console (within the Azure portal), under the **Manage** section, click on **Roles and administrators**, then select **Global administrator**. There are multiple Azure AD built-in roles that we can assign to users and we can also create custom roles:

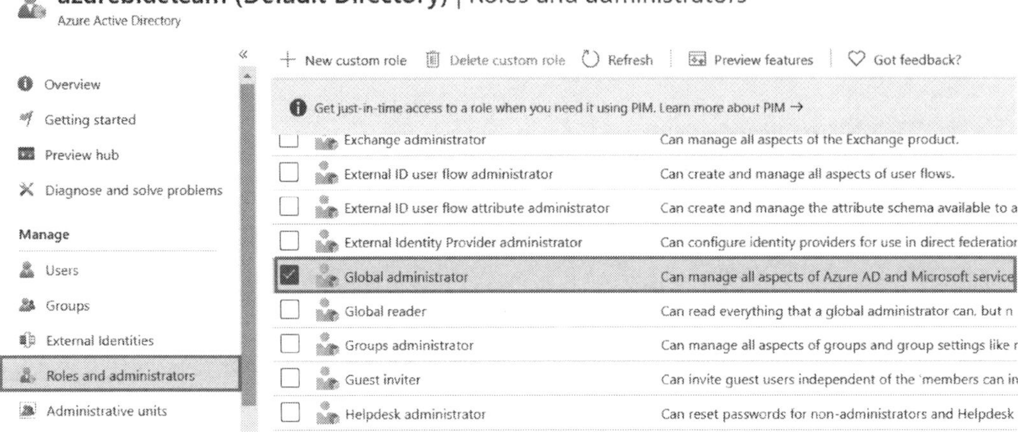

Figure 2.32 – Select an Azure AD role

2. In the **Global administrator | Assignments** window, click on **Add assignments**, select **Brenda Tao**, and click on **Add**:

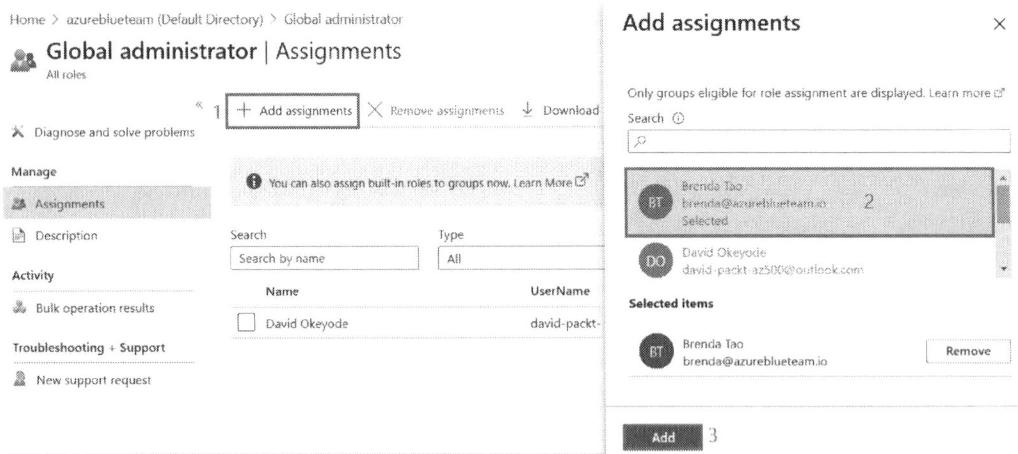

Figure 2.33 – Add an Azure AD role assignment

3. **Brenda Tao** should now be displayed as a **Global Administrator** in Azure AD:

Search

Search by name

Type

All

	Name	UserName	Type	Scope
☐	Brenda Tao	brenda@azureblueteam.io	User	Directory
☐	David Okeyode	david-packt-az500@outlook.com	User	Directory

Figure 2.34 - Azure AD Global Administrators

4. In the Azure portal, click on **Microsoft Azure** in the top-left corner to go to the home page:

Figure 2.35 – Go to the home page

5. On the home page, click on the **Subscriptions** icon:

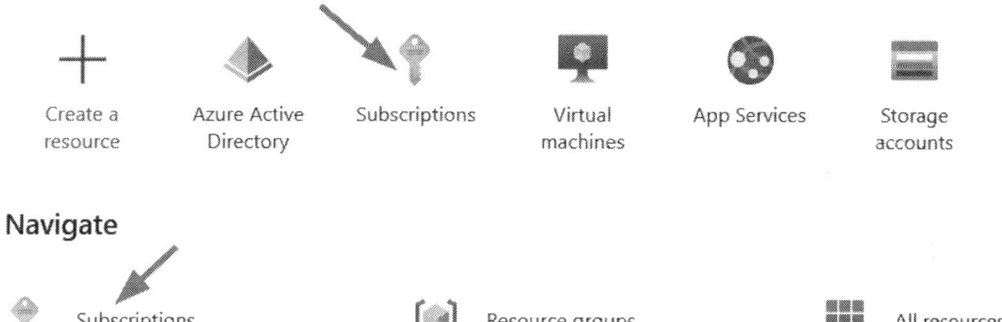

Figure 2.36 – Click on the Subscriptions icon

6. In the **Subscriptions** window, click on your Azure subscription:

Subscriptions

azureblueteam (Default Directory)

\+ Add

View list of subscriptions for which you have role-based access control (RBAC) permissions to manage Azure resources. To view subscriptions for which Showing subscriptions in azureblueteam (Default Directory) directory. Don't see a subscription? Switch directories

My role: 8 selected | Status: 3 selected

Apply

Showing 1 of 1 subscriptions | Show only subscriptions selected in the global subscriptions filter

Search

Subscription name	Subscription ID	My role
Free Trial	5d58…	Account admin

Figure 2.37 – Select your subscription

7. In the **Subscriptions** window, select **Access control (IAM)**, then click on **Add role assignments**:

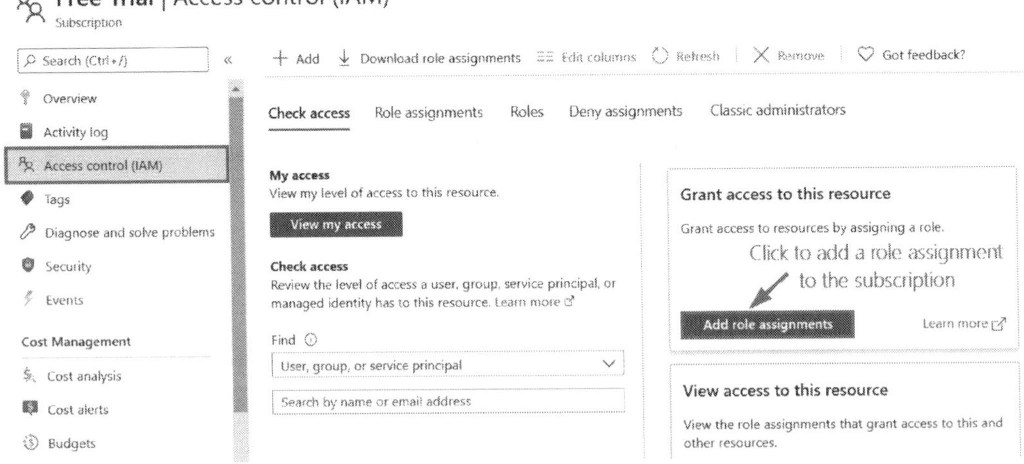

Figure 2.38 – Configure subscription role assignment

8. In the **Add role assignment** window, configure the following:

   Role: **Owner**

   Assign access to: **User, group, or service principal**

   Select the **cloud-architects** group.

   Click on **Save**:

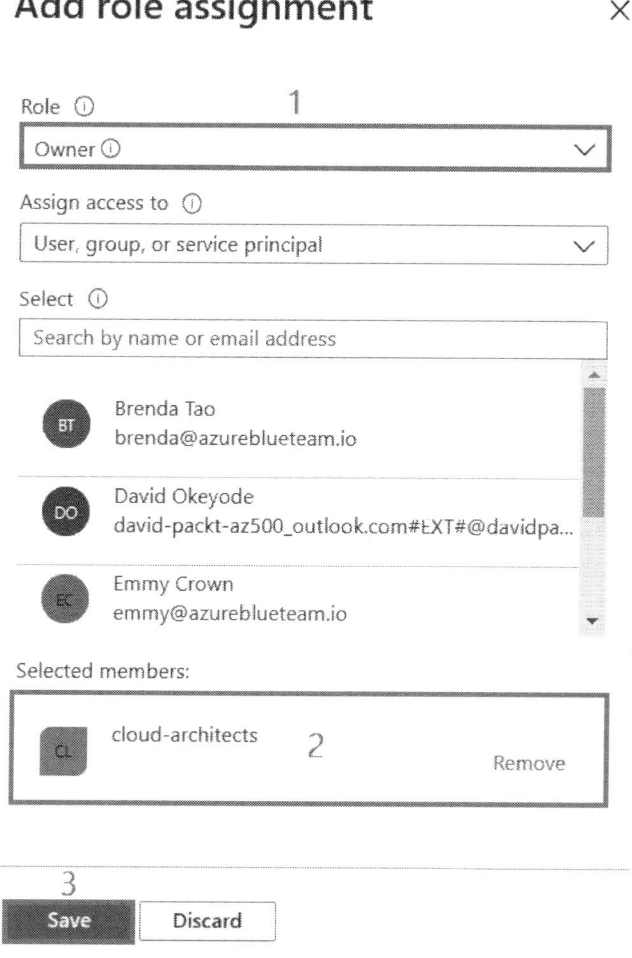

Figure 2.39 – Add role assignment

Congratulations! You have just granted permissions to users and groups in both Azure AD and an Azure subscription.

Summary

In this chapter, we laid a solid foundation of Azure AD that we will be building on in subsequent chapters. We discussed what Azure AD is, the different object types that it supports, and how to manage these object types. This information is necessary before we get into deeper discussions on managing access to Azure resources.

In the next module, we will cover how to integrate an on-premises Active Directory server with Azure AD to create a centralized identity and access framework for both on-premises legacy applications and modern cloud applications.

Questions

As we conclude, here is a list of questions for you to test your knowledge regarding this chapter's material. You will find the answers in the *Assessments* section of the *Appendix*:

1. True or False? Azure AD is on-premises Active Directory on Azure.

   a. True

   b. False

2. Which of the following is *not* a source of user identities in Azure AD?

   a. An internal user created by an administrator.

   b. An internal user synchronized from on-premises.

   c. An external user invited by an administrator.

   d. An internal user imported from ADFS.

3. Which of the following is *not* a valid Azure AD edition?

   a. Free

   b. Office 365

   c. Basic

   d. Premium P1

   e. Premium P2

4. You have the following two groups in your Azure AD tenant (*Figure 2.41*):

Name	Type	Membership
London-Group	Security	Dynamic user membership type that contains all London users
Chicago-Group	Security	Dynamic user membership type that contains all Chicago users

Figure 2.40 – Add role assignment

You have a requirement to add all London users and their devices into `London-Group`. What should you do?

a. Delete `London-Group`. Create a new group named `London-Group` that has a membership type of Office 365. Add users and devices to the group.

b. Add a membership rule to `London-Group`.

c. Change the membership type of `London-Group` to `Assigned`. Create two new groups that have dynamic memberships. Add the new groups to `London-Group`.

d. Modify the membership rule of `London-Group`.

Further reading

To learn more on the topics covered in this chapter, you can refer to the following links:

- Azure AD Built-In Roles: `https://docs.microsoft.com/en-us/azure/active-directory/roles/permissions-reference`
- Azure RBAC Built-In Roles: `https://docs.microsoft.com/en-us/azure/role-based-access-control/built-in-roles`
- Azure Custom Roles: `https://docs.microsoft.com/en-us/azure/role-based-access-control/custom-roles`

3
Azure AD Hybrid Identity

Most organizations are not starting from nothing when they adopt Azure. They already have an identity solution such as **Active Directory Domain Services** (**AD DS**) on-premises to manage identity and access for existing applications. As it is *not* an effective strategy to maintain multiple *independent* silos of user credentials, how should such organizations approach their adoption of Azure and Azure **Active Directory** (**AD**)? Luckily, Azure AD supports the synchronization of identities from existing on-premises AD using a tool called **Azure AD Connect**.

In this chapter, you will learn about this tool, the concepts to consider before deploying it, the different authentication options that it supports, and how to choose the best authentication option for your use case. By the end of this chapter, you will understand by practice how to implement Azure AD Connect to establish a hybrid identity architecture between your on-premises AD and Azure AD.

Here are the topics that we will cover in this chapter:

- Implementing Azure AD hybrid identity
- Selecting a hybrid identity authentication method
- Implementing password writeback in a hybrid identity scenario

Technical requirements

To follow along with the instructions in this chapter, you will need the following:

- A PC with an internet connection.
- An Azure subscription. You can use the same subscription that you set up in the first chapter of this book.
- An on-premises AD domain environment. The first exercise in this chapter will walk you through the setup of an environment.

Implementing Azure AD hybrid identity

Maintaining multiple *independent* silos of user credentials carries with it an increased risk of a data breach. How many times have we heard of security breaches that happened as a result of ex-employees having unrevoked access to sensitive systems after leaving their former organization? The access should have been disabled but because the victim organization had many *independent* access control systems, it was missed. One solution to this is to establish a centralized identity system where the provisioning and de-provisioning of user identities happen in one place. This way, if a user leaves an organization, the user account only needs to be disabled once in the central system! This is exactly what Azure AD Connect can help organizations that already have an on-premises AD DS solution to achieve as they adopt Azure AD.

Azure AD Connect

So, what is Azure AD Connect? It is a tool that can be used to synchronize objects such as user accounts and groups from an on-premises AD DS environment into Azure AD. It can be installed on-premises on any domain-joined Windows Server 2012 or later system.

Once deployed and configured, on-premises AD DS becomes the *source of truth* for digital identities in the organization. What this means is that **users**, **groups**, and **contact objects** in on-premises AD DS are automatically synchronized to Azure AD (*Figure 3.1*). This allows us to centralize digital identity provisioning and management:

- When new objects are created on-premises, they are automatically created in Azure AD.
- When those objects are disabled on-premises, they are automatically disabled in Azure AD.
- When those objects are deleted on-premises, they are automatically deleted in Azure AD.

- When the attributes of those objects are modified on-premises, the modifications are automatically applied in Azure AD.

It is important to clarify that when we use the term *objects* in relation to Azure AD Connect synchronization, this only applies to user, group, and contact objects. For example, computer objects or shared folder objects in on-premises AD DS are not synchronized to Azure AD. We can also configure the scope of synchronization based on domains, **Organizational Units** (**OUs**), group membership, or attribute values (we will cover this in more detail later):

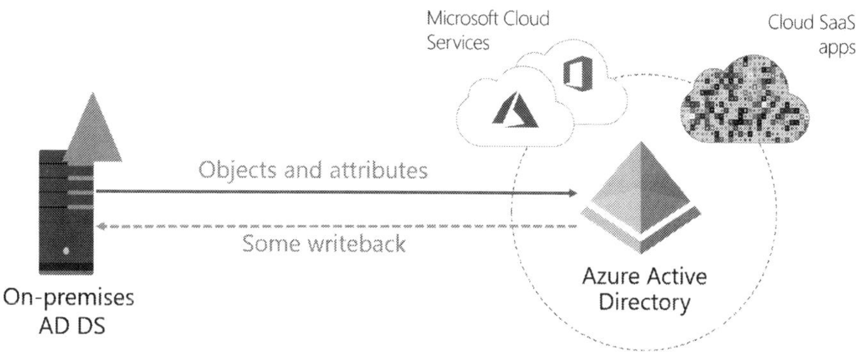

Figure 3.1 – Azure AD Connect

Apart from synchronizing AD DS objects and their attributes to Azure AD, Azure AD Connect can also facilitate some writeback from Azure AD to on-premises AD DS. This opens up interesting use cases, such as self-service password reset.

Preparing for Azure AD Connect installation

Before deploying the Azure AD Connect tool, there are three essential steps that are recommended to prepare for the installation:

- Prepare a system running Windows Server 2012 or above in our on-premises environment. This will be the system that we will deploy the Azure AD Connect tool on. Apart from the operating system requirement, it also needs to be joined to our on-premises domain.
- Prepare two accounts with required permissions in on-premises AD DS and Azure AD. Installing and configuring Azure AD Connect requires *an Azure AD account with the Global Administrator role assignment* and *an on-premises AD DS account with Enterprise Administrator permissions*. The Enterprise Administrator permission in on-premises AD DS is required to create a synchronized user account in AD DS and it is only required when we install and configure Azure AD Connect.

- Perform a health check on the on-premises AD DS objects to identify and remediate potential issues that may lead to synchronization errors later. A good tool to use for this is the free Microsoft **IdFix** tool. The tool can be used to identify common issues such as duplicate or malformed `proxyAddresses` and `userPrincipalName`. We will be using this tool in our hands-on exercise:

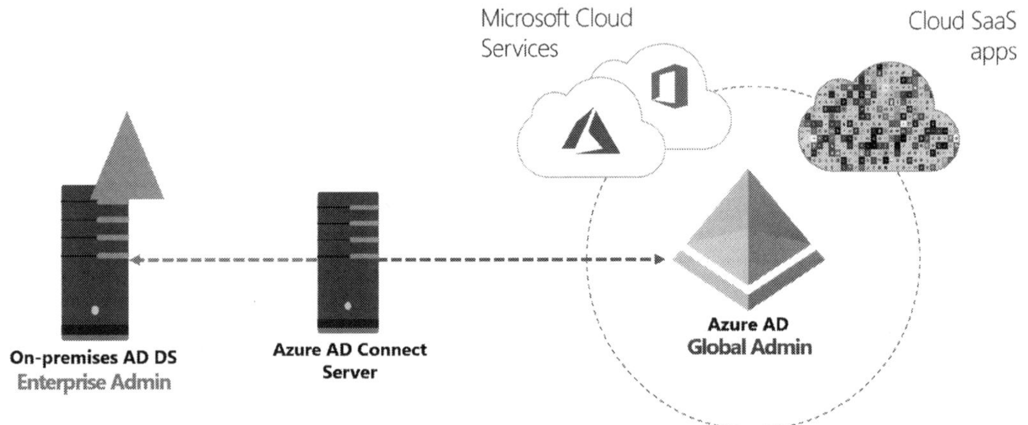

Figure 3.2 – Azure AD Connect pre-deployment preparation

Now that you have an idea of the steps needed to prepare for the implementation of Azure AD hybrid identity, we will proceed to deploy an AD domain controller, which we will use to complete other exercises that we will cover in this chapter.

Hands-on exercise – deploying an Azure VM hosting an AD domain controller

In this hands-on exercise, we will complete the following tasks:

- **Task 1**: Deploy an Azure VM hosting an AD domain controller.
- **Task 2**: Create test users in AD DS.

Task 1 – deploying an Azure VM hosting an AD domain controller

Let's follow these steps:

1. Open a web browser and browse to this GitHub Azure Quickstart template: `https://github.com/Azure/azure-quickstart-templates/tree/master/application-workloads/active-directory/active-directory-new-domain`.

2. On the **Create a new Windows VM and create a new AD Forest, Domain and DC** page, click on **Deploy to Azure**:

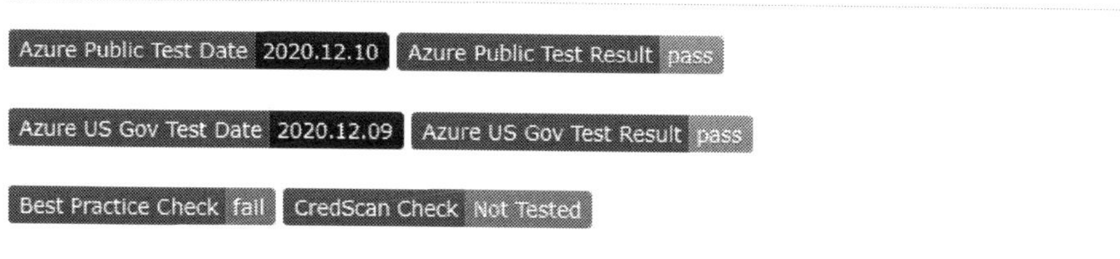

This template will deploy a new VM (along with a new VNet and Load Balancer) and will configure it as a Domain Controller and create a new forest and domain.

Click the button below to deploy

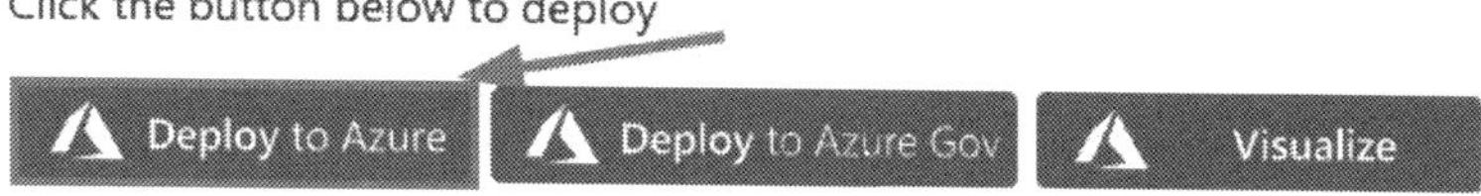

Figure 3.3 – Deploying a template to Azure

3. Sign in to the portal using the account that you used to sign up for your Azure account:

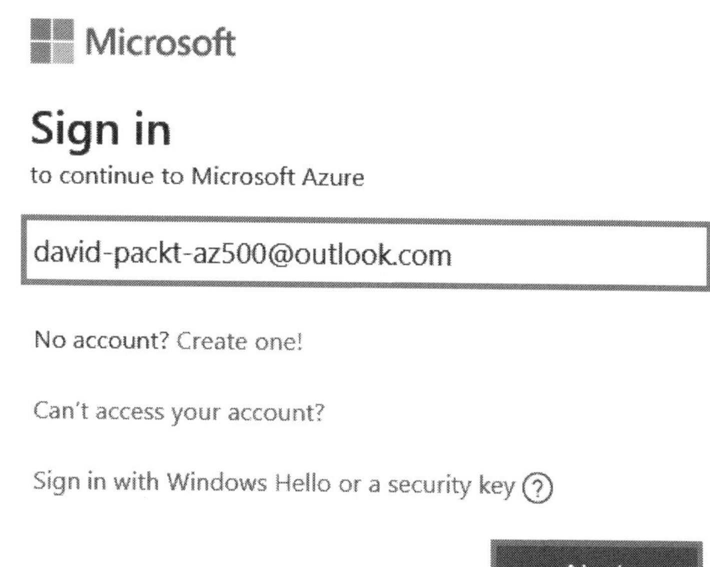

Figure 3.4 – Signing in to the Azure portal

4. On the **Create an Azure VM with a new AD Forest** blade, initiate a template deployment with the following settings:

   Subscription: Select your subscription.

   Resource group: **Create new** | **Name**: `onpremises-rg`.

   Region: Select the Azure region closest to your location.

   Admin Username: `onpremadmin`.

   Admin Password: `QqLXXma6hAfs` (you can enter any complex password. I recommend using the same password for all the exercises to keep things simple).

   Domain Name: `az500lab.com`.

   Dns Prefix: `az500lab-XXXXX` (enter a random number to replace the `XXXXX` placeholder).

   Vm Size: `Standard_D2s_v3`.

5. Accept the default values for the remaining settings.
6. Click **Review + create**:

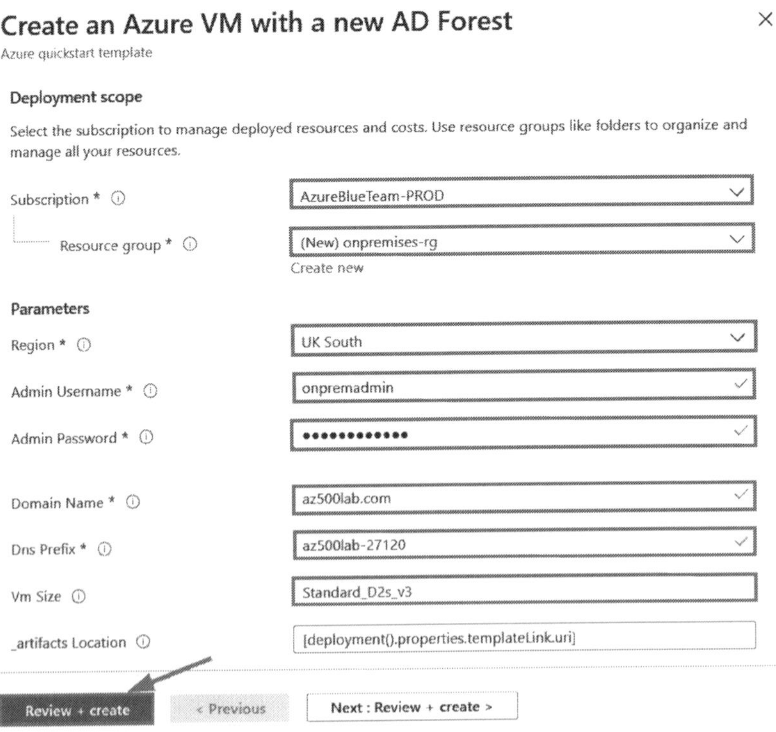

Figure 3.5 – Configuring the template parameters

After the validation has passed, click **Create**:

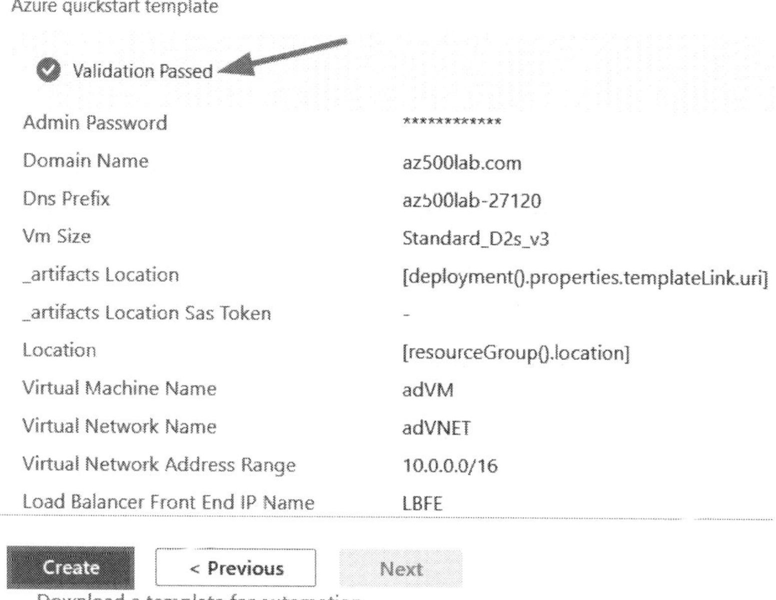

Figure 3.6 – Deploying the template

7. Wait for the deployment to complete. It could take between 15 to 20 minutes to complete so feel free to come back to it later. After the deployment has completed, click on **Go to resource group**:

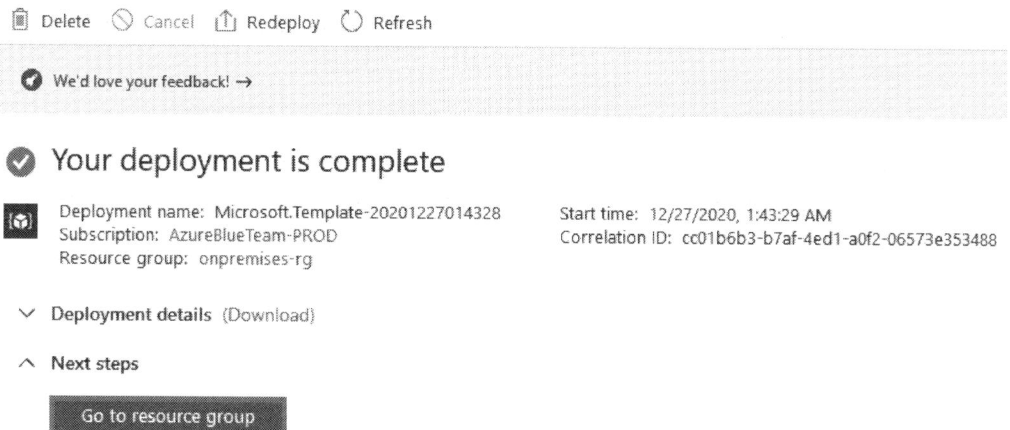

Figure 3.7 – Waiting for the deployment to complete

8. In the **onpremises-rg** resource group blade, click on the deployed **adVM** VM resource:

Filter by name... | Type == **all** | Location == **all** | Add filter

Showing 1 to 8 of 8 records. ☐ Show hidden types

Name	Type	Location
adAvailabiltySet	Availability set	UK South
adLoadBalancer	Load balancer	UK South
adNic	Network interface	UK South
adPublicIP	Public IP address	UK South
adVM	Virtual machine	UK South
adVM_DataDisk	Disk	UK South
adVM_OSDisk	Disk	UK South
adVNET	Virtual network	UK South

Figure 3.8 – Clicking on the adVM VM resource

9. In the **adVM** blade, in the **Overview** section, copy the **DNS name** value:

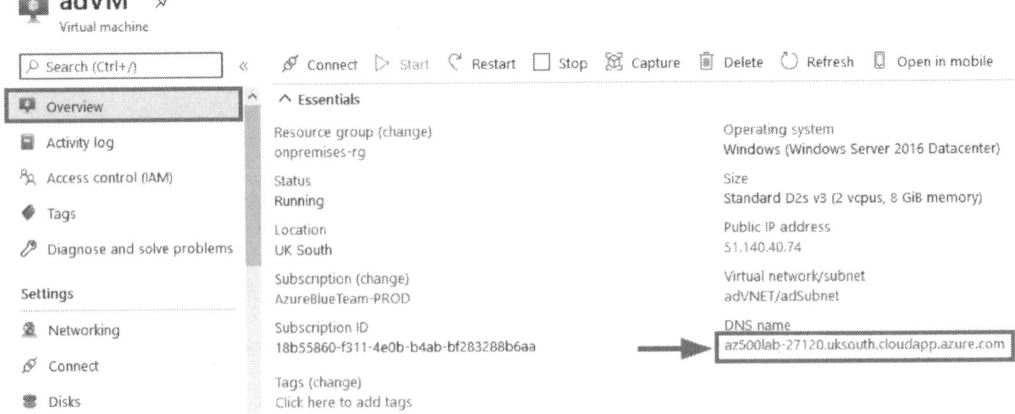

Figure 3.9 – Copying the adVM DNS name

10. On your system, open the **Remote Desktop Connection** (**RDP**) client and enter the DNS name that you copied earlier, then click on **Connect**:

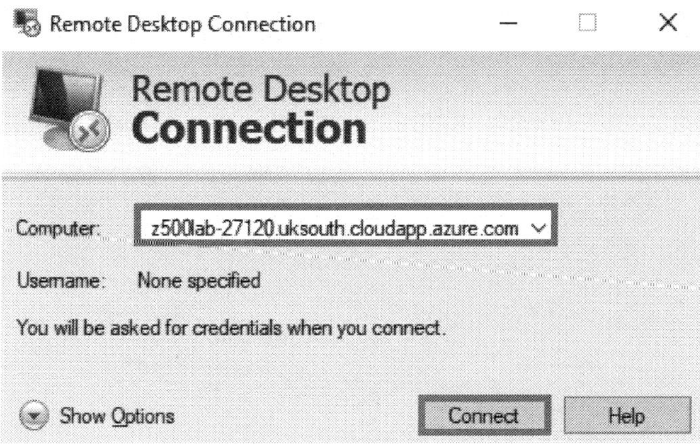

Figure 3.10 – Connecting to the adVM VM using RDP

11. In the **Windows Security** prompt, click on **More choices** | **Use a different account** and enter the following details:

    Username: `onpremadmin`

    Password: `QqLXXma6hAfs` (or the password that you entered in *Step 4*)

12. Click **OK** to connect:

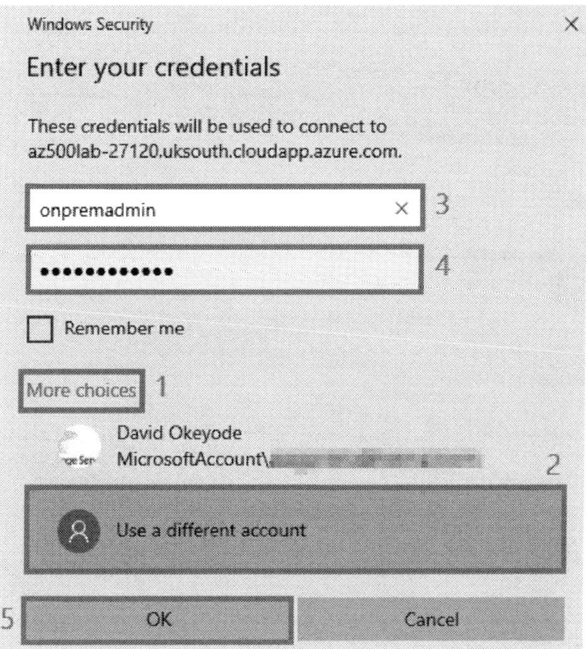

Figure 3.11 – Connecting to the adVM VM using RDP

13. In the security prompt that comes up, select **Don't ask me again for connections to this computer** to prevent future prompts on certificate trust. Click **Yes**:

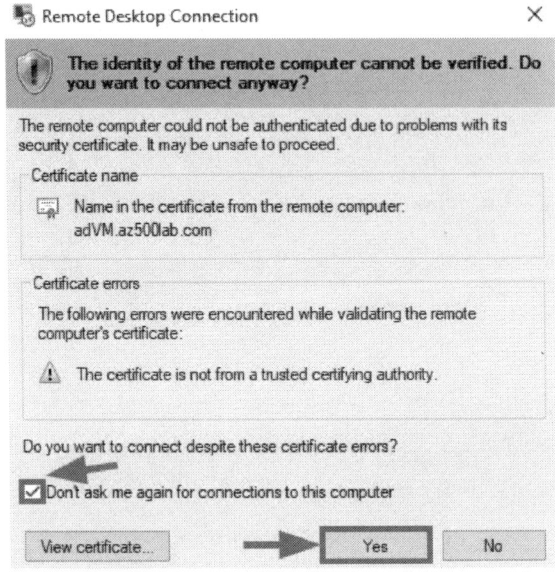

Figure 3.12 – Skipping future certificate trust prompts

You should now be connected to the VM using RDP:

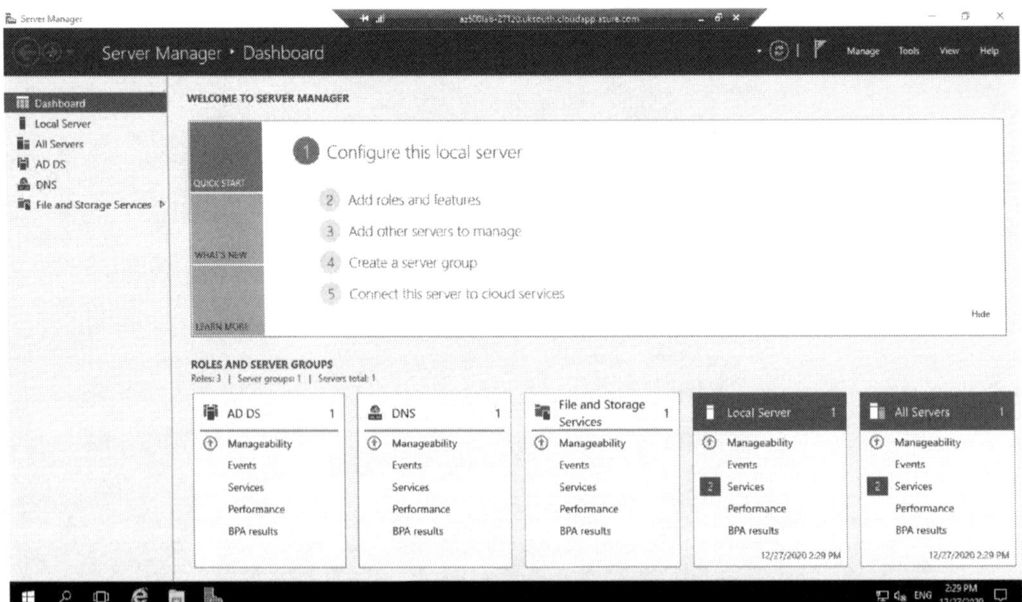

Figure 3.13 – Connected to the adVM VM

Now that we've completed *Task 1*, let's move on to *Task 2*.

Task 2 – creating test users in AD DS

Let's follow these steps:

1. Within the RDP session to the **adVM** VM, right-click the Start button (lower-left corner) and click on **Command Prompt (Admin)** to open the command console as an administrator:

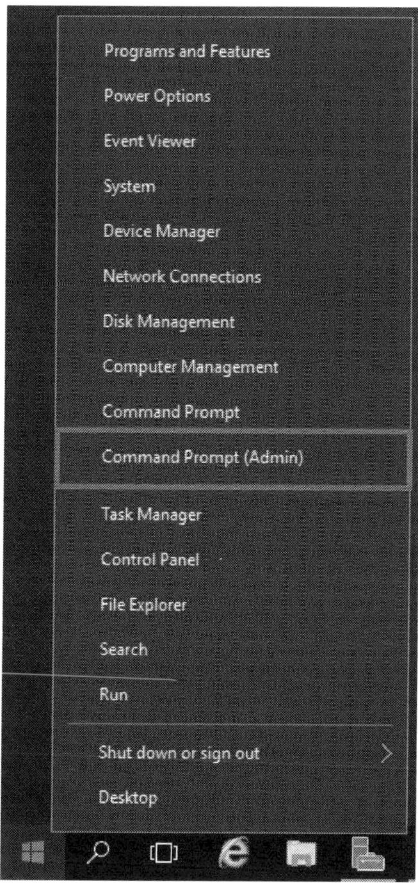

Figure 3.14 – Opening the command console as an administrator

2. Within the command-line console, type `powershell` and press *Enter* to switch to the PowerShell console:

```
powershell
```

This is what it looks like in the console:

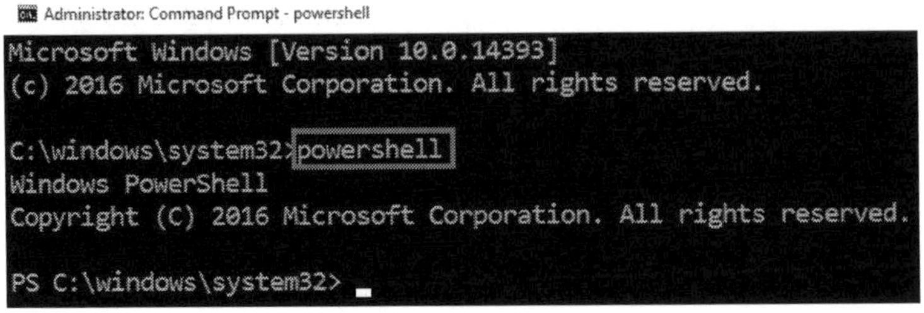

```
Administrator: Command Prompt - powershell
Microsoft Windows [Version 10.0.14393]
(c) 2016 Microsoft Corporation. All rights reserved.

C:\windows\system32>powershell
Windows PowerShell
Copyright (C) 2016 Microsoft Corporation. All rights reserved.

PS C:\windows\system32>
```

Figure 3.15 – Switching to the PowerShell console

3. Within the PowerShell console, run the following commands to download and run a script that will create test users and groups. Note that the script assumes that you used the `az500lab.com` domain name when you deployed the domain controller:

```
New-Item -Path "c:\" -Name "packtaz500" -ItemType
"directory"

Set-Location -Path "c:\packtaz500"

Invoke-WebRequest -Uri "https://raw.githubusercontent.
com/davidokeyode/azure-offensive/master/
packtaz500testusers.ps1" -OutFile "packtaz500testusers.
ps1"

.\packtaz500testusers.ps1
```

When prompted to enter a password for the test users, enter the password `QqLXXma6hAfs` (or any other complex password. It is recommended to use the same password as earlier to keep things simple):

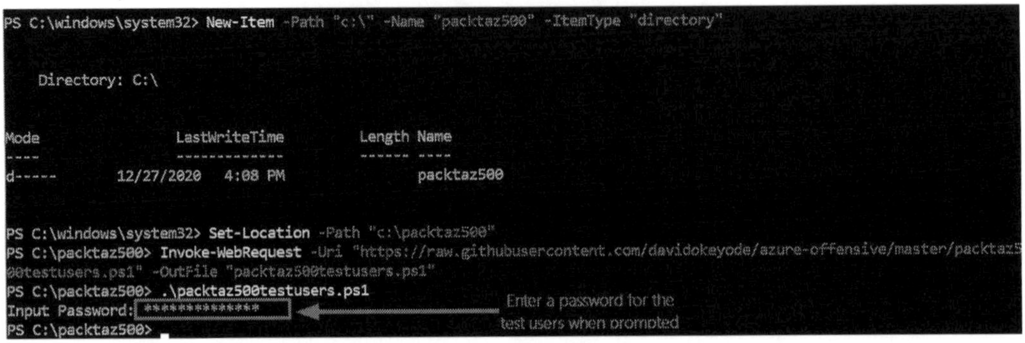

```
PS C:\windows\system32> New-Item -Path "c:\" -Name "packtaz500" -ItemType "directory"


    Directory: C:\


Mode                LastWriteTime         Length Name
----                -------------         ------ ----
d-----       12/27/2020   4:08 PM                packtaz500


PS C:\windows\system32> Set-Location -Path "c:\packtaz500"
PS C:\packtaz500> Invoke-WebRequest -Uri "https://raw.githubusercontent.com/davidokeyode/azure-offensive/master/packtaz5
00testusers.ps1" -OutFile "packtaz500testusers.ps1"
PS C:\packtaz500> .\packtaz500testusers.ps1
Input Password: ************
PS C:\packtaz500>
```

Enter a password for the test users when prompted

Figure 3.16 – Entering a password when prompted

4. In the PowerShell console, enter `dsa.msc` and press *Enter* to open Active Directory Users and Computers:

Figure 3.17 – Opening Active Directory Users and Computers

5. Review the OU called **OrgUsers** to see the OUs, groups, and users created by the script:

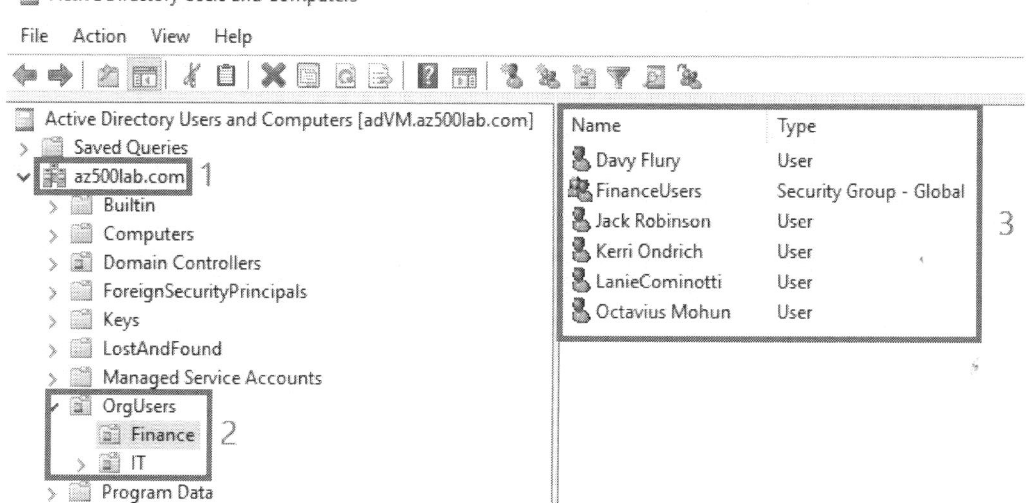

Figure 3.18 – Reviewing AD objects

Leave the RDP session open for later exercises in this chapter.

Hands-on exercise – preparing for Azure AD Connect deployment

In this section, we'll carry out two tasks:

- **Task 1**: Create an Azure AD user with the Global Administrator role.
- **Task 2**: Run IdFix to identify and remediate potential object synchronization issues.

Unlike in the previous section, we'll cover both tasks in one set of instructions:

1. In the Azure portal, go to the Azure AD console:

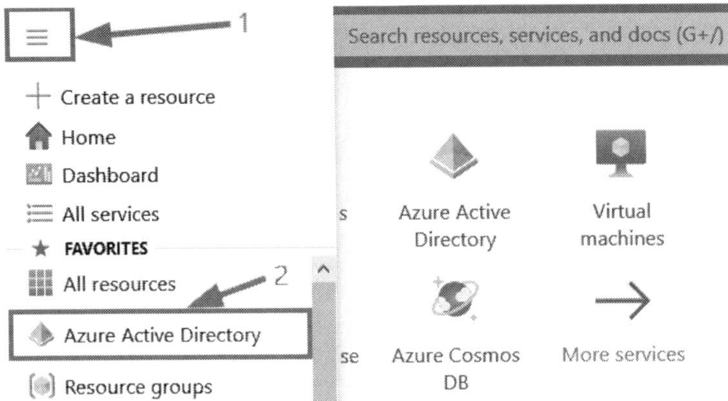

Figure 3.19 – Deploying the template

2. In the Azure AD console, click on **Users** and then click on **New user**:

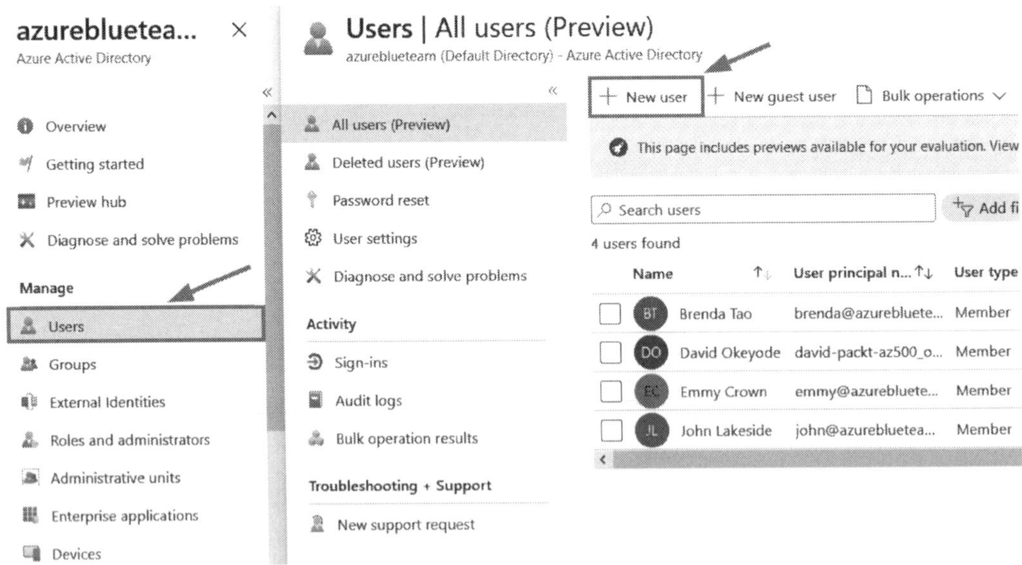

Figure 3.20 – Creating a syncadmin user

3. In the **New user** blade, create a new user with the following settings:

   User name: `syncadmin`, and select **@<Azure-AD-DNS-domain-name>** where **<Azure-AD-DNS-domain-name>** represents the default Azure AD primary DNS domain. You will need it later in this lab.

Name: `syncadmin`.

Password: Click **Let me create the password** and type `QqLXXma6hAfs` (you can enter any complex password in the initial password text box).

Groups: **0 groups selected**.

Roles: Click **User** and select **Global administrator**.

> **Important Note**
> An Azure AD user with the Global Administrator role is required to implement Azure AD Connect.

4. Accept the default values for the remaining settings.
5. Click **Create**:

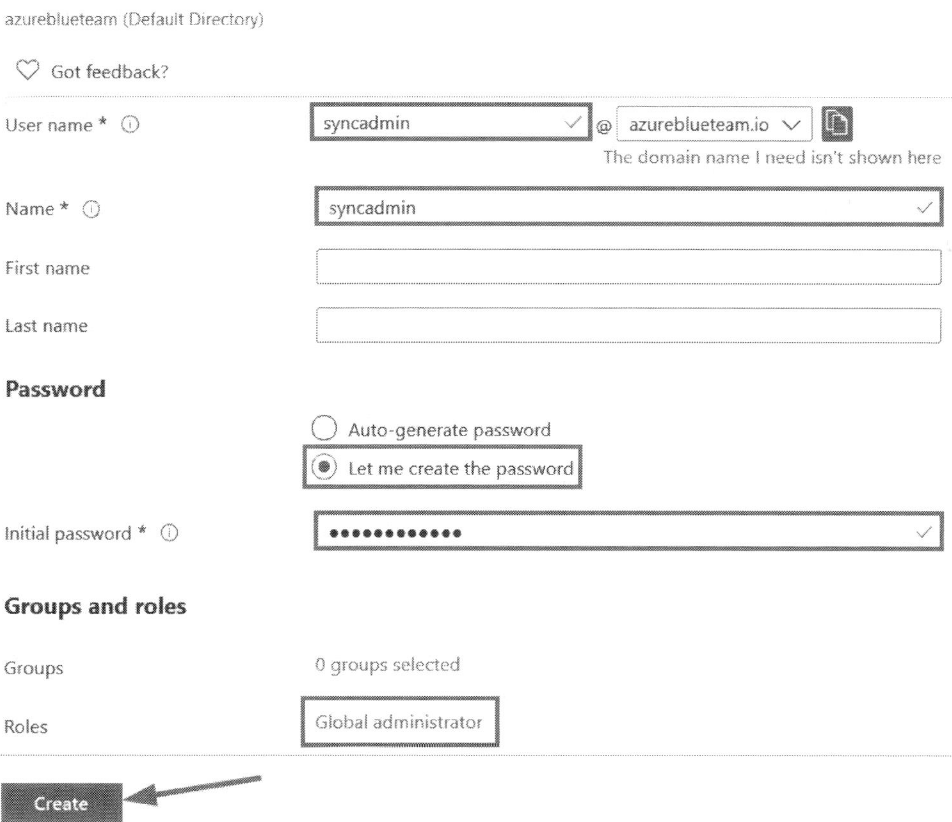

Figure 3.21 – Creating the syncadmin user

6. Open an InPrivate browser window (or Incognito if you are using Chrome), browse to the Azure portal, `https://portal.azure.com`, sign in with the `syncadmin` temporary credentials, and update it when prompted:

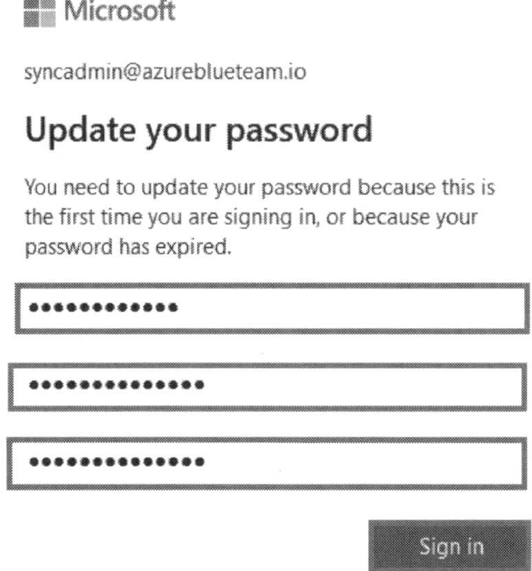
Microsoft
syncadmin@azureblueteam.io
Update your password
You need to update your password because this is the first time you are signing in, or because your password has expired.
Sign in

Figure 3.22 – Updating the syncadmin credentials

7. In the RDP session to the **adVM** VM, open PowerShell as an administrator if you have closed the previous session, then run the following commands to download and run the **IdFix** tool:

```
Set-Location -Path "c:\packtaz500"

[Net.ServicePointManager]::SecurityProtocol
= [Net.SecurityProtocolType]::Tls, [Net.
SecurityProtocolType]::Tls11, [Net.
SecurityProtocolType]::Tls12, [Net.
SecurityProtocolType]::Ssl3

[Net.ServicePointManager]::SecurityProtocol = "Tls,
Tls11, Tls12, Ssl3"

Invoke-WebRequest -Uri "https://github.com/microsoft/
idfix/raw/master/publish/setup.exe" -OutFile "idfix.exe"

.\idfix.exe install
```

8. In the **Application Install - Security Warning** window, click **Install**:

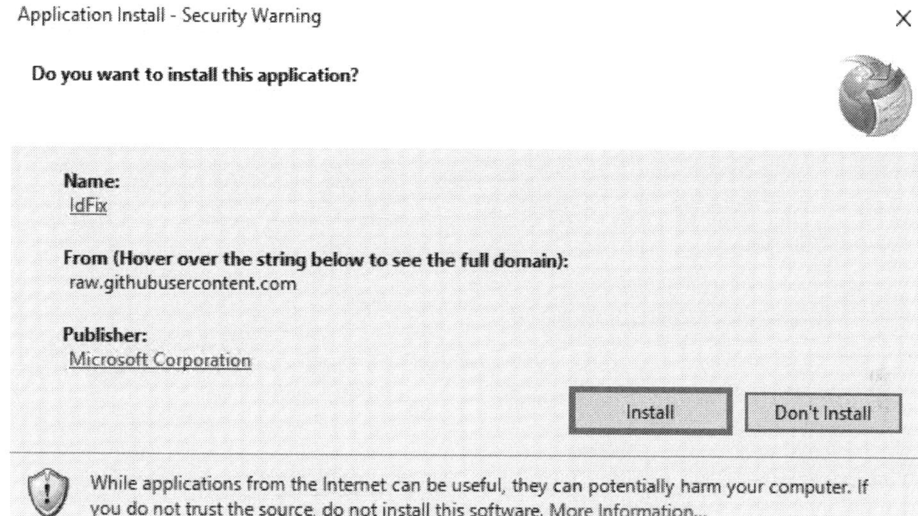

Figure 3.23 – Clicking to install IdFix

9. In the **Open File - Security Warning** window, click on **Run**:

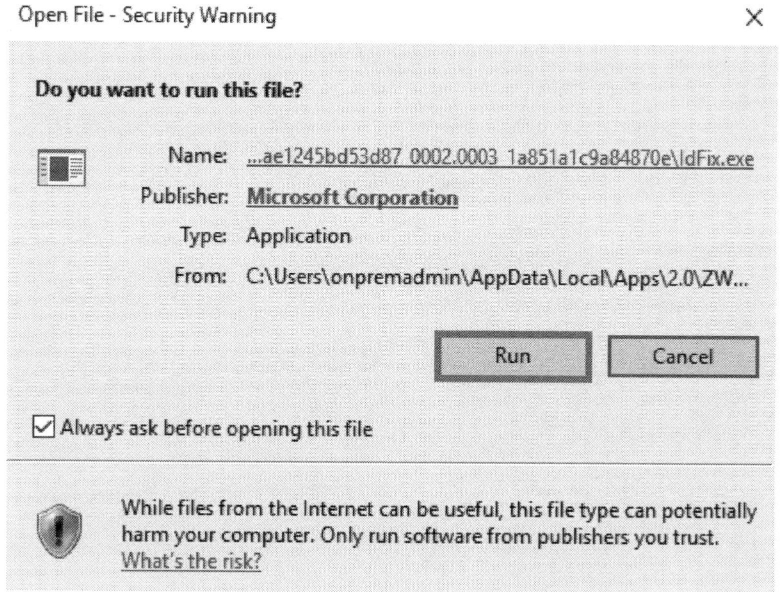

Figure 3.24 – Clicking to run IdFix

10. In the **IdFix Privacy Statement** message box, click **OK**:

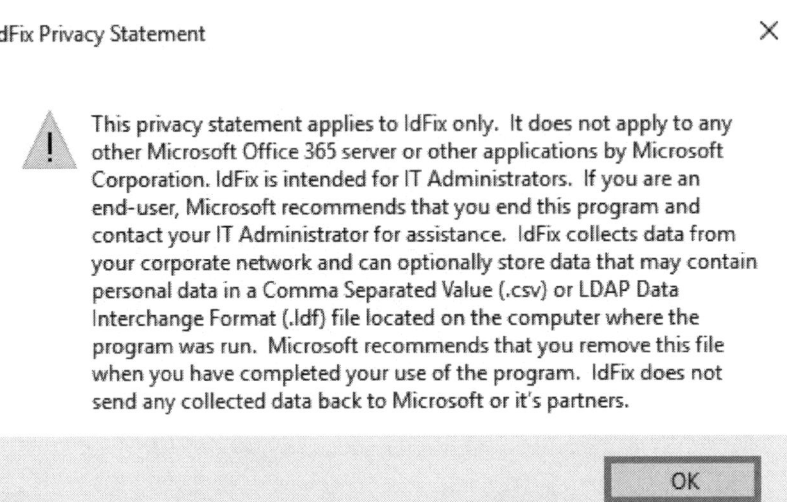

Figure 3.25 – Clicking to accept the privacy terms

In the IdFix toolbar, click **Query**. You should see a few objects with errors but the one that we are concerned with is the error for the user object named `Kerri Ondrich`. You can see that IdFix has identified invalid characters in the **userPrincipalName** attribute and also proposed a fix in the **UPDATE** column.

To apply the fix, set the **ACTION** column for the user object to **EDIT**, then click on **Apply**:

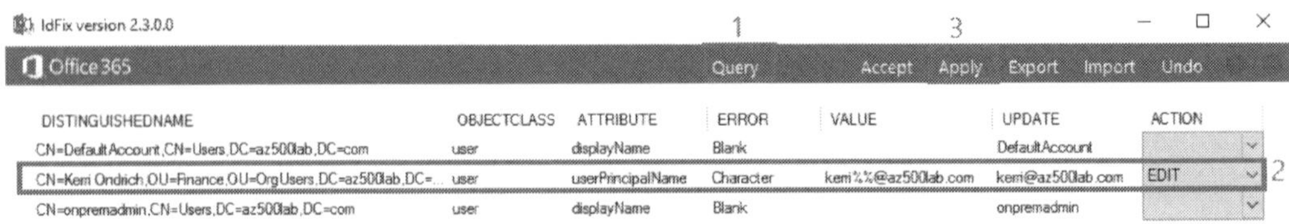

Figure 3.26 – Applying the recommended fix to a user object

11. In the **Apply Pending** dialog box, click **Yes**.:

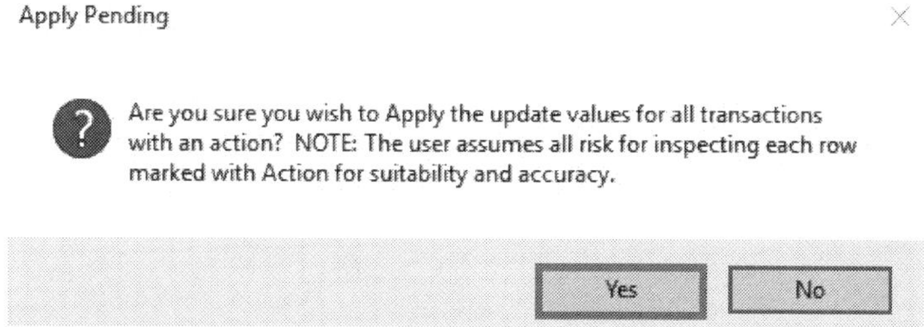

Figure 3.27 – Clicking Yes to apply the update

Notice the **COMPLETE** status in the **ACTION** column, which indicates a successful write

12. In the IdFix toolbar, click **Query** again to verify that the error for the user object named `Kerri Ondrich` is no longer displayed (as it has been corrected).

Congratulations! You have successfully prepared your on-premises AD environment for integration with Azure AD. In the next section, we will start reviewing some of the choices that we need to make when implementing hybrid identity.

Selecting a hybrid identity authentication method

When implementing Azure AD Connect using custom settings, we have the option to choose the authentication method that we want to use. There are three options that are available:

- **Password Hash Synchronization** (**PHS**)
- Federation
- **Pass-Through Authentication** (**PTA**)

PHS is one of the authentication methods that we can implement when we configure hybrid identity using Azure AD Connect. It is the default option. So, how do we implement this authentication method?

1. First, we install Azure AD Connect on-premises. This creates a secure outbound connection between on-premises AD DS and Azure AD.

2. We select the PHS option and configure the scope of synchronization that identifies the boundary of the objects that we want Azure AD Connect to synchronize to Azure AD.
3. Azure AD Connect synchronizes the user objects, attributes, and password hashes from an on-premises AD DS instance to Azure AD:

> **Important Note**
>
> Passwords are never stored in clear text or encrypted with a reversible algorithm in Azure AD but are hashed with a strong one-way hashing algorithm such as SHA256. When Azure AD Connect synchronizes the password hash of user objects, it synchronizes a SHA256 hash of the original MD4 hash that is stored in on-premises AD DS. This is a security measure to prevent an on-premises pass-the-hash attack in the unlikely event that the hash stored in Azure AD is stolen. You can read more about this here: `https://docs.microsoft.com/en-us/azure/active-directory/hybrid/how-to-connect-password-hash-synchronization`.

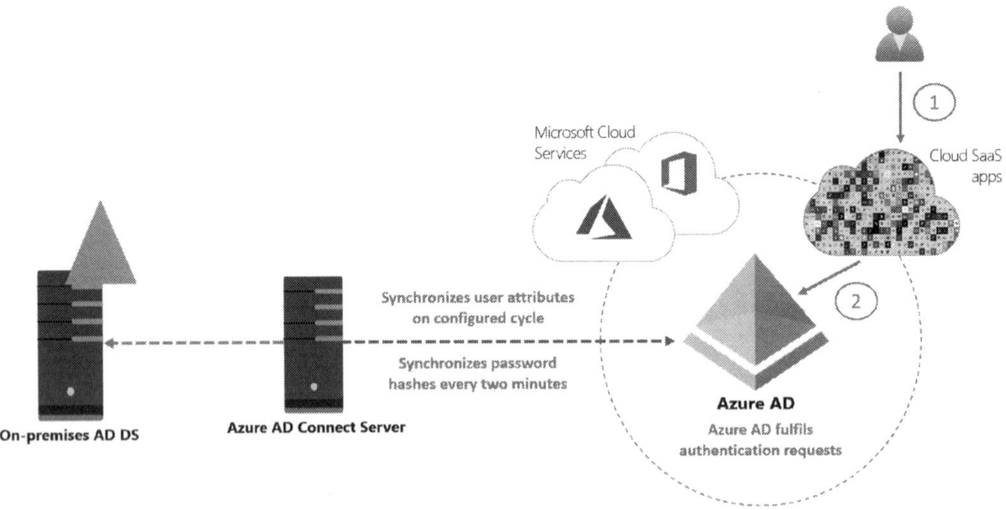

Figure 3.28 – PHS

So, what does the authentication process look like for a user when this authentication method is implemented?

1. When an unauthenticated user tries to access a cloud application, they are redirected to the Azure AD user sign-in page.

2. The user signs in with a username and password. Azure AD fulfills the authentication request as it has the password hash of the user.
3. The user's client receives an access token from Azure AD that they can use to access the cloud application.

The main advantage of using this authentication method is that it does not rely on our on-premises infrastructure to fulfill authentication requests. Even if the connection between on-premises AD DS and Azure AD is broken, Azure AD can still fulfill authentication requests as it has the user password hashes. Another advantage of this method is that we can implement a security feature called **leaked credential detection**. This security feature detects whether our user credentials have been identified in publicly leaked username/password pairs (we will discuss this feature in more detail in *Chapter 4*, *Azure AD Identity Security*, of this book).

The main downside of the PHS authentication method is that it does not support on-premises AD DS user-level security. This means that organizations that want to enforce their on-premises AD DS user security and password policies will not be able to so with this authentication method. This is because authentication requests are not fulfilled on-premises so those policies cannot be applied. Also, on-premises **Multi-Factor Authentication** (**MFA**) servers cannot be used with this authentication method. So, if an organization uses a third-party on-premises MFA server, this will not factor in authentication requests. Another downside is that some organizations may not be allowed to synchronize password hashes outside of their environment to an infrastructure that is not completely in their control. This is especially true for very highly regulated industries. For those special cases, they may not be able to implement this option.

Federation

For those organizations that may not be able to implement PHS due to the compliance requirements of password hash storage, an option that they can implement is **federation**. This option allows organizations to configure a **trust relationship** between their on-premises federation servers and Azure AD. With the federation authentication method, authentication requests are redirected to the on-premises federation servers in order to be fulfilled on-premises. The method currently supports two federation services – **Active Directory Federation Services** (**AD FS**) and **PingFederate** (another federation service similar to AD FS). So, how do we implement this authentication method?

1. First, we install Azure AD Connect on-premises. This creates a secure outbound connection between on-premises AD DS and Azure AD.

2. We select one of the federation options (AD FS or PingFederate) and configure the scope of synchronization, which identifies the boundary of the objects that we want Azure AD Connect to synchronize to Azure AD.
3. Azure AD Connect synchronizes the user objects and attributes from an on-premises AD DS instance to Azure AD. Password hashes are *not* synchronized:

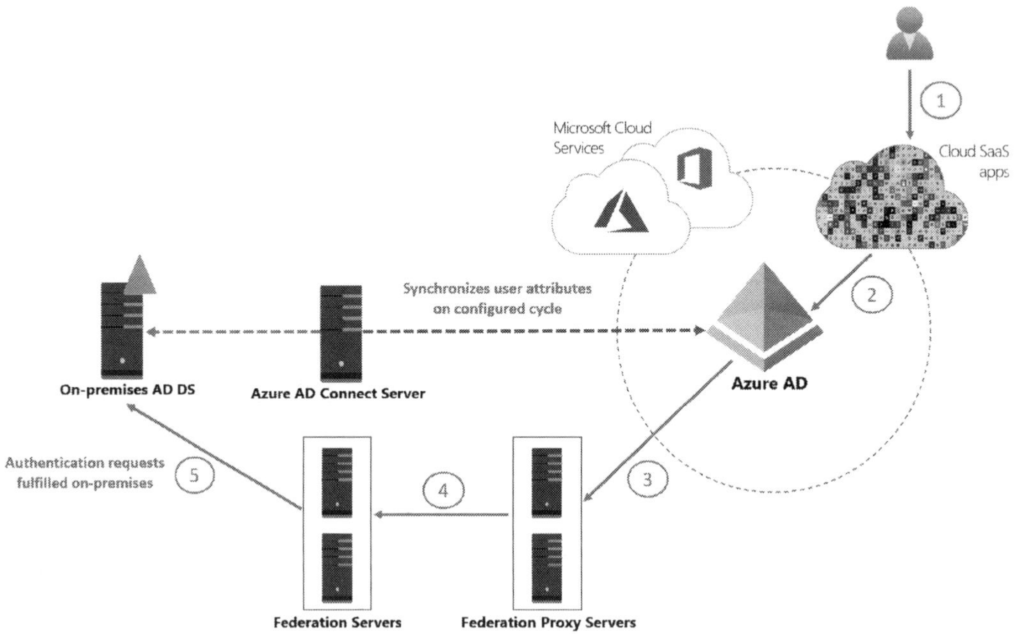

Figure 3.29 – Hybrid identity federation

So, what does the authentication process look like for a user when this authentication method is implemented?

1. When an unauthenticated user tries to access a cloud application, they are redirected to the Azure AD user sign-in page.
2. Azure AD then redirects the user to the federation sign-in page.
3. The user signs in with a username and password.
4. The federation server fulfills the authentication request on-premises.

The main advantage of using this authentication method is that password hashes are not synchronized to Azure AD, which enables certain organizations to fulfill very strict regulatory requirements. Another advantage of this method is that on-premises AD DS user-level security policies will be applied and an on-premises MFA server can be used. This is because authentication requests are fulfilled on-premises.

The main downside of the federation authentication method is that it depends on the availability of the on-premises infrastructure. If the on-premises infrastructure experiences downtime, no one will be able to authenticate to cloud applications! To prevent this, organizations end up having a redundant implementation of the federation proxy server and the federation server, which increases the complexity and the ongoing management overhead of the implementation. Another downside of this method is that the **leaked credential detection** security feature cannot be used for hybrid identity as Azure AD does not have the user password hashes.

Pass-Through Authentication (PTA)

PTA is another option that can be implemented by organizations that have a compliance requirement to keep password hash storage in-house. This is achieved using a lightweight agent that can be installed on one or more on-premises servers (it can even be installed on the same server that Azure AD Connect is installed on). So, how do we implement this authentication method?

First, we install Azure AD Connect on-premises. This creates a secure outbound connection between on-premises AD DS and Azure AD.

We select one of the PTA options and configure the scope of synchronization that identifies the boundary of the objects that we want Azure AD Connect to synchronize to Azure AD.

Azure AD Connect synchronizes the user objects and attributes from an on-premises AD DS instance to Azure AD. Password hashes are *not* synchronized.

We download and install the PTA agent on-premises:

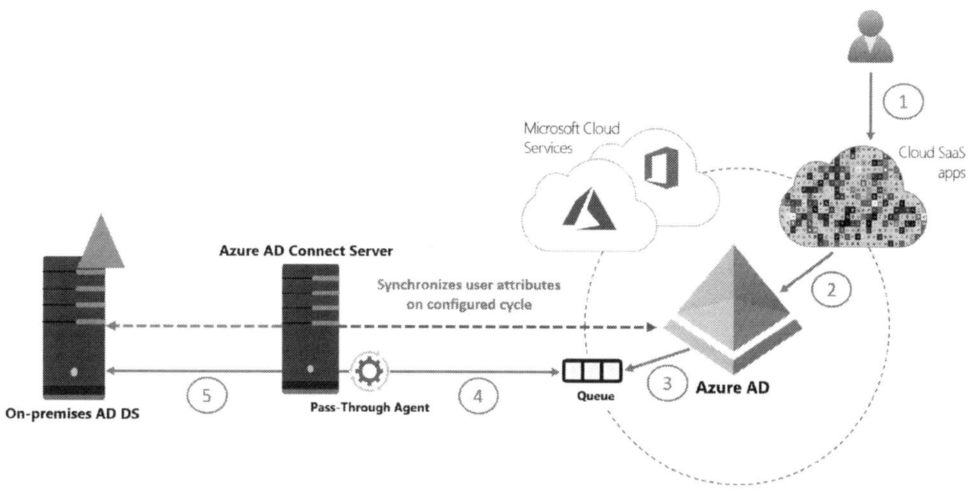

Figure 3.30 – PTA

So, what does the authentication process look like for a user when this authentication method is implemented?

1. When an unauthenticated user tries to access a cloud application, they are redirected to the Azure AD user sign-in page.
2. The user signs in with a username and password.
3. Azure AD collects the user's authentication information, encrypts the password using the public key of the on-premises authentication agent, and temporarily places it in a queue.
4. An on-premises PTA agent retrieves the username and encrypted password from the queue over a pre-established persistent connection. The agent then decrypts the password by using its private key.
5. The agent validates the username and password against an on-premises AD DS server.
6. The agent returns the authentication response back to Azure AD.

PTA allows us to keep our password hashes on-premises without the management overhead of AD FS. However, it still has the disadvantage of relying on customer infrastructure. What you will usually see is that customers use PTA as their primary option with PHS as a backup option (for disaster recovery).

Azure AD Connect deployment options

When installing Azure AD Connect, we have the option to use **Express Settings** or **Custom Settings**. The **Express Settings** option automatically uses certain defaults, such as PHS (instead of presenting us with an option to select the authentication method that we want to implement), synchronization of all users in a single domain (instead of giving us filtering options to decide which objects we want to sync), and the use of SQL Express for the synchronization database.

The **Custom Settings** option gives us the flexibility to select our implementation options and customize the tool for our specific requirements:

- We can select the authentication method that we want to implement (PHS, PTA, or federation).
- If we select federation or PTA, we can choose to use the PHS option as a backup in the event that our on-premises infrastructure experiences downtime.
- We can choose to use the built-in SQL Express database or a licensed SQL server for the synchronization database implementation.

- We can customize our setup to work for a multi-domain scenario.
- We can choose to filter the objects that Azure AD Connect synchronizes to Azure AD by domain, OU, group, or even object attributes.
- We can choose the object attributes that we want Azure AD Connect to synchronize from on-premises AD DS to Azure AD.

Figure 3.31 shows the window where we are presented with the choice of selecting either the **Express Settings** option or the **Custom Settings** option:

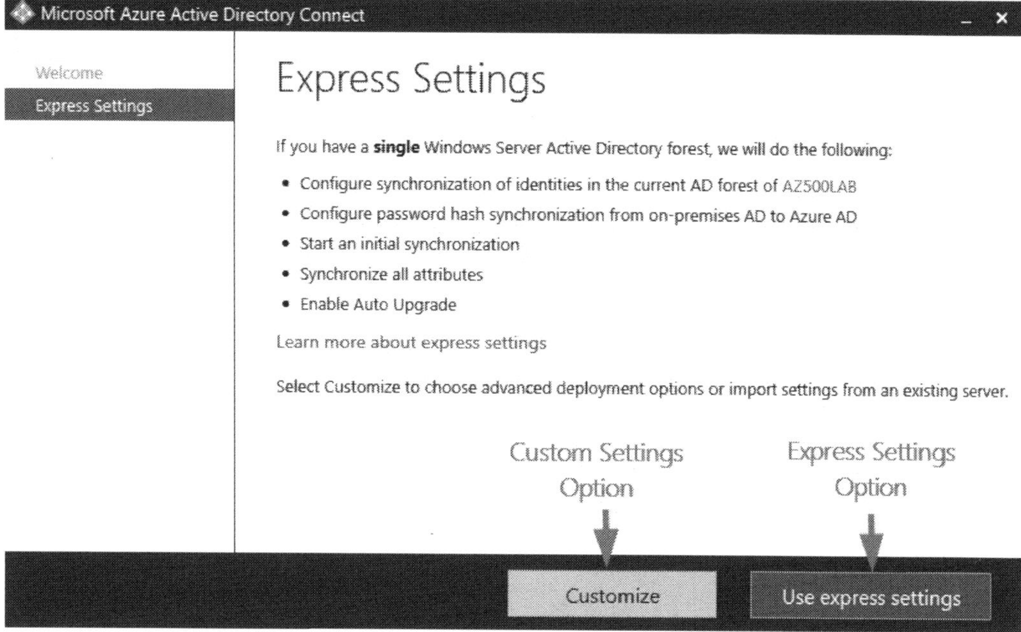

Figure 3.31 – Azure AD Connect deployment options

Now that we have an understanding of Azure AD hybrid identity authentication and deployment options, we will proceed to set this up in the next exercise.

Hands-on exercise – deploying Azure AD Connect PHS

In this exercise, we will complete the following tasks:

- **Task 1**: Install Azure AD Connect.
- **Task 2**: Verify directory synchronization.

Let's follow these steps:

1. Within the RDP session to **adVM**, from **Server Manager**, click on the **Start** button, then click on **Server Manager** to open the Server Manager console:

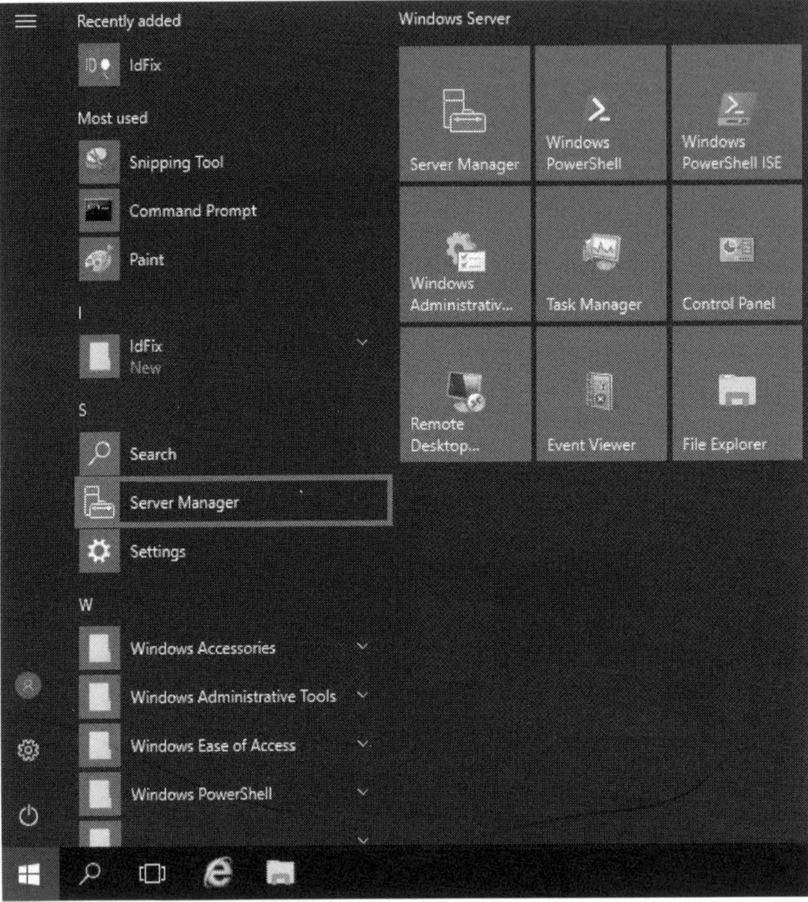

Figure 3.32 – Opening Server Manager

2. In the **Server Manager** console, click on **Local Server** in the left-hand tab, then click **On** in front of the **IE Enhanced Security Configuration** option:

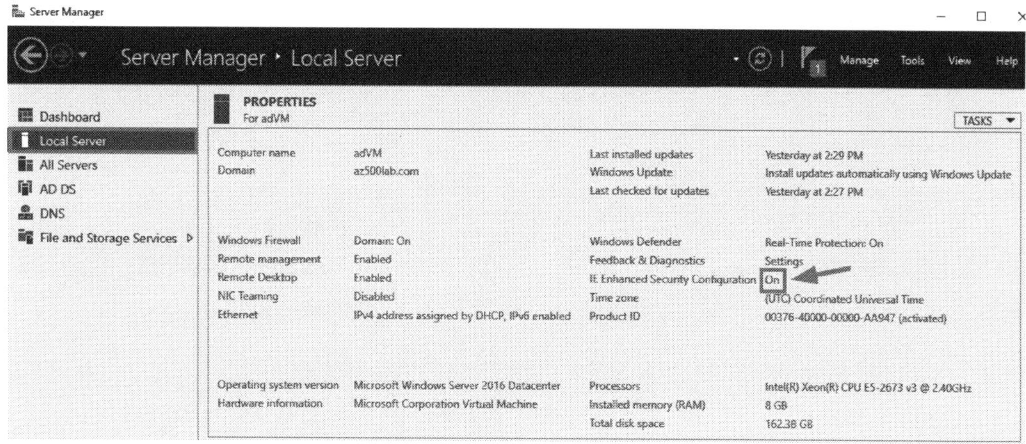

Figure 3.33 – Configuring IE Enhanced Security Configuration

3. In the **Internet Explorer Enhanced Security Configuration** window, set both options to **Off** and click **OK**:

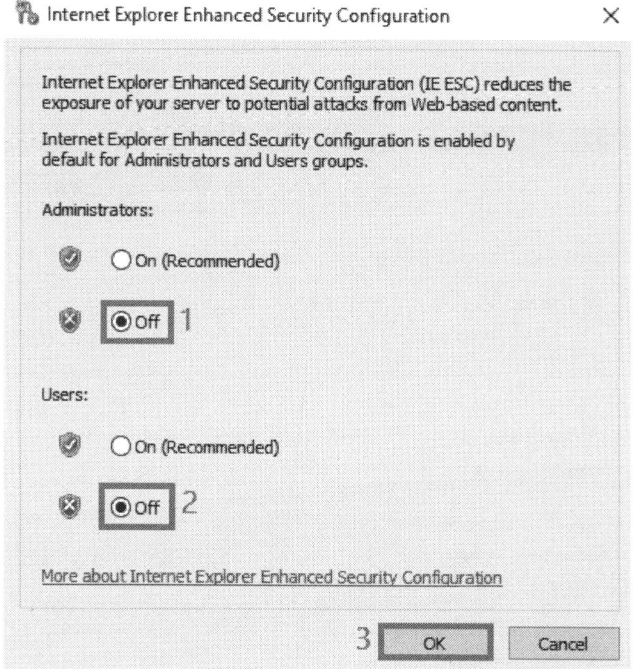

Figure 3.34 – Setting Internet Explorer Enhanced Security Configuration to Off

4. Within the RDP session to **adVM**, open a web browser and browse to `https://www.microsoft.com/en-us/download/details.aspx?id=47594`.

5. Click on **Download** on the web page that opens:

Microsoft Azure Active Directory Connect

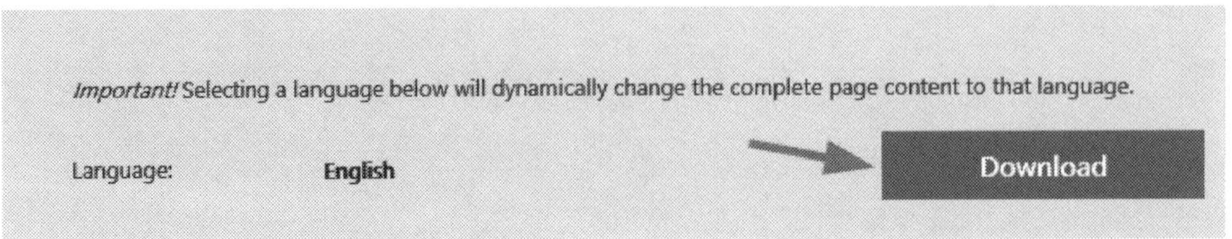

Figure 3.35 – Clicking to download Azure AD Connect

6. On the download prompt, click on **Run** to both download and run the installer:

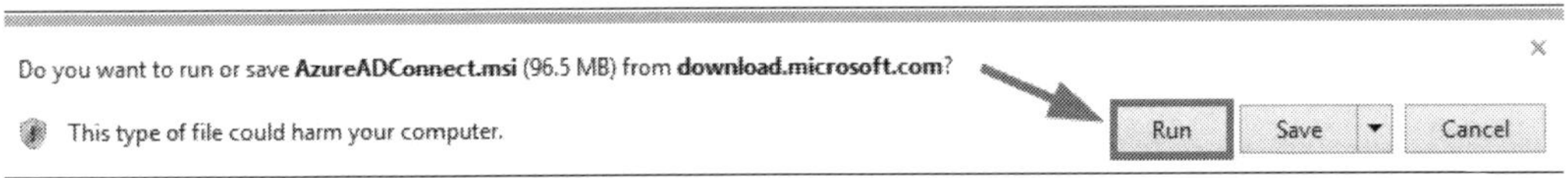

Figure 3.36 – Downloading and running the installer

7. In the **Microsoft Azure Active Directory Connect** wizard that opens, select the option to agree to the license terms and privacy notice, then click **Continue**:

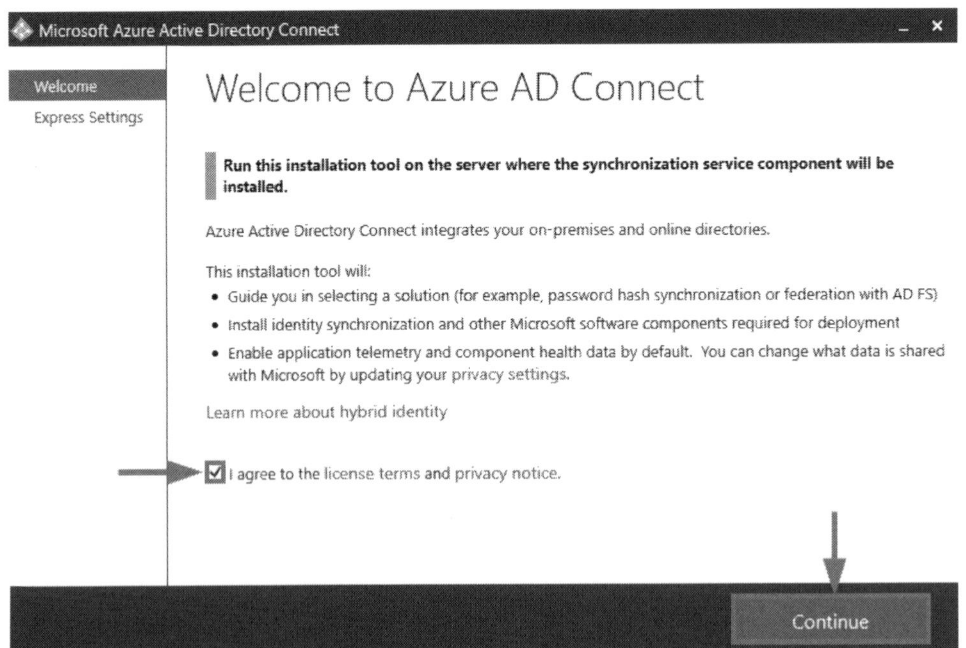

Figure 3.37 – Downloading and running the installer

8. On the **Express Settings** page, select the **Customize** option:

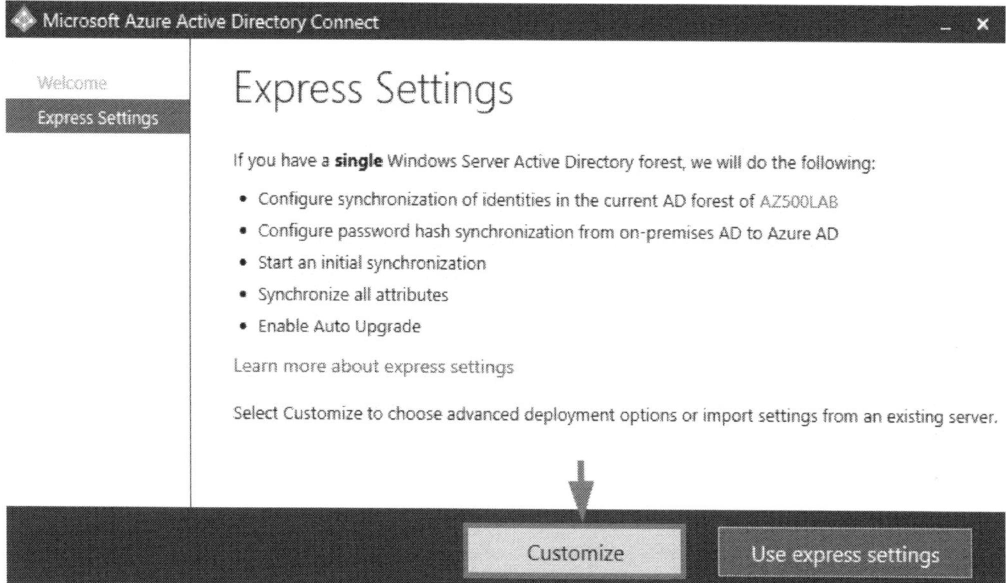

Figure 3.38 – Selecting Customize

9. On the **Install required components** page, leave all the optional configuration options deselected and click **Install**:

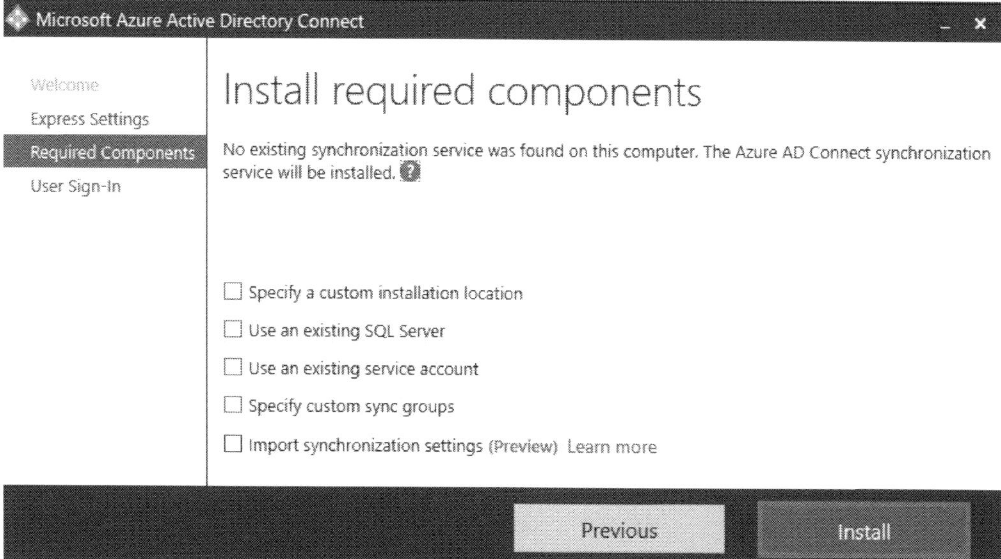

Figure 3.39 – Installing Azure AD Connect

10. On the **User sign-in** page, review the available options. These are the options that we discussed earlier in this chapter. Ensure that only **Password Hash Synchronization** is selected and click **Next**:

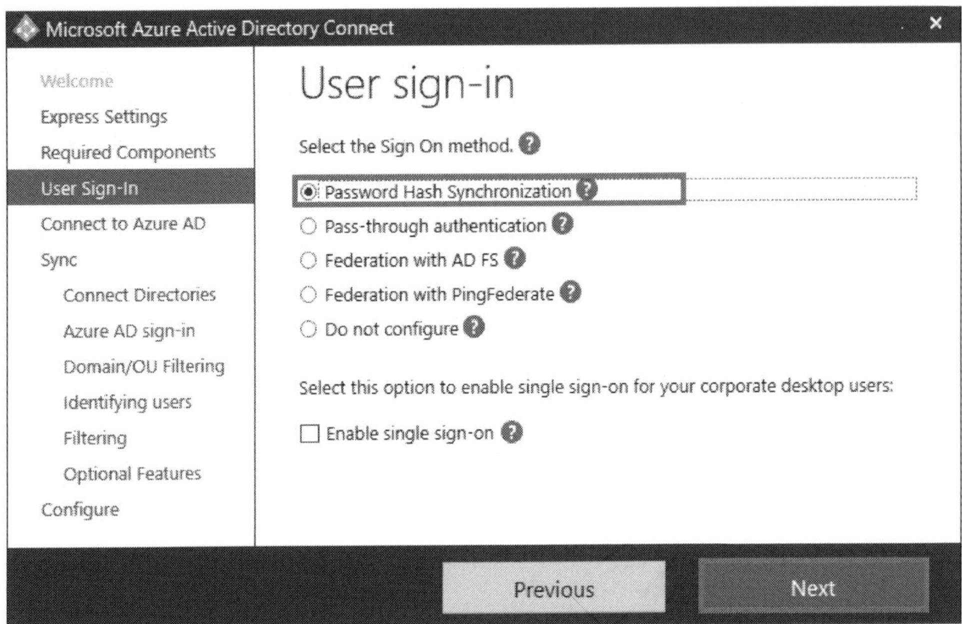

Figure 3.40 – Selecting Password Hash Synchronization

11. On the **Connect to Azure AD** page, enter the credentials of the `syncadmin` account that was created earlier:

    USERNAME: `syncadmin@<Azure-AD-DNS-domain-name>`

    PASSWORD: `QqLXXma6hAfs` (or the complex password that you used earlier):

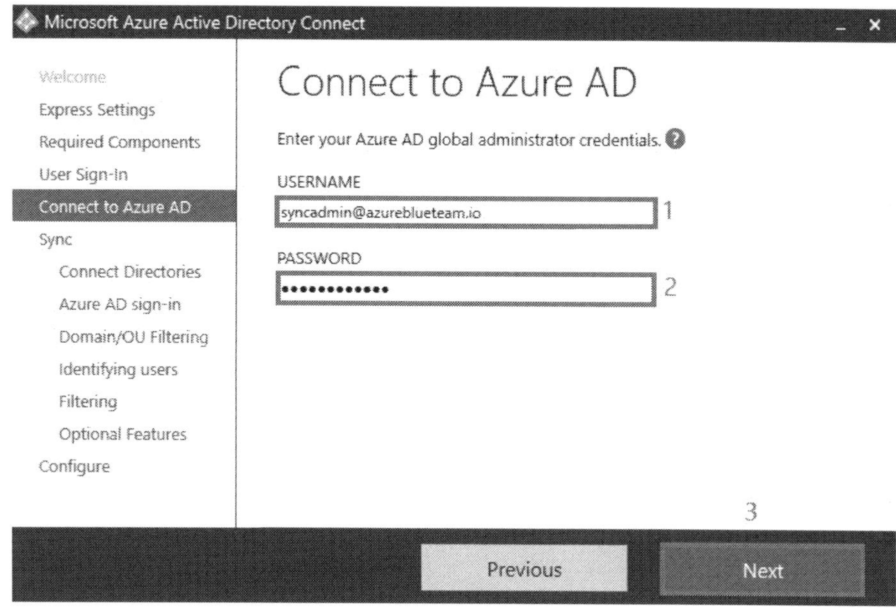

Figure 3.41 – Entering Azure AD credentials

12. When prompted to connect your directories, click on **Add Directory** to add the `az500lab.com` forest:

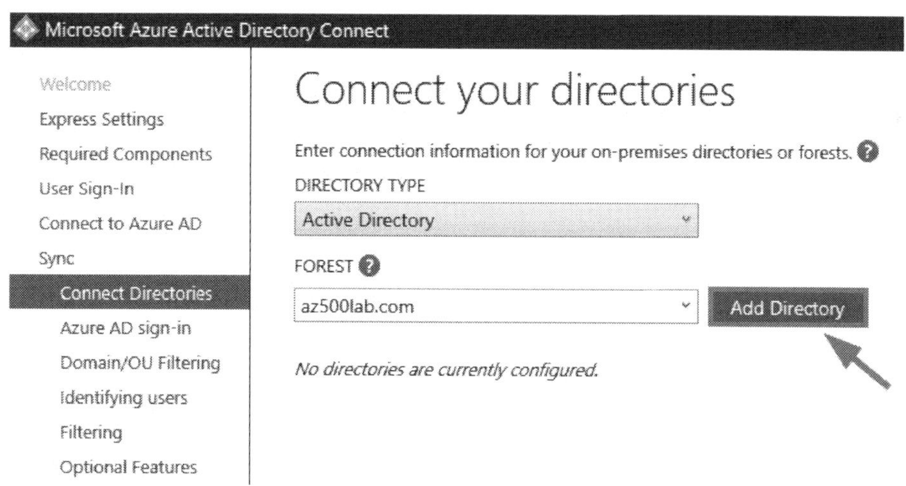

Figure 3.42 – Adding the on-premises forest

13. In the **AD forest account** window, configure the following:

    Select account option: **Create new AD account**

    ENTERPRISE ADMIN USERNAME: `AZ500LAB\onpremadmin`

PASSWORD: `QqLXXma6hAfs` (or the complex password that you used earlier)

Click **OK**:

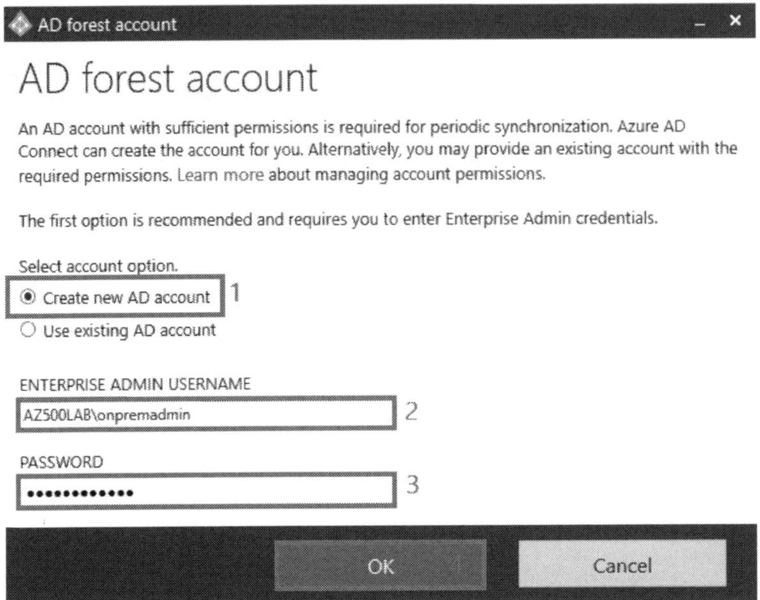

Figure 3.43 – Configuring the on-premises Enterprise Admin account

14. Once the directory is successfully added, click **Next**:

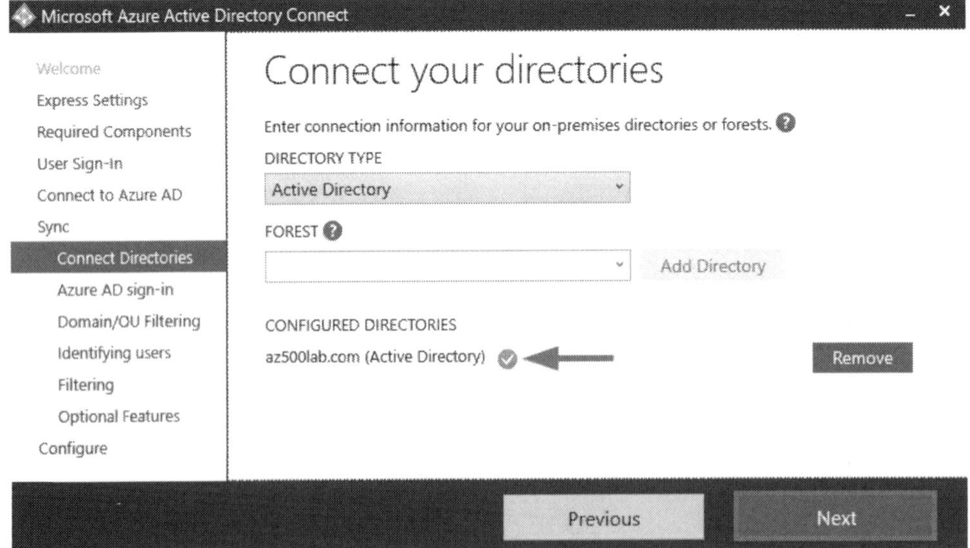

Figure 3.44 – Verifying that the on-premises domain was added

15. On the **Azure AD sign-in configuration** page, note the warning stating users will not be able to sign in to Azure AD with on-premises credentials if the UPN suffix does not match a verified domain name, and enable the **Continue without matching all UPN suffixes to verified domains** checkbox:

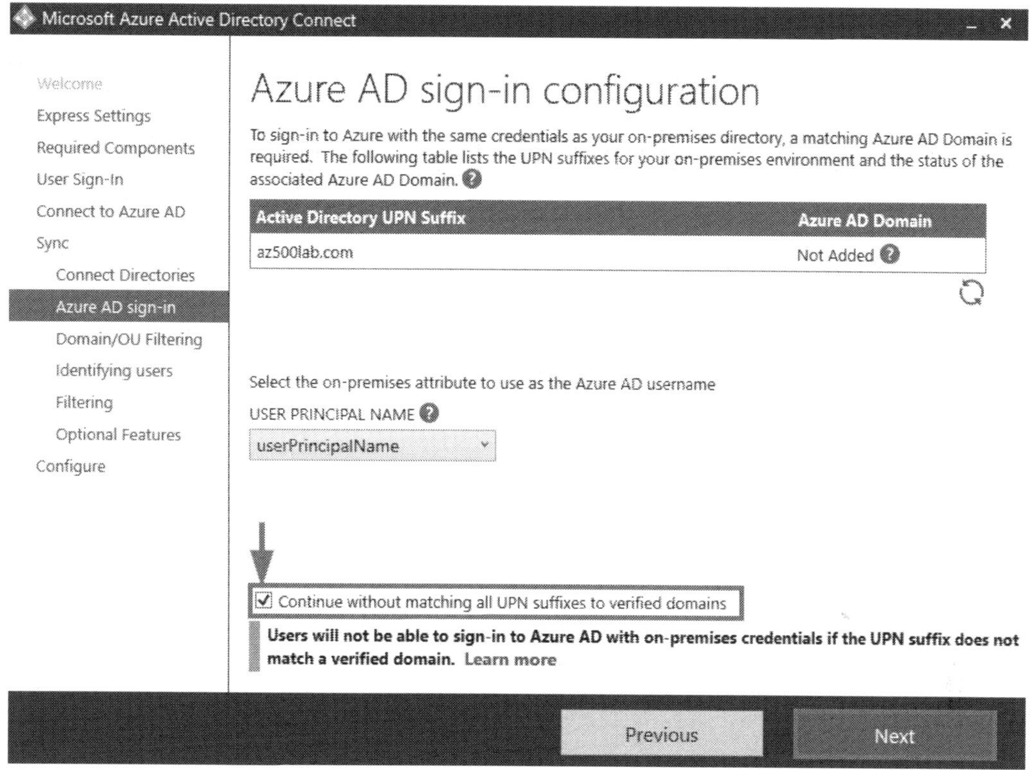

Figure 3.45 – Continuing without matching UPN suffixes

16. On the **Domain and OU filtering** page, select the **Sync selected domains and OUs** option and ensure that only the **OrgUsers** OU is selected. This option allows us to filter the scope of objects that we want Azure AD Connect to synchronize to Azure AD based on the domain and OU:

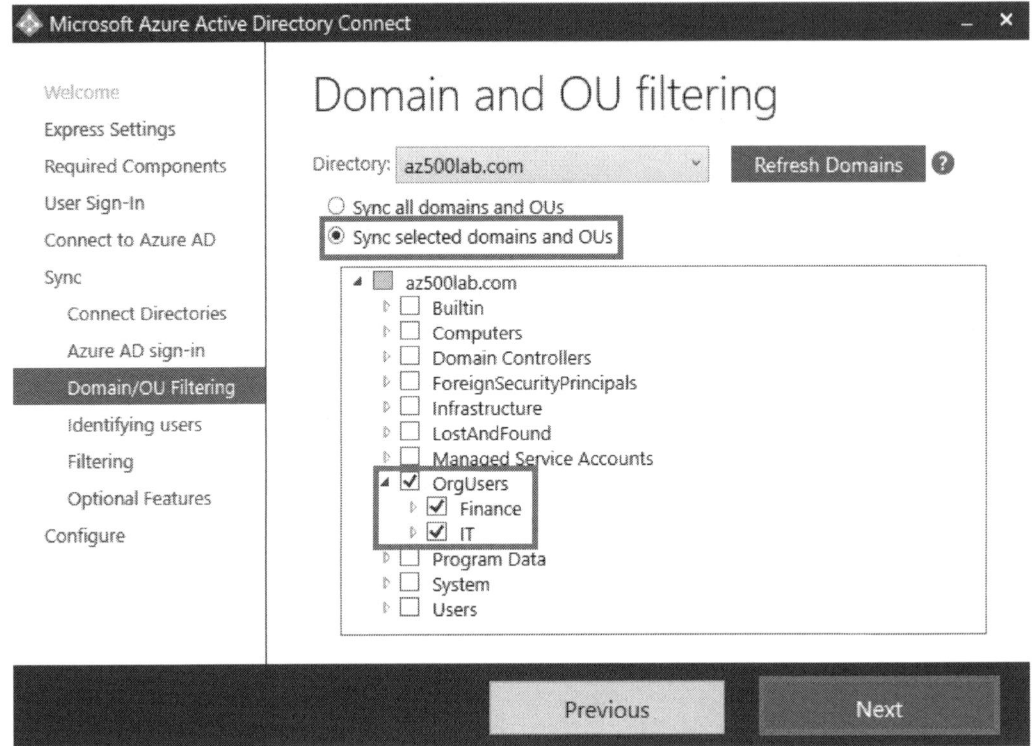

Figure 3.46 – Continuing without matching UPN suffixes

17. On the **Uniquely identifying your users** page, accept the default settings.
18. On the **Filter users and devices** page, accept the default settings.

19. On the **Optional features** page, select **Password writeback** and click **Next**. We will complete the configuration of the password writeback feature in a later exercise and test it:

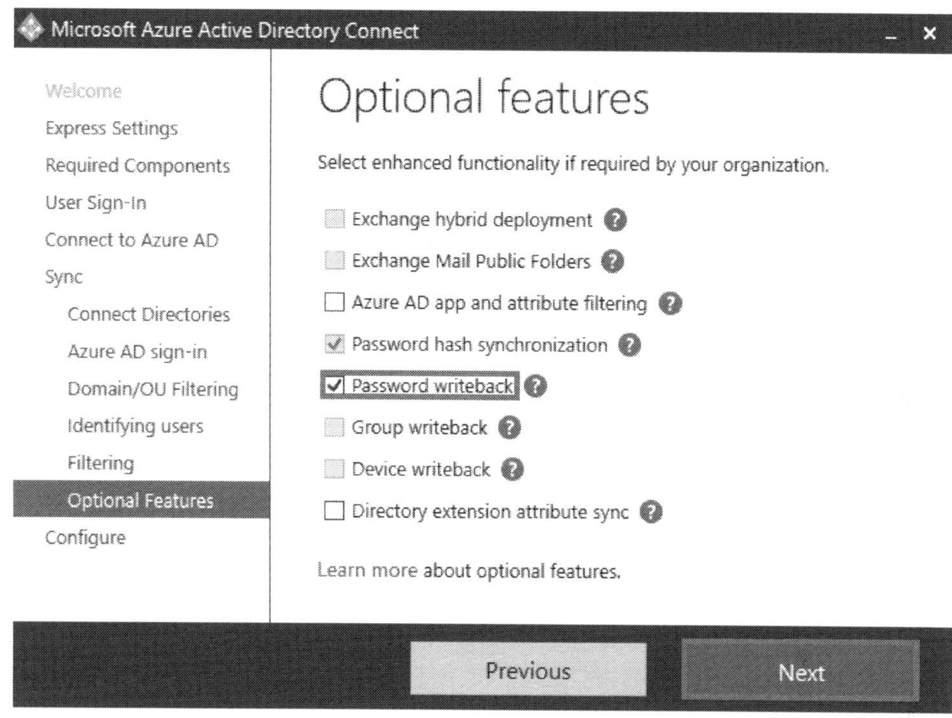

Figure 3.47 – Enabling password writeback in Azure AD Connect

20. On the **Ready to configure** page, ensure that the **Start the synchronization process when configuration completes** checkbox is selected, then click **Install** to continue with the installation process:

> **Important Note**
> Installation should take about 2 minutes.

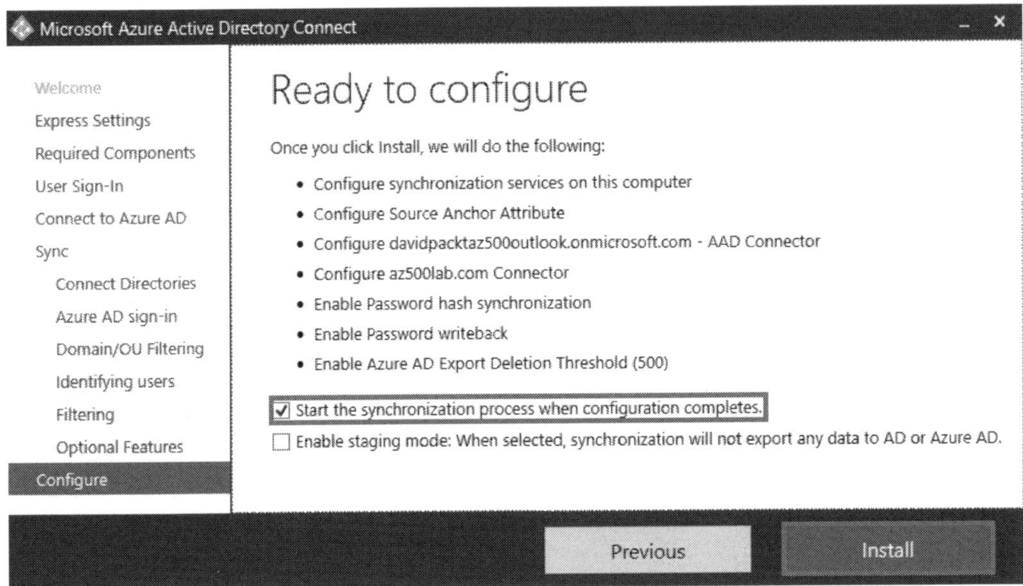

Figure 3.48 – Concluding the configuration and installing

21. Click **Exit** to close the **Microsoft Azure Active Directory Connect** window once the configuration is completed:

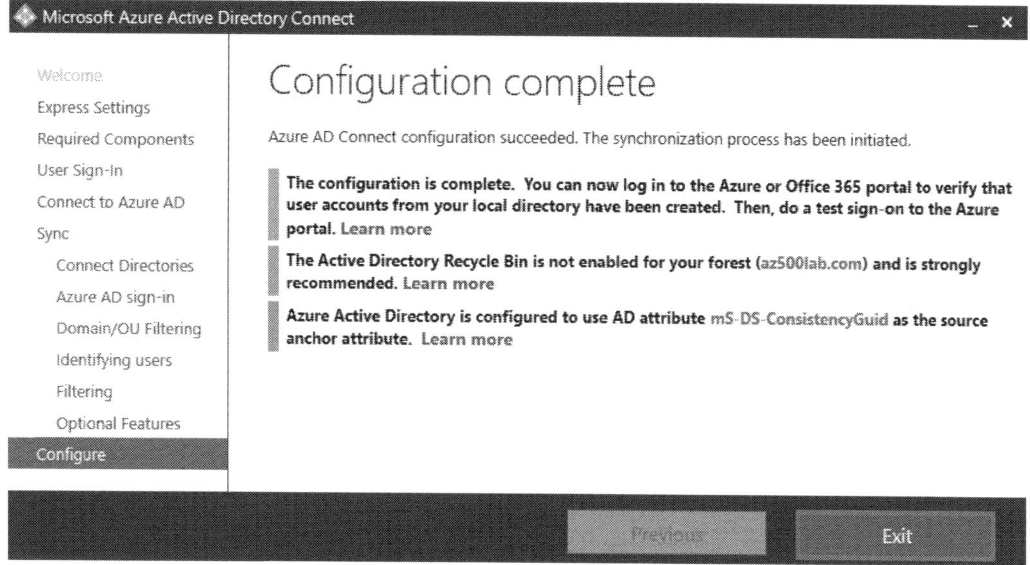

Figure 3.49 – Exiting after the installation has completed

22. Open a web browser and navigate to the Azure portal, `https://portal.azure.com`, then open the Azure AD console.

23. In the Azure AD console, click on **Users**. Notice that the list of user objects includes user accounts that were synchronized from on-premises AD DS. Review the **Directory synced** column to identify the synchronized users:

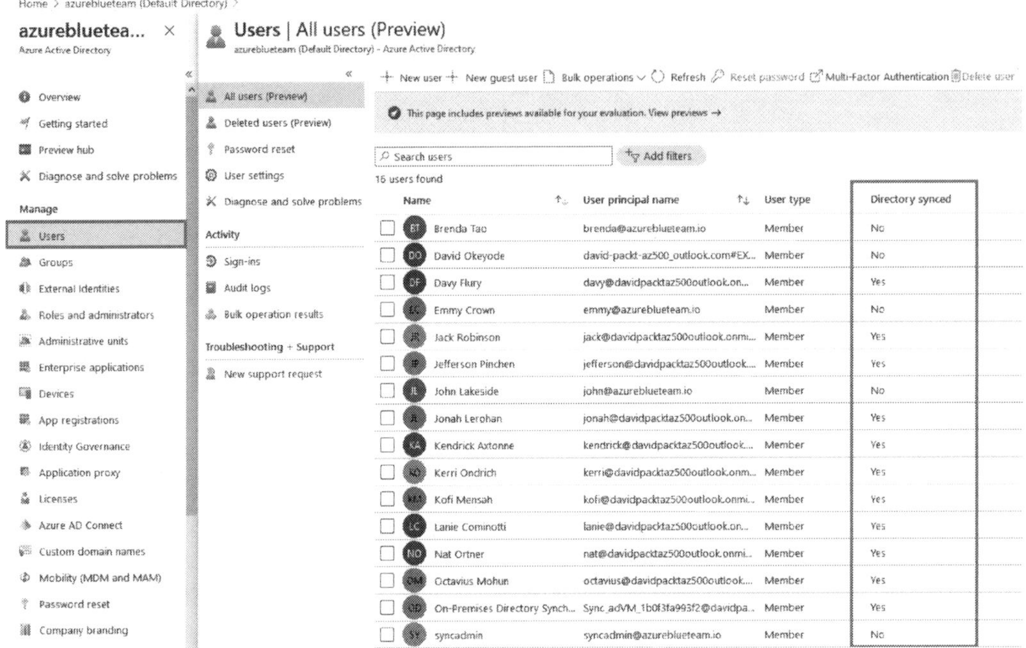

Figure 3.50 – Reviewing the Directory synced column

Congratulations! You have now successfully implemented a hybrid identity setup with on-premises AD and Azure AD.

> **Synchronization Rules Editor**
>
> The synchronization of objects from on-premises AD to Azure AD can be managed using another tool called the Synchronization Rules Editor. This tool is installed by default when we install Azure AD Connect. It can be used to configure complex synchronization rules such as preventing users with certain attributes from being synchronized to Azure AD. You can learn more about it from this document: `https://docs.microsoft.com/en-us/azure/active-directory/hybrid/how-to-connect-sync-change-the-configuration`.

Implementing password writeback

Password writeback is a popular feature of Azure AD Connect. It allows us to write password changes in Azure AD back to on-premises AD, provided that the password does not violate the on-premises AD password policy. It is supported for all three hybrid identity authentication methods (PHS, federation, and PTA).

The main use case of this feature is to implement a self-service password reset solution. This way, a user can reset their password using the **Forgot Password** option from a cloud application, and the password is written to Azure AD and then written back to on-premises AD!

It is worth noting that administrators control the scenarios where this will be possible. For example, we can choose the users/groups that will be able to use this feature and we can configure the additional authentication methods that will be required for a reset request (*Figure 3.51*). For security reasons, you may choose not to enable this feature for highly privileged user accounts:

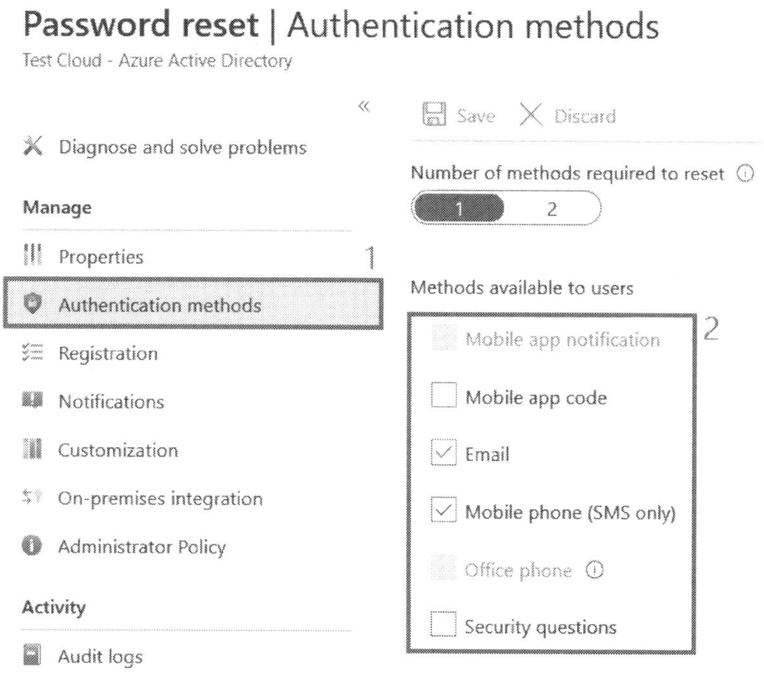

Figure 3.51 – Reviewing the Directory synced column

I strongly recommend going through this link by Microsoft to find out how this feature works: `https://docs.microsoft.com/en-us/azure/active-directory/authentication/concept-sspr-writeback`.

Summary

In this chapter, we covered the necessary steps to plan for an Azure AD hybrid identity implementation and what to consider when selecting the right authentication method for your implementation. We also covered the different deployment options of the Azure AD Connect tool and the implementation of password writeback for self-service password reset scenarios. The knowledge that you gained in this chapter has equipped you with how to create a centralized identity and access framework using Azure AD and on-premises AD.

In the next chapter, we will start to cover how to secure our Azure identities using the built-in security capabilities of Azure AD.

Questions

As we conclude, here is a list of questions for you to test your knowledge regarding this chapter's material. You will find the answers in the *Assessments* section of the *Appendix*:

1. Which of the following is *not* a hybrid identity authentication method when implementing Azure AD Connect?

   a. Password hash synchronization

   b. Active Directory Federation Services

   c. Pass-through authentication

   d. Instant authentication

2. You need to recommend a hybrid identity implementation that ensures that password policies and user login restrictions applied to user accounts in on-premises AD are applied to users when authenticating to cloud applications that use Azure AD. Your solution should use the least amount of servers possible. Which authentication method should you recommend?

   a. Password hash synchronization

   b. Federated identity with Active Directory Federation Services

   c. Password hash synchronization with seamless single sign-on

   d. Pass-through authentication with seamless single sign-on

3. You have implemented hybrid identity using Azure AD Connect. Your implementation currently synchronizes all on-premises identities to Azure AD. You need to prevent users who have a `givenName` attribute that starts with `DEMO` from being synced to Azure AD. Your solution must minimize administrative effort. What should you use?

   a. The Azure AD Connect wizard

   b. Active Directory Users and Computers

   c. The Synchronization Rules Editor

   d. The Web Service configuration tool

4. True or false: Passwords stored in Azure AD are stored with a reversible encryption algorithm.

   a. True

   b. False

5. You plan to deploy Azure AD Connect using the Express Settings deployment option. Which two roles and groups are required to perform this installation? You must use the principle of least privilege.

   a. The Domain Admins group in Active Directory

   b. The Security Administrator role in Azure AD

   c. The Global Administrator role in Azure AD

   d. The Enterprise Admins group in Active Directory

Further reading

To learn more on the topics covered in this chapter, you can refer to the following links:

- Password hash synchronization: `https://docs.microsoft.com/en-us/azure/active-directory/hybrid/whatis-phs?WT.mc_id=AZ-MVP-5003870`
- Pass-through authentication: `https://docs.microsoft.com/en-us/azure/active-directory/hybrid/how-to-connect-pta?WT.mc_id=AZ-MVP-5003870`
- Azure AD authentication methods: `https://docs.microsoft.com/en-us/azure/active-directory/authentication/concept-authentication-methods?WT.mc_id=AZ-MVP-5003870`

4
Azure AD Identity Security

A common attack entry point to Azure environments is by compromising Azure AD identities and credentials. The risk is greater if the compromised identity belongs to a privileged account, which has broader access in the environment. Mitigating identity security risks and configuring secure access is a key objective of the Azure Security Engineer certification exam.

In previous chapters, we covered Azure AD and how to manage its identities. In this chapter, we will explore how to secure those Azure identities using the advanced security features of Azure AD. By the end of this chapter, you will understand how to configure protection against common identity-related attacks in Azure AD.

Here are the topics that we will cover in this chapter with accompanying hands-on exercises:

- Implementing Azure AD Password Protection
- Securing Azure AD users with **multi-factor authentication** (**MFA**)
- Implementing Conditional Access policies
- Protecting identities with Azure AD Identity Protection

Technical requirements

To follow along with the instructions in this chapter, you will need the following:

- A PC with an internet connection.
- The Tor Browser downloaded and installed on your computer.
- An Azure subscription. You can use the same subscription that you set up in the first chapter of this book.

Implementing Azure AD Password Protection

Many identity systems rely on **password complexity requirements** to protect against password-related attacks such as password guessing and brute force. While this can provide a level of protection by forcing users to select passwords that are difficult to crack, it can also give a false sense of security. The reason for this is that there are passwords that users can select that may satisfy password complexity requirements but can still be easily guessed by attackers.

Take a password such as `Pa$$w0rd1`, for example. This password meets most complexity requirements (nine characters; includes uppercase and lowercase characters; includes special characters; includes digits). However, it is a common password that attackers are aware of, and this makes accounts that use it vulnerable to password spray attacks. The mitigation, in this case, is to ensure that your users cannot choose weak and vulnerable passwords like this even if they meet the required complexity policy. This is where the feature of Azure AD called **Password Protection** can help us!

So, what is Azure AD Password Protection? It is a native feature of Azure AD that has three main functionalities:

1. **Global banned password list**:

   This is essentially an *automatically generated* list of vulnerable passwords that Azure AD users are banned from using regardless of whether they satisfy complexity requirements. This list is compiled and regularly updated by the Azure AD Identity Protection team (not by the customer) based on their intelligence-gathering activities. To prevent cyber criminals from using this list for attacks, Microsoft does not publish it. The list is automatically used as a password filter for every password **SET** or **RESET OPERATION** in Azure AD.

   So how do we enable this functionality of password protection? The good thing is that it is enabled by default for all Azure AD tenants regardless of the edition (Free, Office 365, Premium P1 and P2) and cannot be disabled (*Figure 4.2*).

2. **Custom banned password list**:

    In addition to the global banned password list, a customer with an Azure AD Premium P1 or P2 license may add their own custom list of a thousand banned passwords. This way, administrators can manage their own list of vulnerable passwords to block.

    When implemented, the combined global and custom banned password list is used as a password filter for every password **SET** or **RESET OPERATION** to prevent the variants of the passwords from both lists from being chosen by users/admins (*Figure 4.1*).

    This functionality of Azure AD Password Protection is only available in Azure AD Premium P1 or P2 editions (*Figure 4.2*).

    Figure 4.1 highlights how the global and custom banned password list functionalities of Password Protection work:

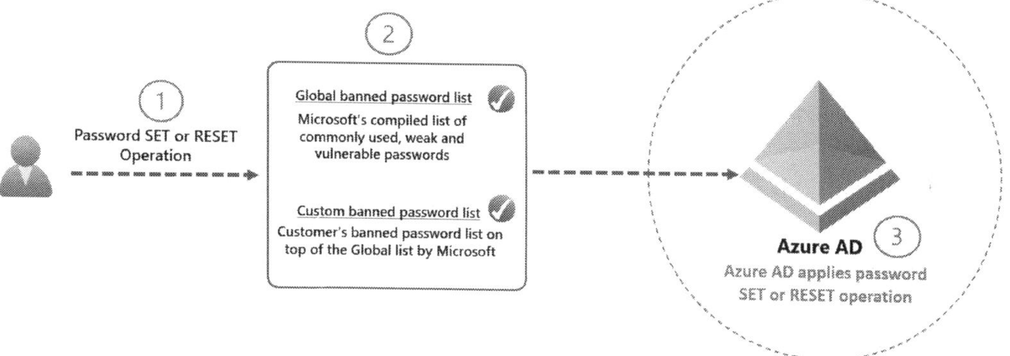

Figure 4.1 – Azure AD Password Protection

Step 1: User or administrator initiates a password set or reset operation.

Step 2: The specified password is validated against password variants in both the **Global banned password list** and the **Custom banned password list**.

Step 3: If the specified password does not match any password or variant in both lists, the password is accepted and applied by Azure AD. If the specified password matches any password or variant in any of the lists, the user or admin is blocked from choosing that password.

3. **Active Directory Domain Services** (**ADDS**) integration:

   The functionality of Password Protection allows us to extend both global and custom banned password lists to our on-premises Active Directory environments. Similar to the custom banned password list capability, it requires Azure AD Premium P1 or P2 editions (*Figure 4.2*):

	Azure AD Free	Azure AD Office 365	Azure AD Premium P1	Azure AD Premium P2
Global banned password	✓	✓	✓	✓
Custom banned password			✓	✓
Active Directory Domain Services (AD DS) Integration			✓	✓

Figure 4.2 – Azure AD Password Protection licensing

Figure 4.3 highlights how the ADDS integration capability of Password Protection works:

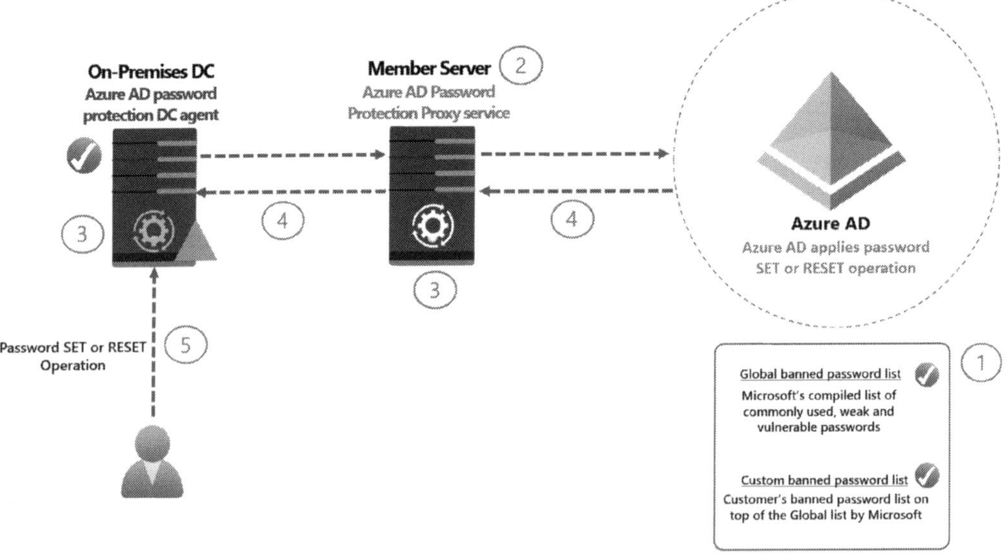

Figure 4.3 – Azure AD Password Protection ADDS integration

Step 1: Configure the password protection custom banned password list in Azure AD (remember that the global banned password list is enabled by default and cannot be disabled).

Step 2: Prepare a member server that is joined to the on-premises domain. This is a mandatory requirement. The member server will be used as the password protection proxy service. This server will download the banned password lists directly from the Azure AD (via the internet) to avoid the domain controller having to connect outbound to the internet.

Step 3: Install the Azure AD Password Protection DC agent on the domain controller and the Azure AD Password Protection proxy service on the member server.

Step 4: The Password Protection agent on the domain controller through the password protection proxy service requests that the password protection policy be downloaded from Azure AD (it does this at startup and on an hourly schedule).

Step 5: Whenever there is a password change operation performed on-premises, the password will be validated against the downloaded banned password list.

Now that you have some understanding of Azure AD Password Protection, you will implement and verify one of its features – the custom banned password list, in the next exercise.

Hands-on exercise – Configuring the custom banned password list feature of Azure AD Password Protection

Here are the tasks that will be completed in this exercise:

- Reviewing Azure AD licensing
- Enabling and configuring the custom banned password list
- Disabling Azure AD security defaults
- Verifying custom banned password lists

Let's now complete the aforementioned tasks by performing the following steps:

1. Open a web browser and browse to the Azure portal URL: `https://portal.azure.com`.
2. Sign in to the portal using the account that you used to sign up in the previous chapter.

3. Click the portal menu icon in the top-left corner and select **Azure Active Directory**:

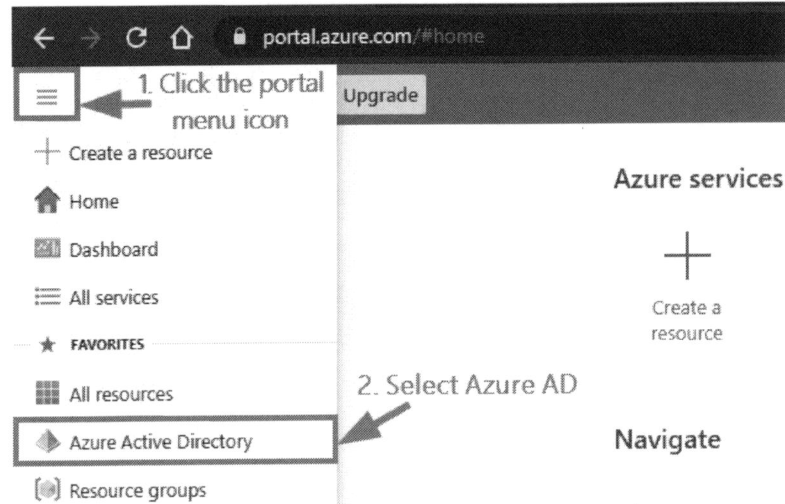

Figure 4.4 – Selecting Azure AD

4. In the **Default Directory | Overview** blade, click on **Licenses** and then click on **Licensed Features**:

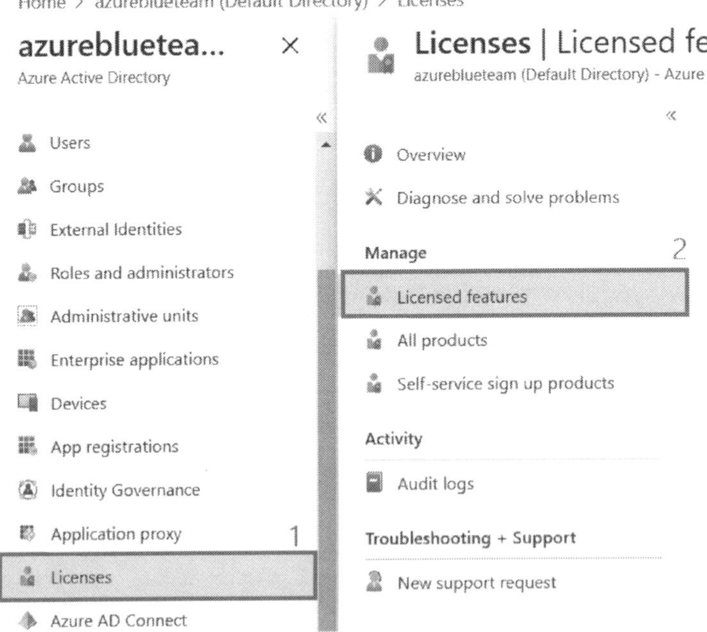

Figure 4.5 – Selecting Azure AD licenses

5. In the **Licenses | Licensed features** blade, search for `password protection` (lowercase). Review the **Feature available** column. You should see that the three password protection features are available. Close the **Licenses | Licensed features** blade:

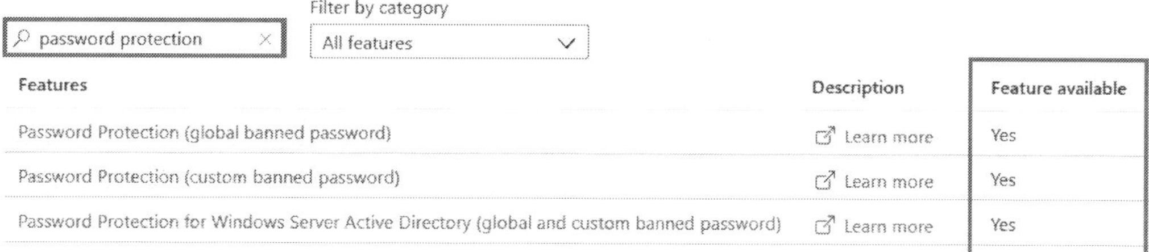

Figure 4.6 – Verifying the Password Protection feature

6. In the **Default Directory | Overview** blade, click on **Security** and then click on **Authentication Methods** and **Password protection**:

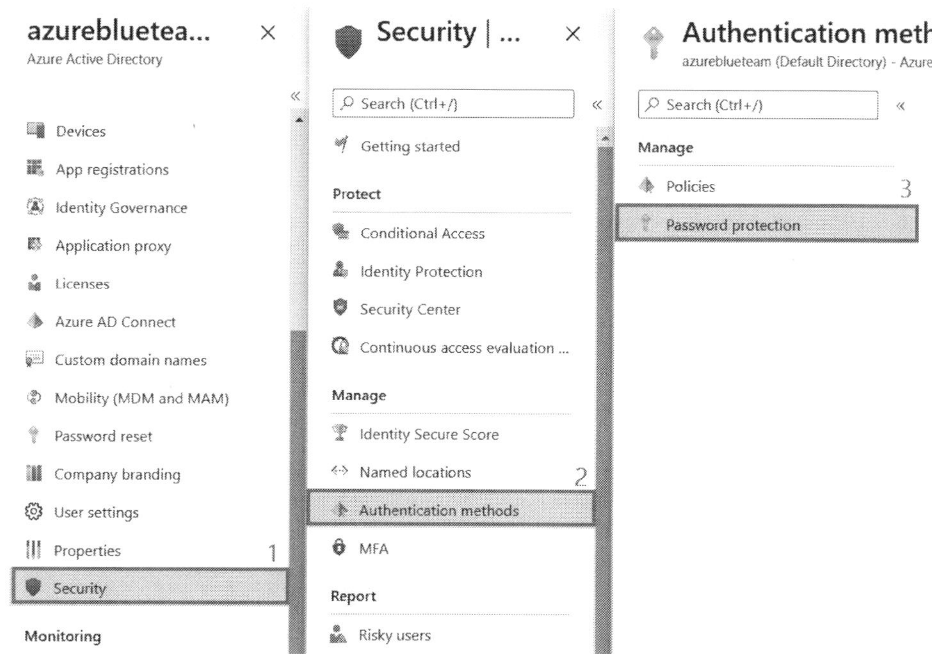

Figure 4.7 – Configuring password protection

7. In the **Authentication methods | Password protection** blade, configure the following:

   Custom banned passwords

   Enforce custom list: Yes

   Custom banned password list: `superclouds`

   Password protection for Windows Server Active Directory

   Enable password protection on Windows Server Active Directory: No

   Leave the other settings as their default settings and then click on **Save**.

   Close the **Authentication methods | Password protection** blade.

   Close the **Security | Getting started** blade:

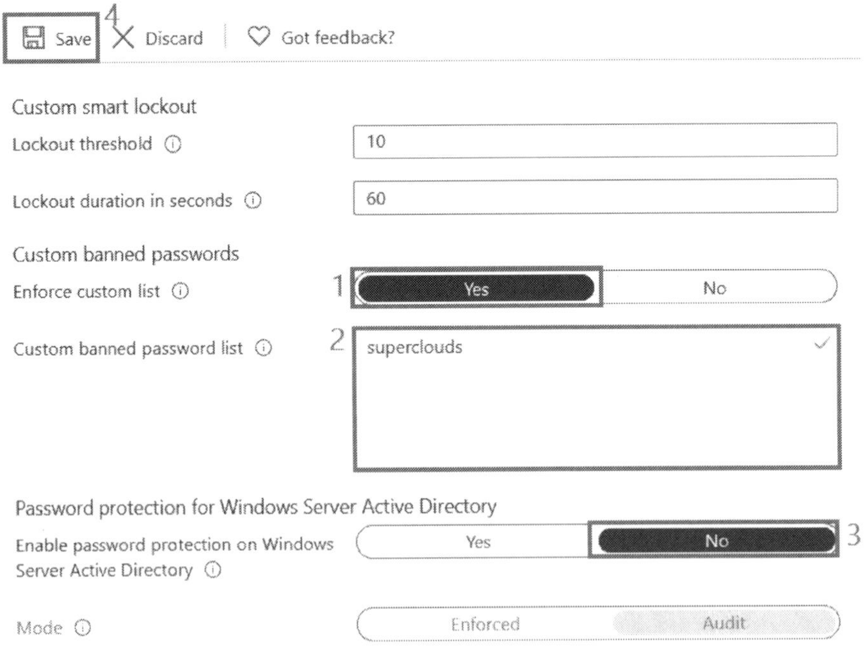

Figure 4.8 – Configuring the custom banned password list

> **Important note**
> When a password is added to the custom banned password list, variants of the password are also automatically blocked. For example, adding `superclouds` to the list automatically blocks variants such as `$upercl0ud$` and `$upercl0uds123`.

8. In the **Default Directory | Overview** blade, click on **Properties** and then click on **Manage Security defaults**:

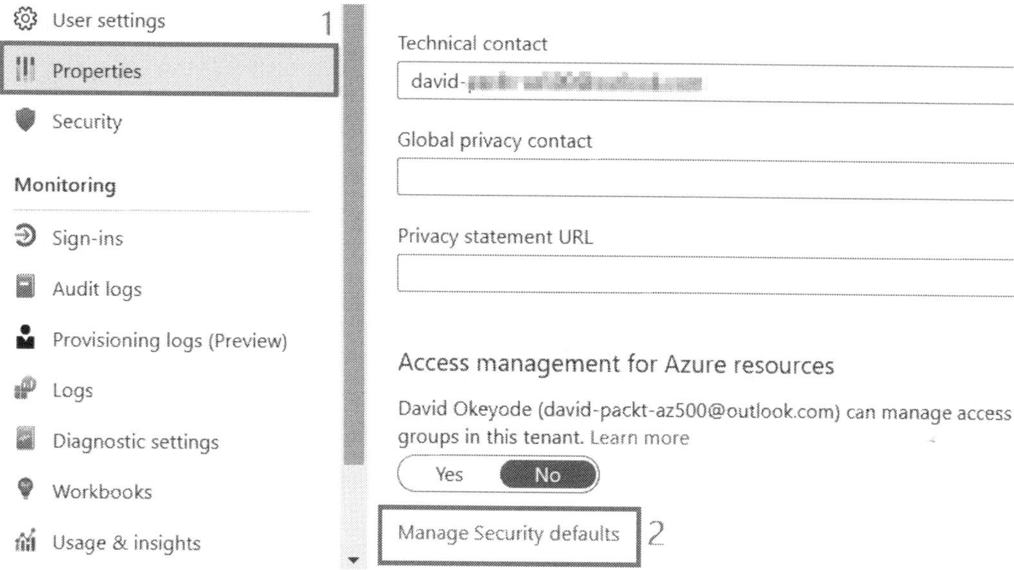

Figure 4.9 – Azure AD Properties

9. In the **Enable Security Defaults** blade, configure the following:

   Enable Security Defaults: No.

   We'd love to understand why you're disabling Security defaults so we can make improvements: Select **Other**.

   In the textbox, enter `Testing`.

Click **Save**:

> **Important note**
>
> **Security defaults** is a setting that is automatically enabled on new Azure AD tenants. It configures Microsoft-managed identity security settings that enforce the following: It requires all users and admins to register for MFA; it challenges users with MFA when they log in using a new device or app; it disables authentication from legacy authentication clients that have no MFA support. As we will be implementing customer-managed identity security capabilities in this chapter, we should disable this setting to avoid a conflict with the features that we will be implementing and testing.

Enable Security defaults
Security defaults is a set of basic identity security mechanisms recommended by Microsoft. When enabled, these recommendations will be automatically enforced in your organization. Administrators and users will be better protected from common identity related attacks.
Learn more
Enable Security defaults
Yes
No
1
We'd love to understand why you're disabling Security defaults so we can make improvements.
My organization is using Conditional Access
My organization is unable to use critical business applications
My organization is getting too many MFA challenges
2
Other
3
Testing
Save
4

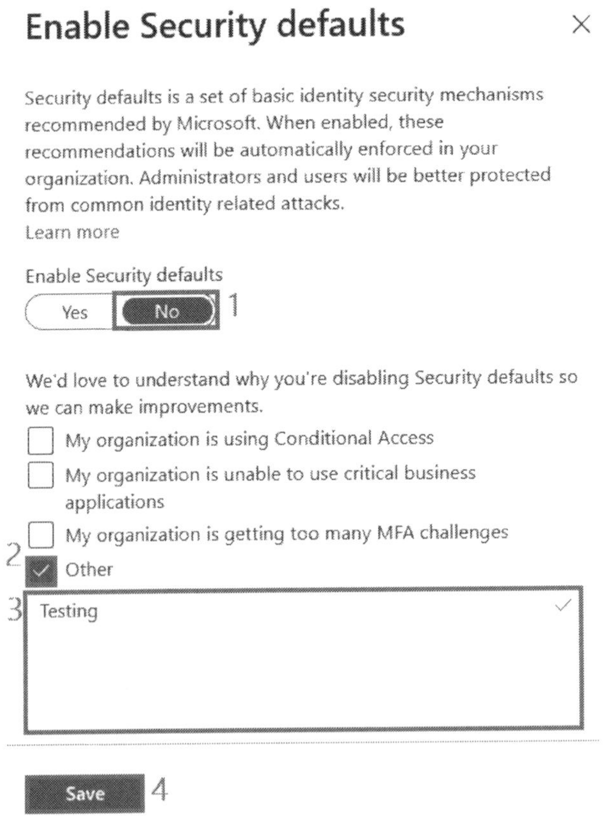

Figure 4.10 – Disabling security defaults

10. Open a new InPrivate or Incognito browser window and browse to the Azure portal: `https://portal.azure.com`.
11. In the **Sign in** window, enter the username of the user named `Brenda` that you created in *Chapter 2, Understanding Azure AD*, and then click **Next**:

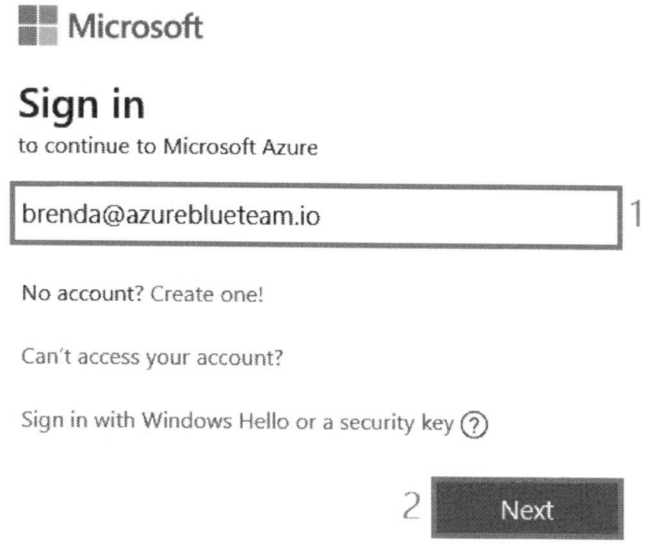

Figure 4.11 – Signing in as Brenda

12. In the **Enter password** window, enter the initial password that you configured for the user in *Chapter 2, Understanding Azure AD*. The recommended password was `QqLXXma6hAfs` (if you used a different password, make sure you enter this instead). Click **Sign in**.
13. In the **Update your password** window, enter the following:

    Current password: Enter the initial password again.

    New password: `superclouds`.

    Confirm password: `superclouds`.

    Click **Sign in**.

    You should receive an error message about the password being banned.

You can try using variations of the banned password, such as `$upercl0ud$` and `$upercl0uds123`. You should receive the same message:

Microsoft
brenda@azureblueteam.io
Update your password
You need to update your password because this is the first time you are signing in, or because your password has expired.

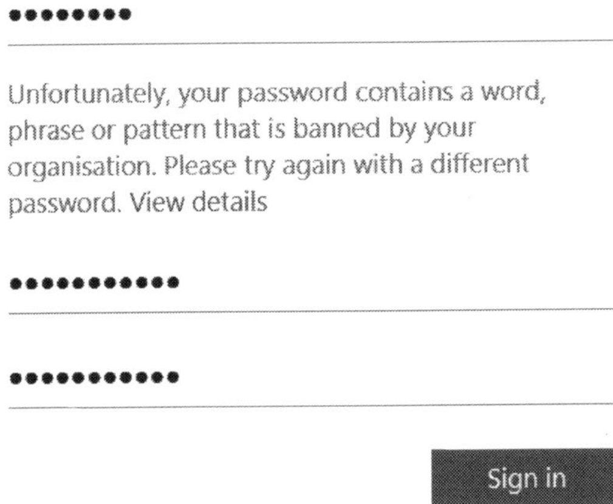

••••••••
Unfortunately, your password contains a word, phrase or pattern that is banned by your organisation. Please try again with a different password. View details
•••••••••••
•••••••••••
Sign in

Figure 4.12 – Blocked banned password error message

14. In the **Update your password** window, enter the following:

    Current password: Enter the initial password again.

    New password: Enter a complex password. Make a note of this password as you will need it later.

    Confirm password: Re-enter the complex password.

    Click **Sign in**.

    Leave the browser open for the next exercise.

In this exercise, you enabled and configured the custom banned password list for Azure AD. This is one of the functionalities of password protection that we discussed earlier. In the next section, we will discuss how to protect Azure AD identities using the native MFA capabilities of Azure AD.

Securing Azure AD users with multi-factor authentication (MFA)

If we look at the threat landscape against user identities today, there are few types of attacks where having a complex password can help. Complex passwords could provide some mitigation against threats such as *password spray* and *brute-force* attacks, but they offer no mitigation against other prominent identity threats such as *credential stuffing*, *breach replay*, *phishing*, *database extraction*, and *malware sniffing*. Why? Because in all those cases, the password is already exposed! For example, in the case of a successful phishing attack, the attacker already has the password! This is why **MFA** is critical to identifying security. Luckily for us, Azure AD comes with native MFA capabilities that are easy to implement.

Azure AD MFA enables users to validate their identities using an additional form of authentication (beyond username and password) during sign-in. When implemented, users have the option of validating their identities using any of the methods below in combination with their passwords:

- **Phone call**: The Azure AD MFA service places a call to the user's registered phone number. The user then approves the authentication using their phone keypad.
- **Text message**: The Azure AD MFA service sends a six-digit code to the user's registered mobile phone number. The user then enters the verification code into the sign-in interface to complete the authentication.
- **Mobile app notification**: The Azure AD MFA service sends a verification request to a user's smartphone, which asks them to complete the verification by selecting **Verify** in the mobile app.
- **Mobile app verification code**: The Azure AD MFA service sends a six-digit OATH verification code to the user's mobile app. The user then enters this code on the sign-in page. This code is changed every 30 seconds.
- **Open Authentication (OATH) compliant tokens** (hardware or software): The Azure AD MFA service prompts the user to enter the one-time password code displayed on their OATH device. The user enters this code on the sign-in page to complete authentication.

There are different ways to implement MFA in Azure AD. **The basic method** is to enable *MFA by changing a user state*. This is also referred to as *per user* MFA and you will configure this in the next exercise. The downside to this method is that the user will be prompted for MFA for all applications that they access (except if their source IP is configured as a trusted IP for exclusion). Users getting prompted for MFA for every application may result in a poor user experience.

A better option is to *enable MFA with conditional access policies*. This option allows us to only prompt users for MFA based on the conditions that we define, providing a more granular MFA experience. For example, we can configure a policy to challenge users for MFA only if they are connecting from an unexpected or unusual location, but if they are working from a trusted office network, they are not prompted. We will cover conditional policies in more detail later in this chapter, but for now, just know that this option requires Azure AD Premium editions (P1 or P2).

Hands-on exercise – Enabling MFA by changing user state

In this exercise, we will enable MFA for users by using the basic method of changing a user's state. Here are the tasks that we will complete:

- **Task 1**: Enable MFA for the user – Brenda Tao.
- **Task 2**: Complete the MFA registration process for the user.

Let's now complete the aforementioned tasks by performing the following steps:

1. Open a web browser and browse to the Azure portal URL: `https://portal.azure.com`.
2. Sign in to the portal using the account that you used to sign up in the previous chapter.
3. Click the portal menu icon in the top-left corner and select **Azure Active Directory**:

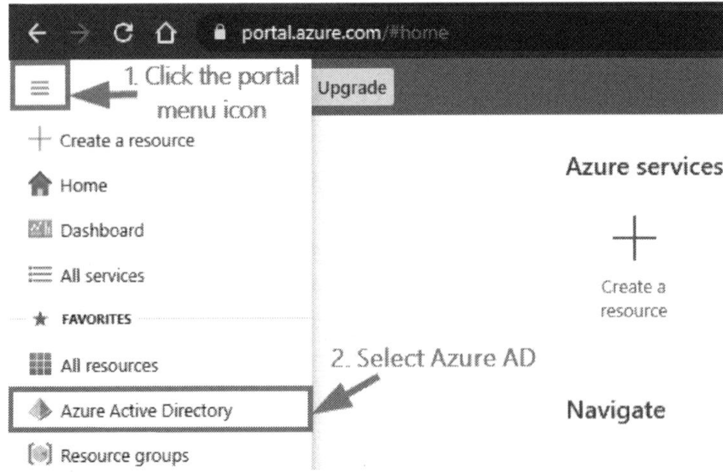

Figure 4.13 – Selecting Azure AD

4. In the **Default Directory | Overview** blade, click on **Security** and then click on **MFA**:

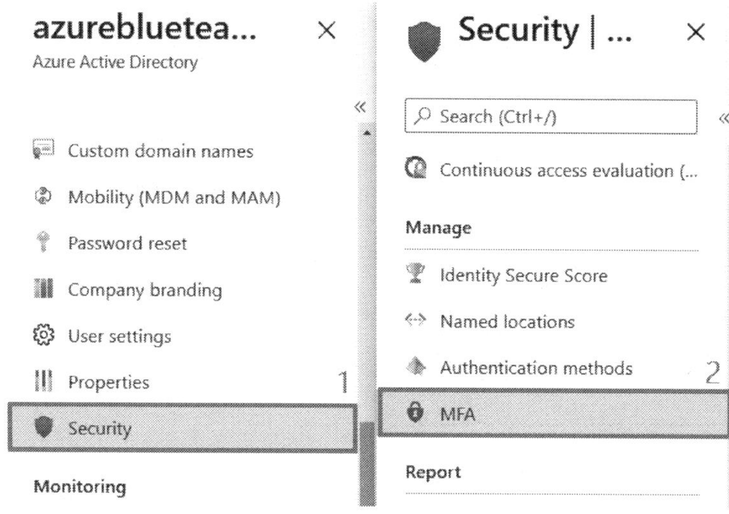

Figure 4.14 – Azure AD MFA option

5. In the **Multi-Factor Authentication | Getting started** blade, click on **Additional cloud-based MFA settings**. This will open a new browser page where you can see the MFA configuration options.

   This is where we can enable or disable app passwords that allow users to create unique account passwords for apps that do not support MFA. We can also configure trusted IPs for which to skip MFA:

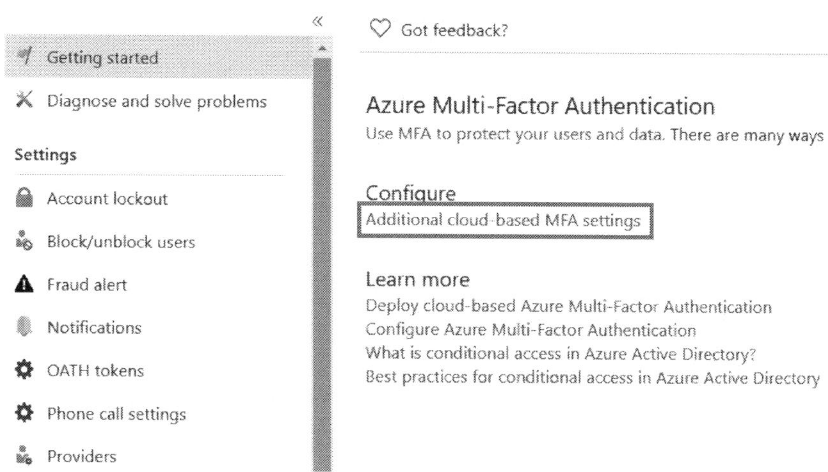

Figure 4.15 – Configuring MFA settings

6. In the **multi-factor authentication service settings** page, scroll down to the **verification options** section, ensure that only the **Text message to phone** and **Notification through mobile app** options are selected. Click on **Save** and then click on **Close**:

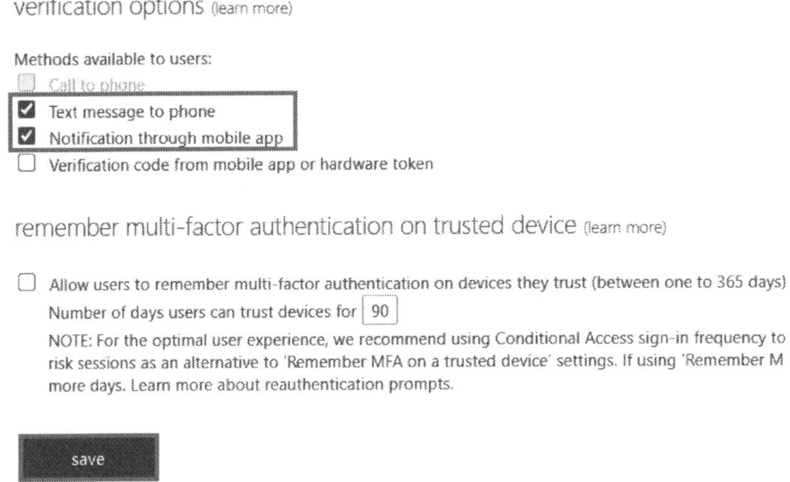

Figure 4.16 – MFA verification options

7. On the **multi-factor authentication service settings** page, click on **users**, select **Brenda Tao**, and then click on **Enable**. Click on **enable multi-factor auth** and then click on **Close**:

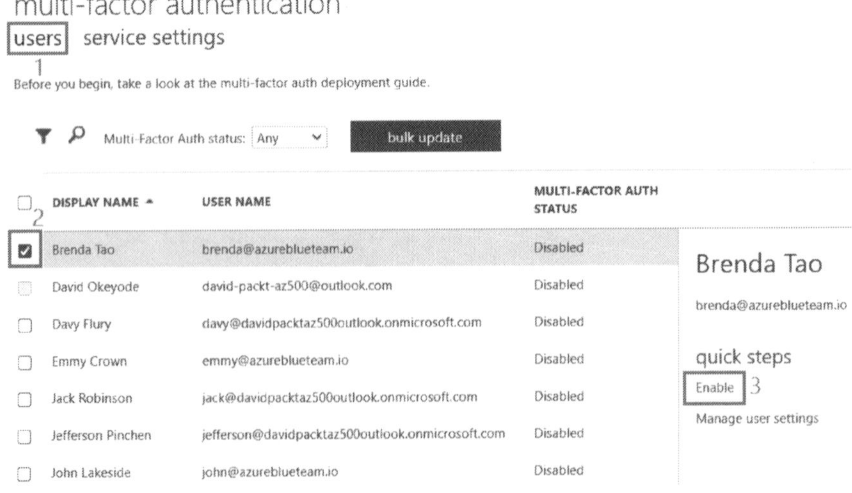

Figure 4.17 – Enabling user MFA

8. Open a different browser in InPrivate or incognito mode and browse to the Azure Portal: `https://portal.azure.com`.
9. In the **Sign in** window, enter Brenda's username and then click **Next**:

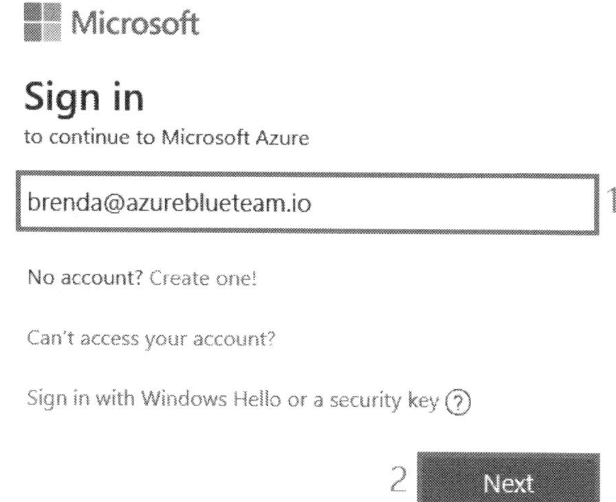

Figure 4.18 – Signing in as Brenda

10. In the **Enter password** window, enter the password that you set for Brenda earlier. Click **Sign in**.
11. In the **More information required** window, click **Next**:

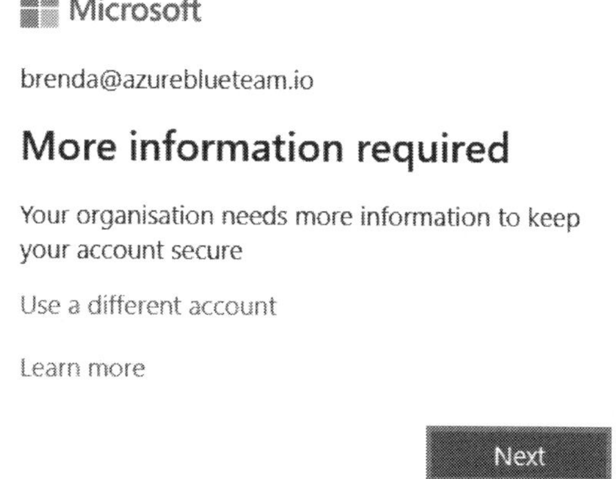

Figure 4.19 – MFA registration prompt

12. In the **Keep your account secure** window, click on **Next**. Then, click on **Next** again:

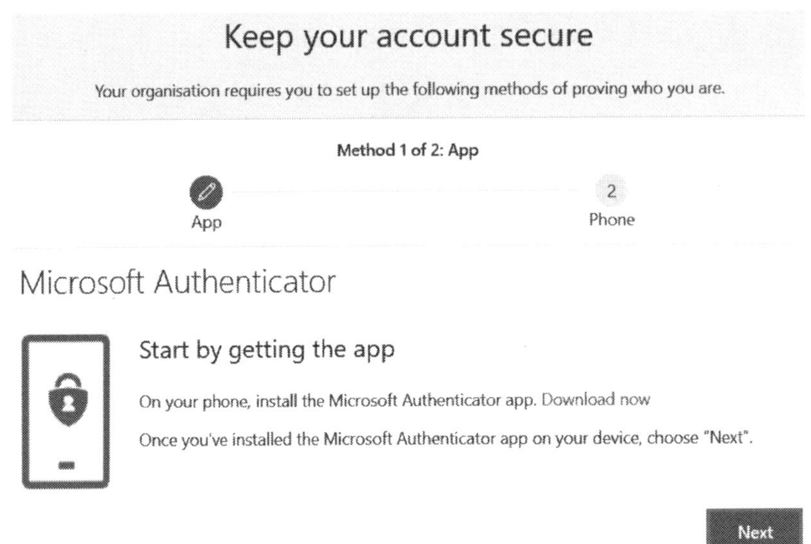

Figure 4.20 – MFA registration setup

13. Open the Microsoft Authenticator app on your mobile phone and click on **Add Account → Work or school account → Scan QR code → Click Next**.
14. In the **Scan the QR Code** window, scan the QR code and then click **Next**:

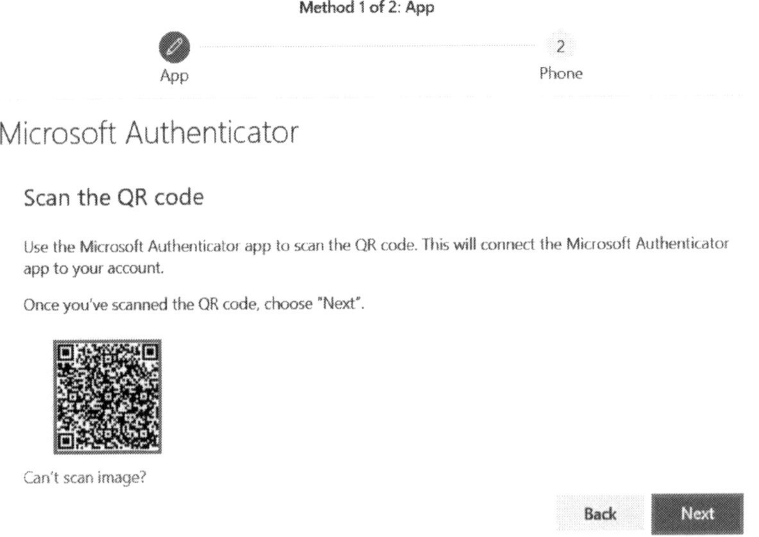

Figure 4.21 – MFA device QR code scan

15. A notification will be sent to your mobile phone, approve the notification, and then click **Next**:

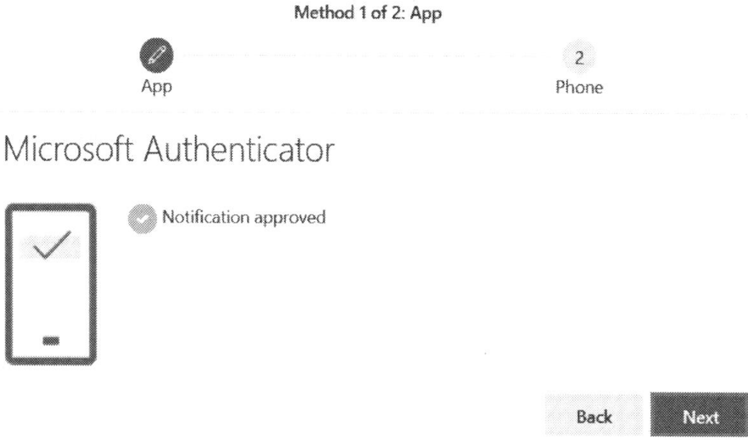

Figure 4.22 – MFA device notification approved

16. In the **Phone** window, select your country code and enter your phone number. Click **Next**:

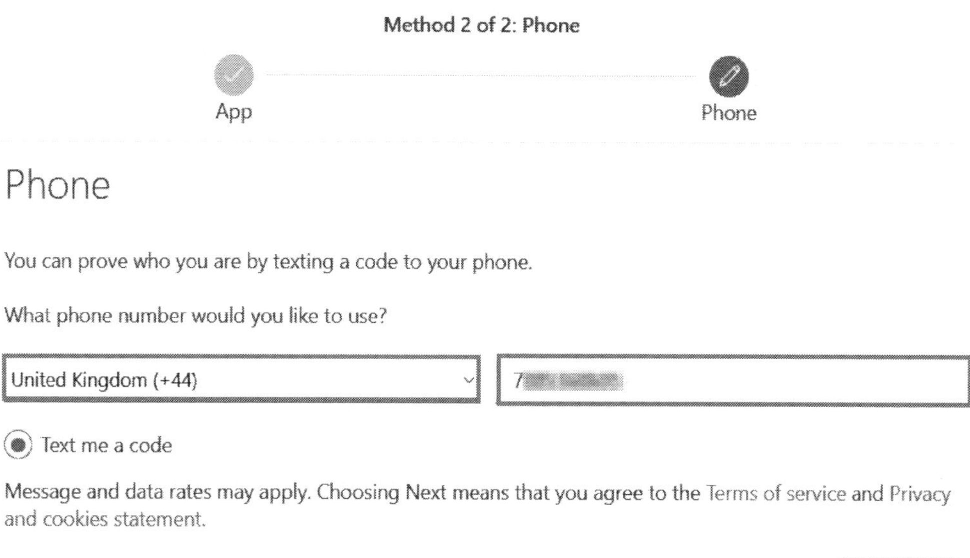

Figure 4.23 – MFA phone registration

17. Enter the verification code sent to your phone and click **Next**. Click **Next** again, and then click **Done**:

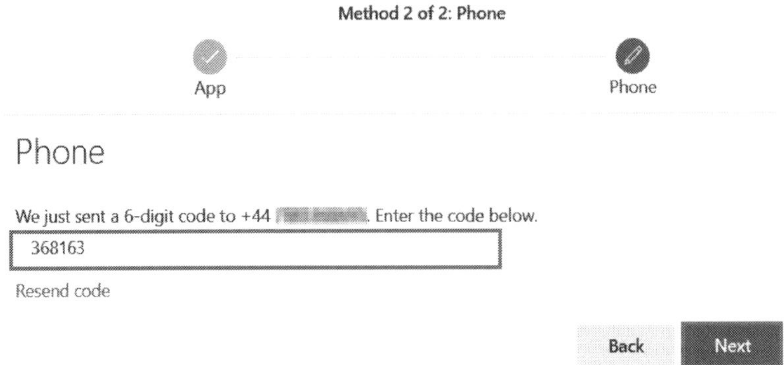

Figure 4.24 – MFA registration verification code

We have now successfully enabled MFA for a user and completed the registration of the user's device for MFA verification. In the next section, we will start to look at the more advanced security capabilities of Azure AD, starting with conditional access.

Implementing conditional access policies

Conditional access is an Azure AD feature that protects applications by requiring certain criteria (beyond identity authentication) to be met before access is granted. What exactly does this mean? For us to understand how conditional access works, let's review how normal application access works with Azure AD and then compare the process to how it works when we implement conditional access:

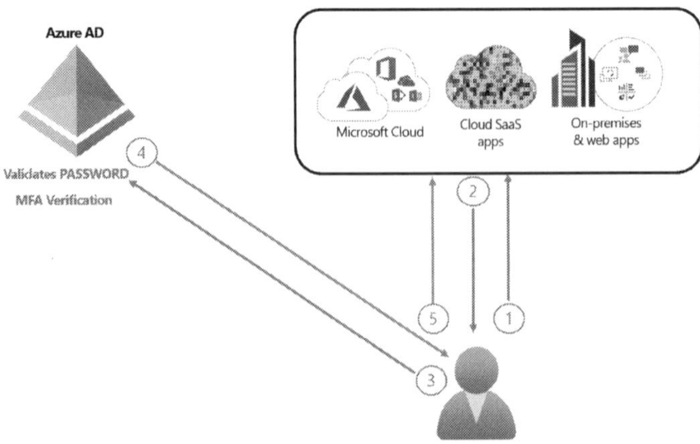

Figure 4.25 – Normal application access (without conditional access)

Figure 4.25 illustrates the normal application access flow (without conditional access):

- **Step 1**: A user accesses an application that uses Azure AD as its identity provider.
- **Steps 2 and 3**: The user's client is redirected to Azure AD, which validates the first factor of authentication – the user's password. If MFA is required, MFA will also be verified.
- **Steps 4 and 5**: Following successful verification, the user's client is granted an access token for the application.

Now, let's compare this with the flow using conditional access:

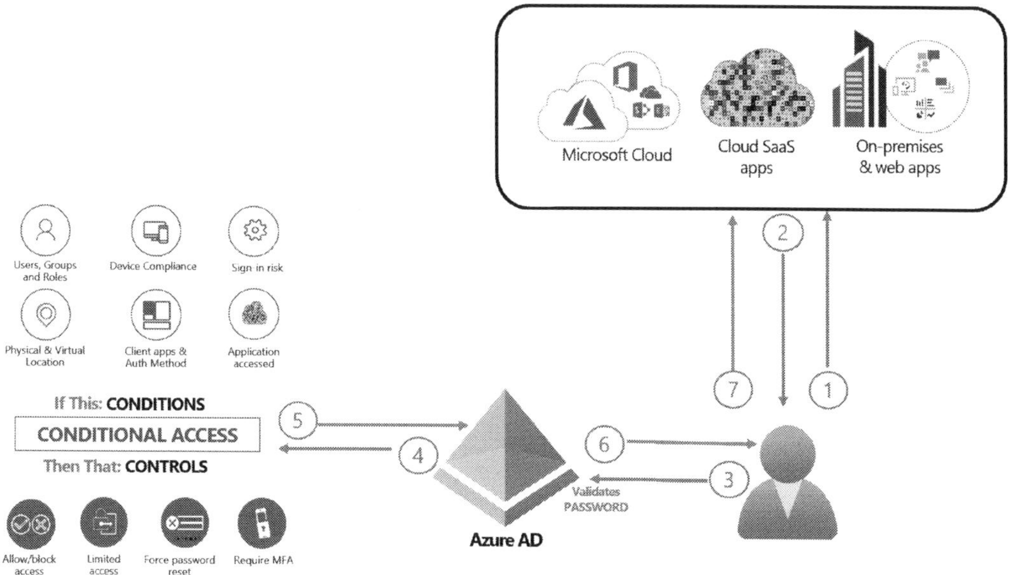

Figure 4.26 – Normal application access (with conditional access)

Figure 4.26 illustrates the following:

- **Step 1**: A user accesses an application that uses Azure AD as its identity provider.
- **Steps 2, 3**: The user's client is redirected to Azure AD, which validates the first factor of authentication – the user's password.
- **Step 4**: Following successful password verification, the request is evaluated using the configured conditional access policies. We can have one or more conditional access policies configured. A conditional access policy is made up of two main parts: the **conditions to match** and the **control to apply**.

The **conditions** are based on information signals relating to the specific authentication request. Common conditions include **user information** (for example, role assignment or group membership), **user location** (source IP address), **user device information**, and **client application**, which the user is trying to access.

The **control** could be to allow access, block access, or require MFA if the defined conditions are matched in the authentication request.

- **Steps 5, 6, and 7**: The result of the conditional access policy evaluation is passed on to the user's client.

Here are some of the common use cases of conditional access:

- Requiring MFA: For administrators only; per application (for example, when accessing Azure management portals); only for access attempts from untrusted networks
- Blocking legacy authentication
- Requiring trusted locations for MFA registration
- Blocking access by location
- Requiring compliant devices

> **Important note**
>
> **Legacy authentication** is a term used to describe authentication requests made from *older Office clients* such as an Office 2010 client and any application client that uses legacy mail protocols such as `IMAP/SMTP/POP3`.
>
> Legacy authentication clients pose a major security risk as they do not support MFA. An attacker could use legacy clients to bypass configured MFA policies. The best way to mitigate this risk is to block attempts from clients using legacy authentication.

Now that you have some understanding of conditional access policies, let's look at how policies are evaluated if we have multiple conditions in a policy or multiple policies in a tenant.

Conditional access – How policies are evaluated

Certain rules govern how conditional access policies are evaluated when determining whether an access attempt will be allowed or blocked. Here are the two critical rules to be aware of:

1. Here is the first rule: If a policy has multiple conditions, all conditions MUST be met in order for the policy control to be applied. What does this statement mean? Let's try to understand it using an example.

   Figure 4.27 shows a single conditional policy called **Policy-1**. **Policy-1** has three conditions defined – **Member of HR-Group**; **Windows OS**; and **Browser Client**. The policy also has the control set to allow access:

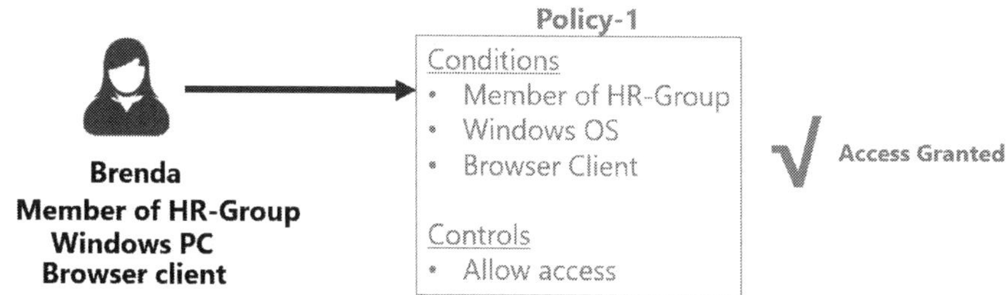

Figure 4.27 – Multi-condition conditional access policy

   For this policy to apply to an authentication request, all three conditions must be met by that request. In our example, the user Brenda's authentication request matches the three configured conditions, therefore, this policy will match, and the defined control (allow access) will be applied. If Brenda's authentication request only matches one of the three defined conditions, this policy will not be applied to the request and the next policy will be evaluated.

2. Here is the second rule: If there are multiple conditional access policies, all matching policies will be applied, and if there is a conflict in resulting controls, the **Block access** control always wins. What does this mean? Let's look at an example to try to make sense of it.

Figure 4.28 shows two conditional access policies called **Policy-1** and **Policy-2**:

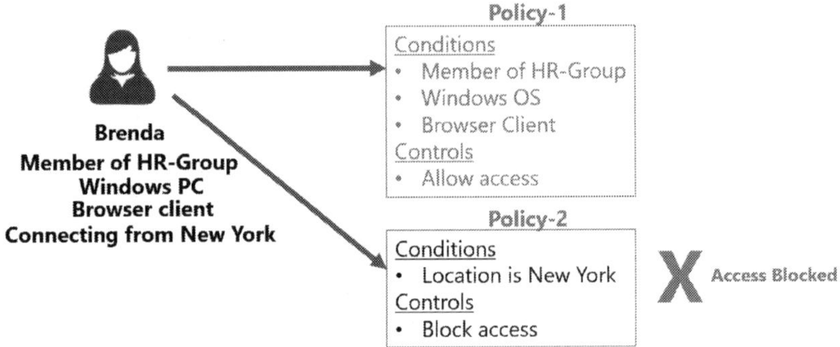

Figure 4.28 – Multi-condition conditional access policy

Policy-1 has three conditions defined – **Member of HR-Group**; **Windows OS**; and **Browser Client**. The defined control is to allow access.

Policy-2 has a single condition defined – the New York location. The defined control is to block access.

Because the user Brenda's authentication request matches the three defined conditions of **Policy-1**, the policy will match. But because the authentication request also matches the defined condition of **Policy-2**, it will match also. In this situation, the net effective control that will apply will be a combined result of all matching policies. In this case, access will be blocked for Brenda because a **Block access** control result always wins when conflicting controls apply. Hopefully, that makes sense to you.

Next, let's review the best practices.

Conditional access best practices

As you can see from previous explanations, conditional access is a powerful feature that we can use to implement. However, to avoid issues down the line, there are best practices that it is recommended to follow. A failure to follow these best practices can have severe consequences, including the risk of locking everyone in your organization out from being able to access applications. Here are the five key ones:

1. Do not use the block access control for any policy that includes all users or all applications. This configuration blocks access to your entire organization, and it is not a good idea.

2. Avoid the use of the `require domain join` or `require compliant device` access controls for any policy that includes all users or all applications. If you are yet to have a domain-joined device or a compliant device in your organization, this will lock everyone out.
3. Before configuring conditional access policies, it is highly recommended to create two emergency access or break-glass accounts that you can use to roll back an organization-wide misconfiguration. The two emergency accounts should be excluded from conditional access policies that block access or that require further compliance.
4. Use the `what-if` tool to test policies before enabling them. You can read more at this link: `https://docs.microsoft.com/en-gb/azure/active-directory/conditional-access/what-if-tool`.
5. And finally, roll out new policies in phases. It is recommended to have a group of users that can act as your pilot group to evaluate the impact before rolling out to the wider organization. This way, you can verify that your policies behave as expected.

Now that you have some understanding of conditional access policies and best practices to follow, we will implement conditional access in the next exercise.

Hands-on exercise – Implementing conditional access

Here are the tasks that will be completed in this exercise:

- **Task 1**: Configure a conditional access policy.
- **Task 2**: Test the conditional access policy.

Let's now complete the aforementioned tasks by performing the following steps:

1. Open a web browser and browse to the Azure portal URL: `https://portal.azure.com`.
2. Sign in to the portal using the account that you used to sign up in the previous chapter.

3. Click the portal menu icon in the top-left corner and select **Azure Active Directory**:

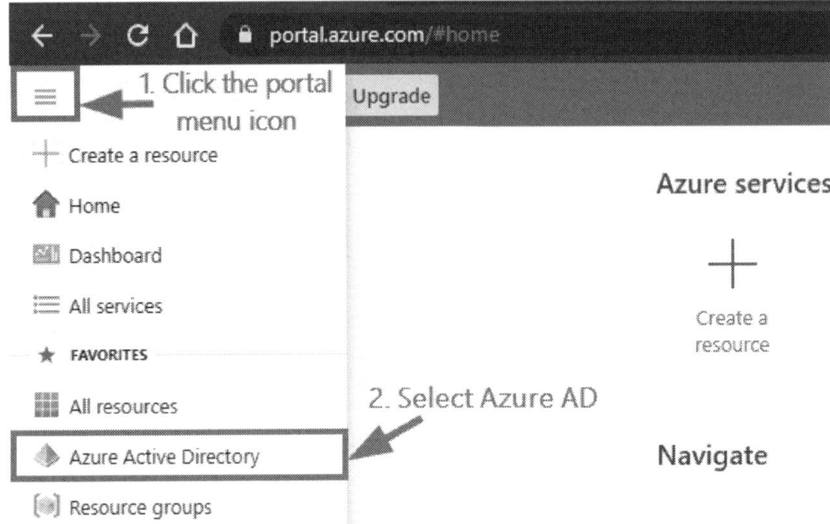

Figure 4.29 – Selecting Azure AD

4. In the **Default Directory | Overview** blade, in the **Manage** section, click **Security**. In the **Protect** section, click **Conditional Access**:

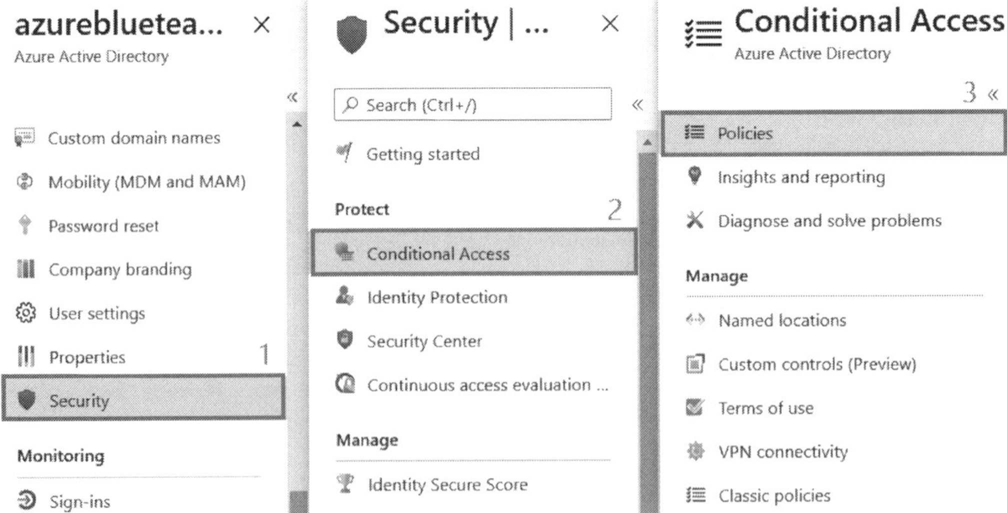

Figure 4.30 – Selecting conditional access policies

5. On the **Conditional Access | Policies** blade, click **+ New policy**:

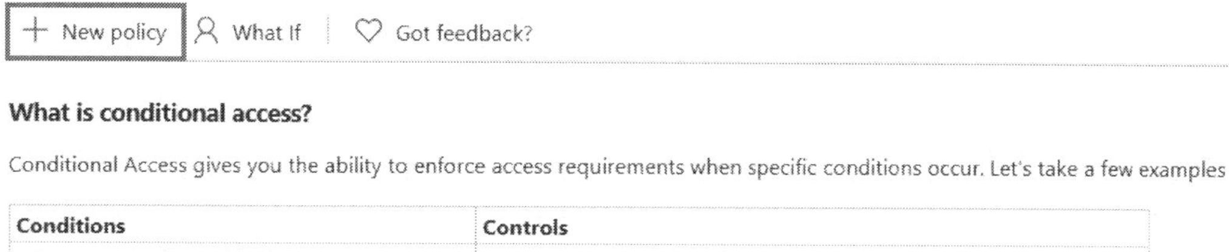

Figure 4.31 – Creating a new conditional access policy

6. On the **New** blade, configure the following settings:

   Name: `Azure-Management-External-Policy`

   Assignments

   Click **Users and groups**, select the **Users and Groups** checkbox, and then, on the **Select** blade, click **Brenda Tao** and then click **Select**:

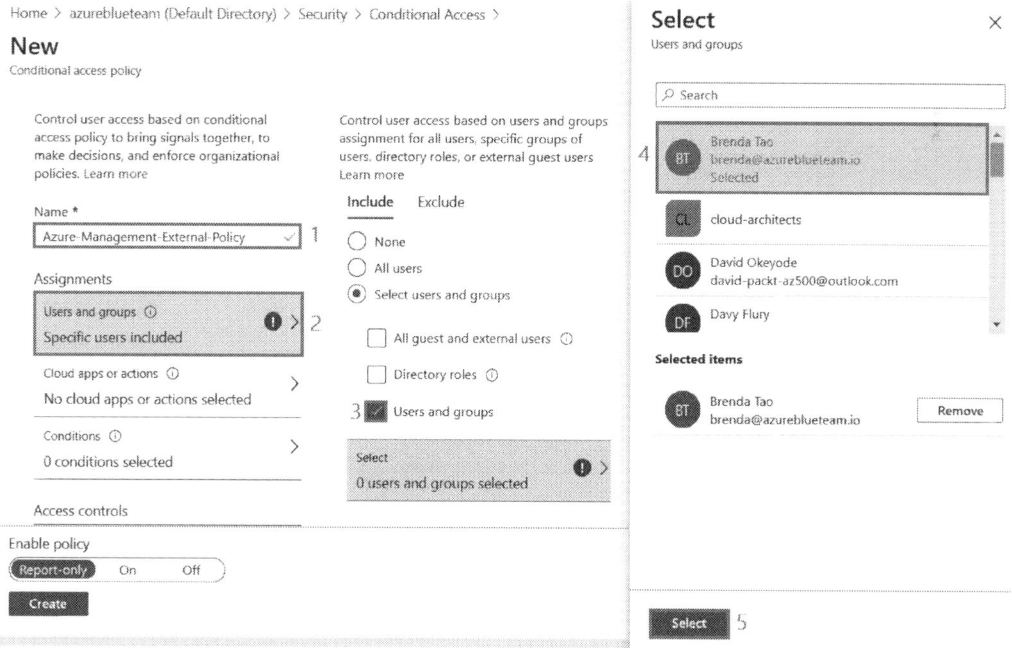

Figure 4.32 – Configuring a conditional access policy

7. Click **Cloud apps or actions**, click **Select apps**, click **Microsoft Azure Management**, and then click **Select**:

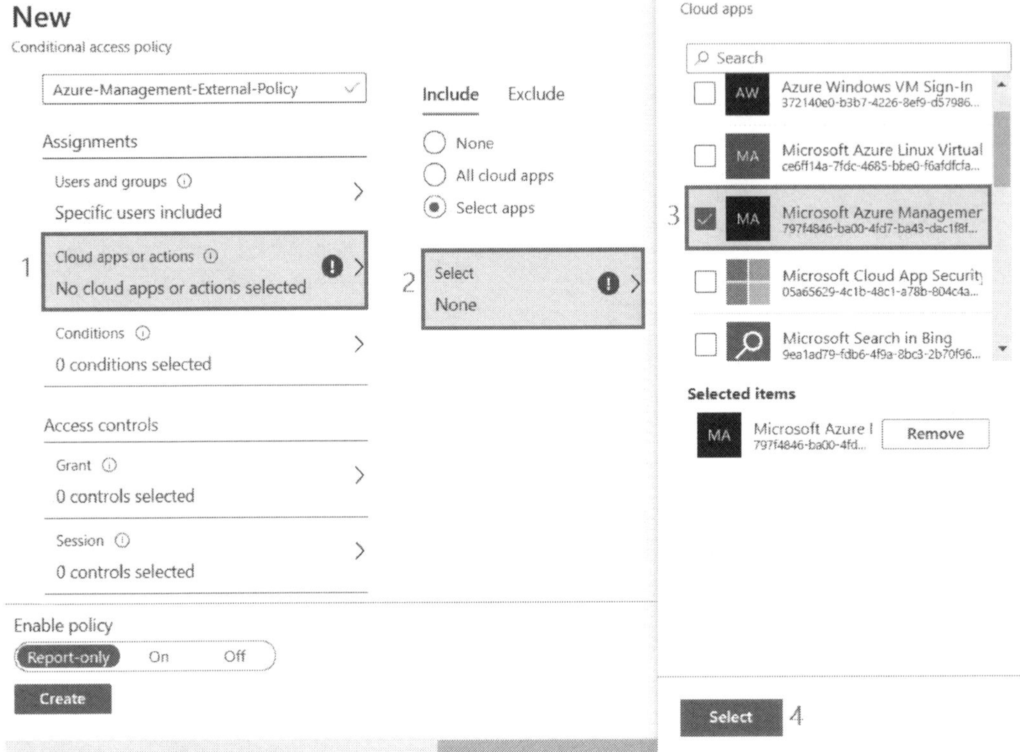

Figure 4.33 – Conditional access cloud apps configuration

8. Review the warning that this policy impacts access to the Azure portal:

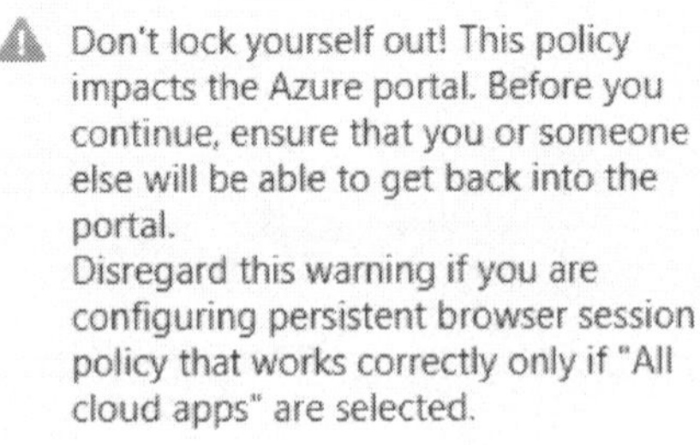

Figure 4.34 – Conditional policy lockout warning

9. Click **Conditions**, followed by **Sign-in risk**, and then, on the **Sign-in risk** blade, review the risk levels but do not make any changes and then close the **Sign-in risk** blade:

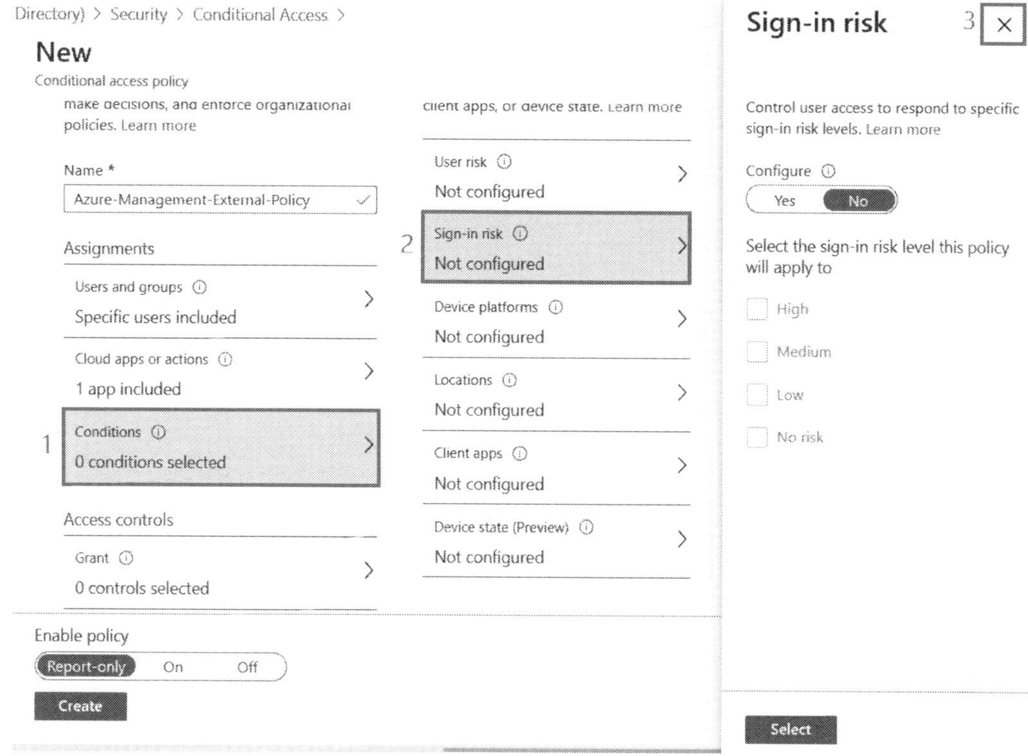

Figure 4.35 – Configuring conditional access sign-in risk configuration

10. Click **Device platforms**, review the device platforms that can be included, and then click **Done**:

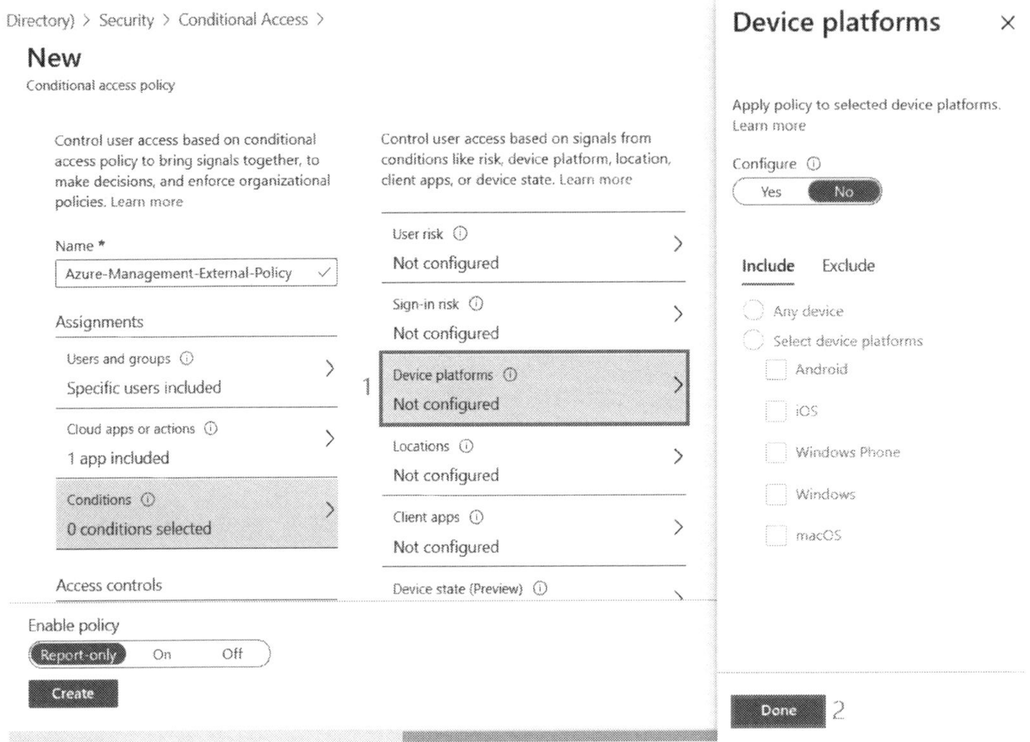

Figure 4.36 – Conditional access device platform configuration

11. Click **Locations** and review the location options without making any changes:

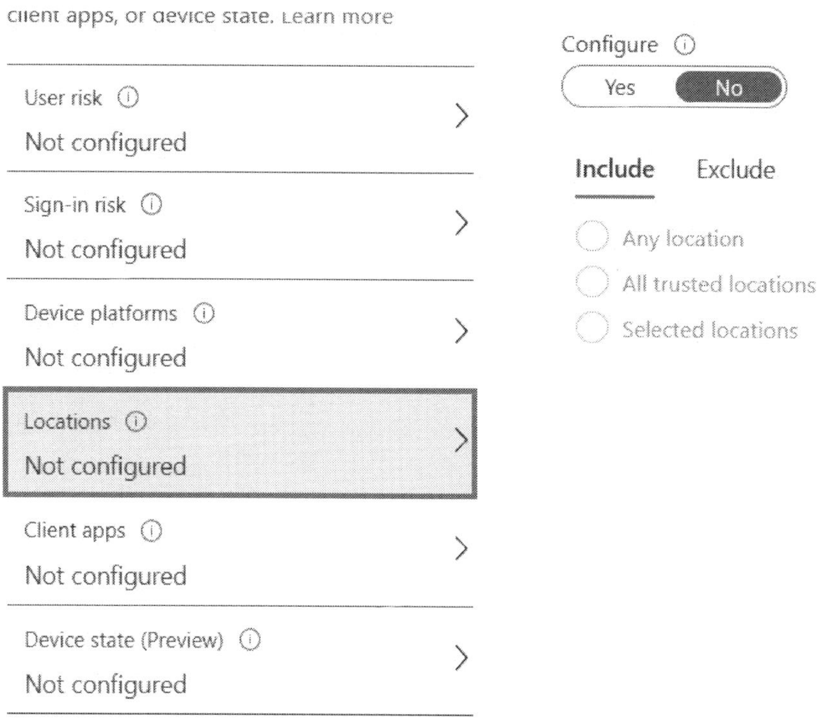

Figure 4.37 – Conditional access location configuration

12. Click **Grant** in the **Access controls** section and then, on the **Grant** blade, review the control options and then select **Block access**. You can see that conditional access can be used to apply MFA on a granular basis. Click **Select**:

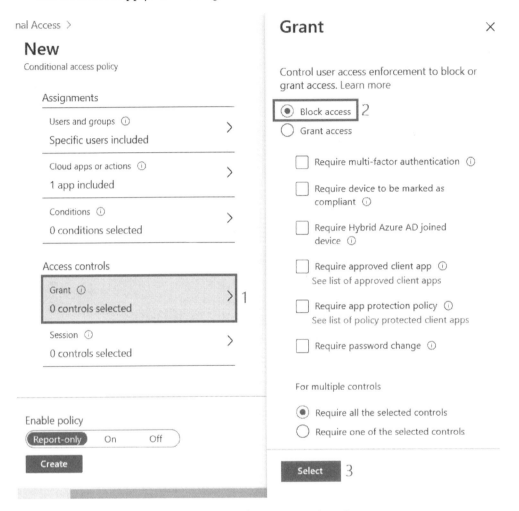

Figure 4.38 – Conditional access control configuration

13. Set **Enable policy** to **On**. Then, click **Create**:

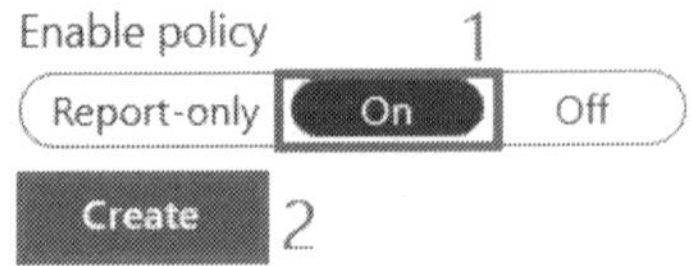

Figure 4.39 – Conditional access enable policy

At this point, you have a conditional access policy that blocks the user Brenda from signing in to the Azure portal. In the remaining steps, you will sign in to the Azure portal as Brenda to verify that access is now blocked. You will also delete the policy before proceeding.

14. Open an InPrivate or Incognito window.
15. In the new browser window, navigate to the Azure portal: `https://portal.azure.com`. Sign in with Brenda's user account. You will receive a message about the user not having permission:

brenda@azureblueteam.io

You don't have access to this

Your sign-in was successful, but you don't have permission to access this resource.

Sign out and sign in with a different account

More details

Figure 4.40 – Conditional access block message

16. Close the InPrivate/Incognito browser window. You have now verified that the newly created conditional access policy blocks access when Brenda signs in to the Azure portal.
17. Back in the browser window, in the **Conditional Access | Policies** blade, click on the ellipsis next to the conditional access policy that was created earlier and then click on **Delete**. When prompted to confirm, click **Yes**:

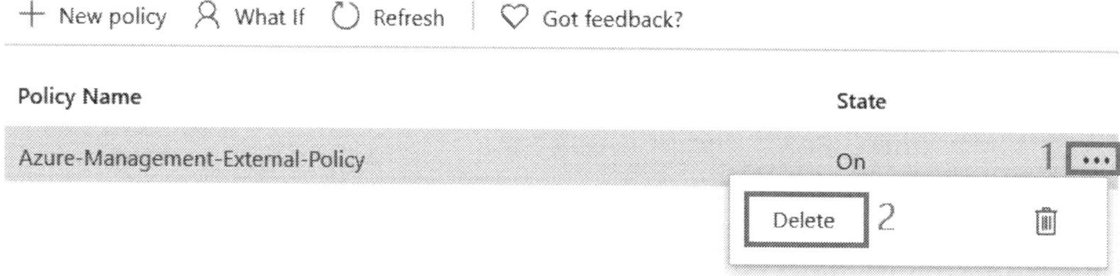

Figure 4.41 – Deleting a conditional access policy

In this exercise, you implemented a conditional access policy to block access when a user signs in to the Azure portal. In the next section, we will cover another advanced security capability of Azure AD – identity protection.

Protecting identities with Azure AD Identity Protection

So, what is identity protection? Here is my definition – **It is an automated identity risk detection service provided by Microsoft**. But what does this mean?

If you think about it, there is a wealth of useful security information in Azure AD sign-in activities. By analyzing sign-in activities, we can uncover suspicious events that indicate that a user's identity has been compromised. For example, if we notice a sign-in event that deviates from a user's normal sign-in behavior, this could indicate that the user's identity is being used by someone other than the user.

The issue is that manual analysis to uncover these types of incidents involves a lot of administrative effort and may be practically impossible depending on the size of the environment. This is where identity protection comes in. **It can help us to automate the detection of indicators of compromise and suspicious actions (for our user identities) in Azure AD sign-in activities.**

The great thing about identity protection is that it is not only about *detection*, but we can also *investigate* any risks that have been identified using its reports. We can even *export* the detections to third-party systems for further analysis and we can configure policies to react to risks that are detected.

Using identity protection requires an Azure AD Premium P2 license. To understand identity protection, there are four main concepts that we need to grasp – risk categories, detection types, risk levels, and policies.

Identity protection – risk categories

One term that you will often hear when discussing identity protection is **risk**. Risk describes a suspicious activity or event related to a user identity. Identity protection can detect two categories of risks – **User risks** and **Sign-in risks**.

A **user risk** represents the likelihood that a user account has been compromised. Identity protection can detect the following user risk types:

User Risk Type	Description	Detection Type
Leaked credentials	Detects whether a user's valid credentials have been leaked on the dark web, public paste sites, or other sources such as law enforcement agencies. The detection is powered by the Microsoft Identity Security team.	Offline
Azure AD threat intelligence	Detects unusual user sign-in activity that is either not consistent with the user's normal sign-in behavior or that is consistent with known attack patterns identified by Microsoft's threat intelligence sources.	Offline

> **Important note**
>
> If you are using a hybrid identity configuration with Azure AD Connect as described in *Chapter 3, Azure AD Hybrid Identity*, leaked credential detection will only work with the password hash sync option enabled.

The two user risk types are detected *offline*, as indicated in the preceding table. We will get into what *offline* means in the next sub-section.

A **sign-in risk** represents the likelihood that a given sign-in request is coming from someone else other than the legitimate user. In other words, it goes beyond detecting the fact that a user's credentials have been compromised to detecting that the credentials are actively being used by someone else to sign in as the user. Identity protection uses different techniques to detect sign-in risks. Identity protection can detect the following sign-in risk types:

Sign-in Risk Type	Description	Detection Type
Anonymous IP address	Detects user sign-in activities from an anonymous IP address such as the TOR network or an anonymous VPN service. These sorts of events usually indicate someone trying to hide their activities.	Real-time

Sign-in Risk Type	Description	Detection Type
Atypical travel	Detects sign-in activities by the same user that originates from geographically distant locations within a short period of time; for example, if the same user signs in from Australia and Canada within a short timeframe. The machine learning algorithm that detects this risk avoids false positives by taking into consideration previous sign-in behavior by that user and legitimate factors that could contribute to this behavior, such as signing in from a company VPN or locations regularly used by other users in the organization. The algorithm has an initial learning period of either 14 days or 10 logins, during which it learns a user's sign-in behavior.	Offline
Malware linked IP address	Detects sign-in activities from an IP address that Microsoft threat intelligence systems have identified as being in communication with a known active bot server. This could indicate that the device that the user is connecting from has been compromised with malware.	Offline
Unfamiliar sign-in properties	Detects unfamiliar sign-in activities by a user; for example, a user signing in from a location that they have never connected from in the past or a user signing in with a client that uses basic authentication or legacy protocols. The machine learning algorithm that detects this risk stores information about previous locations that a user connects from and considers these "familiar" locations. Sign-in activity from a location that is not already in the list of familiar locations will then be flagged.	Real-time
Malicious IP address	Detects sign-in activities from an IP address that is considered to be suspicious by Microsoft threat intelligence sources. This is based on IP reputation intelligence.	Offline
Password spray	Detects sign-in activities that match a password spray attack pattern where multiple usernames are attacked using common passwords.	Offline
Admin confirms user compromised	This is a manual detection procedure based on admin confirmation. An administrator can mark a user account as being compromised in the Azure portal, based on investigations done using other means.	Offline

> **Important note**
>
> If you are using a hybrid identity configuration with Azure AD Connect as described in *Chapter 3, Azure AD Hybrid Identity*, password spray detection will only work with the password hash sync option enabled.

The sign-in risk types can either be detected *offline* or in *real time*, as indicated in the preceding table. In the next section, we will discuss what these detection types mean.

Identity protection – detection types

Detection types in identity protection indicate the reporting latency between when suspicious activity happens and when the risk is flagged by identity protection. There are two types of detection as shown in the tables in the previous section: real-time or offline.

Real-time detection means that there is a latency of 5-10 minutes between when suspicious activity occurs and when it is flagged.

Offline detection means there is a latency of 2-4 hours between when suspicious activity occurs and when it is flagged; for example, the **leaked credential** user risk detection type that detects user leaked credentials on the dark web or paste bin sites happens offline. This means that there could be a latency of 2-4 hours between when the leak is identified and when it is flagged by identity protection.

Identity protection – risk levels

Identity protection categorizes risks in three levels: low, medium, and high. You can think of the risk level as a confidence indicator that the user or sign-in has been compromised:

- A **High-risk level** event means there is a strong indicator that the user's identity has been compromised, and any user accounts impacted should be remediated immediately.
- A **Medium-risk level** event means there is a potential risk, and any user accounts impacted should be remediated, but the urgency is lower.
- A **Low-risk level** event means that immediate action may not be required, but when combined with other risk detections, it may provide a strong indication that the identity has been compromised.

Microsoft disclosed information on how risk levels were calculated in the past, but this is no longer the case. This information is now kept confidential. The risk level is useful when we configure identity protection policies to respond to risk events. For example, we could configure a risk policy to block sign-in for high-risk level detections.

Identity protection - policies

The previous concepts of identity protection that we have discussed are about detecting risks. The other aspect is to respond to the risks that have been detected. **Identity protection policies** can be configured to automate the response to risk detections in your environment. There are three default policies in identity protection that administrators can choose to enable:

1. **Sign-in risk policy**: This policy can be used to **automate the response to sign-in risk detections** based on the risk level.

   First, we decide the level of risk that we are willing to accept – **High**, **medium**, or **low**. We then configure the control that we want to apply to the risk. There are three options: **block access**, **allow access**, or **allow access but require MFA**.

   For example, we can configure this policy to require MFA for users if a medium-level sign-in risk is detected.

   Microsoft's recommendation is to set the sign-in risk threshold to **Medium**. This way, the policy is only triggered for medium and high severity sign-in risk detections, thereby reducing user interruptions. We always want to strike the right balance between security and user experience. If we trigger this policy for low-level sign-in risk detections, we will introduce additional user interruptions, but increase our security posture.

   > **Important note**
   >
   > Using the sign-in risk policy automates the response to sign-in risk detections on a global level for all applications. Another method that we can use to respond to detected sign-in risks is to configure a conditional access policy to automate the response to sign-in risk detections on a per-application basis.

2. **User risk policy**: This policy can be used to automate the response to user risk detections based on the risk level.

   First, we decide the level of risk that we are willing to accept – **High**, **medium**, or **low**. We then configure the control that we want to apply if the risk level is detected. We have three options: **block access**, **allow access**, or **allow access but require a password change**.

   For example, we can require users to change their passwords if their accounts are flagged for a high-level user risk. Microsoft's recommendation is to set the user risk threshold to **High**. This way, the policy is only triggered for high severity user risk detections, thereby reducing user interruptions.

3. **Azure AD MFA registration policy**: This third policy is not really about automating the response to risk detections. It can be used to roll out MFA across an organization.

   You may be thinking, why is this option under identity protection then? This is a valid question. The reason is to allow for user self-remediation. For example, if we configure a sign-in risk policy to **allow access but require MFA** for medium sign-in risk detections, sign-in attempts that are identified as suspicious will fail for users who are yet to register their MFA device, and they may need to call the help desk, leading to an increased workload.

   Enabling this policy is a great way to ensure that new users in our organization have registered for MFA on their first day so that they are ready for the interruptions that may be caused when suspicious activities are detected.

   Figure 4.42 illustrates the user access flow with identity protection policies configured:

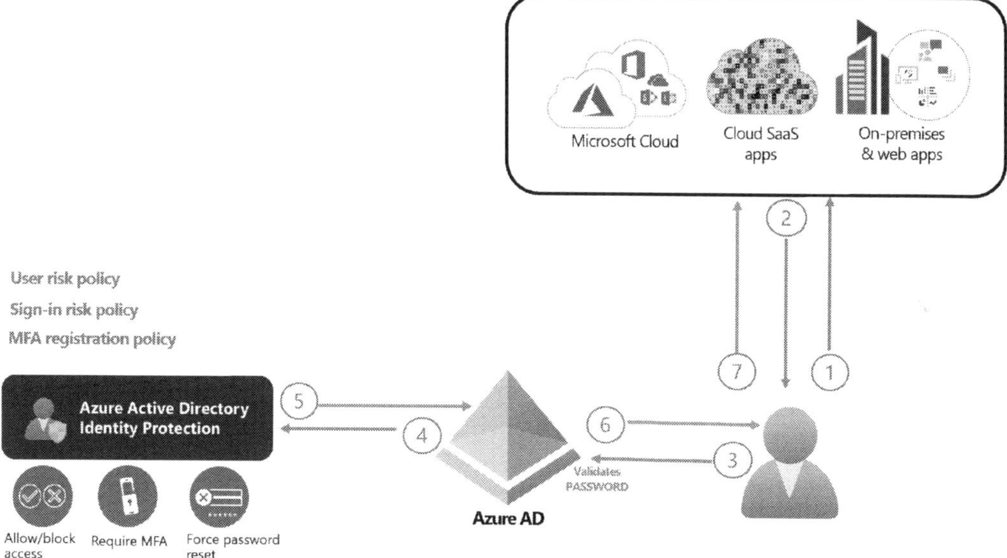

Figure 4.42 – Identity protection flow

- **Step 1**: A user accesses an application that uses Azure AD as its identity provider.
- **Steps 2, 3**: The user's client is redirected to Azure AD, which validates the first factor of authentication – the user's password.
- **Step 4**: Following successful password verification, the user and sign-in risk levels are evaluated by identity protection.

- If no user or sign-in risk is detected and the MFA registration policy does not apply, the flow continues.
- If a user or sign-in risk is detected, access can either be blocked, allowed without interruptions, allowed with MFA (for sign-in risk), or allowed with a password change required (for user risk). The control that will be applied is based on the risk level detected and the control that is configured in the identity protection policies.
- **Steps 5, 6, and 7**: The result of the identity protection policy evaluation is passed on to the user's client.

Now that you have some understanding of Azure AD identity protection, in the next exercise, you will configure its policies (user risk and sign-in risk) to respond to risk detections.

Exercise – Implementing Azure AD Identity Protection

Here are the tasks that will be completed in this exercise:

- Viewing Azure AD Identity Protection options in the Azure portal
- Configuring a user risk policy
- Configuring a sign-in risk policy
- Simulating risk events against the Azure AD Identity Protection policies
- Reviewing the Azure AD Identity Protection reports

Let's now complete the aforementioned tasks by performing the following steps:

1. Open a web browser and browse to the Azure portal URL: `https://portal.azure.com`.
2. Sign in to the portal using the account that you used to sign up in the previous chapter.
3. Click the portal menu icon in the top-left corner and select **Azure Active Directory**:

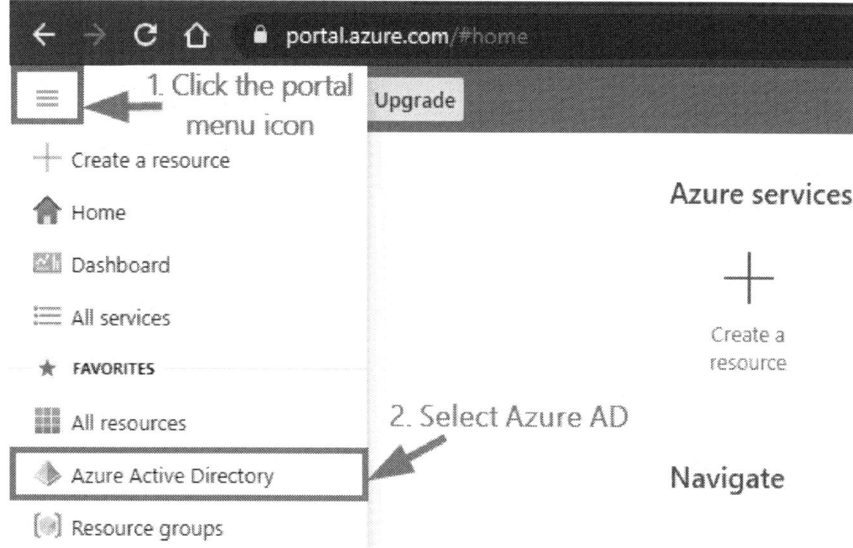

Figure 4.43 – Selecting Azure AD

4. In the **Default Directory | Overview** blade, in the **Manage** section, click **Security** followed by **Identity Protection**:

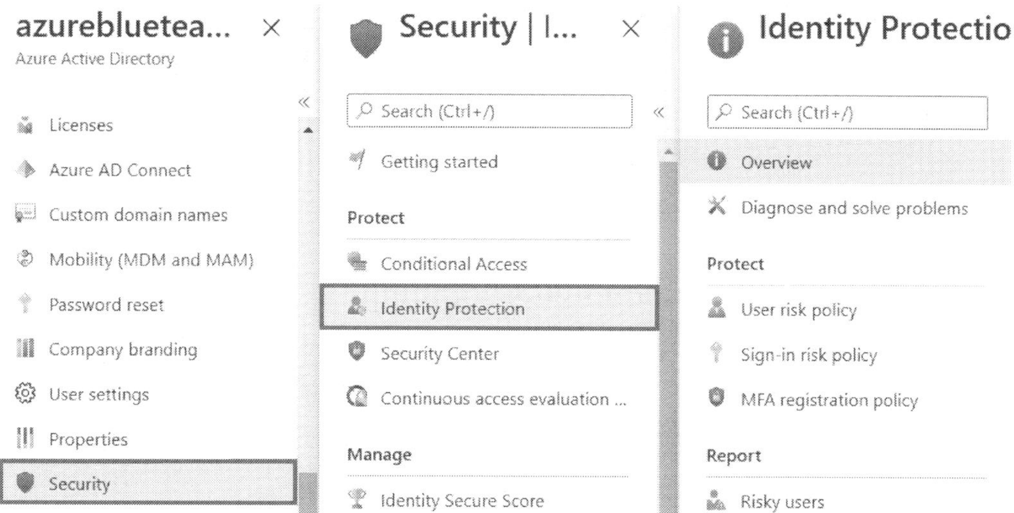

Figure 4.44 – Selecting Identity Protection

5. In the **Identity Protection | Overview** blade, review the **Protect**, **Report**, and **Notify** sections:

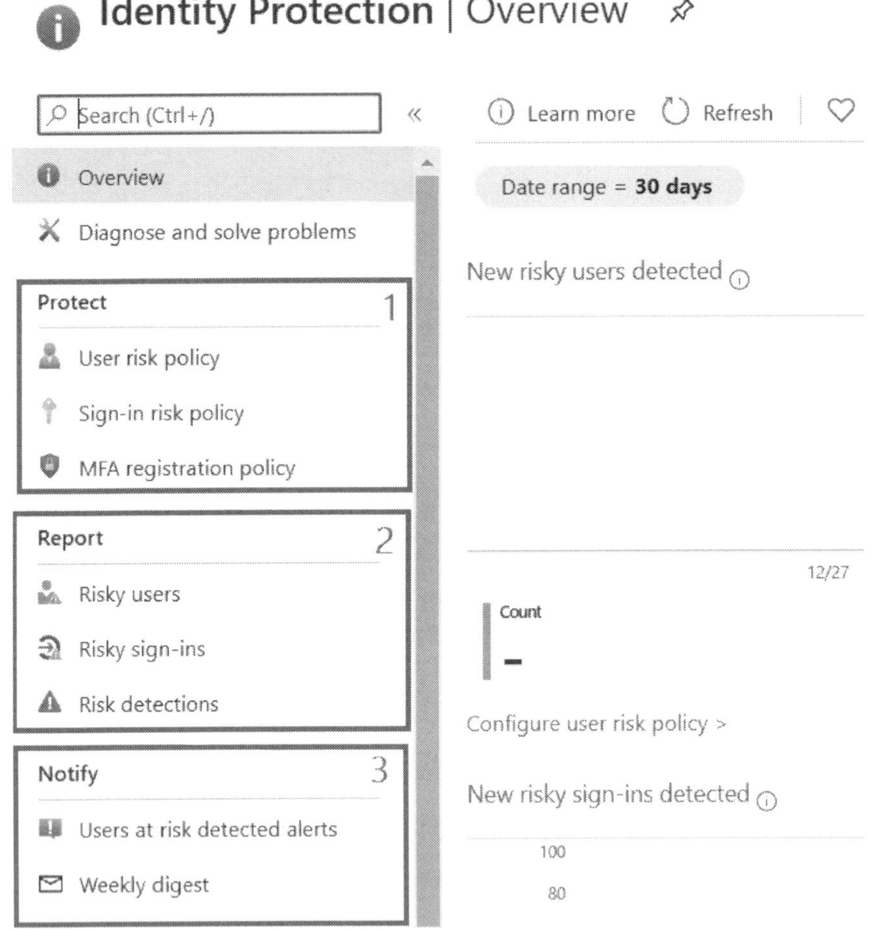

Figure 4.45 – Reviewing Identity Protection configuration options

6. In the **Identity Protection | Overview** blade, in the **Protect** section, click **User risk policy**. Configure **User risk remediation policy** with the following settings:

   Assignments:

   Click **Users**. On the **Include** tab of the **Users** blade, ensure that the **All users** option is selected.

Still on the **Users** blade, switch to the **Exclude** tab, click **Select excluded users**, select your current user account, and then click **Select**. This is an important step to ensure that we do not lock ourselves out!

User risk:

Click **User risk**. On the **User risk** blade, select **Low and above**, and then click **Done**.

Controls:

Click **Access**. On the **Access** blade, ensure that the **Allow access** option and the **Require password change** checkbox are selected and then click **Done**.

Set **Enforce policy** to **On** and click **Save**:

Figure 4.46 – Configuring a user risk remediation policy

7. On the **Identity Protection | User risk policy** blade, in the **Protect** section, click **Sign-in risk policy**. Configure the **Sign-in risk remediation policy** with the following settings:

   Assignments:

   Click **Users – All users**. On the **Include** tab of the **Users** blade, ensure that the **All users** option is selected.

On the **Users** blade, switch to the **Exclude** tab, click **Select excluded users**, select your user account, and then click **Select**. This is an important step to ensure that we do not lock ourselves out!

Sign-in risk:

Click **Sign-in risk**. On the **Sign-in risk** blade, select **Low and above**, and then click **Done**.

Controls:

Click **Access**. On the **Access** blade, ensure that the **Block access** option is selected and then click **Done**.

Set **Enforce Policy** to **On** and then click **Save**.

Leave the browser open:

Figure 4.47 – Configuring a sign-in risk remediation policy

8. On your PC, open an InPrivate or Incognito browser window and then navigate to the ToR Browser Project page at `https://www.torproject.org/projects/torbrowser.html.en`.

9. Download the version of the ToR browser for your operating system. Install it with the default settings:

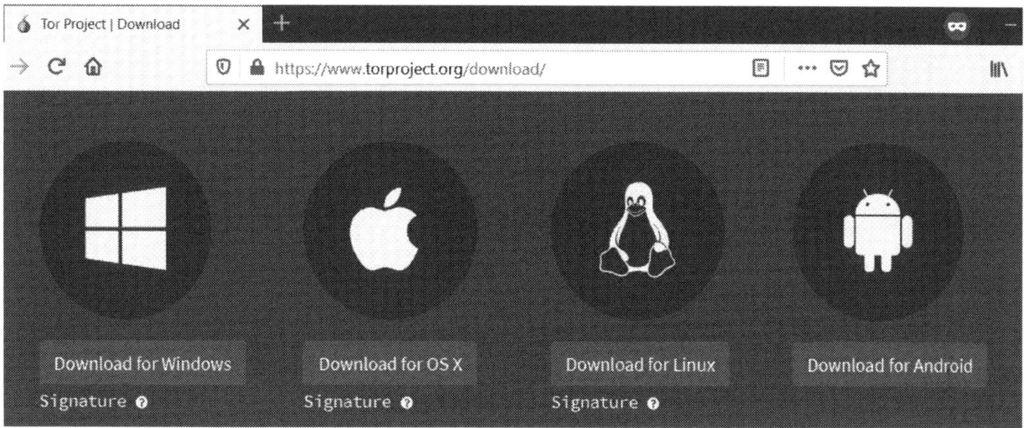

Figure 4.48 – Downloading the ToR browser

10. Once the installation completes, start the ToR browser and use the **Connect** option on the initial page to connect to the ToR network:

Figure 4.49 – Connecting to the ToR network

11. In the ToR browser, browse to the Application Access Panel URL: `https://myapps.microsoft.com`.

12. In the sign-in window, sign in with *Brenda's* account:

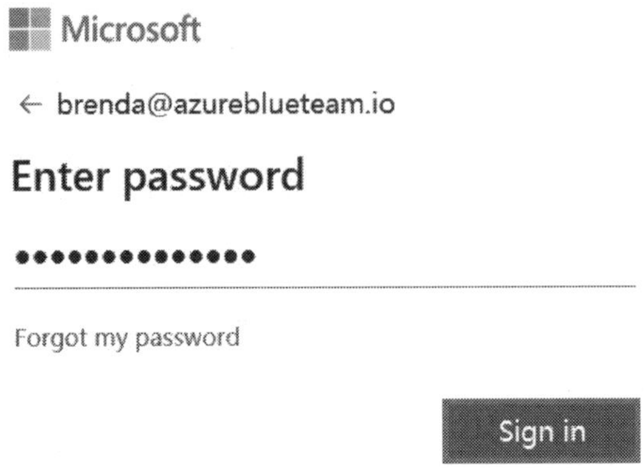

Microsoft

← brenda@azureblueteam.io

Enter password

••••••••••••••

Forgot my password

Sign in

Figure 4.50 – Authenticating with Brenda's account

13. You will be presented with the message **Your sign-in was blocked**. This is expected since the sign-in risk policy that we configured blocks any sign-in risk level with the low-risk level and above. Close the ToR browser:

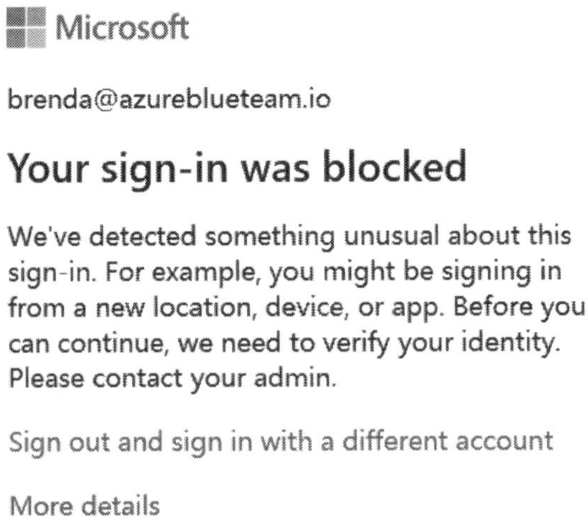

brenda@azureblueteam.io

Your sign-in was blocked

We've detected something unusual about this sign-in. For example, you might be signing in from a new location, device, or app. Before you can continue, we need to verify your identity. Please contact your admin.

Sign out and sign in with a different account

More details

Figure 4.51 – Identity protection block message

14. Back in the Azure portal, in the **Report** section, click **Risky users**. Review the report and identify any entries referencing Brenda's user account. Note that it could take a few minutes for the risk event to be visible in the portal:

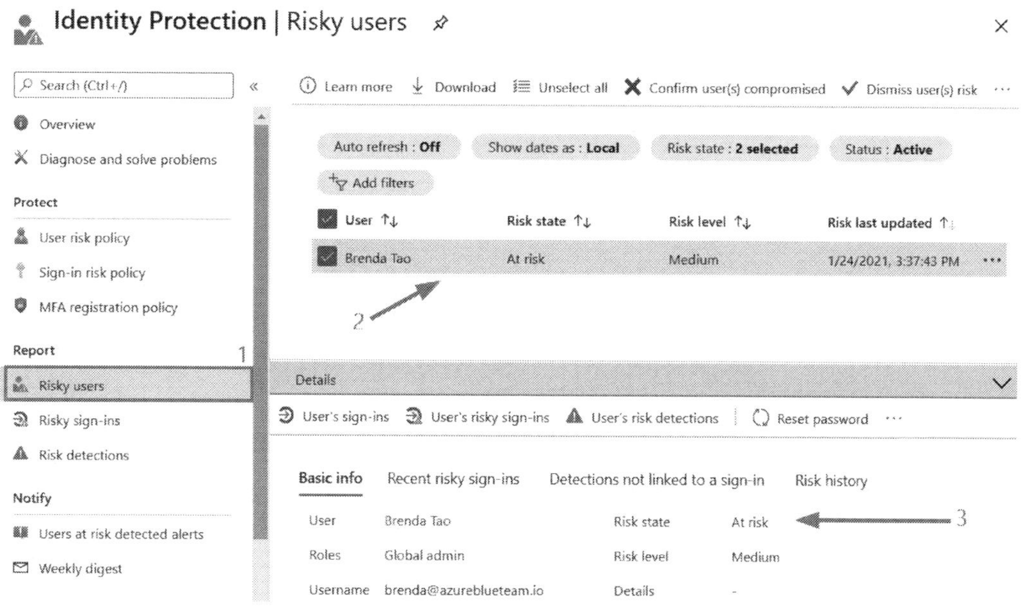

Figure 4.52 – Identity protection risky users report

15. In the **Reports** section, click **Risky sign-ins**. Review the report and identify any entries corresponding to the sign-in with Brenda's user account:

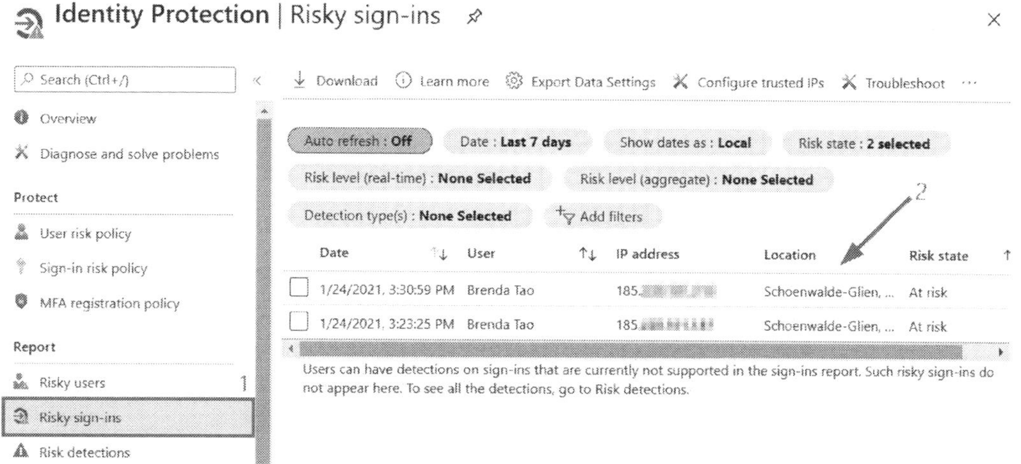

Figure 4.53 – Identity protection risky sign-ins report

16. In the **Reports** section, click **Risk detections**. Review the report and identify any entries representing the sign-in from an anonymous IP address generated by the ToR browser. Note: It may take 10-15 minutes for risks to show up in the reports:

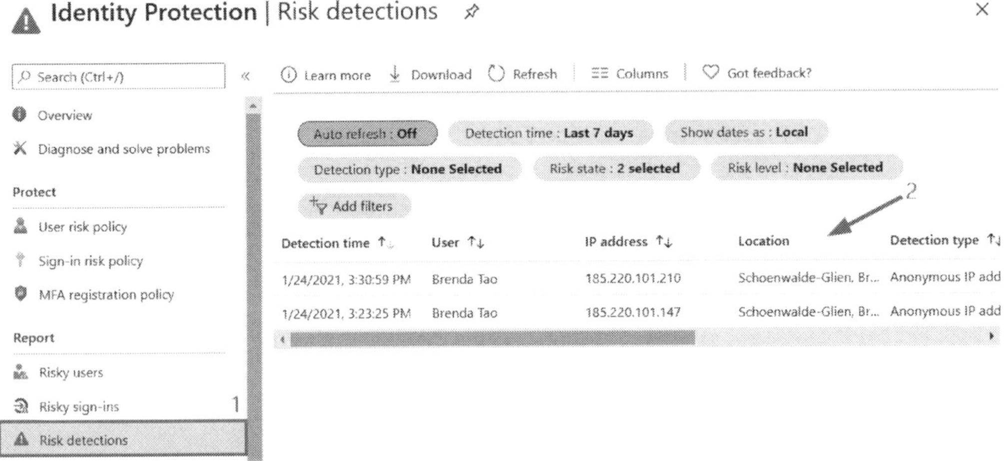

Figure 4.54 – Identity Protection risk detections

Now that you have tested Identity Protection, let's clean up our account to prevent conflicts in later exercises.

17. In the **Protect** section, click **User risk policy**. Set **Enforce policy** to **Off**. Click **Save**.
18. In the **Protect** section, click **Sign-in risk policy**. Set **Enforce policy** to **Off**. Click **Save**.

At this point, you have enabled Azure AD Identity Protection and configured its built-in policies (user risk policy and sign-in risk policy) to respond to identity risk events. You have also validated the effectiveness of the configuration by simulating risk events.

It is worth highlighting that the sign-in risk policy that we configured in this exercise applies on a global level for all applications. There is an option to integrate Identity Protection and conditional access by creating **Risk-based Conditional Access Policies**. This approach uses Identity Protection risk-detection sign-in events as a condition in a conditional access policy. For example, if Identity Protection detects a risky sign-in, a conditional access policy can be used to require the affected user to authenticate with MFA.

Summary

In this chapter, we covered how to configure protection against password-related attacks using Azure AD Password Protection and MFA. We also discussed how to implement conditional access policy controls and assignments to ensure that only authentication requests that meet organization policies are allowed access. And finally, we walked through how to implement identity protection to detect and respond to risky identity events.

In the next chapter, we will take this further by covering how to properly govern privileged access in our Azure environments using Azure AD **Privileged Identity Management** (**PIM**) and Access Reviews. See you in the next chapter!

Question

As we conclude, here is a question for you to test your knowledge regarding this chapter's material. You will find the answer in the *Assessments* section of the *Appendix*:

1. Which of the following is *not* a best practice for implementing conditional access?

    a. Excluding break-glass accounts from conditional access policies that block access

    b. Applying policies to "all users" and "all cloud apps"

    c. Evaluating your policy using the `what if` tool

    d. Rolling out new policies in phases (pilot group)

Further reading

To learn more on the topics covered in this chapter, you can refer to the following links:

- Identity Protection policies: `https://docs.microsoft.com/en-us/azure/active-directory/identity-protection/concept-identity-protection-policies?WT.mc_id=AZ-MVP-5003870`.
- Simulating risk detections in Identity Protection: `https://docs.microsoft.com/en-us/azure/active-directory/identity-protection/howto-identity-protection-simulate-risk?WT.mc_id=AZ-MVP-5003870`.

5
Azure AD Identity Governance

Privileged identities are attractive to attackers because they can be used to gain broad access to an environment, often resulting in a significant business impact. Identity governance ensures that the risk to an organization is reduced even if a user account is compromised. To achieve this, processes need to be in place to ensure that privileged access is granted to the right people only for the duration that it is needed and removed when that duration expires. This way, the chances of an adversary gaining privileged access that could be used to cause significant damage are reduced.

This chapter will equip you with an understanding of how to implement the principles of identity governance using two features of Azure AD Premium P2 – Azure AD **Privileged Identity Management** (**PIM**) and **Access Review**.

Here are the topics that we will cover in this chapter with accompanying hands-on exercises:

- Protecting privileged access using Azure AD Privileged Identity Management (PIM)
- Configuring PIM access reviews

Let's get started!

Technical requirements

To follow along with the instructions in this chapter, you will need the following:

- A PC with an internet connection.
- An Azure subscription. You can use the same subscription that you set up in the first chapter of this book.

Protecting privileged access using Azure AD Privileged Identity Management (PIM)

A **privileged identity** has administrative permissions for our Azure environments. These identities have more permissions for our Azure environments than a typical user. They are usually limited to a small number of users, which may include IT administrators or business users responsible for managing a line of business applications.

As you can imagine, these identities are high-value targets for attackers because of the level of access that is granted to them. If we fail to protect privileged access, an attacker that compromises a privileged user's identity could take advantage of the user's permissions to move laterally within our environments.

When thinking about protecting privileged access, here are some principles that we may want to adopt. Comprehensive privileged identity protection requires the following:

- Access should only be granted to people that require it.
- Access should only be granted when needed (just in time).
- Access should only be granted at the level that is needed (just enough).
- Access should only be granted for the duration that it is needed (time-bound).

These principles fall into the category of what some security professionals refer to as *zero trust principles*. It may sound like simple common sense to you, but managing this type of access protection at scale is complicated. This is where a service such as Azure AD PIM can help us.

What is Azure AD PIM?

So, what is Azure AD PIM? It is an Azure service that helps us to **manage privileged administrative role assignments to Azure AD and Azure resources**. With PIM configured, we can minimize the number of people who have privileged access to Azure AD and Azure resources and only grant the required access when needed and for the duration that it is needed.

To use Azure AD PIM, we need to have and assign Azure AD Premium P2 licenses for users who will be using PIM.

How does Azure AD PIM work?

To get a clearer understanding of how PIM can help us, let's check out some information on how role assignment works with PIM.

Let's say that an admin, **David**, wants to ensure that a user, **Brenda**, can be assigned to the **Global Admin role in Azure AD** by PIM whenever she needs to perform a task that requires the role. He also wants to ensure that the user **Bradley** can be assigned to the **subscription owner role** by PIM whenever he needs it to perform a task:

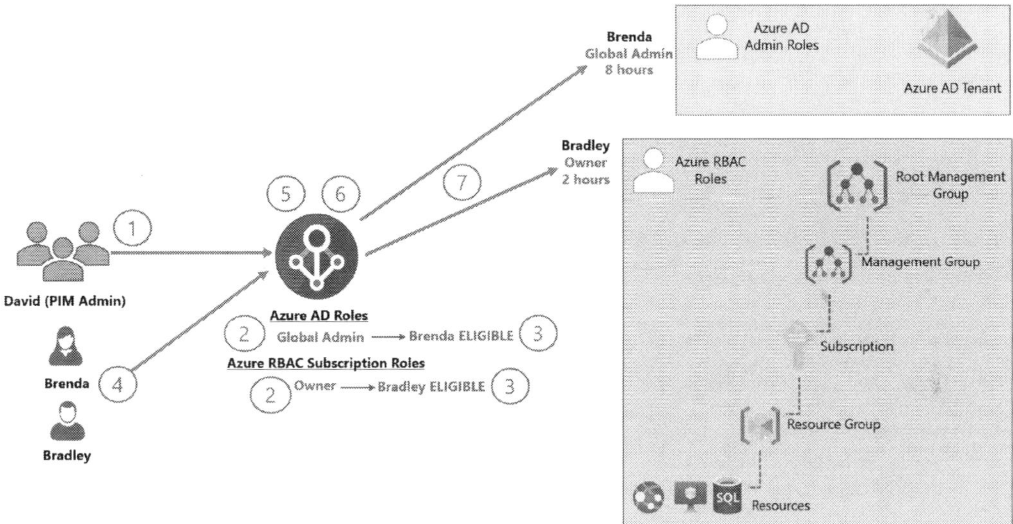

Figure 5.1 – Azure AD PIM workflow

Figure 5.1 shows the flow for this:

- **Step 1**: The admin, David, will need administrative privileges in PIM to be able to complete the configuration process.
- **Step 2**: Once the admin has the right privilege, they will need to onboard the roles that they want to protect into PIM, in this case, the **Azure AD Global Admin** role and the **Azure resource owner** role. David can configure a time limit for which the onboarded roles can be assigned. For example, he can configure the Global Admin role in Azure AD to be assignable for a maximum of 8 hours.

- **Step 3**: David can make Brenda eligible for the global admin role and Bradley eligible for the subscription owner role. Eligible means that the user can request to be assigned the role by PIM whenever they need it to perform a task.
- **Step 4**: Eligible users can then request to take on a role in PIM whenever they need it to perform a task.
- **Step 5**: PIM verifies their eligibility based on what the administrator configured earlier.
- **Step 6**: If configured, PIM can request the user to provide a justification and also forward the request to an approver.
- **Step 7**: If the requesting user satisfies the configured requirements, PIM configures the requested role assignment for the user only for the duration that is allowed or requested. Once the assignment time expires, PIM automatically removes the role assignment.

A great way to understand any concept is to use it. In the next exercise, you will walk through the implementation of Azure AD PIM from the perspectives of the administrator, user, and approver.

Exercise – Azure AD Privileged Identity Management

Here are the tasks that will be completed in this exercise:

- **Task 1**: Configure PIM users and roles.
- **Task 2**: Activate PIM roles with approval.

Here are the steps to complete these tasks:

1. Open a web browser and browse to the Azure portal URL: `https://portal.azure.com`.
2. In the Azure portal, in the **Search resources, services, and docs** textbox at the top of the Azure portal page, type `Azure AD Privileged Identity Management` and then press the *Enter* key:

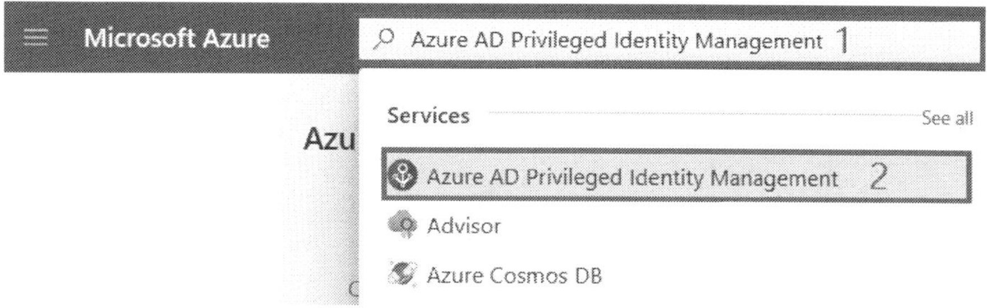

Figure 5.2 – Searching for Azure AD PIM

3. On the **Azure AD Privileged Identity Management** blade, in the **Manage** section, click **Azure AD roles**. In the **Manage** section, click **Roles**. Then, click **+ Add assignments**:

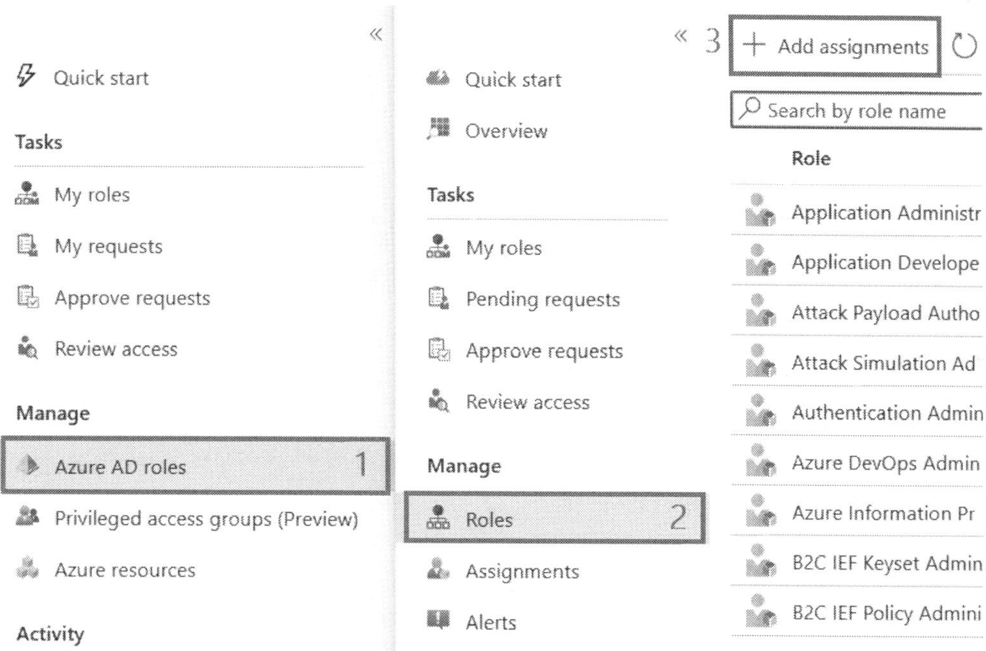

Figure 5.3 – Adding a PIM assignment

4. On the **Add assignments** blade, in the **Select role** dropdown, select **Billing Administrator**. Click the **No member selected** link, on the **Select member(s)** blade, click **Brenda Tao**, and then click **Select**:

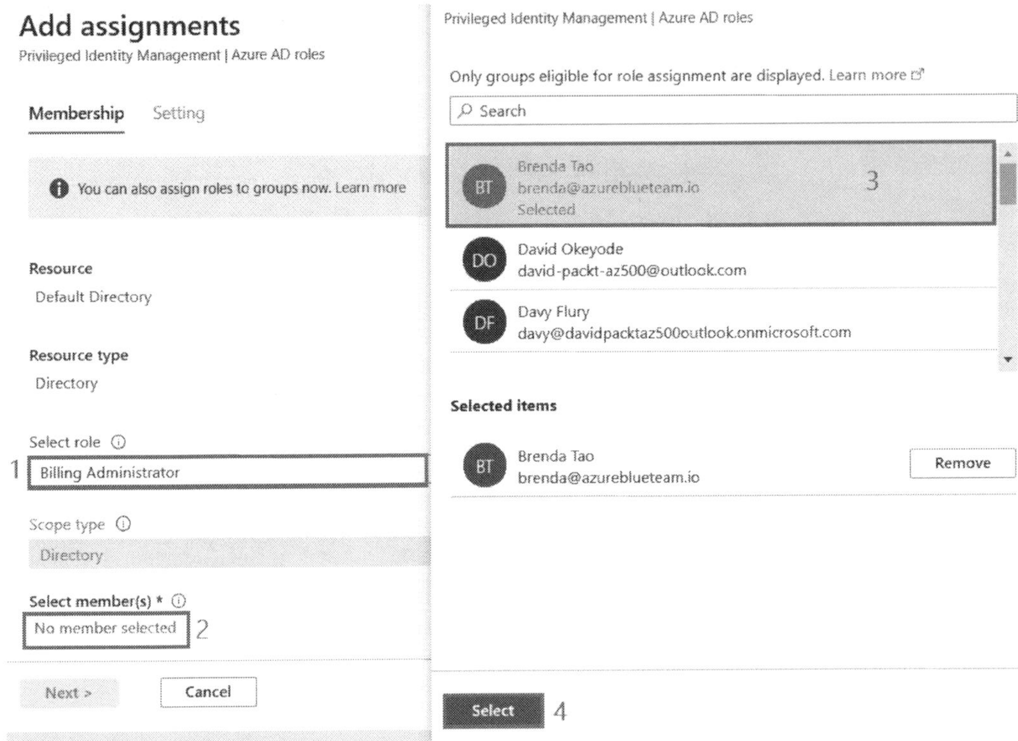

Figure 5.4 – Assigning a user to a role in PIM

5. Back on the **Add assignments** blade, click **Next**. Ensure that **Assignment type** is set to **Eligible** and then click **Assign**:

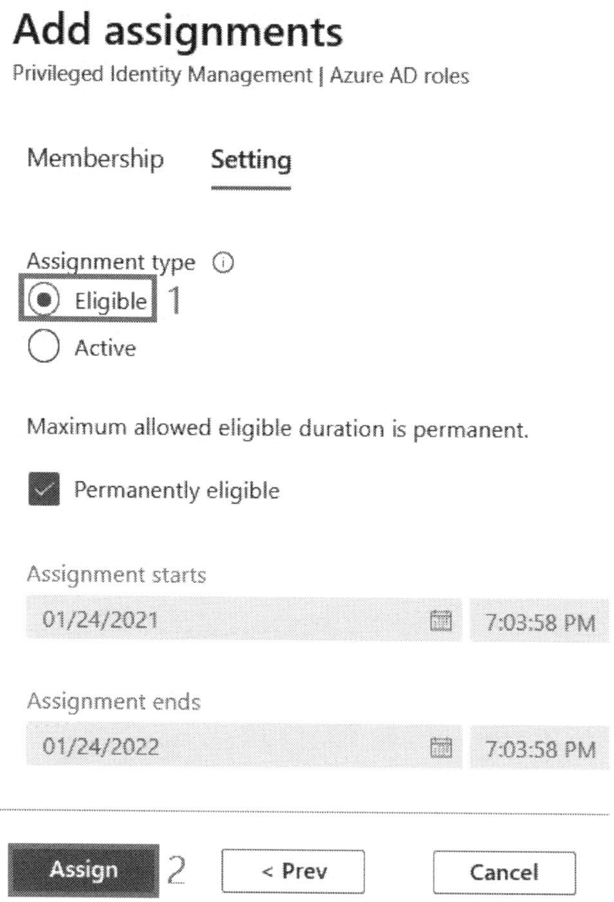

Add assignments

Privileged Identity Management | Azure AD roles

Membership Setting

Assignment type

Eligible 1

Active

Maximum allowed eligible duration is permanent.

Permanently eligible

Assignment starts

01/24/2021 7:03:58 PM

Assignment ends

01/24/2022 7:03:58 PM

Assign 2 < Prev Cancel

Figure 5.5 – Configuring PIM role assignment settings

> **Note**
>
> Eligible assignment type means that the user needs to go through a request process in PIM to be assigned to the role. Active assignment type means that the role is automatically assigned to the user without the need to go through a request process.

6. Back on the **Default Directory | Roles** blade, in the **Manage** section, click **Assignments**. Verify on the **Eligible assignments** tab that **Brenda Tao** is shown as a billing administrator:

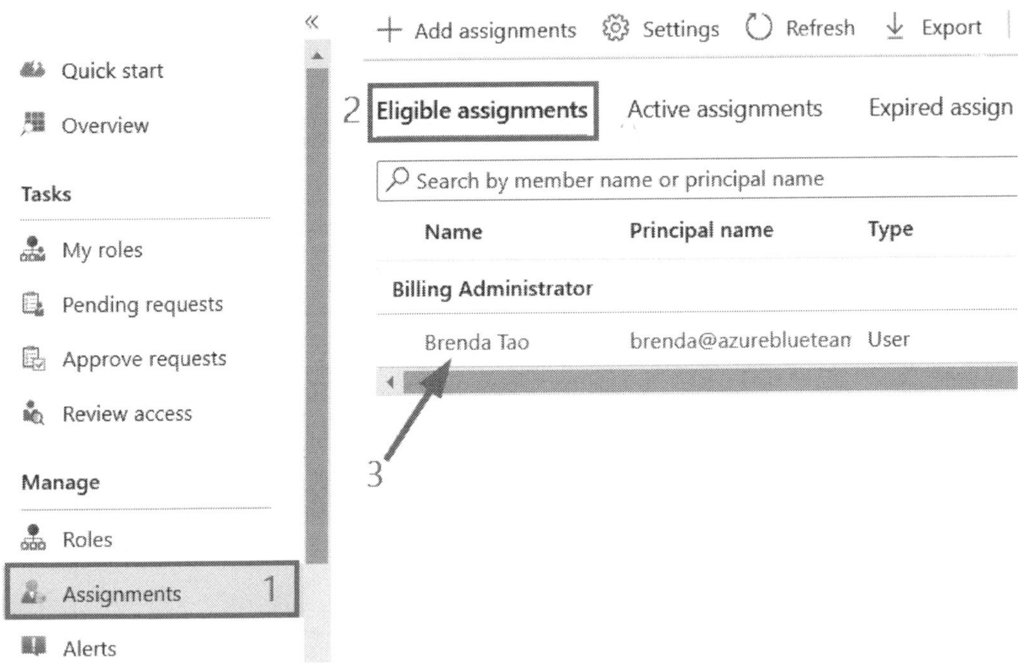

Figure 5.6 – Verifying PIM role assignment

7. In the **Manage** section, click **Roles**. Then, click the **Billing Administrator** role:

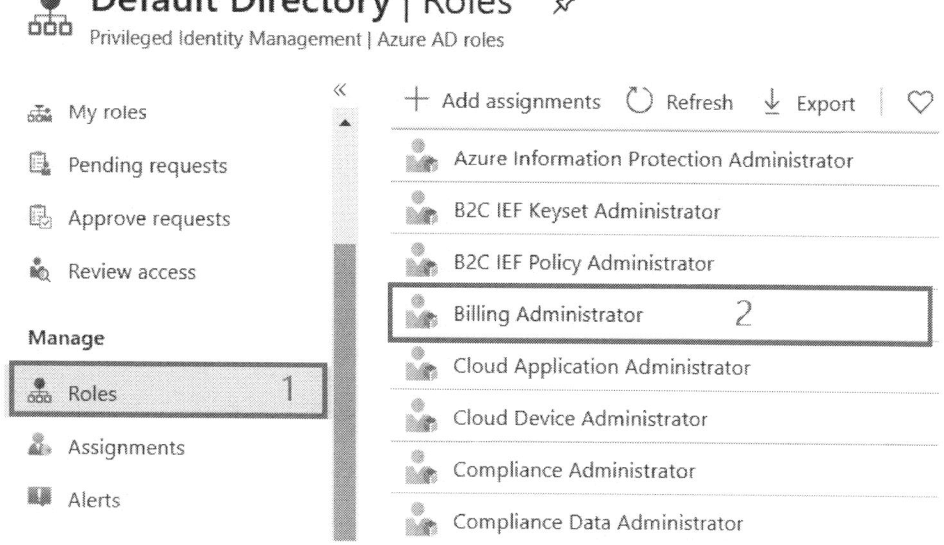

Figure 5.7 – Selecting a role in PIM

8. On the **Billing Administrator | Assignments** blade, click the **Role settings** icon in the toolbar of the blade and review the configuration settings for the role. Click **Edit**:

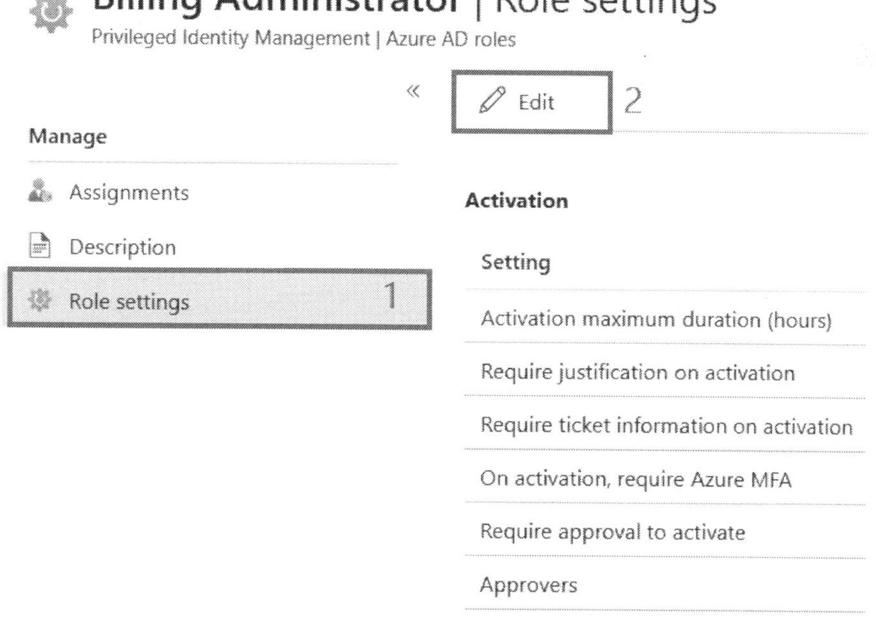

Figure 5.8 – Editing role settings in PIM

9. On the **Activation** tab, configure the following:

   Activation maximum duration (hours): 3.

   On activation, require: None.

   Require justification on activation: Selected.

   Require ticket information on activation: Not selected.

   Require approval to activate: Selected.

   Select approver(s): Select your current user account.

   Then, click **Next: Assignment**:

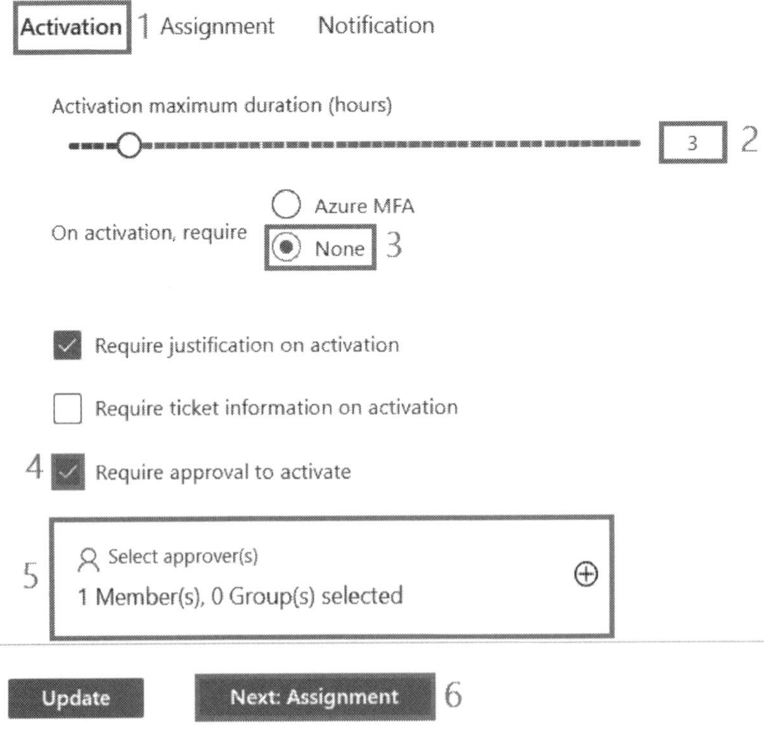

Figure 5.9 – Configuring role setting activation in PIM

10. In the **Assignment** tab, clear the **Allow permanent active assignment** checkbox, leaving all the other settings as their default values. Then, click **Next: Notification**:

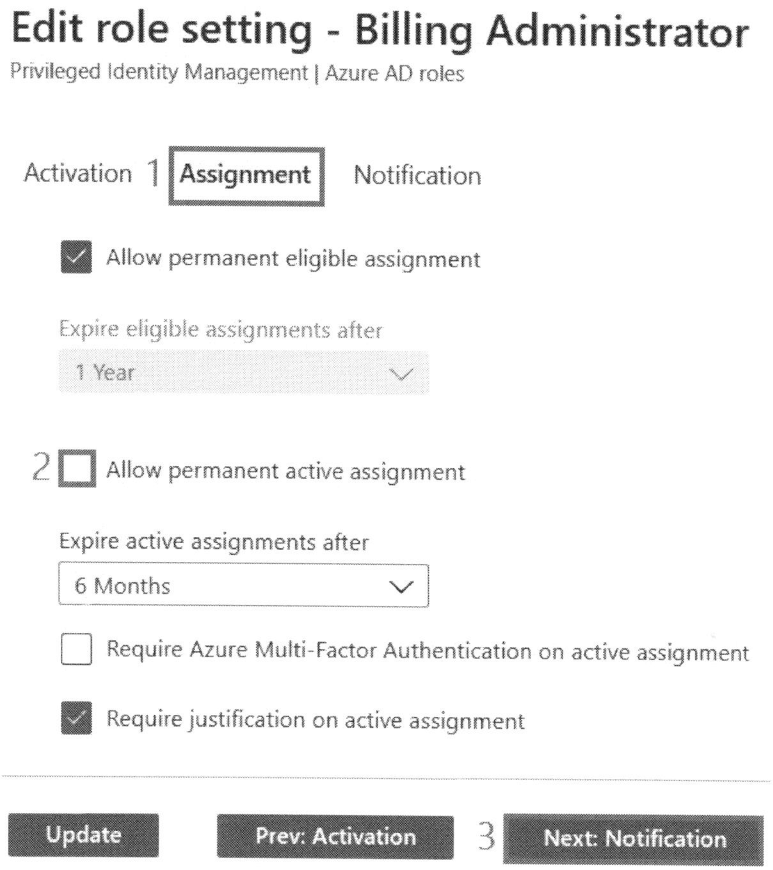

Figure 5.10 – Configuring role setting assignments in PIM

11. In the **Notification** tab, review the configuration and then click **Update**:

> **Important note**
>
> Anyone trying to use the Billing Administrator role will now require approval from your user account before they can be assigned to the role.

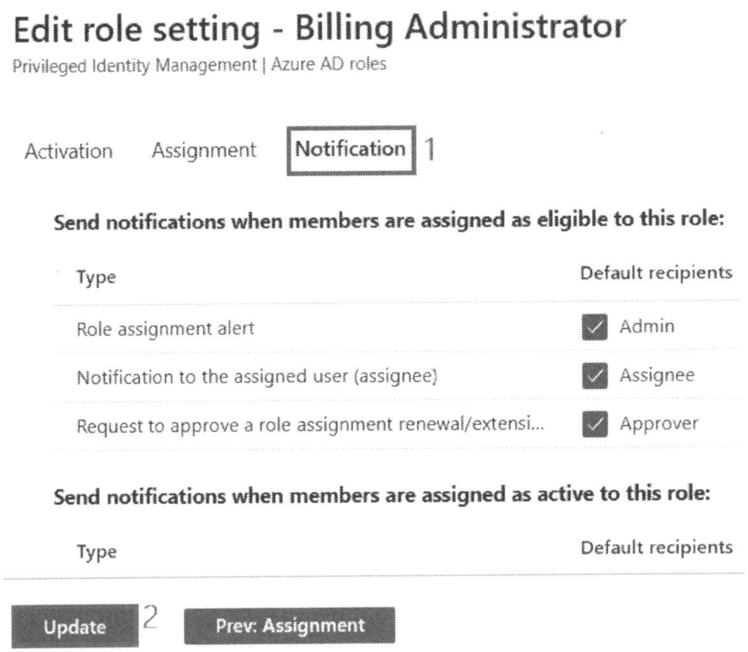

Figure 5.11 – Configuring a role setting notification in PIM

12. Open a new InPrivate or Incognito browser window and sign in to the Azure portal as the user Brenda Tao. You will also need to complete the MFA verification.
13. While signed in as Brenda Tao, navigate to the **Privileged Identity Management** blade.
14. On the **Privileged Identity Management | Quick start** blade, in the **Tasks** section, click **My roles**.

    You will see just the roles that Brenda is eligible to request here.

15. On the **My roles | Azure AD roles** blade, in the **Eligible assignments** list, in the row displaying the **Billing Administrator** role, click **Activate**:

Refresh | Got feedback?

Eligible assignments | Active assignments | Expired assignments

Search by role

Role	Scope	Membership	End time	Action
Billing Administrator	Directory	Direct	Permanent	Activate

Figure 5.12 – Activating a role as a PIM user

16. On the **Activate – Billing Administrator** blade, in the **Reason** textbox, type the following text to justify the activation: `Role needed for some tasks`. Click **Activate**.

Leave the browser window open as we will come back to it for verification. For now, we will switch back to our user browser session to approve Brenda's request:

Activate - Billing Administrator
Privileged Identity Management | Azure AD roles

Roles | Activate | Status

Custom activation start time

Duration (hours) 3

*Reason (max 500 characters) 1

Role needed for some tasks

2 Activate | Cancel

Figure 5.13 – Adding justification for role activation

17. Switch back to the browser window where you are logged in to the Azure portal with your user account. In the **Tasks** section, click **Approve requests**.
18. On the **Approve requests** blade, in the **Requests for role activations** section, select the checkbox for the entry representing the role activation request to the **Billing Administrator** role by **Brenda Tao**. Then, click **Approve**:

Figure 5.14 – Approving a role activation request as a PIM approver

19. On the **Approve Request** blade, in the **Justification** textbox, type the following text to provide a reason for activation as an approver: `Role approved to complete needed tasks for three hours`. Note the start and end times, and then click **Confirm**:

> **Note**
> You also have the option of denying requests.

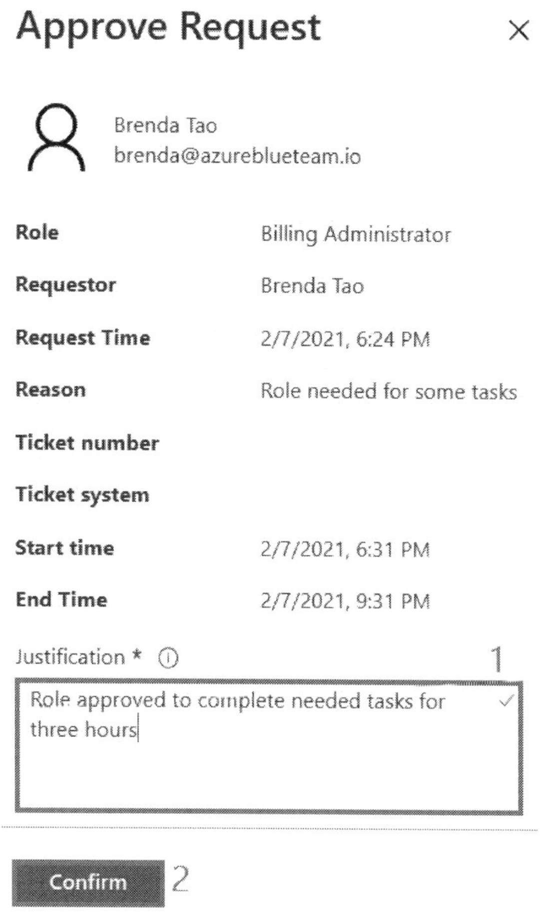

Figure 5.15 – Adding justification for the role activation approval

20. You should see a successful notification in the top-right corner:

Figure 5.16 – Reviewing a notification

21. Switch back to the InPrivate/InCognito browser window where you are logged in to the Azure portal as Brenda Tao.
22. On the **My roles | Azure AD roles** blade, click the refresh button. Then, click the **Active Assignments** tab and verify that the **Billing Administrator** role is now activated for Brenda. Note the end time also:

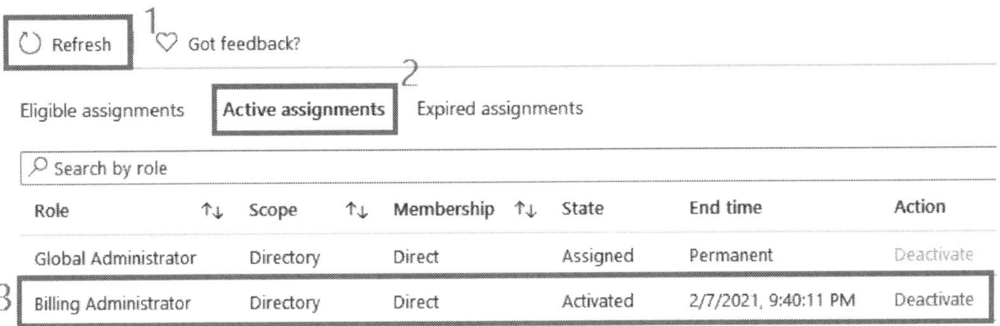

Figure 5.17 – Verifying active role assignments

23. Sign out and close the InPrivate browser window.

In this exercise, you implemented Azure AD PIM and a verified privileged role activation workflow with approval. In the next section, we will cover how to extend PIM with a capability referred to as access review.

Configuring PIM access reviews

It is a security best practice to regularly review privileged access that has been assigned. This is because required access for employees and guests changes over time as people move teams or leave organizations and we want to ensure that old access permissions are cleaned up when this happens. Azure AD PIM has a functionality called **access review** that allows us to implement this. *The core use case of this Azure AD PIM feature is to reduce the risk associated with stale access assignments.*

Access review allows us to assign designated reviewers for sensitive Azure AD and Azure resource roles in our organizations. Reviewers will then be reminded to either approve or revoke role assignments at review time. If a reviewer approves the role for a user, the assignment is extended until the next review period. If the reviewer revokes the role for a user, access is removed. We can also configure **self-review**, which allows users to approve or revoke their own access at review time based on whether access is still required.

We can also configure the default behavior if the designated reviewer fails to complete the review. Here are the four options that we have:

- **No change**: Unreviewed access will be left unchanged (extended).
- **Remove access**: Unreviewed access will be revoked and removed.
- **Approve access**: Unreviewed access will be approved and extended.
- **Take recommendations**: Take the system's recommendation on approving or revoking unreviewed access. The recommendation is usually based on usage (whether a user has signed in recently within the past month).

Now that you have an idea of what the PIM access review feature entails, in the next exercise, you will configure a monthly recurring access review for the Azure AD Global Administrator role to reduce the risk associated with *stale* role assignments. You will do this by creating a PIM access review to ensure that the role assignments are still valid.

Exercise – Create an access review and review PIM auditing features

Here are the tasks that will be completed in this exercise:

- **Task 1**: Create an access review and review PIM auditing features.
- **Task 2**: Review PIM alerts, summary information, and detailed audit information.

Here are the steps to complete the tasks:

1. Open a web browser and browse to the Azure portal URL:`https://portal.azure.com`. Sign in with your user account.
2. In the Azure portal, in the **Search resources, services, and docs** textbox at the top of the Azure portal page, type `Azure AD Privileged Identity Management` and press the *Enter* key:

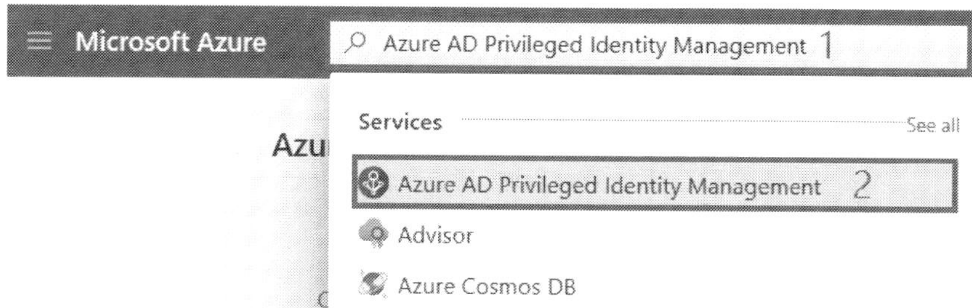

Figure 5.18 – Searching for Azure AD PIM

3. On the **Azure AD Privileged Identity Management** blade, in the **Manage** section, click **Azure AD roles**. Then, click **Access reviews**:

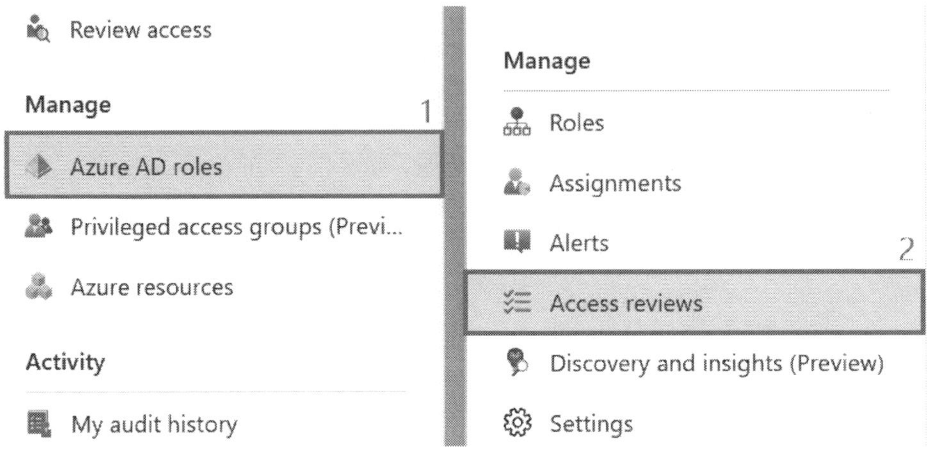

Figure 5.19 – Selecting Access reviews

4. On the **Default Directory | Access reviews** blade, click **New**. On the **Create an access review** blade, specify the following settings (leave others with their default values):

   Review name: `Global Administrator Review`.

   Description: Monthly review of the global administrator role.

   Start date: Today's date.

   Frequency: Monthly.

   Duration (in days): 14 (This defines the number of days that the review will be open for input from reviewers. You cannot set a number that causes overlapping reviews. For example, the maximum duration that can be set for a monthly review is 27 days to avoid overlap).

   End: Never.

   Review role membership (permanent and eligible): Global Administrator.

   Reviewers: Selected users.

   Select reviewers: Your current user account.

Expand and review the **Upon completion settings** and **Advanced settings** sections.

Click **Start**. It will take about a minute for the review to deploy:

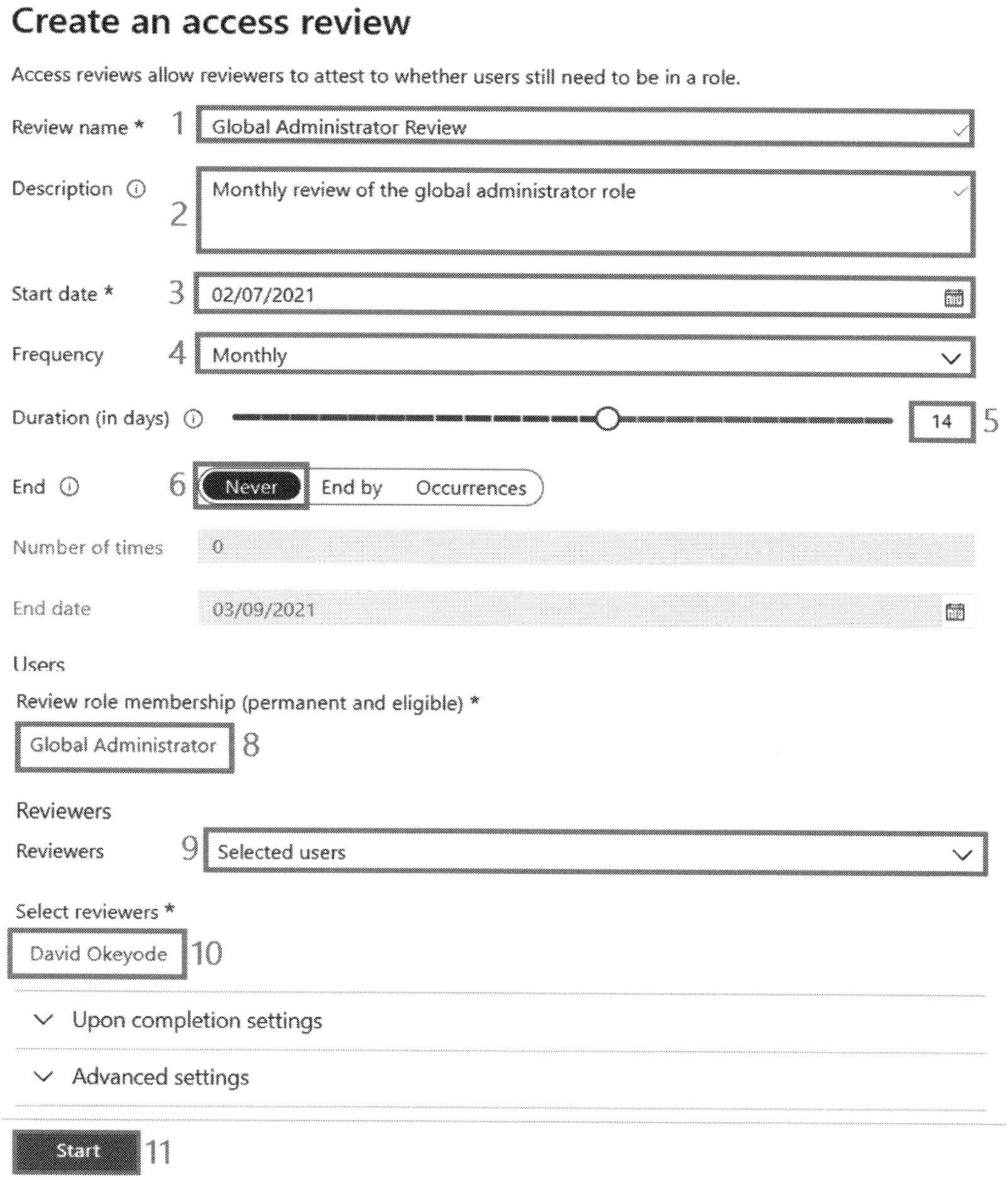

Create an access review

Access reviews allow reviewers to attest to whether users still need to be in a role.

Review name * 1 Global Administrator Review

Description 2 Monthly review of the global administrator role

Start date * 3 02/07/2021

Frequency 4 Monthly

Duration (in days) 14 5

End 6 Never End by Occurrences

Number of times 0

End date 03/09/2021

Users

Review role membership (permanent and eligible) *

Global Administrator 8

Reviewers

Reviewers 9 Selected users

Select reviewers *

David Okeyode 10

Upon completion settings

Advanced settings

Start 11

Figure 5.20 – Configuring access review parameters

5. On the **Default Directory | Access reviews** blade, under the **Global Administrator Review** header, click the **Global Administrator** entry:

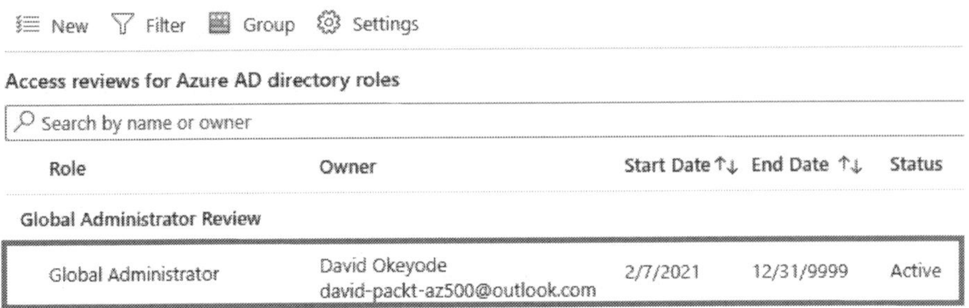

Figure 5.21 – Verifying existing reviews

6. On the **Global Administrator Review** blade, examine the **Overview** page and note that the **Progress** chart shows users in the **Not reviewed** category:

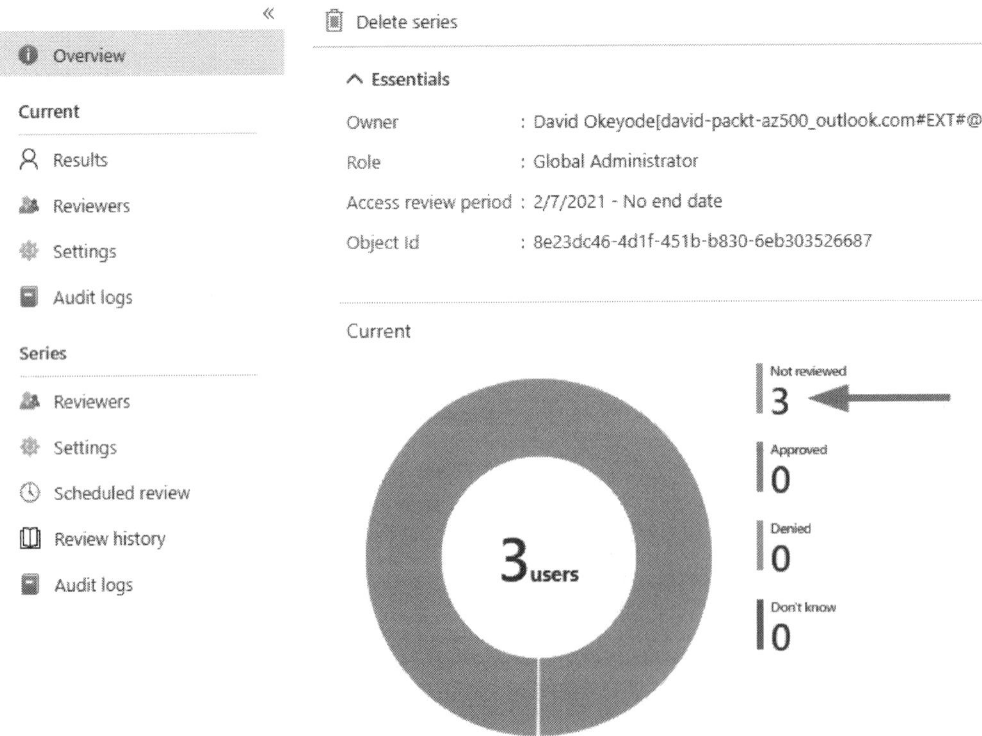

Figure 5.22 – Verifying the review status

7. On the **Global Administrator Review** blade, in the **Current** section, click **Results**. Note that your user account and Brenda Tao's account are listed as having access to this role. Notice the **Recommended action** column. This provides recommendations on whether to keep the user's access based on usage:

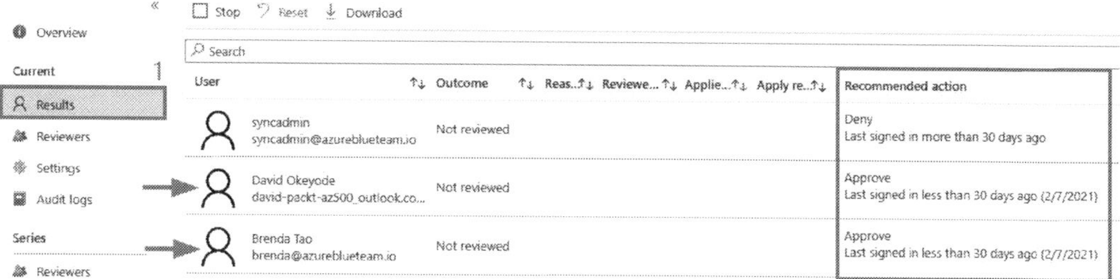

Figure 5.23 – Verifying the review results

8. Click **Brenda Tao** to view a detailed audit log with entries representing PIM activities that involve the user. Close the blade to return to the previous blade:

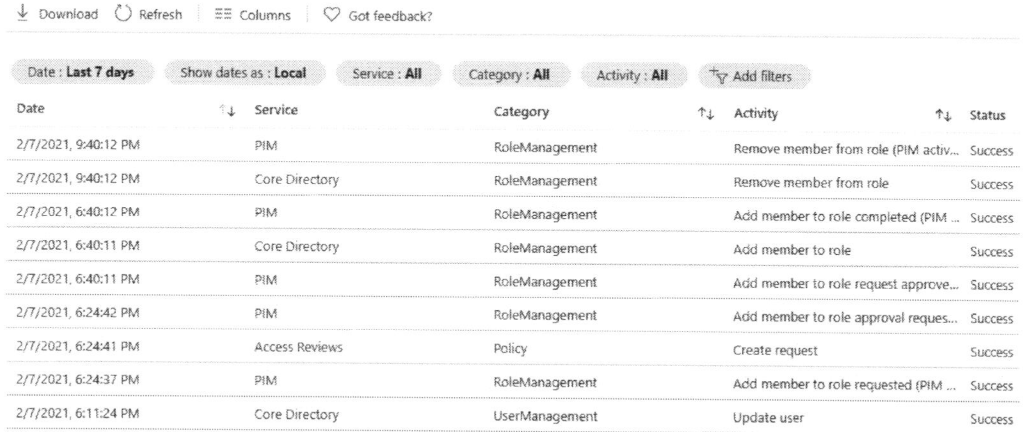

Date	Service	Category	Activity	Status
2/7/2021, 9:40:12 PM	PIM	RoleManagement	Remove member from role (PIM activ...	Success
2/7/2021, 9:40:12 PM	Core Directory	RoleManagement	Remove member from role	Success
2/7/2021, 6:40:12 PM	PIM	RoleManagement	Add member to role completed (PIM ...	Success
2/7/2021, 6:40:11 PM	Core Directory	RoleManagement	Add member to role	Success
2/7/2021, 6:40:11 PM	PIM	RoleManagement	Add member to role request approve...	Success
2/7/2021, 6:24:42 PM	PIM	RoleManagement	Add member to role approval reques...	Success
2/7/2021, 6:24:41 PM	Access Reviews	Policy	Create request	Success
2/7/2021, 6:24:37 PM	PIM	RoleManagement	Add member to role requested (PIM ...	Success
2/7/2021, 6:11:24 PM	Core Directory	UserManagement	Update user	Success

Figure 5.24 – Reviewing audit logs

9. On the **Default Directory | Access reviews** blade, in the **Current** section, click **Settings**. Review the **Reviewers** tab and the **When completed** tab. The **When completed** tab allows us to configure the behavior if reviewers do not complete the review before the time expiry:

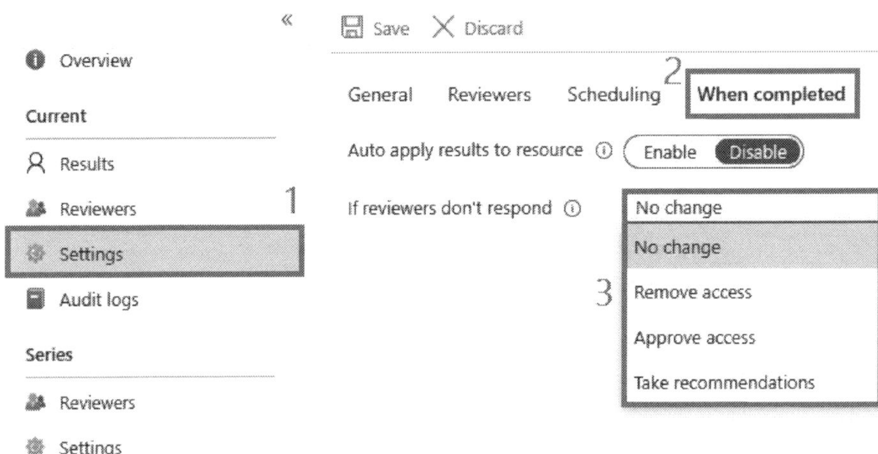

Figure 5.25 – Configuring review settings

10. Close the **Global Administrator Review | Settings** blade.
11. On the **Default Directory | Access reviews** blade, in the **Tasks** section, click **Review access**. Then, click on the **Global Administrator Review** option:

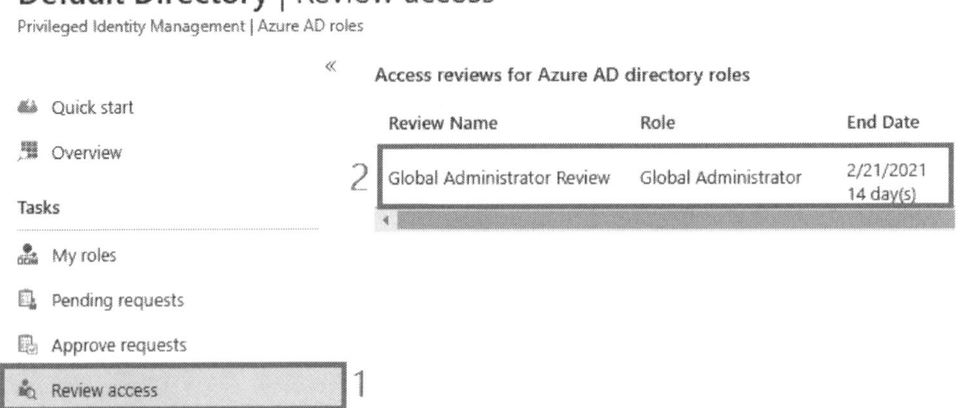

Figure 5.26 – Reviewing role access

12. On the **Global Administrator Review** blade, select **Brenda Tao**. In the **Reason** textbox, type `role still needed`. Click **Approve** to keep the role assignment to Brenda for another 30 days:

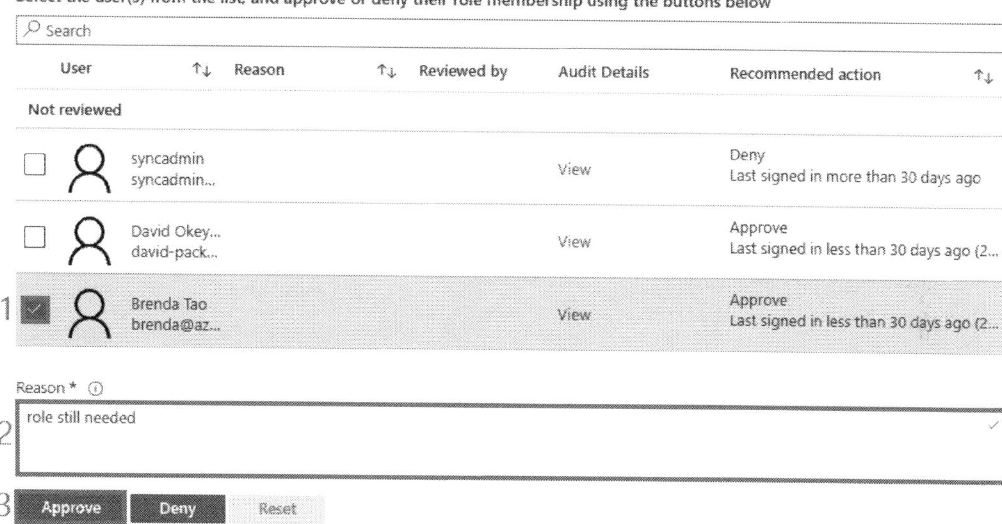

Figure 5.27 – Completing an access review as a user

13. Close the **Global Administrator Review** blade.
14. In the **Default Directory | Access reviews** blade, in the **Manage** section, click **Access reviews**, and then select the **Global Administrator** review:

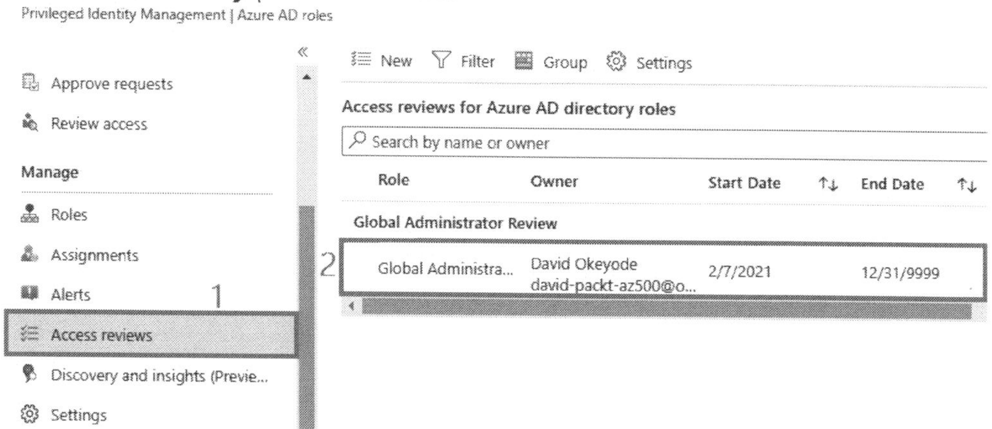

Figure 5.28 – Selecting an access review

15. Note that the **Progress** chart has been updated to show your review:

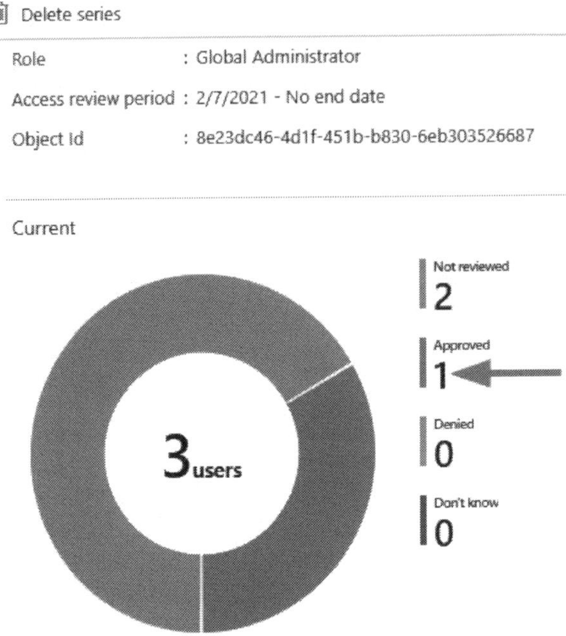

Figure 5.29 – Verifying the access review results

Close the **Global Administrator Review** blade.

16. In the **Default Directory | Access reviews** blade, in the **Manage** section, click **Alerts**, and then click **Settings**.
17. On the **Alert settings** blade, review the preconfigured alerts and risk levels.

Congratulations! You have successfully configured and validated a PIM access review. The skill that you learned in this section will help you to mitigate the risk of stale access in your Azure environment.

Summary

In this chapter, you learned how to implement identity governance using Azure AD PIM and Azure AD PIM access reviews. The information in this chapter has equipped you with the skills needed to reduce the risks associated with compromised privileged identity and stale access. This helps to reduce the blast radius in the event of an identity security breach.

In the next chapter, we will begin to cover the concept of network perimeter security in Azure.

Questions

As we conclude, here is a list of questions for you to test your knowledge regarding this chapter's material. You will find the answers in the *Assessments* section of the *Appendix*:

1. If a user fails to complete an access review before the end date and the default behavior is configured as "Take recommendations," what will happen if the user has not signed in within the past month?

   a. The user's access will be left unchanged.

   b. The user's access will be revoked and removed.

   c. The user's access will be approved and extended.

   d. The administrator will be presented with an option to revoke the user's access.

2. If a user is made eligible for a role in PIM, which of the following statements describes what this means?

   a. It means that the user is automatically assigned to the role.

   b. It means that the user can request to be assigned the role by PIM whenever they need it to perform a task.

   c. It means that the user cannot request to be assigned to the role.

Further reading

To learn more on the topics covered in this chapter, you can refer to the following links:

- Azure AD PIM overview: `https://docs.microsoft.com/en-us/azure/active-directory/privileged-identity-management/pim-configure?WT.mc_id=AZ-MVP-6003870`.
- Activate Azure AD roles in PIM: `https://docs.microsoft.com/en-us/azure/active-directory/privileged-identity-management/pim-how-to-activate-role?WT.mc_id=AZ-MVP-6003870&tabs=new`.
- Activate Azure resource roles in PIM: `https://docs.microsoft.com/en-us/azure/active-directory/privileged-identity-management/pim-resource-roles-activate-your-roles?WT.mc_id=AZ-MVP-6003870`.
- Zero Trust Resource Center: `https://docs.microsoft.com/en-us/security/zero-trust/`.

Section 2: Implement Azure Platform Protection

The Azure cloud platform offers multiple options to organizations for hosting their workloads, including virtual machines and containers in both private and public networks. This section will cover how to secure your workloads in the cloud, from the perimeter (the outer boundary between the untrusted public internet and your workloads) to the actual services that host our applications. We will walk through many hands-on scenarios, including the implementation of DDoS protection, Web Application Firewall, Disk Encryption, just-in-time virtual machine access, Kubernetes RBAC with Azure Active Directory, and more. By the end of this section, you will have a solid understanding of how to secure your cloud workloads using a multi-layered approach.

This part of the book comprises the following chapters:

- *Chapter 6, Implementing Perimeter Security*
- *Chapter 7, Implementing Network Security*
- *Chapter 8, Implementing Host Security*
- *Chapter 9, Implementing Container Security*

6
Implementing Perimeter Security

The Azure cloud platform allows customers to create logically isolated private networks called **virtual networks**. These isolated networks are used to host IaaS and PaaS services, which require network isolation or traffic control measures managed by the customer. Securing these private networks from attacks and unauthorized access starts at the perimeter (the outer boundary between the untrusted public internet and your Azure virtual network resources).

In this chapter, we will look at what perimeter security looks like for Azure virtual networks, and how to use services and features of the platform to implement perimeter protection. Here are the topics that we will cover in this chapter, along with accompanying hands-on exercises:

- Securing the Azure virtual network perimeter
- Implementing Azure **Distributed Denial of Service (DDoS)** Protection
- Implementing Azure Firewall
- Implementing a **Web Application Firewall (WAF)** in Azure

Technical requirements

To follow along with the instructions in this chapter, you will need the following:

- A PC with an internet connection.
- An Azure subscription. You can use the same subscription that you set up in the first chapter of this book.

Securing the Azure virtual network perimeter

A network perimeter is the outer boundary between the untrusted public internet and our Azure virtual network resources (*Figure 6.1*). This is where we have to start in any discussion regarding securing our Azure virtual networks. There are two main objectives of network perimeter security:

- To filter **Distributed Denial of Service** (**DDoS**) attacks before they can cause a denial of service for legitimate users of services hosted in our networks. The Azure platform has a service that we can use to achieve this objective – the **Azure DDoS Protection** service.
- To protect virtual network workloads against malicious ingress and egress network traffic originating from external networks. The Azure platform has various services that we can use to achieve this objective. The ones that we will cover in this chapter are the ones that we can use depending on our requirements: **Azure Firewall**, **Azure Web Application Firewall**, and **Network Virtual Appliance** (**NVA**):

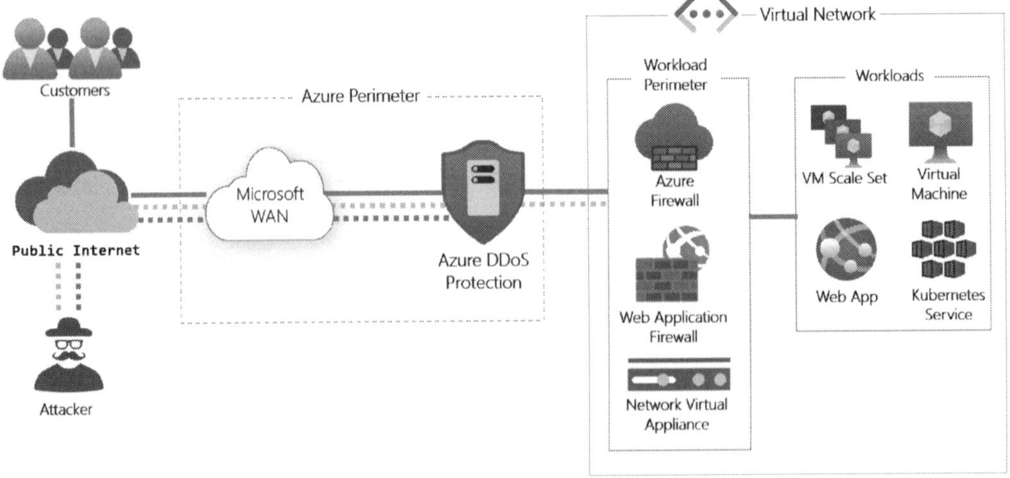

Figure 6.1 – Azure network perimeter security

Figure 6.1 highlights the main perimeter security services that we will cover in this chapter and how they are positioned in an Azure network architecture.

In the next section, we will start with a discussion of the Azure DDoS protection service.

Implementing Azure Distributed Denial of Service (DDoS) Protection

A **DDoS attack** is a collection of attack types aimed at disrupting the availability of a target by overwhelming it with malicious traffic. The Azure DDoS protection service enables us to protect our *internet-facing* virtual network workloads from DDoS attacks before the availability of our service is impacted (*Figure 6.1*).

The service identifies malicious attempts to overwhelm the network and blocks them before they reach our Azure resources. Legitimate traffic from customers still flows into Azure without any interruption (*Figure 6.1*). It uses the scale and elasticity of Microsoft's global network to mitigate DDoS attacks at the Azure network edge.

Before we get into more details on this service, let's review the different categories of DDoS attacks so that we are clear on what this service protects against and what it does not. There are three main categories of common DDoS attacks:

- **Volumetric DDoS attacks**: These attacks create congestion by overwhelming the network bandwidth capabilities of a target to make it inaccessible. This is the equivalent of what happens in a *traffic jam* – when vehicles cannot move forward because there is too much traffic. Examples of volumetric DDoS attacks are amplification floods and UDP floods. Mitigating this category of DDoS attack usually involves having a large enough bandwidth to absorb the traffic and scrub them with a network that scales on demand. *The Azure DDoS protection service can protect against this category of DDoS attack.*
- **Protocol DDoS attacks**: These attacks abuse weaknesses in layers 3 and 4 of the network protocol stack (OSI model) to render a target inaccessible. They are sometimes referred to as state-exhaustion attacks. Examples include reflection attacks and SYN flood attacks. Mitigating this type of attack usually involves the use of client probing techniques to differentiate between legitimate clients and malicious clients. *The Azure DDoS protection service can protect against this category of DDoS attack.*

- **Application DDoS attacks**: These attacks are designed to exploit application-level weaknesses and vulnerabilities with the intent of making them unavailable. They are also referred to as Layer 7 DDoS attacks because they target application-layer processes (Layer 7 refers to the **Open Systems Interconnect (OSI)** model). Mitigation usually involves deep behavioral analysis of application network traffic. Examples include HTTP protocol violation attacks such as slowloris, low, and slow attacks. *The Azure DDoS protection service* **DOES NOT** *protect against this category of DDoS attack.* A **Web Application Firewall** (**WAF**) in Azure can be used to protect against these. We will cover the implementation of a WAF later in this chapter.

Now that you have an understanding of what the Azure DDoS protection service can do and what it cannot do, let's review the service tiers that it offers. The service offers two service tiers – Basic and Standard.

The **Basic tier** is what we get by default when we deploy internet-facing workloads in our Azure virtual networks. It automatically protects our public-facing virtual network workloads for free! No customer intervention or configuration is required. It just works transparently in the background when we assign a public IP to a virtual network resource. It continually looks for indicators of DDoS attacks and automatically mitigates the attack once it is detected.

The **Standard tier** also automatically protects our public-facing virtual network workloads from DDoS attacks, but it adds extra capabilities, such as the following:

- Intelligently learning the traffic patterns of our applications and tuning the DDoS protection profile appropriately
- Providing detailed metrics, alerts, and reports in the case of an attack
- Customer access to the Microsoft **DDoS Rapid Response** (**DRR**) team, who can help with attack investigation during an ongoing attack or in a post-attack analysis
- Cost protection to ensure that we receive service credits if a successful DDoS attack results in us incurring costs due to scaled-out workloads or outbound data transfer

Now that you have some understanding of how the Azure DDoS protection service can help to protect against DDoS attacks at the perimeter of our virtual networks, let's go ahead and implement it. However, before we can do this, we need to set up resources that we can use to follow along with the exercises in this chapter and the next one.

Hands-on exercise – provisioning resources for the exercises in Chapters 6 and 7

To follow along with the exercises in this chapter and the next one, we will provision some Azure resources to work with. We have prepared an Azure ARM template in the GitHub repository of this book for this purpose. The template will deploy an Azure virtual network with two subnets as shown in *Figure 6.2*. The public subnet will have a Windows Server 2019 VM that is reachable from the public internet. The private subnet will have an Ubuntu Linux VM that is not reachable directly from the internet. Here are the tasks that we will complete in this exercise:

- **Task 1**: Initialize template deployment in GitHub.
- **Task 2**: Complete the parameters and deploy the template to Azure:

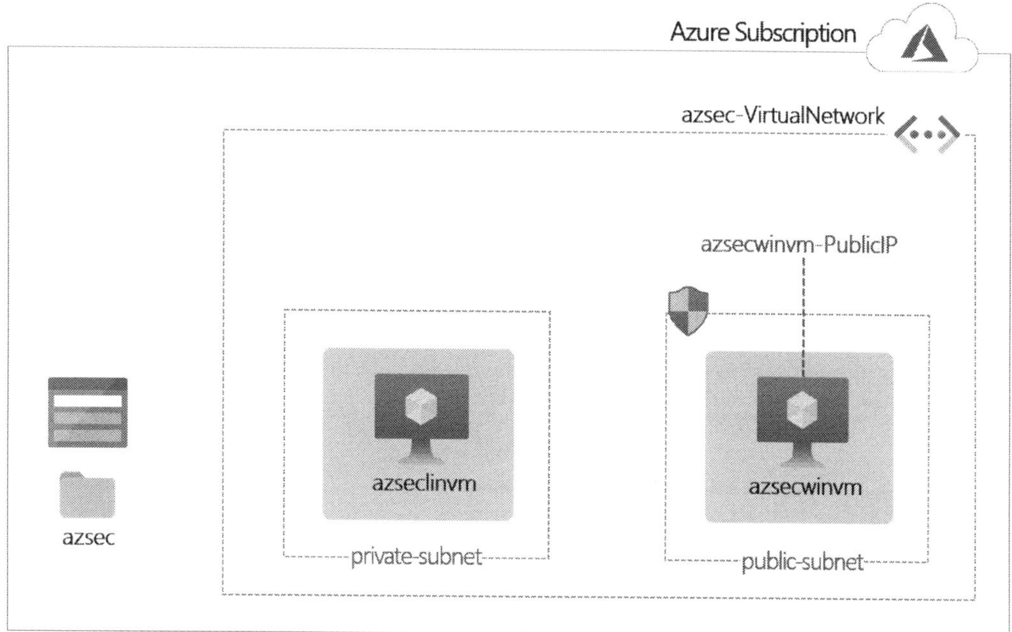

Figure 6.2 – Chapter 6 exercises scenario

Let's begin deploying our template:

1. Open a web browser and browse to `http://bit.ly/az600-c6-template`. This link will open the GitHub repository that has an ARM template to deploy the resources that we need.

2. In the GitHub repository that opens, click on **Deploy to Azure**:

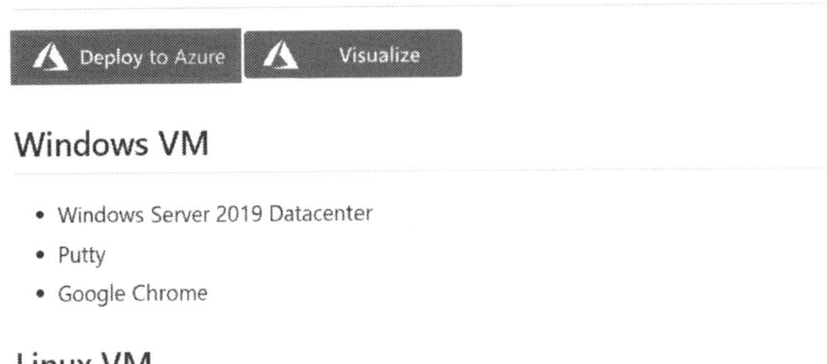

Figure 6.3 – Clicking on the "Deploy to Azure" option

3. In the **Sign in** window, enter your administrative username and password to authenticate to your Azure subscription:

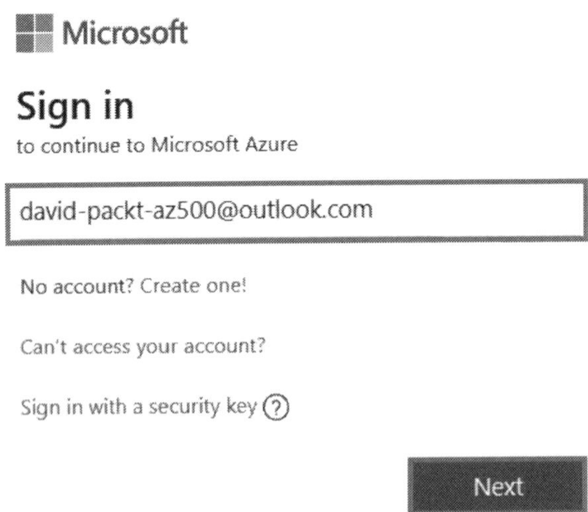

Figure 6.4 – Authenticating to Azure

4. In the **Custom Deployment** window, configure the following:

   Subscription: Select the subscription that you want to deploy the resources to.

   Resource group: **Create New** | **Name**: `azuresec-c6-rg` | **OK**.

   Region: Select an Azure region close to your location.

Storagename: Leave the default value.

Vm-dns: Leave the default value.

Admin User: Leave the default value.

Admin Password: Enter a complex password. Make a note of the password that you use. We recommend that you select one complex password that you use throughout the scenarios in this book to keep things simple.

Vmsize: Leave the default value.

Location: Leave the default value.

_artifacts Location: Leave the default value.

_artifacts Location Sas Token: Leave the default value.

Click on **Review + create**:

Custom deployment ...
Deploy from a custom template
Subscription * 1 AzureBlueTeam-PROD (1c63ad39-68ee-444a-90a8-a2ccaf67f671)
Resource group * 2 (New) azuresec-c6-rg
Create new
Instance details
Region * 3 UK South
Storagename [concat('azsecvmstrg', uniqueString(resourceGroup().id))]
Vm-dns [concat('azsecwinvm-',uniqueString(resourceGroup().id))]
Admin User azureadmin
Admin Password * 4 ••••••••••••••
Vmsize * 1x Standard B2ms
2 vcpus, 8 GB memory
Change size
Location [resourceGroup().location]
_artifacts Location [deployment().properties.templateLink.uri]
_artifacts Location Sas Token
Review + create 5 < Previous Next : Review + create >

Figure 6.5 – Configuring template parameters

5. After the template validation has passed, click on **Create**. This will begin the deployment process, which takes about 7 to 10 minutes to complete. Grab yourself a cup of water, tea, or coffee and wait for the deployment to complete:

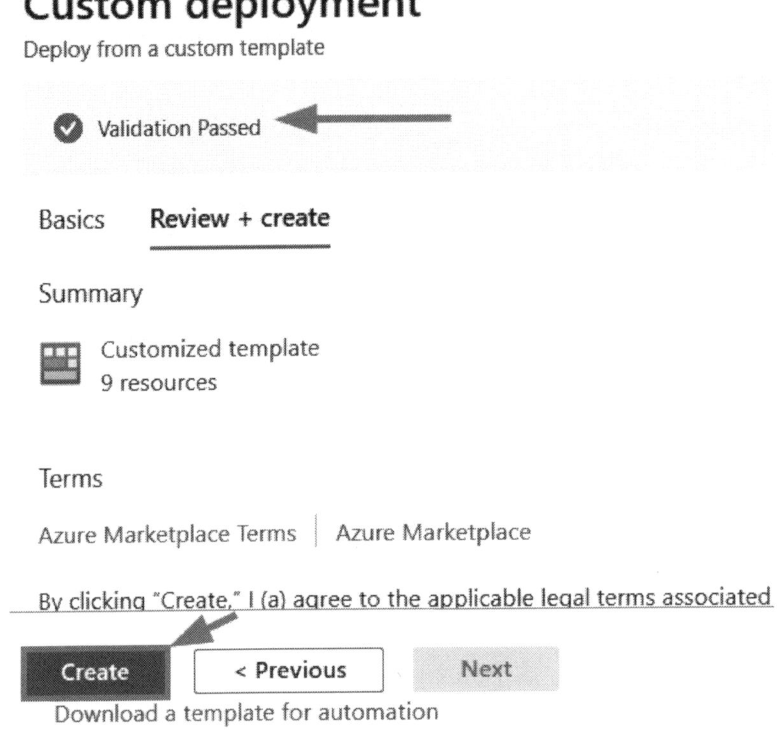

Figure 6.6 – Deploying the Pentest VM template

6. Once the deployment is complete, click on the **Outputs** tab. Make a note of the **winvm-dns** value. This is the public DNS name of the public Windows VM that we just deployed:

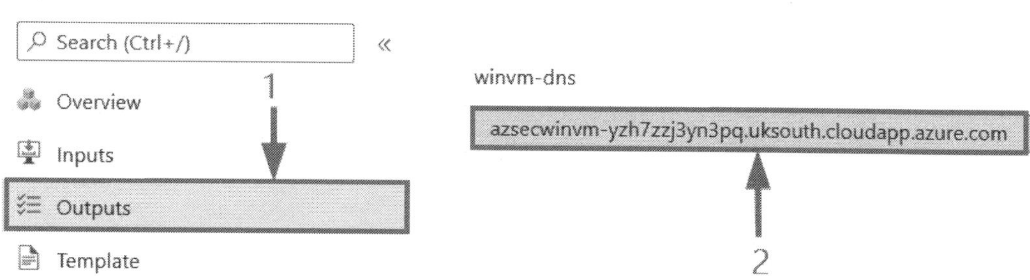

Figure 6.7 – Obtaining the Windows VM DNS name

7. On your client system, open an RDP client and enter the **winvm-dns** value that you made a note of earlier. Click on **Connect**. The instructions here describe the use of a Windows RDP client. If you are using a different RDP client, the instructions may vary.

   To open the Windows RDP client, execute `mstsc` from the Windows run dialog, or type `mstsc` in the Windows Start menu:

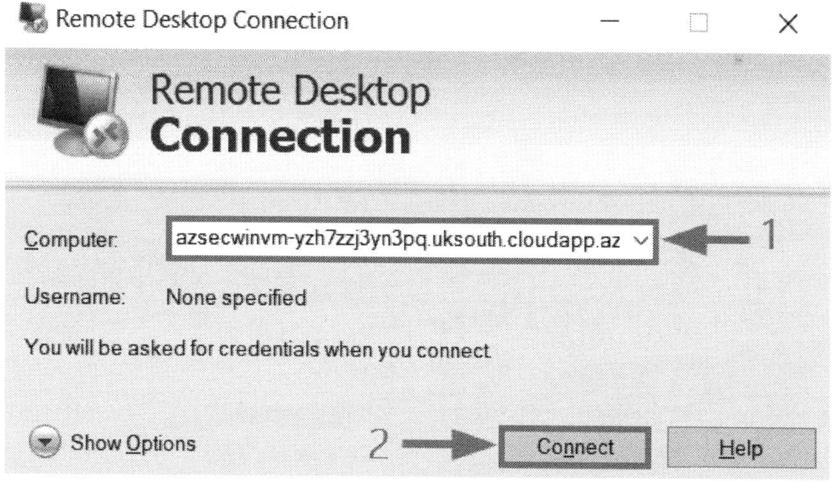

Figure 6.8 – Connecting to the Windows VM using RDP

8. When prompted to sign in, click on **More choices | Use a different account**. Enter the following information:

   Username: `azureadmin.`

   Password: Enter the password that you configured during template deployment:

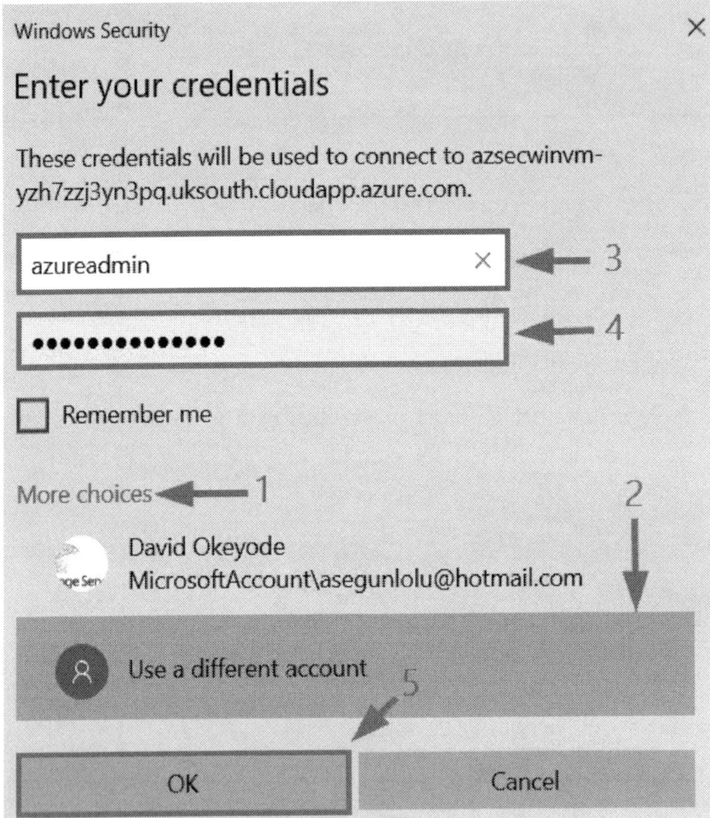

Figure 6.9 – Authenticating using the RDP client

9. When prompted about the certificate warning, select the **Don't ask me again for connections to this computer** option and then click **Yes**:

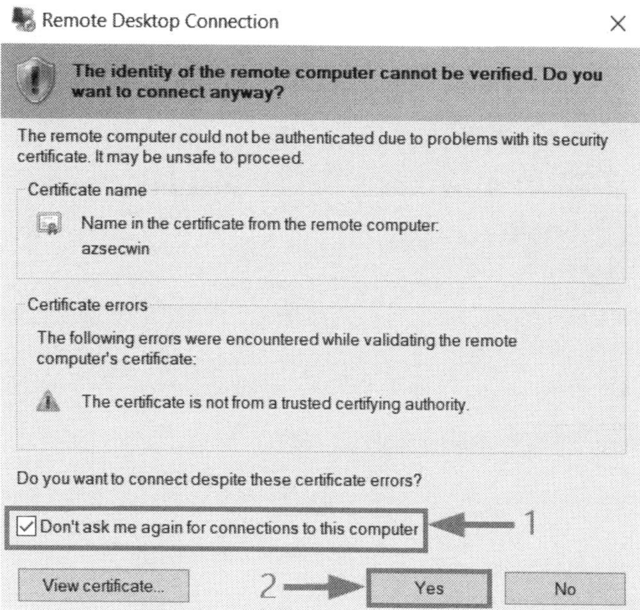

Figure 6.10 – Skipping the certificate warning

10. You should now have an RDP session to the public Windows VM! Keep this session open as you will need it for the later exercises:

Figure 6.11 – RDP session to the public Windows VM

In this exercise, we provisioned some Azure resources that we need for the rest of the exercises in this chapter. In the next section, we will implement the Azure DDoS protection service as our first line of perimeter defense.

Hands-on exercise – implementing the Azure DDoS protection Standard

Here are the tasks that we will complete in this exercise:

- **Task 1**: Create a DDoS protection plan.
- **Task 2**: Enable DDoS for a new virtual network.
- **Task 3**: Disable DDoS for a virtual network.

Let's now complete the aforementioned tasks by performing the following steps:

1. Open a web browser and browse to `https://portal.azure.com`.
2. On the left-hand side, click on the portal menu and then click on **Create a resource**:

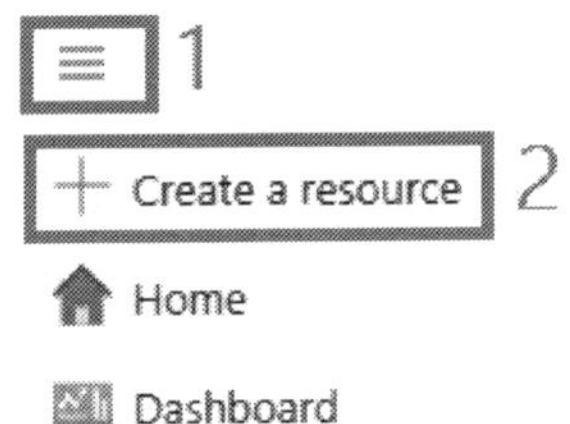

Figure 6.12 – Clicking to create a resource

3. In the search area at the top of the screen, type `DDoS protection plan` and click it. Then, click on the **Create** button:

Figure 6.13 – Entering "DDoS protection plan"

4. In the **Create a DDoS protection plan** blade, configure the following:

   Name: `azsec-DdoS`.

   Subscription: Select your subscription.

Resource group: `azuresec-c66-rg`.

Location: Select the same region that you set when you deployed the template earlier.

Click on **Create**:

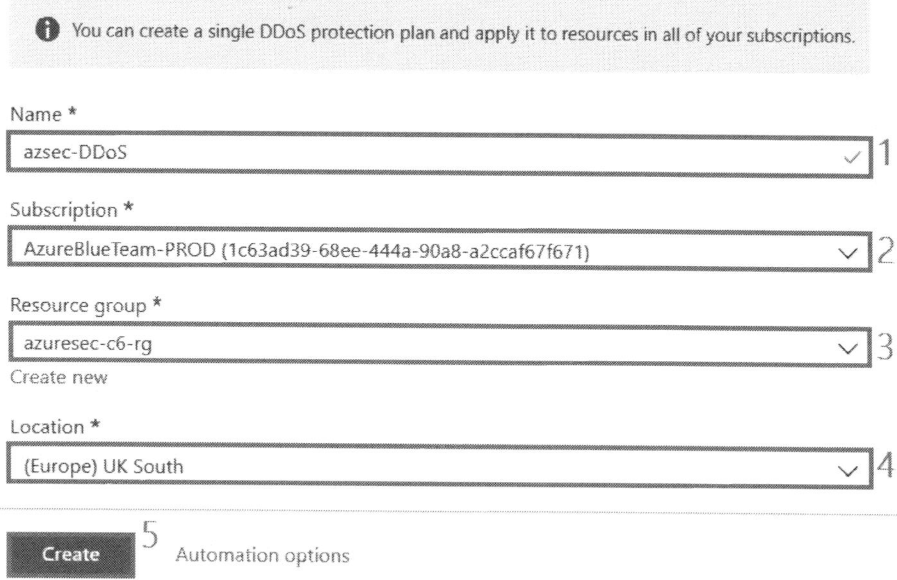

Figure 6.14 – Entering the DDoS protection plan parameters

5. In the **Search resources, services, and docs** box at the top of the portal, type `virtual network` and select the **Virtual networks** option:

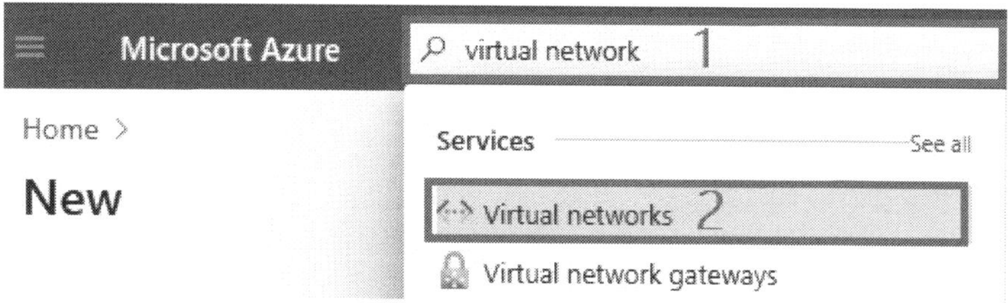

Figure 6.15 – Entering and selecting "virtual network"

6. In the **Virtual networks** blade, click on **azsec-VirtualNetwork**, and then click on DDoS protection:

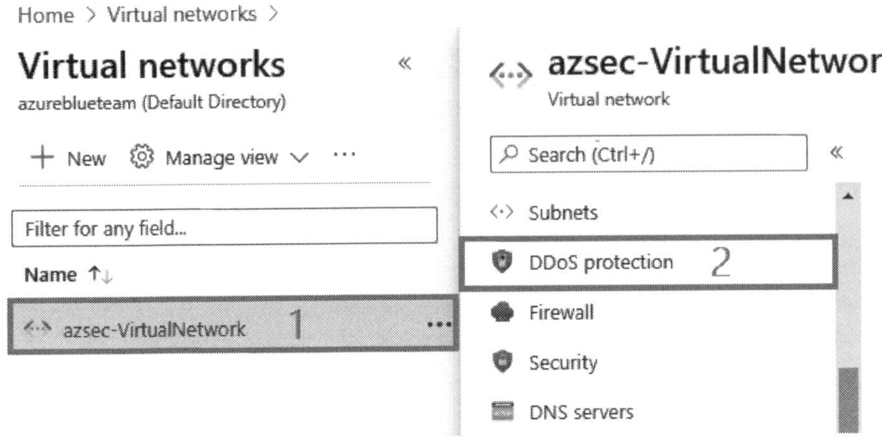

Figure 6.16 – Selecting the virtual network DDoS configuration

7. In the **azsec-VirtualNetwork | DDoS protection** blade, select the **Enable** option and configure the following:

   DDoS protection plan: `azsec-DDoS`

   Click **Save**:

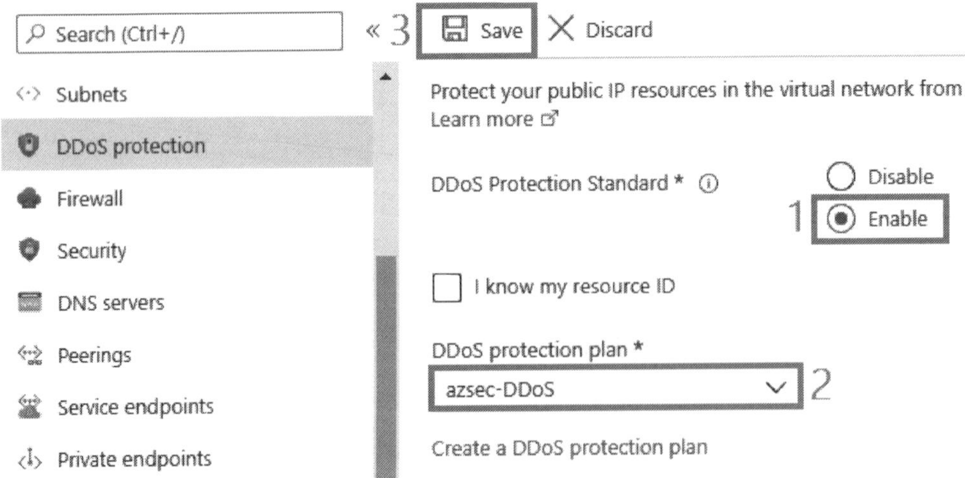

Figure 6.17 – Configuring the virtual network DDoS option

This applies the DDoS plan that we created earlier to our virtual network. In the next step, we will remove the DDoS plan from the network as the service can be expensive!

1. In the **azsec-VirtualNetwork | DDoS protection** blade, select the **Disable** option and click on **Save**:

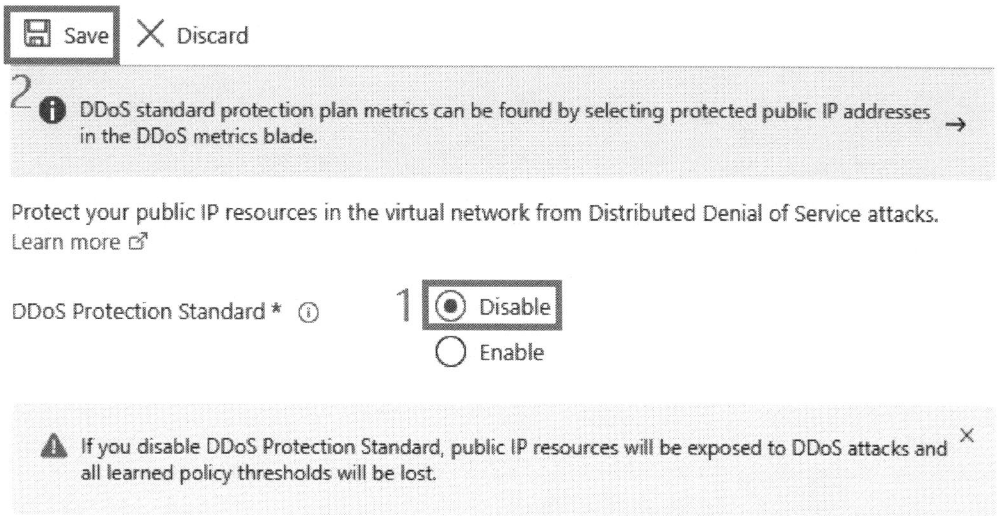

Figure 6.18 – Disabling DDoS protection

2. In the **Search resources, services, and docs** box at the top of the portal, type `DDoS` and then select the **DDoS protection plans** option:

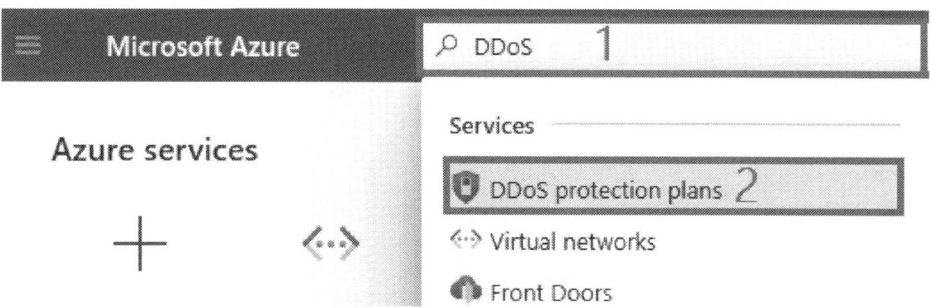

Figure 6.19 – Searching for DDoS protection plans

3. In the **DDoS protection plans** blade, click on **azsec-DDoS** and then click on **Delete**:

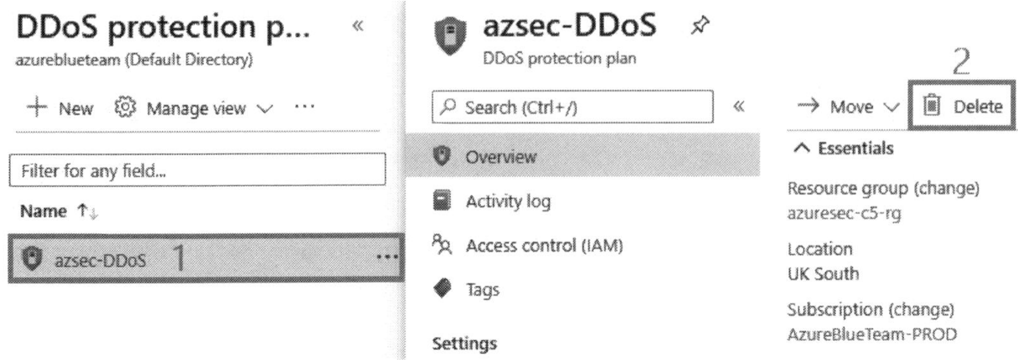

Figure 6.20 – Deleting a DDoS protection plan

4. Click **Yes** when prompted to delete the plan:

Delete the DDoS protection plan

Do you want to delete the DDoS protection plan 'azsec-DDoS'?

Figure 6.21 – Confirming DDoS protection plan deletion

So, in the preceding exercise, we created an Azure DDoS plan and enabled DDoS protection for an Azure virtual network to establish perimeter security. We also disabled the plan to avoid a huge cost to our subscription.

From a central governance perspective, we can configure an Azure policy to auto enable and apply a DDoS protection plan when new virtual networks are created in our subscription. To learn more about this approach, you can refer to this documentation: `https://aka.ms/ddosvnetpolicy-techcommunity`.

In the next section, we will look at the next layer of perimeter defense that we can configure for an Azure virtual network using Azure Firewall.

Implementing Azure Firewall

Azure Firewall is a perimeter network security solution in Azure. It inspects incoming and outgoing virtual network connections to protect against malicious traffic before they impact our workloads. The main difference between Azure Firewall and a third-party firewall appliance deployed as a VM in Azure (called a **network virtual appliance** - **NVA**) is that it is a managed service. This means that we do not have to worry about managing the underlying OS updates, application updates, high availability, and scalability for Azure Firewall as these are managed for us by Microsoft. We simply deploy the service, configure it, use it, and pay for what we use. From a security perspective, Azure Firewall offers the following capabilities:

- Define **application rules** to allow or deny connections to specified domain names. For example, `Allow access to github.com`; `Block access to gambling.com`. This is solely URL filtering. No TLS termination or deep packet inspection is taking place.
- Define **network rules** to allow or deny connections based on the source IP address, destination IP address, source port, destination port, and protocol; for example, `Block access for connections with a source IP of 1.1.1.1`; `Allow internet connections to port 80 of an internal web server`.
- Define **Network Address Translation (NAT) rules** to translate inbound network requests for delivery to internal services.
- Alert or block network connections to or from malicious IP addresses and domains based on Microsoft's threat intelligence information. This is referred to as **threat intelligence-based filtering**.

Microsoft recommends implementing Azure Firewall in a **hub and spoke** topology as shown in *Figure 6.22* for workload perimeter security. However, if you have multiple Azure subscriptions and are implementing services in multiple Azure regions, you may have to deploy so many instances of Azure Firewall that it becomes ineffective to manage them individually. This is where **Azure Firewall Manager** can help us. Firewall Manager provides centralized firewall management across subscriptions and regions. We manage our configuration and policies from one place and deploy them to multiple firewall instances. This significantly reduces the complexity of deploying policies to multiple Azure firewalls:

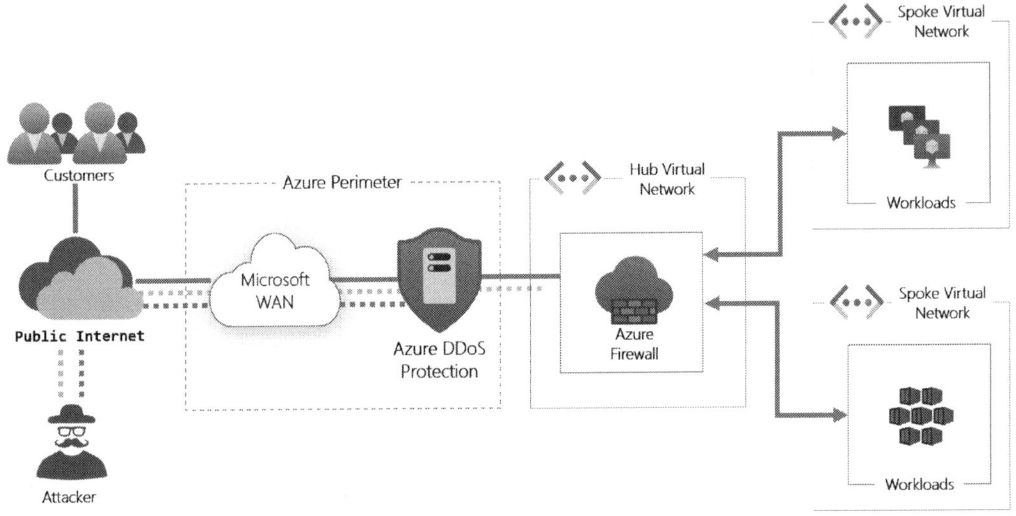

Figure 6.22 – Hub and Spoke Virtual Network architecture

You may also have noticed that the security capabilities of Azure Firewall are very limited when compared with the capabilities of a next-generation firewall, such as a Palo Alto appliance. Customers can choose to implement a third-party firewall appliance as a VM for virtual network perimeter security. These appliances are called **NVAs** in Azure and we can choose to implement these instead of Azure Firewall. In the next exercise, we will implement an Azure firewall for workload perimeter security. Note that the process of implementing Azure Firewall or an NVA is very similar, so the steps in the next exercise are applicable in either scenario.

Hands-on exercise – implementing Azure Firewall

Here are the tasks that we will complete in this exercise:

- **Task 1**: Create an Azure firewall subnet.
- **Task 2**: Deploy an Azure firewall in the subnet.

- **Task 3**: Create a default route and associate it with the private subnet.
- **Task 4**: Configure an egress application and network rules on the firewall.
- **Task 5**: Test the firewall.

Let's get into the steps to complete this:

1. In the **Search resources, services, and docs** box at the top of the portal, type `virtual network` and select the **Virtual networks** option:

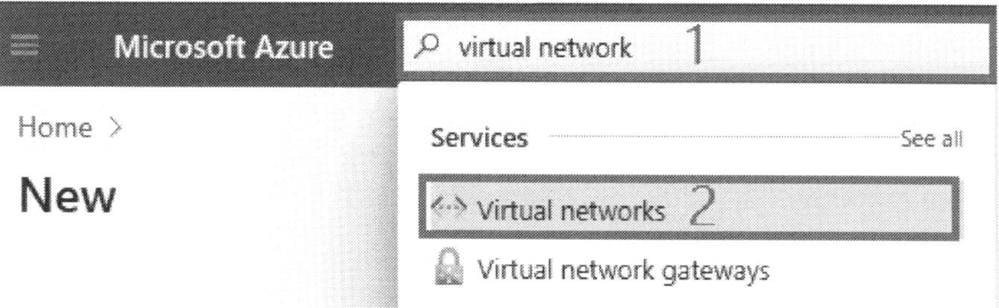

Figure 6.23 – Searching for "virtual network"

2. In the **Virtual networks** blade, click on **azsec-VirtualNetwork** and then click on **Subnets**:

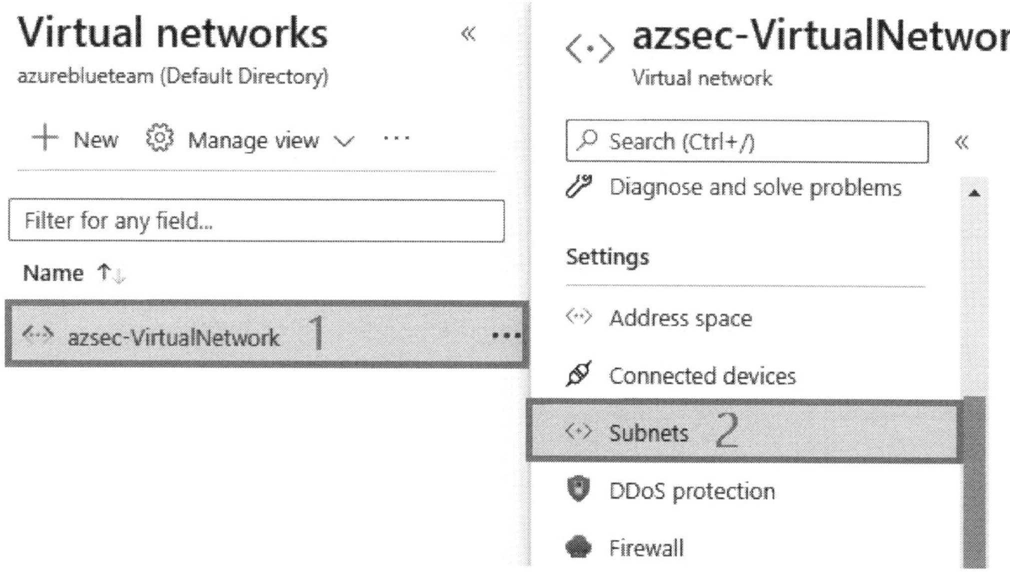

Figure 6.24 – Selecting virtual network subnets

3. In the **azsec-VirtualNetwork | Subnets** blade, click on **+ Subnet** to create a new subnet that we will deploy Azure Firewall to:

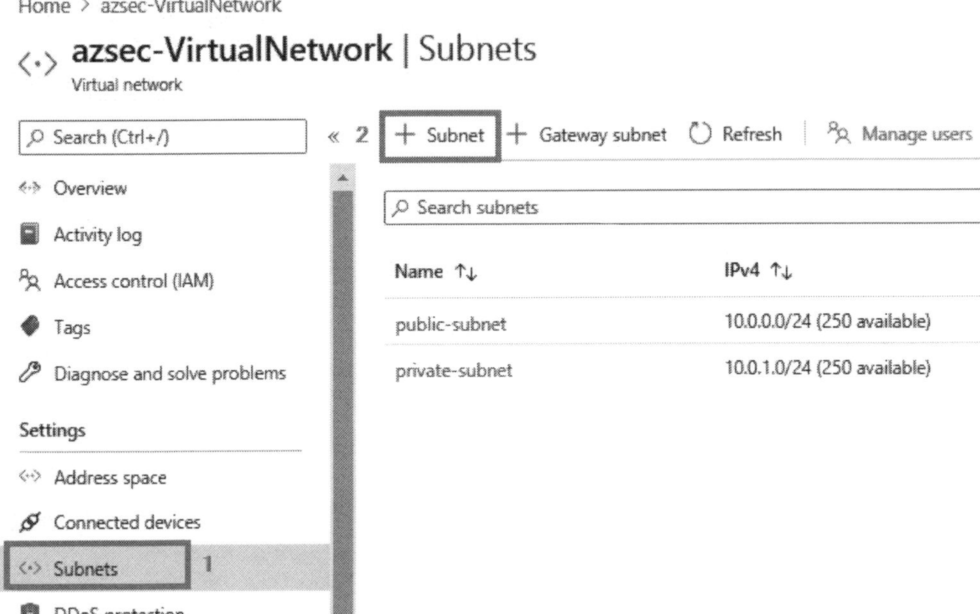

Figure 6.25 – Creating a new subnet

4. In the **+ Subnet** blade, configure the following:

   Name: `AzureFirewallSubnet` (note that the name must be exactly `AzureFirewallSubnet` otherwise you will get errors when creating the firewall)

   Subnet address range: `10.0.2.0/24`

   Leave the other settings as their default values and then click **Save**:

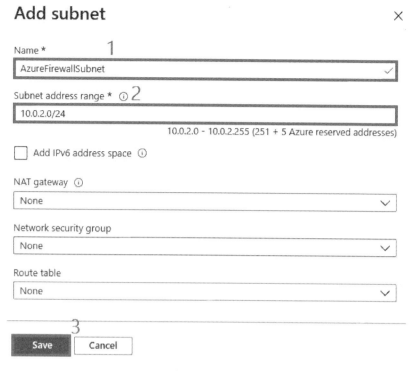

Figure 6.26 – Configuring new subnet parameters

5. You should get a notification in the top-right corner informing you that the subnet has been successfully created. Close the **Add subnet** blade. You should now see the new **AzureFirewallSubnet**:

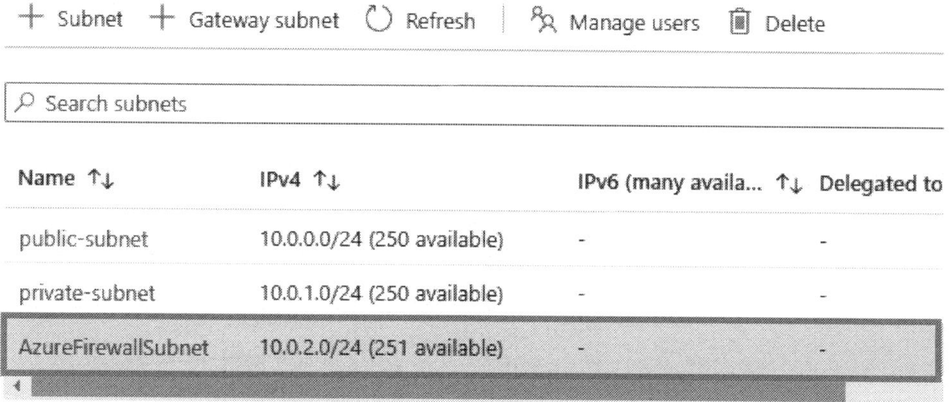

Figure 6.27 – Selecting the Azure Firewall subnet

6. In the **Search resources, services, and docs** textbox at the top of the portal, type `Firewall` and then select the **Firewalls** option:

Figure 6.28 – Searching for Firewalls

7. Click on the **Create firewall** button that appears and configure the following:

   Subscription: Select your subscription.

   Resource group: `azuresec-c5-rg`.

   Name: `azsec-Firewall`.

   Region: Select the same region that you set when you deployed the template earlier.

   Choose a virtual network: The **Use existing** setting.

   Virtual network: `azsec-VirtualNetwork (azuresec-c5-rg)`.

   Public IP address: **Add new**: `azsec-FirewallIp`

   Leave the other settings as their default values.

   Click **Review + create**.

   Then, click **Create**.

   This will create the Azure Firewall service in the subnet that we created earlier. Wait for the deployment to complete:

Home > Firewalls >

Create a firewall

virtual network. The service is fully integrated with Azure Monitor for logging and analytics. Learn more.

Project details

Subscription * 1 AzureBlueTeam-PROD (699f5153-f723-4d1c-9bfa-bb173c35ec53)

Resource group * 2 azuresec-c5-rg

Create new

Instance details

Name * 3 azsec-Firewall

Region * 4 UK South

Availability zone None

Choose a virtual network Create new Use existing 5

Virtual network 6 azsec-VirtualNetwork (azuresec-c5-rg)

Public IP address * 7 (New) azsec-FirewallIp

Add new

Forced tunneling Disabled

8

Review + create Previous Next : Tags > Download a template for automation

Figure 6.29 – Configuring new firewall parameters

8. Once the deployment is complete, click on the **Go to resource** button:

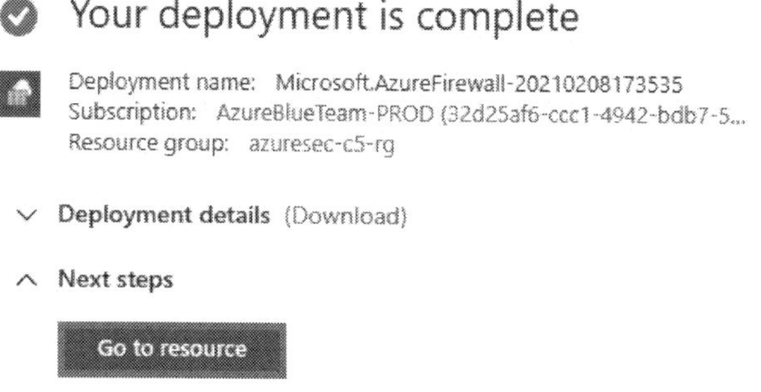

Figure 6.30 – Firewall deployment completion

9. In the **azsec-Firewall** blade, make a note of the **Firewall private IP** value. We will need this value in later steps:

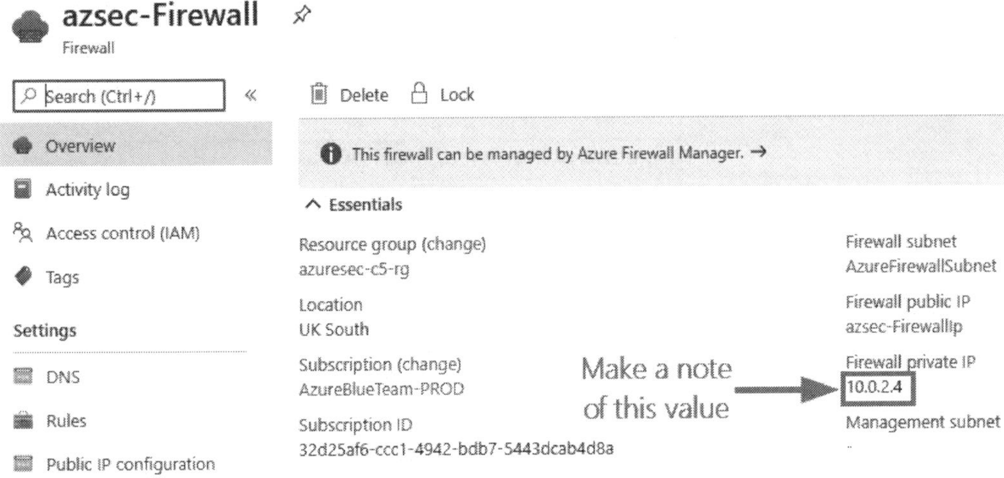

Figure 6.31 – Recording the firewall's internal IP

In the next step, we will begin the creation of a custom route table with a default route to direct traffic to `AzureFirewallSubnet`. This route will configure outbound traffic through the firewall:

1. In the Azure portal, in the **Search resources, services, and docs** textbox at the top of the Azure portal page, type `route tables` and then press the *Enter* key:

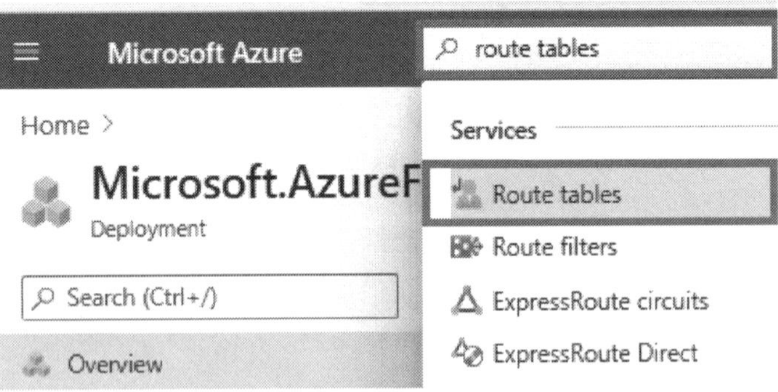

Figure 6.32 – Searching for Route tables

2. On the **Route tables** blade, click **+ Add**. Configure the following settings in the **Create Route table** blade:

   Subscription: Select your subscription.

   Resource group: `azuresec-c5-rg`.

   Region: Select the same region that you set when you deployed the template earlier.

   Name: `private-subnet-routetable`.

   Propagate gateway routes: **No**.

   Click **Review + create**.

   Then, click **Create**:

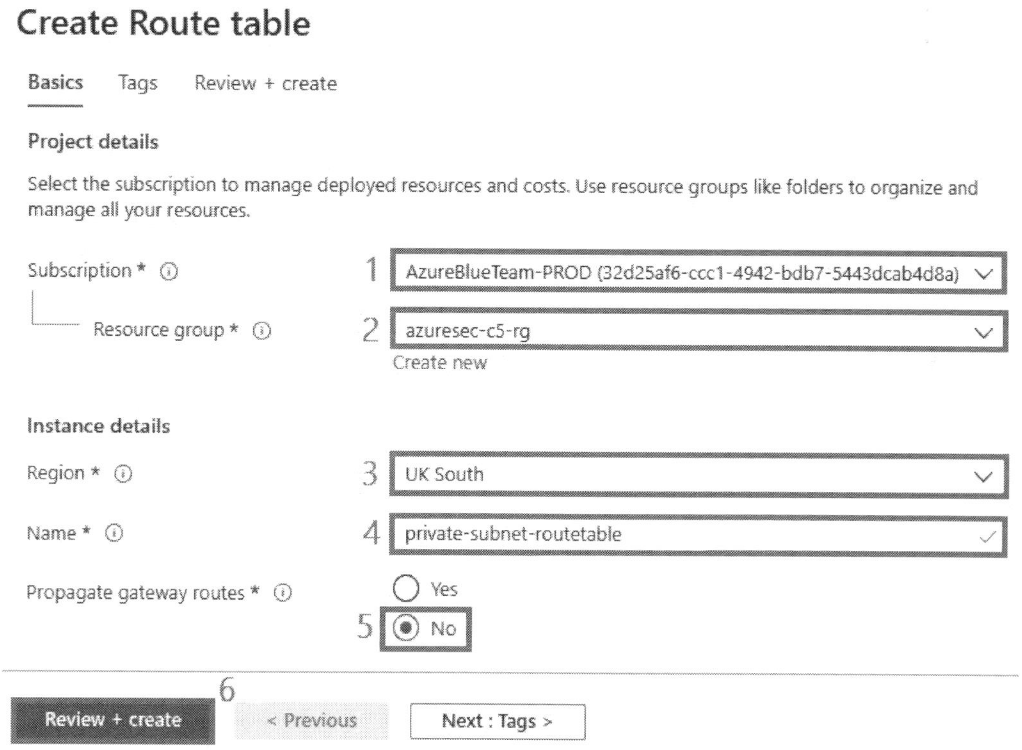

Create Route table

Basics Tags Review + create

Project details

Select the subscription to manage deployed resources and costs. Use resource groups like folders to organize and manage all your resources.

Subscription * 1 AzureBlueTeam-PROD (32d25af6-ccc1-4942-bdb7-5443dcab4d8a)

Resource group * 2 azuresec-c5-rg

Create new

Instance details

Region * 3 UK South

Name * 4 private-subnet-routetable

Propagate gateway routes * Yes 5 No

Review + create 6 < Previous Next : Tags >

Figure 6.33 – Configuring new route table parameters

3. Once the deployment is complete, click on the **Go to resource** button:

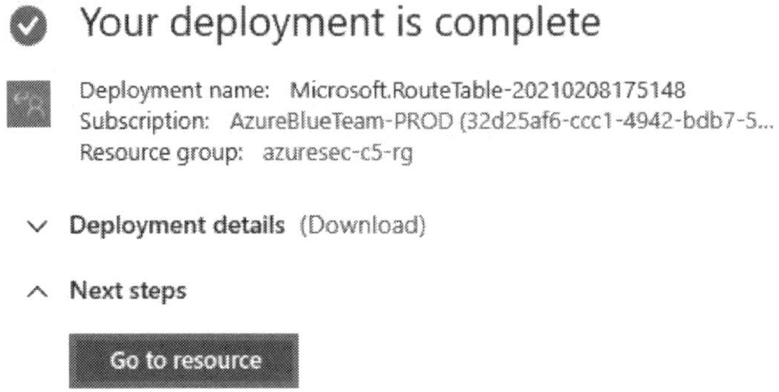

Figure 6.34 – Route table deployment completion

4. Now that we have created a route table, we need to add a "user-defined route" entry to route selected traffic to the firewall. To do this, on the **private-subnet-routetable** blade, in the **Settings** section, click **Routes** and then click **+ Add**:

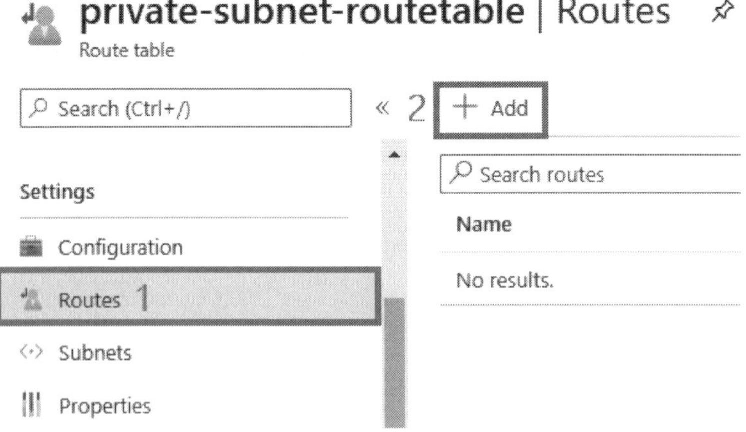

Figure 6.35 – Adding routes to the route table

> **Note**
>
> In the previous step, we created a user-defined route entry to send traffic that we specify to the firewall. A user-defined route is a custom route entry configured by us. This contrasts with system route entries that are automatically created by the platform to implement default routing behaviors and cannot be modified by a user. User-defined route entries will override conflicting system routes.

5. On the **Add route** blade, configure the following settings:

   Route name: `internet-route`

   Address prefix: `0.0.0.0/0`

   Next hop type: **Virtual appliance**

   Next hop address: The value that you made a note of in *step 9*

   Then, click **OK**:

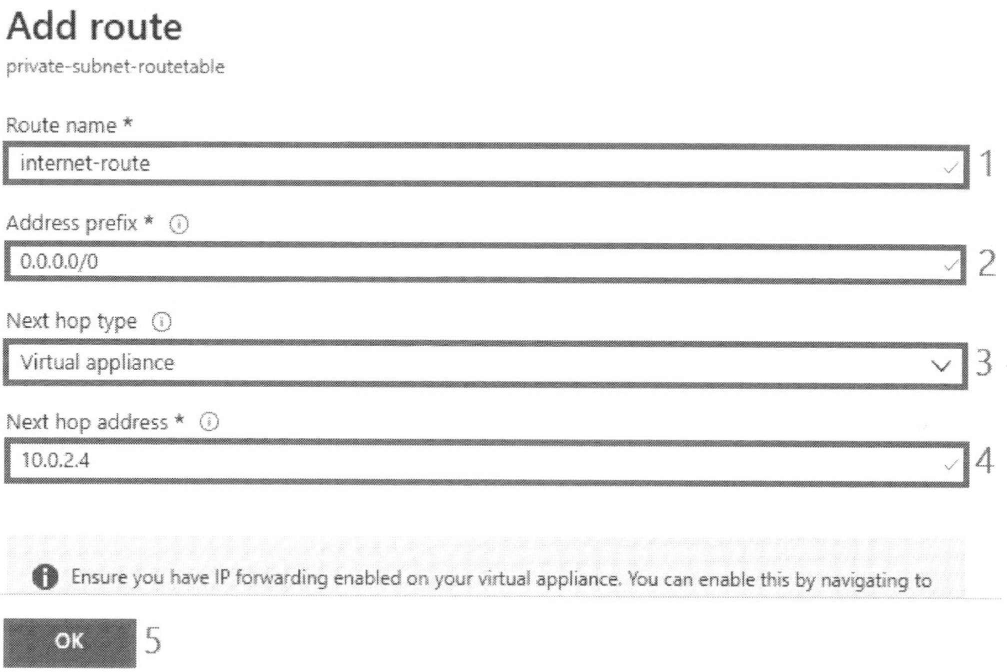

Add route
private-subnet-routetable
Route name *
internet-route 1
Address prefix *
0.0.0.0/0 2
Next hop type
Virtual appliance 3
Next hop address *
10.0.2.4 4
Ensure you have IP forwarding enabled on your virtual appliance. You can enable this by navigating to
OK 5

Figure 6.36 – Configuring new route parameters

6. On the **private-subnet-routetable** blade, in the **Settings** section, click **Subnets** and then click **+ Associate**:

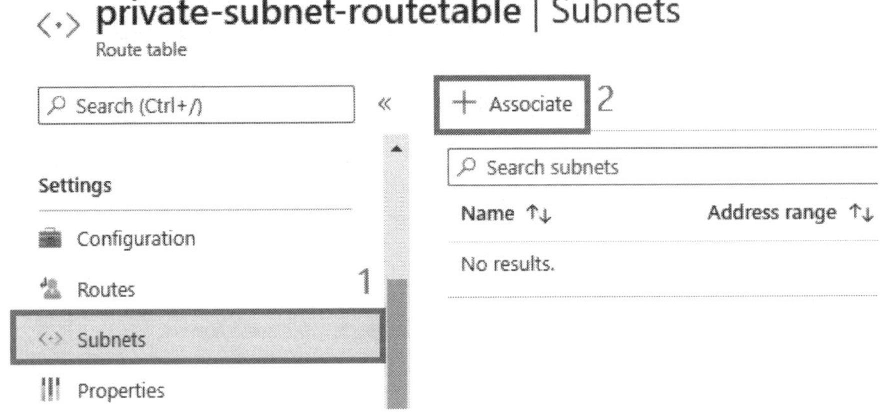

Figure 6.37 – Associating a route table with subnet

7. On the **Associate subnet** blade, configure the following settings:

   Virtual network: `azsec-VirtualNetwork`

   Subnet: `private-subnet`

   Then, click **OK**:

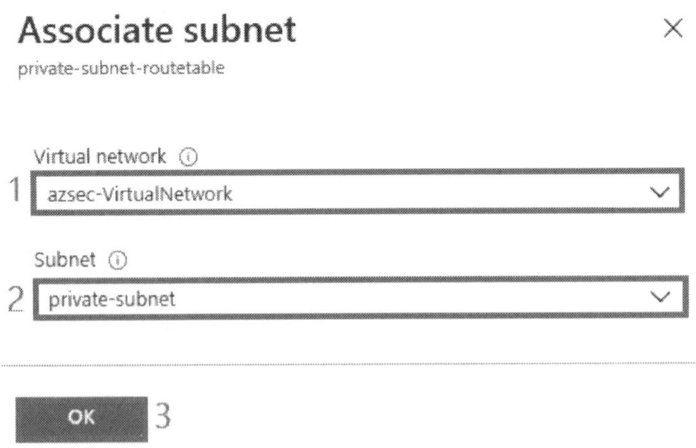

Figure 6.38 – Configuring route association parameters

This will associate the route table with the private subnet. In the next steps, we will create application and network rules on the firewall for egress traffic that we want to allow from our private subnet.

8. In the **Search resources, services, and docs** textbox at the top of the portal, type `Firewall` and then select the **Firewalls** option. Click on **azsec-Firewall**.
9. On the **azsec-Firewall** blade, in the **Settings** section, click **Rules**. Then, click the **Application rule collection** tab, and then click **+ Add application rule collection**:

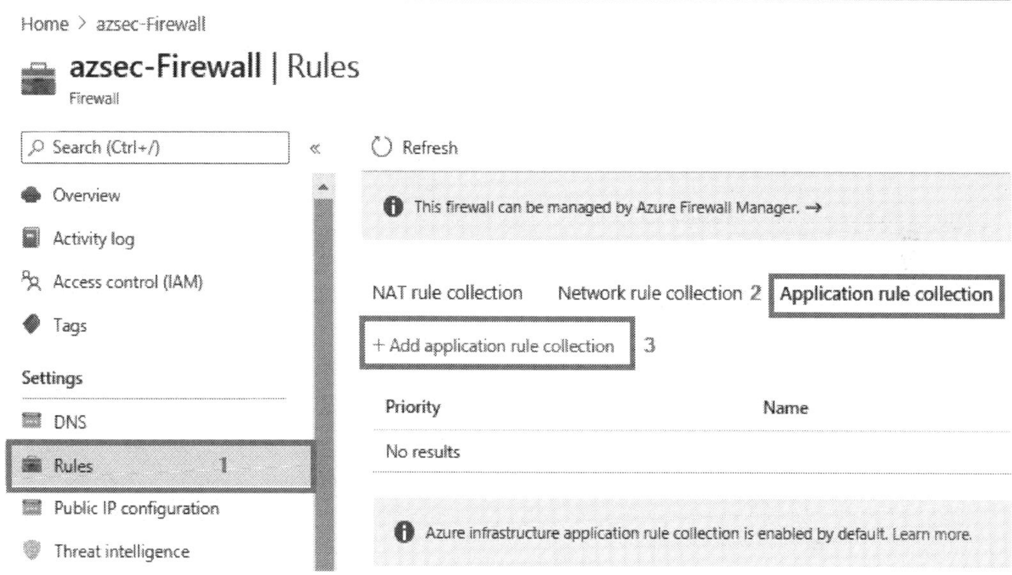

Figure 6.39 – Adding an application rule

10. On the **Add application rule collection** blade, configure the following settings:

    Name: `egress-firewall-app-rule`

    Priority: `200`

    Action: `Allow`

    Target FQDNs

    name: `allow-bing-search-engine`

    Source type: **IP address**

    Source: `10.0.0.0/16`

    Protocol:Port: `http:80, http:443`

    Target FQDNs: `www.bing.com`

    Leave the others as their default values.

Then, click **Add**:

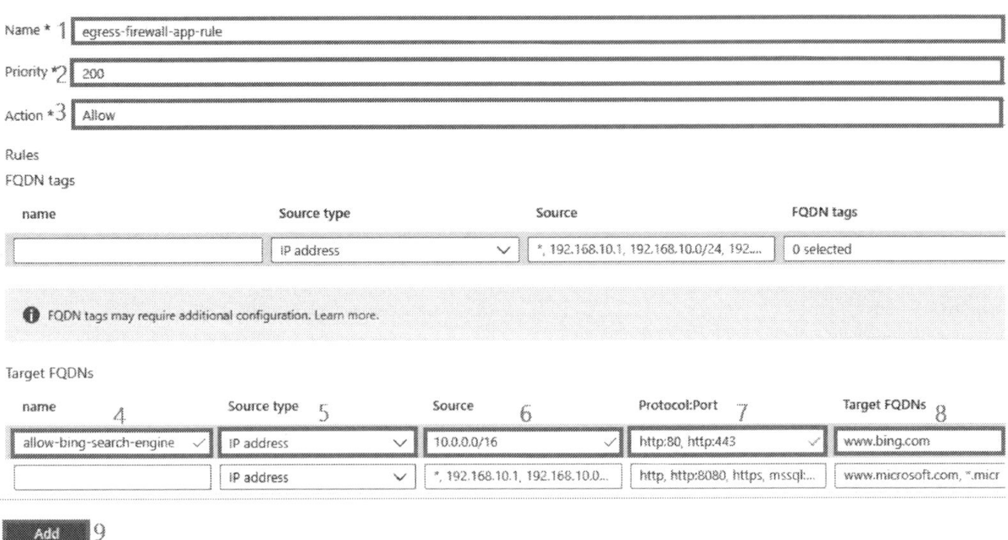

Figure 6.40 – Configuring application rule parameters

11. On the **azsec-Firewall | Rules** blade, click the **Network rule collection** tab and then click **+ Add network rule collection**:

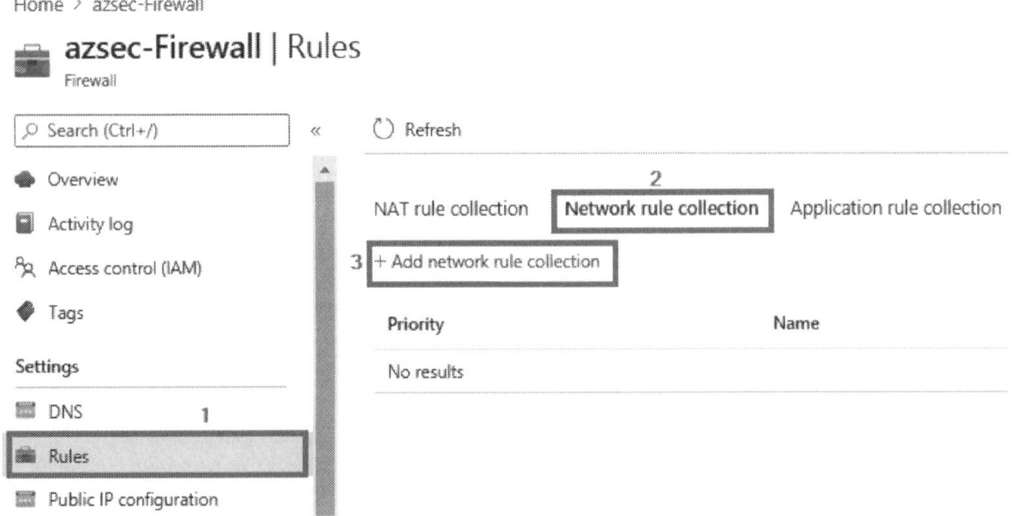

Figure 6.41 – Adding a network rule

12. On the **Add network rule collection** blade, specify the following settings (leave the others as their default values):

    Name: `egress-firewall-network-rule`

    Priority: `200`

    Action: `Allow`

    IP Addresses

    name: `allow-dns`

    Protocol: **UDP**

    Source type: **IP address**

    Source: `10.0.0.0/16`

    Destination type: **IP address**

    Destination Address: *

    Destination Ports: `53`

    Leave the others as their default values.

    Click **Add**:

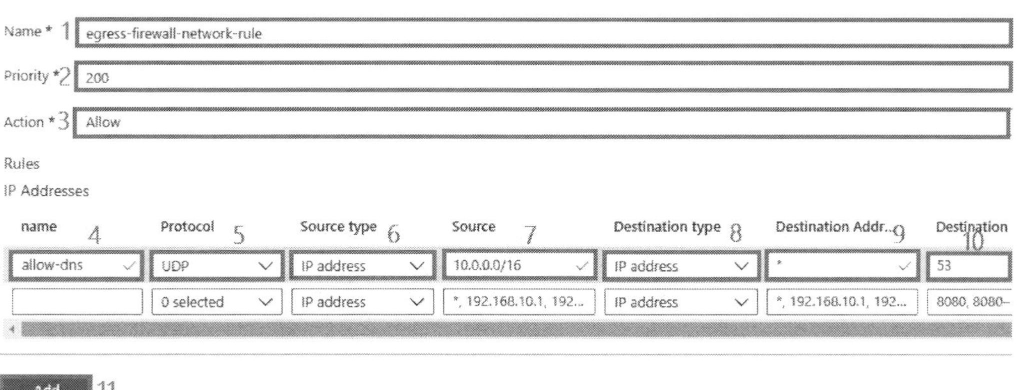

Figure 6.42 – Adding network rule parameters

Now that we have configured the egress firewall rules, we will be testing the behavior from the private Linux VM that was deployed as part of our template.

13. In the Azure portal, in the **Search resources, services, and docs** textbox at the top of the Azure portal page, type `azsecwinvm` and then press the *Enter* key:

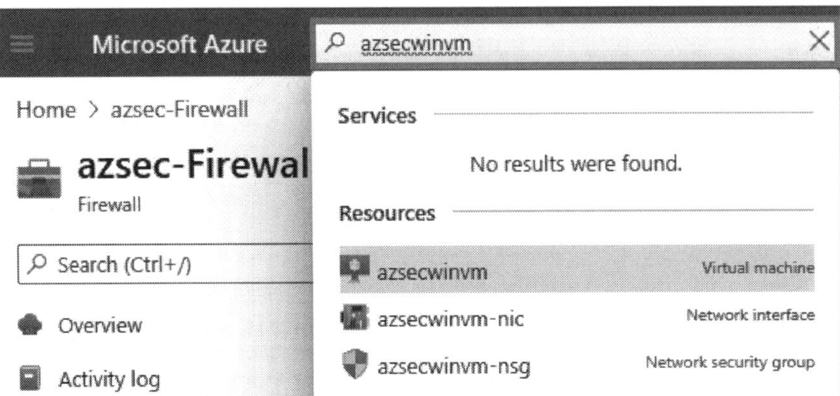

Figure 6.43 – Searching for azsecwinvm

14. On the **azsecwinvm** blade, click **Connect** and, in the drop-down menu, click **RDP**. Click **Download RDP File** and use it to connect to the azsecwinvm Azure VM via Remote Desktop.
15. When prompted to authenticate, provide the following credentials:

    Username: `azureadmin`.

    Password: Enter the password that you configured during template deployment.
16. Within the RDP session, click the **Start** button and then type `putty 10.0.1.4`:

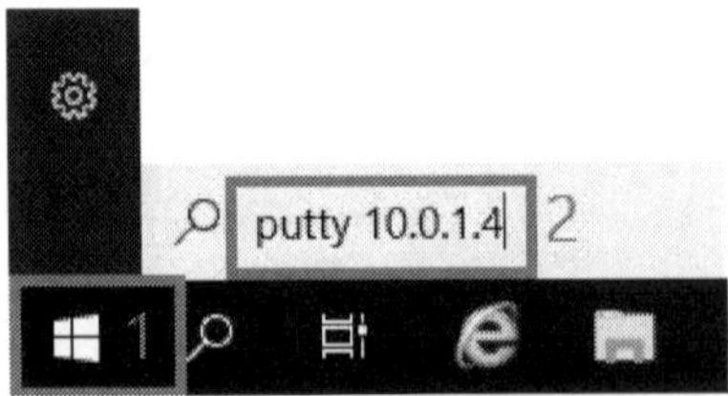

Figure 6.44 – Opening an SSH session using PuTTY

17. In the PuTTY window, authenticate using the following credentials:

    Username: `azureadmin`.

    Password: Enter the password that you configured during template deployment:

```
azureadmin@azseclinvm: ~
login as: azureadmin
azureadmin@10.0.1.4's password:
Welcome to Ubuntu 18.04.5 LTS (GNU/Linux 5.4.0-1039-azure x86_64)
```

Figure 6.45 – Entering Linux VM credentials

18. In the shell session, type the following command and press *Enter* to test egress access to a destination that is not allowed. You should receive a deny message due to `No rule matched`:

    ```
    curl www.google.com
    ```

    Here is a screenshot of the output:

```
azureadmin@azseclinvm:~$
azureadmin@azseclinvm:~$ curl www.google.com
HTTP  request from 10.0.1.4:43142 to www.google.com:80. Url: www.google.com. Act
ion: Deny. No rule matched. Proceeding with default actionazureadmin@azseclinvm:
~$
```

Figure 6.46 – Testing connectivity using curl

19. In the shell session, type the following command and then press *Enter* to test egress access to a destination that is not allowed. This should be successful:

    ```
    curl www.bing.com
    ```

    Here is a screenshot of the output:

```
azureadmin@azseclinvm:~$
azureadmin@azseclinvm:~$ curl www.bing.com
<!doctype html><html lang="en" dir="ltr"><head><meta name="theme-color
" content="#4F4F4F" /><meta name="description" content="Bing helps you
 turn information into action, making it faster and easier to go from
searching to doing." /><meta http-equiv="X-UA-Compatible" content="IE=
edge" /><meta name="viewport" content="width=device-width, initial-sca
```

Figure 6.47 – Testing connectivity using curl

Close the PuTTY SSH session, but leave the RDP session open as we will need it for later exercises.

Congratulations! You have just implemented an Azure firewall with network and application rules. In the next section, we will look at the implementation of another perimeter security defense service – Web Application Firewall.

Implementing a Web Application Firewall (WAF) in Azure

Web and API applications are popular workload types to host in Azure virtual networks. They are also increasingly targeted by malicious attacks that exploit commonly known vulnerabilities, such as SQL injection and cross-site scripting.

Apart from getting developers to follow good coding security practices when developing web applications, a WAF can also be deployed at the network perimeter as an added layer of protection against these exploits and vulnerabilities. WAF can be deployed with three services in Azure:

- **The Azure Application Gateway WAF SKU**: This is a regional-level WAF that can be deployed in Azure virtual networks to protect public-facing or private workloads.
- **Azure Front Door WAF**: This is a WAF service that is integrated with the Azure Front Door global service.
- **Azure Content Delivery Network (CDN)**: Similar to the WAF on Azure Front Door, this is a global service that is integrated with the Azure CDN service. This capability is currently under public preview at the time of writing this book.
- For the purpose of the exam objectives, we will look at both the Application Gateway and the Front Door services. We will configure the application gateway in our hands-on exercise.

Application Gateway WAF

Azure Application Gateway is a web traffic load balancer that enables us to manage traffic to our web applications. Traditional load balancers operate at the transport layer (OSI Layer 4 – TCP and UDP) and route traffic based on the source IP address and port to a destination IP address and port. Application Gateway operates on Layer 7 and can route traffic based on additional attributes of an HTTP request, for example, the URI path or host headers:

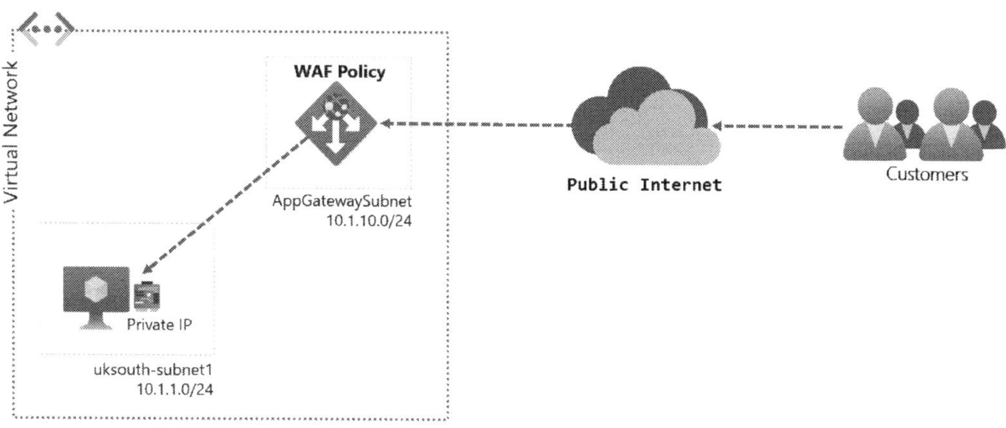

Figure 6.48 – Azure Application Gateway architecture

As mentioned earlier, the Application Gateway service can be deployed in a designated subnet within our Azure virtual networks.

WAF on Application Gateway supports three rule sets: core rule sets 3.1, 3.0, and 2.2.9 from the **Open Web Application Security Project** (**OWASP**). These rules protect our web applications from malicious activity.

WAF on Application Gateway can be set to either detection mode or prevention mode. In detection mode, the WAF monitors and logs all threat alerts, but it does not block them. In prevention mode, the WAF blocks intrusions and attacks that the rules detect, but it also logs them in the WAF logs.

Front Door WAF

Azure Front Door is a highly scalable, globally distributed application and CDN. It uses the anycast protocol with split TCP and Microsoft's global network to improve global connectivity and performance for our web applications:

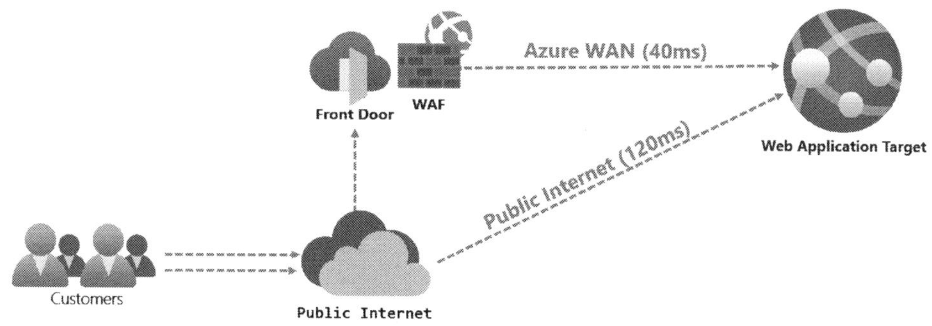

Figure 6.49 – Azure Front Door WAF

Figure 6.49 shows how Front Door receives client requests through a point of presence that is close to end users, and uses the Microsoft high throughput backbone network to accelerate delivery to the backend application instead of the traffic being routed entirely over the public internet. Azure WAF, when integrated with Front Door, stops application denial-of-service and targeted application attacks at the Azure network edge.

In the next section, you will configure an application gateway WAF to protect a web application in Azure.

Hands-on exercise – configuring a WAF on Azure Application Gateway

Here are the tasks that we will complete in this exercise:

- **Task 1**: Create a subnet for Azure Application Gateway.
- **Task 2**: Create an application gateway.
- **Task 3**: Add a health probe.
- **Task 4**: Configure path-based routing.
- **Task 5**: Test the application gateway.

Here are the steps to complete the tasks:

1. In the Azure portal, locate the **azsec-VirtualNetwork virtual network**, select **Subnets**, and then click on **+ Subnet**:

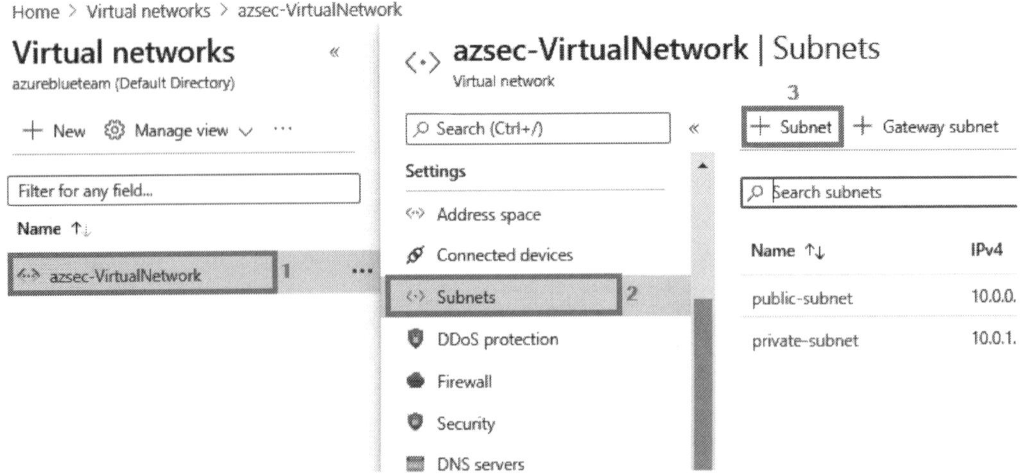

Figure 6.50 – Adding a new subnet

2. In the **+ Subnet** blade, configure the following:

   Name: `AppGwSubnet`

   Subnet address range: `10.0.3.0/24`

   Leave the other settings as their default values and then click **Save**:

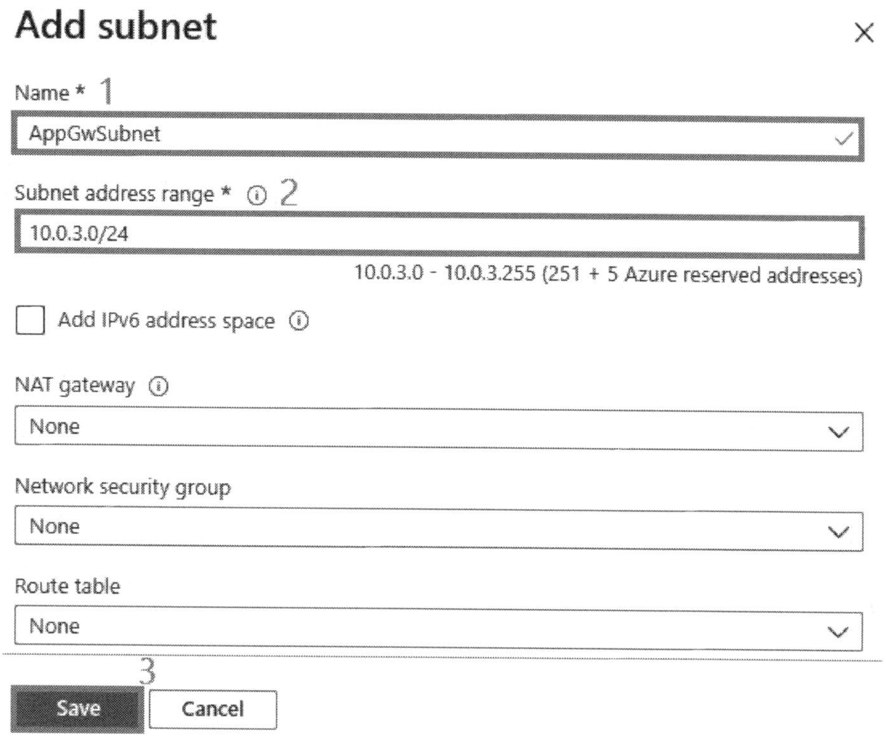

Add subnet
Name * 1
AppGwSubnet
Subnet address range * 2
10.0.3.0/24
10.0.3.0 - 10.0.3.255 (251 + 5 Azure reserved addresses)
Add IPv6 address space
NAT gateway
None
Network security group
None
Route table
None
3
Save
Cancel

Figure 6.51 – Configuring the subnet parameters

3. In the Azure portal, in the **Search resources, services, and docs** textbox at the top of the Azure portal page, type `Application gateway` and then press *Enter*:

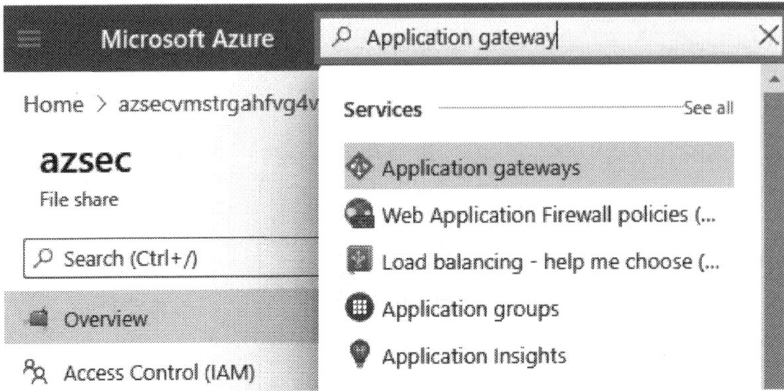

Figure 6.52 – Searching for the application gateway

4. Click on the **Create application gateway** button and configure the following:

Subscription: Select your subscription.

Resource group: `azuresec-c5-rg`.

Application gateway name: `azsec-app-gw`.

Region: Select the same region that you set when you deployed the template earlier.

Tier: **WAF V2**.

Enable autoscaling: **Yes**.

Minimum instance count: `1`.

Maximum instance count: `2`.

Firewall status: **Enabled**.

Firewall mode: **Prevention**.

Availability zone: **None**.

HTTP2: **Disabled**.

Virtual network: **azsec-VirtualNetwork**.

Subnet: **AppGwSubnet (10.0.3.0/24)**.

Click **Next : Frontends** >.

Then, click **Create**:

Create application gateway

your resources.

Subscription * — 1 — AzureBlueTeam-PROD (32d25af6-ccc1-4942-bdb7-5443dcab4d8a)

Resource group * — 2 — azuresec-c5-rg

Create new

Instance details

Application gateway name * — 3 — azsec-app-gw

Region * — 4 — UK South

Tier — 5 — WAF V2

Enable autoscaling — 6 — Yes / No

Minimum instance count * — 7 — 1

Maximum instance count — 8 — 2

Firewall status — Disabled / Enabled — 9

Firewall mode — Detection / Prevention — 10

Availability zone — None

HTTP2 — 11 — Disabled / Enabled

Configure virtual network

Virtual network * — 12 — azsec-VirtualNetwork

Create new

Subnet * — 13 — AppGwSubnet (10.0.3.0/24)

Manage subnet configuration

Previous | Next : Frontends > 14

Figure 6.53 – Configuring the application gateway parameters

5. In the **Frontends** tab, configure the following:

   Frontend IP address type: **Public**

   Public IP address: **Add new**: `azsec-app-gw`

Click **Next : Backends >**:

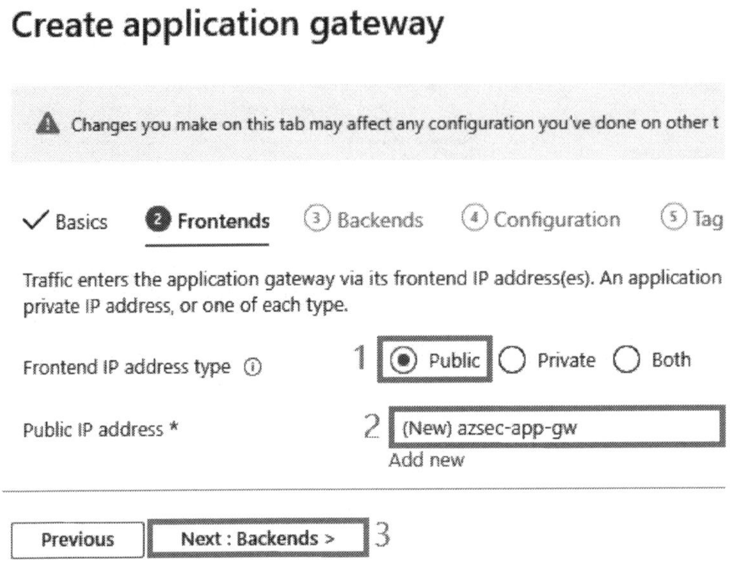

Create application gateway

Changes you make on this tab may affect any configuration you've done on other t

✓ Basics 2 Frontends 3 Backends 4 Configuration 5 Tag

Traffic enters the application gateway via its frontend IP address(es). An application private IP address, or one of each type.

Frontend IP address type 1 Public Private Both

Public IP address * 2 (New) azsec-app-gw
Add new

Previous Next : Backends > 3

Figure 6.54 – Configuring the application gateway frontend

6. On the **Backends** tab, select **Add a backend pool**:

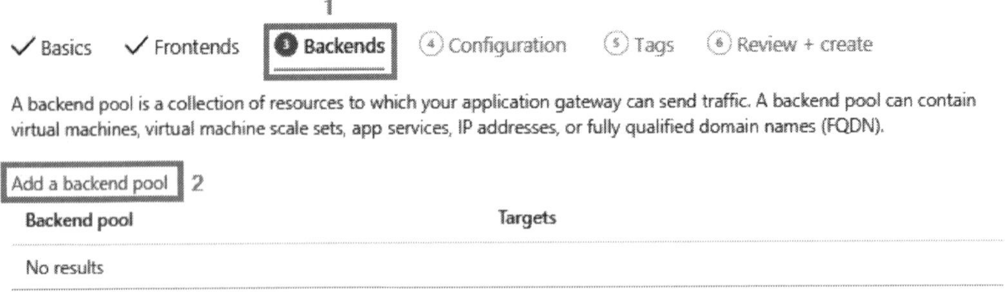

Figure 6.55 – Configuring the application gateway backend

7. In the **Add a backend pool** blade, configure the following settings:

   Name: `linux-web-server`

   Add backend pool without targets: **No**

   Target type: **Virtual machine**

   Target: **azseclinvm-nic (10.0.1.4)**

   Then, click **Add**:

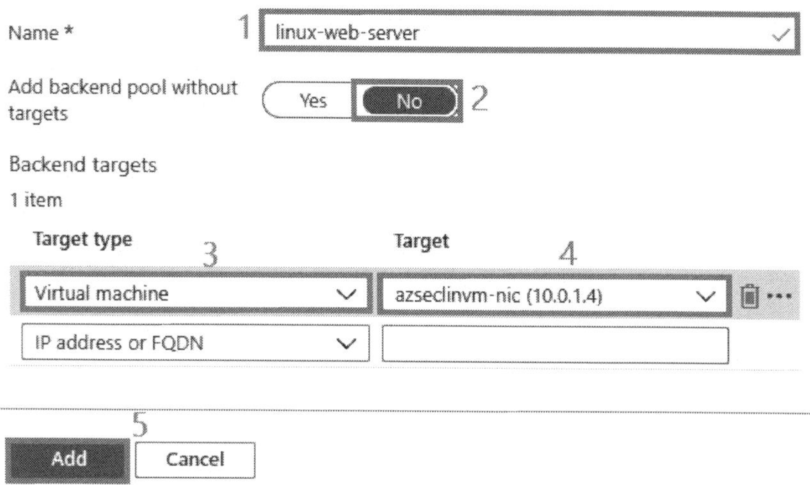

Figure 6.56 – Adding a backend pool

8. Back in the **Backends** tab, click on **Next : Configuration >**:

Create application gateway

✓ Basics ✓ Frontends ❸ Backends ④ Configuration ⑤ Tags

A backend pool is a collection of resources to which your application gateway can send virtual machines, virtual machine scale sets, app services, IP addresses, or fully qualified

Add a backend pool

Backend pool	Targets
linux-web-server	> 1 target

Previous | Next : Configuration >

Figure 6.57 – Clicking on "Next : Configuration >"

9. In the **Configuration** tab, select **Add a routing rule**:

✓ Basics ✓ Frontends ✓ Backends ❹ Configuration ⑤ Tags ⑥ Review + create

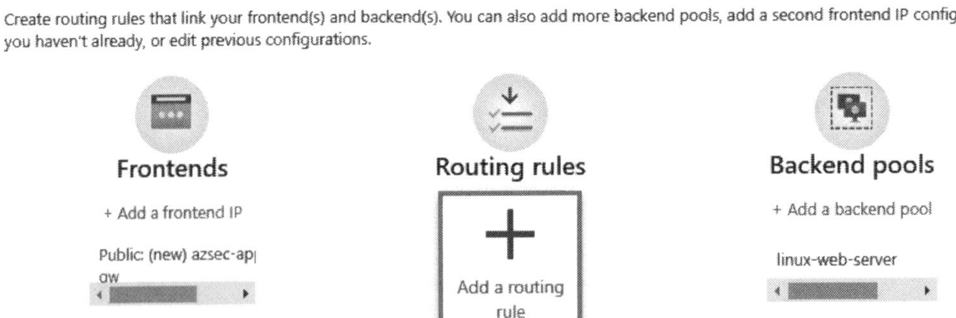

Figure 6.58 – Adding a routing rule

10. In the **Add a routing rule** blade, configure the following:

    Rule name: `webapp-http-rule`

    Listener

    Listener name: `webapp-http-rule-listener`

    Frontend IP: **Public**

    Protocol: **HTTP**

    Port: `80`

    Listener type: **Basic**

    Error page url: **No**:

Add a routing rule

Configure a routing rule to send traffic from a given frontend IP address to one or more backend targets. A routing rule must contain a listener and at least one backend target.

Rule name * 1 webapp-http-rule

2 * Listener * Backend targets

A listener "listens" on a specified port and IP address for traffic that uses a specified protocol. If the listener criteria are met, the application gateway will apply this routing rule.

Listener name * 3 webapp-http-rule-listener

Frontend IP * 4 Public

Protocol 5 HTTP HTTPS

Port * 6 80

Additional settings

Listener type 7 Basic Multi site

Error page url Yes No 8

Add Cancel

Figure 6.59 – Configuring routing rule parameters

11. Click on the **Backend targets** tab and then configure the following:

    Target type: **Backend pool**

    Backend target: **linux-web-server**

    HTTP settings: Click **Add new**:

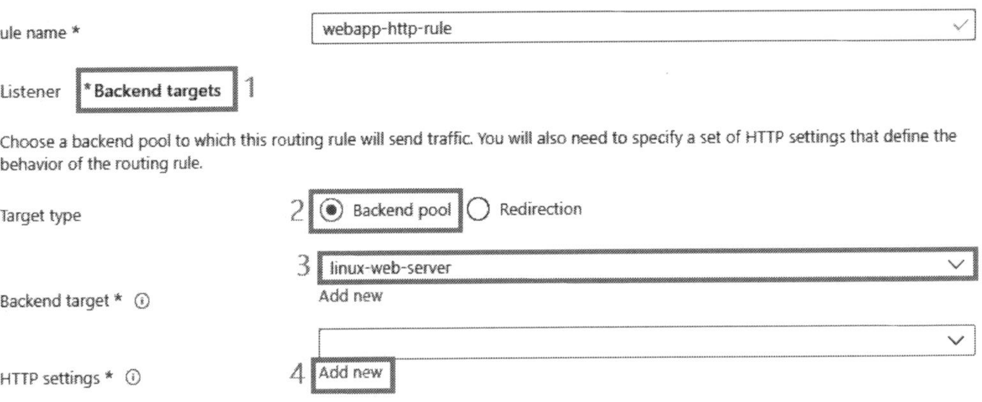

Figure 6.60 – Adding the backend target

12. In the **Add a HTTP setting** blade, configure the following:

    HTTP settings name: `webapp-http-setting`

    Leave the other settings as their default values.

    Click **Add**.

    Then, click **Add** again:

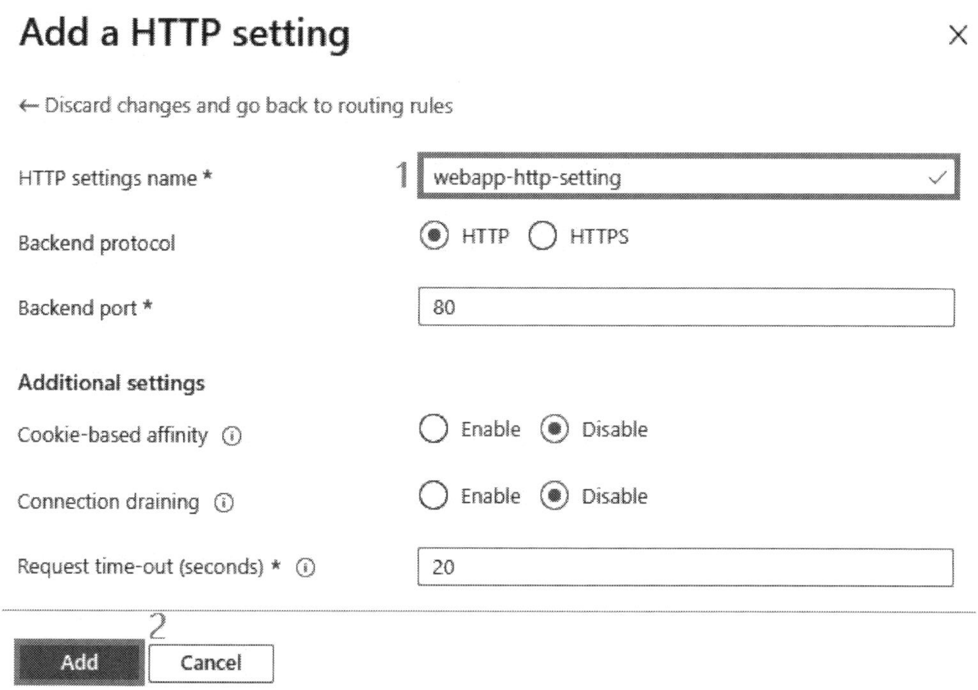

Add a HTTP setting

← Discard changes and go back to routing rules

HTTP settings name * 1 webapp-http-setting

Backend protocol HTTP HTTPS

Backend port * 80

Additional settings

Cookie-based affinity Enable Disable

Connection draining Enable Disable

Request time-out (seconds) * 20

2

Add Cancel

Figure 6.61 – Adding an HTTP setting

13. Back in the **Create application gateway** blade, click **Next : Tags** >. Then, click **Next : Review + create**:

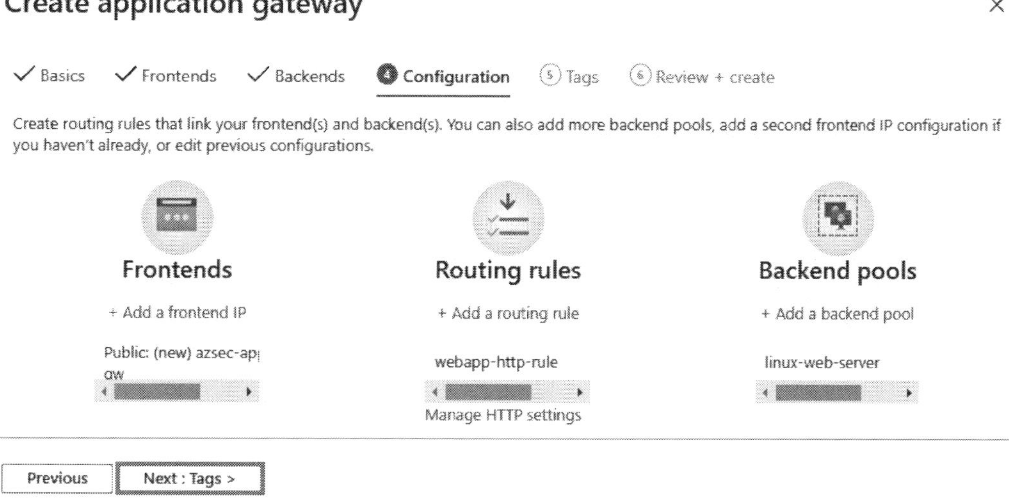

Figure 6.62 – Clicking on "Next : Tags >"

14. After the validation has passed, click on **Create**. Wait for the deployment to complete:

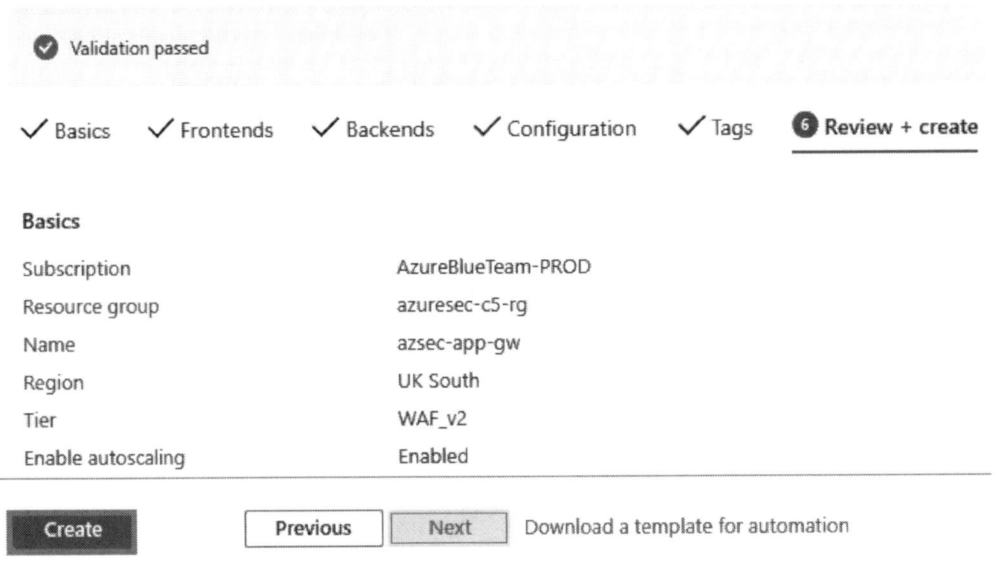

Figure 6.63 – Clicking to create the application gateway

15. Once the deployment is complete, click on **Go to resource group**:

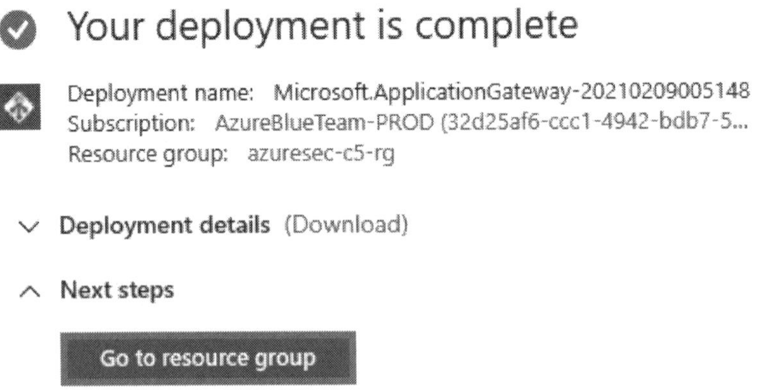

Figure 6.64 – Application gateway deployment completion

16. In the **Resource group** blade, select `azsec-app-gw`. Copy the **Frontend public IP address** value:

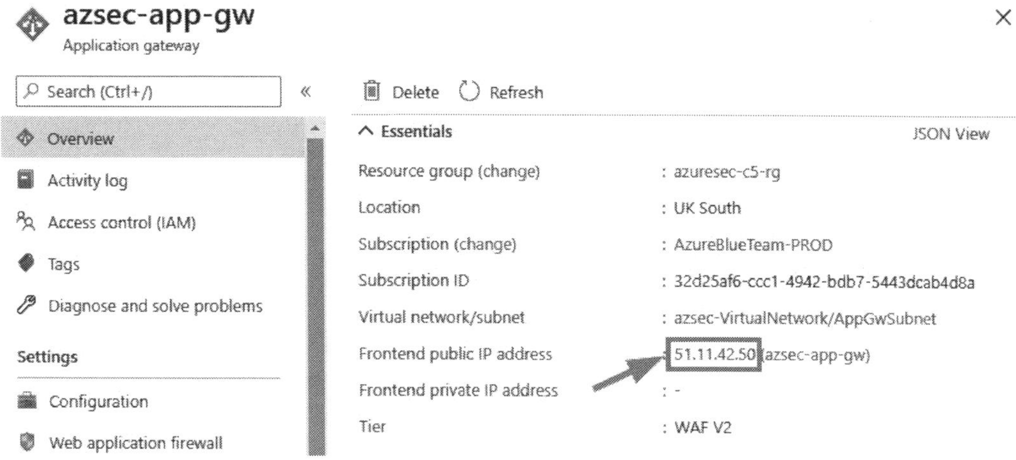

Figure 6.65 – Recording the application gateway's public IP

17. Open a new browser tab and browse to the public IP that you copied in *step 16*. You should reach the default Apache server page. This means that traffic is passing through the application gateway to the backend web server hosted on the Linux VM:

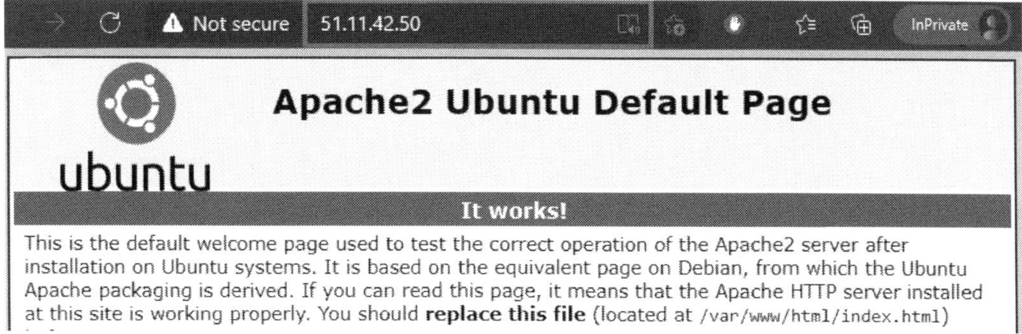

Figure 6.66 – The Ubuntu default page

Congratulations! You have successfully configured the Azure Application Gateway WAF.

Summary

In this chapter, you learned how the Azure DDoS protection service can be implemented to mitigate DDoS threats against applications and resources deployed in our virtual networks.

You also learned how Azure Firewall can be used to inspect incoming and outgoing virtual network connections to protect against malicious traffic before it impacts our application workloads. We also covered how Azure Firewall Manager can reduce the complexity of deploying policies to multiple firewalls from a centralized management service.

And finally, we covered how WAF (in Application Gateway or Azure Front Door) can be implemented to secure web applications against common exploits, such as SQL injection and cross-site scripting.

The information in this chapter has equipped you with the skills required to secure the perimeter of your Azure virtual networks from attacks and unauthorized access. In the next chapter, we will take this further by looking at network security for our virtual network workloads. We will be using the same resources that we deployed in this chapter for the exercises. See you in the next chapter!

Questions

As we conclude, here is a list of questions for you to test your knowledge regarding this chapter's material. You will find the answers in the *Assessments* section of the *Appendix*:

1. You need to deploy the Azure Firewall service in a virtual network in Azure. What should you do first?

   a. Create a new subnet in the virtual network.

   b. Create an NSG and associate it with the virtual network.

   c. Delete and recreate the virtual network.

   d. Configure DDoS protection for the virtual network.

2. You have a web app named `customapp`. You need to protect `customapp` using a WAF. What should you do?

   a. Deploy Azure Front Door.

   b. Add an extension to `customapp`.

   c. Deploy Azure Firewall.

   d. Deploy DDoS Protection.

3. You deployed an Azure VM named `web-vm1` in an Azure virtual network subnet. You need to ensure that all outbound traffic from the VM is routed through a network virtual appliance. What should you configure?

    a. A user-defined route

    b. A network security group

    c. An application security group

    d. A system route

Further reading

To learn more on the topics covered in this chapter, you can refer to the following links:

- Azure DDoS Protection standard documentation: `https://docs.microsoft.com/en-us/azure/ddos-protection/?WT.mc_id=AZ-MVP-6003870`
- Azure Firewall Manager documentation: `https://docs.microsoft.com/en-us/azure/firewall-manager/?WT.mc_id=AZ-MVP-6003870`
- Azure Web Application Firewall on Azure Application Gateway: `https://docs.microsoft.com/en-us/azure/web-application-firewall/ag/ag-overview?WT.mc_id=AZ-MVP-6003870`
- Web Application Firewall core rule sets: `https://docs.microsoft.com/en-us/azure/web-application-firewall/ag/application-gateway-crs-rulegroups-rules?WT.mc_id=AZ-MVP-6003870`

7
Implementing Network Security

In the previous chapter, we covered the options that we have to secure the perimeters of our virtual networks in Azure. However, not all threats come from outside the network! We also need to ensure that we have a reduced network attack surface and can contain breaches to a reduced blast radius even if an attacker gains a foothold on our network. This is in line with the principles of zero trust and micro-segmentation.

In this chapter, we will look at what network security looks like in Azure from both the IaaS and PaaS perspectives. We will also cover how to implement Azure platform features to deliver a highly secure network architecture. Here are the topics that we will cover in this chapter, with accompanying hands-on exercises:

- Implementing virtual network segmentation
- Implementing platform service network security
- Securing Azure network hybrid connectivity

Technical requirements

To follow along with the instructions in this chapter, you will need the following:

- A PC with an internet connection
- An Azure subscription. You can use the same subscription that you set up in the first chapter of this book.

Implementing virtual network segmentation

Let's assume for a minute that you work for a global financial organization that is looking to perform a lift-and-shift migration of key systems into virtual networks in Azure. Part of the requirements that they have is to ensure that only required network connections can reach these key systems even if the connection originates from within the same network. How do you implement this level of control? There are two Azure network security capabilities that we can use to achieve this – **Network Security Group (NSG)** and **Application Security Group (ASG)**.

Implementing NSGs

An NSG is a simple packet filter that we can use to filter network traffic to and from Azure resources in a virtual network. The terminology that I used here is intentional. An NSG is a packet filter, not a firewall! It does not have the capabilities that the Azure firewall or a **Network Virtual Appliance** (**NVA**) has because the use cases are different. With NSGs, we have a mechanism for controlling traffic between resources within a virtual network. We can allow or deny inbound or outbound network traffic on a subnet or individual resource basis, making it a great candidate for implementing micro-segmentation *(Figure 7.1)*:

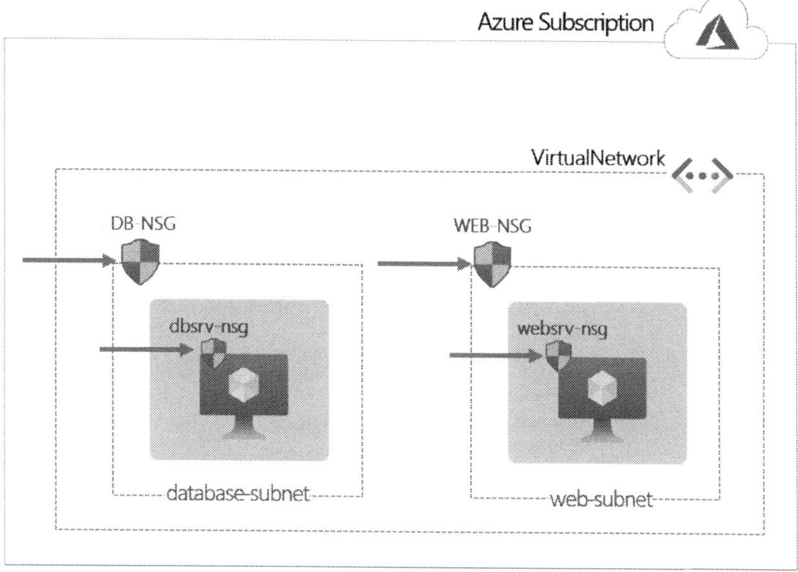

Figure 7.1 – NSGs can be applied to a subnet or individual resources

For each rule in an NSG, we can specify any combination of source/destination IP, source/destination port, and protocol (*Figure 7.2*). Each rule has a priority number that determines the order of evaluation (refer to the first column in *Figure 7.2*). The rules with the lower priority numbers will be evaluated first. For example, if I have a deny rule with a priority number of 2000 and an allow rule for the same traffic with a priority number of 3000, the traffic will be denied as rule 2000 will be evaluated first and once there is a match, evaluation stops (similar to typical firewall behavior):

Priority ↑↓	Name ↑↓	Port ↑↓	Protocol ↑↓	Source ↑↓	Destination ↑↓	Action ↑↓
∨ Inbound Security Rules						
100	⚠ nsgRule1	3389	Tcp	Any	Any	Allow
65000	AllowVnetInBound	Any	Any	VirtualNetwork	VirtualNetwork	Allow
65001	AllowAzureLoadBalancerInBound	Any	Any	AzureLoadBalancer	Any	Allow
65500	DenyAllInBound	Any	Any	Any	Any	Deny
∨ Outbound Security Rules						
65000	AllowVnetOutBound	Any	Any	VirtualNetwork	VirtualNetwork	Allow
65001	AllowInternetOutBound	Any	Any	Any	Internet	Allow
65500	DenyAllOutBound	Any	Any	Any	Any	Deny

Figure 7.2 – NSG rules

When we create an NSG, it comes with certain default rules that we cannot delete or modify. However, we can override those rules by specifying rules with lower priority numbers ahead of them. The default rules are those with very high priority numbers (65000 and above) in *Figure 7.2*.

While NSGs are great, using an IP address to define that segmentation could be difficult to manage as IP addresses are usually transient in a cloud environment and could change. Also, in an autoscaling scenario where new instances are constantly provisioned and deprovisioned, using IP addresses to define our NSG rules means that we constantly have to be keeping our rules updated with the latest IP information. This is where ASGs can help us. We will look at what ASGs are in the next section.

Implementing ASGs

ASG allows us to group a set of VMs under an application tag and define NSG traffic rules based on that. This may not make sense to you now, but it will all become clear once you do the hands-on exercise. The primary use case of ASGs is to implement simplified micro-segmentation in Azure virtual networks.

In *Figure 7.3*, you can see that ASGs are associated with VMs. The first VM is associated with an ASG called **WebServer**, the second VM is associated with an ASG called **AppServer**, while the third VM is associated with an ASG called **DBserver**:

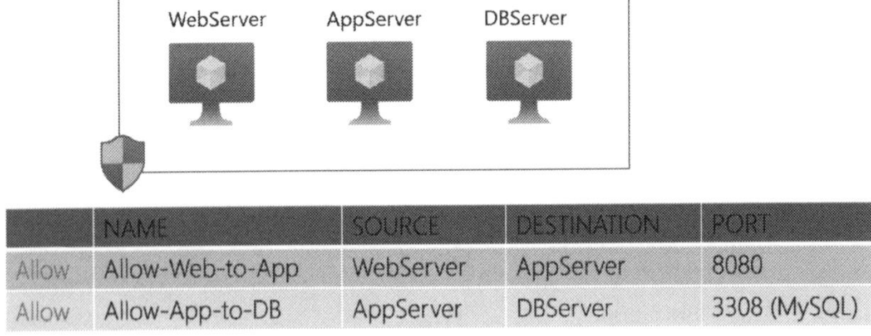

	NAME	SOURCE	DESTINATION	PORT
Allow	Allow-Web-to-App	WebServer	AppServer	8080
Allow	Allow-App-to-DB	AppServer	DBServer	3308 (MySQL)

Figure 7.3 – ASG sample scenario

Now, when we apply our NSG rules, instead of using IP addresses that could change, we use the ASGs to specify our source and destination targets. For example, the first rule allows traffic to port `8080` from any VM associated with the **WebServer** ASG to any VM associated with the **AppServer** ASG, while the second rule allows traffic to port `3308` from any VM associated with the **AppServer** ASG to any VM associated with the **DBServer** ASG. This is what ASGs allow us to implement!

This setup also makes it easy to implement security policies for dynamic workloads as we mentioned earlier. So, if we bring up a new web server, for example, all we need is to make sure that it is associated with the **WebServer** ASG and the right rules will automatically apply. We do not need to update the NSG rules with the IP address of the new instance.

One last thing to note about ASGs is that they are limited to a single virtual network, so we cannot use them across virtual network peers, only within a virtual network. In the next exercise, we will implement NSGs and ASGs in a virtual network.

Hands-on exercise – Configuring NSGs and ASGs

Here are the tasks that we will complete in this exercise:

- **Task 1**: Create an ASG and associate it with the private Linux VM.
- **Task 2**: Create an NSG.
- **Task 3**: Add inbound block and allow rules to the NSG.
- **Task 4**: Attach the NSG to the private subnet.
- **Task 5**: Verify that the NSG rule is working.

An ASG enables you to group servers with similar functions, such as web servers:

1. In the Azure portal, in the **Search resources, services, and docs** textbox at the top of the Azure portal page, type **Application security groups** and press the *Enter* key:

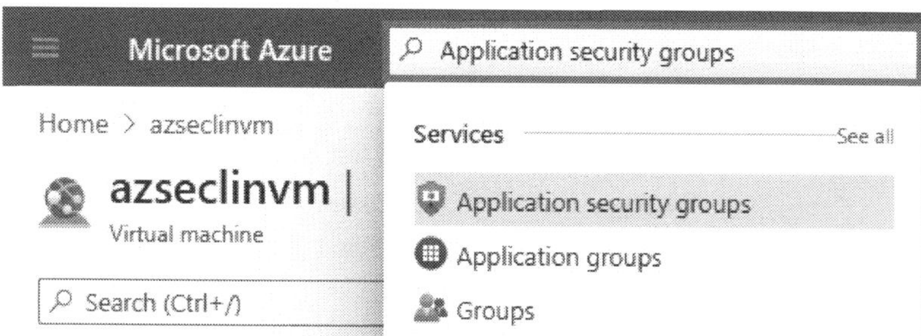

Figure 7.4 – Searching for ASGs

2. Click on **Create an application security group** and configure the following settings:

   Subscription: Select your subscription.

   Resource group: `azuresec-c6-rg`.

   Name: `web-server-asg`.

Region: Select the same region that you set when you deployed the template earlier.

Click **Review + create**.

Then, click **Create**:

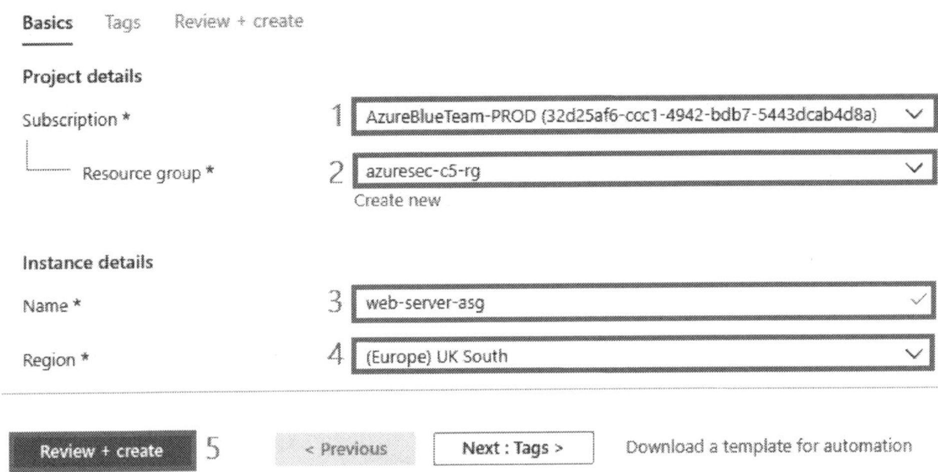

Figure 7.5 – Configure ASG parameters

Wait for the deployment to complete. In the next steps, we will associate the newly created ASG with the private Linux VM.

3. In the Azure portal, in the **Search resources, services, and docs** textbox at the top of the Azure portal page, type `azseclinvm` and press the *Enter* key:

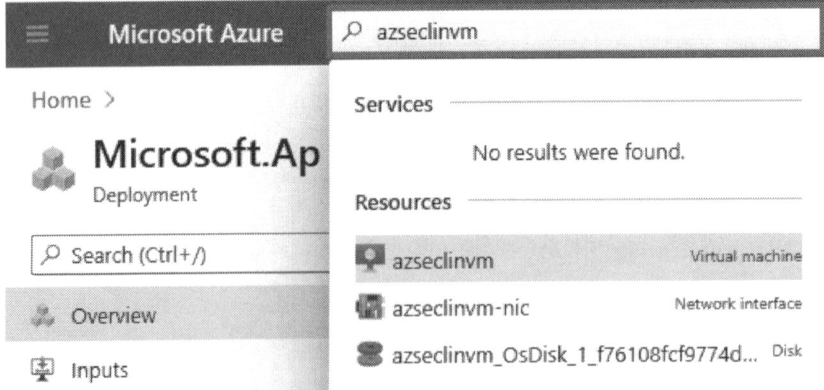

Figure 7.6 – Searching for the Linux VM

4. In the **Settings** section, click on **Networking**, and then click on the **Application Security Groups** tab. Click on **Configure the application security groups** and configure the following settings:

   Application security groups: `web-server-asg`

   Click **Save**:

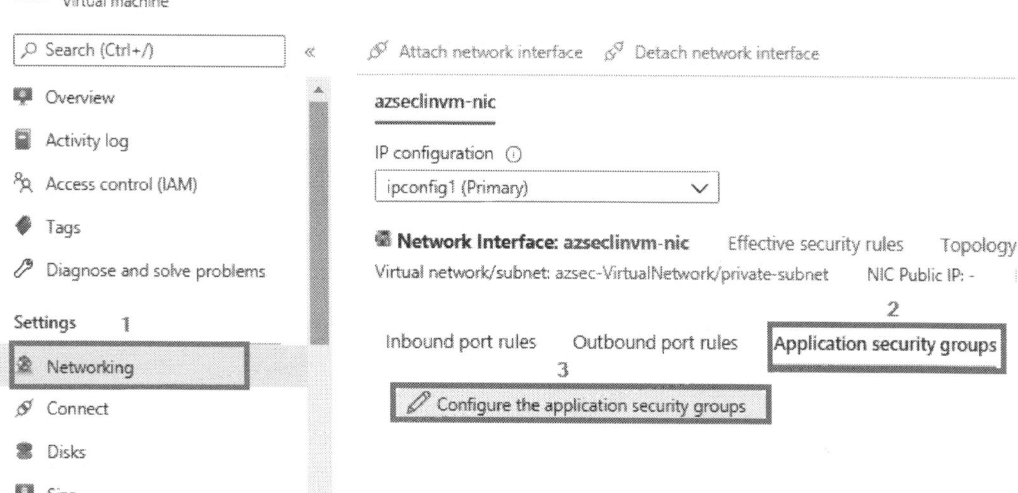

Figure 7.7 – Associating the ASG with the Linux VM

The ASG should now be associated with the Linux VM, as shown here:

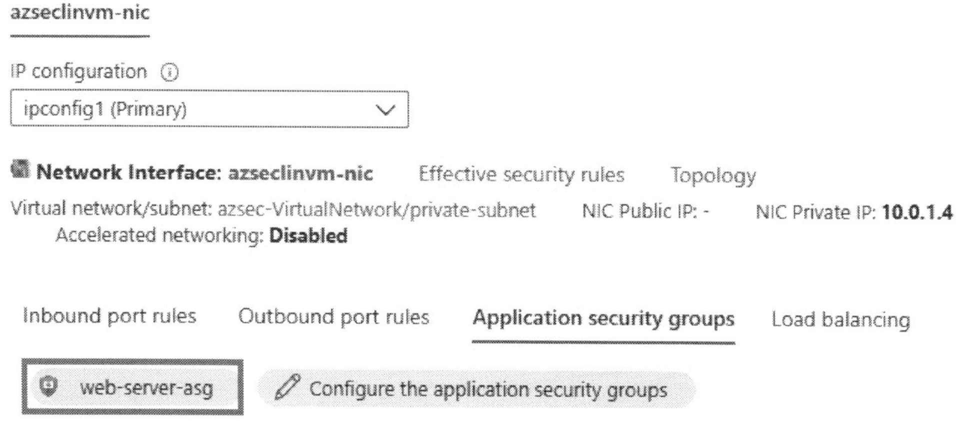

Figure 7.8 – Reviewing the associated ASG

In the next steps, we will use our NSG to implement micro-segmentation.

5. In the Azure portal, in the **Search resources, services, and docs** textbox at the top of the Azure portal page, type **Network security groups** and then click on **Network security groups**:

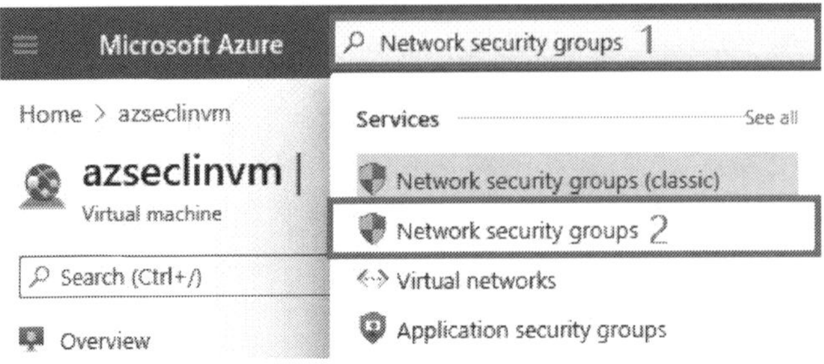

Figure 7.9 – Searching for NSGs

6. In the **Network security groups** blade, click on **+ Add** and configure the following settings:

   Subscription: Select your subscription.

   Resource group: `azuresec-c6-rg`.

   Name: `private-vm-nsg`.

   Region: Select the same region that you set when you deployed the template earlier.

   Click **Review + create**.

   Then, click **Create**:

Create network security group

Basics Tags Review + create

Project details

Subscription * 1 AzureBlueTeam-PROD (32d25af6-ccc1-4942-bdb7-5443dcab4d8a)

Resource group * 2 azuresec-c5-rg

Create new

Instance details

Name * 3 private-vm-nsg

Region * 4 (Europe) UK South

Review + create 5 < Previous Next : Tags > Download a template for automation

Figure 7.10 – Configuring NSG parameters

7. Once the deployment completes, click on **Go to resource**. In the **private-vm-nsg** blade, click on **Inbound security rules** and then click on **+ Add**:

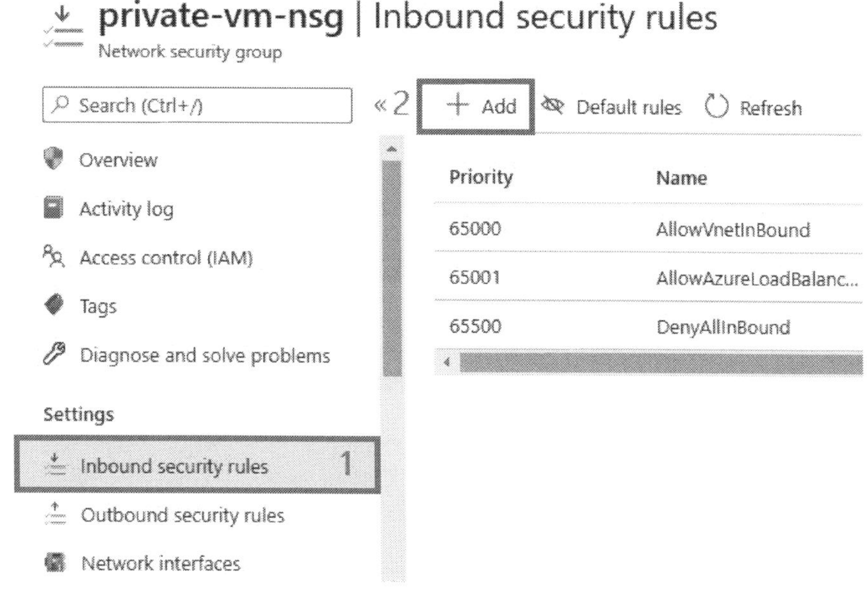

Figure 7.11 – Adding an inbound security rule to the NSG

8. In the **Add inbound security rule** blade, configure the following:

   Source: Any

   Source port ranges: *

   Destination: Application security group

   Destination application security group: `web-server-asg`

   Destination port ranges: 80, 443

   Protocol: TCP

   Action: Allow

   Priority: 1000

   Name: allow-web-traffic

   Description: Allow web traffic to web servers

Then, click **Add** to create the rule:

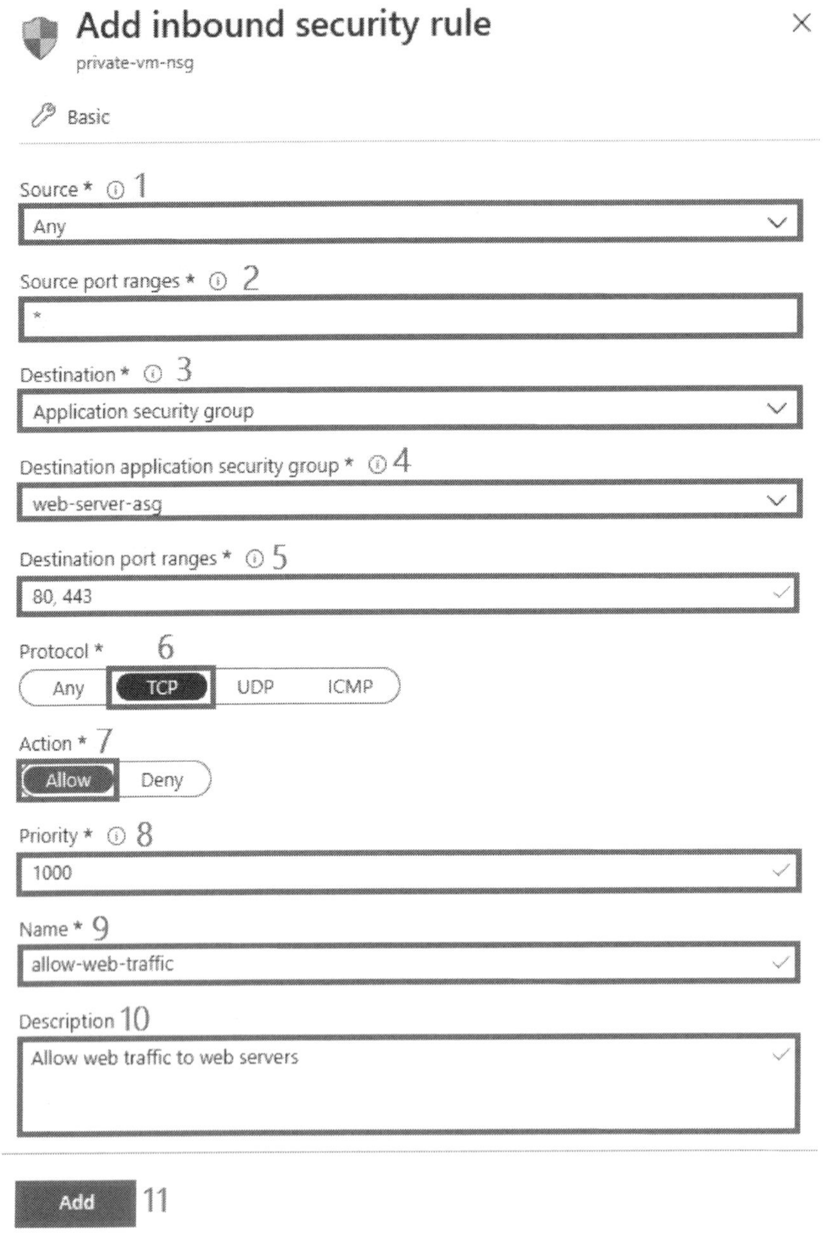

Figure 7.12 – Configuring inbound security rule parameters

9. Repeat *steps 7* and *8* to add the following security rule:

   Source: Any

   Source port ranges: *

   Destination: Application security group

   Destination application security group: `web-server-asg`

   Destination port ranges: 22

   Protocol: TCP

   Action: Deny

   Priority: 900

   Name: deny-ssh-traffic

   Description: Deny SSH traffic to web servers

   Then, click **Add** to create the rule.

10. On the **private-vm-nsg | Inbound security rules** blade, in the **Settings** section, click on **Network interfaces** and then click on the **+ Associate** tab:

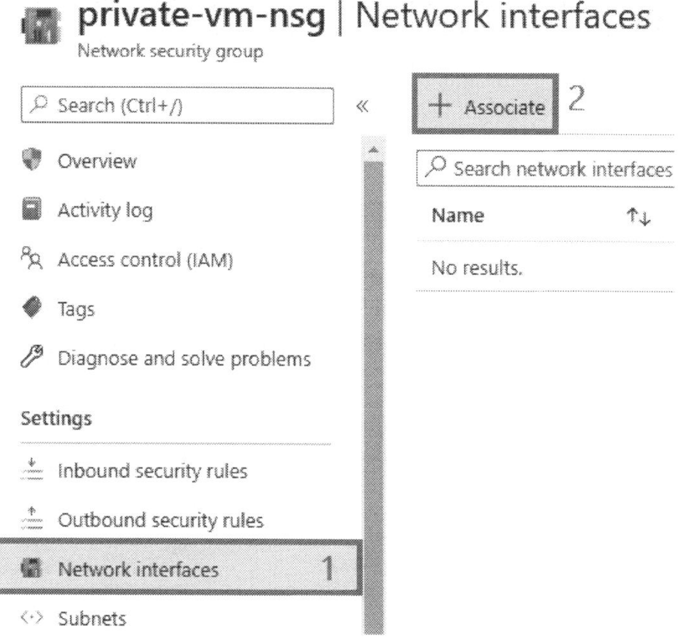

Figure 7.13 – Associating an NSG with the VM's network interface

11. In the **Associate network interface** blade, click on **azseclinvm-nic** to associate the NSG with the network interface of the Linux VM:

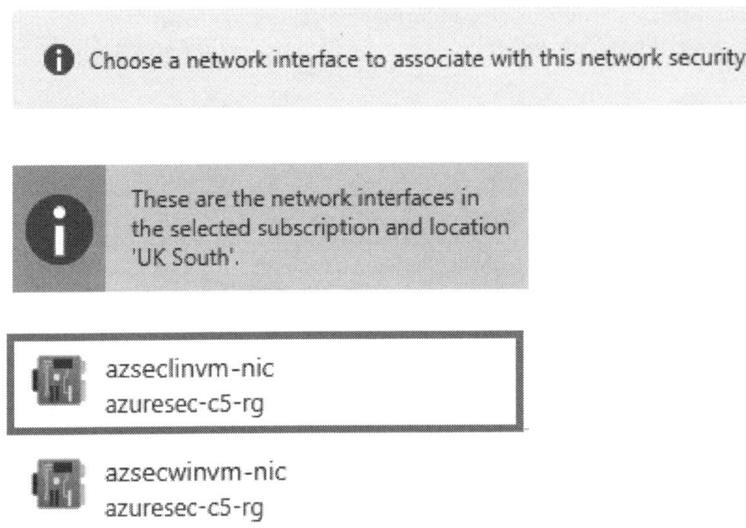

Figure 7.14 – Selecting a network interface with which to associate the NSG

In the next steps, we will verify that our NSG is working by checking that we can connect to it over TCP port `80` (HTTP), but that we can no longer connect to it over TCP port `22` (SSH).

12. In the RDP session of the **azsecwinvm** Windows VM, click the **start** button and type *putty 10.0.1.4*. **This should fail as we have an NSG rule to deny an SSH connection** to any VM that is associated with the **web-server-asg** ASG:

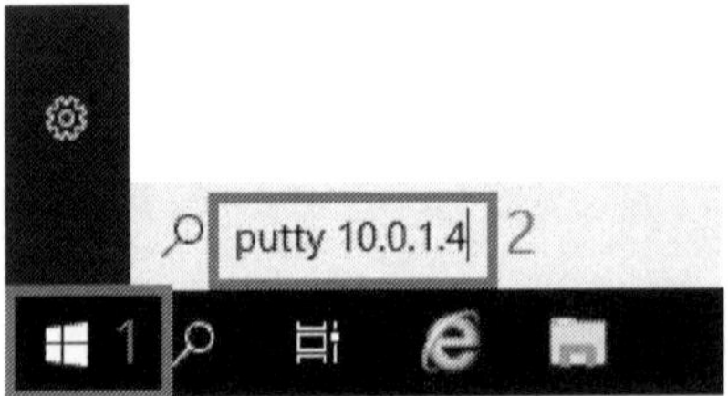

Figure 7.15 – Attempt to connect to a Linux VM via SSH (using PuTTY)

13. Still in the RDP session of the **azsecwinvm** Windows VM, on the desktop, double-click the Google Chrome icon to open the browser. Browse to `http://10.0.1.4`. You should be able to reach the Apache server hosted on the Linux VM:

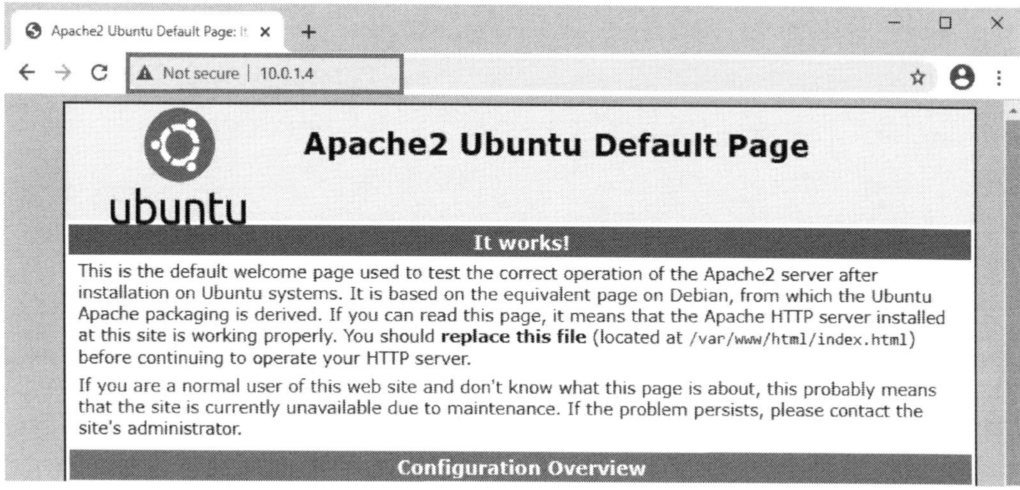

Figure 7.16 – Connecting to the Linux VM using HTTP

14. In the Azure portal, in the **Search resources, services, and docs** textbox at the top of the Azure portal page, type **Network security groups,** and then click on **Network security groups**:

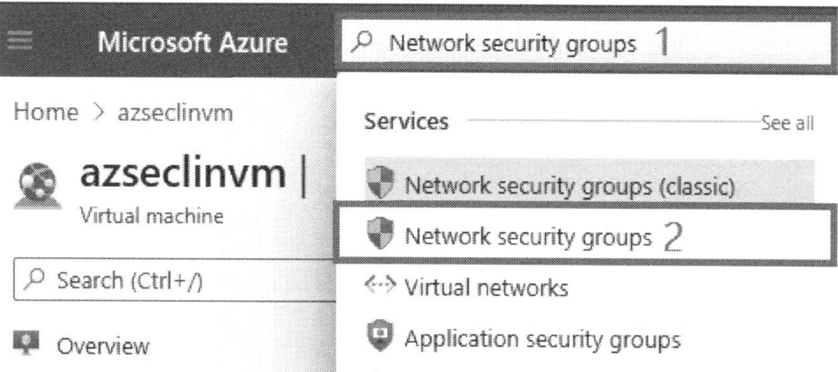

Figure 7.17 – Searching for NSGs

15. In the **Network security groups** blade, click on **private-vm-nsg**. Click on **Network interfaces**. Click on the **ellipsis** in front of **azseclinvm-nic** and click **Dissociate**. Then, click **Yes** when prompted for confirmation:

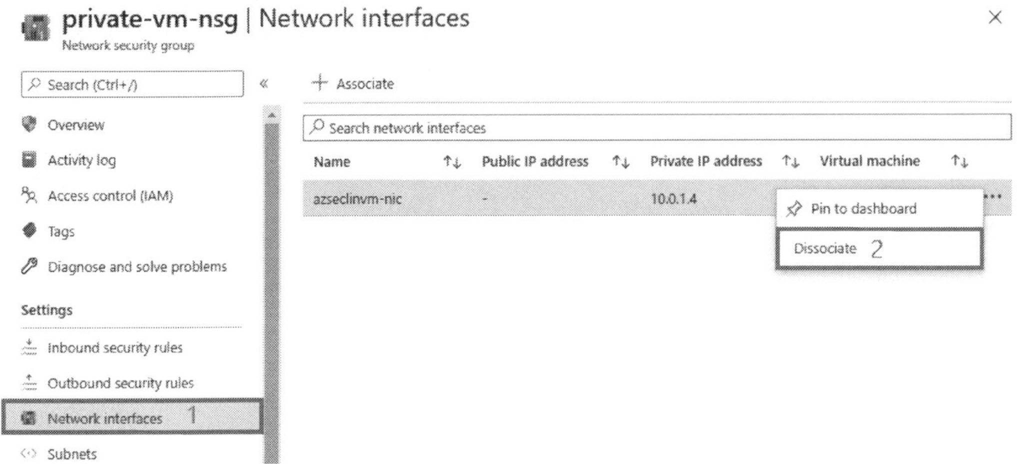

Figure 7.18 – Dissociating an NSG from the Linux VM's network interface

Congratulations! You have now successfully implemented an NSG that uses an ASG in its security rule. This can be implemented at scale to achieve very granular segmentation in your Azure virtual networks. In the next section, we will take a slightly different direction to discuss how to implement network firewall rules for our Azure PaaS services that are not deployed in a virtual network.

Implementing platform service network security

Earlier in this chapter, we covered how the Azure firewall or third-party NVAs can be used to protect services within a virtual network. The question here is, what if the service is not in a virtual network? Many platform services, such as Azure Storage and Azure Key Vault, cannot be deployed in an Azure virtual network, so how do we secure them from the network perspective?

Firewall for PaaS services (and firewall exceptions)

By default, platform services have public endpoints that accept connections from clients on any network, and this includes the internet! There is an option to limit that network access by allowing ONLY network traffic originating from specified, trusted IP addresses or IP ranges (*Figure 7.19*):

Allow access from
All networks | Selected networks
Configure network security for your storage accounts. Learn more
Virtual networks
+ Add existing virtual network + Add new virtual network

Virtual Network	Subnet	Address
No network selected.		

Firewall
Add IP ranges to allow access from the internet or your on-premises networks. Learn more
Add your client IP address ('109.145.121.23')

Address range
1.1.1.1
2.2.2.2
IP address or CIDR

Figure 7.19 – Sample firewall rule for an Azure PaaS service

Even though we can configure this restriction for some platform services, we need to be a bit careful with the implementation. Why, you may ask? The reason is that when we configure a firewall for supported PaaS services, all requests that are not explicitly allowed are blocked. You may be thinking to yourself, this is exactly what I want! But you have to consider that this also includes network traffic from other Azure services, and this could affect the functionality of certain features that rely on interactions with other services.

For example, if we have our VM disks in a storage account and we want to use the Azure backup service to protect those disks, without explicitly allowing the IP addresses of the Azure backup service, the backup process will fail! However, it is a tricky thing to keep IP addresses used by Microsoft services up to date in our rules as they are dynamic and could change. So how do we handle this? We do this by configuring the exception to **Allow trusted Microsoft services** (*Figure 7.20*):

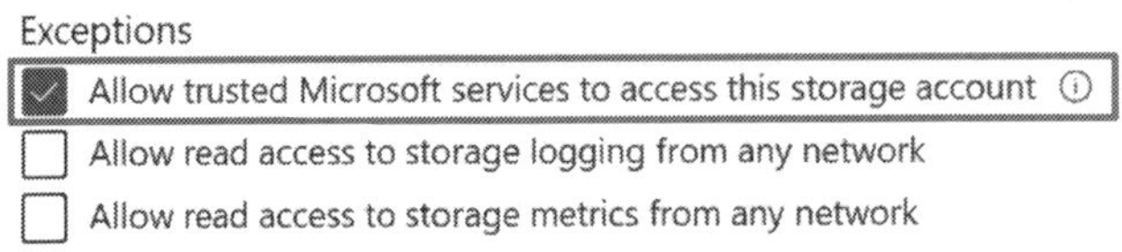

Figure 7.20 – Adding PaaS firewall exceptions

Any time you implement a platform service in Azure, always verify whether this option exists in its firewall settings and consider if you need to implement it.

Service endpoints

There are situations where services hosted in our virtual networks need to access platform services such as Azure Storage. This could be for a variety of reasons, for example, to store data in a storage account. For these scenarios, a virtual network service endpoint provides secure and direct connectivity to Azure services over an optimized route using the Azure backbone network instead of the internet (*Figure 7.21*):

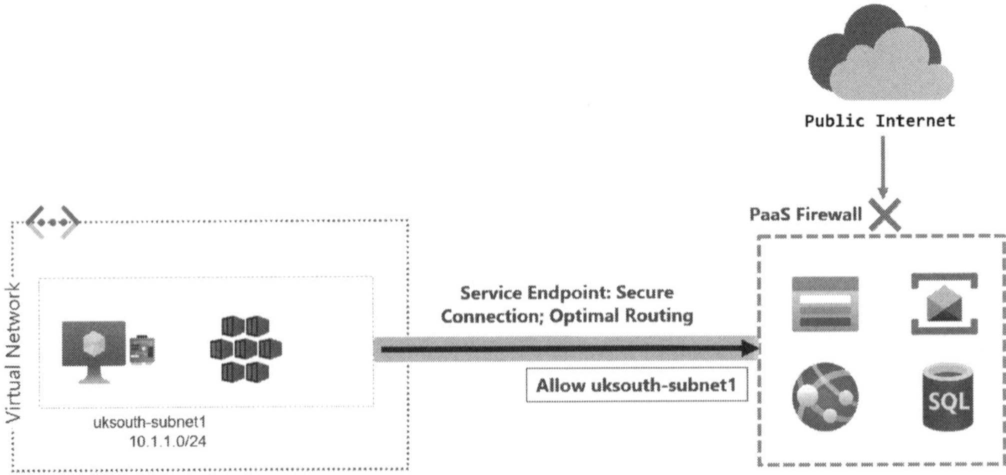

Figure 7.21 – Azure PaaS firewall with service endpoint scenario

Using service endpoints together with a firewall for PaaS services allows us to isolate platform services only for private network access, as shown in *Figure 7.21*. In the next hands-on exercise, you will configure the PaaS firewall and service endpoint to ensure that a storage account can only be accessed privately.

Hands-on exercise: Configuring a firewall and service endpoints on a storage account

Here are the exercises that we will complete in this exercise:

- **Task 1**: Obtain file share mounting information and store in a notepad.
- **Task 2**: Service endpoint configuration.
- **Task 3**: Test the storage connection from the private subnet that is connected to the Linux VM to confirm that access is allowed.
- **Task 4**: Test the storage connection from the public subnet to confirm that access is denied.

Let's go through the steps to accomplish these tasks:

1. In the Azure portal, in the **Search resources, services, and docs** textbox at the top of the Azure portal page, type *azsecvmstrg*, and then press *Enter*:

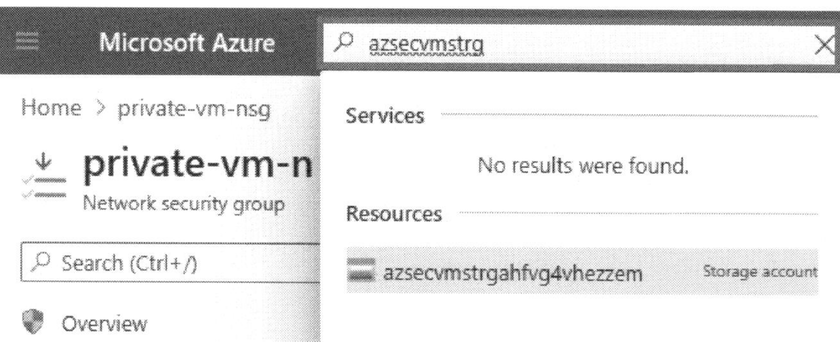

Figure 7.22 – Searching for the storage account

2. In the **File service** section, click on **File shares** and then select the **azsec** share:

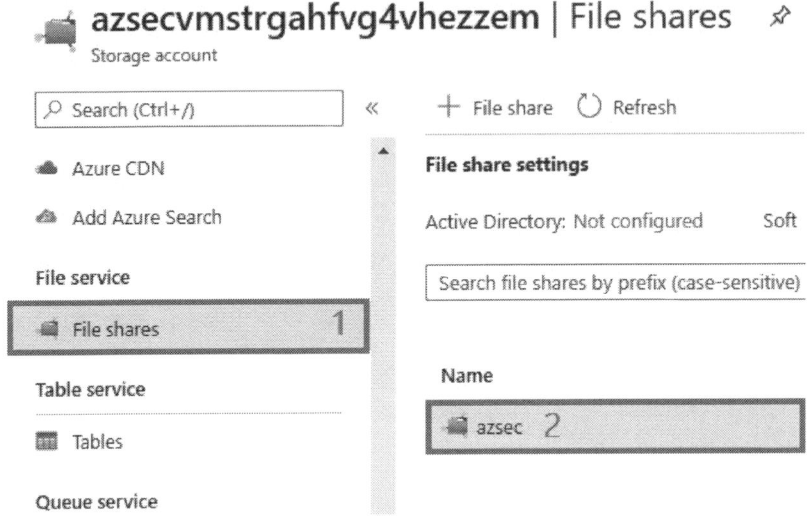

Figure 7.23 – Selecting the azsec file share

3. In the **azsec** window, click on **Connect**, select the **Linux** tab, and make a note of the mount command. You can copy the information into a notepad document. This information will be required in the later steps of this exercise. Close the **Connect** blade, and then close the **azsec** blade:

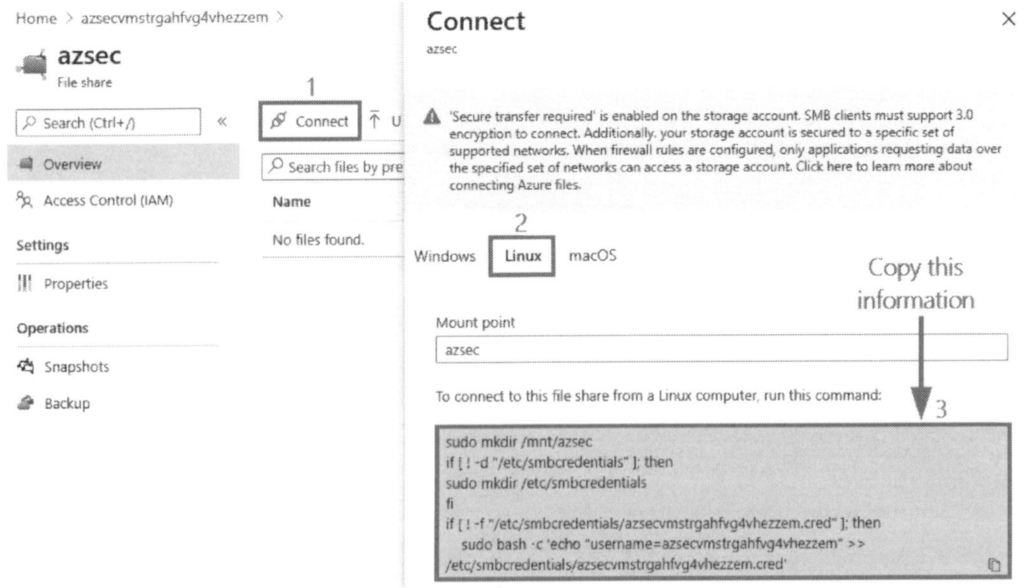

Figure 7.24 – Copying the connection information for the file share

4. On the **Storage account** blade, in the **Settings** section, click on **Networking**, click on **Selected networks**, and then click on the **+ Add existing virtual network** tab:

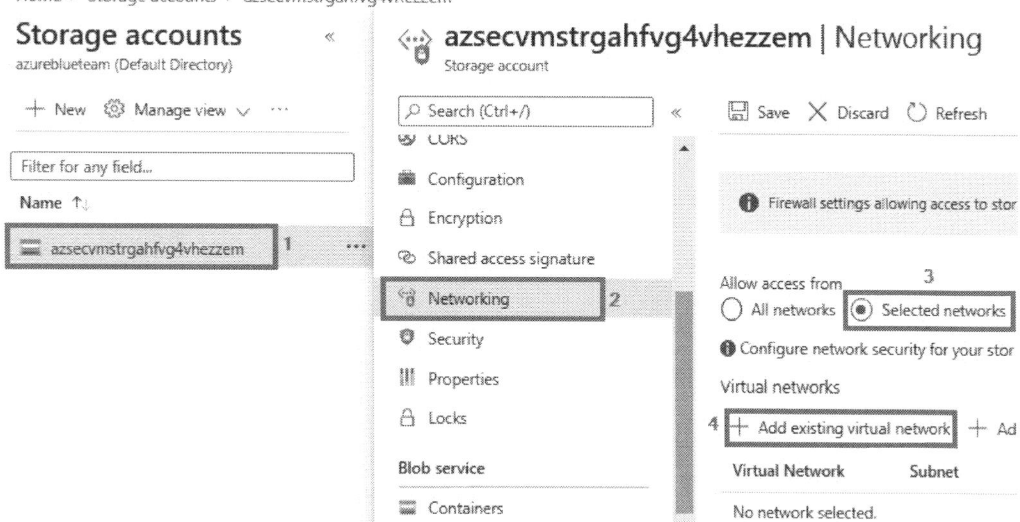

Figure 7.25 – Adding a service endpoint connection

5. In the **Add networks** blade, configure the following:

 Subscription: Select your subscription.

 Virtual network: **azsec-VirtualNetwork**.

 Subnets: private-subnet.

Then, click on **Enable**:

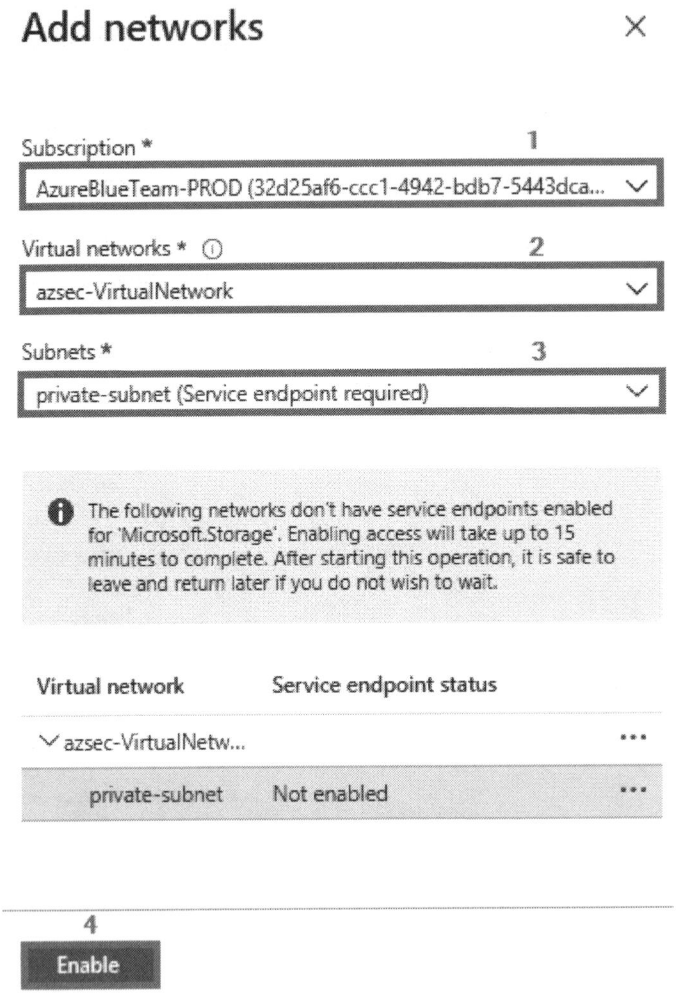

Figure 7.26 – Configuring service endpoint parameters

6. This will enable a service endpoint for **private-subnet**. You will get a confirmation when this is completed, as shown here. Click on **Add** to proceed with the process:

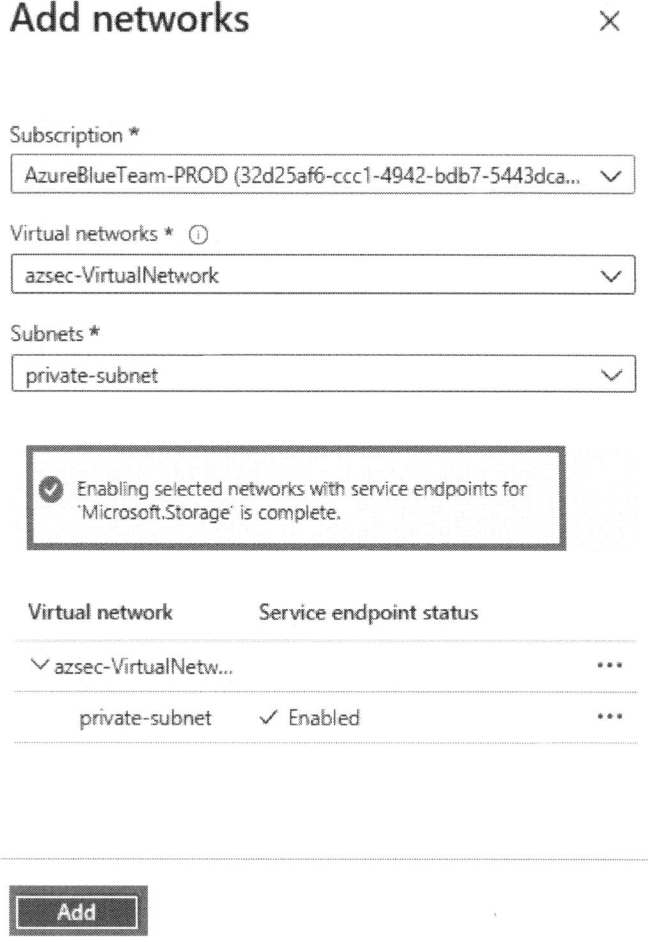

Figure 7.27 – Adding the new service connection

7. Click on **Save** to complete the process:

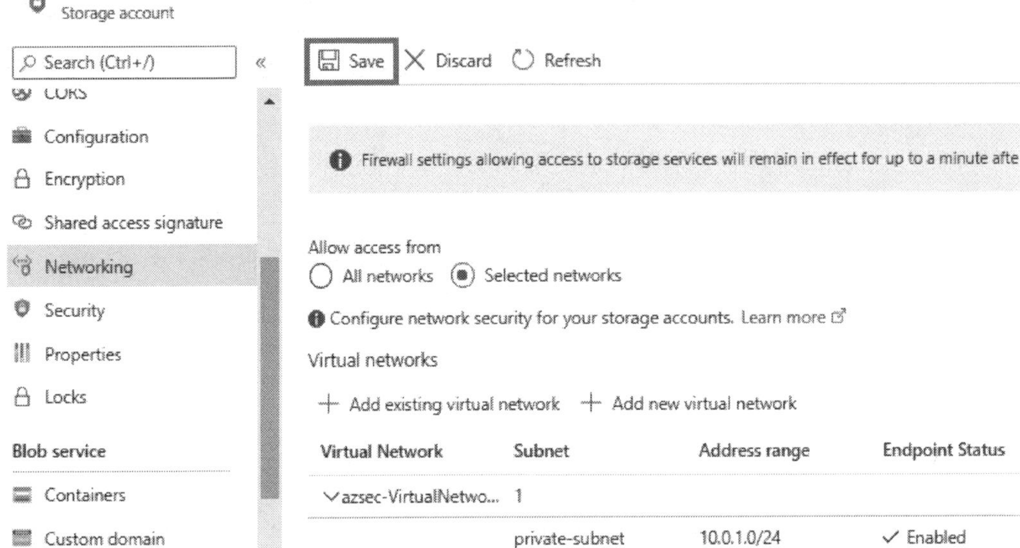

Figure 7.28 – Saving the configuration

Now that we have the service endpoint configured, we will test access to the storage account by mounting the **azsec** file share on the Linux VM since it is connected to the private subnet. If the mounting process is successful, this means that the private subnet has access to the storage account. Leave the Azure portal open.

8. In the RDP session of the **azsecwinvm** Windows VM, click the **start** button and type *putty 10.0.1.4* to connect to the Linux VM over SSH. Authenticate to the Linux VM with the following credentials:

   Username: `azureadmin`.

   Password: Enter the password that you configured during the template deployment.

9. Confirm that there is currently no file share mounted on the Linux VM by running the `sudo df -Th` command. As can be seen here, no file share is currently mounted:

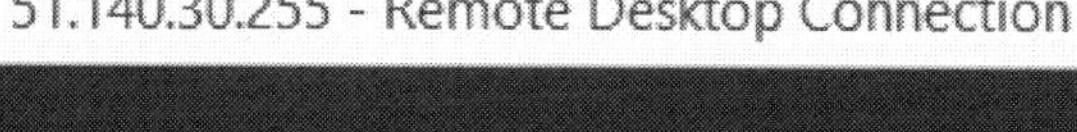

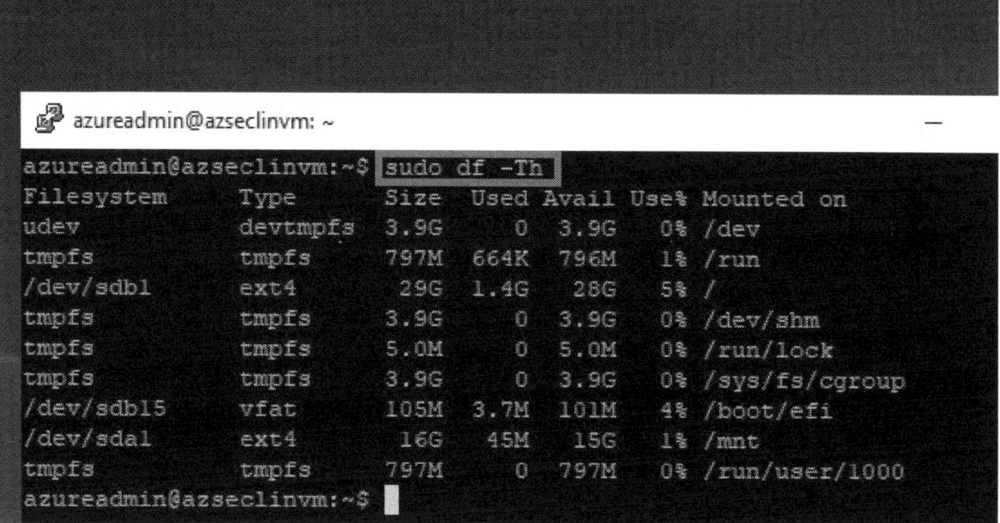

Figure 7.29 – Confirming a mounted file share

10. Run the commands copied in *step 3* to mount the **azsec** file share on the Linux VM:

```
sudo mkdir /mnt/azsec
if [ ! -d "/etc/smbcredentials" ]; then
sudo mkdir /etc/smbcredentials
fi
if [ ! -f "/etc/smbcredentials/azsecvmstrgahfvg4vhezzem.cred" ]; then
    sudo bash -c 'echo "username=azsecvmstrgahfvg4vhezzem" >> /etc/smbcredentials/azsecvmstrgahfvg4vhezzem.cred'
    sudo bash -c 'echo "password=deobh44cwqKsr8XtXPt0oPoa54sffFQ37FDic7jxFQBJQ2EsrnqiT4a36VeDtOBn1KVUiXhDZYduw0AeGmG72g==" >>
/etc/smbcredentials/azsecvmstrgahfvg4vhezzem.cred'
fi
sudo chmod 600 /etc/smbcredentials/azsecvmstrgahfvg4vhezzem.cred

sudo bash -c 'echo "//azsecvmstrgahfvg4vhezzem.file.core.windows.net/azsec /mnt/azsec cifs
nofail,vers=3.0,credentials=/etc/smbcredentials/azsecvmstrgahfvg4vhezzem.cred,dir_mode=0777,file_mode=0777,serverino" >> /etc/fstab'
sudo mount -t cifs //azsecvmstrgahfvg4vhezzem.file.core.windows.net/azsec /mnt/azsec -o
vers=3.0,credentials=/etc/smbcredentials/azsecvmstrgahfvg4vhezzem.cred,dir_mode=0777,file_mode=0777,serverino
```

Figure 7.30 – Running the commands to mount the file share

11. To confirm that the `azsec` file share was successfully mounted on the Linux VM, run the `sudo df -Th` command and, as can be seen in the following screenshot, the file share mounted successfully:

```
azureadmin@azseclinvm:~$ sudo df -Th
Filesystem                                           Type      Size  Used Avail Use% Mounted on
udev                                                 devtmpfs  3.9G     0  3.9G   0% /dev
tmpfs                                                tmpfs     797M  664K  796M   1% /run
/dev/sdb1                                            ext4       29G  1.4G   28G   5% /
tmpfs                                                tmpfs     3.9G     0  3.9G   0% /dev/shm
tmpfs                                                tmpfs     5.0M     0  5.0M   0% /run/lock
tmpfs                                                tmpfs     3.9G     0  3.9G   0% /sys/fs/cgroup
/dev/sdb15                                           vfat      105M  3.7M  101M   4% /boot/efi
/dev/sda1                                            ext4       16G   45M   15G   1% /mnt
tmpfs                                                tmpfs     797M     0  797M   0% /run/user/1000
//azsecvmstrgahfvg4vhezzem.file.core.windows.net/azsec cifs   5.0T     0  5.0T   0% /mnt/azsec
azureadmin@azseclinvm:~$
```

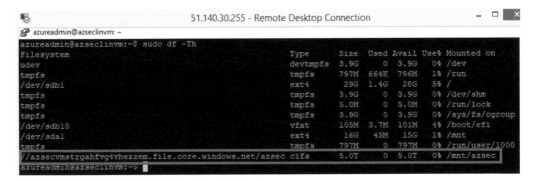

Figure 7.31 – Verifying the mounted file share

The preceding screenshot confirms that the private subnet has access to the storage account. To confirm that the public internet does not have access to the storage account, we will try to access the storage account from the Azure portal.

12. Back in the Azure portal, in the **Storage account** blade, select **File shares** and then click on **azsec** to attempt to access the file share:

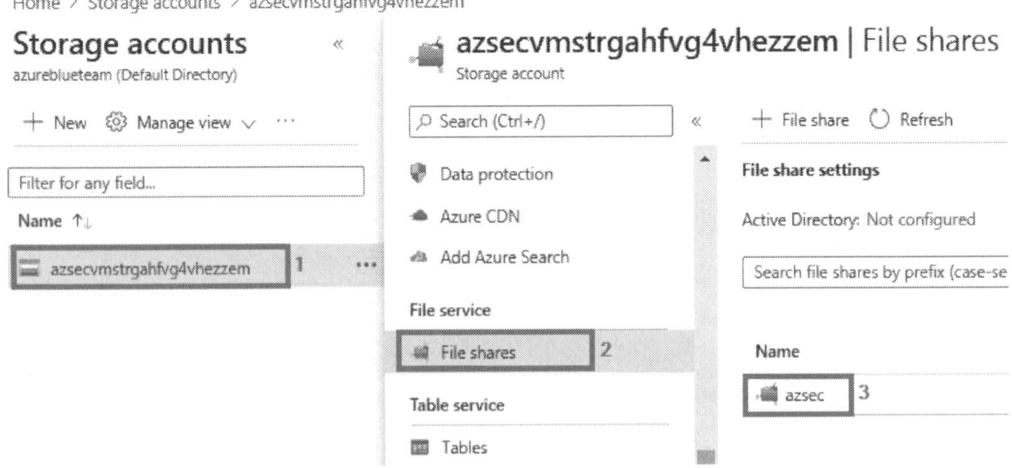

Figure 7.32 – Attempting to access the file share from the portal over the internet

13. You should get an error informing you that you do not have access to the file share, as seen here. This confirms that access from the public internet is now restricted:

This machine doesn't seem to have access.
This storage account is located in a VNET.
Recent changes to "Firewalls and virtual networks" settings may not be in effect yet. If you expect this machine to be able to connect to the content of this file share, check that this machine is a part of the VNET or try waiting a few minutes for changes in settings to take effect, and then refresh this page.
Learn more
Summary
Session ID
2aecdcca799141198493cd690603a468
Resource ID
/subscriptions/32d25af6-ccc1-4942-bdb7-5443dcab4d8...
Extension
Microsoft_Azure_FileStorage
Content
FilesGridBladev2
Error code
403

Figure 7.33 – Reviewing the denied access message

In this hands-on exercise, you learned how to implement platform service firewall and service endpoints on a storage account. Even though we focused on the storage account, implementation for other platform services follows a similar process. In the next section, we will cover the implementation of Azure Bastion!

Securing Azure network hybrid connectivity

Exposing our VM management ports to the public internet carries with it some inherent risks; for example, the VMs are exposed to threats such as port scanning, vulnerability scanning, and brute-force attacks from malicious hosts on the internet (*Figure 7.34*):

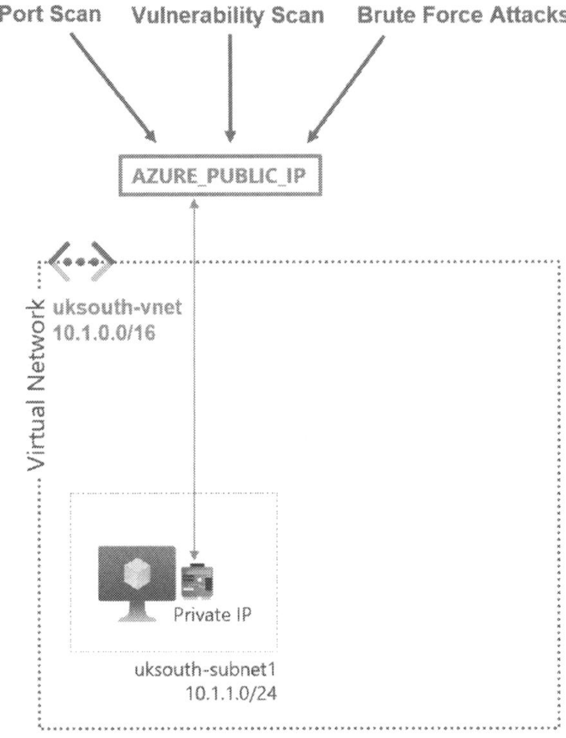

Figure 7.34 – Threats to publicly exposed virtual network workloads

To contain this threat surface, we could deploy a jump box at the public side of our perimeter network, but this creates extra management overhead as we have to update, back up, and troubleshoot the jump box going forward. This is where Azure Bastion can help us. In the next section, we will introduce Azure Bastion and explain how to implement it.

Implementing Azure Bastion

So, what is Azure Bastion? It is a fully managed service that provides a way for us to seamlessly connect to our private VMs using RDP and SSH over a web browser (using the Azure portal). In *Figure 7.35*, the user connects to Azure Bastion through the Azure portal, and the Bastion service then provides that private RDP and SSH connection to the VMs in the virtual network. The result of this is that our VMs do not need to have public IP addresses assigned to them. RDP and SSH RDP connections are contained within a customer's network and the connections are secured using TLS to prevent man-in-the-middle attacks:

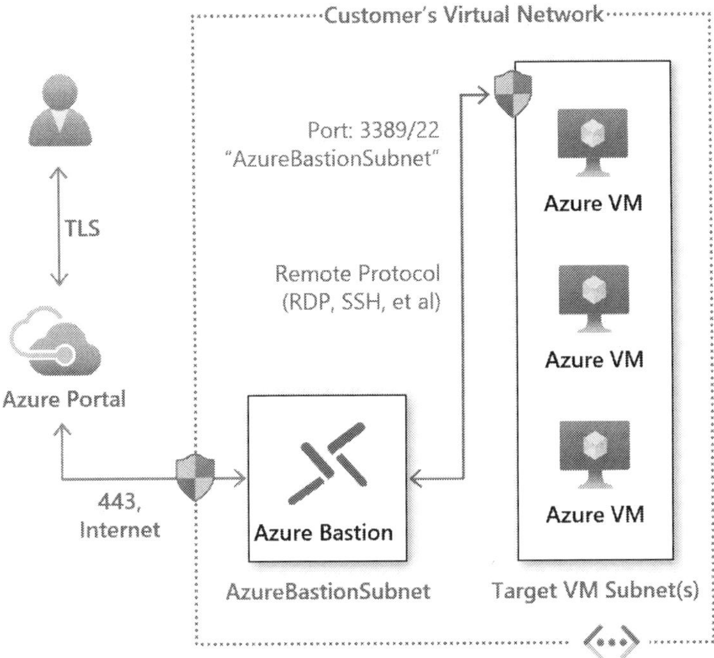

Figure 7.35 – Azure Bastion implementation

The service is also fully managed by Microsoft even though it is deployed in our network, so we do not need to manage infrastructure or software updates and patches. Supported virtual network resources for Azure Bastion include VMs, VM Scale Sets, and Dev-Test Labs. In the next hands-on exercise, we will walk through how to configure Azure Bastion to securely manage our virtual network resources.

Hands-on exercise: Configuring Azure Bastion

Here are the tasks that we will complete in this exercise:

- **Task 1**: Create a subnet for Azure Bastion.
- **Task 2**: Deploy Azure Bastion.
- **Task 3**: Connect to the Windows VM using Azure Bastion.
- **Task 4**: Monitor and disconnect a remote session.

Before you can use Azure Bastion, you need to create a subnet on the virtual network that the `azsecwinvm` VM uses:

1. In the Azure portal, locate and select the **azsec-VirtualNetwork** virtual network, click on **Subnets**, and then click on **+ Subnet**:

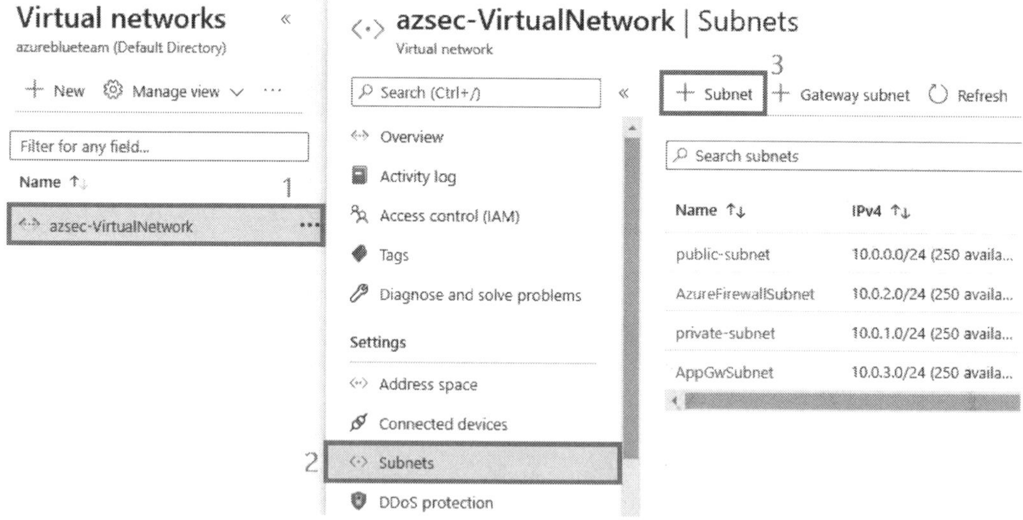

Figure 7.36 – Adding a new subnet

2. In the **Add subnet** blade, configure the following:

   Name: `AzureBastionSubnet` (note that you need to use the subnet name, `AzureBastionSubnet`, exactly as it is otherwise you will experience errors when creating Azure Bastion)

   Subnet address range: 10.0.3.0/24

Leave the other settings as their default values and then click **Save**:

Add subnet

Name * 1

AzureBastionSubnet

Subnet address range * 2

10.0.4.0/24

10.0.4.0 - 10.0.4.255 (251 + 5 Azure reserved addresses)

Add IPv6 address space

NAT gateway

None

Network security group

None

Route table

None

3

Save Cancel

Figure 7.37 – Configuring subnet parameters

3. In the Azure portal, select or search for *Virtual machines*, select the **azsecwinvm** VM, select **Connect**, and then select **Bastion** and **Use Bastion**:

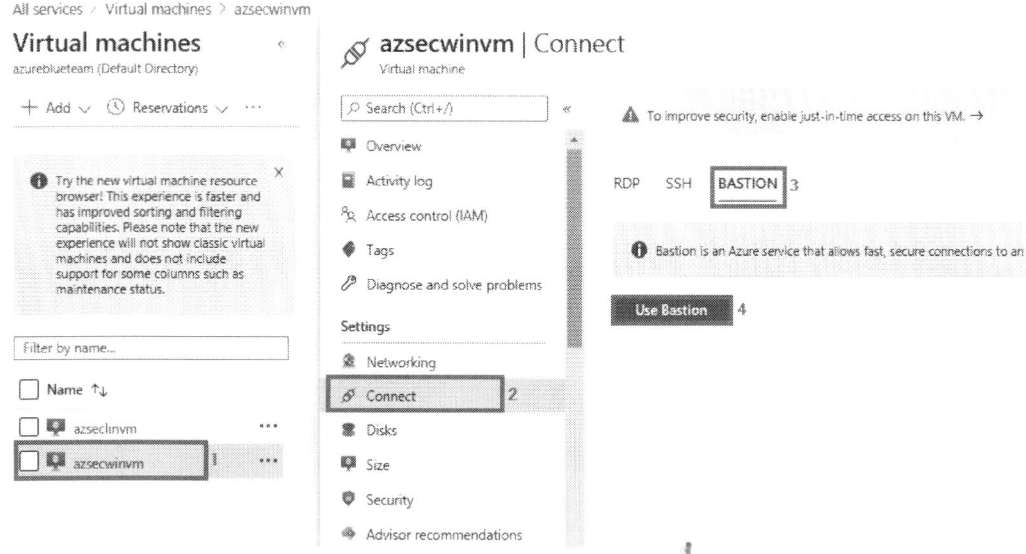

Figure 7.38 – Selecting the option to use Azure Bastion

4. Review and use the default values, such as the Azure Bastion resource name, subnet, and the option to create a new public IP address. Select **Create**, and then wait a few minutes for the Azure Bastion resource to be created:

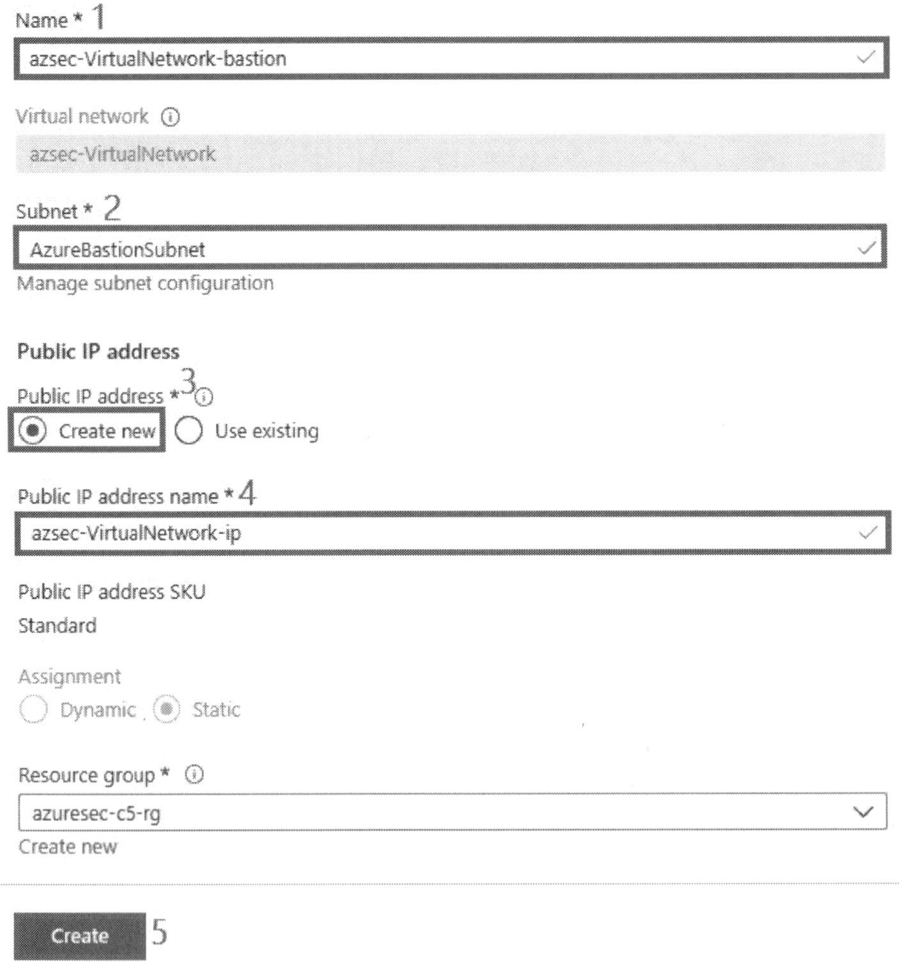

Figure 7.39 – Configuring Azure Bastion parameters

5. After the Azure Bastion resource has been created, you are prompted to enter credentials to connect to the VM.

6. Enter the `azureadmin` username and password that you specified during the template deployment. Then, click on **Connect** to proceed:

Connect using Azure Bastion
Azure Bastion Service enables you to securely and seamlessly RDP & SSH to your VMs in your Azure virtual network, without exposing a public IP on the VM, directly from the Azure portal, without the need of any additional client/agent or any piece of software. Learn more about Azure Bastion.

Using Bastion: **azsec-VirtualNetwork-bastion**, Provisioning State: **Succeeded**

Please enter username and password to your virtual machine to connect using Bastion.

Open in new window

Username *

azureadmin

Password *

Connect

Figure 7.40 – Connecting to the VM using Azure Bastion

7. Once you click on **Connect**, you should see a screen like the following, which shows that you have been able to connect to the VM using Azure Bastion:

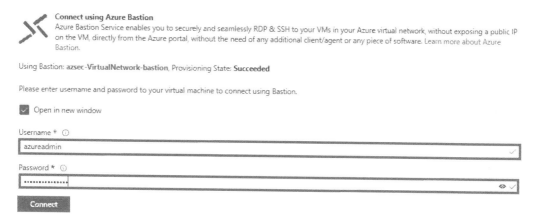

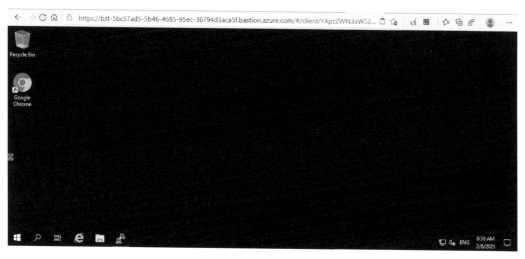

Figure 7.41 – Connecting to the Azure VM

8. To disconnect from the session, close the current browsing tab and the session will be disconnected.

Congratulations! You have now completed the hands-on exercises in this chapter. In the next section, we will clean up all the resources that we have created in the last two chapters.

Hands-on exercise: Cleaning up resources

Here is the task that we will complete in this exercise:

- **Task 1**: Delete the `azuresec-c6-rg` resource group.

Here are the steps to complete the task:

1. In the Azure portal, in the **Search resources, services, and docs** textbox at the top of the Azure portal page, type *Resource groups* and then press *Enter*:

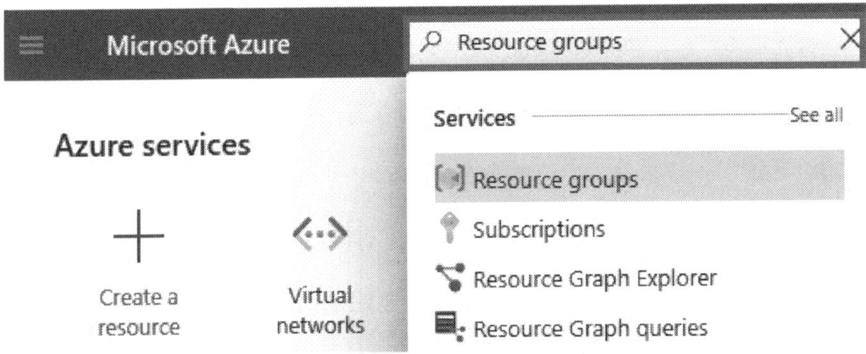

Figure 7.42 – Searching for Resource groups

2. In the **Resource groups** blade, click on **azuresec-c6-rg**:

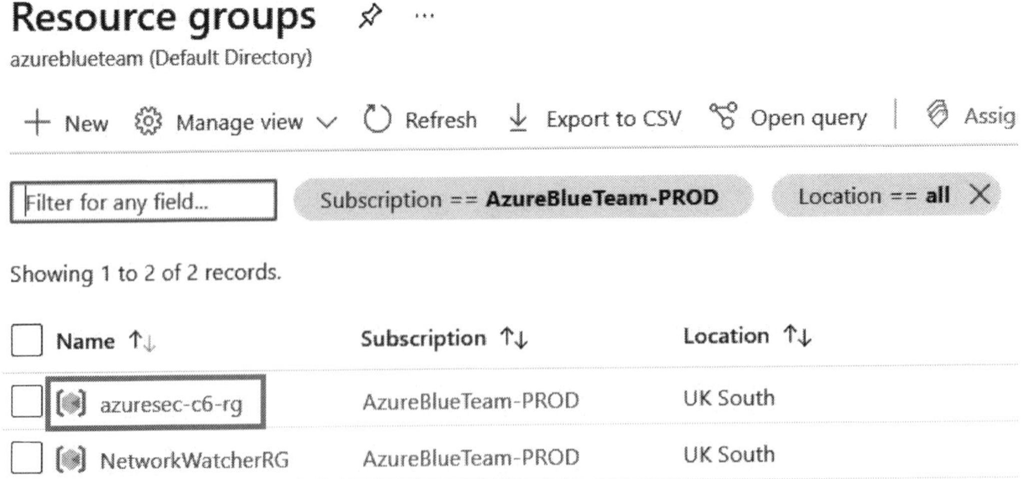

Figure 7.43 – Selecting the resource group

3. In the **azuresec-c6-rg** blade, click on **Delete resource group**. When prompted for confirmation, type `azuresec-c6-rg` and then click **Delete**:

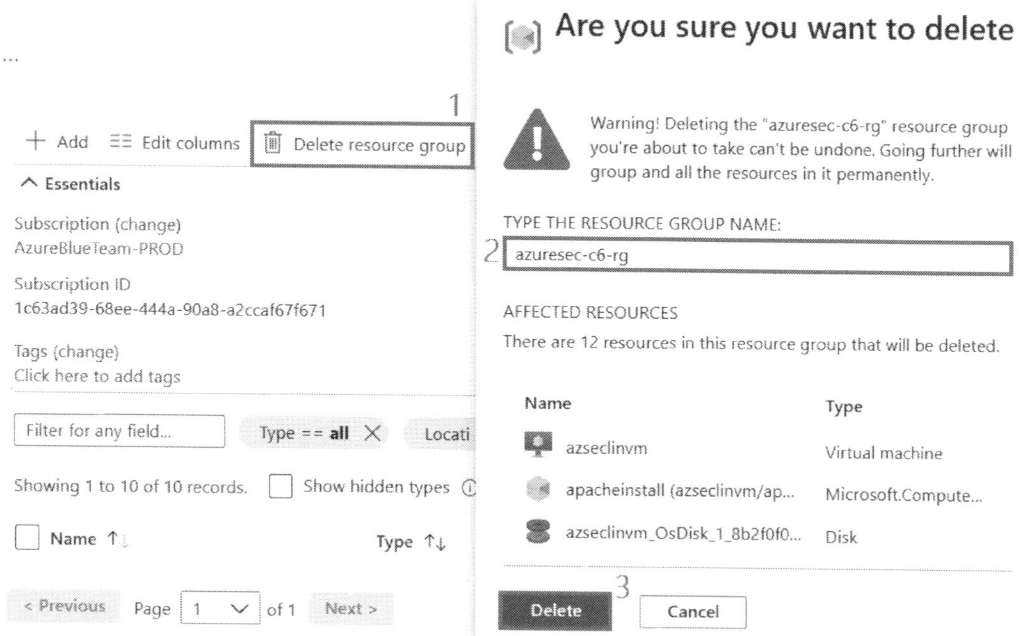

Figure 7.44 – Deleting the resource group

Congratulations! You have now cleaned up the resources that we deployed for the exercises in this chapter.

Summary

In this chapter, you learned how to implement network segmentation for Azure virtual network workloads using NSGs and ASGs. You also learned how the Azure PaaS Firewall can restrict public access to supported PaaS services such as Azure Storage, and how service endpoint features can be used to access supported PaaS services privately over the Azure backbone network.

Finally, we covered how the Azure Bastion service can be used to securely connect to virtual network VMs over the internet without publicly exposing them.

The information in this chapter has equipped you with the skills needed to implement secure access to your Azure virtual network workloads. In the next chapter, you will learn how to implement host security best practices in Azure. See you in the next chapter!

Question

As we conclude, here is a question for you to test your knowledge regarding this chapter's material. You will find the answer in the *Assessments* section of the *Appendix*:

1. You have attached an NSG to an Azure subnet that has a VM deployed in it. An NSG rule with priority number 104 denies traffic to the Azure Storage destination prefix. Another NSG rule with priority number 106 allows traffic to the Azure Storage UK South destination prefix. Will traffic destined for a storage account in the UK South region be allowed?

   a. Yes, it will be allowed.

   b. No, it will not be allowed.

Further reading

To learn more on the topics covered in this chapter, you can refer to the following links:

- Azure service endpoint: `https://docs.microsoft.com/en-us/azure/virtual-network/virtual-network-service-endpoints-overview?WT.mc_id=AZ-MVP-6003870`
- Azure Storage firewall exceptions: `https://docs.microsoft.com/en-us/azure/storage/common/storage-network-security?tabs=azure-portal#exceptions?WT.mc_id=AZ-MVP-6003870`

8
Implementing Host Security

The Azure cloud platform offers a broad range of computing services, including user-managed options such as **Virtual Machines (VMs)**, **Virtual Machine Scale Sets (VMSSes)**, and **Windows Virtual Desktops (WVDs)**. User-managed compute options provide a greater level of flexibility when we host applications on them. This is because we can install any application or dependency that is needed since we have control of the operating system. This also means that we are responsible for securing the services from the operating system level and upward in the stack.

In this chapter, we will focus on the key security best practices that we can implement to protect user-managed computing resources in Azure. The following are the main topics that we will cover alongside this chapter's hands-on exercises:

- Using hardened baseline VM images
- Protecting VMs from viruses and malware
- Implementing system update management for VMs
- Implementing vulnerability assessment for VMs
- Encrypting VM disks with Azure Disk Encryption
- Securing management ports with just-in-time access

As you can see, each topic has been structured to align with a security best practice for securing hosts in Azure. Let's get into this!

Technical requirements

To follow along with the instructions in this chapter, you will need the following:

- A PC with an internet connection.
- An Azure subscription. You can use the same subscription that you set up in *Chapter 1, Introduction to Azure Security.*

Before we proceed and cover security best practices, let's prepare our Azure subscription for the hands-on exercises that we will be completing later in this chapter.

Hands-on exercise – provisioning resources for this chapter's exercises

To follow along with the exercises in this chapter, we will provision some Azure resources to work with. We have prepared an Azure ARM template in this book's GitHub repository for this purpose. The template will deploy an Azure virtual network with a single subnet. This subnet will have a Windows Server 2019 VM that can be reached from the public internet. Here are the tasks that we will complete in this exercise:

- **Task 1**: Initialize template deployment in GitHub.
- **Task 2**: Complete our parameters and deploy the template to Azure:

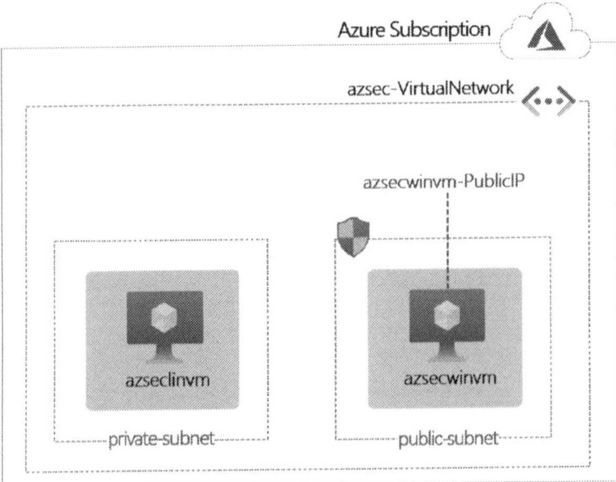

Figure 8.1 – Hands-on exercise resources

Let's start deploying our template:

1. Open a web browser and browse to `http://bit.ly/az500-c6-template`. This link will open this book's GitHub repository, which contains an ARM template for deploying the resources that we need.
2. In the GitHub repository that opens, click on **Deploy to Azure**:

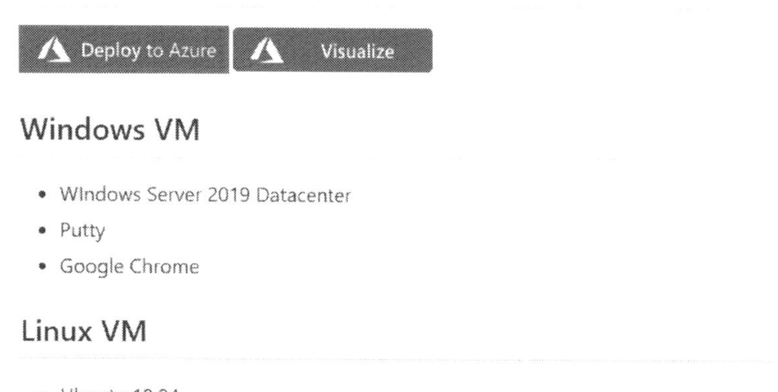

Figure 8.2 – Deploying the template to Azure

3. In the **Sign in** window, enter your administrative username and password to authenticate to your Azure subscription:

Figure 8.3 – Authenticating to Azure

4. In the **Custom Deployment** window, configure the following:

   Subscription: Select the subscription that you want to deploy the resources to.

   Resource group: **Create New** → **Name**: `azuresec-c6-rg` → **OK**.

   Region: Select an Azure region close to your location.

   Storagename: Leave as the default value.

   Vm-dns: Leave as the default value.

   Admin User: Leave as the default value.

   Admin Password: Enter a complex password. Make a note of the password that you use. We recommend that you select one complex password that you will use throughout the scenarios in this book to keep things simple.

   VMsize: Leave as the default value.

   Location: Leave as the default value.

   _artifacts Location: Leave as the default value.

   _artifacts Location Sas Token: Leave as the default value.

   Then, click on **Review + Create**:

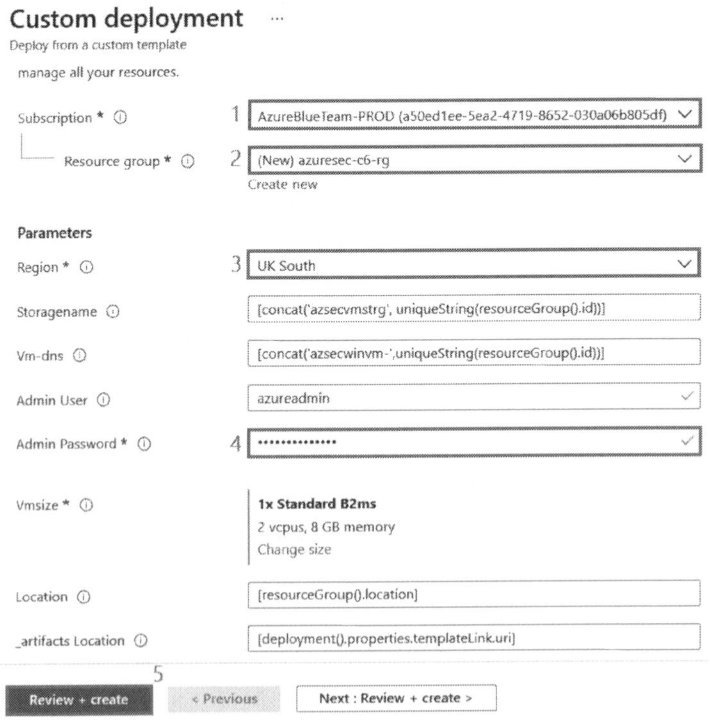

Figure 8.4 – Configuring template parameters

5. Once the template validation has passed, click on **Create**. This will begin the deployment process, which takes about 7 to 10 minutes to complete. Grab yourself a cup of water, tea, or coffee and wait for the deployment to complete.

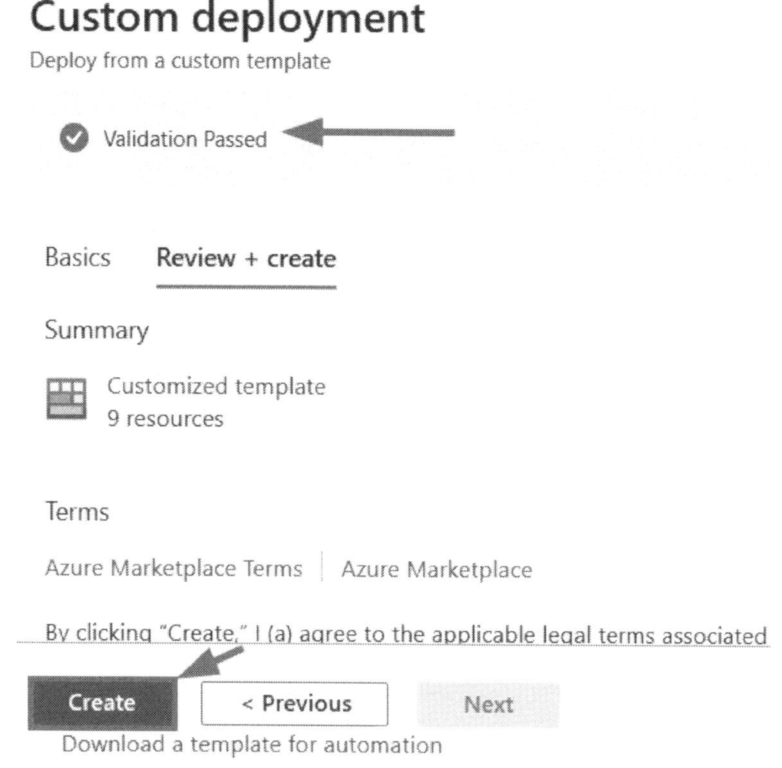

Figure 8.5 – Creating the resources

Wait for the deployment to complete. At the end of the deployment, you can review the resources that were created. In the next section, we will start looking at the first security best practice of using hardened baseline VM images.

Using hardened baseline VM images

One of the first choices that we need to make when deploying a VMs in Azure is the image that it will be based on. We have three options to choose from:

- Microsoft-provided marketplace image
- Third party-provided marketplace image
- Customer-provided image

The decision that we make here has an impact on the security posture of the virtual machine after deployment! The image that users choose when deploying VMs in Azure could be one that has vulnerable binaries and configurations that need to be patched or reconfigured after deployment.

The best practice here is to choose a hardened image that already has baseline security configurations and the most recent patches applied. But where can we get this? Customers who are willing could build the hardened images themselves using an automation tool such as Packer or a service such as Azure Image Builder.

> **Information**
>
> Packer is an open source tool created by Hashicorp that can be used to automate the creation of any type of machine image, including Azure VM images. The Azure Image Builder service, which does something similar, is built on Packer. A walkthrough on how to use Packer to automate the creation of an Azure Linux image can be found here: `https://docs.microsoft.com/en-us/azure/virtual-machines/linux/build-image-with-packer`.
>
> The Shared Image Gallery is an Azure service that can be used to store and distribute VM images with users or user groups within and across Azure subscriptions.

The images can then be distributed across the organization using a service called the Shared Image Gallery. For other customers, who are willing to pay for this, **Center for Internet Security (CIS)** hardened images are also available in the Azure marketplace, as shown in the following screenshot:

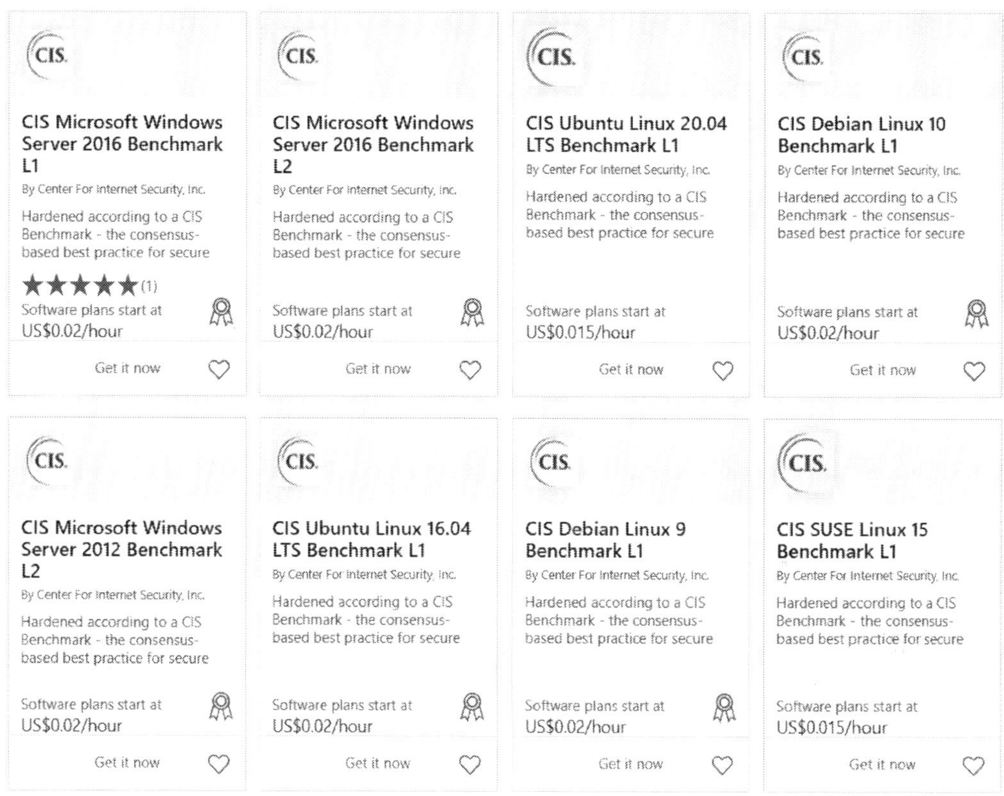

Figure 8.6 – CIS hardened images in the Azure marketplace

So, now that we know where we can get hardened images from, how do we enforce their use? The easiest way to enforce this is to use Azure Policy, which defines a list of trusted images that users can choose from. If you are wondering what Azure Policy is, don't worry – we will cover this in detail in *Chapter 13, Azure Cloud Governance and Security Operations*. For now, just know that it provides a way for us to monitor and enforce resource configuration in our Azure subscriptions. The following is a screenshot of an Azure Policy definition in GitHub that can be used for this (`https://github.com/Azure/azure-policy/tree/master/samples/Compute/allowed-custom-images`):

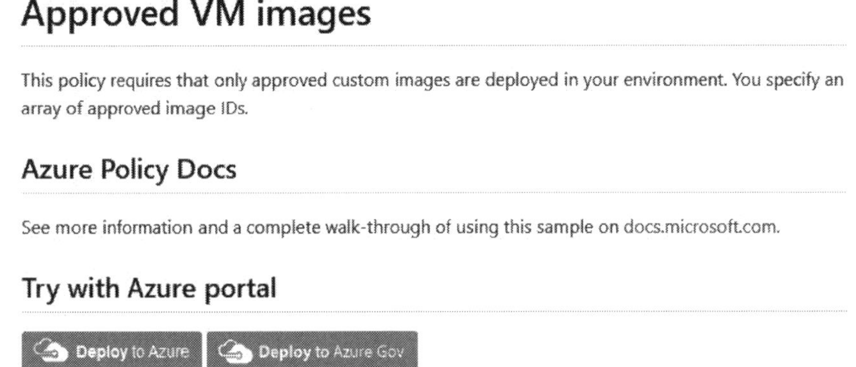

Figure 8.7 – Approved VM images policy

In this section, we discussed the importance of using a hardened VM image for the virtual machines that you deploy in Azure. We will learn how to protect VMs from malicious software in the next section.

Protecting VMs from viruses and malware

VMs, **VM Scale Sets** (**VMSSes**), and **Windows Virtual Desktops** (**WVDs**) in Azure, just like any other computer system, can be vulnerable to malicious software attacks. The recommendation is to install antimalware protection on all user-managed systems in Azure to protect against compromise due to viruses, worms, spyware, and other malicious software.

We can either use a Microsoft-provided endpoint protection solution such as the free Microsoft Antimalware for Azure, or an endpoint protection solution from third-party security vendors such as Palo Alto, Symantec, Trend Micro, and more.

Microsoft Antimalware for Azure is a free endpoint protection solution that can be used in the absence of an alternative. It has very limited capabilities compared to paid alternatives such as Microsoft Defender for Endpoint or third-party security offerings. Its capabilities are very much limited to signature-based runtime protection against malware for Windows VMs (Linux VMs are not supported). It also has no support for **Endpoint Detection and Response** (**EDR**) capabilities.

To install the Microsoft Antimalware agent for a Windows VM in Azure, we can deploy the Microsoft antimalware extension (*Figure 8.8*). Security events will be logged in the Windows Event system logs and can be collected using the Azure Diagnostic agent or the Microsoft Monitoring Agent:

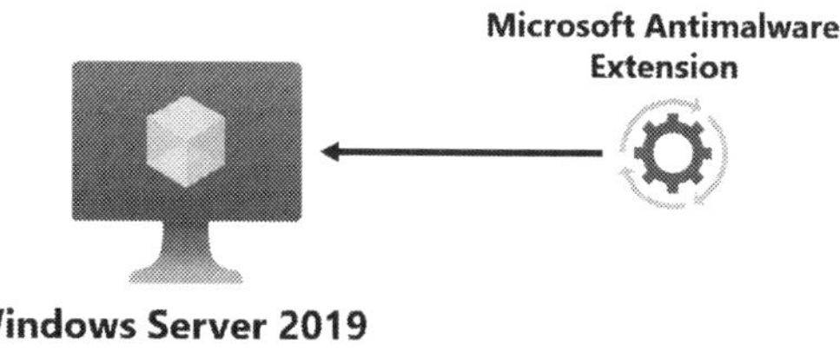

Figure 8.8 – Approved VM images policy

If you are planning to use a third-party antimalware offering, you can deploy the solution using a custom script extension, which can be used to run a PowerShell script (Windows) or a Bash script (Linux) on a VM, post-deployment. You can also deploy the solution using a VM configuration management tool such as Chef, Puppet, or Microsoft Endpoint Manager.

Azure Policy has built-in policy definitions that can be used to monitor and enforce the deployment of an antimalware extension on Windows VMs, as shown in the following screenshot:

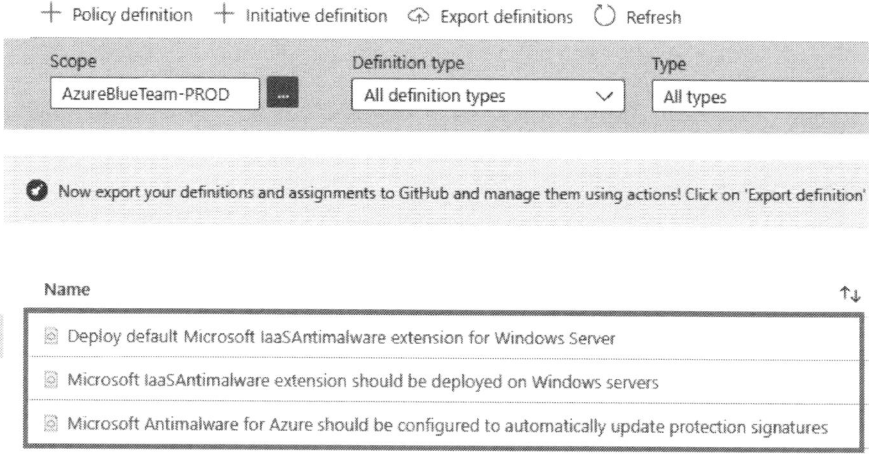

Figure 8.9 – Approved VM images policy

In the next section, you will learn how to implement and configure the Microsoft Antimalware solution for a VM in Azure.

Hands-on exercise deploying the Microsoft Antimalware extension for Azure

Here is what we will complete in this exercise:

- **Task 1**: Deploy the Microsoft Antimalware extension on a Windows Server VM.

Let's look at the steps:

1. In the Azure portal, in the **Search resources, services, and docs** text box at the top of the Azure portal home page, type `azsecwinvm` and press *Enter*:

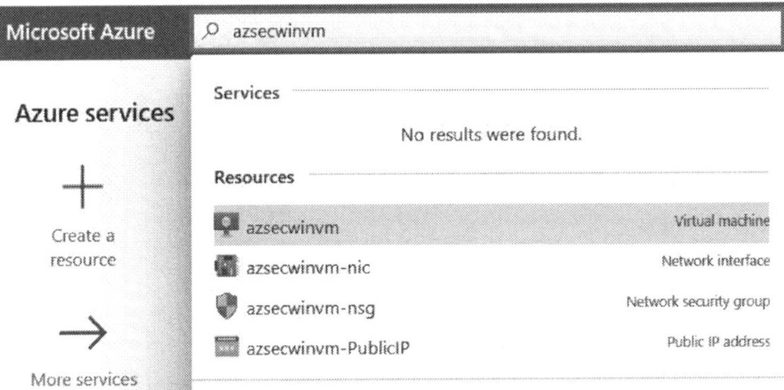

Figure 8.10 – Searching for the Windows VM by name

2. In the **Virtual machine** blade, click on **Extensions**, and then click on + **Add**:

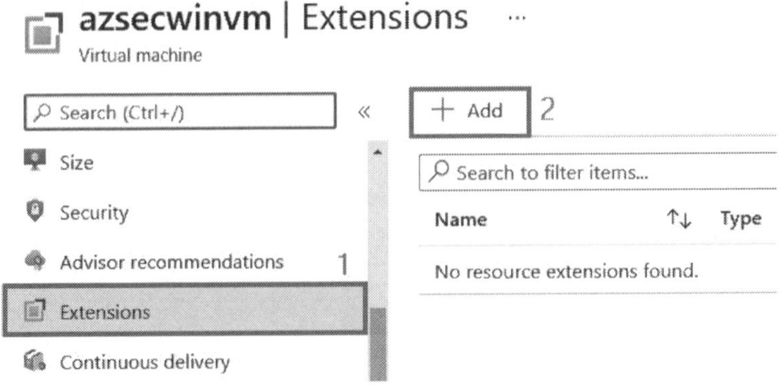

Figure 8.11 – Adding a new VM extension

3. In the **New resource** blade, click on the **Microsoft Antimalware** option:

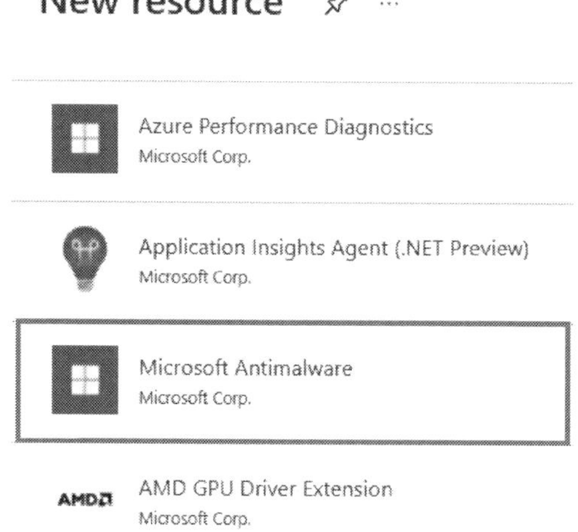
New resource
Azure Performance Diagnostics
Microsoft Corp.
Application Insights Agent (.NET Preview)
Microsoft Corp.
Microsoft Antimalware
Microsoft Corp.
AMD GPU Driver Extension
Microsoft Corp.

Figure 8.12 – Selecting the Microsoft Antimalware extension

4. In the **Microsoft Antimalware** blade, click on **Create**:

Microsoft Antimalware
Microsoft Corp.
Microsoft Antimalware for Azure Virtual Machines is a real-time protection capability that helps identify and remove viruses, spyware, and other malicious software, with configurable alerts when known malicious or unwanted software attempts to install itself or run on your system. The solution can be enabled and configured from the Azure Portal, Service Management REST API, and Microsoft Azure PowerShell SDK cmdlets.
To enable antimalware with the default configuration, click Create on the Add Extension blade without inputting any configuration setting values.
To enable antimalware with a custom configuration, input the supported values for the configuration settings provided on the Add Extension blade and click Create. Please refer to the tooltips provided with each configuration setting on the Add Extension blade to see the supported configuration values.
To enable antimalware event collection for a virtual machine, click any part of the Monitoring lens in the virtual machine blade, click Diagnostics command on Metric blade, select Status ON and check Windows Event system logs. The antimalware events are
Create

Figure 8.13 – Creating the extension

5. In the **Install extension** blade, configure the following:

   Real-time protection: Enable.

   Run a scheduled scan: Enable.

   Scan type: Quick.

   Leave the other settings as their default values.

   Click **OK**:

Install extension ...

Real-time protection
Enable Disable

Run a scheduled scan
Enable Disable

Scan type
Quick Full

Scan day
Saturday

Scan time
120

OK

Figure 8.14 – Configuring the antimalware parameters

6. Wait for a few minutes for the extension to be deployed:

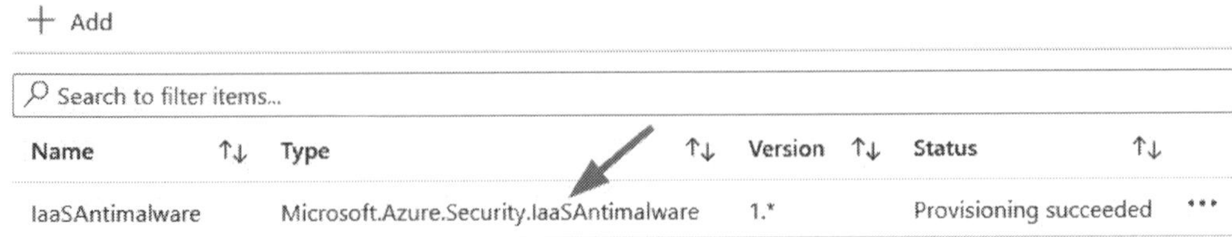

Figure 8.15 – Reviewing the installation of the extension

Congratulations! You have successfully configured the Microsoft Antimalware extension for an Azure VM. The same process can be followed to install a third-party antimalware solution using a custom script extension. In the next section, we will discuss how to manage system updates.

Implementing system update management for VMs

Update management is one of the most important security processes in any environment. Unpatched operating systems or software puts organizations at risk of serious security breaches. This is further complicated by the unpredictable nature of updates for different software. Updates can come quickly and frequently when newly discovered security flaws or attack vectors are addressed.

Azure has a service called Azure Automation that we can use to manage operating system updates for Windows and Linux systems, regardless of where they are hosted – in Azure, in other public cloud environments, or in on-premises data centers.

The update management feature of Azure Automation supports multiple OS platforms, including Windows Server (2008 and newer), CentOS 6 and 7 (x64), Red Hat Enterprise 6 and 7 (x64), SUSE Linux Enterprise Server 12, 15, and 15.1 (x64), Ubuntu 14.04 LTS, 16.04 LTS, and 18.04 LTS (x64). At the time of writing this book (early 2021), Windows clients and Azure Kubernetes Service nodes are not supported.

There are three main components of this solution:

- An Azure Automation account
- A Log Analytics workspace
- The Microsoft Monitoring Agent

As shown in the following diagram, the Monitoring Agent collects information about missing updates and sends them to a Log Analytics workspace. The updates are then installed by runbooks in Azure Automation:

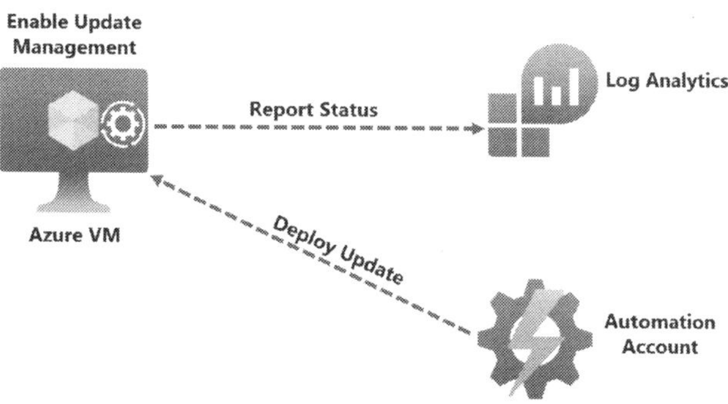

Figure 8.16 – System update management for Azure VMs

When an update deployment is created, the deployment creates a schedule that starts a master update runbook at the specified time for the included computers.

The master runbook then starts a child runbook on each agent to install the required updates. To reduce this attack surface, the recommendation is to keep management ports such as RDP and SSH closed, and only open them when needed for administrative tasks. This is exactly what **just-in-time (JIT)** VM access allows us to do, without the management overhead of closing and opening these ports manually.

Hands-on exercise – implementing Azure Automation Update Management

Here is what we will complete in this exercise:

- **Task 1**: Create a Log Analytics workspace.
- **Task 2**: Create an automation account.
- **Task 3**: Enable update management for an Azure VM.

Let's get started.

1. In the Azure portal, in the **Search resources, services, and docs** text box at the top of the Azure portal home page, type `log analytics workspace` and press *Enter*:

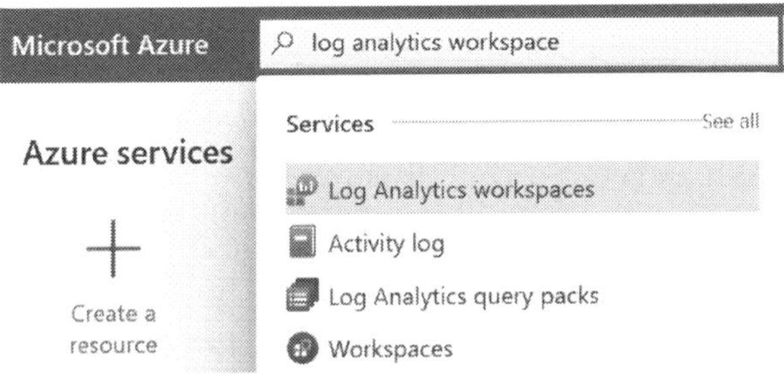

Figure 8.17 – Searching for Log Analytics workspaces

2. In the **Log Analytics workspaces** blade, click on **+ New**, and then click on **+ Add**:

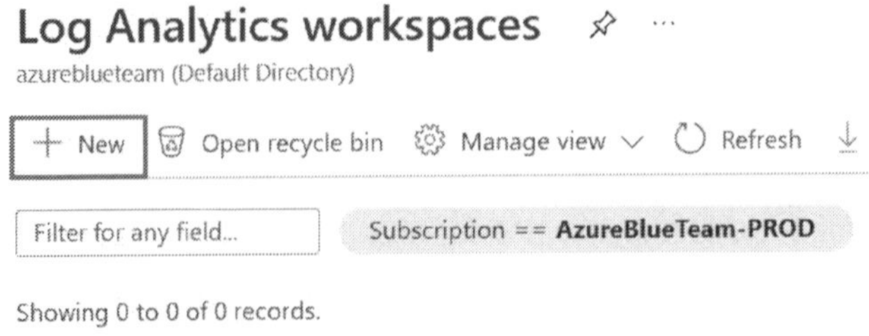

Figure 8.18 – Creating a new workspace

3. In the **Create Log Analytics workspace** blade, configure the following:

   Subscription: Select your Azure subscription.

   Resource group: `azuresec-c6-rg`.

   Name: `update-mgmt-workspace`.

   Region: Select the same region that you deployed resources in earlier in this chapter.

   Click **Review + Create**, and then click on **Create**:

Create Log Analytics workspace ...

Project details

Select the subscription to manage deployed resources and costs. Use resource groups like folders to organize and manage all your resources.

Subscription * 1 AzureBlueTeam-PROD (a50ed1ee-5ea2-4719-8652-030a06b805df)

Resource group * 2 azuresec-c6-rg

Create new

Instance details

Name * 3 update-mgmt-workspace

Region * 4 UK South

5 Review + Create « Previous Next : Pricing tier >

Figure 8.19 – Configuring the parameters for the workspace

   Wait for the deployment to complete.

4. In the Azure portal, in the **Search resources, services, and docs** text box at the top of the Azure portal home page, type `automation accounts` and press *Enter*:

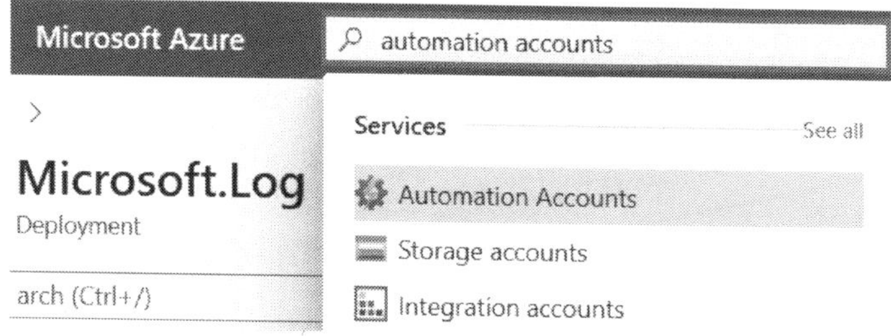

Figure 8.20 – Searching for Automation Accounts

5. In the **Automation Accounts** blade, click on **+ New**, and then click on **+ Add**.
6. In the **Add Automation Account** blade, configure the following:

   Name: update-mgmt-aac.

   Subscription: Select your Azure subscription.

   Resource group: `azuresec-c6-rg`.

   Location: Select the same region that you deployed resources in earlier in this chapter.

   Create Azure Run As account: Yes.

   Click on **Create**:

   Figure 8.21 – Configuring the parameters for the Automation Account

   Wait for the deployment to complete.

7. In the Azure portal, in the **Search resources, services, and docs** text box at the top of the Azure portal home page, type `virtual machines` and press *Enter*:

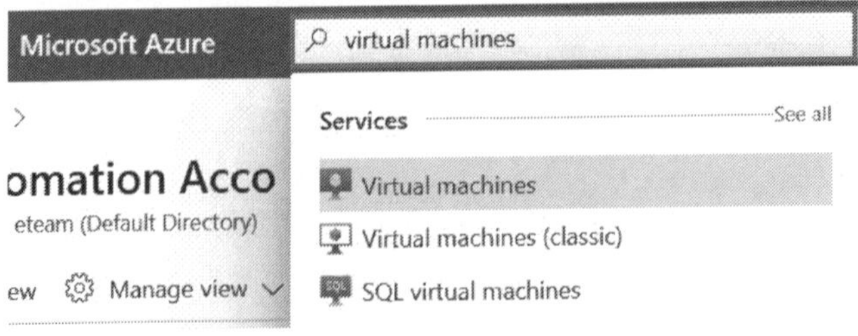

Figure 8.22 – Searching for virtual machines

8. In the **Virtual machines** blade, select all VMs. In the top-right corner, click the **ellipsis** icon, click on **Services**, and then click on **Update Management**:

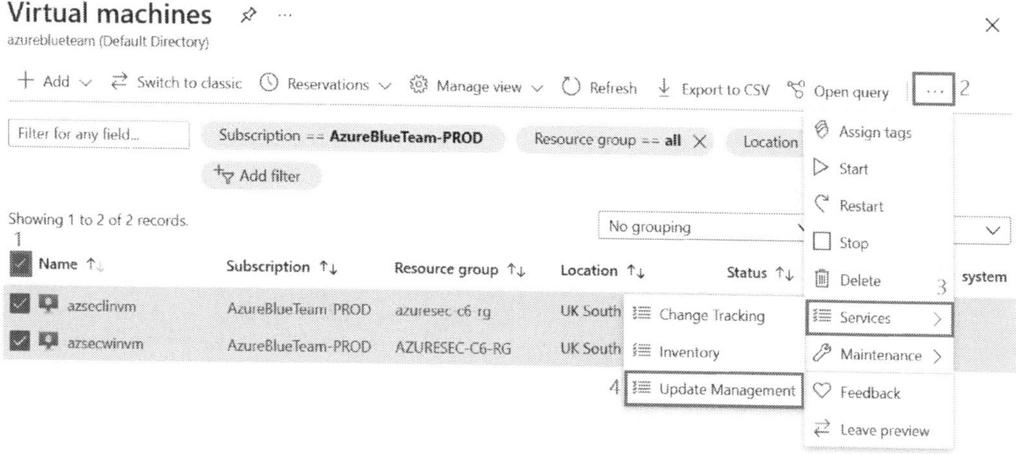

Figure 8.23 – Configuring update management for VMs

9. In the **Enable Update Management** blade, select **CUSTOM**, then click to change the Log Analytics workspace to the one you created earlier:

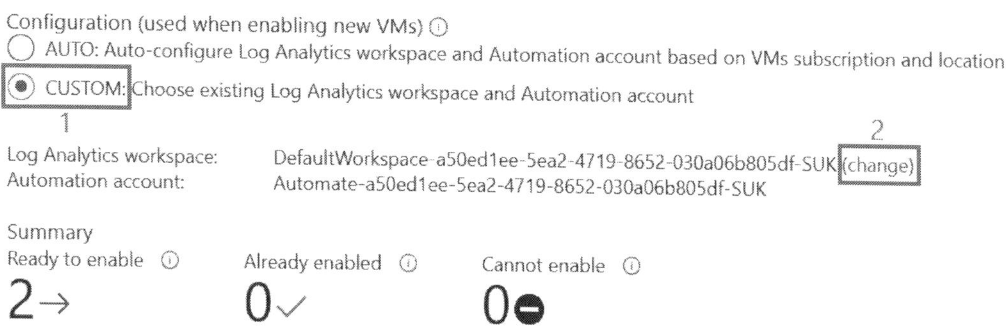

Figure 8.24 – Changing the workspace for Update Management

10. In the **Custom** configuration blade, configure the following:

    Log Analytics workspace Subscription: Select your subscription.

    Location: Select the same region that you deployed resources in earlier in this chapter.

    Workspace: `update-mgmt-workspace`.

    Automation account Subscription

    Account: `update-mgmt-aac`.

    Click **OK**.

    Ignore the warning message that appears:

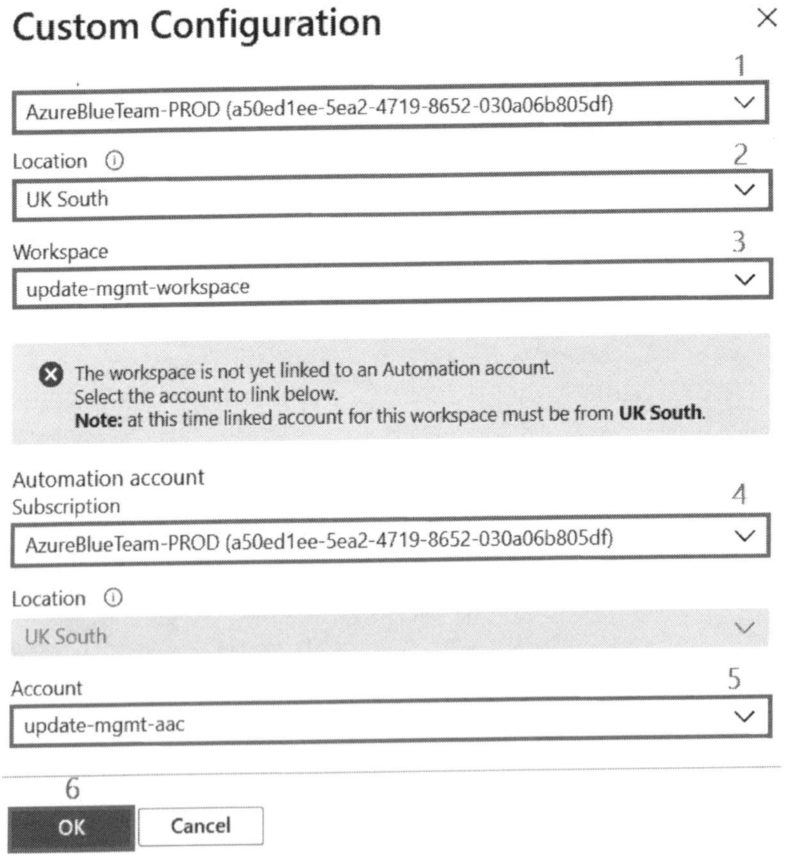

Figure 8.25 – Selecting the workspace and Automation Account

11. Back in the **Enable Update Management** blade, ensure all VMs are selected, and then click **Enable**:

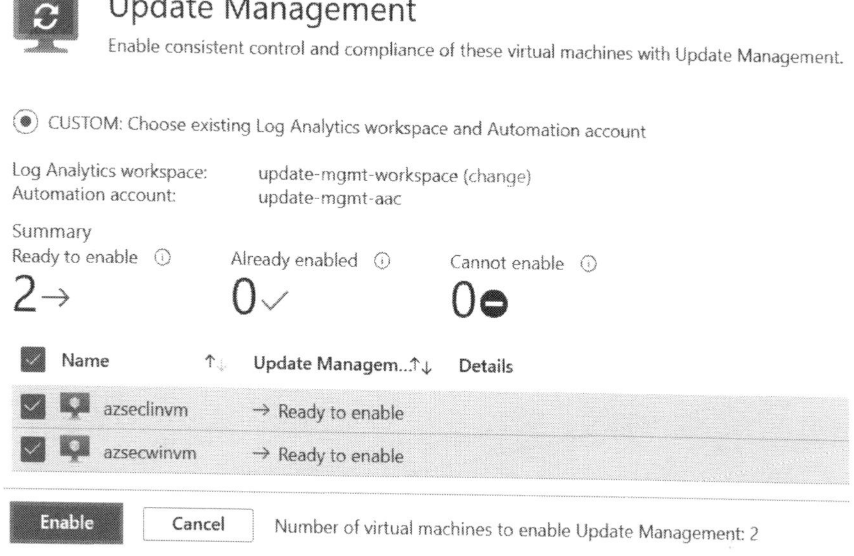

Figure 8.26 – Enabling VM update management

Congratulations! You have successfully configured update management for Azure VMs. After a while, you will begin to see the update statuses of the VMs in the **Update Management** section of Azure automation. You can also configure a schedule for the update installation from there. In the next section, we will look at vulnerability management for VMs in Azure.

Implementing vulnerability assessment for VMs

When we talk about VM vulnerability scanning, the Azure Defender plan of Security Center has functionality that we can use for this. This functionality is called **Azure Defender for Servers**. It uses a third-party solution known as Qualys in the background, but the process and integration are abstracted from us.

Even though Qualys is used, we do not need to obtain a Qualys license or have a relationship with Qualys. Everything is handled seamlessly inside Security Center:

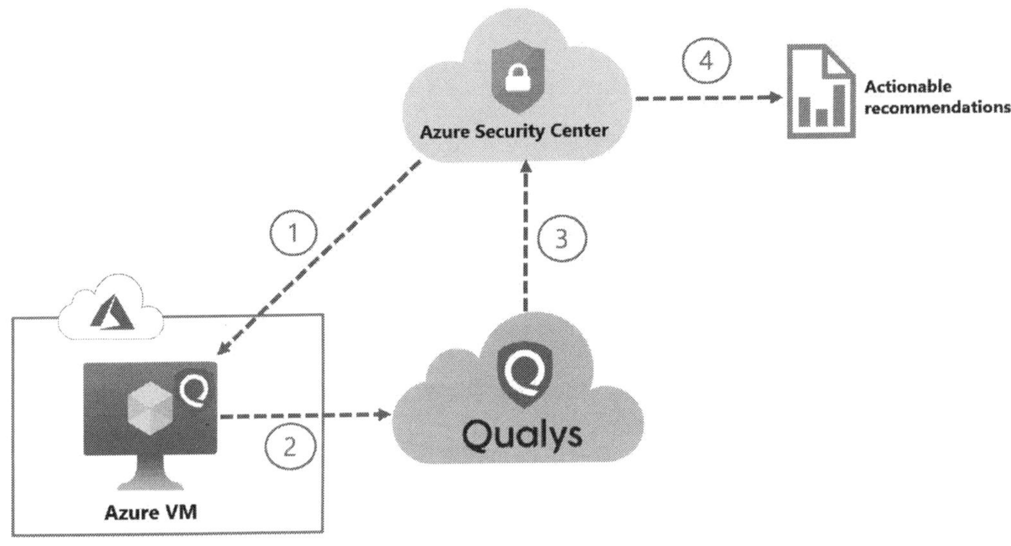

Figure 8.27 – Azure Defender for VMs

There are four stages to using this functionality:

1. Deploy the Qualys vulnerability scanner extension. The extension can be deployed to Azure VMs from Azure Security Center.
2. The extension gathers information and artifacts concerning the VM and sends them to the Qualys cloud service. Network communication between the VM and the Qualys cloud service is needed for this.
3. The Qualys cloud service conducts the vulnerability assessment and sends its findings to Security Center.
4. Recommendations can be accessed in Security Center via the console or through the API.

A customer can also choose to use other solutions for VM vulnerability assessment. For example, the Palo Alto Prisma Cloud compute solution can be used to consolidate vulnerability management for code, configuration, VMs, containers, and serverless functions.

Encrypting VM disks with Azure Disk Encryption

VM disks are encrypted at rest in Azure data centers. While this will protect against data theft if someone breaks into one of the Microsoft data centers and steals a bunch of disks (an unlikely scenario), it will not prevent an attacker or a malicious insider with the right credentials from taking a snapshot of a VM disk, and then mounting it on another system to access its data (a more likely scenario). The recommendation to prevent this likely scenario is to enable volume-level encryption, and the easiest way to implement this is to utilize a feature called **Azure Disk Encryption** (**ADE**).

ADE leverages built-in OS encryption capabilities to provide volume-level encryption for your OS and its data disks. For Windows VMs in Azure, ADE uses the built-in BitLocker feature. For Linux VMs in Azure, ADE uses the DM-Crypt feature. To store the encryption secrets and keys, ADE uses Azure Key Vault (which we will cover in *Chapter 12, Implementing Secrets, Keys, and Certificate Management with Key Vault*).

Regarding pricing, there are charges associated with the use of Azure Key Vault, but the disk encryption feature itself is not charged for use.

Regarding supported operating systems, Windows 8 and later are supported for the Windows client family, Windows Server 2008 R2 and later are supported for the Windows server family, and most official Linux distributions in the Azure marketplace are also supported, including Ubuntu, RedHat, Centos, and SUSE.

So, how does ADE work? When ADE is enabled on an Azure VM, an extension is deployed to the VM. This extension enables and configures volume encryption on the VM and stores the symmetric key used for encryption as a secret in an Azure Key Vault resource. This secret will be unique for each VM. To add an extra layer of protection for the encryption secret, we can protect or wrap it using an RSA 2048 asymmetric key, referred to as the **Key Encryption Key** (**KEK**). This key will be used to encrypt the secret before it is stored in the Key Vault (*Figure 8.28*). This also makes it easier to rotate the keys as we only need to rotate the KEK instead of all the unique symmetric keys:

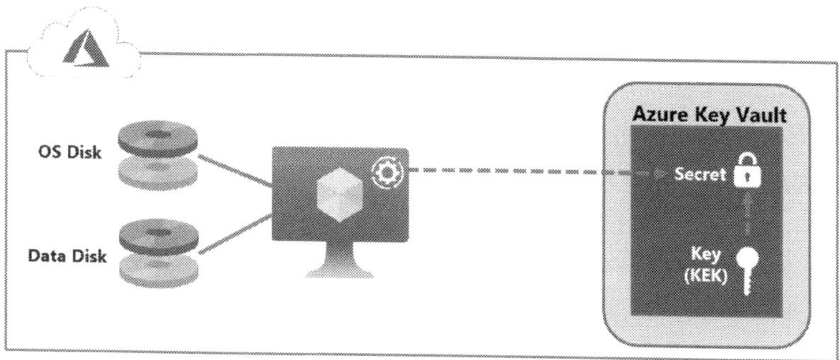

Figure 8.28 – Azure Disk Encryption integration with Key Vault

There are some additional points to note when implementing ADE:

- Basic A-series VMs, or VMs with less than 2 GB of memory, are not supported.
- A VM in Azure has an OS disk and could have one or more data disks attached. The OS disk must be encrypted to be able to encrypt the data disks.
- It is not enough for data disks to be attached to a VM from the Azure platform – the volumes must also be mounted within the OS before they can be encrypted with ADE.
- Using ADE does not prevent VM backups from working. VMs with encrypted disks using Azure Disk Encryption can be backed up using Azure Backup. The main thing to watch out for is that the Recovery Services Vault must reside on the same subscription and region.
- For a more comprehensive list of considerations when using ADE, please refer to this FAQ document: `https://docs.microsoft.com/en-us/azure/virtual-machines/windows/disk-encryption-faq`.

To implement VM disk encryption at scale, ADE can be enabled using a resource manager template. This way, we can ensure that our VM disks are encrypted at the point of deployment.

Hands-on exercise – implementing Azure Disk Encryption

Here is what we will complete in this exercise:

- **Task 1**: Create an Azure Key Vault resource.
- **Task 2**: Create a key that will be used to protect the encryption secrets.
- **Task 3**: Enable Azure Disk encryption on a VM.

Here are the steps to complete these tasks:

1. In the Azure portal, in the **Search resources, services, and docs** text box at the top of the Azure portal home page, type `key vault` and press *Enter*:

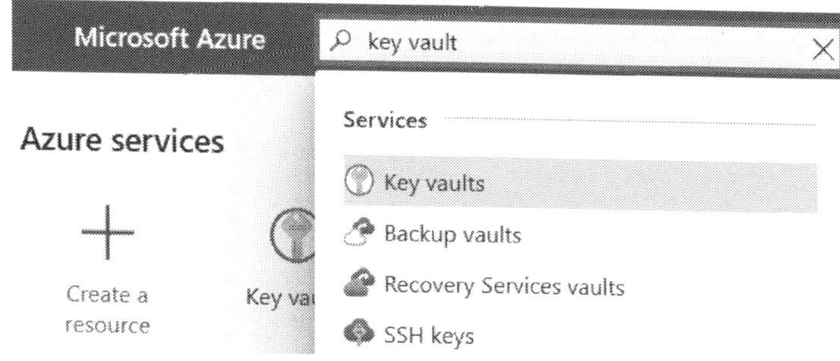

Figure 8.29 – Searching for key vault

2. In the **Key vaults** blade, click on **+ New** to create a new key vault:

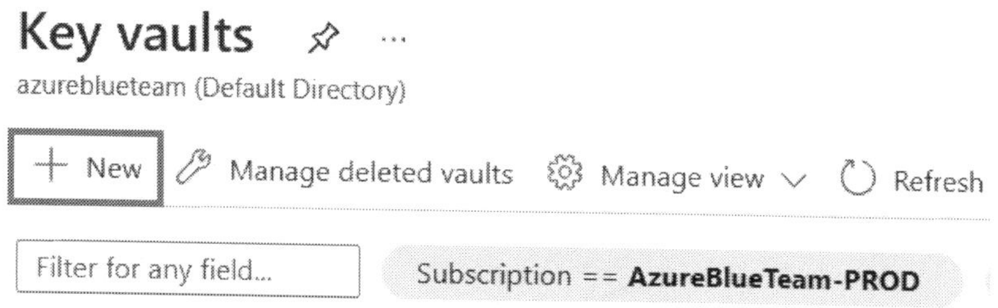

Figure 8.30 – Creating a new key vault resource

3. In the **Create key vault** blade, configure the following:

   Subscription: Select your Azure subscription.

   Resource group: azuresec-c6-rg.

   Key vault name: `azsec-<random_number>`. Replace `<random_number>` with a randomly selected number to ensure that the name is unique in the `vault.azure.net` DNS zone; for example, `azsec-120321`.

   Region: Select the same region that you deployed the template to earlier. The key vault must be in the same subscription and region as the encrypted disks.

   Pricing tier: Standard.

   Days to retain deleted vaults: Leave as the default setting.

   Purge protection: Leave as the default setting.

Click **Next: Access policy** >. It will take about a minute for the review to deploy:

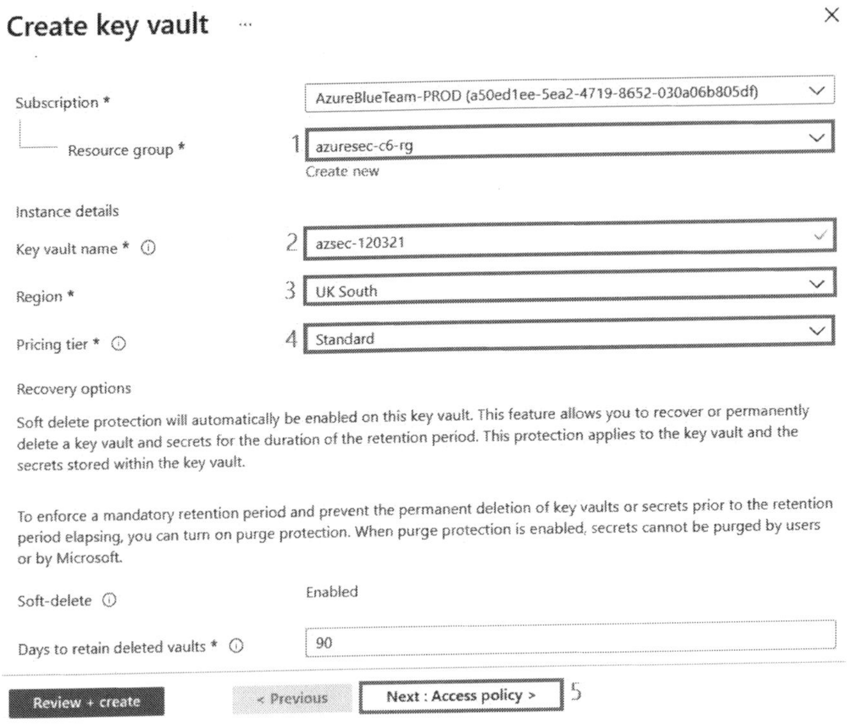

Figure 8.31 – Configuring the parameters for the new key vault

4. In the **Access policy** tab, ensure that the option for **Azure Disk Encryption for volume encryption** is selected. Selecting this option will grant ADE the permission it needs to retrieve secrets from the vault and unwrap keys. Then, click on **Review + create**:

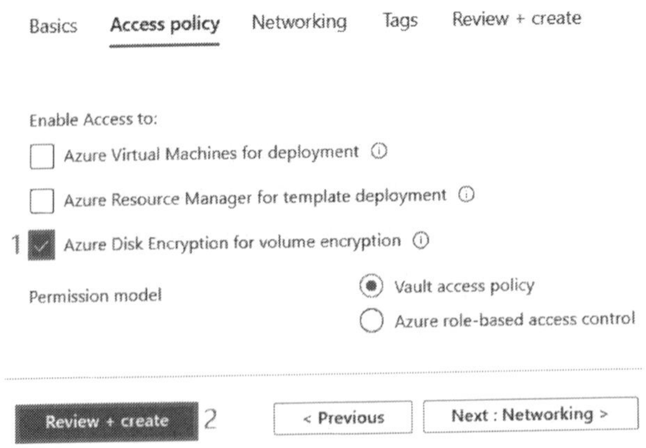

Figure 8.32 – Configuring the key vault for ADE

5. In the **Review + create** tab, after the validation has passed, click on **Create**. Wait for the deployment to complete:

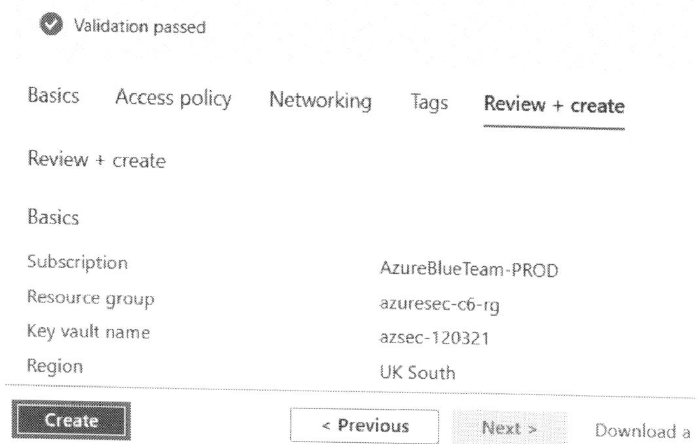

Figure 8.33 – Creating a key vault with the configured parameters

The Key Vault resource that you just created will be used to store the VM encryption secrets! But before we enable encryption, let's generate an RSA 2048 key that will be used to protect the encryption secrets before they are stored in the Key Vault.

6. Once the deployment has been completed, click on **Go to resource**:

Figure 8.34 – Viewing the deployed resources

7. In the **Key vault** resource blade, click on **Keys**, and then select **+ Generate/Import**:

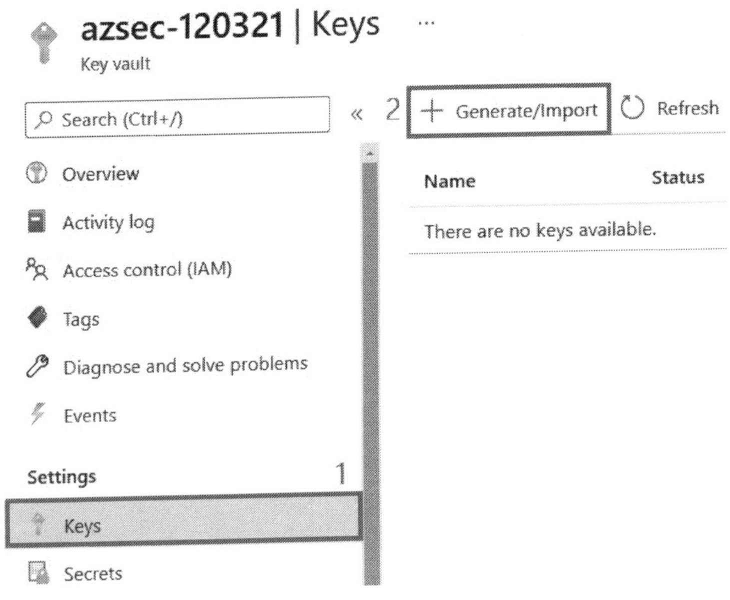

Figure 8.35 – Generating a new key in the key vault

8. In the **Create a key** blade, configure the following:

   Options: **Generate.**

   Name: **Disk-Encryption-KEK.**

   Key Type: **RSA.**

   RSA Key Size: 2048.

   Leave other options as their default settings.

   Click **Create**:

Create a key ...

Options

1 Generate

Name *

2 Disk-Encryption-KEK

Key Type

3 RSA EC

RSA Key Size

4 2048 3072 4096

Set activation date?

Set expiration date?

Enabled?

Create 5

Figure 8.36 – Configuring the parameters for the new key

Now that we have created our key vault and the encryption key, we can proceed to enable ADE throughout.

9. In the Azure portal, in the **Search resources, services, and docs** text box at the top of the Azure portal home page, type `azsecwinvm` and press *Enter*.
10. Open the Windows VM resource that was created as part of the deployment template earlier in this chapter:

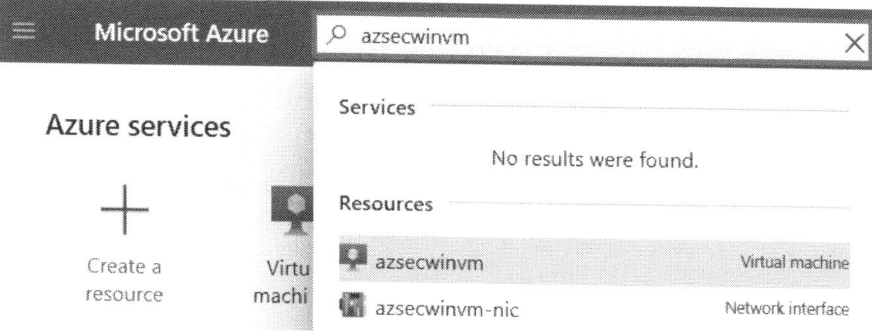

Figure 8.37 – Searching for the Windows VM by name

11. In the **azsecwinvm** virtual machine blade, click on **Disks**, and then click on **Additional settings**:

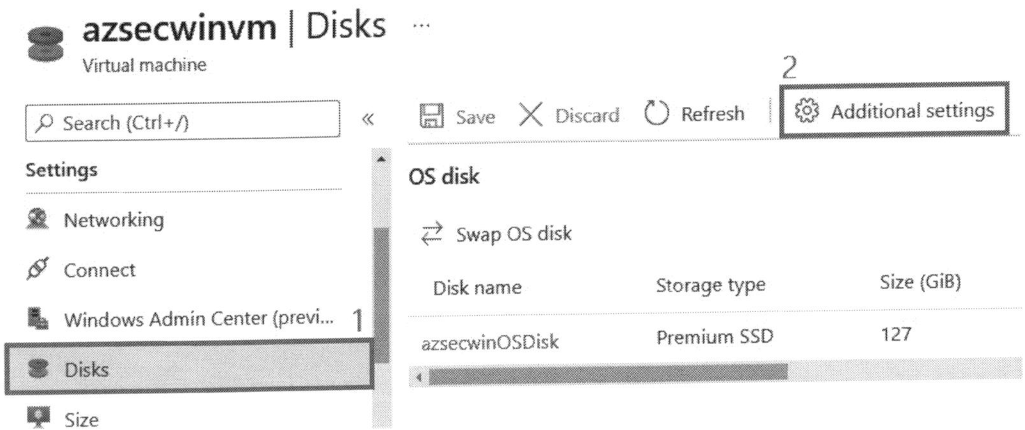

Figure 8.38 – Configuring the VM's disk settings

12. In the **Disk settings** blade, configure the following:

    Disks to encrypt: OS and data disks

    Key vault and key: Click on the **Click to select a key** link:

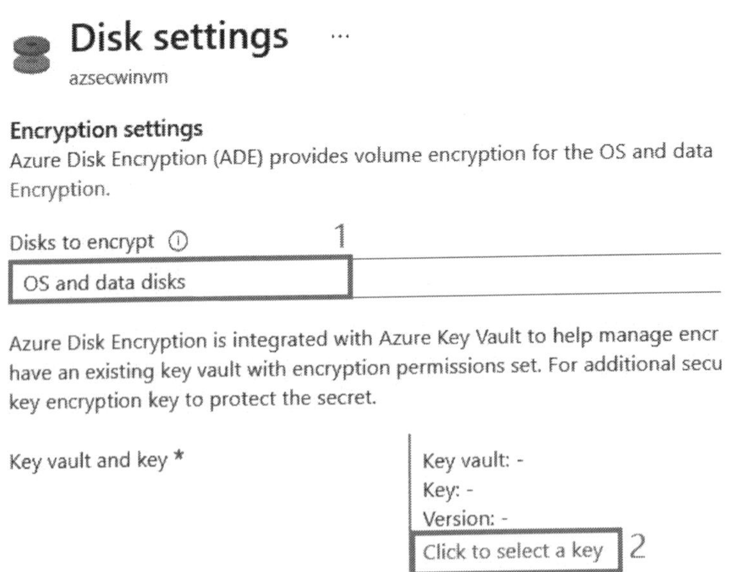

Figure 8.39 – Encrypting both OS and data disks

13. In the **Select key from Azure Key Vault** blade, configure the following:

    Key vault: Select the key vault resource that you created earlier.

    Key: **Disk-Encryption-KEK**.

    Version: Select the latest key version that's displayed.

    Click on **Select**:

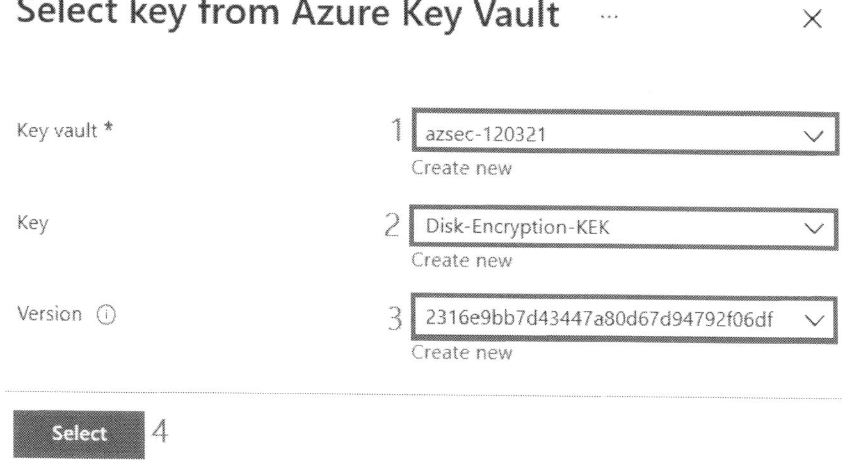

Figure 8.40 – Configuring the key vault and key to use

14. Back in the **Disk settings** blade, click on **Save**. This will begin the encryption process.
15. On the left-hand pane, select **Extensions**. You should see two extensions that were provisioned as part of the process:

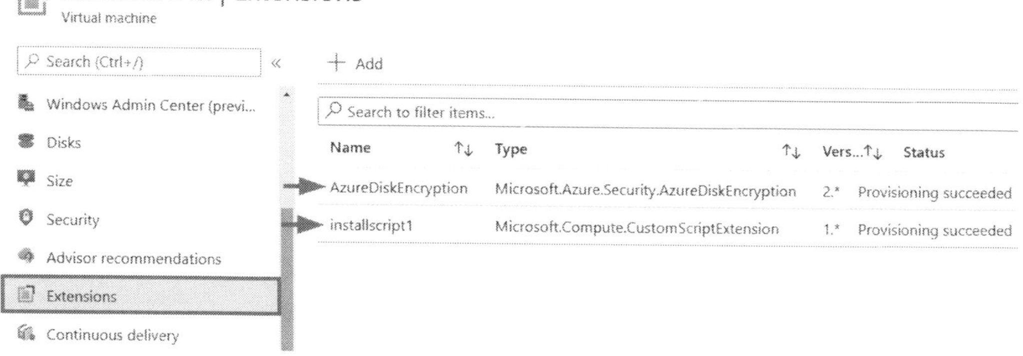

Figure 8.41 – Reviewing the VM extensions

16. If you review the secrets repository of the key vault resource, you will also see a wrapped BitLocker encryption secret that was used for volume encryption:

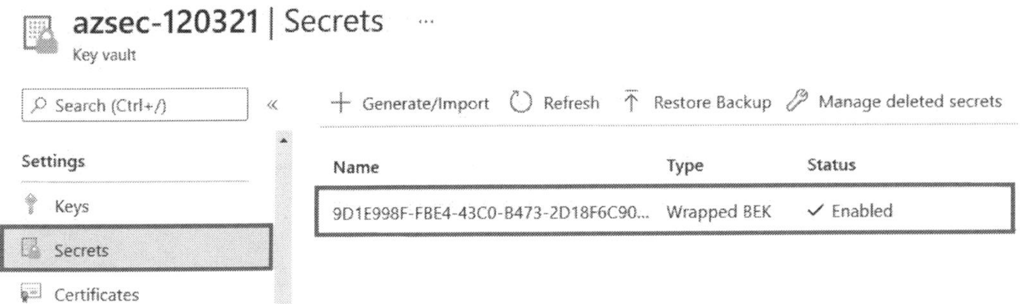

Figure 8.42 – Reviewing the secret in the key vault

Congratulations! You have successfully protected sensitive data stored in an Azure VM disk using the Azure disk encryption feature. You now know how to configure the key vault resource needed to store the secrets, generate the encryption key needed to encrypt the secrets, and then implemented the feature. We will cover the Key Vault resource in more detail in *Chapter 12, Implementing Secrets, Keys, and Certificate Management with Key Vault*. In the next section, we will cover how to secure the management ports of our VMs using JIT VM access.

Securing management ports with JIT VM access

Internet attackers are always hunting for connected systems with open management ports. Once a target has been identified, it can be scanned for vulnerabilities that could be exploited, or a brute-force login attack could be performed. If the host is successfully compromised, it can be used as the entry point to proceed further in an attack chain or even used as a landing zone to compromise other victims!

To reduce this attack surface, the recommendation is to keep management ports such as RDP and SSH closed and only open them when needed for administrative tasks. This is exactly what JIT VM access allows us to do, without the management overhead of closing and opening these ports manually.

To use JIT, we need to enable the Azure Defender pricing tier of Azure Security Center (you will be doing this in the following hands-on exercise). To enable JIT for a VM, you must be a resource manager VM (classic VMs are not supported), the VM must have an associated **Network Security Group** (**NSG**), and it should be powered on.

So, how does JIT VM access work? The first thing we need to do is enable the feature for a VM that we want to protect. We can enable it from Security Center (**Security Center → Just in time VM access → Not configured → Select VM → Enable JIT → Save**) or from the VM configuration (**Virtual Machine → Configuration → Enable JIT**).

When we enable the feature, we can specify the management port that we want to protect, the approved IP address that can access the port, and the maximum time that the port can be kept open for, as shown here:

Add port configuration ×

Port *

3389

Protocol

Any TCP UDP

Allowed source IPs

Per request CIDR block

IP addresses

*

Max request time

3

(hours)

Figure 8.43 – Configuring the management port options

After enabling JIT, Security Center ensures that the protected ports are blocked in the NSG associated with that VM, as shown in the following diagram:

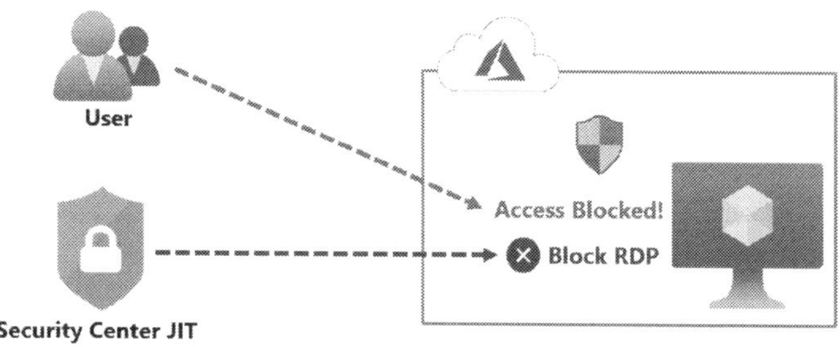

Figure 8.44 – Security Center JIT adding a block rule

Whenever a user needs to connect to the VM on the protected management port, they can authenticate to the Azure portal and request access to the management port for a limited time (**Virtual Machine → Connect → Request Access**). Security Center will then auto-configure the NSG to allow the inbound traffic. Once the maximum time has expired, the access will be automatically removed, as shown here:

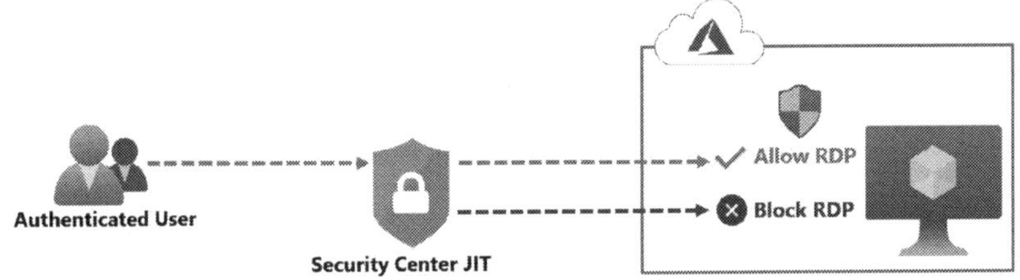

Figure 8.45 – Authenticated users can request temporary access

Now that we have some understanding of JIT VM access and how it works, in the next section, we will head on over to the Azure portal to see this capability in action!

Hands-on exercise – enabling JIT VM access

This is what we will complete in this exercise:

- **Task 1**: Enable Security Center – Azure Defender plan.
- **Task 2**: Enable and configure JIT for a Windows VM.
- **Task 3**: Verify JIT network security group rules and audit log.

Here are the steps to complete these tasks:

1. In the Azure portal, in the **Search resources, services, and docs** text box at the top of the Azure home portal page, type `security center` and press *Enter*. This will open the **Security Center** management pane:

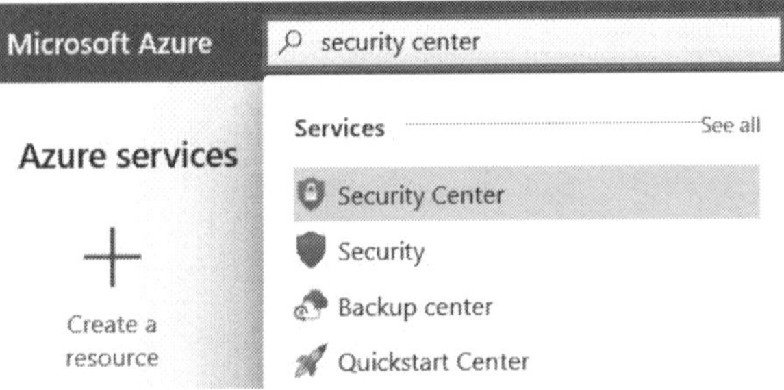

Figure 8.46 – Searching for Security Center

2. In the **Security Center | Getting started** blade, scroll down and click on **Upgrade** to upgrade to the Azure Defender plan. You will need this to use the JIT feature that we are about to implement:

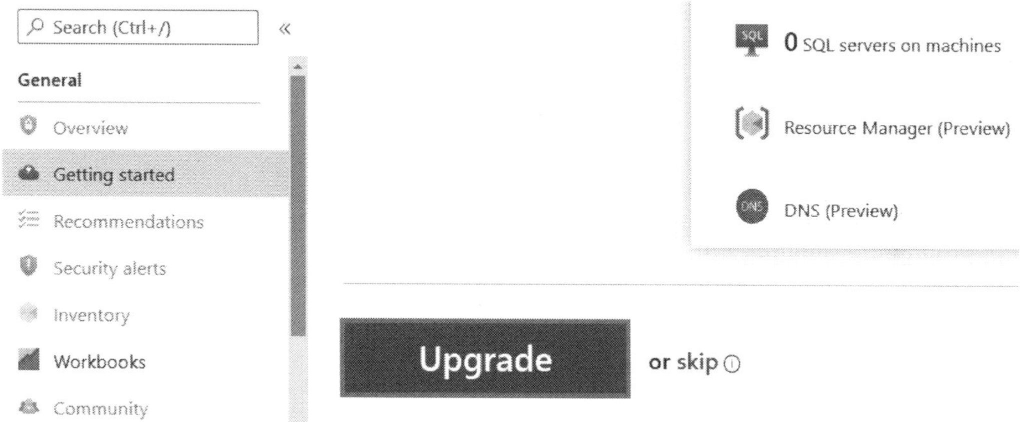

Figure 8.47 – Upgrading the Security Center plan

3. Wait for the upgrade to complete. Do not click on the option to **Install agents** for now. Once the upgrade is complete, you should see a **Trial started** notification in the top-right corner:

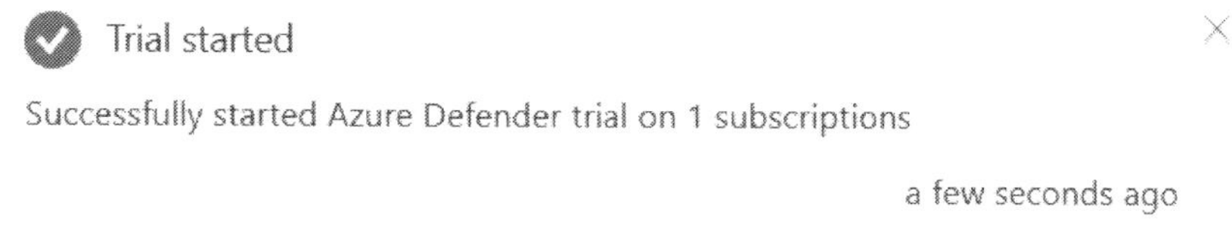

Figure 8.48 – Trial started notification

4. In the Azure portal, in the **Search resources, services, and docs** text box at the top of the Azure portal home page, type `azsecwinvm` and press *Enter*. This will open the **Windows VM** management pane:

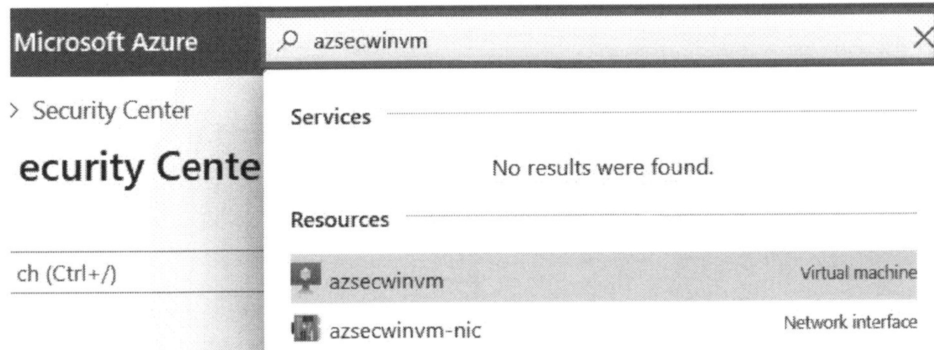

Figure 8.49 – Searching for the Windows VM by name

5. In the **Virtual machine** blade, click on **Configuration**, and then click on **Enable just-in-time**. This will enable JIT protection for the VM:

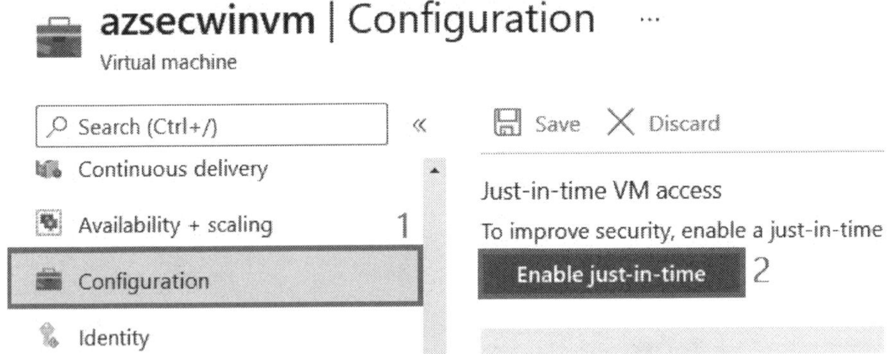

Figure 8.50 – Enabling just-in-time VM access

6. In the left pane, click on **Networking**. Review the **Inbound port rules** section. You will notice that Security Center has added a deny rule to block the RDP management port:

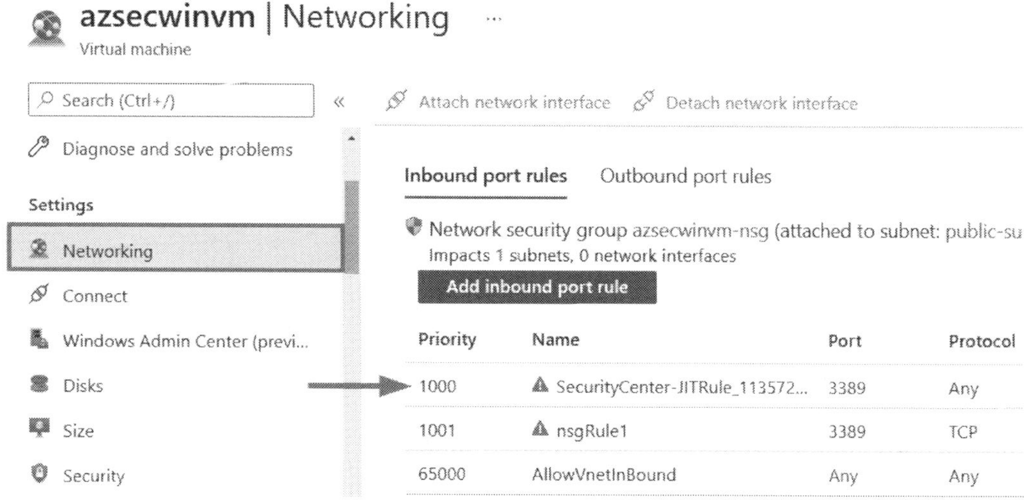

Figure 8.51 – Reviewing the security center block rule

7. To request temporary access, click on **Configuration** in the left-hand pane, and then click on **Open Azure Security Center**:

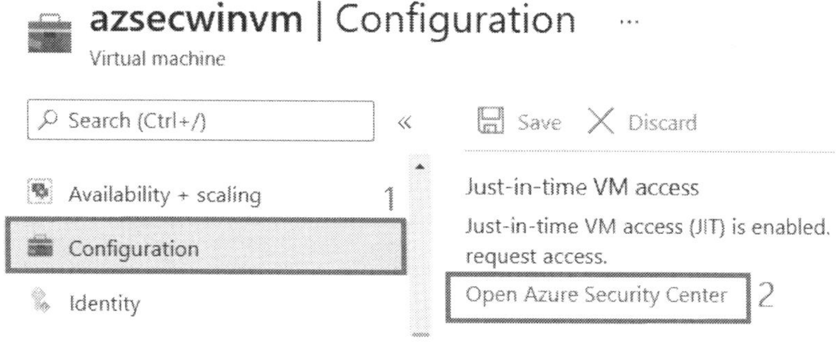

Figure 8.52 – Opening Azure Security Center from the VM blade

8. In the **Just-in-time VM access** blade, you can review VMs that have JIT enabled, VMs that do not have JIT enabled, and VMs that do not support JIT. In the **Configured** tab, click on the **ellipsis** icon in front of **azsecwinvm**, and then click on **Edit**:

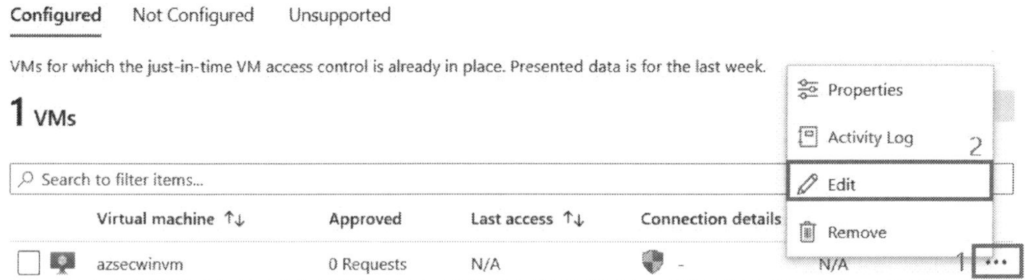

Figure 8.53 – Editing VM JIT configuration

9. In the **JIT VM access configuration** blade, click on **port 3389** and review the current settings. You will see that we can configure the allowed source IP address block when users request temporary access to connect to the VM using this management port. We can also configure the maximum allowed time per request before access will be removed. Click on **Discard**, then close the **JIT VM access configuration** blade to return to the previous blade:

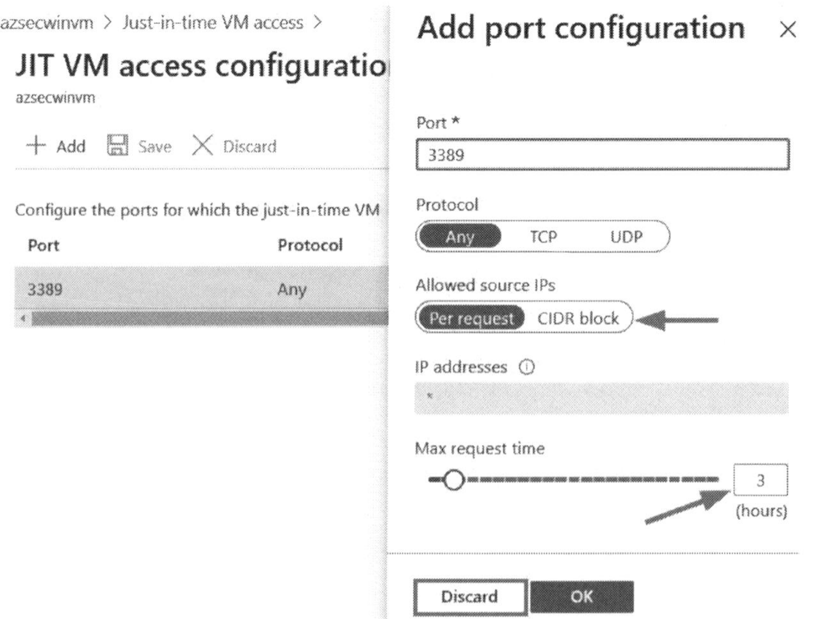

Figure 8.54 – Configuring the management port options for JIT

10. Back in the **Just-in-time VM access** blade, select **azsecwinvm**, and then click on **Request access**:

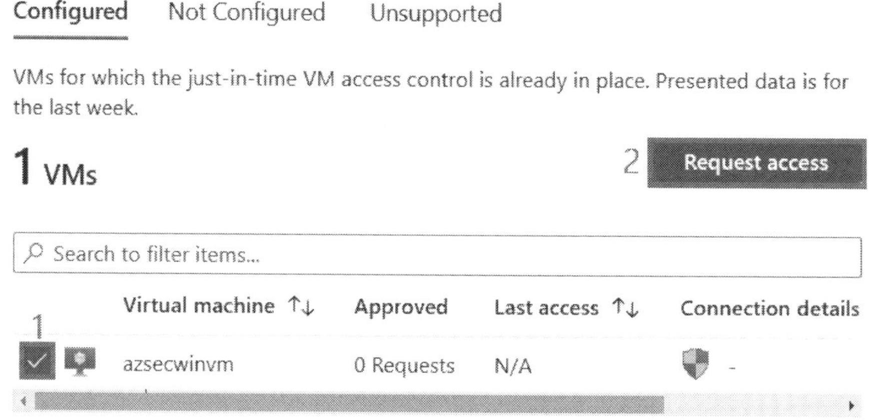

Figure 8.55 – Requesting JIT VM access

11. In the **Request access** blade, configure the following for port 3389:

    Toggle: **On**

    Allowed Source IP: **My IP**

    Time Range: Leave as the default setting

    Enter request justification: Needed for admin tasks

    Click on **Open ports**. Then, close the **Just-in-time VM access** blade to return to the previous blade:

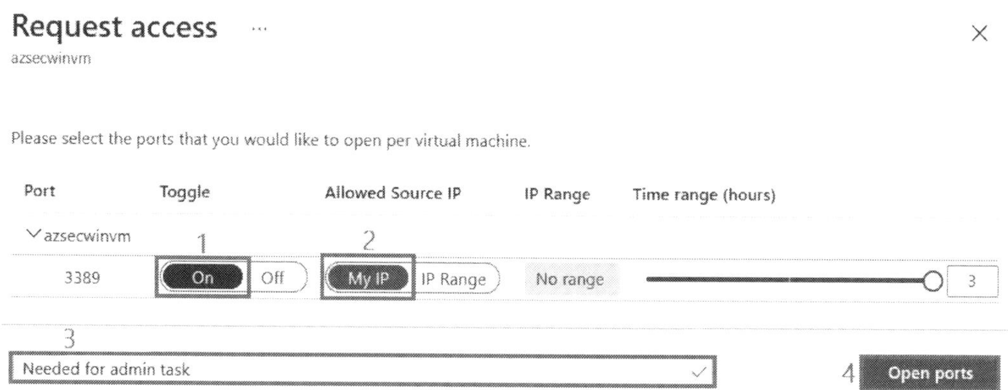

Figure 8.56 – Completing the request parameters

12. Back in the **azsecwinvm** blade, click on the **Networking** tab. Review the **Inbound port rules** section. You will notice that Security Center has added an allow rule on top of the deny rule to allow the RDP management port from your single source IP. This access will be automatically removed after the request time expires:

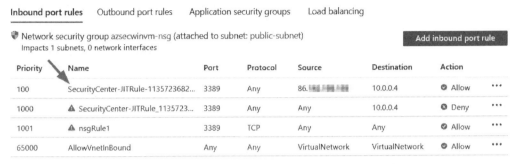

Inbound port rules | Outbound port rules | Application security groups | Load balancing

Network security group azsecwinvm-nsg (attached to subnet: public-subnet)
Impacts 1 subnets, 0 network interfaces

Add inbound port rule

Priority	Name	Port	Protocol	Source	Destination	Action
100	SecurityCenter-JITRule-1135723682...	3389	Any	86.	10.0.0.4	Allow
1000	SecurityCenter-JITRule_1135723...	3389	Any	Any	10.0.0.4	Deny
1001	nsgRule1	3389	TCP	Any	Any	Allow
65000	AllowVnetInBound	Any	Any	VirtualNetwork	VirtualNetwork	Allow

Figure 8.57 – Reviewing the Security Center JIT allow rule

13. In the left pane, click on **Activity log**. You should see the audit trail of JIT access being requested and granted. You can click on each event to review the full JSON log entry:

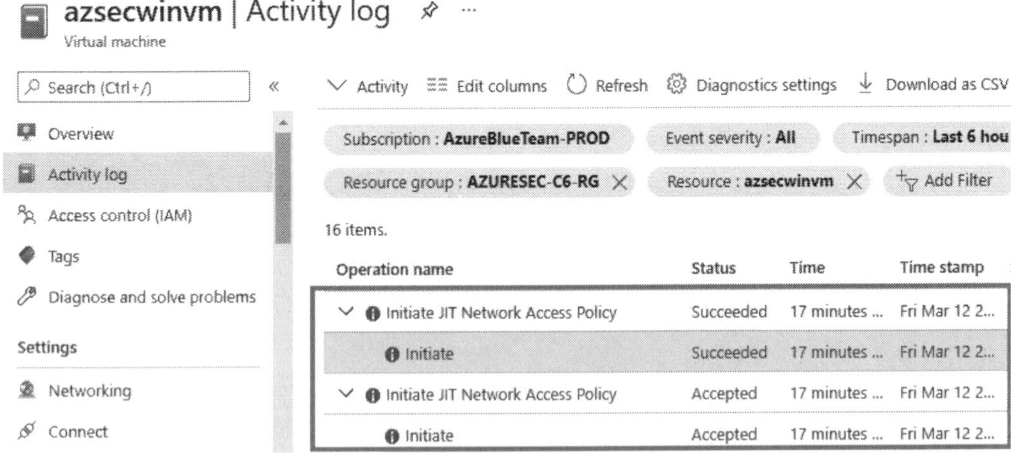

Figure 8.58 – Reviewing the audit logs for JIT

Congratulations! You have successfully protected the management port of an Azure VM with JIT access capabilities in Security Center. This is one of the objectives that is called out in the Azure Security Engineer certification guideline, and it will also be useful in the real world. Remember to clean up the resources that we created for the exercises by deleting the **azuresec-c6-rg** resource group in the Azure portal. This will remove all the resources that we created in this chapter.

Summary

In this chapter, we covered how to implement best practices for host security in Azure. We learned about reducing the risks of introducing vulnerabilities by choosing a hardened VM image, implementing an update management process, and continuously scanning VMs for vulnerabilities. We also learned how to implement disk encryption to protect against data exfiltration.

Finally, we covered how to implement JIT access for sensitive VM management ports to reduce the attack surface that's exposed to external adversaries.

The information in this chapter has equipped you with the skills needed to protect your VM workloads in Azure.

See you in the next chapter!

Questions

As we conclude, here is a list of questions for you to test your knowledge regarding this chapter's material. You will find the answers in the *Assessments* section of the *Appendix*:

1. You have two Windows VMs in Azure. **Win-VM1** is an F-Series Windows Server 2008 R2 VM with 4 GB of memory. **Win-VM2** is an A-Series Windows Server 2016 VM with 8 GB of memory. Which of these VMs can be protected with **Azure Disk Encryption** (**ADE**)?

   a. Win-VM1 only

   b. Win-VM2 only

   c. Both Win-VM1 and Win-VM2

   d. None of the VMs

2. You have an Azure subscription. The subscription contains 100 VMs that run Windows Server 2016 or Windows Server 2019. You need to deploy Microsoft Antimalware on these VMs. What should you do?

   a. Connect to each VM and add a Windows feature.

   b. Add an extension to each VM using an automation script.

   c. Recreate the VMs.

Further reading

To learn more on the topics covered in this chapter, you can refer to the following links:

- Azure Disk Encryption for Linux VMs: https://docs.microsoft.com/en-us/azure/virtual-machines/linux/disk-encryption-overview?WT.mc_id=AZ-MVP-6003870
- Azure Disk Encryption for Windows VMs: https://docs.microsoft.com/en-us/azure/virtual-machines/windows/disk-encryption-overview?WT.mc_id=AZ-MVP-6003870
- ASC Just-In-Time VM Access: https://docs.microsoft.com/en-us/azure/security-center/security-center-just-in-time?WT.mc_id=AZ-MVP-6003870
- ASC VM Vulnerability Scanning: https://docs.microsoft.com/en-us/azure/security-center/deploy-vulnerability-assessment-vm?WT.mc_id=AZ-MVP-6003870
- Security Best Practices for IaaS in Azure: https://docs.microsoft.com/en-us/azure/security/fundamentals/iaas?WT.mc_id=AZ-MVP-6003870

9
Implementing Container Security

Containers have been around for a long time. However, recently, they have become commonplace within an enterprise. The Azure platform continues to extend services that we can use to host containerized applications (for example, Container Registry, Kubernetes Service, Container Instances, App Service, "Functions", and Batch). In this chapter, we will be going over containerization in Azure, the container security threat landscape for Azure, and how to implement security across three key services – **Azure Container Registry** (**ACR**), **Azure Container Instances** (**ACI**), and **Azure Kubernetes Services** (**AKS**). We will cover the following main topics with accompanying hands-on exercises:

- An overview of containerization in Azure
- Introducing ACR
- ACR security best practices
- Introducing AKS
- AKS security best practices

As you can see, each topic has been structured to align with a security best practice for securing hosts in Azure.

Let's get started!

Technical requirements

To follow along with the instructions in this chapter, you will need the following:

- A PC with an internet connection.
- An Azure subscription. You can use the same subscription that you set up in the first chapter of this book.
- A GitHub template to deploy test resources: `http://bit.ly/az500-c9-template`.

Before we proceed to cover the security best practices, let's prepare our Azure subscription for the hands-on exercises that we will be implementing later in the chapter.

An overview of containerization in Azure

A container is a portable way in which to package and run software packages. It provides an efficient way to package application code, and all the necessary dependencies, to run in any computing environment. In general, when we talk about containerization, there are three main aspects to it. These three aspects are clearly highlighted in *Figure 9.1*:

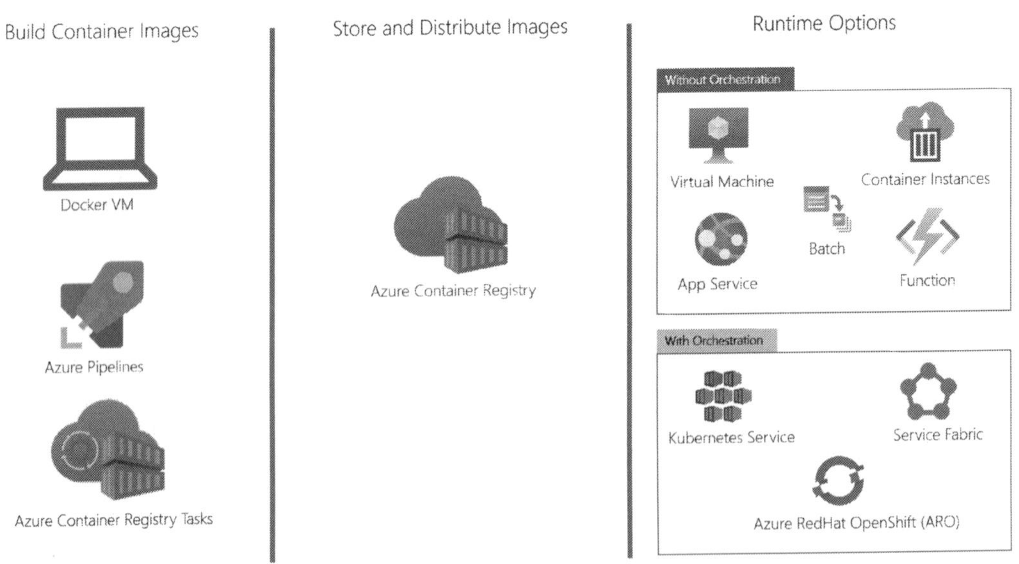

Figure 9.1 – An overview of containerization in Azure

The first aspect is to `BUILD` container images that contain application code, dependencies, and runtime. This is sometimes referred to as the `BUILD TIME`. Building container images is beyond the scope of this course, but it is important to mention it as security decisions begin at this stage. In Azure, there are different options that can be used to build container images. A developer could spin up a **virtual machine** (**VM**) in Azure, install Docker on it, and use it to build container images. A service called ACR can also be used. However, the most likely option is to automate everything using Azure Pipelines.

From a security perspective, the objective should be to reduce the risk of an attacker compromising our environment using containers running from this image. To achieve this objective, we can follow good security practices such as the following:

- Only use trusted base images. Images can contain malicious code or vulnerable components, so be extra careful with images from untrusted sources such as public registries.
- Avoid including sensitive information such as passwords or secrets in an image. This is because anyone with access to the image at any time in its life cycle can access any file or information included in it.

After the container images are ready, they need to be **STORED** and **DISTRIBUTED**. Images are stored in repositories called **container registries**. Docker clients can connect to registries to upload images (which is referred to as *push*) or to download images (which is referred to as *pull*). If you are familiar with Docker, you have probably interacted with the most popular container registry platform in the world – Docker Hub. **Docker Hub** is most popular for its public registry, which is accessible to everyone, but it also has a private option that allows organizations to implement access control policies.

Additionally, the Azure cloud platform has a service that we can use as a public or private container registry. The service is called ACR, and we will learn how to secure it later in this chapter.

The third aspect is to **RUN** images as containers in an environment. The Azure platform has multiple options that we can use to run container images. These runtime options are generally divided into two categories (please refer to *Figure 9.1*). The first category is **runtime options without orchestration** (or **standalone container runtime options**). Services such as VMs, ACI, App Service, Functions, and Batch fall under this category. These services do not support orchestration capabilities and are tailored toward running single container workloads. This does not mean that they cannot run multiple container instances – they can. It just means that they are not designed to make the running of multiple container workloads easy.

The second category is **runtime options with orchestration**. Services such as AKS, Azure Service Fabric, and **Azure RedHat for OpenShift** (**ARO**) fall under this category. These options are designed to simplify the running of distributed containerized workloads across multiple hosts. This is referred to as orchestration. Here are some capabilities of container orchestration options that standalone options do not have:

- **Scheduling**: This enables us to automatically find a suitable machine with sufficient resources to run our container on.
- **Affinity/Anti-affinity**: This means that we can specify a set of containers that run close to each other (for performance reasons) or sufficiently far apart from each other (for availability reasons). The orchestrator will manage the enforcement of this configuration for us.
- **Health monitoring**: The orchestrator watches out for container failures and automatically reschedules them in the case of a failure.
- **Failover**: The orchestrator constantly keeps track of what is running on each cluster node and reschedules containers from failed nodes to healthy nodes.
- **Scaling**: The orchestrator can add or remove container instances to match demand, either manually or automatically.
- **Networking**: The orchestrator provides a shared overlay network to facilitate container communication across multiple hosts (such as cluster nodes).
- **Service discovery**: The orchestrator implements a simplified way for containers to automatically locate each other even as they are moved between host machines and change IP addresses.
- **Coordinated application upgrades**: The orchestrator manages container workload upgrades in a way that prevents application downtime and enables a rollback if there are any issues.

In this chapter, we will cover the security of AKS; however, before we go any further, let's go over to our Azure environment to prepare a scenario that we can use to follow along with the exercises in this chapter.

Hands-on exercise – providing resources for the chapter exercises

To follow along with the exercises in this chapter, we will provide some Azure resources to work with. We have prepared an ARM template in the GitHub repository of this book for this purpose. The template will deploy an Azure virtual network with a public subnet, as shown in *Figure 9.2*. The subnet will have an Ubuntu Linux VM that can be accessed over SSH. Here are the tasks that we will complete in this exercise:

- **Task 1**: Initialize the template deployment in GitHub.
- **Task 2**: Complete the parameters and deploy the template to Azure:

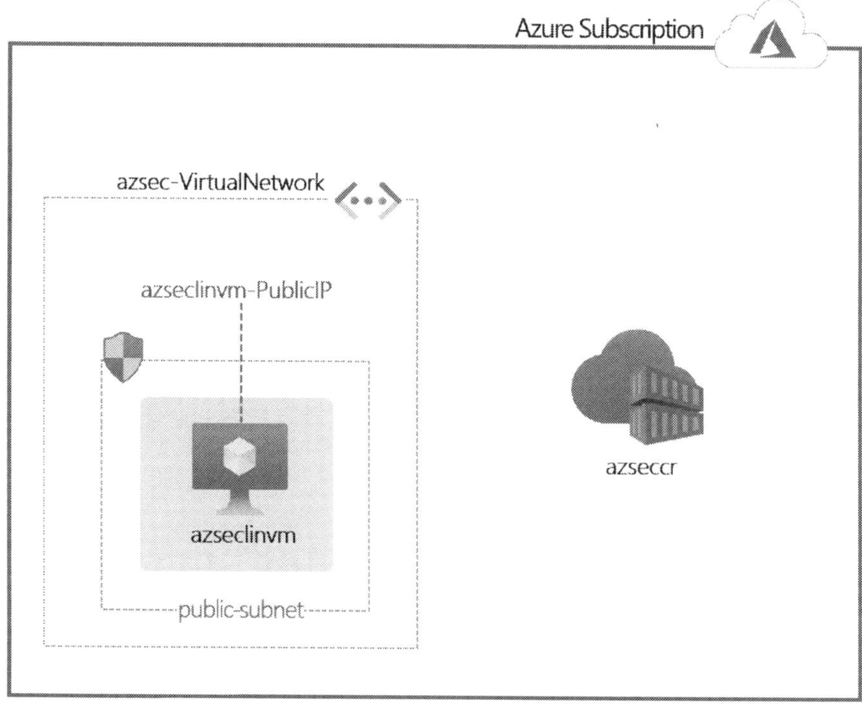

Figure 9.2 – Resources created for the exercise scenarios

Let's begin deploying our template deployment:

1. Open a web browser and browse to `http://bit.ly/az500-c9-template`. This link will open the GitHub repository that has an ARM template to deploy the resources we need.
2. In the GitHub repository that opens, click on **Deploy to Azure**:

Azure Security Engineer Book - Chapter 9

Linux VM

- Ubuntu 18.04
- Azure CLI Installed
- Docker Installed
- Kubernetes CLI Installed

Figure 9.3 – Deploying the template to Azure

3. If required, sign in with your administrative username and password to authenticate your Azure subscription.
4. In the **Custom Deployment** window, configure the following:

   Subscription: Select the subscription that you want to deploy the resources to.

   Resource Group: Navigate to **Create New** → **Name**: `azuresec-c9-rg` → **OK**.

   Region: Select an Azure region that is close to your location.

   Vm-dns: Leave the default value.

   Admin User: Leave the default value.

   Admin Password: Enter a complex password. Make a note of the password that you use. We recommend that you select one complex password that you can use throughout the scenarios in this book to keep things simple.

Vmsize: Leave the default value.

Location: Leave the default value.

Resource Tags: Leave the default value.

_artifacts Location: Leave the default value.

_artifacts Location Sas Token: Leave the default value.

Click on **Review + Create**:

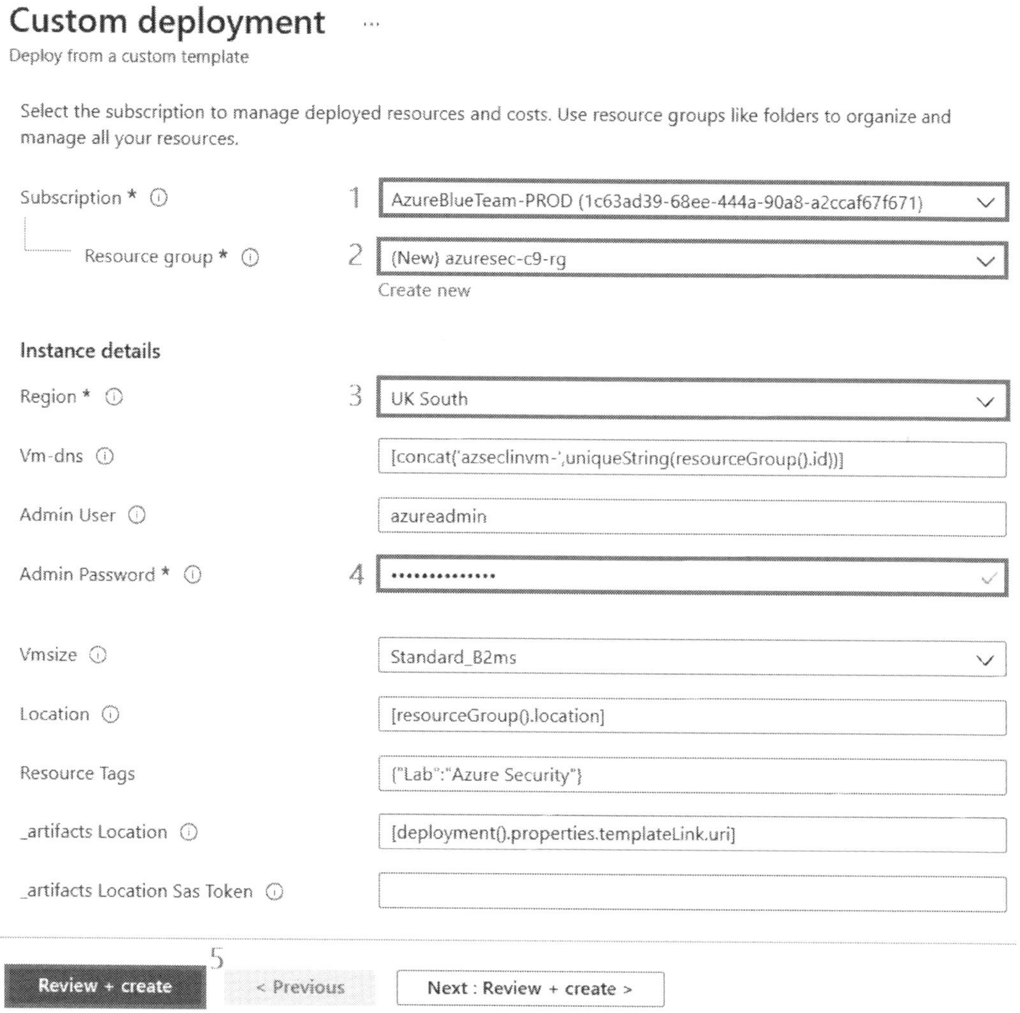

Figure 9.4 – Configuring the template parameters

5. After the template validation has passed, click on **Create**. This will begin the deployment process, which takes about 7 to 10 minutes to complete. Grab yourself a cup of water, tea, or coffee, and wait for the deployment to complete:

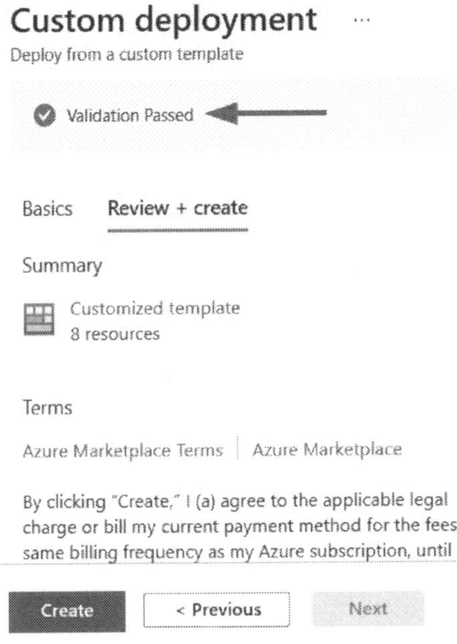

Figure 9.5 – Deploying the template

6. After the deployment has been completed, click on the **Outputs** tab. Make a note of the **linvm-dns** value. This is the public DNS name of the Linux VM that we just deployed:

Figure 9.6 – Obtaining the Linux VM DNS name

In this exercise, we provisioned some Azure resources that we need for the rest of the exercises in this chapter. In the next section, we will begin to look at ACR and examine how to secure it.

Introducing ACR

ACR is a managed Docker registry service that we can use to store and distribute container images and other containerization artifacts. Other artifacts that we can store in ACR include Helm, which is a packaging format that is used to deploy applications for Kubernetes, such as Helm charts.

ACR is based on the open source Docker Registry 2.0 service, which is the same service that the popular Docker Hub registry (`https://hub.docker.com/`) is based on.

Because ACR is a managed service, we do not need to manage the underlying infrastructure, **operating system** (**OS**), or application; this gives us fewer security responsibilities to fulfill. Before we explore how to implement security for ACR, let's discuss how this service works. *Figure 9.7* illustrates this clearly:

1. First, we create a container registry with the Azure portal, Azure CLI, or Azure PowerShell. The registry will receive a fully qualified domain name that should be unique in the `acr.net` domain.
2. Then, we use the Docker client's `login` and `push` commands to authenticate and upload our container images into the registry.
3. We can then reference our images that are stored in ACR when deploying to services that run container images. The runtime engine will pull and run the images from our registry:

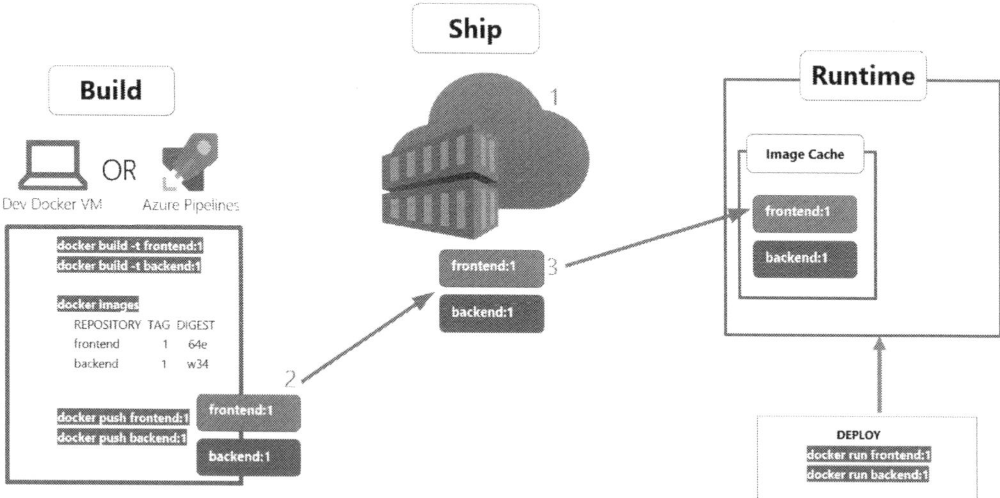

Figure 9.7 – Container image flow

Now that you understand how the container registry works, let's take a look at the different pricing tier options and the impact of our selection on the security capabilities that we can implement.

ACR pricing tiers

ACR is available in three tiers, and we need to specify a tier during creation. The pricing tier that we select has an impact on the security capabilities that we can implement. The three tiers are Basic, Standard, and Premium.

The **BASIC tier** is a cost-optimized entry point for developers looking to learn about Container Registry, while the **STANDARD tier** is an entry-level production option with more storage capacity and throughput than the basic tier. From a security perspective, both tiers support the same security capabilities:

- **Webhook integration**: This is useful when we want to trigger container scans in a third-party service based on registry events. Security services such as the Palo Alto Prisma Cloud Compute service leverages this capability to scan container images on image push events.
- **Azure Active Directory (Azure AD) authentication**: This allows us to control authentication and access to the registry using Azure AD credentials.
- **Microsoft-managed platform encryption**: This ensures that our images are encrypted at rest in the Azure data centers using keys that are managed by the Azure platform.

The **PREMIUM tier** has more storage capacity and throughput than the standard tier. From a security perspective, it supports advanced security functionalities such as geo-replication, private endpoints, content trust, and encryption using customer-managed keys. **Geo-replication** provides registry resilience in the case of a regional outage. We will cover private endpoints, content trust, and encryption using customer-managed keys when we discuss the security best practices.

ACR security best practices

To protect container image assets in our registries, there are certain security configurations that we should implement. In this book, we will cover the following security best practices:

- Configuring service firewall rules (premium only)
- Restricting access using a private endpoint (premium only)

- Using Azure AD **role-based access control** (**RBAC**) for secure authentication and access control
- Implementing container image vulnerability and compliance scanning

In the following sections, we will cover these best practices in detail so that you can gain an understanding of them and the risks they help us to mitigate. Additionally, you have an upcoming hands-on exercise to complete where you will be able to implement some of these best practices.

Configuring service firewall rules for ACR

To pull or push images to ACR, a client, such as a Docker daemon running on a developer's laptop, or an Azure pipeline agent needs to interact with its REST endpoint over HTTPS. By default, ACR accepts connections over the internet from hosts on any network (*Figure 9.8*):

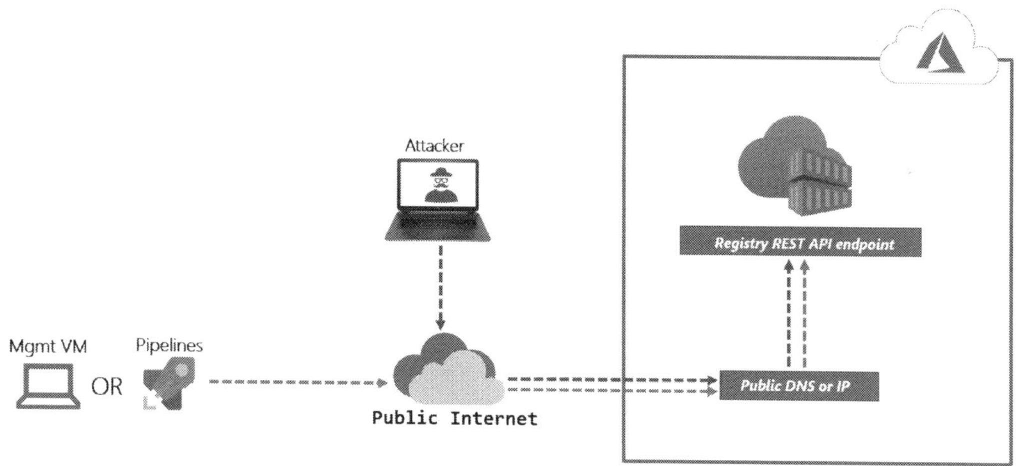

Figure 9.8 – ACR's public endpoint

Here, the risk is that an attacker could start to probe the container registry for weak credentials, or if an authorized identity is already compromised, an attacker could access the contents of the registry from any network on the internet.

The best practice here is to restrict this access to trusted public IP addresses only, as shown in *Figure 9.9*:

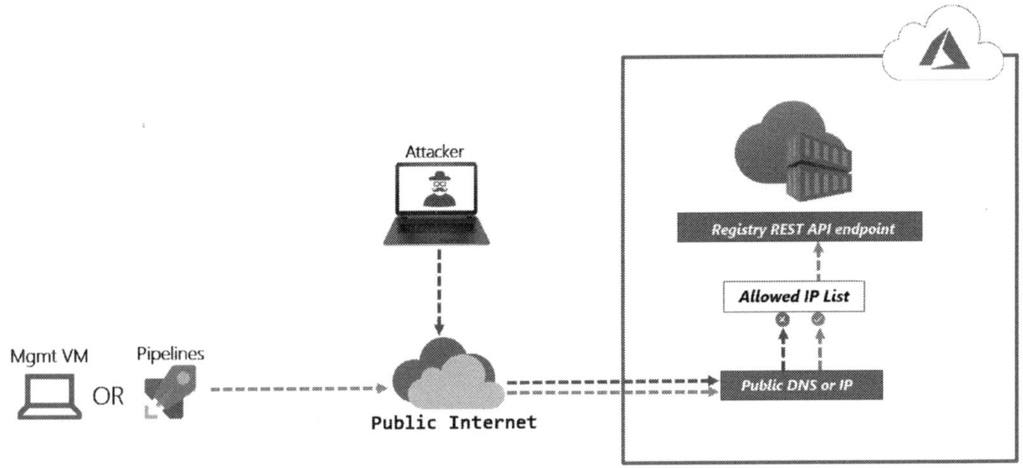

Figure 9.9 – ACR service firewall rules

This feature is only available to the premium container registry service tier, and there is a limit of 100 network access rules. To implement this feature from the Azure portal, we can modify the network settings, as shown in *Figure 9.10*:

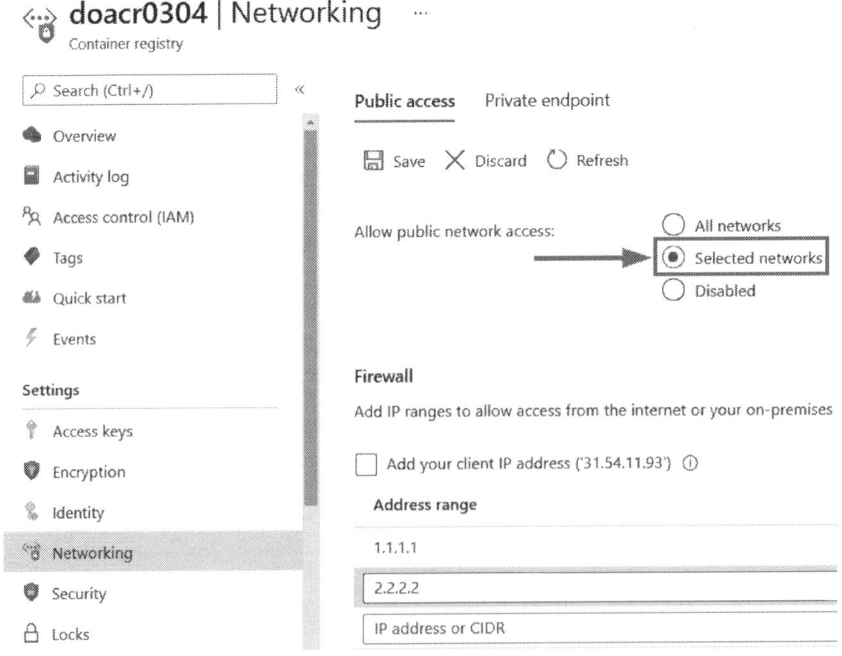

Figure 9.10 – Configuring the service firewall rule

Additionally, we can use the Azure CLI command-line tool to implement this in two steps. First, we need to change the default action to deny access. Second, we need to allow our trusted IP address. Here are the commands to complete this:

```
az acr update --name <acr_name> --default-action Deny
az acr network-rule add --name <acr_name> --ip-address
<trusted-ip-address>
```

In some cases, we might want to go further than simply restricting access through the registry's public endpoint. For instance, we might want to eliminate exposure to the public internet. This is where the next best practice of using a private endpoint can be of help.

Restricting access using a private endpoint

A private endpoint allows clients located in our private networks to securely access the registry over a private link using a private IP address (please refer to *Figure 9.11*). This feature eliminates exposing our container registry to the internet and reduces the risk of data exfiltration.

To use this capability, we require the premium container registry service tier. It is important to note that once this capability has been enabled, **Azure Security Center** (**ASC**) cannot perform image vulnerability scanning for that registry. Enhanced container security solutions such as Palo Alto Prisma Cloud Compute (formerly known as Twistlock) can still scan images for this scenario:

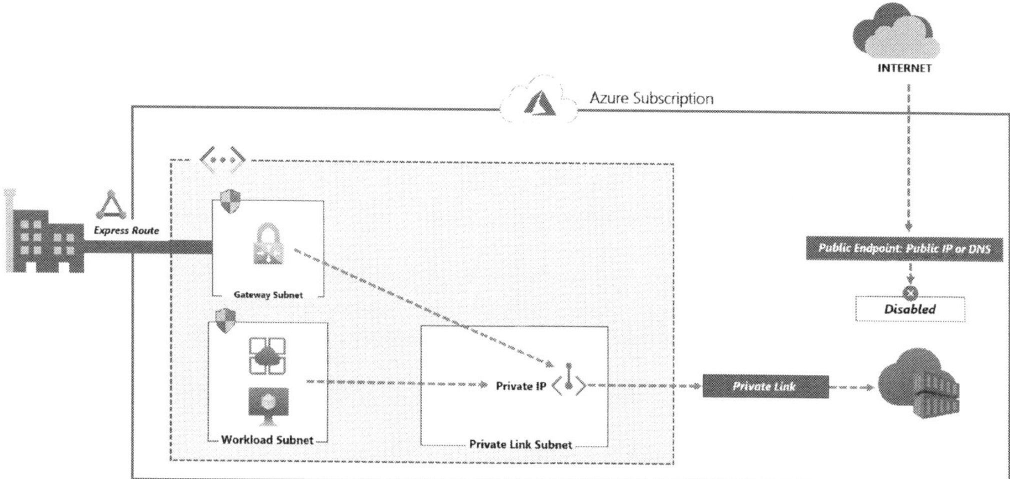

Figure 9.11 – ACR's private endpoint

To implement this feature from the Azure portal, we can modify the network settings of the container registry. We can also implement it using Azure CLI or Azure PowerShell. The process is covered in the official documentation, which can be found at `https://docs.microsoft.com/en-us/azure/container-registry/container-registry-private-link`.

Using Azure AD RBAC for secure authentication and access control

To perform registry management operations against the ACR's API endpoint, the client needs to be authenticated and authorized to perform the operation that is being requested. There are three main ways to authenticate with ACR:

- Using the admin user
- Using an Azure AD identity
- Using an authentication token

The first authentication method is to use the admin user. Every container registry includes an admin user account that has unrestricted permissions to perform any operation. Because the account has full access, it should be treated with extreme care. It is disabled by default, but it can be enabled using the Azure portal, as shown in *Figure 9.12*. It can also be enabled using other management tools, such as Azure CLI and Azure PowerShell:

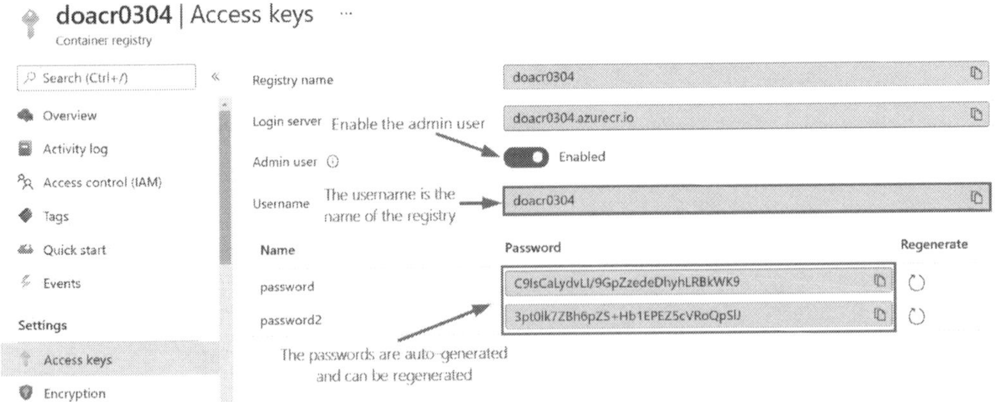

Figure 9.12 – Enabling the ACR admin user

To authenticate with the admin user account, we can specify the name of our registry as the username and one of the automatically generated passwords (*Figure 9.12*). The primary downside of this authentication method is that all clients that authenticate with this account will appear as a single user in the logs. This is not good for auditing in the case of an incident.

The best practice is to keep this account disabled and use an authentication method, such as Azure AD, that supports an individual identity per client. This can be governed at scale using Azure Policy. We will cover Azure Policy in *Chapter 13, Azure Cloud Governance and Security Operations.*

The second authentication method is to use an Azure AD identity admin user. This could be a user identity, a service principal, or a managed identity. **Service principals** are great for non-interactive clients such as **Continuous Integration** (**CI**) pipelines that are used to automate the build of container images and publish them to the registry. **Managed identities** are great for non-interactive clients that run on Azure services that support managed identities such as a Docker VM or Kubernetes service cluster. **User identities** are great for developers and DevOps engineers that need to interact with the container registry.

To assign permissions to Azure AD identities, we use Azure RBAC. When assigning permissions, the best practice is to follow the principle of least privilege, that is, do not assign more permissions than what is needed for the task:

Role/Permission	Access Resource Manager	Create/delete registry	Push image	Pull image	Delete image data	Change policies	Sign images
Owner	X	X	X	X	X	X	
Contributor	X	X	X	X	X	X	
Reader	X			X			
AcrPush			X	X			
AcrPull				X			
AcrDelete					X		
AcrImageSigner							X

Figure 9.13 – ACR RBAC roles

For example, if a container runtime node needs to be able to pull images from the registry, the **AcrPull** role is sufficient for that (the **Reader** role gives permissions to the management plane, which, in this case, is not needed). *Figure 9.13* shows the built-in roles and the associated permissions.

RBAC for container registries can be configured from the Azure portal, as shown in *Figure 9.14*. Additionally, we can configure RBAC using other Azure management tools such as PowerShell and CLI:

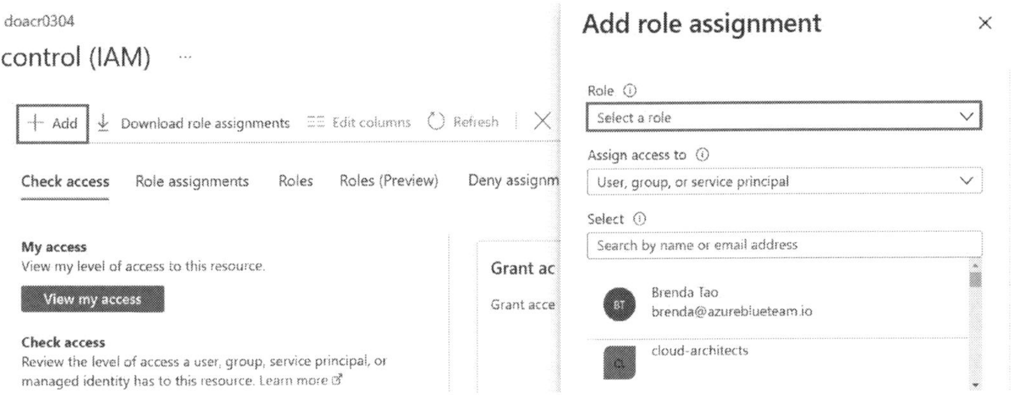

Figure 9.14 – Add role assignment

While the built-in roles are sufficient for most use cases, we can also create custom roles to use for permission assignments.

The third option (using an authentication token) is currently in preview as, at the time of writing, it is only available to the premium tier of ACR. It allows us to generate tokens that give permissions on a repository level.

Implementing container image vulnerability and compliance scanning

Container images could include libraries and dependencies that are out of date or vulnerable. They could also include sensitive secrets and keys or insecure configurations. Our objective is to mitigate the risk of deploying vulnerable container images to runtime from our container registries. To achieve this, we can ensure that images stored in the registry are continually scanned for vulnerabilities and compliance.

ASC, which we will cover in the last chapter of this book, has a feature, called **Azure Defender for container registries**, that we can use to implement a container vulnerability assessment. This feature requires the standard tier of ASC and relies on a third-party service (such as Qualys) to perform the vulnerability assessment:

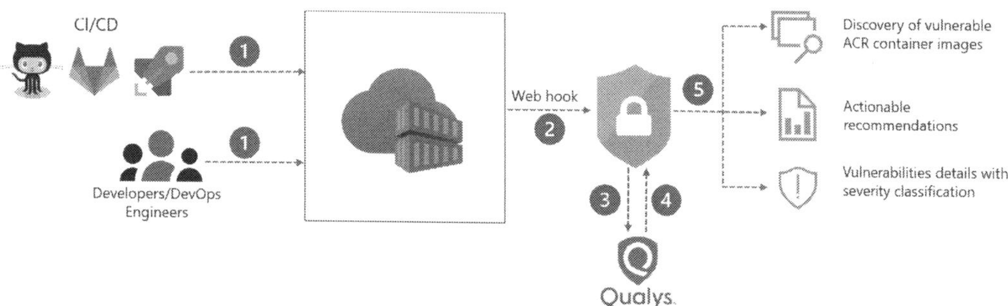

Figure 9.15 – Azure Defender for container registries

Figure 9.15 shows an example flow for this. After a new container image is pushed into the registry (**1**), a webhook is triggered in ASC (**2**), and this triggers an image scan.

The image is pulled from the registry (**3**). It is then run in an isolated sandbox environment with the Qualys scanner, which extracts a list of known vulnerabilities. The results are returned to ASC (**4**), which alerts us to any detected issues along with actionable recommendations (**5**).

While this feature of ASC is better than nothing, it is worth noting that it is also limited in its capabilities. For example, it does not support the scanning of private registries, Windows images, and super-minimalist images. It is also limited in the assessment that it does, as it only supports the scanning of vulnerabilities and not compliance. **To support a more comprehensive container scanning scenario, third-party services such as the Prisma Cloud Compute solution (formerly known as Twistlock) can be implemented.**

This feature can be enabled by enabling the Azure Defender for container registries feature of Security Center; you will be doing this in the hands-on exercise next.

Hands-on exercise – securing ACR

In this exercise, we will complete the following tasks:

- **Task 1**: Disable the Admin user for ACR.
- **Task 2**: Configure RBAC for ACR.
- **Task 3**: Enable Azure Defender for ACR for image vulnerability assessment.
- **Task 4**: Authenticate and push images to ACR.

Here are the steps to complete the preceding tasks:

1. Open a web browser and browse to `https://portal.azure.com`.

   In the search box at the top of the screen, type in `azseccr` and click on the container registry resource:

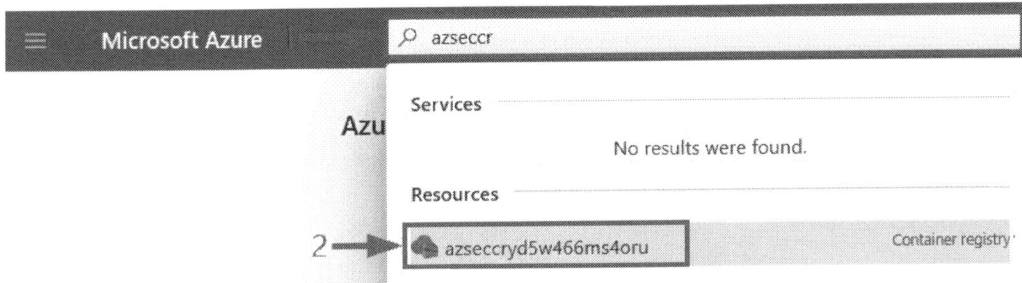

Figure 9.16 – Searching for the container registry

2. In the **Container registry** window, click on **Access keys** underneath the **Settings** section. Review the admin account username and passwords. Note that the passwords can be regenerated:

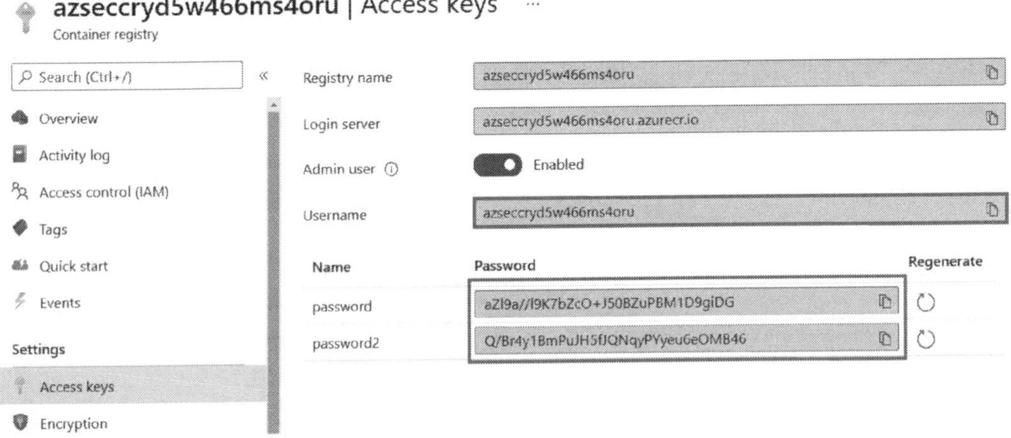

Figure 9.17 – Reviewing the ACR admin credentials

3. Make a note of the registry name and the login server address (you will need them in *steps 14*, *16*, and *17* of this exercise). Then, click to disable the **Admin user**:

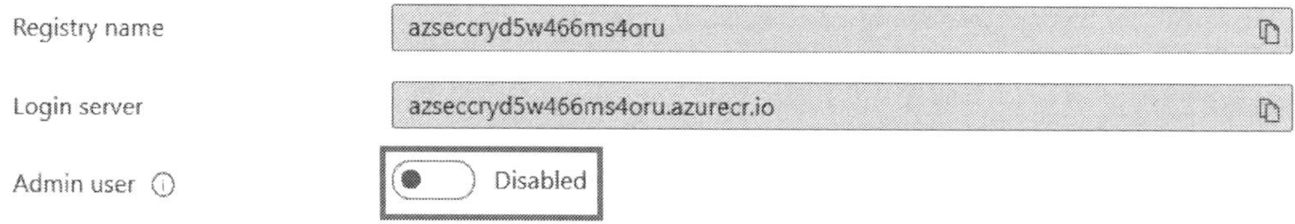

Figure 9.18 – Making a note of the admin credentials

Next, we will configure RBAC to give a system-managed identity the permission to push images to the registry.

4. In the container registry blade, click on **Access control (IAM)**. Then, click on **Add role assignments**:

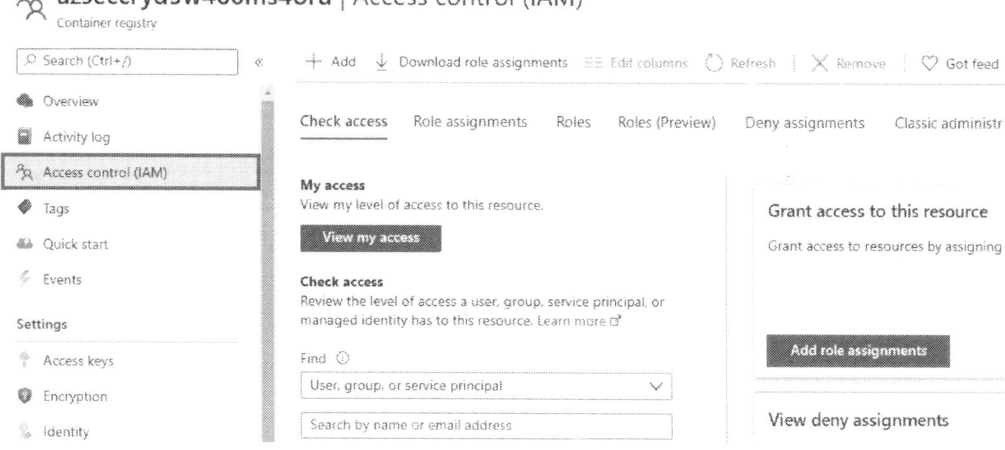

Figure 9.19 – Adding a role assignment

5. In the **Add role assignment** blade, configure the following:

   Role: AcrPush.

   Assign access to: User, group, or service principal.

   Select: Search for and select `azseclinvm`.

   Click on **Save**:

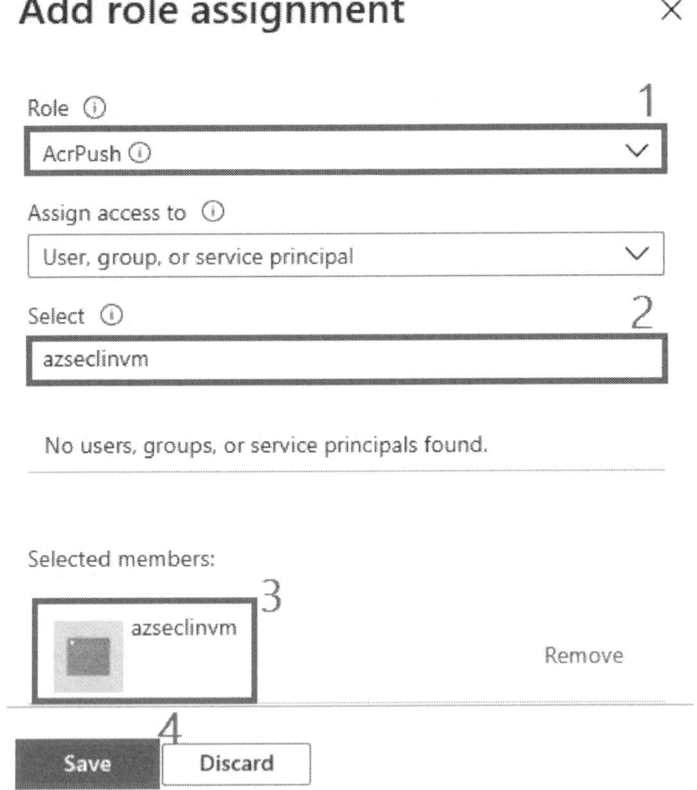

Figure 9.20 – Configuring the role assignment

We have now successfully assigned the AcrPush role to the Linux VM's system-managed identity. This gives it the permission to push images into the registry but nothing else. We will verify this later in this exercise.

Next, we will enable Azure Defender for container registries, which will ensure that images in container registries are assessed for vulnerabilities.

6. In the **Settings** section, click on **Security**. Then, click on the **Security Center** link. This opens Security Center in a new browser tab:

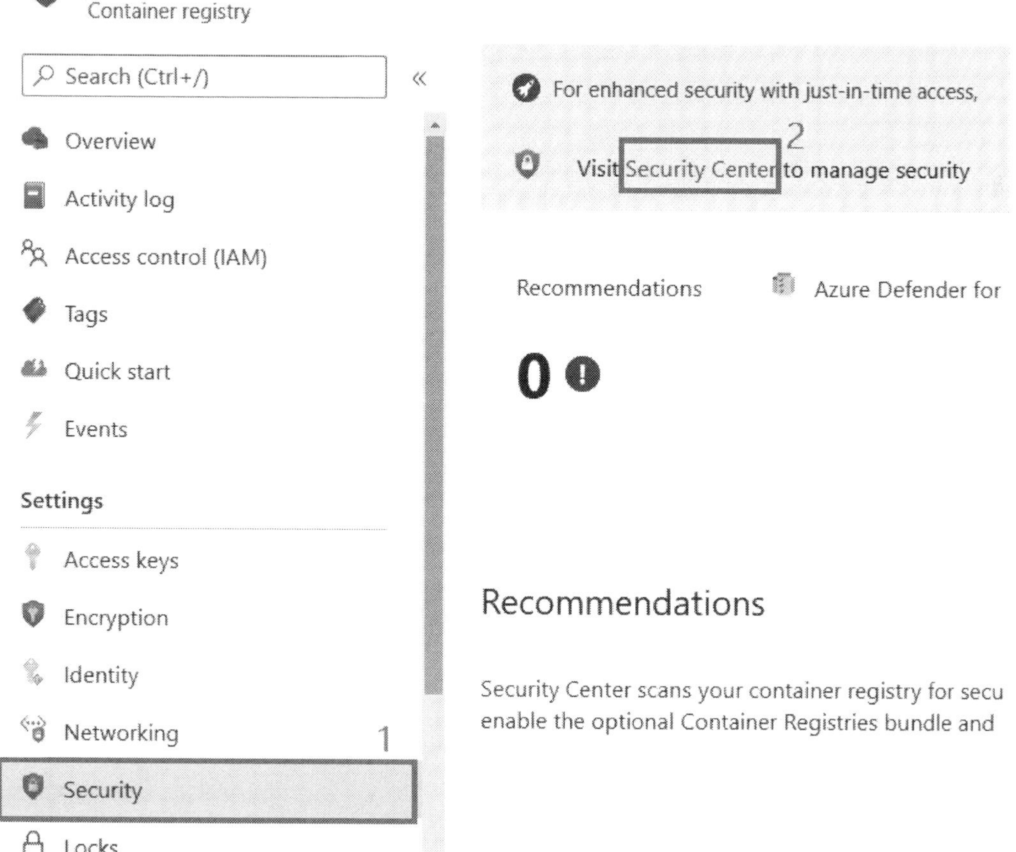

Figure 9.21 – Clicking on Security Center

7. In the **Security Center** window, in the **Cloud Security** section, click on **Azure Defender**. Then, click on **Enable Azure Defender**:

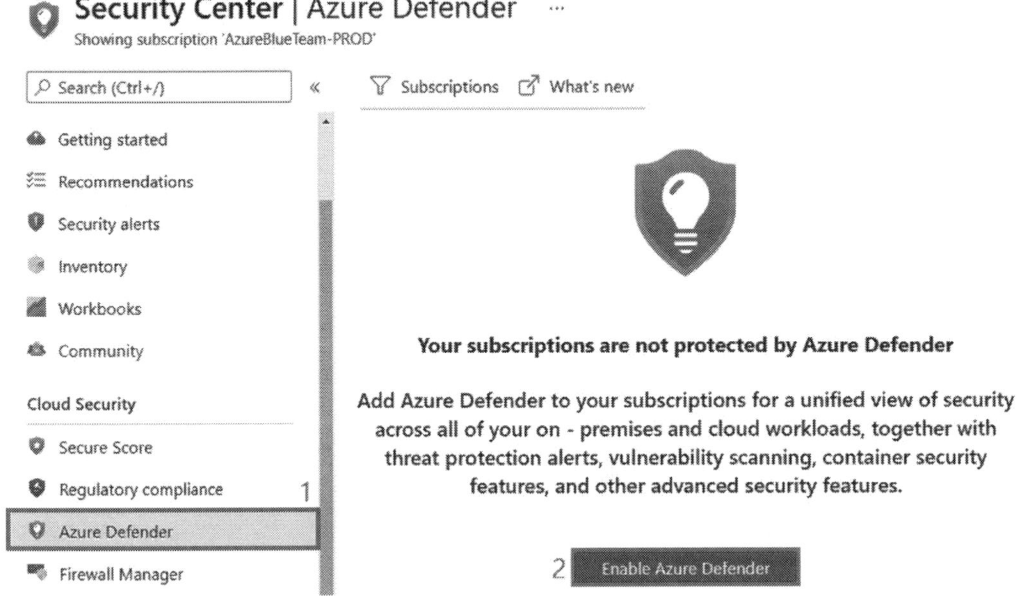

Figure 9.22 – Enabling Azure Defender

8. In the **Getting started** window, ensure that your subscription is selected, then click on **Upgrade**. This enables Azure Defender for supported resources in that subscription. You should be able to view the supported resources listed, including the container registry images:

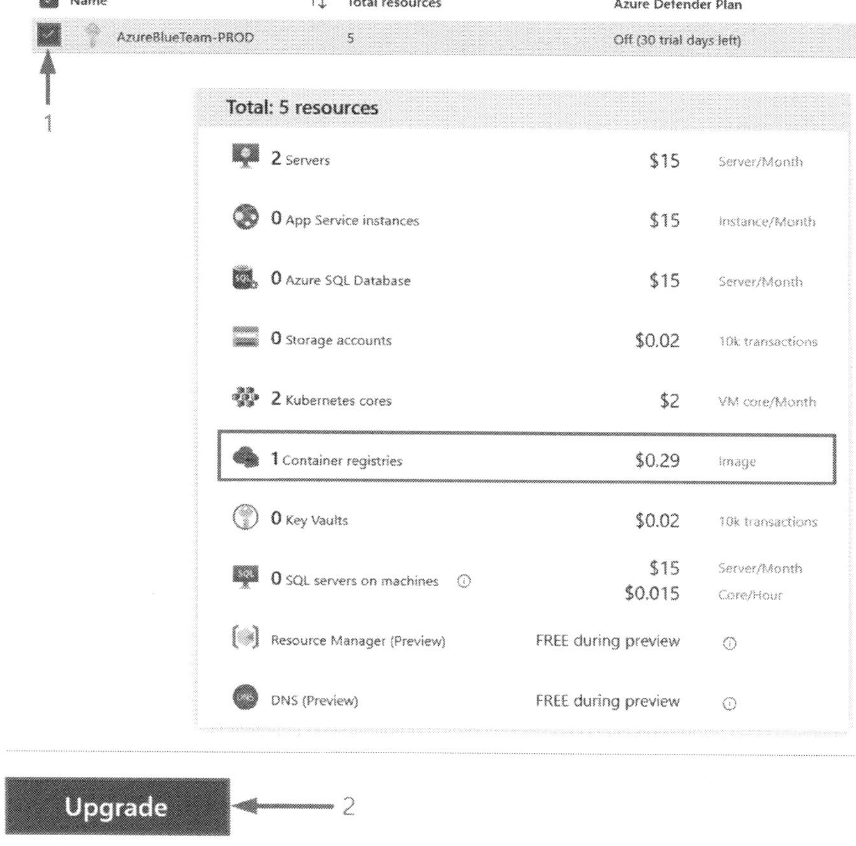

Figure 9.23 – Upgrading the Security Center SKU for subscription

9. Close the **Getting started** window. DO NOT install the agents:

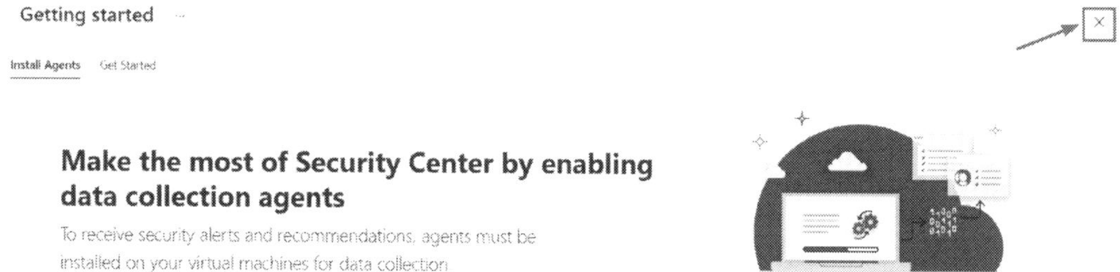

Figure 9.24 – Closing the Getting started window

10. Back in the ASC main window, in the Azure Defender pane (you might need to refresh the browser to get an updated view), pay attention to the container registries that are now protected by Azure Defender. This means we now have vulnerability assessment enabled for images in the container registries:

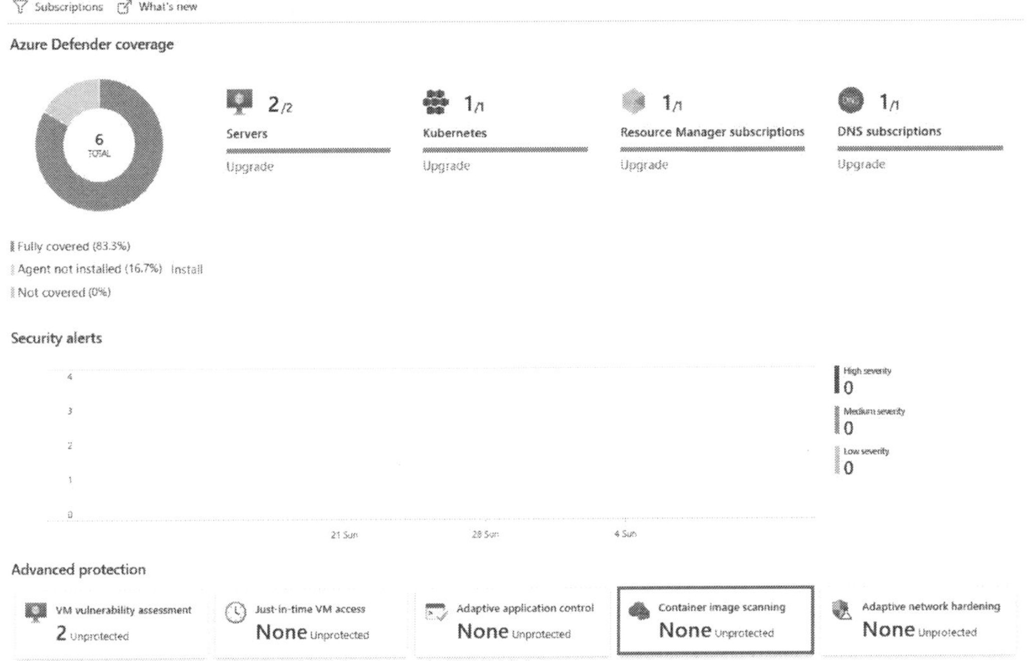

Figure 9.25 – Clicking on Container image scanning

11. Use an SSH client, such as PuTTY, to connect to the Linux VM that was deployed as part of the template earlier in this chapter (please refer to the *Hands-on exercise – providing resources for the chapter exercises* section). Use the DNS name that you made a note of earlier:

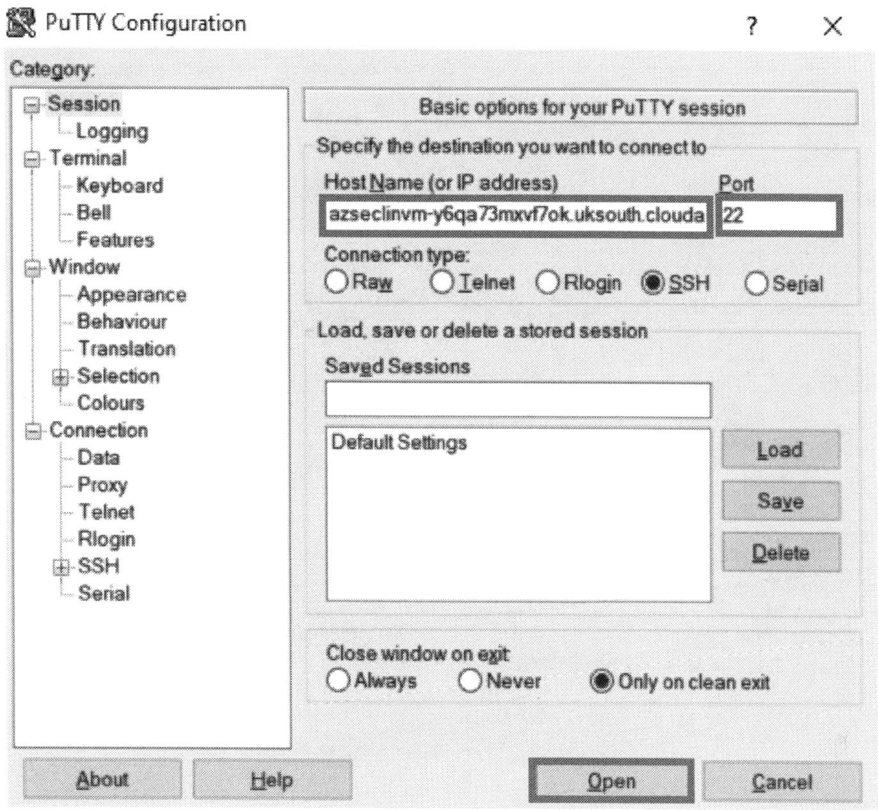

Figure 9.26 – SSHing into the Linux VM

12. When prompted, authenticate using the following credentials:

    Username: `azureadmin`.

    Password: Enter the password that you entered during template deployment.

13. To push images to the registry, first, we need to switch to the root user and authenticate with Azure CLI using the system-assigned identity of the VM. To do this, use the following commands:

```
sudo su -
az login --identity
```

Here is a screenshot of the output:

```
azureadmin@azseclinvm:~$
azureadmin@azseclinvm:~$ sudo su -
root@azseclinvm:~#
root@azseclinvm:~# az login --identity
[
  {
    "environmentName": "AzureCloud",
    "homeTenantId": "7f3e6937-b492-49e7-9856-07d84e1cf2ae",
    "id": "1c63ad39-68ee-444a-90a8-a2ccaf67f671",
    "isDefault": true,
    "managedByTenants": [],
    "name": "AzureBlueTeam-PROD",
    "state": "Enabled",
    "tenantId": "7f3e6937-b492-49e7-9856-07d84e1cf2ae",
    "user": {
      "assignedIdentityInfo": "MSI",
      "name": "systemAssignedIdentity",
      "type": "servicePrincipal"
    }
  }
]
```

Figure 9.27 – Authenticating to Azure CLI

14. Next, we will authenticate to the container registry with `az acr login`. This command uses the token that we created earlier when we ran the `az login` command. Replace `<acrName>` with the name that you made a note of in *step 3* of this exercise:

```
az acr login --name <acrName>
```

You should get a **Login Succeeded** message, as shown in the following screenshot:

```
root@azseclinvm:~#
root@azseclinvm:~# az acr login --name azseccryd5w466ms4oru
Login Succeeded
root@azseclinvm:~#
```

Figure 9.28 – Verifying a successful login

15. To view a list of current local images, switch to the root privilege and use the `docker images` command, as follows:

```
docker images
```

You should see a single node image, as shown in the following screenshot:

```
root@azseclinvm:~#
root@azseclinvm:~# docker images
REPOSITORY          TAG             IMAGE ID          CREATED           SIZE
node                13.5-alpine     e1495e4ac50d      15 months ago     111MB
root@azseclinvm:~#
```

Figure 9.29 – Listing images in the local cache

16. To push the local image to the container registry, first, we need to tag it with the login server address of the registry. Replace `<acrLoginServer>` with the login server value that you made a note of in *step 3*:

```
docker tag node:13.5-alpine <acrLoginServer>/node:13.5-
alpine
```

Here is a screenshot of this:

```
root@azseclinvm:~#
root@azseclinvm:~# docker tag node:13.5-alpine azseccryd5w466ms4oru.azurecr.io/node:13.5-alpine
root@azseclinvm:~#
root@azseclinvm:~# docker images
REPOSITORY                              TAG             IMAGE ID          CREATED
 SIZE
azseccryd5w466ms4oru.azurecr.io/node    13.5-alpine     e1495e4ac50d      15 months ago
 111MB
node                                    13.5-alpine     e1495e4ac50d      15 months ago
 111MB
root@azseclinvm:~#
```

Figure 9.30 – Tagging an image with the registry address

17. Push the image to ACR using the `docker push` command. Replace `<acrLoginServer>` with the login server value that you made a note of earlier:

```
docker push <acrLoginServer>/node:13.5-alpine
```

Here is a screenshot of this:

```
root@azseclinvm:~#
root@azseclinvm:~# docker push azseccryd5w466ms4oru.azurecr.io/node:13.5-alpine
The push refers to repository [azseccryd5w466ms4oru.azurecr.io/node]
efd6e0da275f: Pushed
b352b61d0fe4: Pushed
d06ff5e5272b: Pushed
6b27de954cca: Pushed
13.5-alpine: digest: sha256:990e2a5ecd6419bfd1ae1af8dc585924712614e9cc79999d943c
 1158
```

Figure 9.31 – Pushing the image into the container registry

18. If you go back to the container registry in the Azure portal, in the **Repositories** section, you should now be able to view the image there:

Figure 9.32 – Viewing the image in the registry

19. Go back to the SSH session of the Linux VM. Let's attempt to list the container registries in the Azure subscription using the following command:

```
az acr list
```

The list returned will be empty, as shown in the following screenshot. This is because the assigned role does not have permission to do this:

```
root@azseclinvm:~#
root@azseclinvm:~# az acr list
[]
root@azseclinvm:~#
```

Figure 9.33 – Listing images in the registry

Congratulations! You have now successfully implemented some security best practices for ACR. In the next section, we will take a look at one of the container runtime options that we mentioned earlier, that is, AKS.

Introducing AKS

Kubernetes is an open source container orchestration solution for automating the deployment, scaling, and management of containerized workloads. It offers all the elements of orchestration that we described earlier in this chapter. It was initially designed by Google, but it has now been donated to the **Cloud Native Computing Foundation (CNCF)** who now maintains it.

So, what is the relationship between AKS and native Kubernetes? Put simply, deploying Kubernetes by ourselves and configuring the infrastructure needed from scratch is a complex process. AKS abstracts these complexities from us by providing a managed Kubernetes service. We simply specify what our Kubernetes cluster should look like and the Azure platform builds it for us!

Understanding the AKS architecture

A Kubernetes cluster is divided into two components. The **control plane** provides the core Kubernetes services and orchestration of application workloads (marked in red in *Figure 9.34*), while the **worker nodes** run our containerized application workloads (marked in purple in *Figure 9.34*):

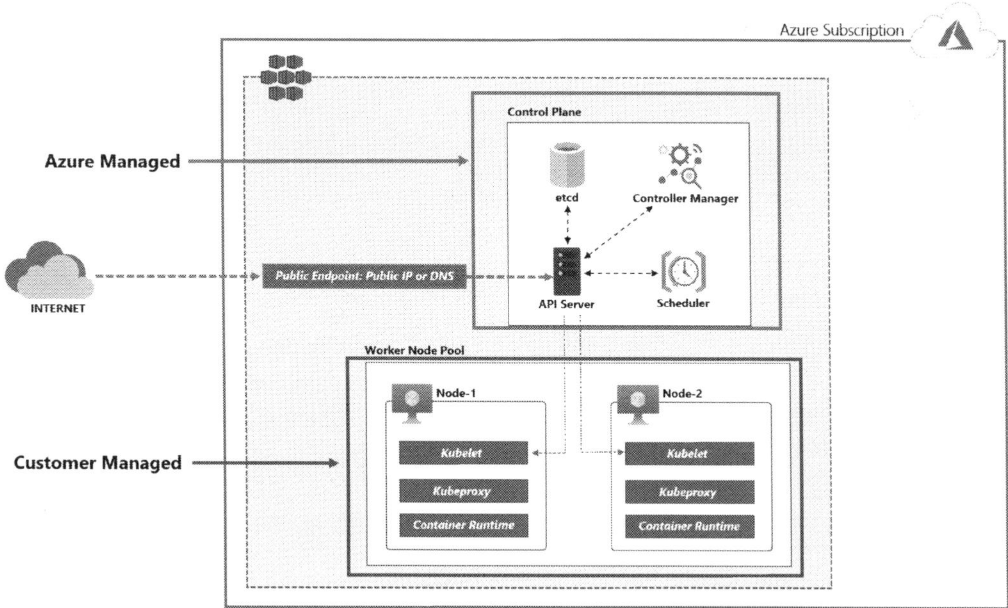

Figure 9.34 – The AKS architecture

The worker node pools can either be a Linux OS pool, a Windows OS pool, or a combination of Linux and Windows pools. For Linux OS pools, the default base image uses Ubuntu 18.04 if the Kubernetes version is 1.18 or higher. If it is less, it uses Ubuntu 16.04 as the default base image.

A container runtime is software that executes containers and manages container images on a node. The runtime helps abstract away sys-calls or OS-specific functionality to run containers on Linux or Windows. AKS clusters using Kubernetes version 1.19 node pools and greater use `containerd` as their container runtime. In comparison, AKS clusters using Kubernetes prior to v1.19 for node pools use Moby (upstream Docker) as their container runtime.

Native Kubernetes has a rich ecosystem of development and management tools such as Helm, Draft, and the Kubernetes extension for Visual Studio Code. These tools work seamlessly with AKS.

AKS security best practices

There are multiple attack vectors that an adversary could exploit to compromise our AKS instances. For this reason, our security strategy should follow a defense-in-depth approach that includes multiple layers of protection. In the following sections, we will cover some of these layers.

Limiting access to the API server using authorized IP address ranges

The Kubernetes API server is the central management endpoint for an AKS cluster. Developers and administrators use client management tools, such as `kubectl`, to connect to it to perform cluster operations such as deploying applications, creating cluster objects, and scaling the number of nodes.

By default, the API server uses a public IP address with access to any IP address. From a security perspective, our objective should be to minimize any attacks on the Kubernetes control plane components. One way to do this is to limit the IP addresses that can communicate with the API server using the authorized IP range feature:

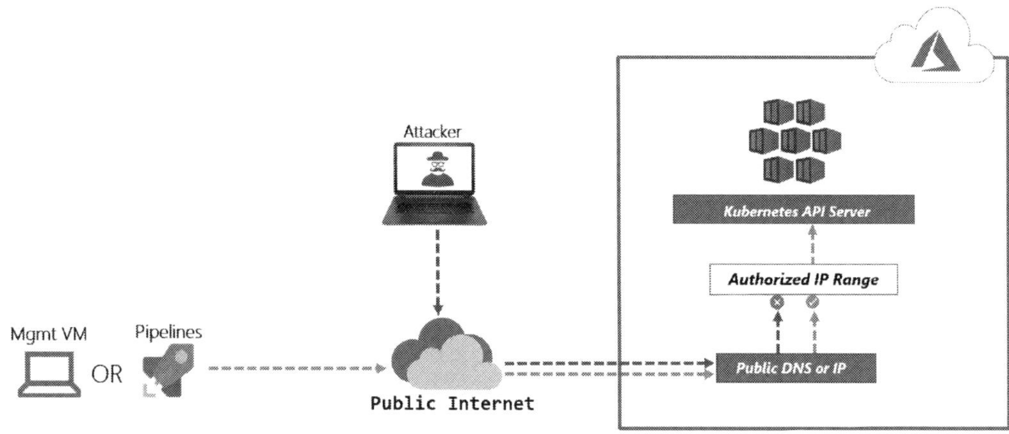

Figure 9.35 – The AKS authorized IP range

This feature enables us to apply an IP filter list that only allows trusted public IP addresses to communicate with the API server. To implement this feature from the Azure portal, we can modify the networking settings of the AKS service, as shown in *Figure 9.36*:

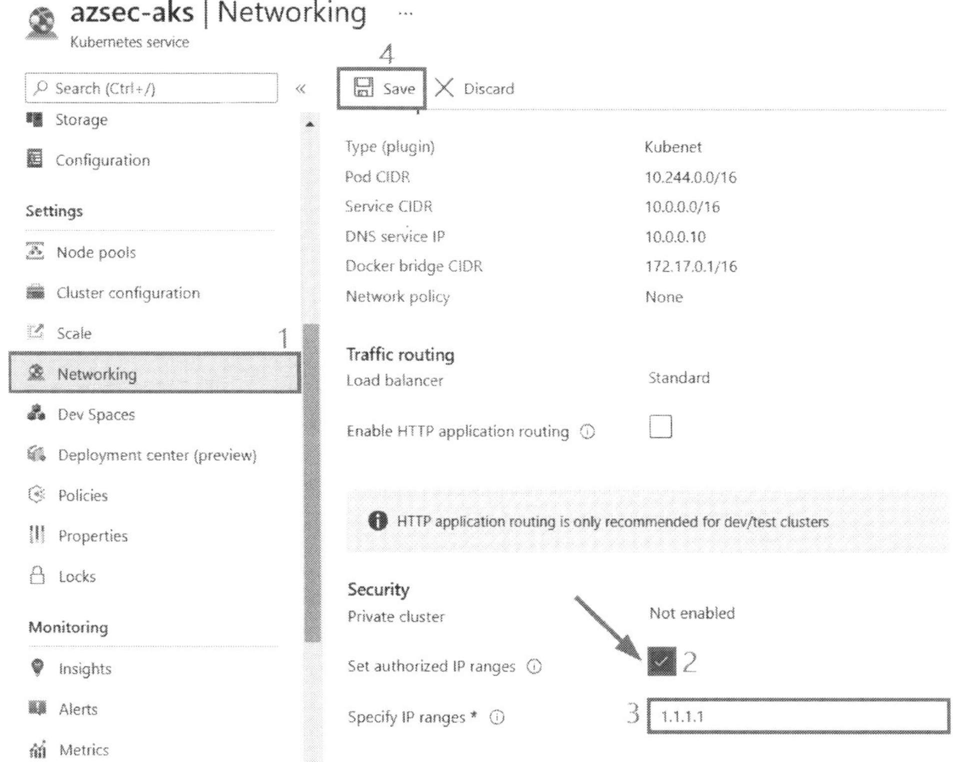

Figure 9.36 – Modifying the AKS authorized IP range

We can also use the Azure CLI command-line tool to implement this feature. For an existing cluster, you can do this using the following commands:

```
az aks update --resource-group <resource_group_name> --name
<aks_cluster_name> --api-server-authorized-ip-ranges  <ip_
address_range>
```

In some cases, we might want to go further than simply restricting access through the API server's public endpoint. For instance, we might want to eliminate any exposure to the public internet altogether. This is where the next best practice of using a private endpoint can be of help.

Implementing a private AKS cluster using a private endpoint

A private endpoint allows clients located in our private networks to securely access the AKS cluster over a private link using a private IP address (*Figure 9.37*). This feature eliminates exposing our cluster to the internet and reduces the risk of data exfiltration:

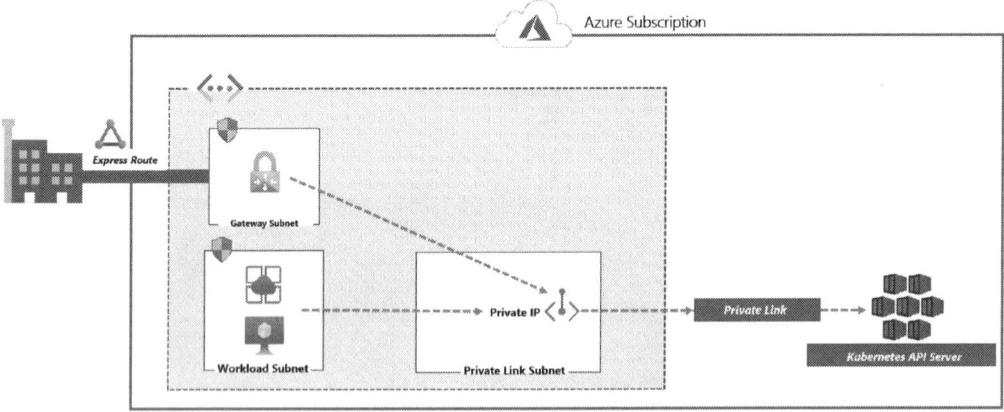

Figure 9.37 – An AKS private endpoint

When enabled, the cluster API server endpoint has no public IP address, as shown in *Figure 9.37*. This way, we can ensure that network traffic remains on the private network. The implementation of this feature can be carried out with the Azure CLI. The process is covered in the official documentation at `https://docs.microsoft.com/en-us/azure/aks/private-clusters`.

Controlling access to cluster resources using Kubernetes RBAC and Azure AD

To perform any cluster operation on the Kubernetes API server (for example, creating or deleting resources), users must be authenticated and authorized to perform the requested action.

AKS can be configured to use Azure AD for user authentication. This helps us to centralize identity management, with Azure AD as the single source of validating user identities. And if you have a hybrid identity set up, as we discussed in *Chapter 4, Azure AD Identity Security*, you can also authenticate with on-premises identities.

When this feature is implemented, we can use Azure AD users, groups, or service principals as subjects in Kubernetes RBAC. To make sense of how Azure AD will work with Kubernetes RBAC, let's spend a few moments reviewing how Kubernetes RBAC works.

Kubernetes uses an RBAC system to define and assign the actions that users can perform in a cluster. The permissions can be defined as either *Roles* or *ClusterRoles*. To grant permissions within a namespace (logical grouping) in a cluster, we define a *Role*. To grant permissions at the cluster level, we define a *ClusterRole*. *Figure 9.38* shows a side-by-side comparison of an example `Role` definition and an example `ClusterRole` definition. You can see that the `ClusterRole` definition does not have namespace metadata defined, as it grants permissions across the cluster:

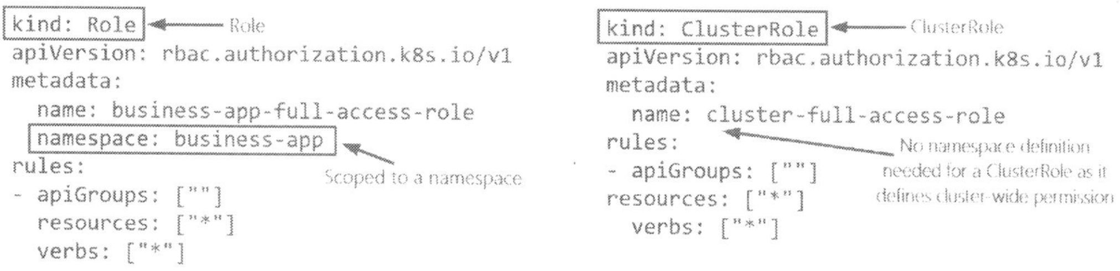

```
kind: Role
apiVersion: rbac.authorization.k8s.io/v1
metadata:
  name: business-app-full-access-role
  namespace: business-app
rules:
- apiGroups: [""]
  resources: ["*"]
  verbs: ["*"]
```

Role

Scoped to a namespace

```
kind: ClusterRole
apiVersion: rbac.authorization.k8s.io/v1
metadata:
  name: cluster-full-access-role
rules:
- apiGroups: [""]
resources: ["*"]
  verbs: ["*"]
```

ClusterRole

No namespace definition needed for a ClusterRole as it defines cluster-wide permission

Figure 9.38 – The Role and ClusterRole definitions

Once we have defined roles to grant permissions to the resources, we can assign the permissions using either a `RoleBinding` or a `ClusterRoleBinding`. To assign permissions to users for a given namespace, we use `RoleBinding`. To assign permissions across the entire cluster, we use `ClusterRoleBinding`. *Figure 9.39* shows examples of `RoleBinding` and `ClusterRoleBinding` with Azure AD identities defined as subjects for both of the bindings:

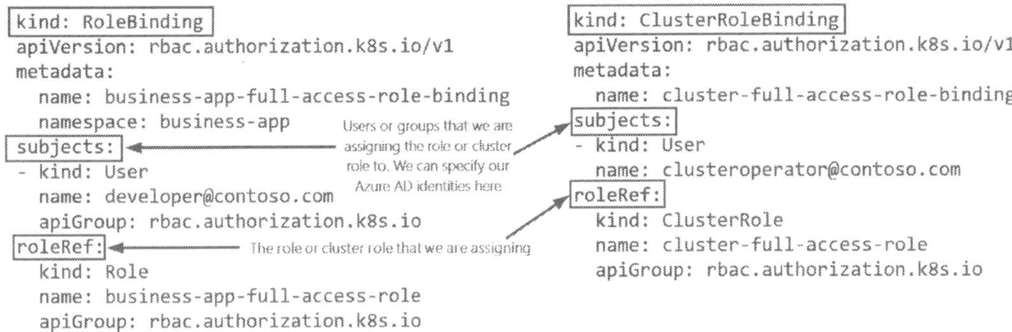

kind: RoleBinding
apiVersion: rbac.authorization.k8s.io/v1
metadata:
name: business-app-full-access-role-binding
namespace: business-app
subjects:
- kind: User
name: developer@contoso.com
apiGroup: rbac.authorization.k8s.io
roleRef:
kind: Role
name: business-app-full-access-role
apiGroup: rbac.authorization.k8s.io
Users or groups that we are assigning the role or cluster role to. We can specify our Azure AD identities here
The role or cluster role that we are assigning
kind: ClusterRoleBinding
apiVersion: rbac.authorization.k8s.io/v1
metadata:
name: cluster-full-access-role-binding
subjects:
- kind: User
name: clusteroperator@contoso.com
roleRef:
kind: ClusterRole
name: cluster-full-access-role
apiGroup: rbac.authorization.k8s.io

Figure 9.39 – The RoleBinding and ClusterRoleBinding definitions

It is worth noting that Microsoft is extending this integration further with a new feature that is currently in preview. This feature will allow us to grant access to the Kubernetes resources using Azure RBAC, which will further simplify access control for AKS. You can read more about this feature at `https://docs.microsoft.com/en-us/azure/aks/manage-azure-rbac`.

Regularly upgrading the cluster control plane

Whenever a new version of Kubernetes is released by the community, Microsoft makes this available to AKS, but we have to upgrade either using the portal or a command-line tool such as Azure CLI. A good security practice is to perform periodic upgrades to the latest Kubernetes version. This ensures that we apply the latest security releases and can use these new features. The window of support from Kubernetes 1.19 is one year, so you will be expected to upgrade once a year to stay in support.

The upgrade process itself should have no impact on our workloads, as the cluster will trigger a cordon and drain of the nodes in a rolling fashion. To perform this operation, we can use the Azure portal or the Azure CLI tool. In the Azure portal, we can review the **Cluster configuration** section of our AKS resource to view any available upgrades and trigger the process (*Figure 9.40*):

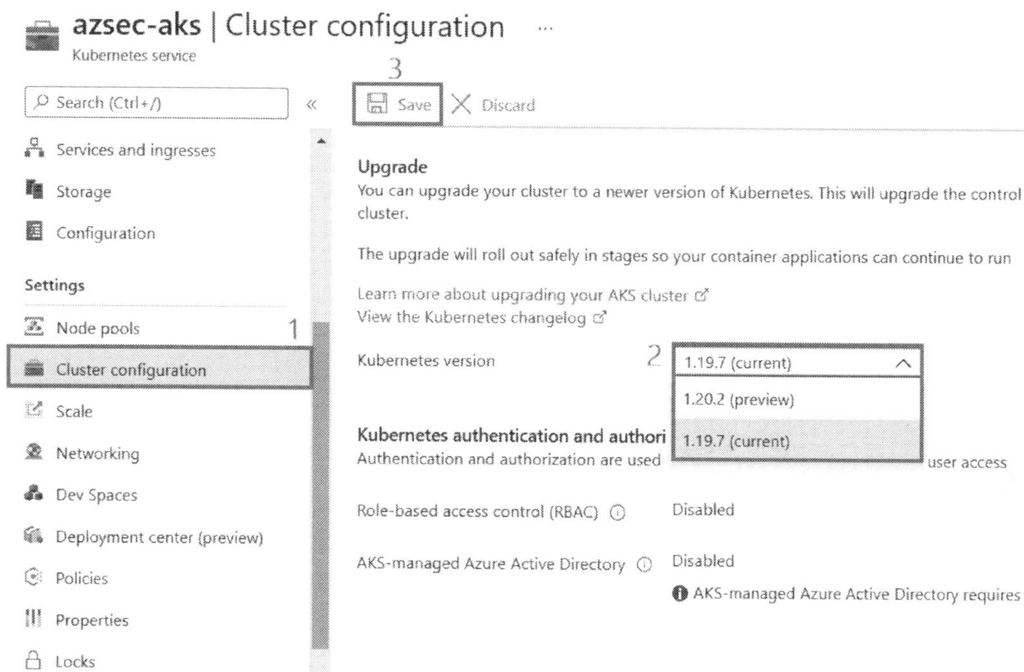

Figure 9.40 – Upgrading the Kubernetes version

If we are using the Azure CLI for the process, we can use the following command to check for available upgrades:

```
az aks get-upgrades --resource-group <resource_group> --name
<aks_cluster_name> --output table
```

We can trigger the upgrade process using the following command:

```
az aks upgrade --resource-group <resource_group> --name <aks_
cluster_name> --kubernetes-version <Kubernetes_version>
```

Another point that is worth noting is that we cannot skip minor upgrades when performing the process. For example, we cannot upgrade from version 1.18.X to version 1.20.X without upgrading to version 1.19.X first.

Regularly applying OS updates to worker nodes

The node OS upgrade process is different depending on which node pools you have implemented – Linux or Windows.

Security updates are automatically downloaded and applied to Linux nodes in AKS. These updates include OS security fixes or kernel updates. Some of these updates might require a node reboot to complete the process. In this case, AKS does not automatically reboot these Linux nodes to complete the update process. To address this scenario, a solution such as **kured** (which is short for **KU**bernetes **RE**boot **D**aemon) can be used to watch the Linux nodes for pending reboots. If a pending reboot is detected, the node is drained and the workloads running on it are moved to other nodes in the cluster. Once the reboot has been completed, the node is added back to the cluster and pods can be scheduled to run on it. To minimize the risk of disruption, kured is permitted to reboot only one node at a time.

For Windows nodes, the latest updates are not automatically applied. We need to monitor for updates and apply them using our own processes.

For both Linux and Windows nodes, there is an alternative to relying on an update process to apply the latest OS security fixes. This alternative is to swap the OS image. AKS provides one new image per week with the latest OS and container runtime patches installed. These releases can be reviewed at `https://github.com/Azure/AKS/releases`. Whenever we upgrade the Kubernetes version of our cluster, as described earlier, the OS images are also swapped with the image version that has the latest OS and runtime updates installed. However, we can trigger this process outside of a Kubernetes version upgrade by specifying the `--node-image-only` parameter, as follows:

```
az aks upgrade --resource-group myResourceGroup --name
myAKSCluster --node-image-only
```

To verify whether our node pool is on the latest node image, we can use the following command:

```
az aks nodepool get-upgrades --nodepool-name <nodepool_name>
--cluster-name <aks_cluster_name> --resource-group <resource_
group>
```

In the next section, we will discuss pod-managed identities.

Implementing pod-managed identities

There are numerous scenarios where pods running in Kubernetes require access to other Azure services. One common scenario is when a pod needs to retrieve secrets or keys in the Azure key vault at runtime. The best practice for this scenario is to use pod-managed identities that are linked in Azure AD. Note that this feature is in preview at the time of writing, and it only works for Linux pods and containers (support for Windows containers is coming soon).

When implemented, this feature enables our applications running in AKS to dynamically obtain an Azure AD token that can be used to access other Azure services. Each pod that requires access, first, needs to be assigned a unique Azure AD managed identity. When pods request access to an Azure service, the traffic is automatically redirected to the **Node Management Identity** (**NMI**) server. NMI identifies the pod that requests access and checks for Azure identity mappings in the AKS cluster. Then, NMI requests an access token from Azure AD based on the pod's identity mapping. Azure AD provides an access token to NMI, which is returned to the pod. This pod can then use the access token to access services in Azure:

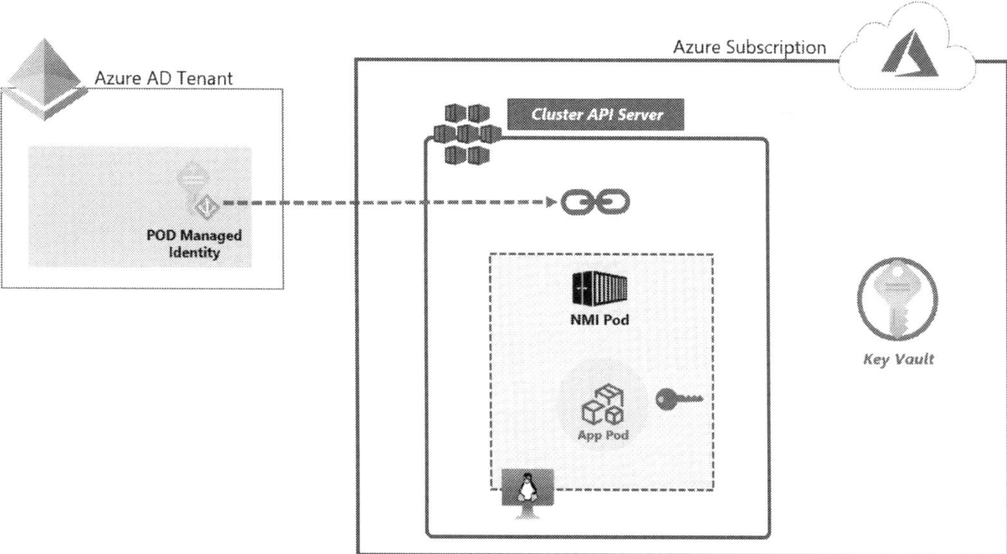

Figure 9.41 – AKS POD Managed Identity

Two components handle the operations that allow our pods to use managed identities. They are as follows:

- **The NMI server**: This is a pod that runs as a DaemonSet on each node in the AKS cluster. The NMI server listens for pod requests to Azure services.
- **The Azure resource provider**: This queries the Kubernetes API server and checks for an Azure identity mapping that corresponds to a pod.

In the next hands-on exercise, we will grant an Azure AD user (Brenda) access to Kubernetes resources using Kubernetes RBAC.

Hands-on exercise – implementing AKS Azure AD integration

In this exercise, we will complete the following tasks:

- **Task 1**: Create AKS cluster resources for development.
- **Task 2**: Interact with cluster resources using Azure AD identities.

Here are the steps to complete the preceding tasks:

1. Open a web browser and browse to the Azure portal at `https://portal.azure.com`. Sign in using the `azureadmin` credentials.
2. In the Azure portal, click on **Create a resource**. In the **Create a resource** blade, search for *Kubernetes service* and then select **Kubernetes service**.
3. In the **Basics** tab, configure the following:

   Subscription: Select your Azure subscription.

   Resource group: `azuresec-c9-rg`.

   Kubernetes cluster name: `azsec-aks`.

   Region: Select a region that is close to you.

   Availability zones: None.

   Node count: 1.

   Leave all the other settings as their default values.

   Click on **Next: Node pools >**:

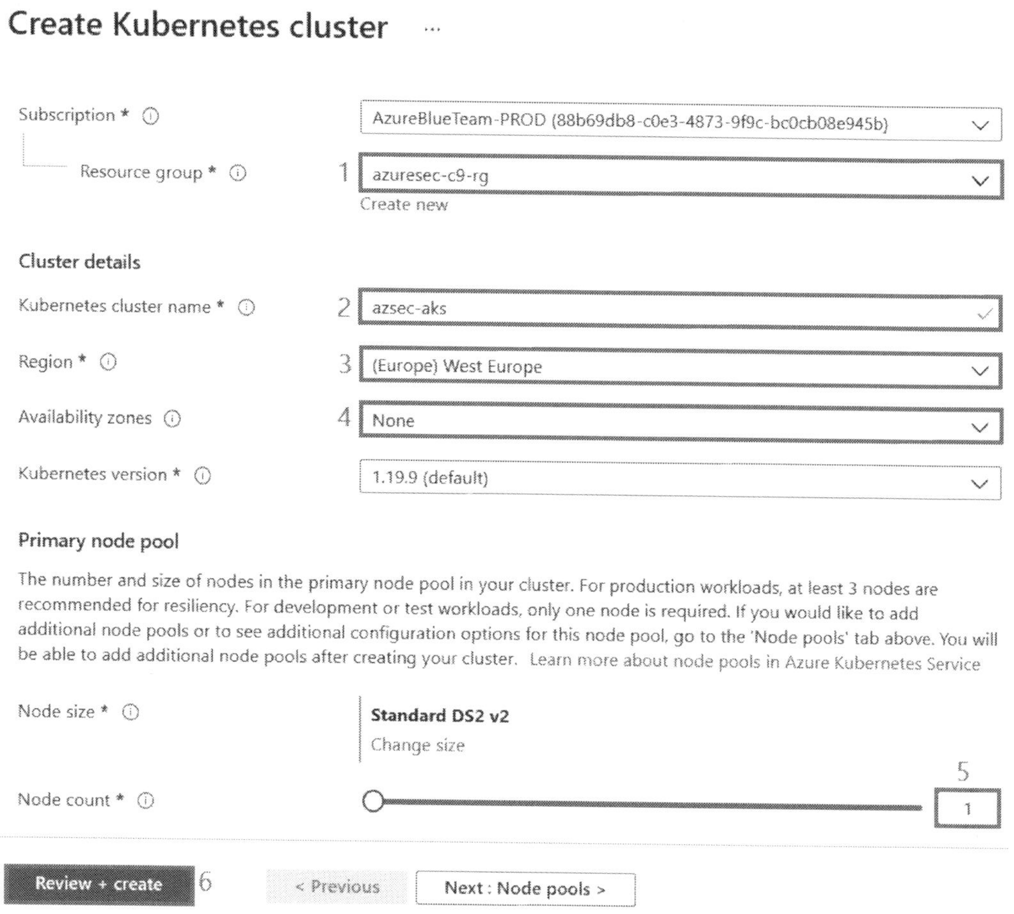

Create Kubernetes cluster ...

Subscription * AzureBlueTeam-PROD (88b69db8-c0e3-4873-9f9c-bc0cb08e945b)

Resource group * 1 azuresec-c9-rg

Create new

Cluster details

Kubernetes cluster name * 2 azsec-aks

Region * 3 (Europe) West Europe

Availability zones 4 None

Kubernetes version * 1.19.9 (default)

Primary node pool

The number and size of nodes in the primary node pool in your cluster. For production workloads, at least 3 nodes are recommended for resiliency. For development or test workloads, only one node is required. If you would like to add additional node pools or to see additional configuration options for this node pool, go to the 'Node pools' tab above. You will be able to add additional node pools after creating your cluster. Learn more about node pools in Azure Kubernetes Service

Node size * Standard DS2 v2

Change size

Node count * 5 1

Review + create 6 < Previous Next : Node pools >

Figure 9.42 – Configuring the AKS cluster details

4. In the **Node pools** tab, click on **Next: Authentication** >.
5. In the **Authentication** tab, configure the following:

   AKS-managed Azure Active Directory: Enabled

   Leave all the other settings at their default values.

Click on **Review + create**:

Create Kubernetes cluster ...

Basics Node pools Authentication Networking Integrations Tags Review + create

Cluster infrastructure

The cluster infrastructure authentication specified is used by Azure Kubernetes Service to manage cloud resources attached to the cluster. This can be either a service principal or a system-assigned managed identity.

Authentication method ○ Service principal ◉ System-assigned managed identity

Kubernetes authentication and authorization

Authentication and authorization are used by the Kubernetes cluster to control user access to the cluster as well as what the user may do once authenticated. Learn more about Kubernetes authentication

Role-based access control (RBAC) ◉ Enabled ○ Disabled

1

AKS-managed Azure Active Directory ◉ Enabled ○ Disabled

Admin Azure AD groups + Add Azure AD groups as administrators on this cluster

Node pool OS disk encryption

By default, all disks in AKS are encrypted at rest with Microsoft-managed keys. For additional control over encryption, you can supply your own keys using a disk encryption set backed by an Azure Key Vault. The disk encryption set will be used to encrypt the OS disks for all node pools in the cluster. Learn more

Encryption type (Default) Encryption at-rest with a platform-managed key

Review + create 2 < Previous Next : Networking >

Figure 9.43 – Enabling AKS-managed Azure AD

6. In the **Review + create** tab, click on **Create**. Wait for the deployment to complete.
7. After the deployment has been completed, click on the **Cloud Shell** icon in the upper-right corner of the Azure portal. Select **Bash**. If prompted, proceed to create a storage account:

Figure 9.44 – Clicking on the icon to open Cloud Shell

8. In the Bash session within the Cloud Shell pane, run the following command to get the cluster admin credentials:

```
az aks get-credentials --resource-group azuresec-c9-rg
--name azsec-aks --admin
```

You should see a message about the context being merged:

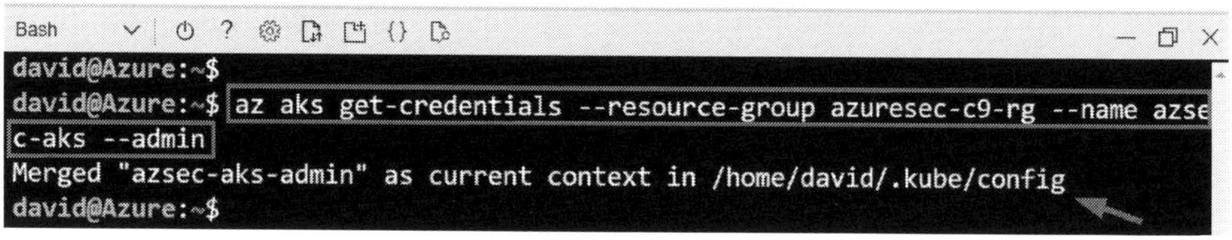

```
Bash
david@Azure:~$
david@Azure:~$ az aks get-credentials --resource-group azuresec-c9-rg --name azse
c-aks --admin
Merged "azsec-aks-admin" as current context in /home/david/.kube/config
david@Azure:~$
```

Figure 9.45 – Authenticating to AKS

9. Create a namespace, called `development`, in the AKS cluster using the following command:

```
kubectl create namespace development
```

You should see a response that verifies that the namespace has been created:

```
david@Azure:~$
david@Azure:~$ kubectl create namespace development
namespace/development created
david@Azure:~$
```

Figure 9.46 – Creating a development namespace

10. Create a role for the development namespace. This role grants full permissions to the namespace. In a production environment, you might want to restrict this further:

```
code role-development-namespace.yaml
```

This will open the code editor. In the open window, copy and paste the following YAML definition and then save it using *Ctrl* + *S*:

```
kind: Role
apiVersion: rbac.authorization.k8s.io/v1
metadata:
  name: development-user-full-access
  namespace: development
rules:
- apiGroups: ["", "extensions", "apps"]
```

```
    resources: ["*"]
    verbs: ["*"]
  - apiGroups: ["batch"]
    resources:
    - jobs
    - cronjobs
    verbs: ["*"]
```

Here is a screenshot of what it looks like:

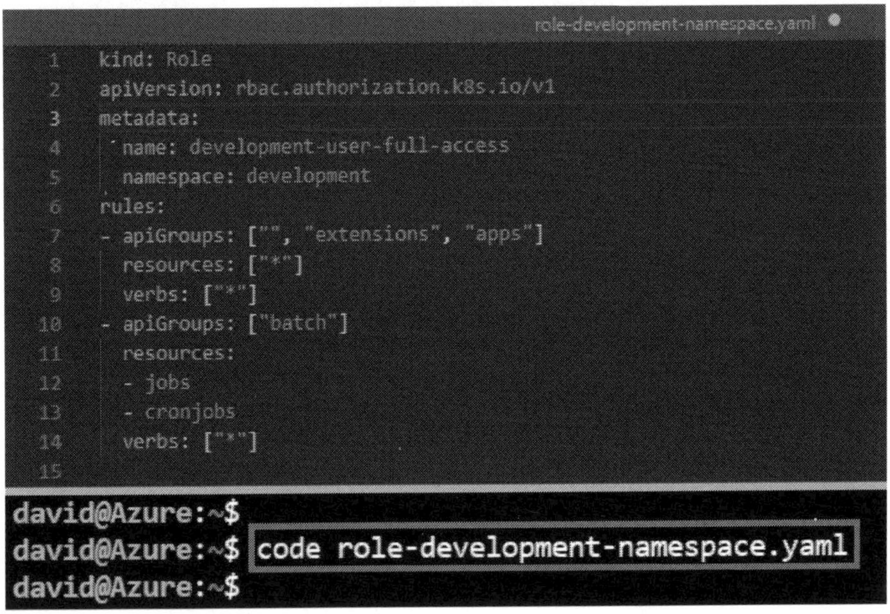

Figure 9.47 – Creating a role definition file

11. Create the role using the following command:

```
kubectl apply -f role-development-namespace.yaml
```

Here is a screenshot of the output:

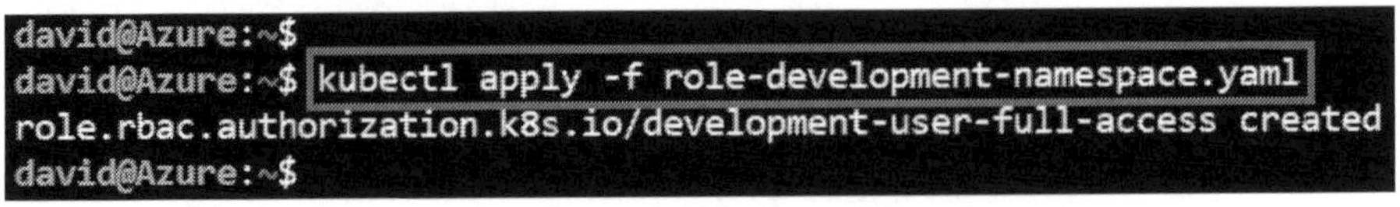

```
david@Azure:~$
david@Azure:~$ kubectl apply -f role-development-namespace.yaml
role.rbac.authorization.k8s.io/development-user-full-access created
david@Azure:~$
```

Figure 9.48 – Creating a role definition

12. In *Chapter 2, Understanding Azure AD*, of this book, we created an Azure AD group, called `cloud-architects`, with both Brenda and Emmy as members. Obtain the object ID of that group using the following command:

```
az ad group show --group cloud-architects --query
objectId -o tsv
```

Here is the output of the command:

```
david@Azure:~$
david@Azure:~$ az ad group show --group cloud-architects --query objectId -o tsv
3ed92323-3235-4102-8a6c-260794ec871a
david@Azure:~$
```

Figure 9.49 – Obtaining an object ID

Make a note of this ID, as we will need it in the next step to grant the group access to Kubernetes resources.

13. Create a `RoleBinding` definition for the `cloud-architects` group to use the previously created role for namespace access. Create a file, named `rolebinding-development-namespace.yaml`, using the following command:

```
code rolebinding-development-namespace.yaml
```

This will open the empty file in the code editor. In the open window, copy and paste the following YAML definition. On the last line, replace `**PLACEHOLDER**` with the group object ID output from the previous command and then save using *Ctrl* + *S*:

```
kind: RoleBinding
apiVersion: rbac.authorization.k8s.io/v1
metadata:
  name: development-user-access
  namespace: development
roleRef:
  apiGroup: rbac.authorization.k8s.io
  kind: Role
  name: development-user-full-access
subjects:
- kind: Group
  namespace: cloud-architects
  name: **PLACEHOLDER**
```

Here is a screenshot of what it looks like:

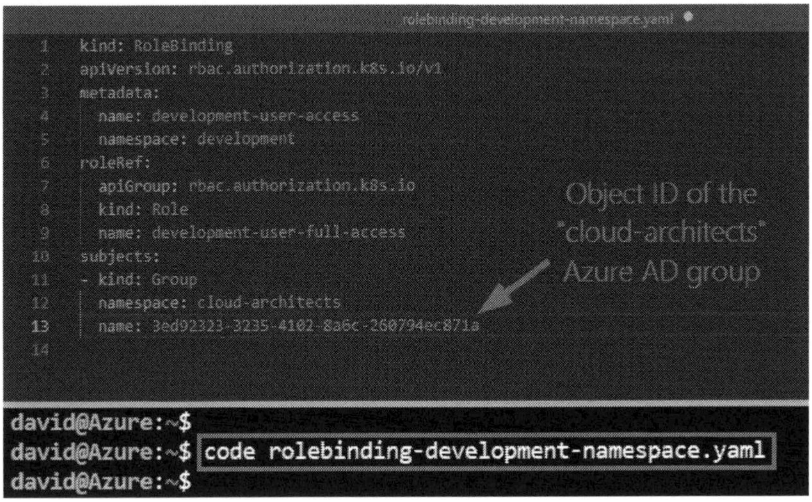

Figure 9.50 – Creating a role binding file

14. Create the RoleBinding using the following command:

```
kubectl apply -f rolebinding-development-namespace.yaml
```

Here is a screenshot of the output:

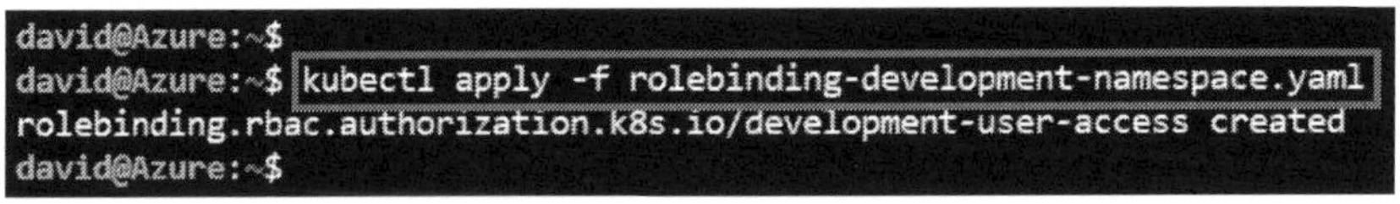

Figure 9.51 – Applying a role binding definition file

15. Create another namespace that the cloud-architects AD group does not have access to using the following command:

```
kubectl create namespace production
```

Now, for everything that we have configured to work, we need to enable AKS-managed Azure AD integration on the AKS cluster.

16. Enable AKS-managed Azure AD integration on the AKS cluster using the following commands. Replace <group_object_id> with the group object ID that you made a note of earlier:

```
tenantId=$(az account show --query tenantId -o tsv)
```

```
az aks update -g azuresec-c9-rg -n azsec-aks --enable-
aad --aad-admin-group-object-ids <group_object_id>
--aad-tenant-id $tenantId
```

17. Now, let's test that a user can authenticate using their Azure AD credentials and authorize:

```
az aks get-credentials --resource-group azuresec-c9-rg
--name azsec-aks --overwrite-existing
```

18. Schedule a basic NGINX pod in the development namespace:

```
kubectl run nginx-dev --image=mcr.microsoft.com/oss/
nginx/nginx:1.15.5-alpine --namespace development
```

19. When prompted, sign in with Brenda's credentials. Once this has been authenticated successfully, the pod will be created:

```
david@Azure:~$ kubectl run nginx-dev --image=mcr.microsoft.com/oss/nginx/nginx:1.15.
To sign in, use a web browser to open the page https://microsoft.com/devicelogin and
pod/nginx-dev created
```

Figure 9.52 – Authenticating as Brenda

20. View pods in the development namespace using the following command:

```
kubectl get pods --namespace development
```

Here is a screenshot of the output:

```
david@Azure:~$ kubectl get pods --namespace development
NAME        READY   STATUS    RESTARTS   AGE
nginx-dev   1/1     Running   0          4m14s
```

Figure 9.53 – Listing pods in the development namespace

21. Try to view pods outside of the development namespace. You should get an error:

```
kubectl get pods --all-namespaces
```

Here is a screenshot of the output:

```
david@Azure:~$ kubectl get pods --all-namespaces
Error from server (Forbidden): pods is forbidden: User "brenda@azureblueteam.io" can
```

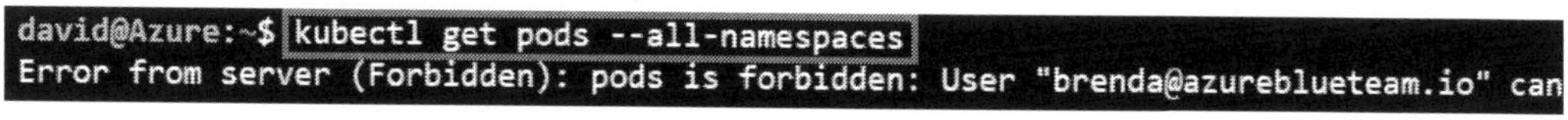

Figure 9.54 – Attempting to list pods for all namespaces

Congratulations! You have successfully configured Azure AD integration with Kubernetes RBAC for the AKS cluster. This information is useful for when you want to implement granular control to Kubernetes resources in an AKS cluster. In the next section, we will remove all the resources that we have created.

Cleaning up the resources

In the Azure portal, delete the `azuresec-c9-rg` resource group. This will remove all the resources that we created for the exercises in this chapter.

Summary

In this chapter, you learned how to secure containerized workloads in Azure. We covered the security best practices that you can implement to secure your images at ship time in a container registry and at runtime in AKS. The skills that you have gained in this chapter will provide a strong foundation that you can build on for further container security studies.

In the next chapter, we will cover Azure storage and how to secure the data stored in it. See you in the next chapter!

Questions

As we conclude, here is a list of questions for you to test your knowledge regarding this chapter's material. You will find the answers in the *Assessments* section of the *Appendix*:

1. From ASC, you enable Azure Defender for container registries for the vulnerability assessment of images in a container registry. You have pushed two container images into the registry – a Windows image and a Linux image. Which of these images will be scanned for vulnerabilities?

   a. The Windows image only

   b. The Linux image only

   c. Both the Windows and Linux images

   d. None of the images

2. You have an Azure AD tenant, named **spicycrabs.xyz**, and an AKS cluster called **AKS1**. You discover that developers cannot sign in with their Azure AD credentials to create Kubernetes resources on AKS1. What can you do to address this while minimizing administrative efforts?

   a. Update the settings of AKS1 to enable Azure AD integration.

   b. Recreate AKS1 with Azure AD integration enabled.

   c. From AKS1, upgrade the version of Kubernetes.

   d. From Azure AD, implement Azure AD Premium.

3. You have an Azure subscription that contains a standard-tier container registry named **ACR-1**. The subscription uses the free tier of ASC. You upload several container images to ACR-1. You discover that vulnerability security scans were not performed. You need to ensure that the images are scanned for vulnerabilities when they are uploaded to ACR-1. What should you do?

   a. From the Azure portal, modify the pricing tier settings of Security Center.

   b. From Azure CLI, lock the container images.

   c. Modify the pricing tier of **ACR-1** to premium.

   d. Push the container images to **ACR-1** by using Docker.

Further reading

To learn more on the subject, please refer to the following resources:

- *Content trust in Azure Container Registry*: `https://docs.microsoft.com/en-us/azure/container-registry/container-registry-content-trust`
- ACR private endpoints: `https://docs.microsoft.com/en-us/azure/container-registry/container-registry-private-link`
- *Azure Container Registry roles and permissions*: `https://docs.microsoft.com/en-us/azure/container-registry/container-registry-roles?tabs=azure-cli`
- AKS security concepts: `https://docs.microsoft.com/en-us/azure/aks/concepts-security`
- AKS cluster security: `https://docs.microsoft.com/en-us/azure/aks/operator-best-practices-cluster-security`
- AKS pod security: `https://docs.microsoft.com/en-us/azure/aks/developer-best-practices-pod-security`

Section 3: Secure Storage, Applications, and Data

Modern applications interact with different types of data stores and external services. As you can imagine, these data stores and external services are prime targets for attackers looking to steal sensitive information from organizations! This section will walk you through how to mitigate risks to your applications and data by implementing encryption at rest and in transit, network and user access management, threat protection capabilities, secrets management, and more. By the end of this section, you will be well equipped to mitigate the risks of your cloud applications being breached and your data being stolen.

This part of the book comprises the following chapters:

10
Implementing Storage Security

Azure Storage is the primary data storage solution in Azure. It offers services that can be used to store different datasets, including files, messages, tables, and other types of information. As you can imagine, this service is a prime target for attackers who are looking to steal sensitive information from organizations! Azure Storage provides multilayered security options to protect our data. Our focus in this chapter will be on how to implement these security options for two primary services of Azure Storage – Blob and Files. Here are the topics that we will cover in this chapter:

- Implementing encryption at rest
- Implementing encryption in transit
- Configuring storage account authorization
- Implementing Azure Defender for Storage

As you will see, each topic has been structured to align with a security best practice for securing storage in Azure. Let's get into this!

Technical requirements

To follow along with the instructions in this chapter, you will need the following:

- A PC with an internet connection.
- An Azure subscription. You can use the same subscription that you set up in the first chapter of this book.

Before we proceed to cover the security best practices, let's familiarize ourselves with the Azure Storage service.

Azure Storage overview

As mentioned earlier, Azure Storage is Microsoft's data storage solution in the cloud. The solution consists of core services that can be used to store different datasets for modern data storage scenarios, as follows (*Figure 10.1*):

- **Blob Service**, which is object-based storage for text and binary data. Data stored in this service is primarily accessed using a REST API.
- **Files Service**, which offers fully managed file shares in the cloud that can be accessed using standard **Server Message Block (SMB)**, **Network File System (NFS)**, or REST APIs. File shares created in this service can be mounted on cloud or on-premises systems as we would mount a typical SMB share.
- **Table Service**, which offers a NoSQL data store for storing semi-structured application datasets accessed over a REST API or OData.
- **Queue Service**, which offers a messaging store for reliable communication between decoupled application components:

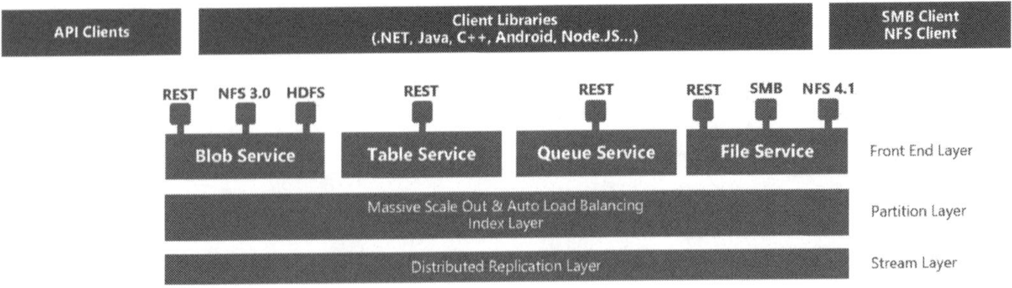

Figure 10.1 – Azure storage services

For our purpose in this chapter, we will focus on two of the services – Azure Blob and Azure Files.

Azure Blob service hierarchy

The Azure Blob service contains the following components as shown in *Figure 10.2*:

- **Storage account**: To use and access the Blob service, we need to create an Azure storage account. This is the parent resource where we define a lot of the configuration options.
- **Container**: The Blob service in a storage account consists of *containers*. These containers are effectively folders that can be used to store objects/data.
- **Blob**: **Blob** stands for **Binary Large Object**. These are the actual objects that we are storing in the containers that we have created. It could be any type of object or file.

Access to objects in the Blob service is through an HTTP/HTTPS endpoint (`blob.core.windows.net`). The URL address is a combination of the storage account name, the container, and the object name.

For example, if we have a storage account with the name `superclouds`, a container named `public`, and a file within the container named `README.txt`, the access URL of the object will be `https://superclouds.blob.core.windows.net/public/README.txt` (*Figure 10.2*):

https://<STORAGE_ACCOUNT_NAME>.blob.core.windows.net/<CONTAINER_NAME>/<BLOB_NAME>

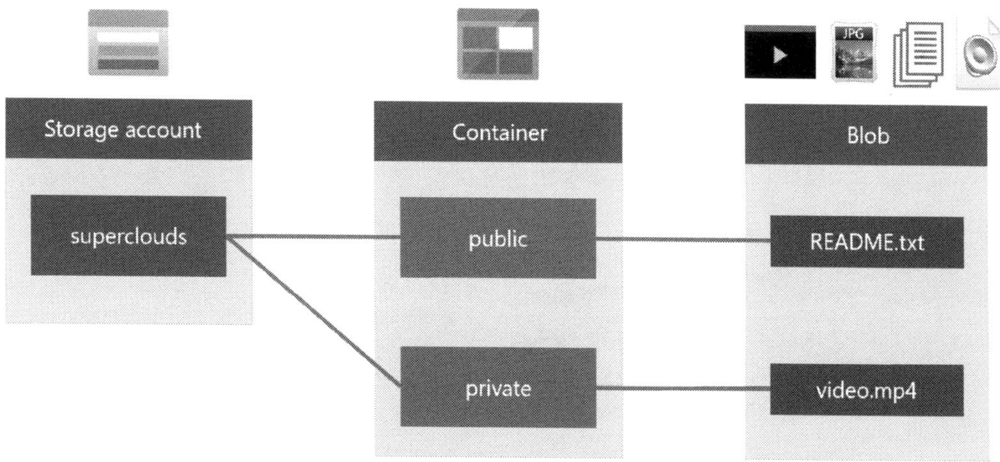

Figure 10.2 – Azure Blob service components and access

The Blob service of a storage account can have multiple containers, but containers cannot be nested. Also, we can have different levels of access configured. We will cover this topic later in this chapter when we discuss authentication and authorization.

Azure Files service hierarchy

The components of the Azure Files service are similar to that of Azure Blob but instead of working with containers, we are working with file shares that can be mounted in Windows or Linux operating systems:

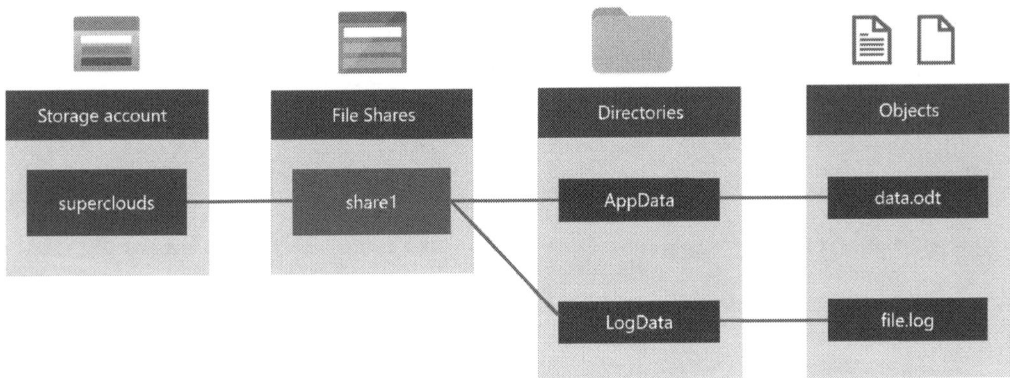

Figure 10.3 – Azure Files service components

In the next sections, we will start to look at security best practices that apply to these two services in Azure storage – Blob and Files.

Implementing encryption at rest

Anytime the topic of storage security comes up, a common concern for organizations is ensuring that data is encrypted at rest and in transit. In many cases, this is a mandatory measure required for compliance with industry and government regulations such as PCI, HIPAA, and FedRAMP.

The great thing about Azure Storage is that encryption at rest is automatic and enabled by default for all services, including Blob and Files. This encryption is powered by a feature called **Storage Service Encryption** (**SSE**). This feature is also referred to as **service-level encryption**. SSE is enabled for all new and existing storage accounts at no additional cost and cannot be disabled.

SSE ensures that data written to any Azure Storage service is encrypted with a 256-bit **Advanced Encryption Standard** (**AES**) cipher, which is one of the strongest block ciphers available. The process transparently decrypts data that is read from Azure Storage before returning it to a client.

By default, SSE uses encryption keys that are managed by the Azure platform. However, customers can enhance this with their own encryption keys stored in Azure Key Vault. This enhancement is only available for the Blob and Files services. A key reason why organizations may want to do this is to meet compliance requirements that mandate for encryption keys to be in the control of the organization. This enhancement can be implemented from the **Encryption** blade of the storage account resource (*Figure 10.4*):

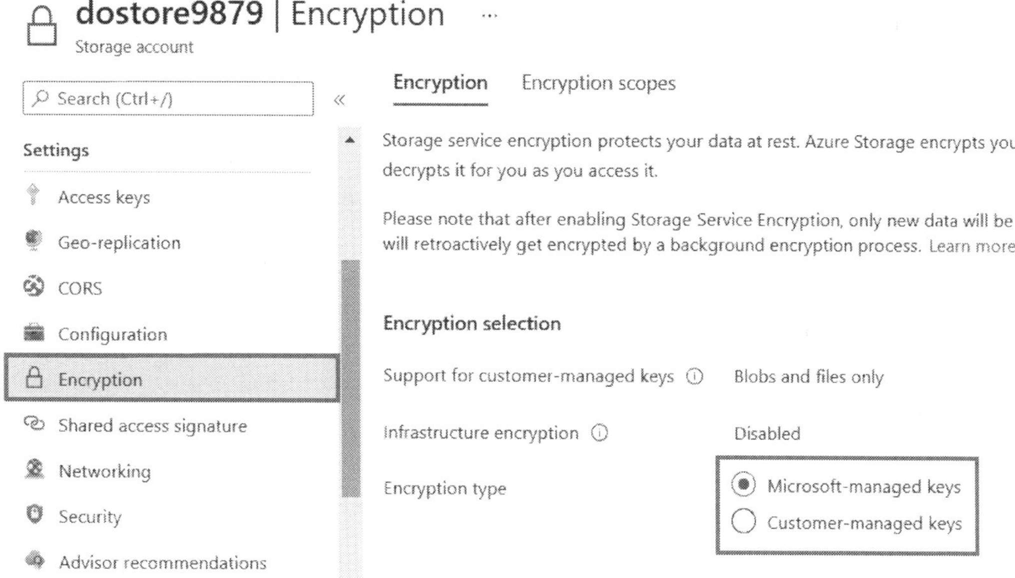

Figure 10.4 – Selecting the encryption type

There is another enhancement option that we can implement called **infrastructure encryption**. As of the time of writing, this option can only be enabled at the time of creation of the storage account and not afterward.

When this feature is configured, data written to services in a storage account is encrypted two times – once at the service level and once at the infrastructure level with different keys (*Figure 10.5*). But why would we want to implement this option with SSE already enabled by default? The answer is simple: to protect against a scenario where one of the encryption keys may be compromised. If this were to happen, the additional layer of encryption continues to protect our data in Azure Storage:

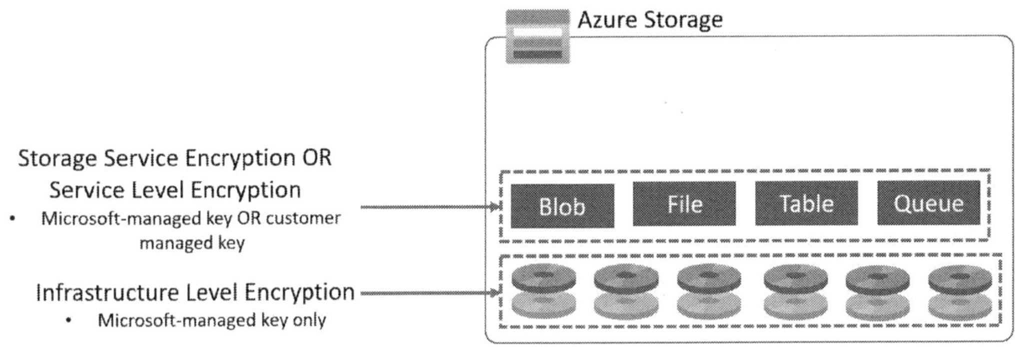

Figure 10.5 – Azure Storage encryption levels

To enable this feature, we must first register to use it using either the Azure CLI or Azure PowerShell. The command to do so with the Azure CLI is as follows:

```
# Register to use the feature
az feature register --namespace Microsoft.Storage --name
AllowRequireInfraStructureEncryption
```

It is worth noting that this can also be done from the **Subscription** blade in the Azure portal.

After registering to use the feature, we can configure it using any of the Azure management options – the portal, CLI, or PowerShell. Here is the Azure CLI command to create a storage account with the feature enabled:

```
# Create a storage account with infrastructure encryption
enabled
az storage account create --name <storage-account-name>
--resource-group <resource-group-name> --location <location>
--sku <storage-account-sku> --kind StorageV2 --require-
infrastructure-encryption
```

To configure the same thing from the Azure portal, we can do this from the **Advanced** tab of the storage account creation process, as shown:

Create a storage account ...

Basics Advanced Networking Data protection Tags Review + create

ⓘ Certain options have been disabled by default due to the combination of storage account

Security

Configure security settings that impact your storage account.

Enable secure transfer ⓘ

Enable infrastructure encryption ⓘ

Enable blob public access ⓘ

Figure 10.6 – Azure Storage encryption levels

There is a final scenario that we need to discuss before we end this section and that is encryption scopes. If we have a storage account that stores data for different customers, we may want to create secure boundaries by encrypting individual containers and objects with different encryption keys. Encryption scopes allow us to achieve this. With encryption scopes, we can manage encryption at rest, at the level of an individual blob or container (*Figure 10.7*). This feature is only available for the Blob service:

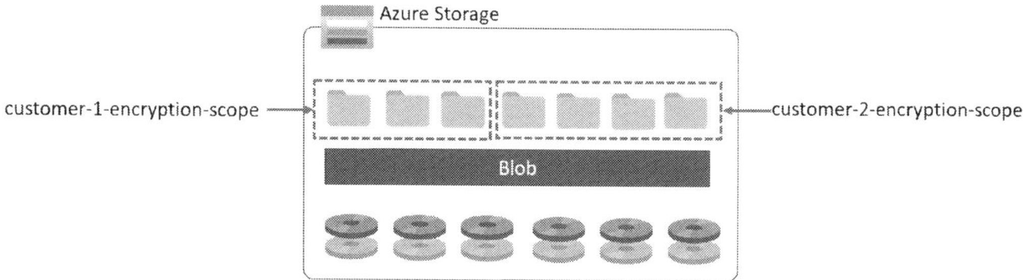

Figure 10.7 – Blob storage encryption scopes

So, in summary, here are the encryption at rest options that we discussed for Azure Storage:

- **Storage service encryption using Microsoft managed keys**: Enabled by default at no additional cost and cannot be disabled.
- **Storage service encryption using customer managed keys**: Enhancement that can be configured by a customer. The customer will need to pay the additional cost of using the Key Vault service.
- **Infrastructure level encryption**: Enhancement that can be configured by the customer only at the time of creation.
- **Encryption scopes**: Enhancement that can be configured by the customer to create secure boundaries in a multi-customer data storage scenario where the data of multiple customers is stored in the same storage account.

In the next section, we will turn our focus to encryption in transit.

Implementing encryption in transit

Another security concern that organizations have is the encryption of data as it moves from one location to another. The Azure platform implements a data link layer encryption method to encrypt all Azure data traffic within an Azure region or between Azure regions. This encryption uses the IEEE 802.1AE **MAC Security** (**MACsec**) standards and requires no action on our part.

However, we will also want to enforce transport-level encryption when data is moved outside network boundaries not controlled by Microsoft. Azure Storage has a **Secure transfer required** option that we can configure to accept requests only from secure connections that support encryption.

When this option is configured, the Blob service will only accept HTTPS requests and will reject HTTP requests. With the option configured, the Files service will also reject insecure connections made over SMB 2.1 and SMB 3.0 without encryption. *Figure 10.8* shows this setting enabled for an existing storage account from the configuration pane of the storage account:

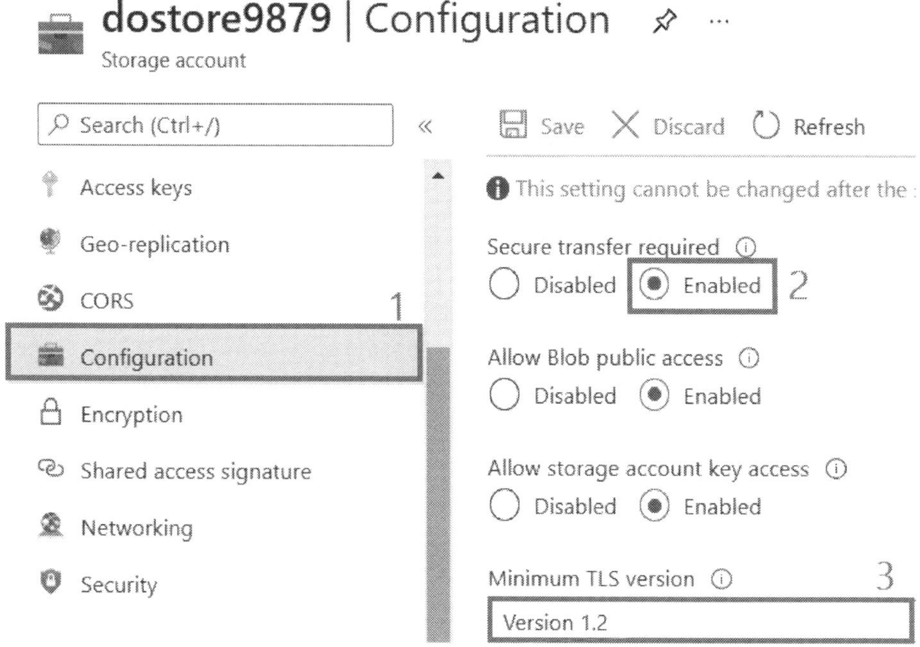

Figure 10.8 – Configuring options for encryption in transit

Another option that we can configure for encryption in transit is to enforce a minimum required version of **Transport Layer Security** (**TLS**) for connection requests to a storage account (*Figure 10.8*). The best practice here is to require TLS 1.2 at a minimum even though TLS 1.0 and 1.1 are supported for backward compatibility.

In the next hands-on exercise, you will implement a storage account that enforces encryption in transit.

Hands-on exercise – provisioning a storage account with encryption in transit enforced

Here are the tasks that we will complete in this exercise:

- **Task 1**: Create a storage account with encryption in transit enforced.
- **Task 2**: Verify encryption in transit.

Here are the steps to complete the tasks:

1. Open a web browser and browse to `http://bit.ly/az500-c10-file`. This will take you to a sample template file. Download and save this file on your PC.
2. Open a web browser and browse to the Azure portal – `https://portal.azure.com`. Sign in with your administrator credentials.
3. On the home page, click on **Create a resource**:

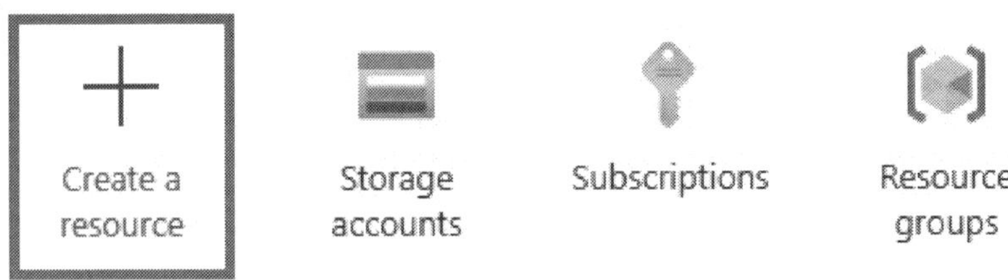

Figure 10.9 – Creating a new Azure resource

4. In the **New** blade, search for `Storage account` and select **Storage account**:

Figure 10.10 – Searching for and selecting Storage account

5. In the **Storage account** blade, click on **Create** to create a new account:

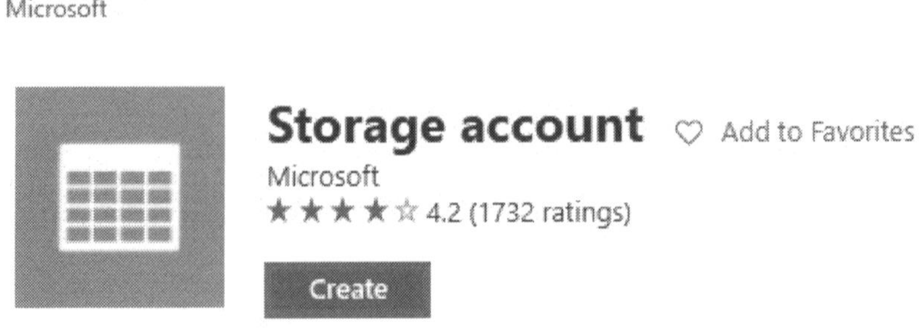

Figure 10.11 – Creating a new storage account

6. In the **Create a storage account** blade, in the **Basics** tab, configure the following:

   Subscription: Select the subscription that you want to deploy the resources into.

   Resource group: **Create new** | **Name**: `azuresec-c10-rg` | **OK**.

   Storage account name: `azsecstorXXXX` (where `XXXX` is a random number).

   Region: Select an Azure region close to your location.

   Performance: **Standard**.

   Redundancy: **Locally-redundant storage (LRS)**.

   Click on **Next: Advanced >** to proceed to the **Advanced** tab.

   Here is a screenshot of the configuration parameters:

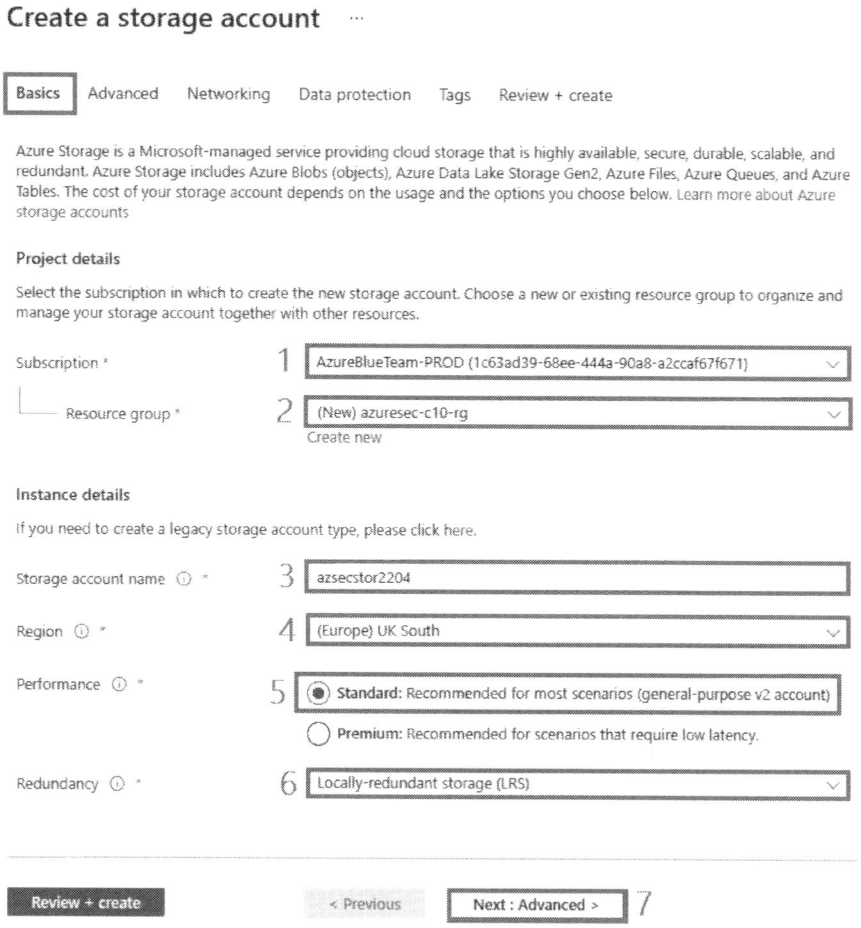

Create a storage account ...

Basics | Advanced | Networking | Data protection | Tags | Review + create

Azure Storage is a Microsoft-managed service providing cloud storage that is highly available, secure, durable, scalable, and redundant. Azure Storage includes Azure Blobs (objects), Azure Data Lake Storage Gen2, Azure Files, Azure Queues, and Azure Tables. The cost of your storage account depends on the usage and the options you choose below. Learn more about Azure storage accounts

Project details

Select the subscription in which to create the new storage account. Choose a new or existing resource group to organize and manage your storage account together with other resources.

Subscription * 1 AzureBlueTeam-PROD (1c63ad39-68ee-444a-90a8-a2ccaf67f671)

Resource group * 2 (New) azuresec-c10-rg
Create new

Instance details

If you need to create a legacy storage account type, please click here.

Storage account name * 3 azsecstor2204

Region * 4 (Europe) UK South

Performance * 5 Standard: Recommended for most scenarios (general-purpose v2 account)
Premium: Recommended for scenarios that require low latency.

Redundancy * 6 Locally-redundant storage (LRS)

Review + create | < Previous | Next : Advanced > 7

Figure 10.12 – New storage configuration settings

7. In the **Advanced** tab, review the following security configurations:

   Enable secure transfer: Ensure that this option is selected to enforce only protocols that support encryption in transit.

   Enable infrastructure encryption: As we discussed earlier in the *Implementing encryption at rest* section, this option will not be configurable until you register the feature for your subscription. Leave it at its current setting.

   Enable blob public access: We will discuss this configuration option later but for now, leave it at its default setting.

   Enable storage account key access: We will discuss this configuration option later but for now, leave it at its default setting.

   Minimum TLS version: **Version 1.2**.

   Leave the other settings at the default values and click on **Next: Networking** > to proceed to the **Networking** tab:

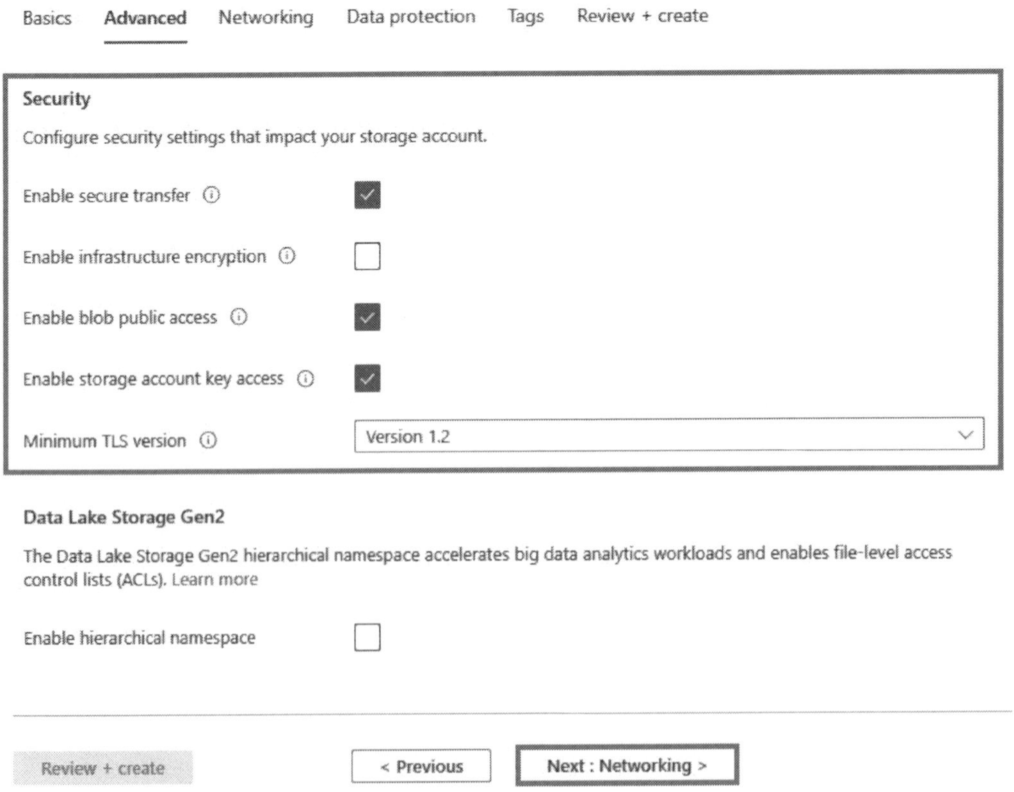

Figure 10.13 – Configuring storage security options

8. In the **Networking** tab, leave all the settings at the default values and click on **Next: Data protection** > to proceed to the **Data protection** tab.
9. In the **Data protection** tab, leave all the settings at the default values and click on **Next: Tags** > to proceed to the **Tags** tab.
10. In the **Tags** tab, leave all the settings at the default values and click on **Next: Review + Create** to proceed to the **Review + create** tab.
11. In the **Review + create** tab, wait for the validation to pass, then click on **Create**. Wait for the deployment to complete:

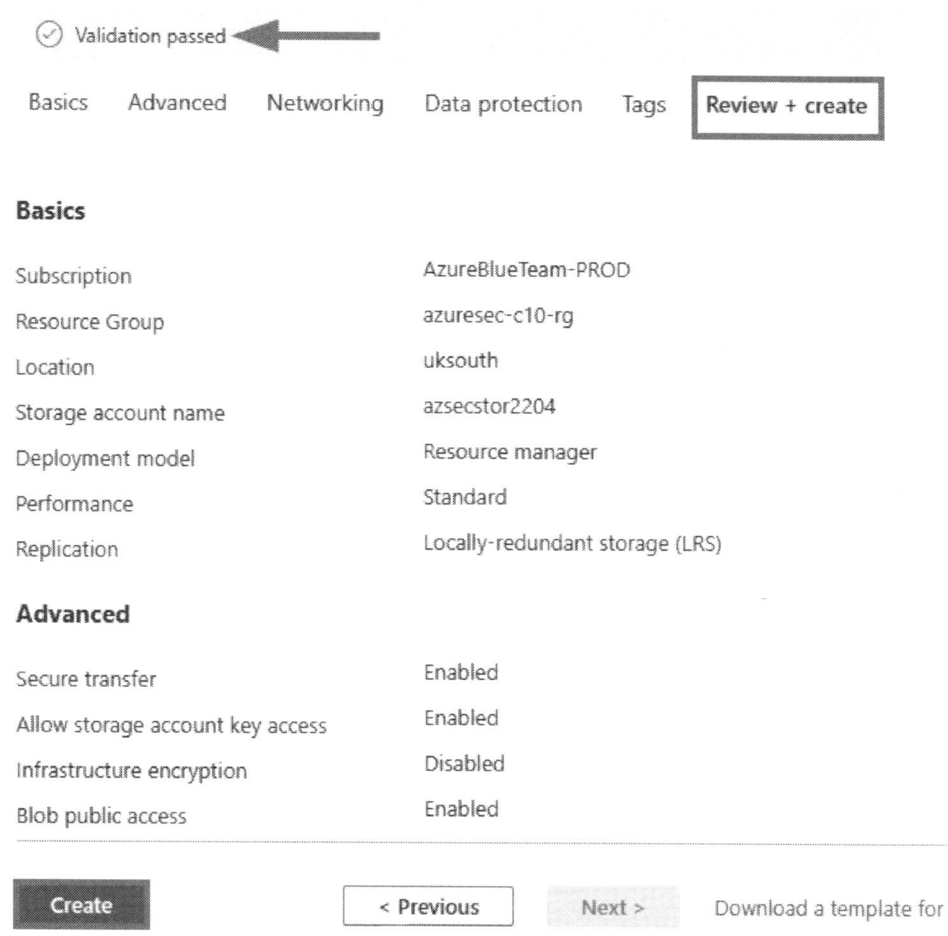

Figure 10.14 – Reviewing settings and deploying a new storage account

12. Once the deployment completes, click on **Go to resource**:

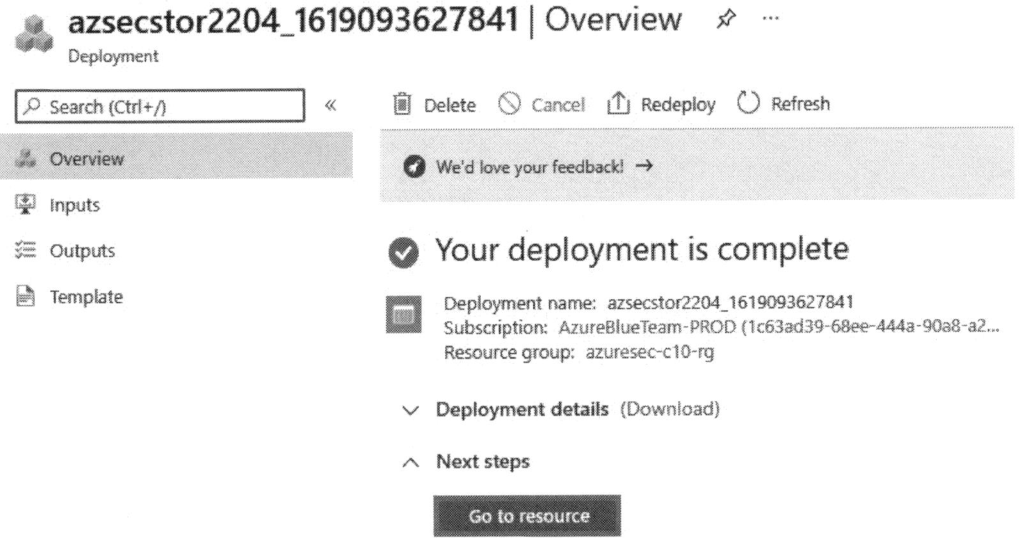

Figure 10.15 – Click to open the newly deployed resource

13. In the storage account resource blade, in the **Blob service** section, click on **Containers**, then click on **+ Container** to create a new container:

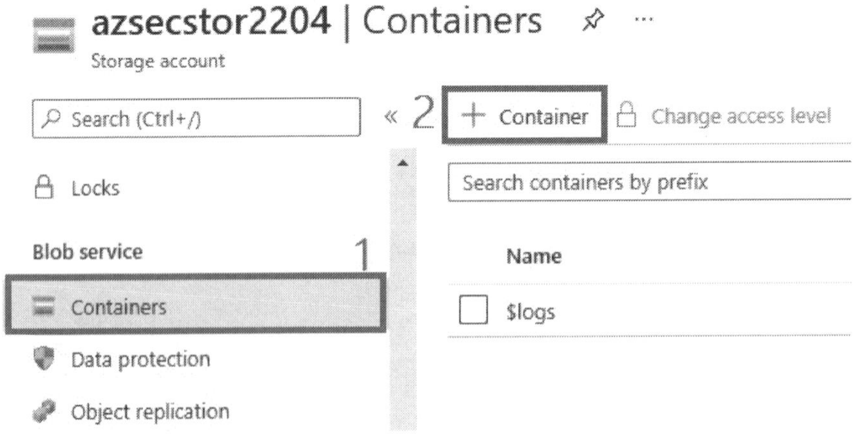

Figure 10.16 – Creating a new container

14. In the **New container** blade, configure the following:

 Name: `public`.

 Public access level: **Blob (anonymous read access for blobs only)**.

Ignore the warning for now. We will come back to it later in this chapter. For now, click on **Create**:

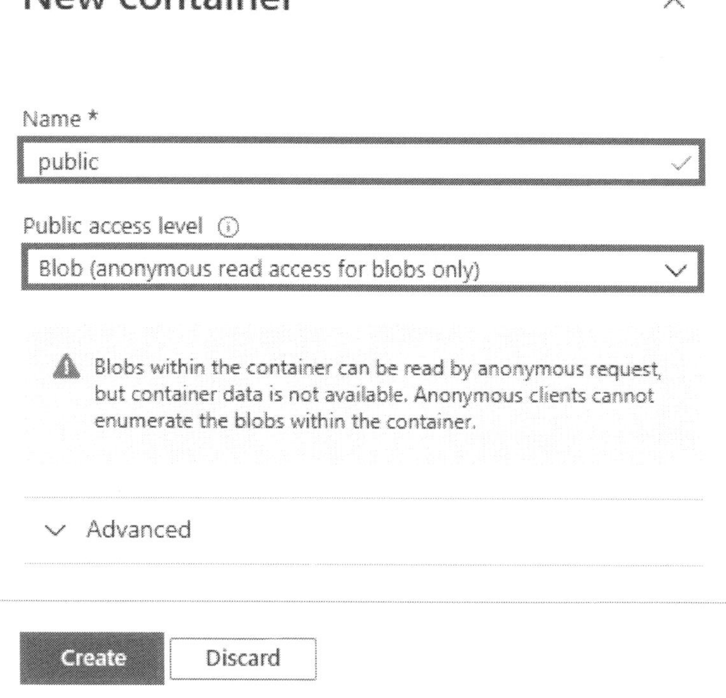

Figure 10.17 – Configuring public access settings and creating a new container

15. Back in the **Containers** blade, click on the **public** container, then click on **Upload**:

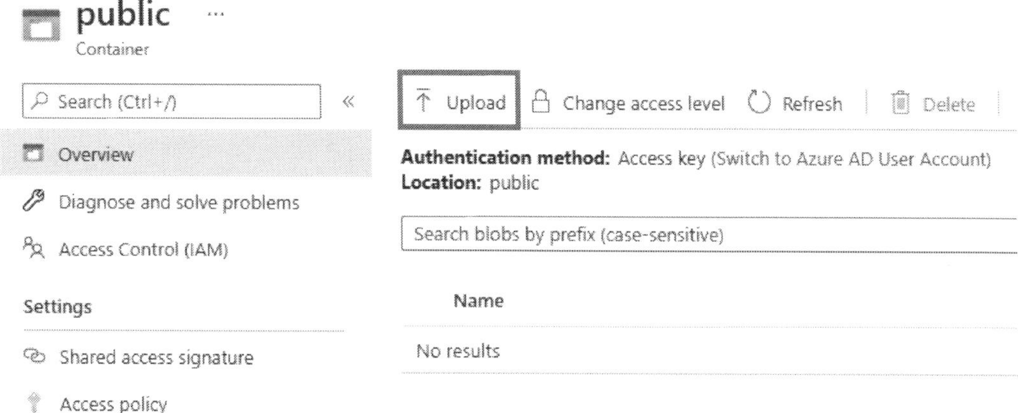

Figure 10.18 – Uploading a new object to a container

16. In the **Upload blob** blade, select the sample template file that you downloaded in *Step 1*, then click on **Upload**:

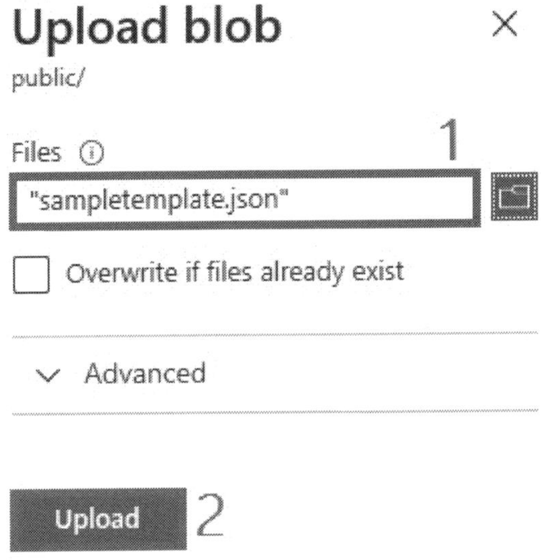

Figure 10.19 – Selecting an object and uploading to a container

17. Back in the **public Container** blade, click on the sample template file, then click to copy the URL of the object as shown in the following screenshot:

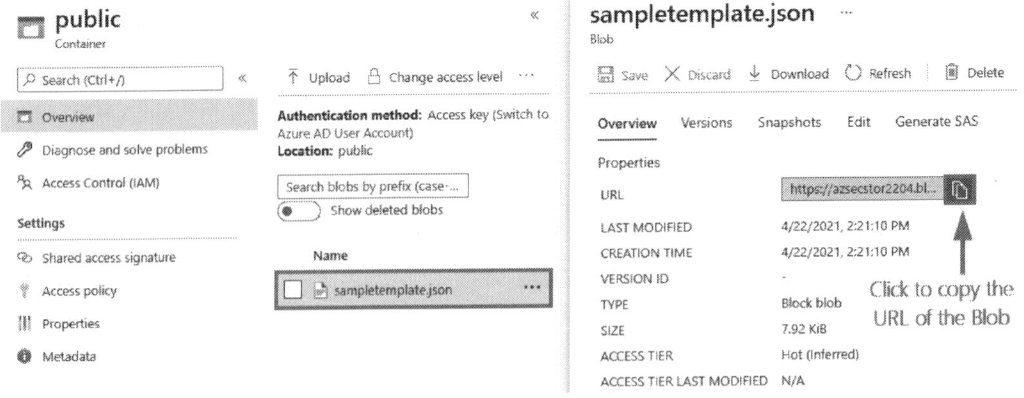

Figure 10.20 – Copying the object URL

18. Open a new browser tab and browse to the object URL that you just copied. This should be successful as the URL should be using HTTPS:

sampletemplate.json - Microsoft ×   https://azsecstor2204.blob.core ×   +

https://azsecstor2204.blob.core.windows.net/public/sampletemplate.json

```
{
  "$schema": "https://schema.management.azure.com/schemas/2019-04-01/deploymentTemplate.json#",
  "contentVersion": "1.0.0.0",
  "parameters": {
    "vmName": {
      "type": "string",
      "defaultValue": "simpleLinuxVM",
      "metadata": {
        "description": "The name of you Virtual Machine."
      }
    },
    "adminUsername": {
      "type": "string",
      "metadata": {
        "description": "Username for the Virtual Machine."
      }
```

Figure 10.21 – Viewing the public blob in the browser using HTTPS

19. In the address bar, modify the URL from HTTPS to HTTP. You should receive an error message that HTTP is not supported, as shown:

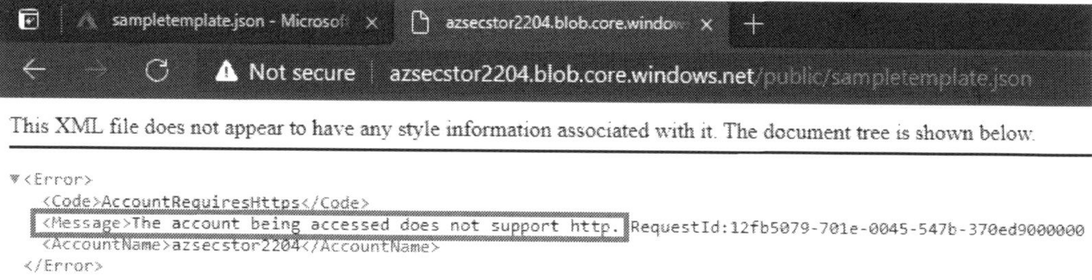

sampletemplate.json - Microsoft
azsecstor2204.blob.core.window
Not secure
azsecstor2204.blob.core.windows.net/public/sampletemplate.json
This XML file does not appear to have any style information associated with it. The document tree is shown below.
<Error>
<Code>AccountRequiresHttps</Code>
<Message>The account being accessed does not support http. RequestId:12fb5079-701e-0045-547b-370ed9000000
<AccountName>azsecstor2204</AccountName>
</Error>

Figure 10.22 – Viewing the public blob in the browser using HTTP

Congratulations! You have successfully created a storage account that enforces encryption in transit, and you verified this configuration. In the next section, we will look at storage account authorization, the options that are available, and security considerations around implementing them.

Configuring storage account authorization

To access data in the Blob or Files service, a client needs to be authenticated and authorized. **Authentication** verifies the identity of a client that is making the connection request while **authorization** grants or denies access to the identified client. Both the Azure Blob and Azure Files services support different authentication and authorization options, as shown in *Figure 10.23*. In general, the authorization options that are supported can be classified into two categories:

- **Key-based authorization** options such as a storage account key and shared access signature
- **Identity-based authorization** options such as Azure AD and on-premises AD

The best practice is to always implement identity-based authorization where possible as it provides better security and auditability:

Azure Storage Service	Storage Account Key	Shared Access Signature (SAS)	Azure Active Directory (Azure AD)	On-premises Active Directory Domain Services	Anonymous public read access
Azure Blobs	Supported	Supported	Supported	Not supported	Supported
Azure Files (SMB)	Supported	Not supported	Supported, only with AAD Domain Services	Supported, credentials must be synced to Azure AD	Not supported
Azure Files (REST)	Supported	Supported	Not supported	Not supported	Not supported

Figure 10.23 – Azure Storage authentication options

> **Important note**
>
> The only exception to the authentication and authorization of connection requests is objects or container resources in the Blob service that have been made available for anonymous access.

In the following sections, we will cover some best practices around implementing the supported authorization options for the Azure Blob and Files services. Here are some authorization best practices that we will cover:

- Protect access to the Storage account keys.
- Grant limited access to using **Shared Access Signatures** (**SAS**).
- Implement Storage account key management with Key Vault.

- Disabling key-based authorization options.
- Disabling anonymous (unauthenticated) Blob access.

Let's now review each of these security practices in detail.

Protect access to the Storage account keys

Every storage account in Azure has two auto-generated access keys – a primary key and a secondary key. The keys grant *full access* to the management plane and the data plane of the storage account and all its resources! Because of the level of access that these keys have, we do not want them to fall into the wrong hands as they could be used to modify any account configuration and gain access to data stored in the storage services (including Blob and Files services).

At a minimum, we want to closely guard these keys by controlling who can read them. One way to do that is by limiting the identities that have this permission in Azure RBAC: `Microsoft.Storage/storageAccounts/listkeys/action`. *Figure 10.24* shows an RBAC role with this permission excluded:

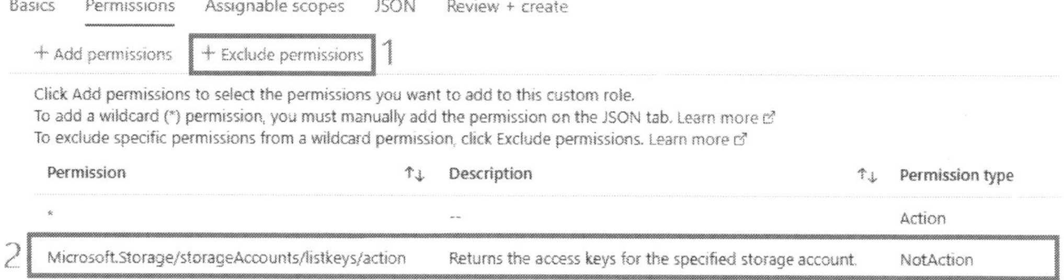

Figure 10.24 – Excluding RBAC permissions

While limiting the identities that can read storage account keys is great, we may want to take this a step further by disabling the option to access Azure Storage using storage account keys. We will discuss this next.

Grant limited access to using Shared Access Signatures (SAS)

As mentioned earlier, it is not recommended to use the storage account keys to access storage resources. There is significant risk involved in distributing a key with an unlimited privilege level. So, what other option can we use in cases where it may not be possible to implement identity-based authorization? We can use a SAS token. The main use case for SAS is to grant access to storage account resources for a limited time range without sharing the storage account key:

Figure 10.25 – Generating a SAS token

A SAS token allows us to use key-based authorization with restrictions that we define. For example, we can define the operations that the token can be used to perform, we can define a start time and an expiry time, we can define the source IP address that the token can be used from, and other configuration parameters (*Figure 10.25*). A SAS token is signed with one of the storage account keys using standard cryptography functionality (SHA-256). If a storage account key is regenerated, all SAS tokens that it was used to sign will be revoked.

Other useful information to know is that SAS tokens can be generated at the account level or the service level. An **account-level SAS** can be used to delegate access to the resources of multiple storage services (that is, Blob, Files, Queue, or Table) while a **service-level SAS** can be used to delegate access to resources within a single service (that is, container or blob). *Figure 10.25* shows the configuration of an account-level SAS. You can see that we have the option to grant access to resources in more than one service.

Ad hoc SAS versus stored access policy SAS

There are two methods that we can use to generate SAS tokens. The first method is **ad hoc**. With ad hoc SAS creation, configuration parameters such as the permissions of the token, its validity start time, and its expiry time are specified with the token itself (*Figure 10.26*). The downside to this method is that once the token is issued, we have no control over the original parameters that we defined. If the token needs to be revoked before its defined expiry time, the storage account key that was used to sign that token needs to be regenerated, which may have a bigger impact if we have used the key to sign other tokens:

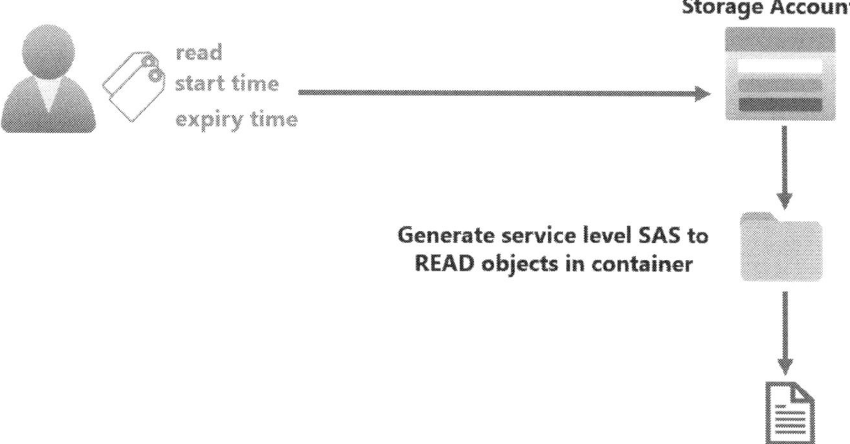

Figure 10.26 – Service-level SAS token

The second method is to use a **stored access policy**. With this method, the configuration parameters such as the permissions of the token, its validity start time, and its expiry time are decoupled from the token and stored on the server side (*Figure 10.27*). This means that we can control the parameters on the server side after the token has been issued. With this method, revoking a token can be done by modifying the expiry time of the access policy in Azure Storage:

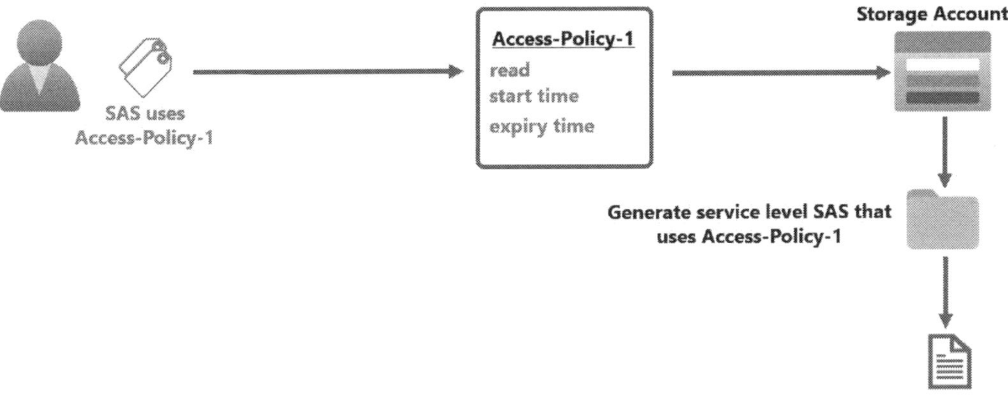

Figure 10.27 – Service-level SAS using an access policy

> **Important note**
>
> SAS tokens are keys that grant permissions to storage resources and they should be protected from malicious or unintended use. Ensure that they are distributed only through secure channels and have a plan in place for identifying and revoking a compromised SAS.

In the next section, we will cover the use of Azure Key Vault for storage account key management.

Implementing storage account key management with Key Vault

We mentioned earlier that the best practice is to use identity-based authorization options. However, there are cases where this may not be possible, for example, in a third-party integration scenario. In such cases, the best practice is to rotate the storage keys periodically. This is something that we can do manually from the Azure portal (*Figure 10.28*), but this is not very efficient:

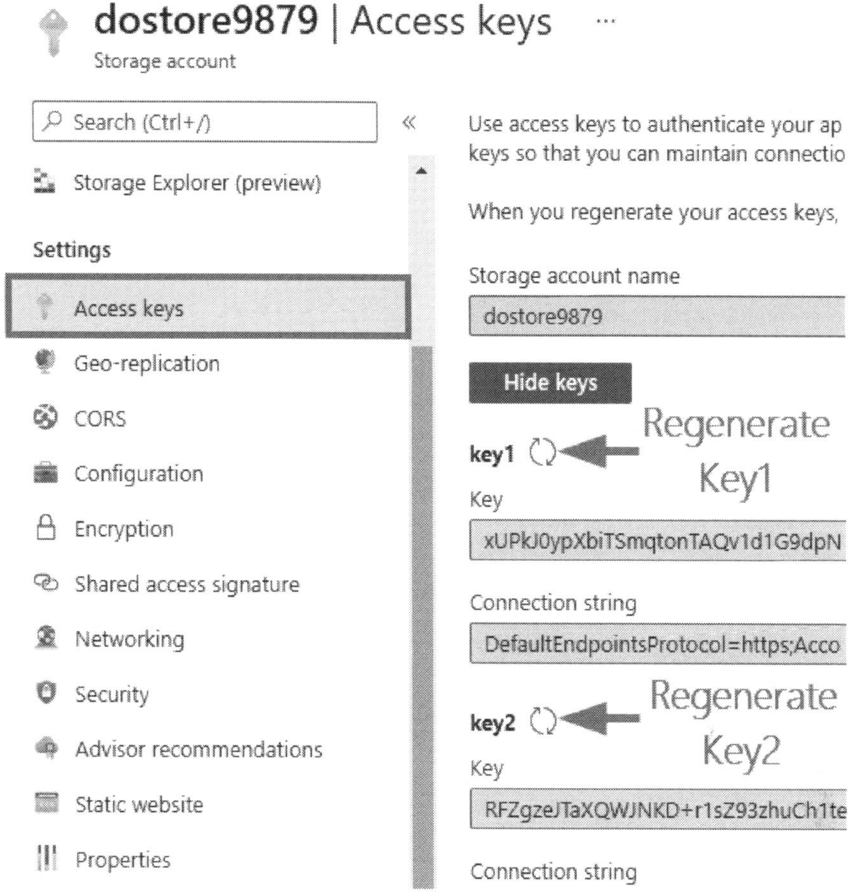

Figure 10.28 – Regenerating storage account access keys

A more effective method is to integrate Azure Storage with Azure Key Vault and let Key Vault handle the periodic automatic key regeneration. At the time of writing, implementing this option is only possible using management command-line tools – the Azure CLI or Azure PowerShell (it is not yet configurable in the portal).

Here are the three main steps to implement this:

1. First, we assign **Storage Account Key Operator Service Role** to the Key Vault service. This gives Key Vault the permissions to list and regenerate the keys.
2. Next, we configure a Key Vault access policy to allow an administrator to configure managed storage accounts in Key Vault and to generate SAS tokens signed by the keys that are managed by Key Vault.
3. We then configure the storage account key management in Key Vault and specify a key regeneration period:

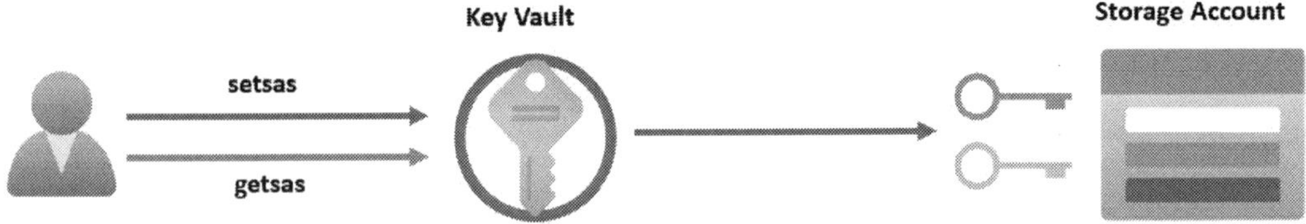

Figure 10.29 – Azure Storage and Key Vault integration

You can follow the instructions here to implement this: `https://docs.microsoft.com/en-us/azure/key-vault/secrets/overview-storage-keys`. Once the keys are managed in Key Vault, clients can gain access by making calls to the Key Vault resource, to generate SAS tokens signed by the storage key.

Disabling key-based authorization options

Using key-based authorization options (storage account key and SAS) to access data in Azure Storage is *not* a best practice. The main reasons for this are security and auditability. Security because it is easier to compromise keys than identities that can be backed by security techniques such as MFA. Auditability because if a key is being used by someone who should not be using it, this cannot be easily identified in the audit logs. For these reasons, we may want to disable the option to use key-based authorization options to access Azure Storage resources. This way, an exposed or stolen storage account key or a compromised SAS token cannot be used by an attacker as the authorization attempt will be rejected by the storage service.

This feature can be implemented in the **Configuration** blade of the Azure Storage resource (*Figure 10.30*) by setting the **Allow storage account key access** option to **Disabled**. It is worth noting that this feature is in preview, at the time of writing:

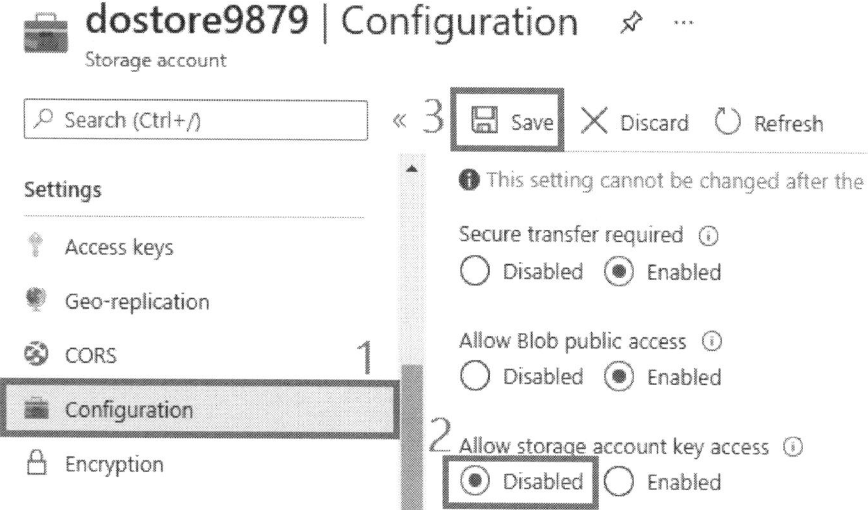

Figure 10.30 – Disabling key-based authentication

Once we have disabled this option, any authorization request with a storage key or SAS tokens will be denied. Authorization to storage services will only be possible with identity-based authorization options.

Disabling anonymous (unauthenticated) Blob access

Earlier in this chapter, we discussed the components of the Azure Blob service. To remind us of what we discussed, here is a short summary: the Blob service exists in a storage account and consists of containers. Containers are effectively folders that can be used to store objects/data:

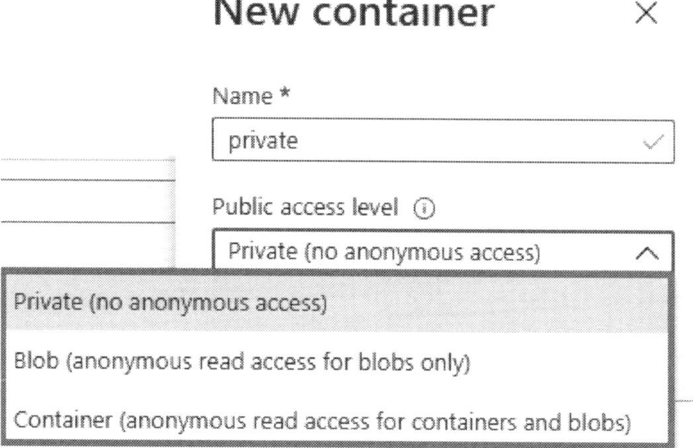

Figure 10.31 – Blob container access levels

When we create a new container, we need to configure a public access level to define whether anonymous (unauthenticated) access will be allowed or not (*Figure 10.31*). We have three options that we can select from:

- **Private**: Does not allow any anonymous access. Access needs to be authenticated.
- **Blob**: Allows anonymous access to a known object URL.
- **Container**: Allows the container files to be listed and accessed anonymously.

While the anonymous options (**Blob** and **Container**) make it convenient for us to share data, they also present a security risk that could lead to a data breach. The best practice is to allow anonymous access *only* when necessary for your scenario (for example, a content store for public websites).

There is a configuration option called **Allow Blob public access** that we can use to disable all anonymous access to storage services, regardless of the public access setting for individual containers. With this option disabled, Azure Storage rejects all anonymous requests to that storage account regardless of the previous configuration of the containers:

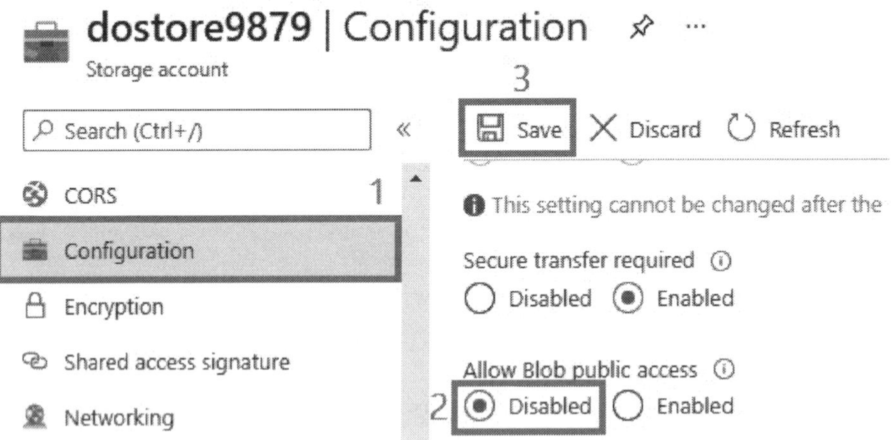

Figure 10.32 – Disabling public blob access

We can configure this option in the **Configuration** blade of the storage account resource (*Figure 10.32*). We can also configure this using command-line management tools and enforce it at scale using Azure Policy. In the next sections, we will discuss how to implement identity-based authorization options for Azure Storage.

Implementing Azure AD authorization for the Blob service

We mentioned earlier in this chapter that the Azure Blob service supports authentication and authorization using Azure AD. We also mentioned that this is the preferred authorization option to use when possible.

For clients to access blob resources with Azure AD identities, they need to be granted permission using Azure RBAC. This permission can be granted to any Azure AD security principal, including users, groups, service principals, and managed identities. The permission can also be granted at any of these scopes: management group, subscription, resource group, storage account, or Blob service container.

Azure provides the following built-in roles that we can use to grant permissions, but we can also create custom roles if the default ones do not fit our requirements:

- **Storage Blob Data Owner**: Gives full access to Azure Storage blob containers and data, including permission to assign POSIX access control
- **Storage Blob Data Contributor**: Gives read, write, and delete access to Azure Storage blob containers and data but no permission to assign access
- **Storage Blob Data Reader**: Gives only read access to Azure Storage blob containers and data

With Azure AD, access to a blob resource is a two-step process. First, a supported identity (user, service principal, or managed identity) authenticates to Azure AD and an OAuth 2.0 token is returned. The token is then used to request access to Azure Blob. You will configure this in the next hands-on exercise in this chapter.

Implementing ADDS or Azure ADDS authentication for Azure Files

Azure Files supports two options for identity-based authentication over SMB. The first option is through on-premises **Active Directory Domain Services** (**AD DS**). The second option is through **Azure AD DS**. For this to work, AD DS users must be synchronized to Azure AD in a hybrid identity scenario as we discussed in *Chapter 3, Azure AD Hybrid Identity*.

Regardless of the option that we implement, authentication works using the Kerberos protocol. When a client requests to access data in Azure file shares, the request is redirected to the domain service that was implemented for authentication. This could be either AD DS or Azure AD DS. If the authentication request is successful, a Kerberos token is returned to the client. The client then uses the Kerberos token to perform authorization against Azure file shares.

Refer to this documentation to see how to implement this: `https://docs.microsoft.com/en-us/azure/storage/files/storage-files-identity-auth-active-directory-enable`.

In the next section, you will implement storage account access controls in a hands-on exercise.

Hands-on exercise – configuring storage account access controls

Here are the tasks that we will complete in this exercise:

- **Task 1**: Disable anonymous (unauthenticated) blob access.
- **Task 2**: Configure SAS key-based authorization.
- **Task 3**: Configure Azure RBAC for blob access.
- **Task 4**: Disable key-based authorization options.

Here are the steps to complete the tasks:

1. Open a web browser and browse to the Azure portal.
2. In the **Search resources, services, and docs** box at the top of the portal, type `azsecstor` and select the storage account that you created earlier in this chapter:

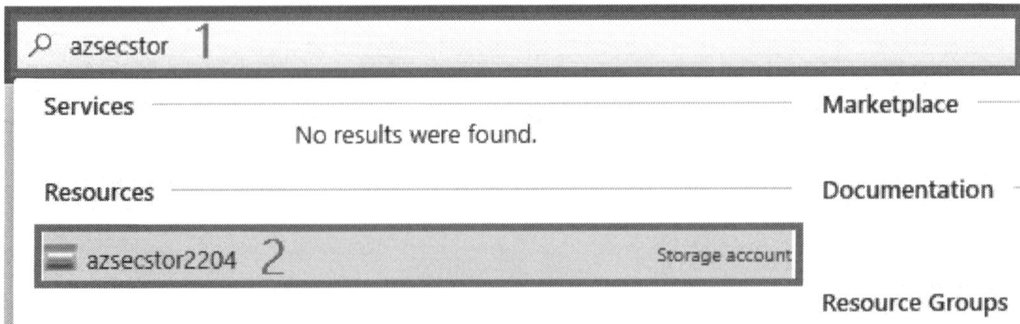

Figure 10.33 – Searching for and selecting a storage account

3. In the **azsecstorXXXX** blade, click on **Configuration** in the **Settings** section. Set the **Allow Blob public access** blade to **Disabled**, then click on **Save**:

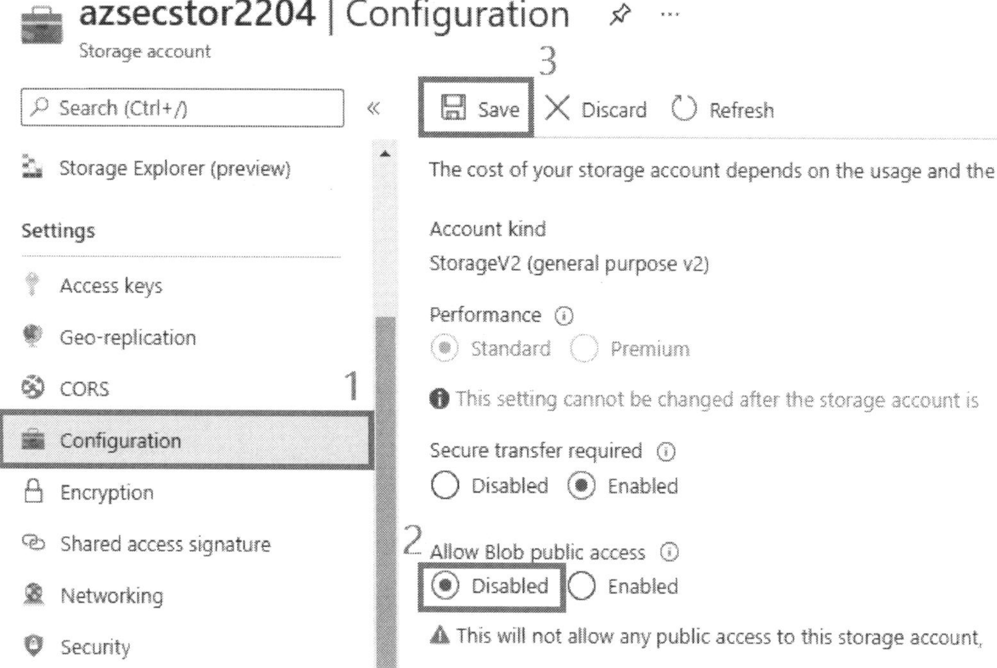

Figure 10.34 – Disabling blob public access

4. On the left-hand side, click on **Containers** in the **Blob service** section, then click on the container named **public** that we created earlier:

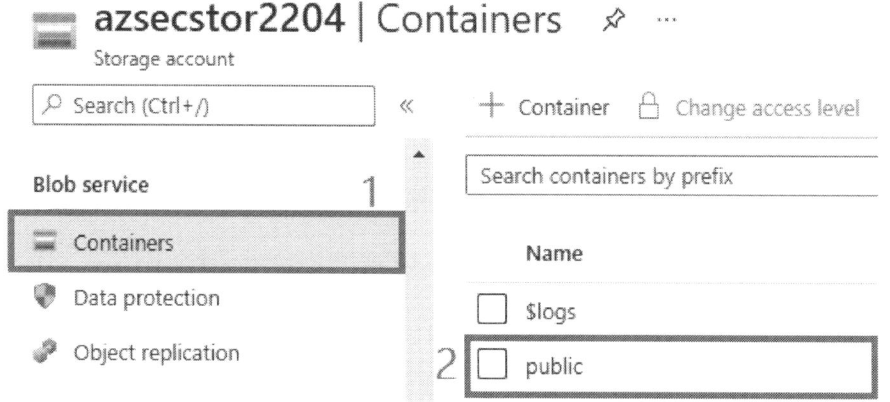

Figure 10.35 – Selecting a blob container

5. In the **public Container** blade, click on **Change access level** and review the message displayed. Notice that you cannot change the configuration to allow anonymous access because we have disabled it for this storage account. Click **OK** to close out of this window:

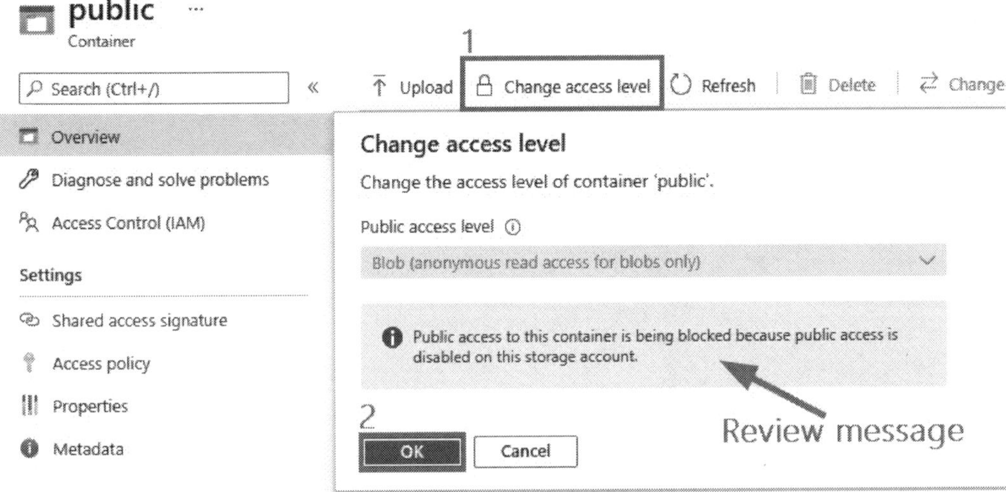

Figure 10.36 – Attempting to change the container access level

6. Click on the `sampletemplate.json` object that you uploaded in the first exercise and copy the URL as shown:

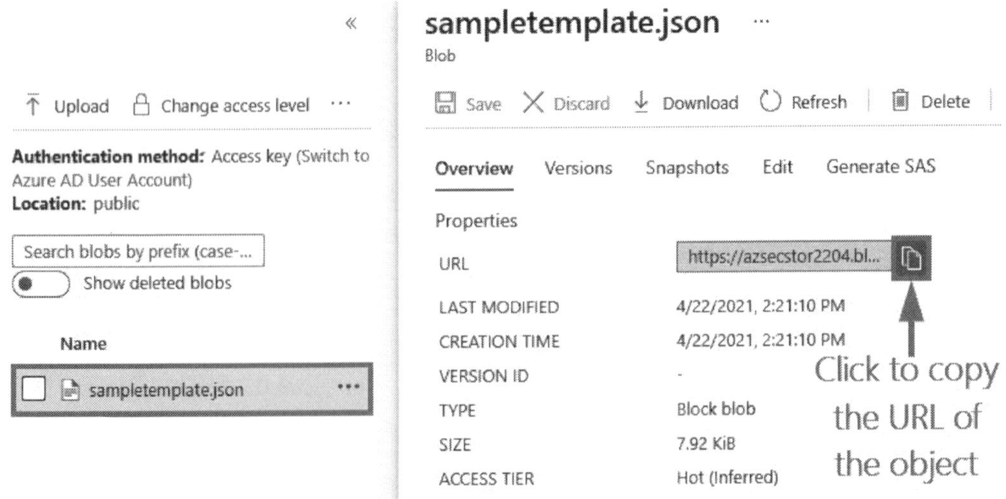

Figure 10.37 – Copying the blob URL

7. Open a new browser tab and browse to the URL that you copied. You should receive an error message that unauthenticated access is not allowed:

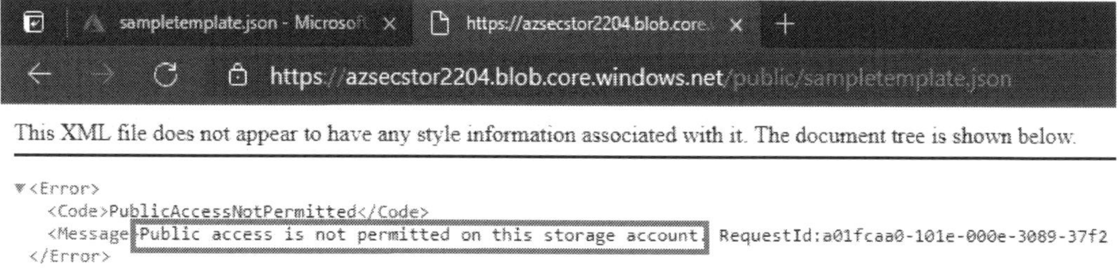

Figure 10.38 – Reviewing the error message

To gain access to this object, we will need to be authorized using key-based authorization or identity-based authorization. Let's go to configure key-based authorization using a SAS token generated via the stored access policy method that we discussed earlier.

8. Go back to the Azure portal tab where you have the `sampletemplate.json` object selected. Click on **Generate SAS** and configure the following:

   Signing method: **Account key**.

   Signing key: **Key 1**.

   Permissions: **Read**.

   Start: Configure a time just before your current time.

   Expiry: Configure any time in the next date from your current date.

   Allowed protocols: **HTTPS only**.

Click on **Generate SAS token and URL**:

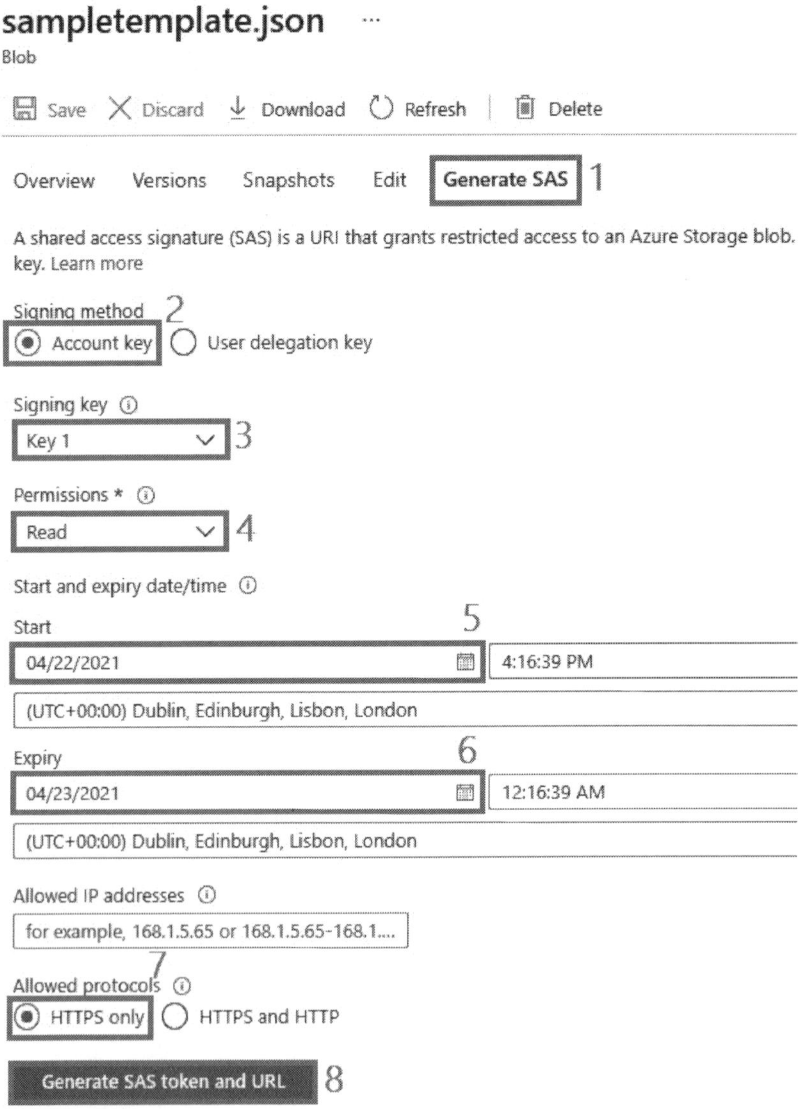

Figure 10.39 – Configuring SAS token settings and generating it

Generating a SAS using this option is called the ad hoc method that we discussed earlier in this chapter.

9. In the output that is returned, copy the Blob SAS URL:

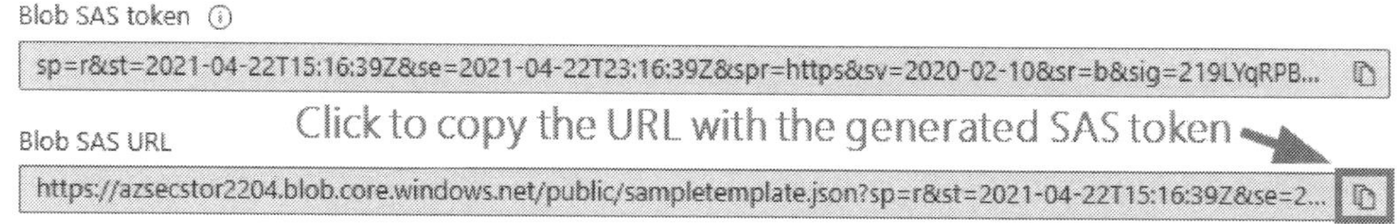

Figure 10.40 – Copying the generated SAS token

10. Open a new browser tab and browse to the URL that you copied. You should be able to access the file. Leave this browser tab open as we will use it to verify the configuration to disable key-based authorization later:

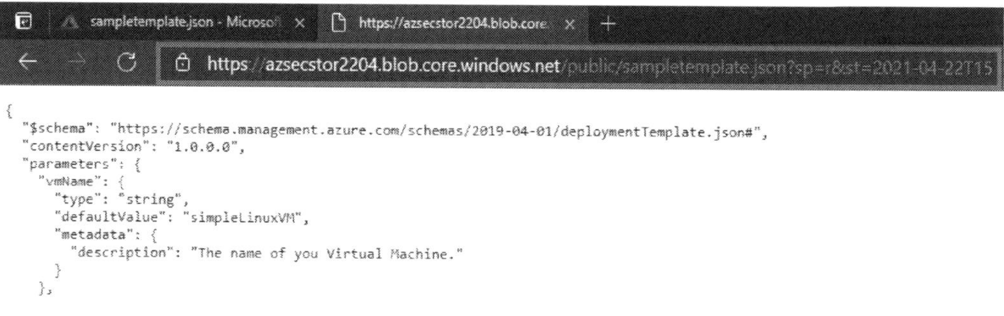

Figure 10.41 – Accessing the blob with the generated SAS token

11. Go back to the Azure portal tab where you generated the SAS. Close the section to return to the container blade:

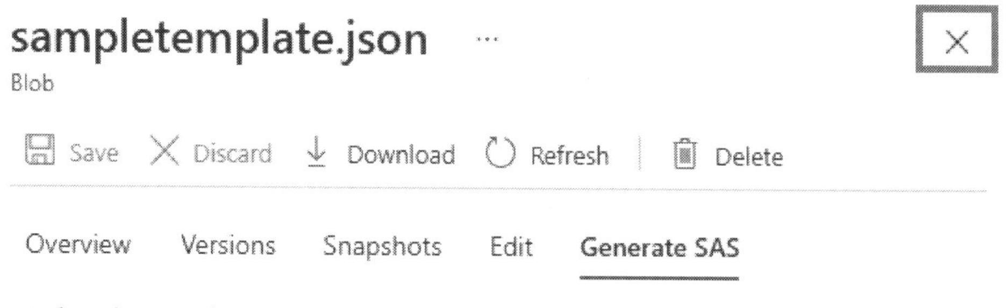

Figure 10.42 – Closing the container blade

12. Back in the **public Container** blade, click on **Switch to Azure AD User Account**:

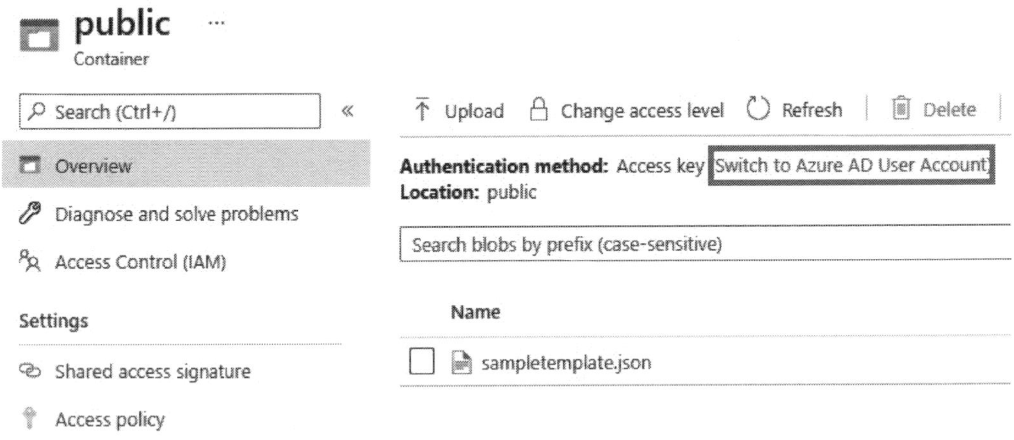

Figure 10.43 – Switch to Azure AD authentication

You should receive an error message that you do not have permission to access blob data with your Azure AD credentials! This is because even as a subscription owner we do not have access to the data plane of Azure Storage by default. The access that we have been using so far has been key-based authorization:

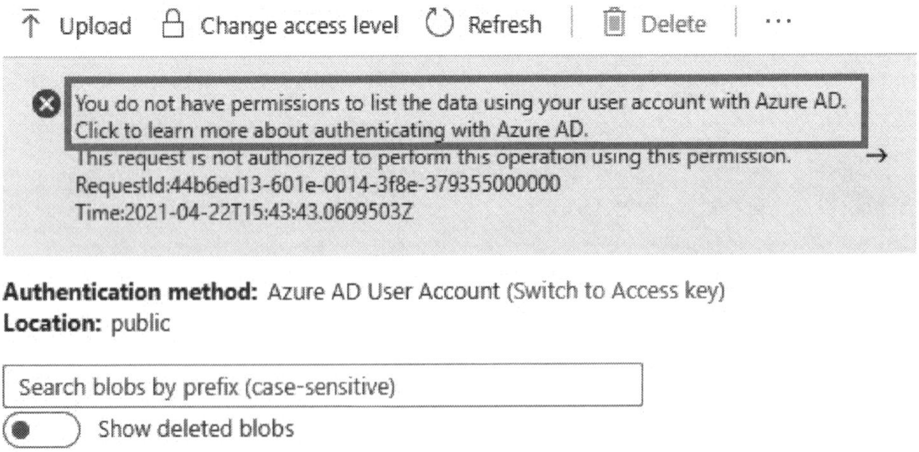

Figure 10.44 – Verifying Azure AD permission

Now, let's go to configure Azure RBAC to grant access.

13. In the current window, click on **Access Control (IAM)** on the left-hand side:

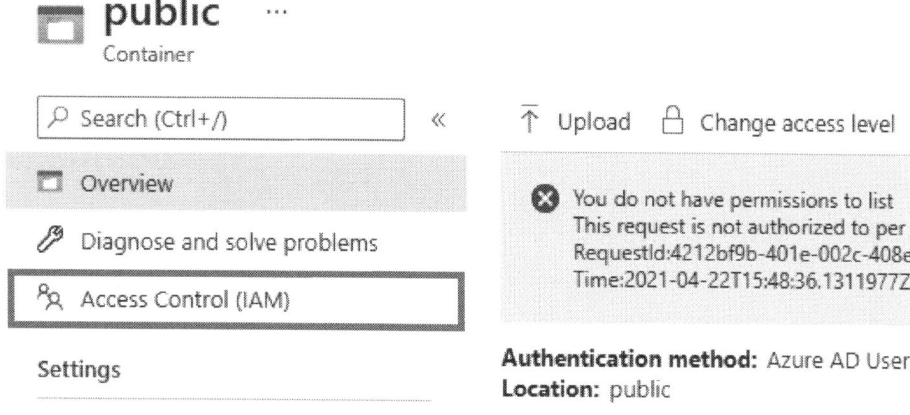

Figure 10.45 – Selecting Access Control (IAM)

14. In the **public | Access Control (IAM)** blade, click on **Add role assignments**:

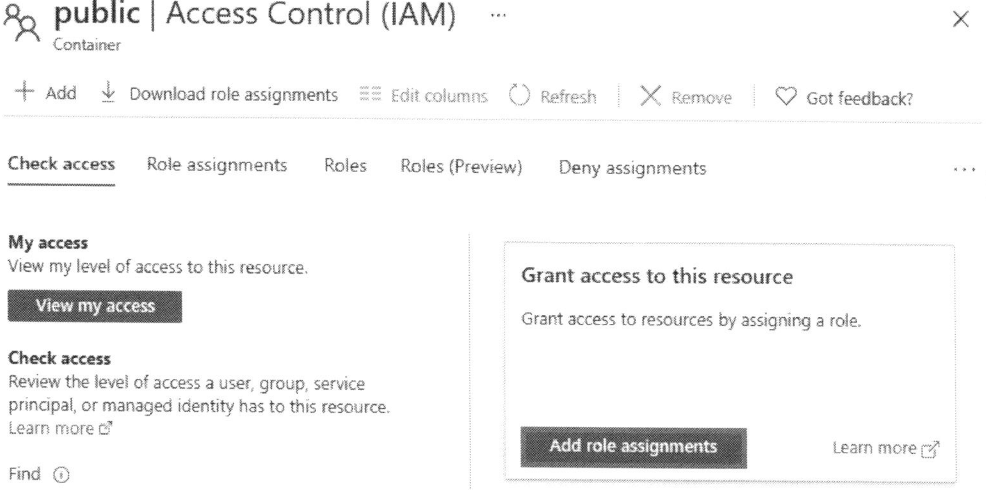

Figure 10.46 – Adding a new role assignment

15. In the **Add role assignment** blade, configure the following:

    Role: **Storage Blob Data Contributor**

    Assign access to: **User, group, or service principal**

    Select: The admin account that you are currently logged in as

    Click on **Save**:

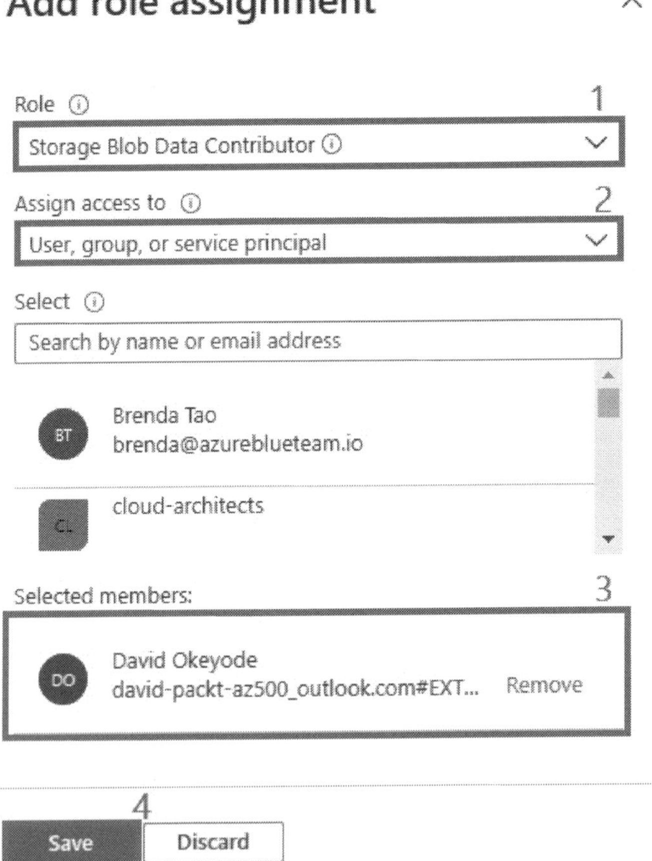

Figure 10.47 – Configuring and assigning a role

16. Once the role is assigned, click on **Overview** on the left-hand side. You should now be able to access container resources using your Azure AD user account:

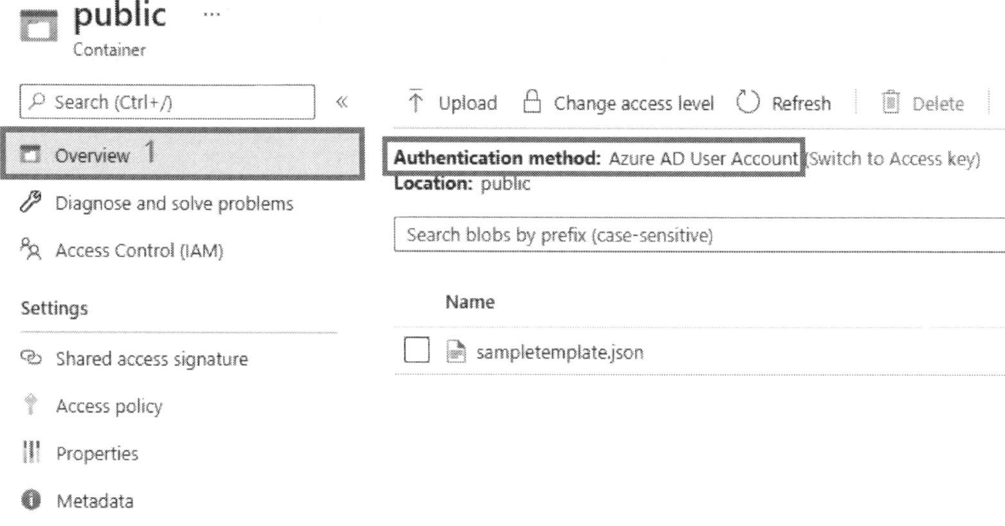

Figure 10.48 – Verifying the Azure AD permission

17. Close the **public Container** blade to go back to the storage account blade:

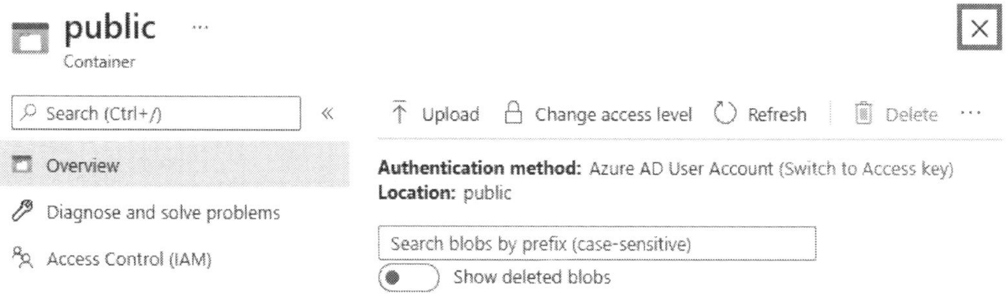

Figure 10.49 – Closing the container blade

18. In the storage account blade, click on **Configuration** and set the option for **Allow storage account key access** to **Disabled**, then click on **Save**. This disables key-based authorization for this storage account:

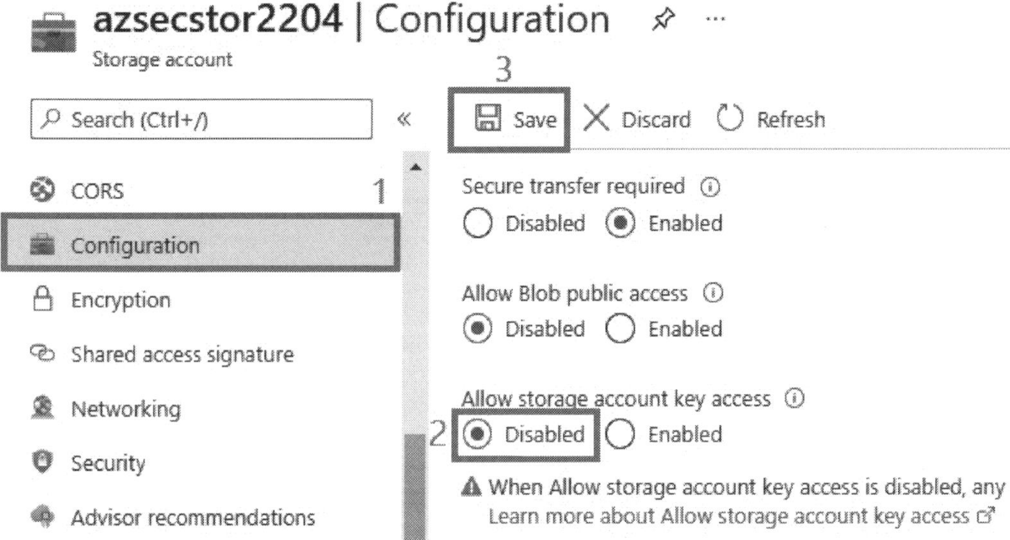

Figure 10.50 – Disabling storage account key access

19. Go back to the browser tab that has the SAS URL open from *Step 10* of this exercise. Refresh the page. You should receive an error message that key-based authorization is now disabled:

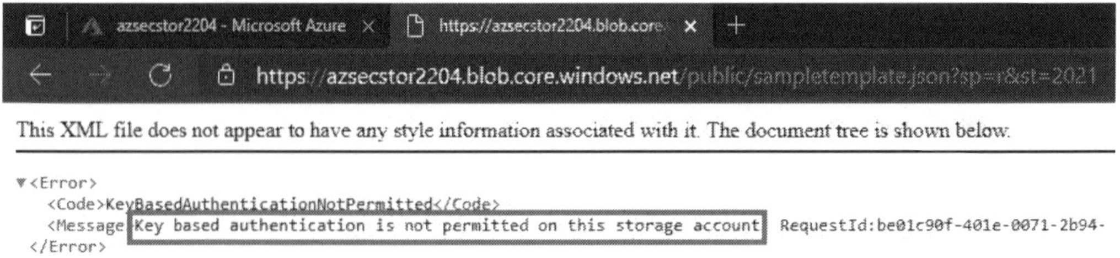

Figure 10.51 – Verifying key-based authentication

Congratulations! You have configured various storage account access control options and verified that your configurations worked.

In the next section, we will cover how to implement Azure Defender for Storage to detect suspicious activities in our storage accounts.

Implementing Azure Defender for Storage

Read, write, and delete requests to the Blob and Files services are logged by the storage service as resource logs. Azure Defender for Storage can ingest these logs and analyze them for suspicious events. Without a service like this, analyzing these logs requires security expertise and a significant amount of time.

When Azure Defender for Storage detects unusual and potentially harmful events, it raises an alert in Security Center for us to investigate and remediate threats. We will cover Security Center in a later chapter:

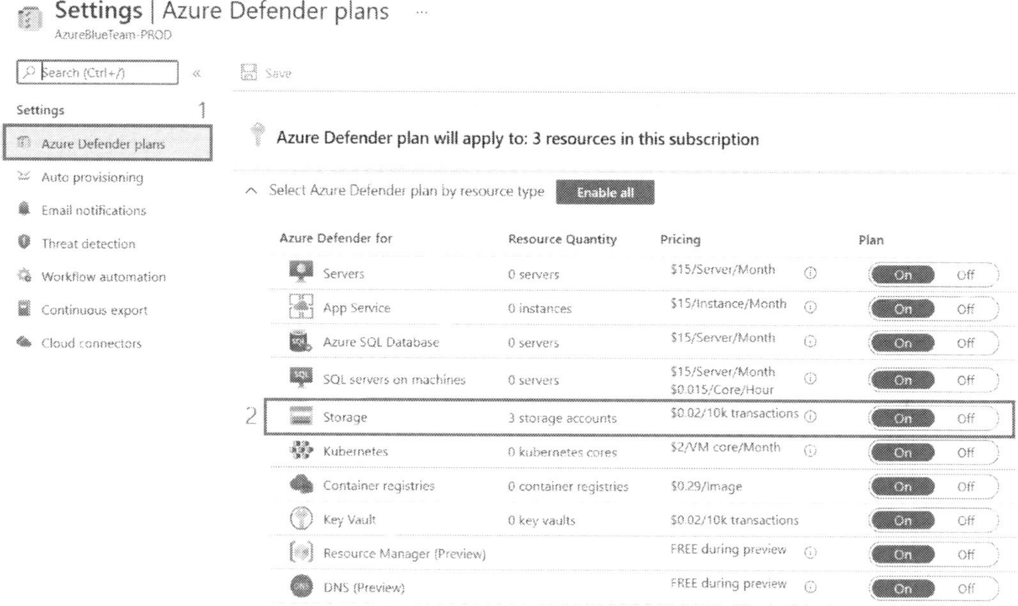

Figure 10.52 – Enabling Azure Defender for Storage

Azure Defender for Storage can be enabled from the **Security** blade of a storage account resource in the Azure portal or from the pricing and settings blade in Security Center (*Figure 10.52*). This can also be enabled at scale using Azure policy.

Cleaning up resources

In the Azure portal, delete the `azuresec-c10-rg` resource group. This will remove all the resources that we created for the exercises in this chapter.

Summary

In this chapter, you learned how to secure storage in Azure. We covered security best practices that you can implement for encryption at rest and in transit, and also how to secure access by implementing recommended authentication options. The skills that you gained in this chapter have equipped you with the knowledge of how to implement multilayered security to protect your critical data in Azure Storage.

In the next chapter, we will cover Azure SQL Database and how to secure data stored in it. See you in the next chapter!

Question

As we conclude, here is a question for you to test your knowledge regarding this chapter's material. You will find the answer in the *Assessments* section of the *Appendix*:

1. You discovered that some ad hoc SAS tokens are compromised and you need to revoke access to all SAS tokens that have been generated. What is the easiest way to accomplish this?

   a. Regenerate the storage account keys.

   b. Manually revoke the SAS tokens.

   c. Inform the users to stop using their SAS tokens.

   d. Delete the storage account.

Further reading

To learn more on the subject, consult the following resources:

- Azure blob security recommendations: `https://docs.microsoft.com/en-us/azure/storage/blobs/security-recommendations`
- Azure storage encryption for data at rest: `https://docs.microsoft.com/en-us/azure/storage/common/storage-service-encryption?toc=/azure/storage/blobs/toc.json`
- Azure Storage SAS: `https://docs.microsoft.com/en-us/azure/storage/common/storage-sas-overview`
- *Manage storage account keys with Key Vault and the Azure CLI*: `https://docs.microsoft.com/en-us/azure/key-vault/secrets/overview-storage-keys`

11 Implementing Database Security

The Azure cloud offers multiple database options to store application data. Customers can choose from a range that includes relational, NoSQL, and in-memory databases. The database technologies on offer also span both **proprietary** database management systems such as Microsoft SQL and **open source** systems such as MySQL, PostgreSQL, and MongoDB. Regardless of the option that we choose to use, we need to implement a comprehensive security strategy to protect our Azure databases from common risks such as unauthorized access, data leakage/theft, and database vulnerabilities. This chapter will cover how to implement this type of holistic database security.

Our focus in this chapter will be on the Azure SQL database options, but the same protection options that we cover can be applied to the other database services in Azure. Here are the topics that we will cover in this chapter:

- Database options in Azure
- Azure SQL deployment options
- Implementing defense in depth for Azure SQL
- Protecting Azure SQL against unauthorized network connections
- Protecting Azure SQL against unauthorized user access
- Protecting Azure SQL against vulnerabilities
- Protecting Azure SQL against data leakage and theft

Each topic has been structured to align with recommended database security best practices in Azure. Let's get into this!

Technical requirements

To follow along with the instructions in this chapter, you will need the following:

- A PC with an internet connection.
- An Azure subscription. You can use the same subscription that you set up in the first chapter of this book.

Before we proceed to cover the security best practices, let's prepare our Azure subscription for the hands-on exercises that we will be completing later in the chapter.

Database options in Azure

Modern business applications rarely interact with a single type of dataset. Increasingly, organizations are adopting a flexible approach that allows them to use different data stores to persist application data based on the workload type or usage pattern of that application. The Azure cloud enables organizations to adopt this approach by offering different database options to fit the needs of modern app developers. *Figure 11.1* shows the range of database options available in Azure:

	Relational Data	Unstructured Data	Semi-Structured Data	Large Data Sets	Small Data Sets	In Memory Database
Azure SQL	✓				✓	
Azure Database for MySQL	✓				✓	
Azure Database for PostgreSQL	✓				✓	
Azure Database for MariaDB	✓				✓	
Azure Cosmos DB		✓	✓	✓	✓	
Azure Table Storage			✓		✓	
Azure Synapse Analytics	✓			✓	✓	
Azure Cache for Redis					✓	✓

Figure 11.1 – Database options in Azure

As you can see from the preceding diagram, there are multiple relational database options that are available, including open source database engines such as PostgreSQL, MySQL, and MariaDB. Before we proceed further in our discussion, let's review the options that we have when we implement Azure SQL.

Azure SQL deployment options

When we talk about Azure SQL, we are referring to a family of products in Azure that is built on Microsoft's popular SQL Server database engine (*Figure 11.2*). This family of products offers two deployment categories based on the use case of the customer – **Infrastructure as a Service** (**IaaS**) and **Platform as a Service** (**PaaS**) (*Figure 11.2*).

In the IaaS category, we have the option to implement SQL Server on an Azure VM. This is similar to what most organizations already do on-premises, only that the VM is hosted in Azure instead of on-premises data centers. The advantage of this option is that the customer has control of the OS and the SQL database engine. This means that the customer has a greater level of flexibility to apply customizations. The downside to this option is that the customer is responsible for managing the OS and the SQL database engine going forward. This means that responsibilities such as OS and SQL Server upgrades, patching, monitoring, and other database management functions are owned by the customer going forward. That is a lot of work! But this is not unusual. This is the standard technology trade-off – flexibility versus management responsibilities:

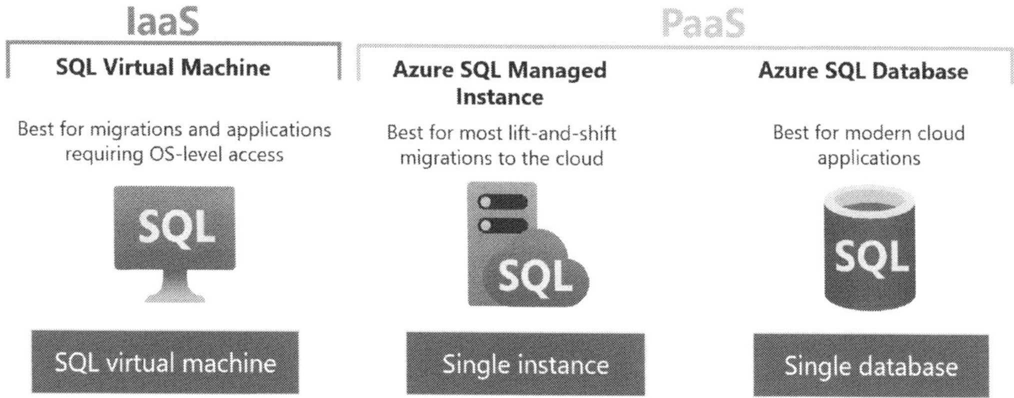

Figure 11.2 – SQL database options in Azure

In the PaaS category, we have two deployment options – **Azure SQL Database** and **Azure SQL Managed Instance**. The **Azure SQL Managed Instance** option gives us an instance of SQL Server but abstracts the overhead of managing the underlying VM from us. Customers do not have access to the OS or the underlying infrastructure as they are managed automatically by the Azure cloud platform! From a security perspective, we have fewer responsibilities to take care of as we do not need to get involved with OS upgrades and patching but it does mean that we have less control and less flexibility to implement customizations. This is the option that Microsoft recommends for customers who are looking to migrate their on-premises SQL workloads to Azure without re-architecting their applications. This is because it has a higher degree of feature compatibility with on-premises SQL Server.

The second option that we have in the PaaS category is **Azure SQL Database**. This option abstracts the overhead of managing both the OS and the SQL Server instance away from us. With that being said, do not think for a minute that we do not have security responsibilities to take care of because of these abstractions – we do! And in the next section, we will highlight what these are before we delve into them in detail.

> **Important note**
>
> For our purpose in this chapter, our focus will be on Azure SQL; however, what we discuss is applicable to other platform database services in Azure.

Implementing defense in depth for Azure SQL

There are multiple attack vectors that an adversary could exploit to compromise our Azure SQL database instances. For this reason, our security strategy should follow a defense-in-depth approach that includes the following layers of protection:

- Protection against unauthorized network access
- Protection against unauthorized user access
- Protection against vulnerabilities and threats
- Protection against data leakage and theft

Figure 11.3 shows this defense:

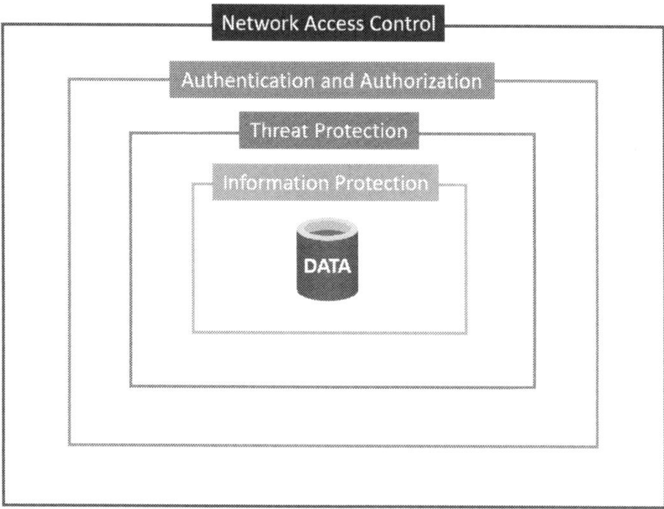

Figure 11.3 – Azure SQL defense in depth

In the following sections in this chapter, we will cover these different layers of protection in detail starting with the mitigation of unauthorized network access.

Protecting Azure SQL against unauthorized network connections

When an Azure SQL database instance is created, it is deployed into an Azure SQL logical server. The logical server acts as the administrative frontend for SQL databases. As shown in *Figure 11.4*, one logical server can contain multiple SQL databases and elastic pool databases:

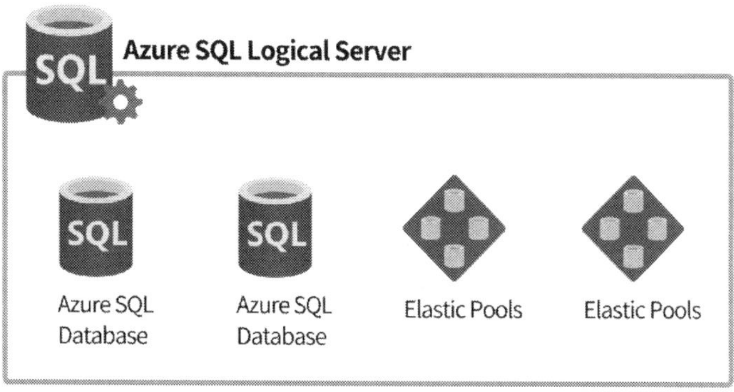

Figure 11.4 – Azure SQL components

To protect data in our SQL databases, we should only allow access from trusted and necessary clients. Here are some ways to control network access to Azure SQL databases.

Implementing IP firewall rules

By default, a logical SQL server has a public endpoint that is reachable on the public internet using the DNS name in the following format:

```
<unique_server_name>.yourservername.database.windows.net.
```

Clients can use this endpoint to connect to databases contained in the server. Azure SQL Database has a built-in firewall that can be used to define trusted network resources that are allowed to establish a connection to our databases. With this feature implemented, connection requests from IP addresses that are not explicitly allowed will be dropped:

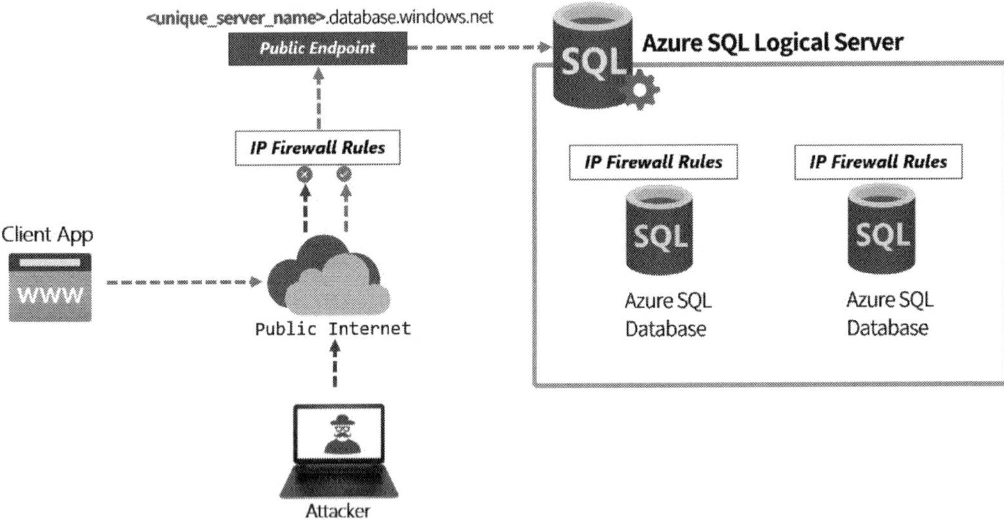

Figure 11.5 – Azure SQL Server and database firewall rules

As shown in *Figure 11.5*, these firewall rules can be configured on the logical server level or on individual database levels for more granular restrictions.

Implementing server-level firewall rules

Server-level firewall rules allow us to define trusted connection sources for all the databases within the same logical server. There are three kinds of rules that we can configure at the server level.

The first kind of rule is the **IP address rule**, which allows us to specify public IP address ranges that are allowed to connect to databases within a logical server (*Figure 11.6*). The second kind of rule is the **virtual network rule**, which allows us to define Azure virtual network subnets that are allowed to connect over the Azure private WAN to databases in the logical server. This second type of rule is similar to the concept of service endpoints that we discussed in previous chapters. It is the **Azure service rule**, which can be used to allow network connection from all Azure public IP addresses including from other Azure customer subscriptions! This is a really broad range!

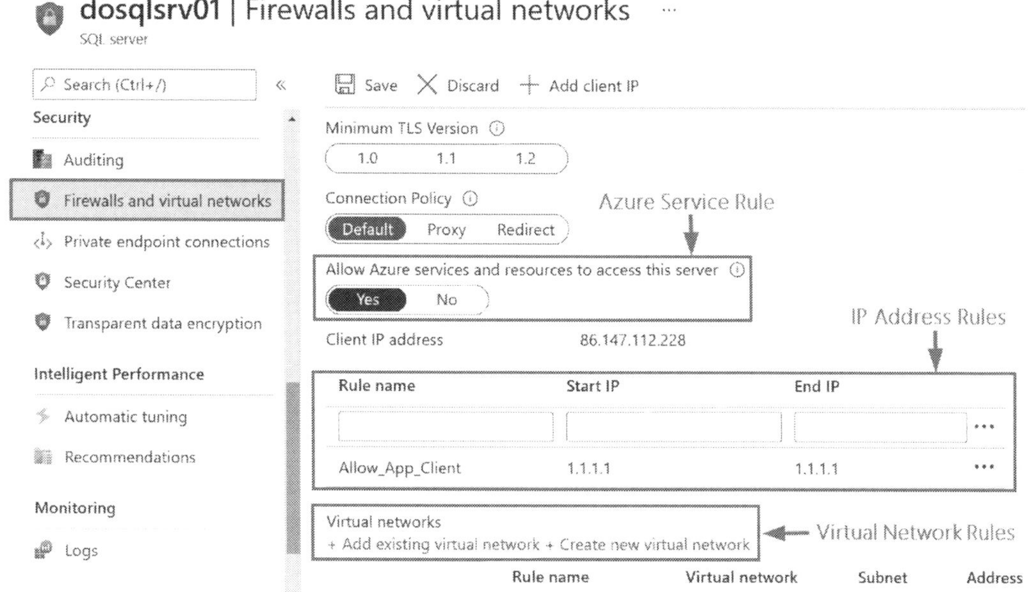

Figure 11.6 – Azure SQL server-level firewall rules

As shown in *Figure 11.6*, we can configure server-level IP firewall rules using the Azure portal, Azure PowerShell, or **Transact-SQL (T-SQL)** statements. To configure this using the Azure portal, we can modify the **Firewalls and virtual networks** setting of the logical server.

Implementing database-level firewall rules

Database-level firewall rules allow access to an individual database on a logical server. This option is useful if we have a need to implement more granular network access control for individual databases in the same logical server. There is only one type of rule that we can configure at the database level – the IP address rule, which can be used to define public IP address ranges that are allowed to connect to a specific database. Another advantage of database-level firewall rules is agility. Because the firewall rules are stored in the database itself, they follow the database wherever it is moved or replicated to.

As of the time of writing (mid-2021), database-level IP firewall rules can only be configured using T-SQL. The following is an example statement that can be used:

```
EXECUTE sp_set_database_firewall_rule @name =
N'DBFirewallRule',
    @start_ip_address = '1.1.1.1', @end_ip_address = '1.1.1.1'
```

Once both or either of the server-level or database-level firewall rules are defined, connection requests from IP addresses that are not explicitly allowed will be dropped (*Figure 11.5*).

Implementing Azure SQL private endpoints

Another option that we can implement for network access control is to configure a private endpoint. This is similar to the implementation of private endpoints that we covered in *Chapter 9*, *Implementing Container Security*, of this book. Configuring this option allows us to connect to a logical server via a private IP address within a specific virtual network and subnet (*Figure 11.7*):

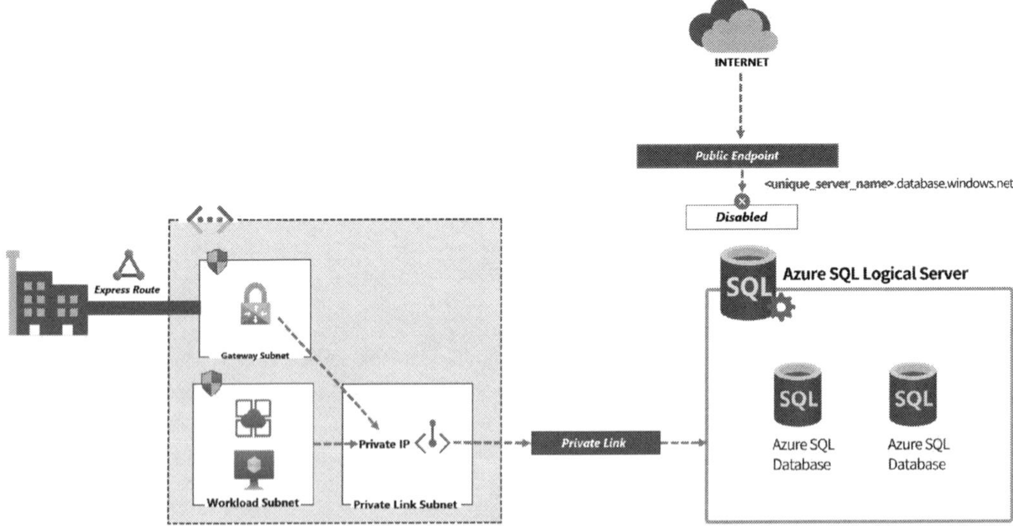

Figure 11.7 – Azure SQL IP private endpoint

With this option configured, we could choose to deny public network access, thereby forcing private-only connectivity (*Figure 11.8*). This option can be configured in the **Firewalls and virtual networks** setting of a logical server:

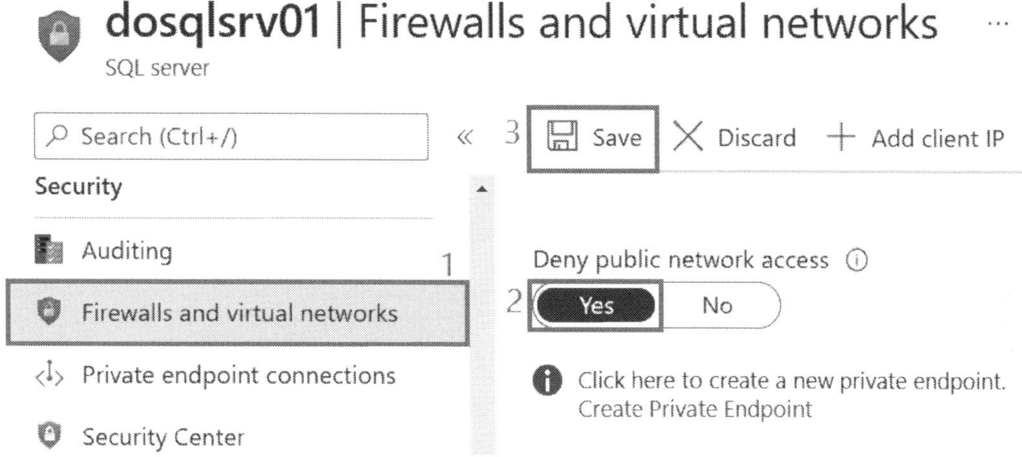

Figure 11.8 – Azure SQL Deny public network access option

One of the best ways to understand a concept is to practice it. In the next two sections, we will provision resources in Azure to use for exercises and we will see some of the concepts that we have discussed in action.

Hands-on exercise – provisioning resources for chapter exercises

To follow along with the exercises in this chapter, we will provision some Azure resources to work with. We have prepared an ARM template in the GitHub repository of this book for this purpose. The template will deploy an Azure virtual network with two subnets as shown in *Figure 11.9*. The public subnet will have a Windows Server 2019 VM that is reachable from the public internet. The private subnet will have an Ubuntu Linux VM that is not reachable directly from the internet. Here are the tasks that we will complete in this exercise:

- **Task 1**: Obtain your user account object ID.
- **Task 2**: Initialize template deployment in GitHub.

- **Task 3**: Complete the parameters and deploy the template to Azure:

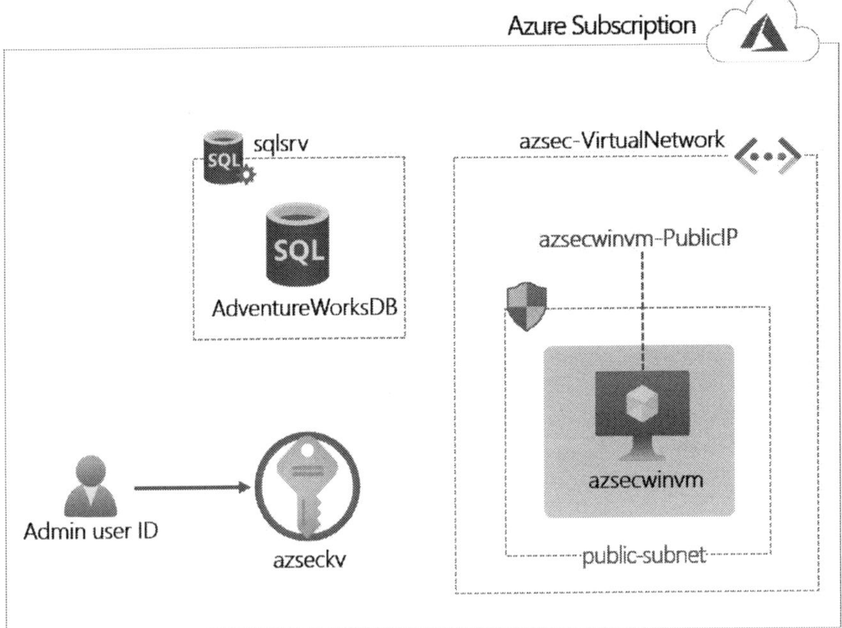

Figure 11.9 – Resources deployed for exercise scenarios

Let's begin the steps to complete the tasks.

In order to grant access to the Key Vault resource that will be deployed in the template, we need to obtain the object ID of our Azure AD user account as we will need to specify it as an input parameter:

1. Open a web browser and browse to the Azure portal (`https://portal.azure.com`). Sign in with your admin user account credentials.
2. In the Azure portal, click on the **Cloud Shell** icon in the top-right corner of the Azure portal. You can select **Bash** or **PowerShell**:

Figure 11.10 – Clicking the icon to open Cloud Shell

3. In the **Bash** or **PowerShell** session within the **Cloud Shell** pane, run the following command to get the object ID of your user account:

```
az ad signed-in-user show --query objectId --output tsv
```

Make a note of the object ID displayed in the output. You will need this information in a later step:

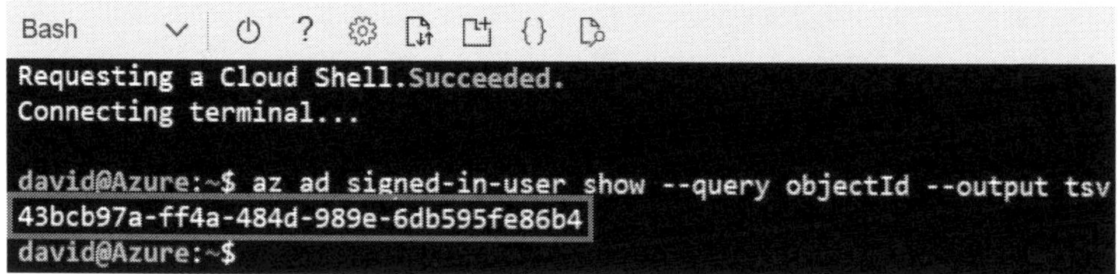

Figure 11.11 – Obtaining the object ID of the user account

4. Open a web browser and browse to `http://bit.ly/az500-c11-template`. This link will open the GitHub repository that has an ARM template to deploy the resources that we need.

5. In the GitHub repository that opens, click on **Deploy to Azure**:

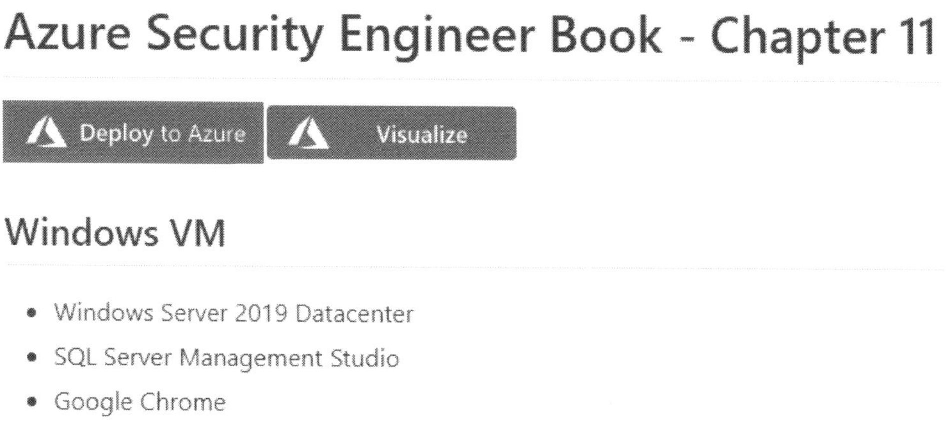

Azure Security Engineer Book - Chapter 11

Windows VM

- Windows Server 2019 Datacenter
- SQL Server Management Studio
- Google Chrome

Figure 11.12 – Starting the template deployment

6. In the **Sign in** window, enter your administrative username and password to authenticate to your Azure subscription:

Figure 11.13 – Authenticating to Azure

7. In the **Custom Deployment** window, configure the following:

   Subscription: Select the subscription that you want to deploy the resources into.

   Resource group: **Create new** | **Name**: `azuresec-c11-rg` | **OK**.

   Region: Select an Azure region close to your location.

   Storagename: Leave default value.

   Vm-dns: Leave default value.

   Admin User: Leave default value.

   Admin Password: Enter a complex password. Make a note of the password that you use. We recommend that you select one complex password that you use throughout the scenarios in this book to keep things simple.

   Vmsize: Leave default value. If no default value is displayed, this is because the default size is not available to deploy in the region selected. Click on **Change size**, and select an available VM size.

   Location: Leave default value.

Object Id: Enter the object ID value that you obtained in the first task of this exercise.

_artifacts Location: Leave default value.

_artifacts Location Sas Token: Leave default value.

Click on **Review + create**:

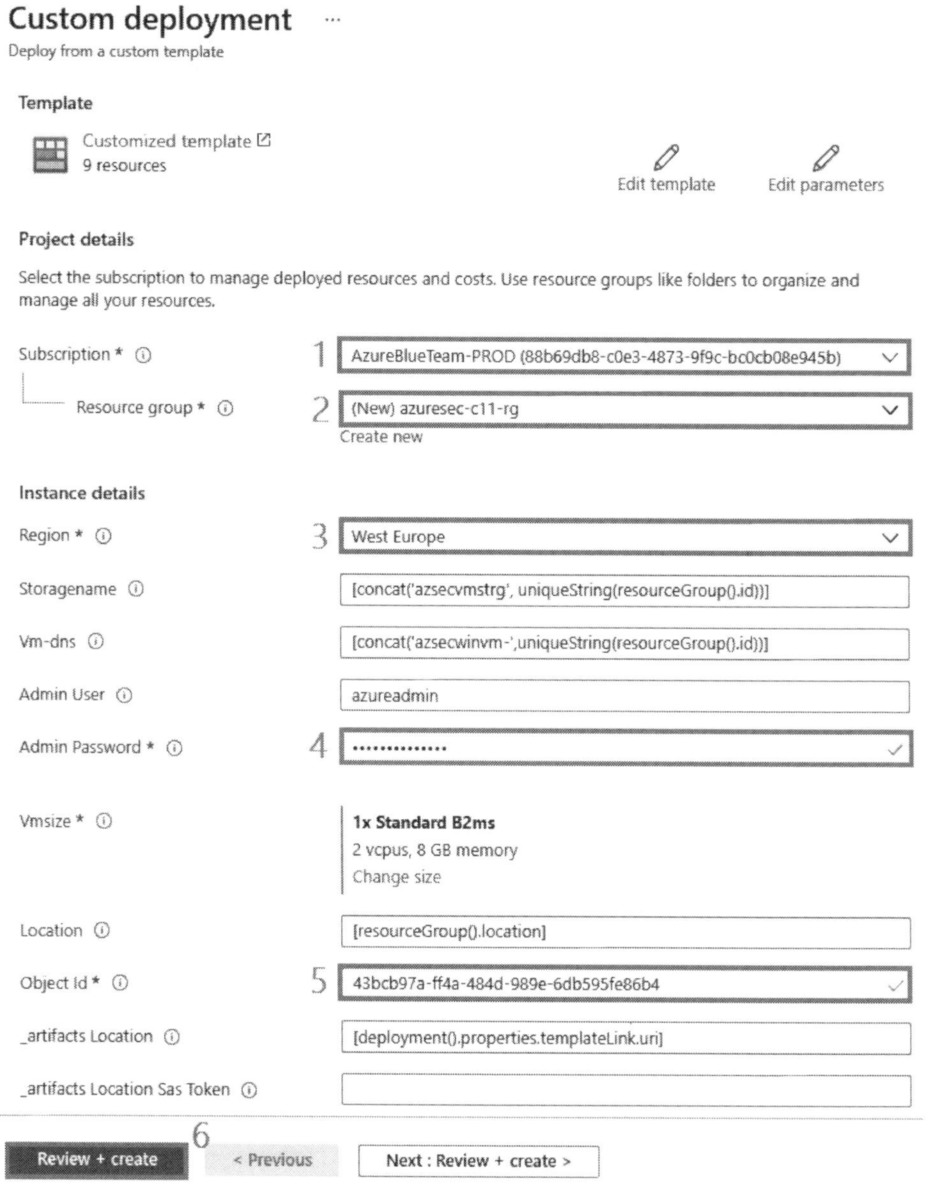

Custom deployment ...
Deploy from a custom template

Template
Customized template
9 resources
Edit template
Edit parameters

Project details
Select the subscription to manage deployed resources and costs. Use resource groups like folders to organize and manage all your resources.

Subscription * 1 AzureBlueTeam-PROD (88b69db8-c0e3-4873-9f9c-bc0cb08e945b)
Resource group * 2 (New) azuresec-c11-rg
Create new

Instance details
Region * 3 West Europe
Storagename [concat('azsecvmstrg', uniqueString(resourceGroup().id))]
Vm-dns [concat('azsecwinvm-',uniqueString(resourceGroup().id))]
Admin User azureadmin
Admin Password * 4 ••••••••••••••
Vmsize * 1x Standard B2ms
2 vcpus, 8 GB memory
Change size
Location [resourceGroup().location]
Object Id * 5 43bcb97a-ff4a-484d-989e-6db595fe86b4
_artifacts Location [deployment().properties.templateLink.uri]
_artifacts Location Sas Token

Review + create 6 < Previous Next : Review + create >

Figure 11.14 – Configuring template parameters

8. After the template validation has passed, click on **Create**. This will begin the deployment process, which takes about 7 to 10 minutes to complete. Grab yourself a cup of water, tea, or coffee and wait for the deployment to complete:

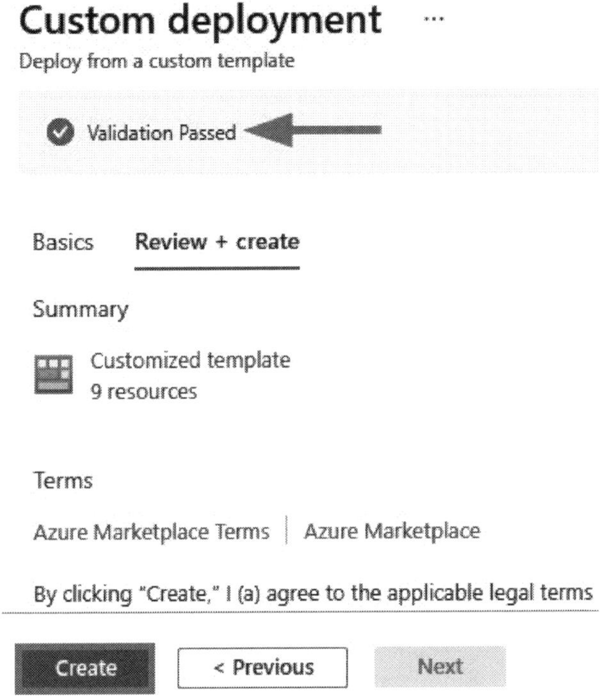

Figure 11.15 – Deploying the template

9. After the deployment has completed, click on the **Outputs** tab. Make a note of the following values:

   winvmdns: This is the public DNS name of the Windows VM that was just deployed.

   winvmuser: This is the administrator username of the Windows VM that was just deployed.

sqlserverName: The DNS of the SQL server.

sqladminuser: The administrator username of the SQL server.

keyVaultName: The name of the Key Vault resource that was deployed:

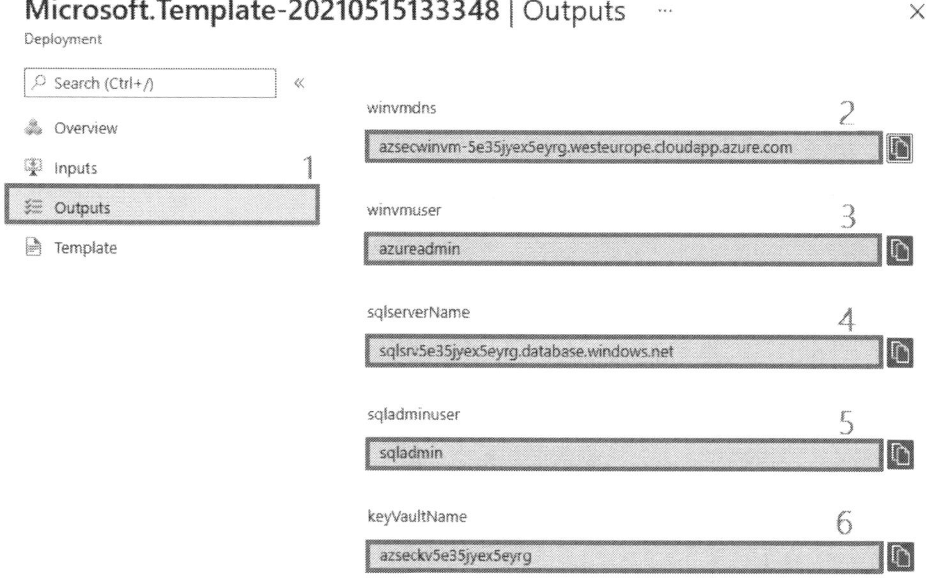

Figure 11.16 – Obtaining the Windows VM DNS name

10. On your client system, open an RDP client and enter the **winvmdns** value that you made a note of earlier and connect to it. Use the following credentials when prompted:

    Username: `azureadmin`.

Password: Enter the password that you configured during the template deployment:

Figure 11.17 – RDP session to the public Windows VM

In this exercise, we provisioned some Azure resources that we need for the rest of the exercises in this chapter. In the next section, we will walk through the implementation of network access control for Azure SQL databases.

Hands-on exercise – implementing network access control

Here are the tasks that we will complete in this exercise:

- **Task 1**: Connect to the SQL server from the Windows VM.
- **Task 2**: Add a server-level firewall rule to allow connections from the Windows VM.
- **Task 3**: Verify the server-level firewall rule that was added.

Here are the steps to complete the tasks:

1. In the RDP session to the Windows VM, click on the Start button, expand **Microsoft SQL Server Tools 18**, and then click on **Microsoft SQL Server Management Studio**:

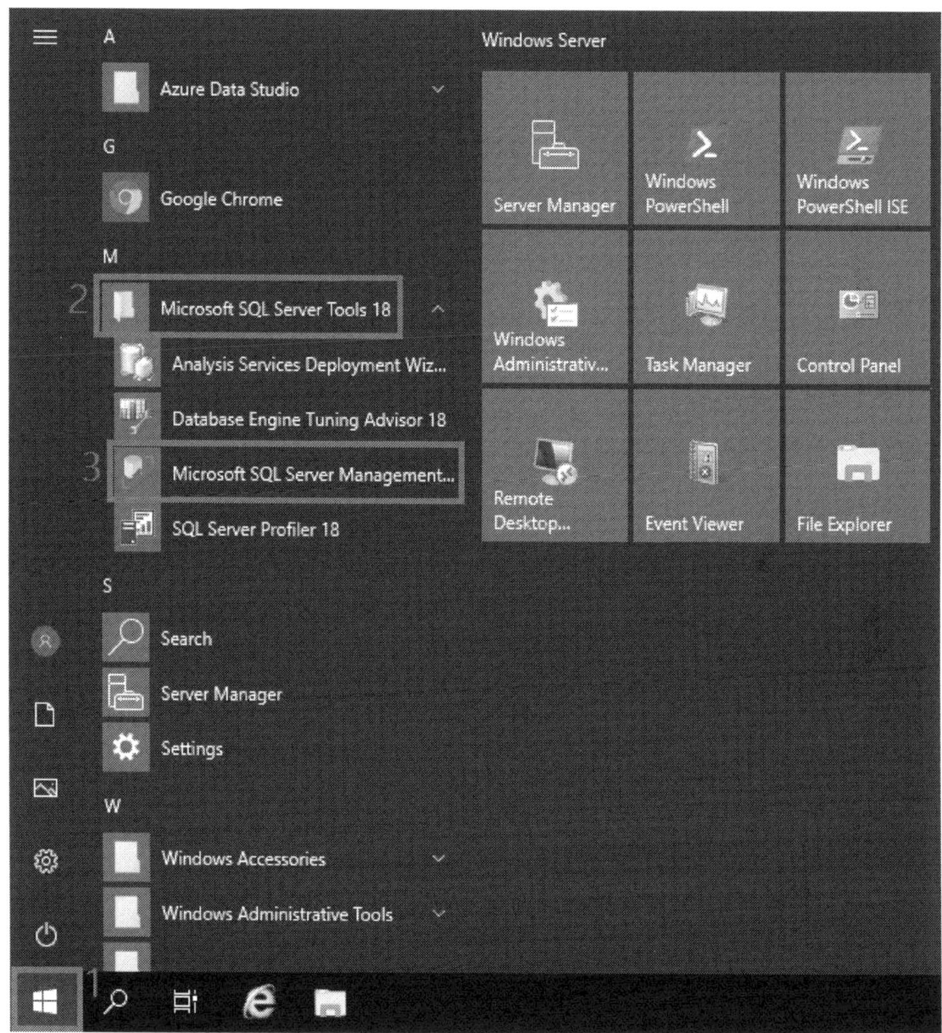

Figure 11.18 – Opening Microsoft SQL Server Management Studio

2. In the **Microsoft SQL Server Management Studio** window, configure the following:

   Server type: **Database Engine**.

   Server name: Enter the value of the **sqlserverName** output that you made a note of in the previous exercise.

   Authentication: **SQL Server Authentication**.

   Login: **sqladmin**.

   Password: The password that you configured during the template deployment.

   Click on **Connect**:

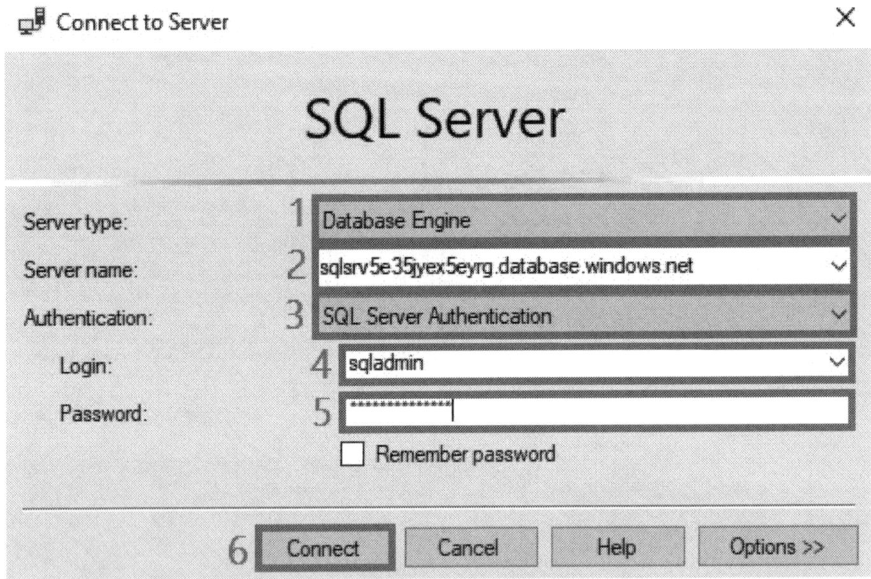

Figure 11.19 – Connecting to the SQL server

   You will receive a message about your client IP not having access to the server. This is because, by default, no IP address is granted access. Because our credentials have permissions to modify the firewall rules for SQL servers, we can sign in from this window and add the rule to allow the Windows VM public IP. We will do this in the next step.

3. In the **New Firewall Rule** window, click on **Sign In…**. When prompted to authenticate, use your Azure administrator sign-in credentials that you used to sign in when you created the resources:

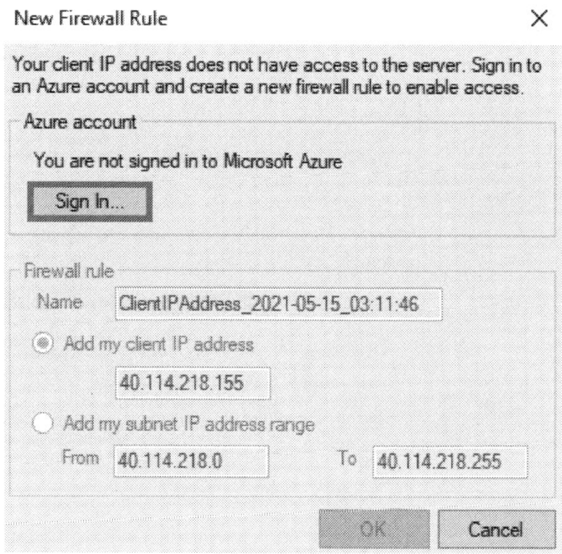

Figure 11.20 – Signing in to create a new firewall rule

4. Still in the **New Firewall Rule** window, configure the following:

   Name: `Allow-Lab-Windows-VM`

   Leave the other settings at the default values and click **OK**:

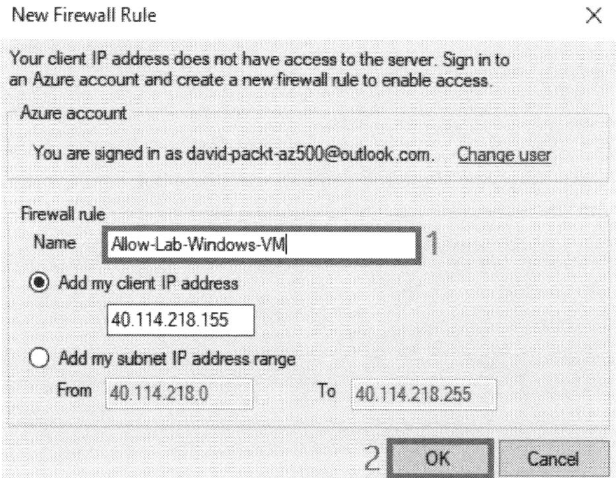

Figure 11.21 – Configuring the name for the firewall

This will automatically add the firewall rule to allow the Windows VM and connect you to the SQL server. In the next steps, we will verify this rule, but for now, close Microsoft **SQL Server Management Studio** (**SSMS**).

5. Open a web browser and browse to `https://portal.azure.com`.
6. In the search area at the top of the screen, type `sqlsrv` and click on the SQL Server resource that was created in the previous exercise:

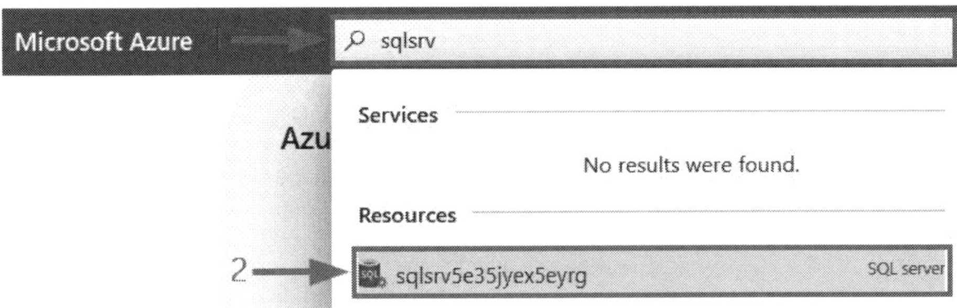

Figure 11.22 – Searching for the SQL server

7. In the SQL Server window, click on **Firewalls and virtual networks** under the **Security** section. Review the rule that was added to allow your Windows VM to connect to the server:

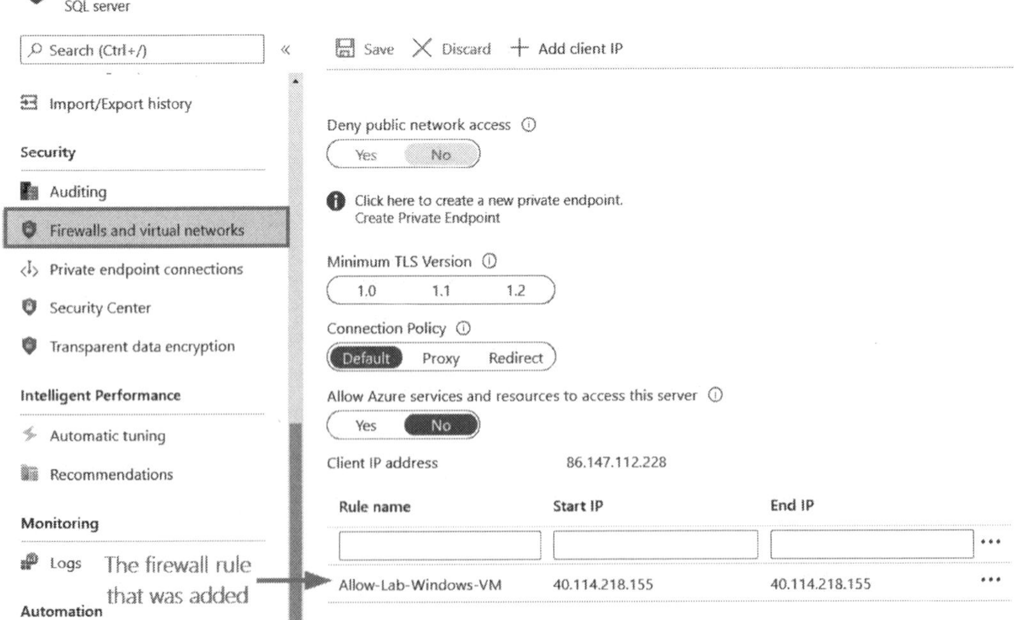

Figure 11.23 – Verifying the firewall rule

Leave the Azure portal open for the next hands-on exercise.

In this section, we covered the first layer of protection – network access control for Azure SQL databases. In the next section, we will cover the second layer of implementing authentication and authorization.

Protecting Azure SQL against unauthorized user access

Preventing unauthorized network connections may be the first layer of security for Azure SQL databases but clients still need to be authenticated and authorized before they can gain access. Authentication validates the identity of the client that is requesting access while authorization validates the *operations that an identity can perform in a SQL database*. Azure SQL Database supports two types of authentication: SQL authentication and **Azure Active Directory** (**Azure AD**) authentication.

SQL authentication uses a username and password that is stored in the master database (for server-wide access) or individual databases. When a new SQL logical server is created in Azure, we need to specify a local server admin credential. This credential is referred to as the **server admin** account. This account can authenticate to any database on that server as the database owner. We can use the initial server admin account to create additional SQL logins and users.

The second option is to implement **Azure AD authentication** so that Azure AD identities (both cloud and hybrid) can be used to authenticate access to our SQL server and databases. When using Azure AD, this can be cloud-only identities or even Azure AD hybrid identities (password hash, pass-through, and federated authentication). The best practice is to implement Azure AD authentication as it means that we could centralize authentication and authorization for SQL databases while leveraging advanced identity security capabilities of Azure AD that we covered in *Chapter 4, Azure AD Identity Security*, and *Chapter 5, Azure AD Identity Governance*, of this book.

Authorization in SQL databases is controlled by permissions granted by assigning a role to a user or a group. Authorization is granted the same way regardless of authentication method – SQL authentication or Azure AD authentication. From a security standpoint, users should only be granted privileges that they need and use to perform their organization functions.

In the next hands-on exercise, we will walk through the implementation of Azure AD authentication for Azure SQL.

Hands-on exercise – implementing Azure AD authentication and authorization

In *Chapter 2, Understanding Azure AD*, we created two Azure AD user accounts named Brenda and Emmy. In this demonstration, we will make Brenda an Azure AD admin for the SQL server that we deployed earlier. We will then use Brenda's account to grant permission to Emmy as a database owner for the `AdventureWorks` database. Here are the tasks that we will complete in this exercise:

- **Task 1**: Configure the Azure AD admin for SQL Server.
- **Task 2**: Add a server-level firewall rule to allow connections from the Windows VM.
- **Task 3**: Connect to a SQL database as an Azure AD user.

Here are the steps to complete the tasks:

1. Open a web browser and browse to `https://portal.azure.com`.
2. In the search area at the top of the screen, type `sqlsrv` and click on the SQL Server resource that was created in the previous exercise:

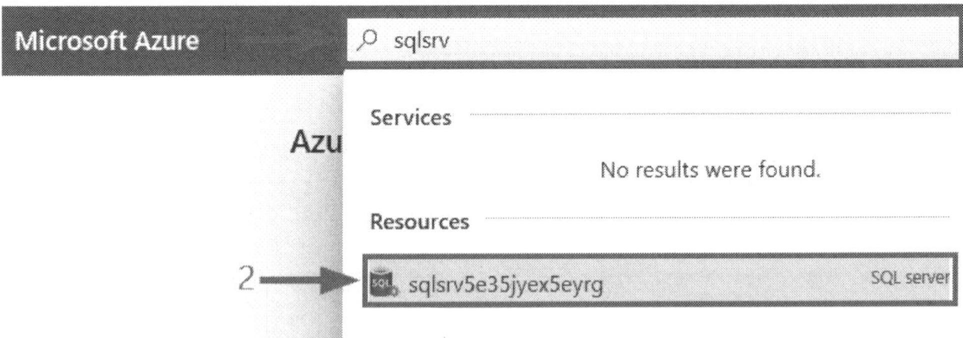

Figure 11.24 – Searching for the SQL server

3. In the SQL Server window, click on **Active Directory admin** in the **Settings** section, then click on **Set admin**:

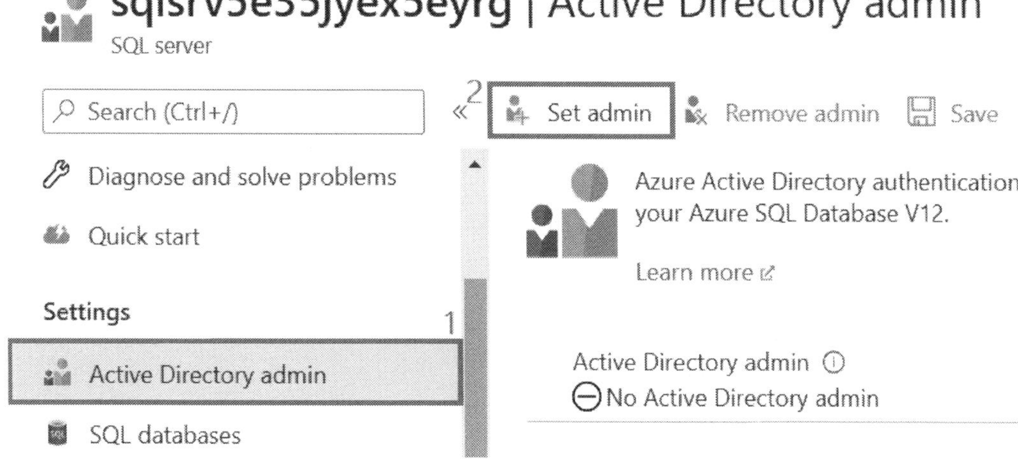

Figure 11.25 – Configuring the Azure AD admin for SQL Server

4. On the **Add admin** page, search for Brenda's Azure AD user account user (note that Microsoft accounts cannot be added). Click to select the account, then click on **Select**:

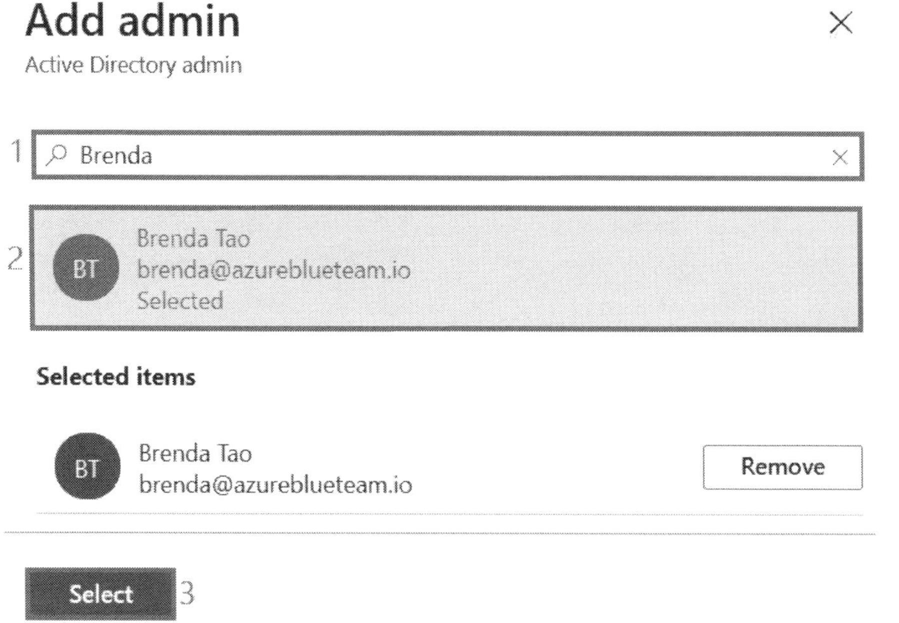

Figure 11.26 – Adding an Azure AD admin user

5. At the top of the **Active Directory admin** page, select **Save**:

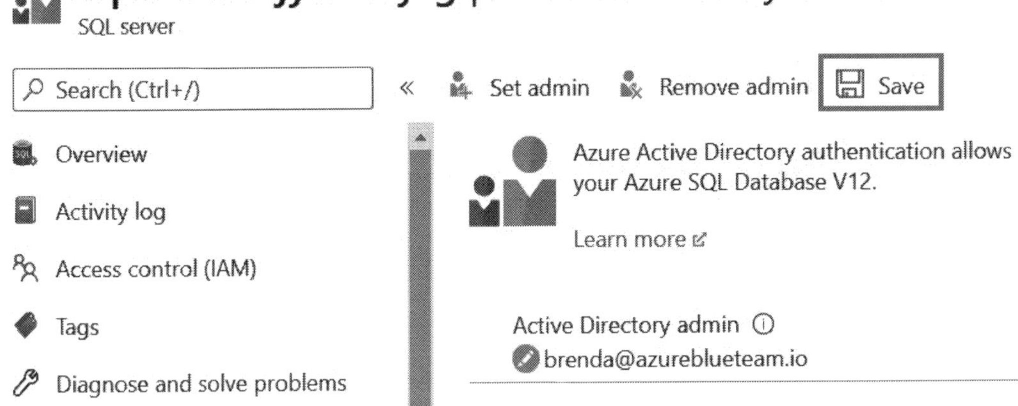

Figure 11.27 – Saving the Azure AD admin configuration

The preceding process will add Brenda's account as a database owner to the master database of the SQL server. This gives her full access to all databases in the SQL logical server. In the next steps, we will use Brenda's new permission to add Emmy's account as a database owner for the `AdventureWorksDB` database.

6. Open the RDP session to the Windows VM and open Microsoft SSMS. In the **Microsoft SQL Server Management Studio** window, configure the following:

   Server type: **Database Engine**.

   Server name: Enter the value of the **sqlserverName** output that you made a note of in the previous exercise.

Authentication: **Azure Active Directory - Universal with MFA** (we are selecting this option because MFA is enabled for Brenda's credentials).

User name: Brenda's UPN information.

Click on **Connect**.

Authenticate with Brenda's credentials and complete the MFA process. If prompted to change Brenda's password, go ahead and change it:

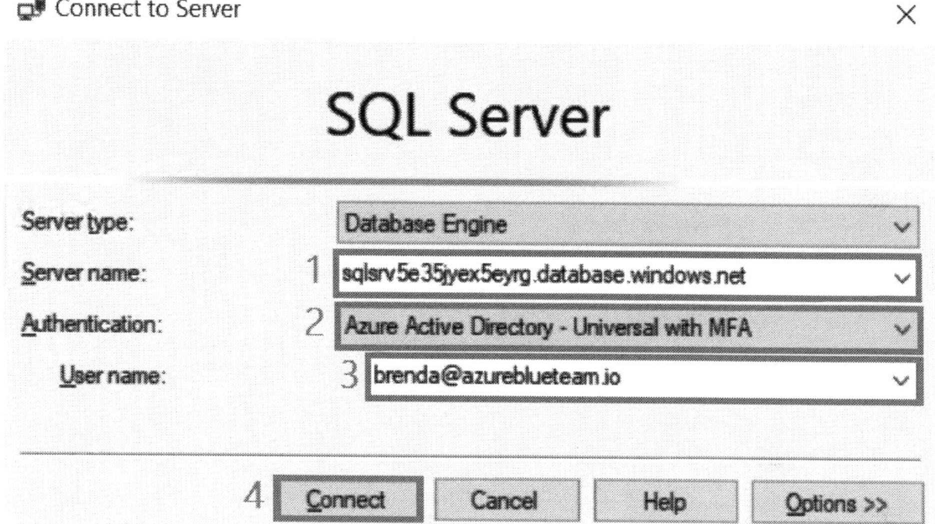

Figure 11.28 – Connecting to SQL Server

You are now connected to the SQL server as Brenda.

7. In the **Microsoft SQL Server Management Studio** window, in the **Object Explorer** pane, expand **Databases**, right-click the **AdventureWorksDB** database, and select **New Query**:

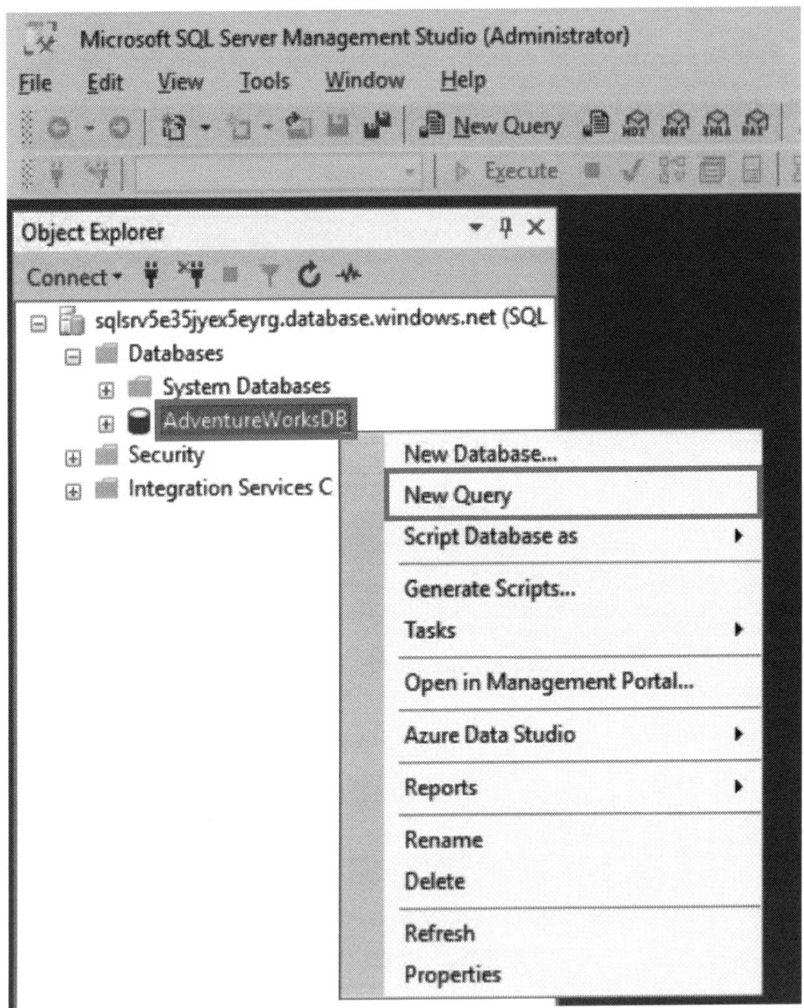

Figure 11.29 – Creating a new query

This will open a new query window.

8. In the query window, enter the following query. Replace <EMMY_UPN> with the user principal name of user Emmy. In my scenario, this will be `emmy@azureblueteam.io`. Proceed to click on **Execute** to execute the SQL query. The first three lines create the user. The last two lines assign roles to the user:

```
CREATE USER "<EMMY_UPN>"
FROM EXTERNAL PROVIDER
WITH DEFAULT_SCHEMA = dbo;

ALTER ROLE db_owner ADD MEMBER "<EMMY_UPN>";
ALTER ROLE db_accessadmin ADD MEMBER "<EMMY_UPN>";
```

Here is a screenshot of this:

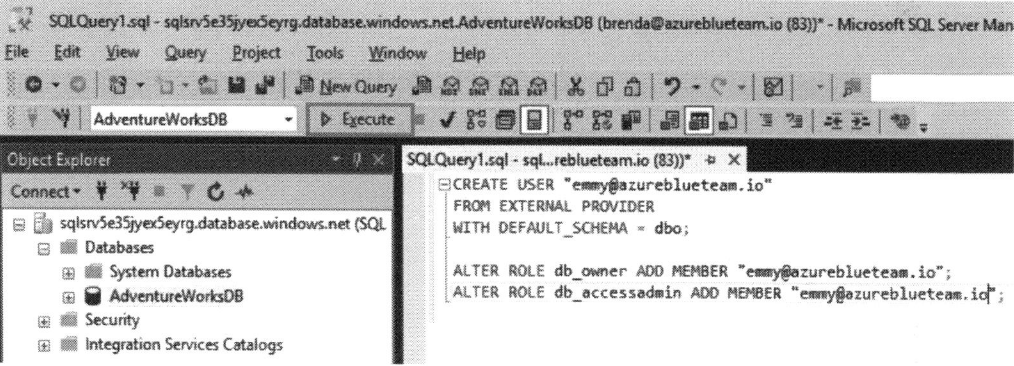

Figure 11.30 – Executing the query

You should receive a message about the commands completing successfully. You can now close SSMS. When prompted about saving the SQL query, select **No**. In the next steps, we will connect as Emmy to the `AdventureWorksDB` database to verify access.

9. In the RDP session to the Windows VM, open Microsoft SSMS. In the **Microsoft SQL Server Management Studio** window, configure the following:

   Server type: **Database Engine**.

   Server name: Enter the value of the **sqlserverName** output that you made a note of in the previous exercise.

   Authentication: **Azure Active Directory - Password** (we are selecting this option because MFA is *not* enabled for Emmy's credentials).

   User name: Emmy's UPN information.

   Click on **Options**:

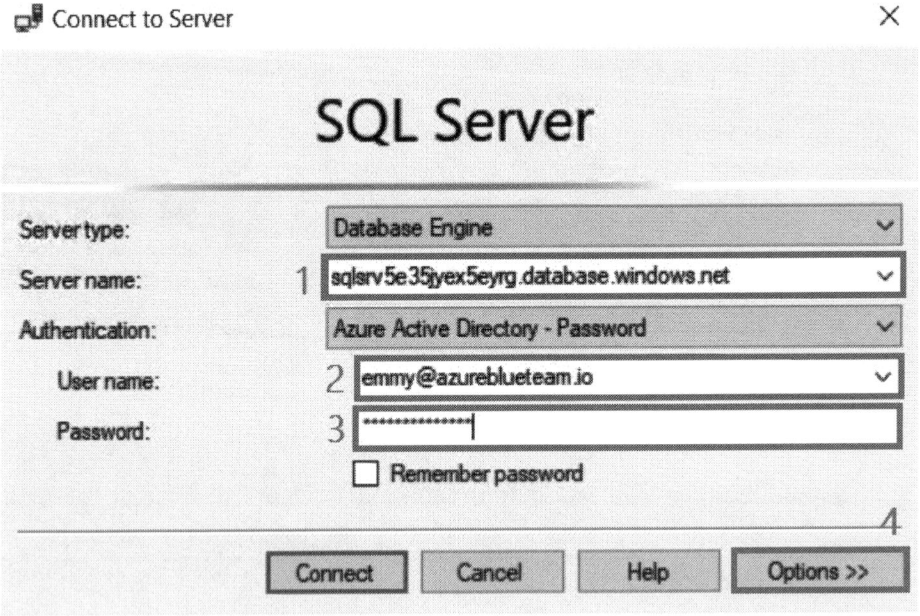

Connect to Server

SQL Server

Server type: Database Engine

Server name: 1 sqlsrv5e35jyex5eyrg.database.windows.net

Authentication: Azure Active Directory - Password

User name: 2 emmy@azureblueteam.io

Password: 3 ***************

Remember password

4

Connect Cancel Help Options >>

Figure 11.31 – Entering SQL Server connection information

10. In the **Connection Properties** menu, configure the following:

    Connect to database: **AdventureWorksDB**

    Click on **Connect**:

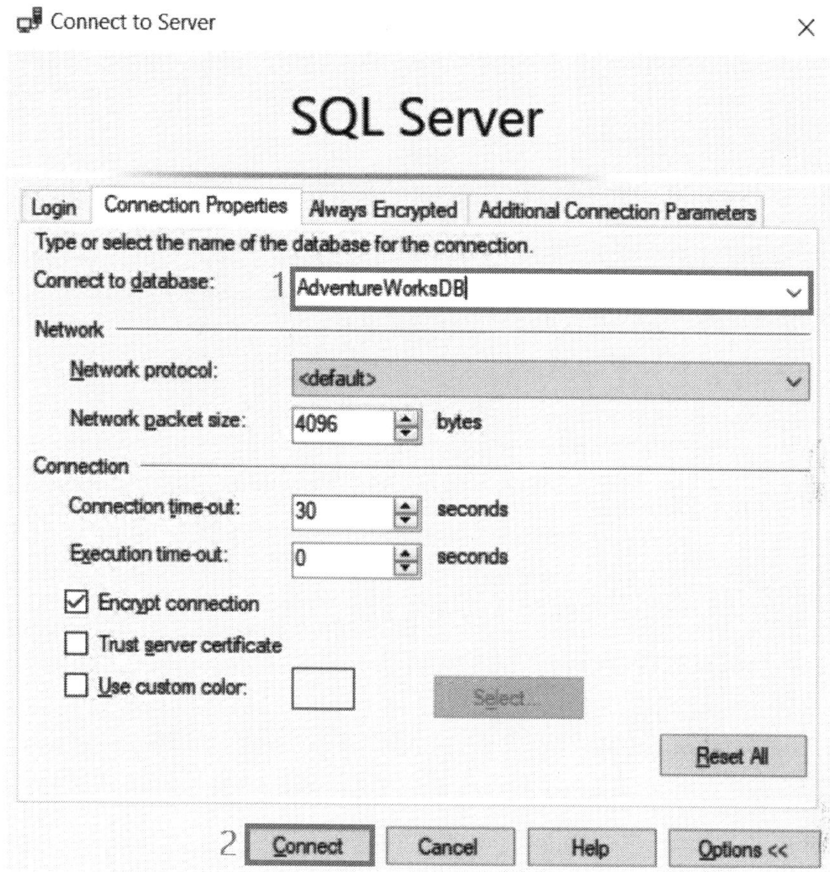

Figure 11.32 – Entering SQL database connection information

Congratulations! You are now authenticated to a SQL database with an Azure AD user credential.

In the next section, we will cover how to implement threat detection and protection for Azure SQL databases.

Protecting Azure SQL against vulnerabilities

A holistic security strategy should not only include *preventing successful attacks*, but should also include *detecting ongoing threats* that may have bypassed existing defenses. There are two sides to implementing this for our SQL databases. The starting point is to **enable Azure SQL database auditing** to record database operations. The other side is to **implement Azure Defender for SQL** to analyze the logs and stay alert for suspicious events.

Enabling Azure SQL database auditing

Azure SQL auditing is a feature that can be used to record database events to an audit log in an Azure Storage account, Log Analytics workspace, or event hub. The main use case of this feature is to record database operations for further analysis. Another use case is for compliance purposes.

This feature is *not* enabled by default. Using the Azure portal, we can enable it at the server or database level from the **Security** section (*Figure 11.33*). Enabling it at the database level enables it only for that specific database. Enabling it at the server level ensures that auditing is enabled for all existing and newly created databases on the server:

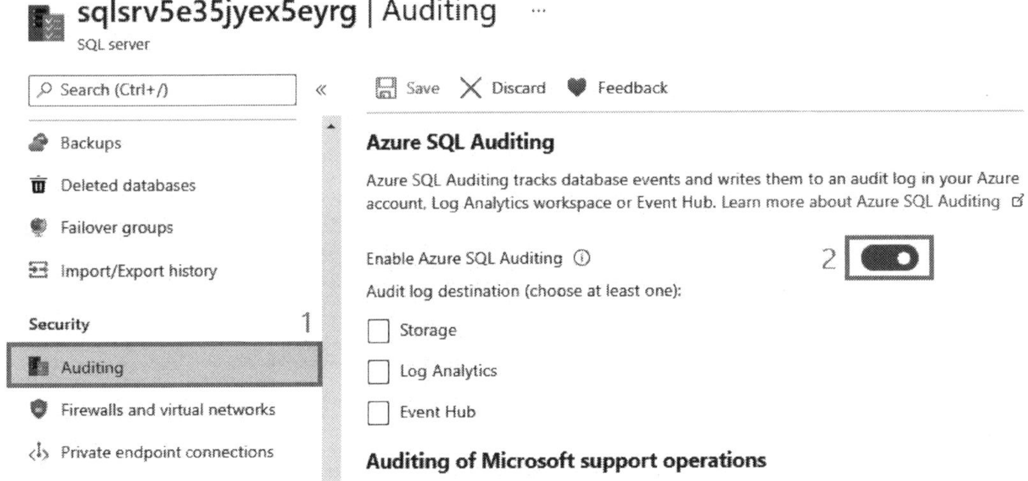

Figure 11.33 – Enabling Azure SQL auditing

After auditing is enabled, we can define the events and operations that we want to be recorded in the logs using an **auditing policy**. By default, all actions, queries, and stored procedures executed against the database, as well as successful and failed logins, will be audited. We can customize audited events by using the `Set-AzSqlDatabaseAudit` Azure PowerShell cmdlet, Azure CLI, or REST API.

Implementing Azure Defender for SQL

After enabling auditing, we can implement Azure Defender for SQL to automate the analysis of the audit logs. This service will detect unusual behavior and potentially harmful attempts to access or exploit databases by using different methods to analyze the logs. Any suspicious or unusual activities detected will raise an alert in Azure Security Center, and we will be able to view details of the detections and recommendations for further investigation.

Azure Defender for SQL is not enabled by default. It can be enabled at the subscription level (in Security Center) or at the server level from the **Security Center** section:

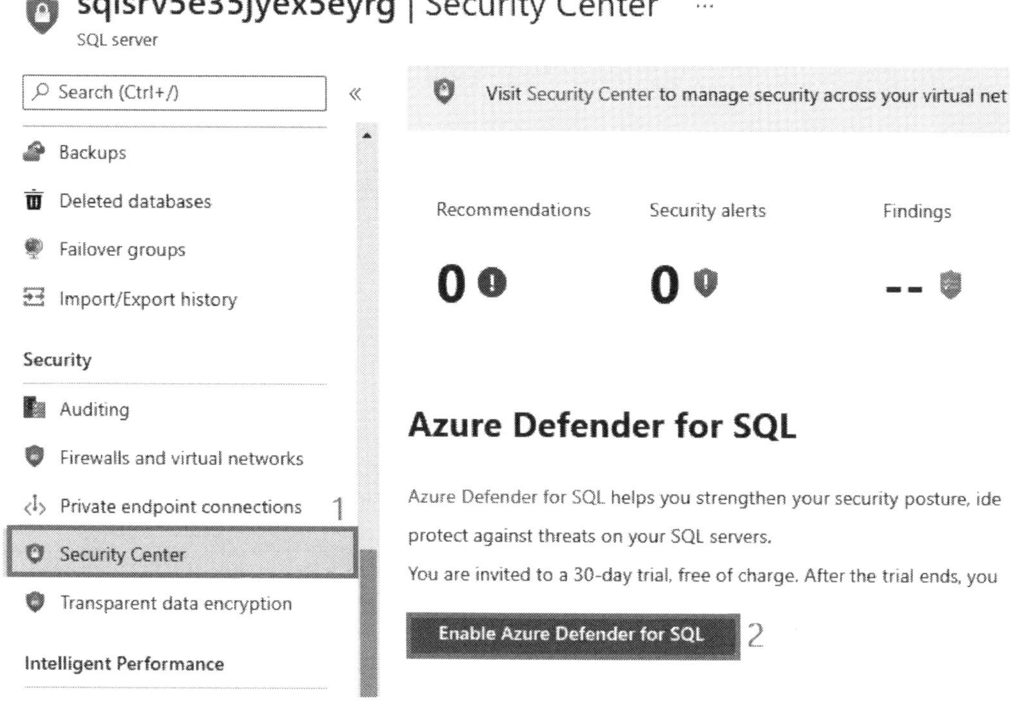

Figure 11.34 – Enabling Azure Defender for SQL

Azure Defender for SQL provides three main functionalities:

- **Data discovery and classification**: Analyzes database data and shows columns within tables that may have sensitive information and need to be further protected.
- **Vulnerability assessment**: Identifies database configurations for vulnerabilities and alerts when found. It also provides remediation instructions for the identified vulnerabilities.
- **Threat detection**: Identifies and alerts on suspicious database activities, such as unusual database access and patterns, SQL injection attacks, and credential brute force attacks.

In the next section, we will cover how data encryption works for Azure SQL databases.

Protecting Azure SQL against data leakage and theft (database encryption)

Databases store sensitive information that should not be exposed. To mitigate the risk of data exposure and theft, we need to ensure that data encryption is enforced at all levels (at rest and in transit). There are different features of Azure SQL that help us to achieve this. Let's look at them.

Implementing Transparent Data Encryption (TDE) – encryption at rest

Data, backups, and logs in Azure SQL databases are stored on storage systems located in Microsoft-managed data centers. To mitigate the risk of data leakage in case of storage disk theft, or unsecured decommissioning of storage media in the data centers, the service transparently encrypts data before storing it on disks. This functionality is referred to as **Transparent Data Encryption** (**TDE**). The great thing is that this functionality is enabled by default!

With TDE, data is transparently encrypted before it is stored on disks. Data is also transparently decrypted when read request operations are performed by authorized clients. To verify TDE, you can view the setting in the **Security** section of a SQL database, as shown in *Figure 11.35*:

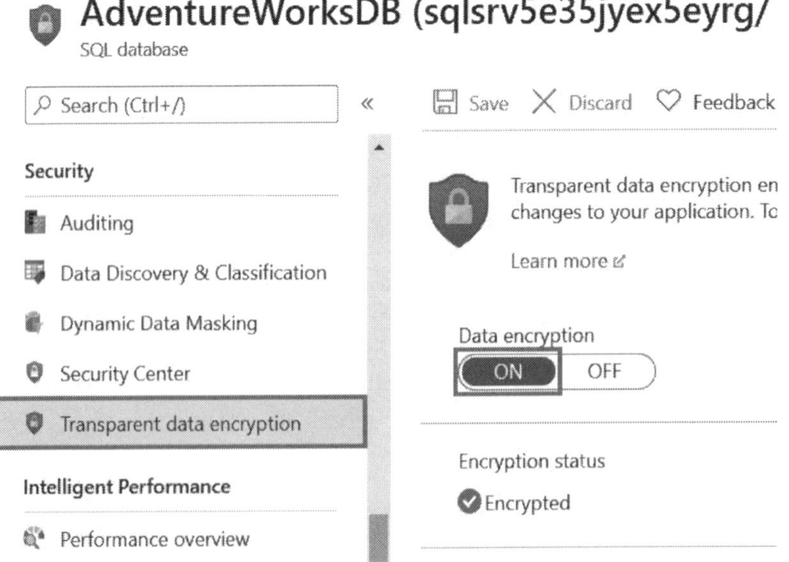

Figure 11.35 – Verifying TDE

TDE uses encryption keys that are managed by the Azure platform by default but a customer with higher compliance requirements could choose to use customer-managed keys for the encryption instead. This option can be configured in the **Security** section of a SQL logical server, as shown in *Figure 11.36*:

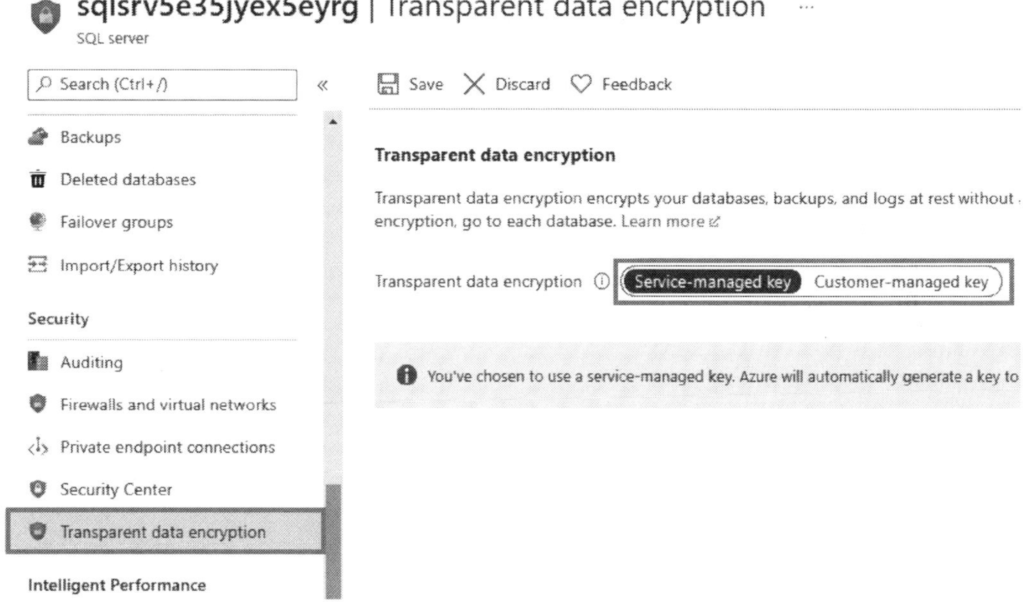

Figure 11.36 – Configuring a customer-managed key

In the next sections, we will review other encryption considerations for Azure SQL databases.

Implementing encryption in transit

Client applications interact with data stored in Azure SQL databases. This could be an administrator using a tool such as SSMS to perform some management operations or application code reading or writing data to the service. In both of these scenarios, there is a risk that malicious actors could intercept data as it flows to and from our databases.

To mitigate this risk, all connections to and from Azure SQL databases enforce **Transport Layer Security** (**TLS**) encryption *by default*. This ensures that data is protected as it flows between clients and our databases. If a malicious actor manages to intercept this traffic, they would not be able to read the data.

To further strengthen this, we should make sure that our clients enforce server certificate validation and newer TLS versions. For example, if your client uses the ADO.NET driver, ensure that the `Encrypt=True` and `TrustServerCertificate=False` options are configured to force the client to verify the server's TLS certificate.

Implementing Azure SQL Database Always Encrypted

A common security and compliance challenge that organizations face is how to ensure separation between those who manage data and those who use data. For example, an administrator may need access to perform management operations on databases, but you might not want them to be able to view sensitive data such as credit card numbers and the health information of your customers. One of the ways to address this is to make sure that sensitive data is always encrypted in our databases and only visible to the client application that uses it. The **Always Encrypted** technology supported by Azure SQL can be used to implement this solution:

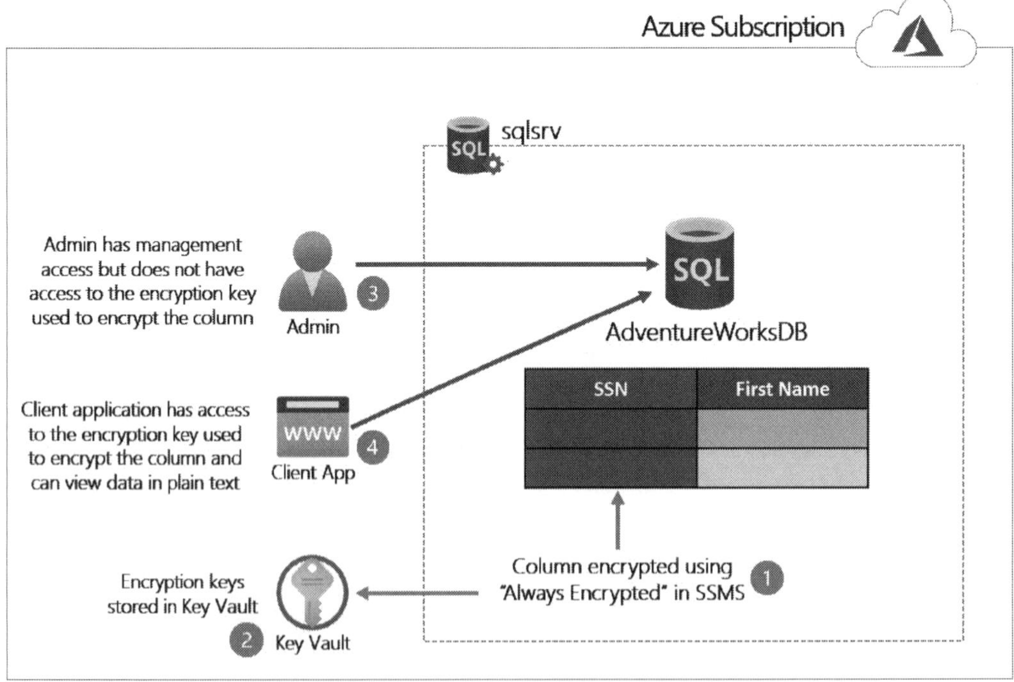

Figure 11.37 – Always Encrypted

With **Always Encrypted**, we enable encryption for columns that contain sensitive data in our databases and make the keys available only to the applications that need to access that data in plain text (*Figure 11.37*). The encryption uses the AES-256 algorithm to encrypt data in the database.

To implement this, we can use the Always Encrypted wizard in SSMS to create Always Encrypted keys. This involves the creation of column encryption keys (that will be used to encrypt columns) and a column master key that will be used to encrypt the column encryption keys. In the next hands-on exercise, we will implement this.

Hands-on exercise – implementing Always Encrypted

Here is the task that we will complete in this exercise:

- **Task 1**: Configure Always Encrypted using SSMS.

Here are the steps to complete this task:

1. In the RDP session to the Windows VM, open Microsoft SSMS.
2. In the **Microsoft SQL Server Management Studio** window, configure the following:

   Server type: **Database Engine**.

   Server name: Enter the value of the **sqlserverName** output that you made a note of in the previous exercise.

   Authentication: **SQL Server Authentication**.

   Login: **sqladmin**.

   Password: The password that you configured during the template deployment.

   Click on **Connect**:

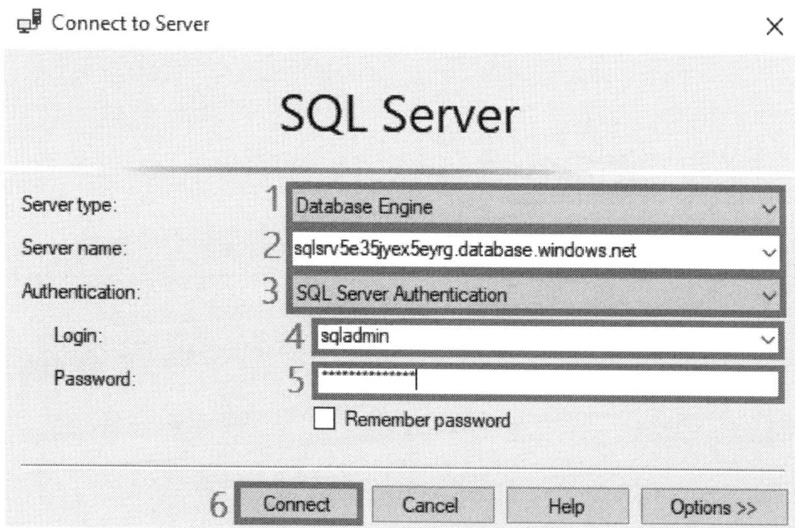

Figure 11.38 – Connecting to the SQL server

You will receive a message about your client IP not having access to the server. This is because by default, no IP address is granted access. Because our credentials have permissions to modify the firewall rules for SQL servers, we can sign in from this window and add the rule to allow the Windows VM public IP. We will do this in the next step.

3. In Object Explorer to the left, expand **Databases** | **AdventureWorksDB** | **Tables**. Right-click on **SalesLT.Customer** and click **Encrypt Columns...**:

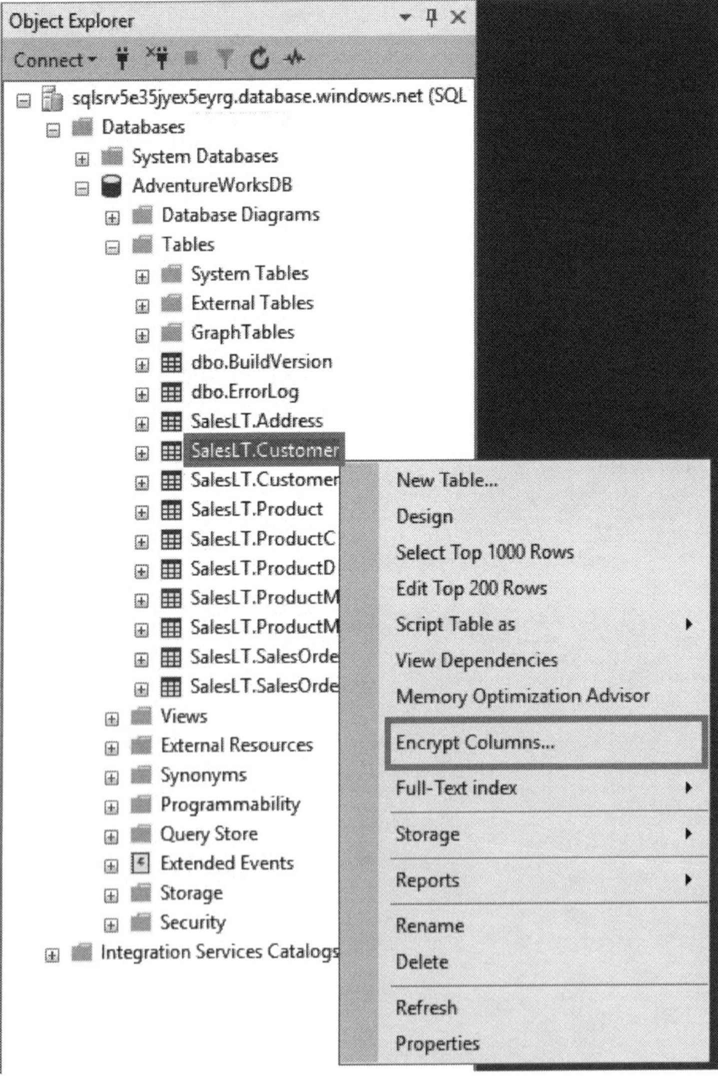

Figure 11.39 – Encrypt database column

4. In the **Always Encrypted** window, click **Next**. In the **Column Selection** section, select **PasswordHash** and **PasswordSalt**. In **Encryption Type**, select **Deterministic** for the two columns and click **Next**:

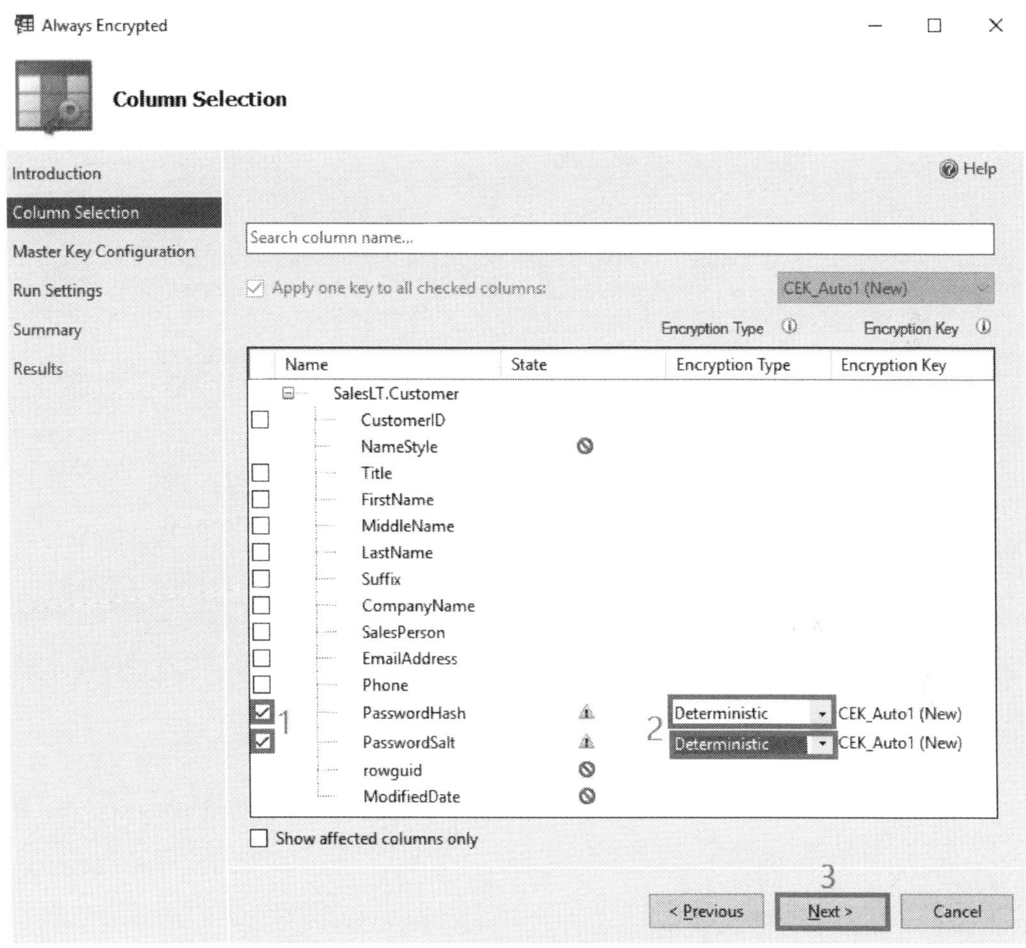

Figure 11.40 – Selecting columns to encrypt

5. In the **Master Key Configuration** section, select **Azure Key Vault** and click **Sign In**. Authenticate with your Azure administrator credentials. Select the key vault that starts with **azsec** in its name. Then click **Next**:

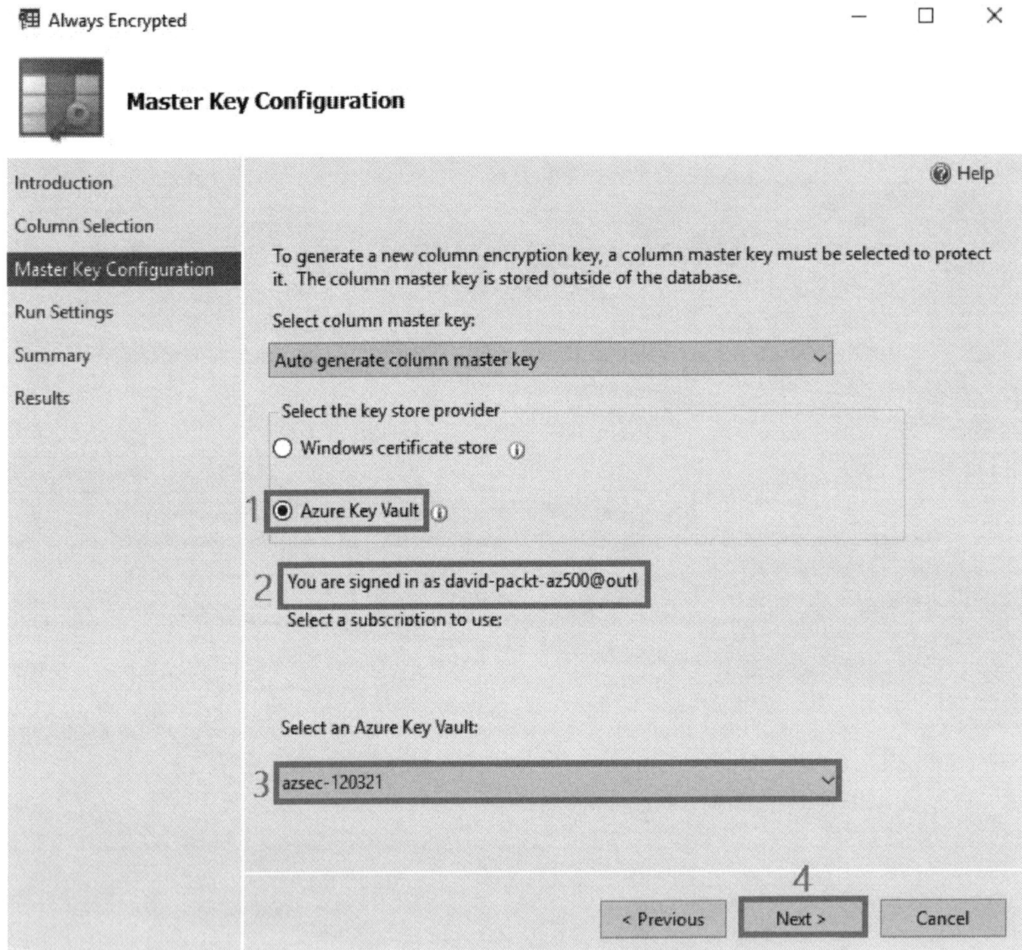

Figure 11.41 – Specifying a Key Vault resource

6. In the **Run Settings** section, click on **Next**. In the **Summary** section, click on **Finish**. When prompted to authenticate, sign in with your Azure.
7. Sign in to the Azure account again. Encryption should now be complete.

Congratulations! You have now implemented Azure SQL Database Always Encrypted to protect against data leakage even from authorized users.

Cleaning up resources

In the Azure portal, delete the `azuresec-c11-rg` resource group. This will remove all the resources that we created for the exercises in this chapter.

Summary

In this chapter, we covered how to implement a comprehensive security strategy for Azure SQL. We discussed, and you implemented, protection against unauthorized network connections, unauthorized user access, data leakage and theft, and database vulnerabilities.

The information and hands-on exercises that we covered in this chapter have equipped you with the knowledge and skills to implement a multi-layered security strategy to protect databases in Azure against common risks. In the next chapter, we will cover Azure subscription governance.

Question

As we conclude, here is a question for you to test your knowledge regarding this chapter's material. You will find the answer in the *Assessments* section of the *Appendix*:

1. You have multiple Azure SQL databases. You need to ensure that administrators cannot view customer-sensitive data in certain columns of the databases that they manage. What functionality do you need to implement?

    a. Implement encryption at rest with TDE.

    b. Switch TDE to customer-managed keys.

    c. Implement column-level encryption with Always Encrypted.

    d. Implement encryption in transit with TLS.

Further reading

To learn more on the topic, refer to the following links:

- Azure SQL security responsibilities – `https://docs.microsoft.com/en-us/azure/azure-sql/database/security-overview?WT.mc_id=AZ-MVP-6003870`
- Azure SQL Advanced Threat Protection – `https://docs.microsoft.com/en-us/azure/azure-sql/database/threat-detection-overview?WT.mc_id=AZ-MVP-6003870`
- Azure AD Authentication for Azure SQL Database – `https://docs.microsoft.com/en-us/azure/azure-sql/database/authentication-aad-overview?WT.mc_id=AZ-MVP-6003870`
- Azure SQL TLS considerations – `https://docs.microsoft.com/en-us/azure/azure-sql/database/connect-query-content-reference-guide#tls-considerations-for-database-connectivity?WT.mc_id=AZ-MVP-6003870`

12 Implementing Secrets, Keys, and Certificate Management with Key Vault

Modern applications often interact with external systems, services, and data stores. These interactions rely on privileged credentials in the form of connection strings, API keys, client secrets, and certificates. Storing these privileged credentials in code or application configuration files is a bad practice and it increases the risk of exposure or leakage.

To mitigate this risk, we need to ensure that this sensitive information is stored and handled securely and is only visible to the application that uses them at runtime. The Azure Key Vault service offers capabilities that we can use to implement this best practice. By the end of this chapter, you will have gained the knowledge, skills, and practical experience to implement Azure Key Vault to secure sensitive application information.

Here are the topics that we will cover:

- Introducing Azure Key Vault
- Understanding secrets, keys, and certificates
- Understanding Key Vault pricing tiers
- Managing access to Key Vault
- Protecting Key Vault resources

Each topic is designed to help your understanding of this service and how you can use it to implement secret management best practices in Azure. Let's get into this!

Technical requirements

To follow along with the instructions in this chapter, you will need the following:

- A PC with an internet connection
- An Azure subscription. You can use the same subscription that you set up in the first chapter of this book.

Introducing Azure Key Vault

At its core, Key Vault is a cloud service that we can use to securely store and safeguard secrets, keys, and certificates that applications use (Figure 12.1).

It allows us to streamline how applications access sensitive configuration parameters. How does it do this? It does this by providing the following capabilities:

- Centralizing the storage of application secrets: This ensures that we only need to make changes in one place instead of on distributed instances of our application.
- Implementing access control to restrict who can access application secrets.
- Implementing audit logging so that we can review how and when application secrets are accessed.

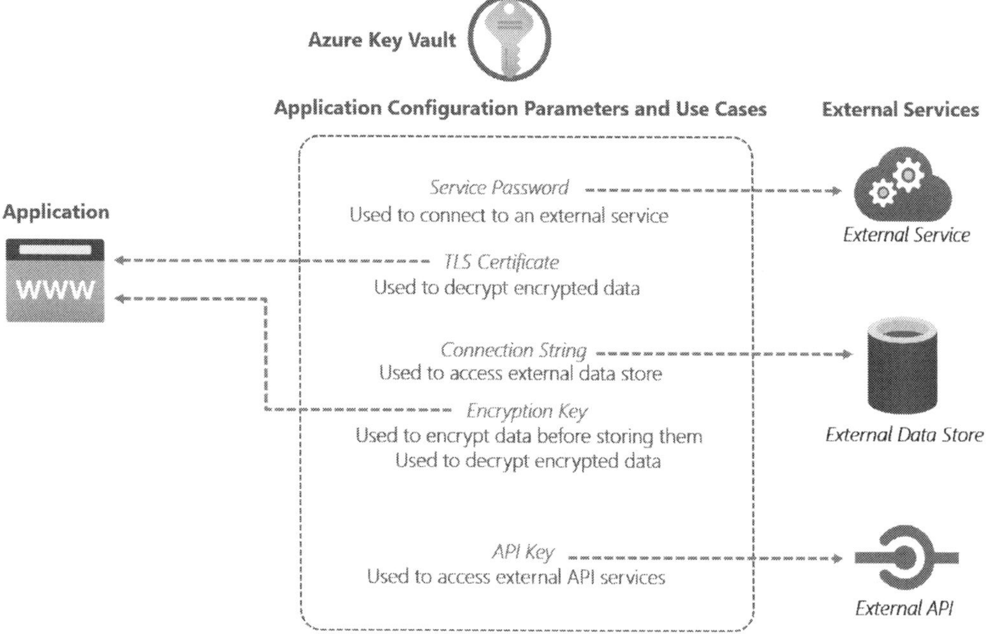

Figure 12.1 – Storing sensitive application configuration parameters

Before we go any further in our discussion, let's take some time to understand what we mean by secrets, keys, and certificates in Key Vault.

Understanding secrets, keys, and certificates

Secrets are data under 25 KB that our applications can store or retrieve in plain text. They are stored as a name-value pair of strings. Passwords, API keys, and connection strings can be stored securely as secrets in Key Vault.

Keys are *cryptographic keys* generated using an algorithm. Key Vault supports multiple sizes and algorithms of the RSA and **Elliptic Curve** (**EC**) key types. We can import RSA keys that we generated elsewhere into our vault, or we can generate RSA and EC keys in the vault itself. Depending on the pricing tier of Key Vault that we deployed (we will cover pricing tiers later in this chapter), the keys could either be software-protected or hardware-protected using **Hardware Security Modules** (**HSMs**).

Certificates refer to SSL/TLS X.509 certificates. These could either be self-signed certificates generated in the vault or certificates generated by external **Certificate Authorities** (**CAs**) that are integrated with Key Vault or that are imported into the vault. It is important to note that Key Vault does not issue publicly trusted certificates or resell them. What Key Vault can provide is the ability to simplify and automate certain tasks such as enrolment and renewal for supported integrated CAs. At the moment, two CAs are supported – DigiCert and GlobalSign.

Key Vault allows us to have multiple versions of the same secret, key, or certificate. This gives us flexibility in how we manage these objects. Client applications have the flexibility to pin the version of a particular secret, key, or certificate by referencing the version number in the object URL as shown here:

```
https://{vault-name}.vault.azure.net/{object-type}/{object-name}/{object-version}
```

If a version number is not referenced, the latest version of the object will be retrieved.

Another important point to note is that secrets, keys, and certificates are immutable in the vault. This means that the value of an existing version cannot be modified once created (metadata such as tags can be modified but not the object values). We will need to create a new version to add a different value. This is great as it provides protection against ransomware attack scenarios where an attacker could look to corrupt existing versions to make them unusable.

Before going any further, let's cover the different pricing tiers of Key Vault and the significance of our selection to the feature capabilities that we can use.

Understanding Key Vault pricing tiers

The first step to protecting sensitive application secrets in Azure is to create a Key Vault resource in an Azure region of our choice. This is the resource that stores our secrets, keys, and certificates. When we create this resource, we need to specify the pricing tier that we want. The pricing tier that we select defines the capabilities that are available for us to use. Azure Key Vault has two pricing tiers – the standard tier and the premium tier.

The main difference between these two tiers is this: the standard tier supports only software-protected keys while the premium tier supports HSM-protected keys.

> Note
>
> **Hardware Security Modules** (**HSMs**) are special hardware that can be used to perform cryptographic operations in a secure environment.

The key advantage of using the premium tier is that HSM keys offer stronger protection against tampering. HSM-protected keys in premium tier vaults are backed by nCipher HSMs, which are **Federal Information Processing Standards** (**FIPS**) 140-2 Level 2 validated. So, if an organization needs to meet that level of compliance, this helps them to achieve that. It is worth mentioning that the HSMs that are used by premium tier vaults are shared with other customers. If you have a requirement to have a dedicated HSM only for your use case, there is another service in Azure called **Azure Dedicated HSM** that you can consider. This service is validated for FIPS 140-2 Level 3 and eIDAS Common Criteria EAL4+ standards.

Now that you understand the different pricing tiers of Azure Key Vault, let's look at how to manage access to the sensitive information that we store in it.

Managing access to Key Vault

Once we have created a Key Vault resource, we can add our application secrets, keys, and certificates to it. When an application needs to access information stored in the vault, it can access it over a REST API (*Figure 12.2*). This access *always* requires authentication and authorization (there is no option to grant anonymous access). Azure Key Vault's REST API uses Azure AD to authenticate requesting applications or clients.

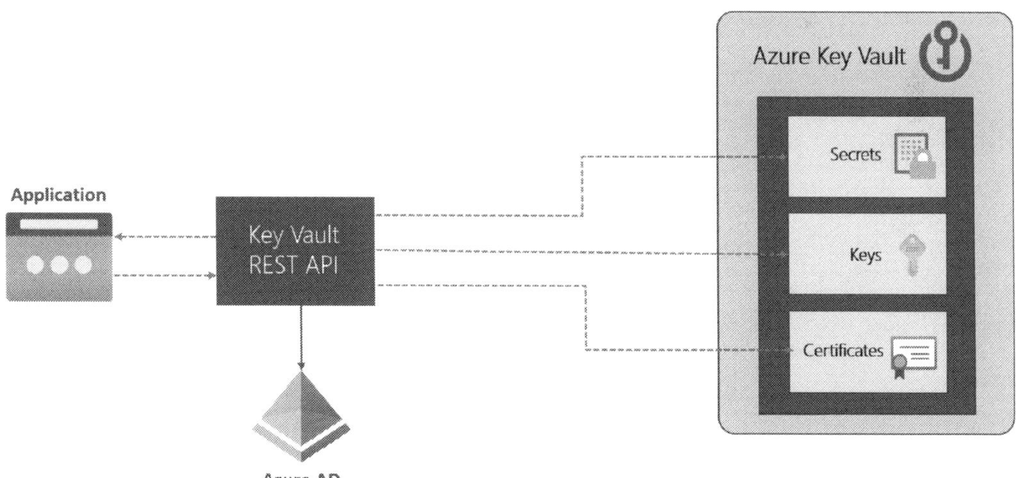

Figure 12.2 – Azure Key Vault REST API

After a requesting client is authenticated using Azure AD and an OAuth token has been granted, the Key Vault API will then verify whether the requesting identity has the required permission to perform the operation that is being requested (authorization). This permission can be granted to Azure AD security principals such as users, service principals, and managed identities. To understand how permission is granted in Key Vault, let's review the two planes of access for Key Vault resources – the **Management plane** and the **Data plane**.

The **Management plane** is where permission is granted to manage the Key Vault resource itself. Access that we can grant in this plane includes permissions to create and delete the vault, retrieve, or modify vault properties, and update access policies. Access to this plane is granted using **Role-Based Access Control** (**RBAC**) as shown in *Figure 12.3*.

The **Data plane** is where permission is granted to the secret information stored in the vault. Access that we can grant in this plane includes permissions to get, list, or update the values of secrets, keys, and certificates in the vault. Access to this plane is granted using an access policy or RBAC as shown in *Figure 12.3*.

The main advantage of this architecture is that we can implement proper separation of roles. *The fact that a user can manage a vault as part of their role does not mean they have automatic access to data in the vault.* This is just like how giving someone the key to access a room does not automatically grant them access to a safe in the room that uses a different key!

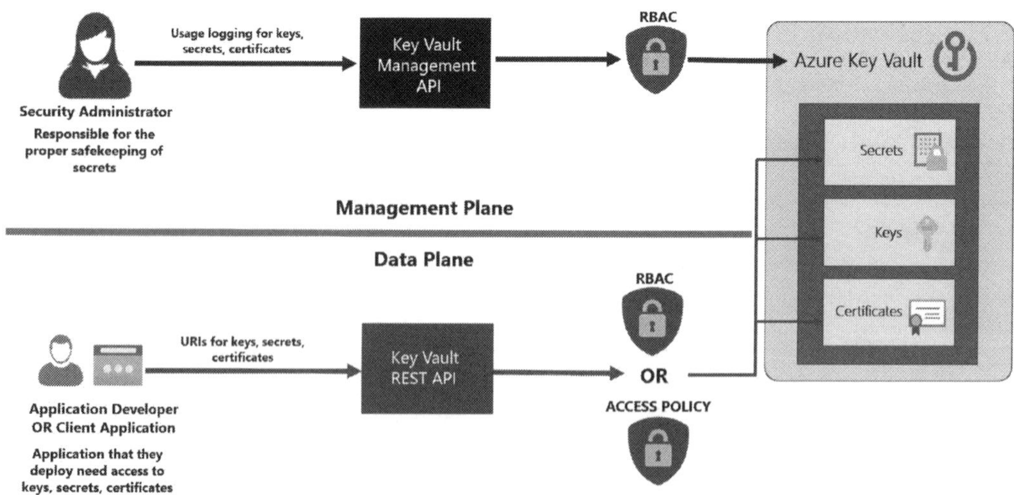

Figure 12.3 – The Key Vault management plane versus the data plane

You might be wondering which option to use to manage permissions to the **Data plane** between the access policy or RBAC. What I will say is that using RBAC has some advantages that are difficult to ignore. The main advantage is that we can manage *ALL* permissions for the vault in one place (a unified management experience). The other advantage of the RBAC model is the ability to scope data plane access to individual secrets, keys, and certificates in the vault, which is not possible with the *access policy* model! You will implement this in your hands-on exercise, so you will see how it works.

When granting access to secrets, keys, and certificates in the vault, we should always follow the principle of least privilege and grant only the minimum set of permissions needed. This helps to reduce the impact radius in the event of a breach. With the access policy model, this can be done by restricting the operations that an identity is allowed to perform, but as mentioned, this model is not granular to individual objects. For example, we can grant an application's service principal permission to `GET` secrets in a vault using the data plane access policy. This will grant that application the permission to `READ` all secrets in that vault but not to `CREATE` or `LIST` them.

With the RBAC model, we can apply the principle of least privilege in the same way as other Azure resources – by assigning roles at a more specific scope. There are eight built-in rules that we can use out of the box (*Figure 12.4*). None of these roles have management plane access by default to keep the planes separate, which is a good idea.

Key Vault Built-In Roles	Description
Key Vault Administrator	Can perform all data plane operations on a key vault and all objects in it, including certificates, keys, and secrets.
Key Vault Reader	Can read metadata of key vaults and its certificates, keys, and secrets. Cannot read sensitive values such as secret contents or key material.
Key Vault Certificates Officer	Can perform any action on the certificates of a key vault, except manage permissions.
Key Vault Crypto Officer	Can perform any action on the keys of a key vault, except manage permissions.
Key Vault Crypto Service Encryption User	Can read metadata of keys and perform wrap/unwrap operations.
Key Vault Crypto User	Can perform cryptographic operations using keys.
Key Vault Secrets Officer	Can perform any action on the secrets of a key vault, except manage permissions.
Key Vault Secrets User	Can read secret contents.

Figure 12.4 – Key Vault's built-in RBAC roles

In many cases, users in developer roles will usually only need `READ`, `CREATE`, and `LIST` permissions to development-environment vault resources ,while only production applications will be granted `READ` permissions to production-environment vault resources.

A scenario that we may encounter is when we need to grant vault data plane access to Azure services to allow them to seamlessly access information stored in the vault as part of an automated process. The way to do this is to configure an **advanced access policy**. There are three main use cases for an advanced access policy as shown in *Figure 12.5*:

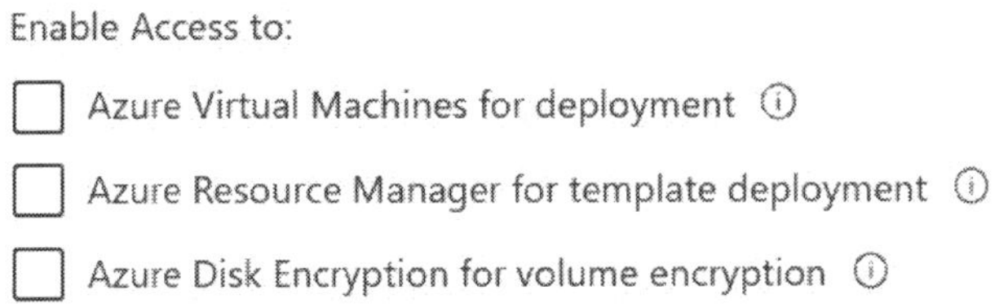

Enable Access to:

- [ ] Azure Virtual Machines for deployment ⓘ
- [ ] Azure Resource Manager for template deployment ⓘ
- [ ] Azure Disk Encryption for volume encryption ⓘ

Figure 12.5 – Advanced access policy options

The first use case is to grant access to Azure Virtual Machines for deployment, which can be used to specify whether Azure Virtual Machines is permitted to retrieve certificates stored as secrets from the key vault. **The second option** is to grant access to Azure Resource Manager for template deployment, maybe to retrieve a secure value (such as a password) as a parameter during deployment. **The third use case** is for Azure Disk Encryption volume encryption to allow VMs to retrieve secrets from the vault to unwrap encryption keys.

In the next hands-on exercise, you will create a Key Vault resource in Azure, and implement access management for it.

Hands-on exercise – managing access to Key Vault resources

Here are the tasks that we will complete in this exercise:

- **Task 1**: Create an Azure AD service principal for testing.
- **Task 2**: Create a key vault with purge protection enabled.
- **Task 3**: Grant Key Vault data plane access to an admin user.
- **Task 4**: Add a secret to the key vault.
- **Task 5**: Grant permission to a single secret to a service principal.
- **Task 6**: Verify access to a secret in the key vault.

Here are the steps to complete the tasks:

1. Open a web browser and browse to the Azure portal `https://portal.azure.com`. Sign in with the `azureadmin` credentials.
2. In the Azure portal, click on the **Cloud Shell** icon in the top-right corner. Select **Bash**.
3. In the **Bash** session within the **Cloud Shell** pane, run the following command to create a service principal that we will use for testing key vault access:

```
az ad sp create-for-rbac --name app-kv-test --skip-
assignment
```

4. In the output of the command, make a note of the values for `appID`, `password`, and `tenant`. You will need these values for a later step in this exercise.

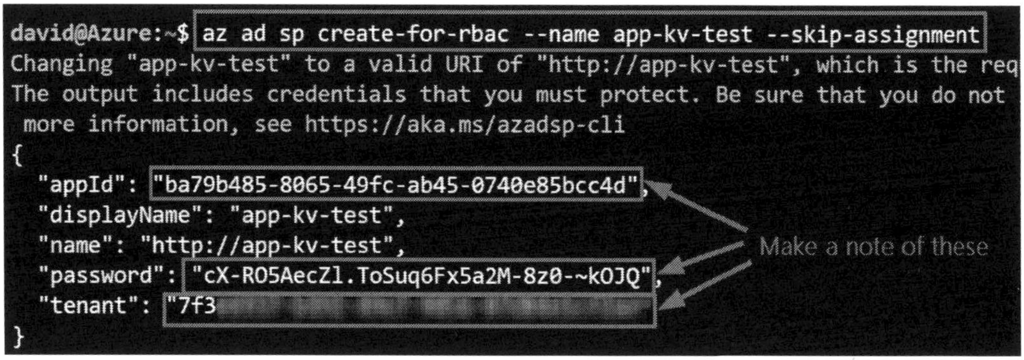
david@Azure:~$ az ad sp create-for-rbac --name app-kv-test --skip-assignment
Changing "app-kv-test" to a valid URI of "http://app-kv-test", which is the req
The output includes credentials that you must protect. Be sure that you do not
more information, see https://aka.ms/azadsp-cli
{
"appId": "ba79b485-8065-49fc-ab45-0740e85bcc4d",
"displayName": "app-kv-test",
"name": "http://app-kv-test",
"password": "cX-RO5AecZl.ToSuq6Fx5a2M-8z0-~kOJQ",
"tenant": "7f3
}
Make a note of these

Figure 12.6 – Create a service principal

5. Open a web browser and browse to the Azure portal – `https://portal.azure.com`. Sign in with your administrator credentials.
6. On the home page, click on **Create a resource**.

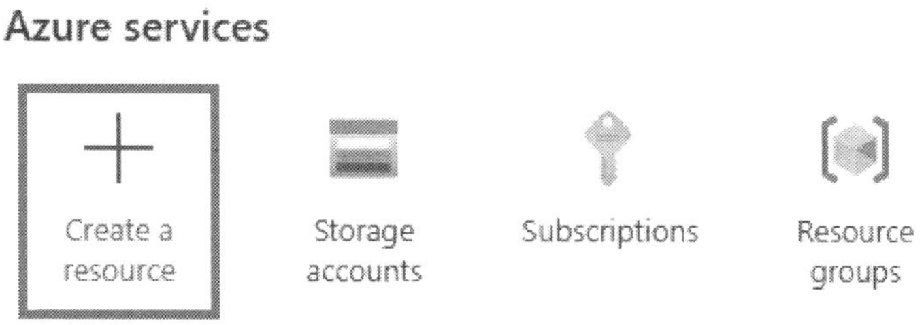
Azure services
Create a resource
Storage accounts
Subscriptions
Resource groups

Figure 12.7 – Create a new Azure resource

7. In the **Create a resource** blade, search for *Key Vault* and select **Key Vault**.

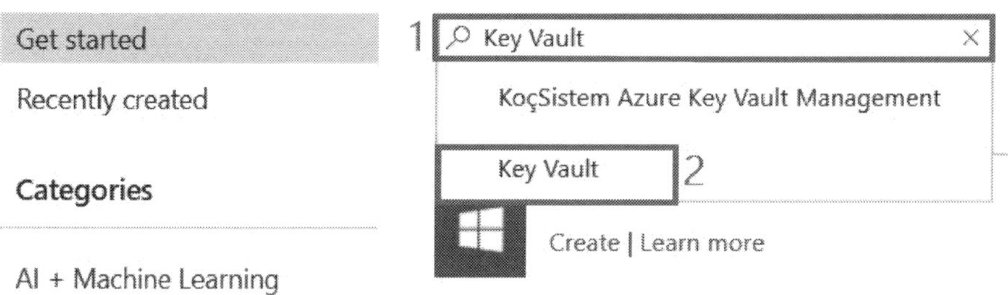

Figure 12.8 – Search for and select Key Vault

8. In the **Key Vault** blade, click on **Create** to create a new vault.
9. In the **Create a key vault** blade, in the **Basics** tab, configure the following:

   Subscription: Select the subscription that you want to deploy the resources into.

   Resource Group: **Create new** → **Name**: `azuresec-c12-rg` → **OK**.

   Key vault name: `azseckvXXXX` (where `XXXX` is a random number).

   Region: Select an Azure region close to your location.

   Pricing tier: Standard

   Soft-delete: Notice that **Soft-delete** is now enabled by default. We will cover **Soft-delete** later in this chapter.

   Days to retain deleted vaults: Leave the default setting of 90 days.

   Purge Protection: Enable purge protection. We will cover purge protection later in this chapter.

   Click on **Next: Access policy** > to proceed to the **Access policy** tab.

   Here is a screenshot of the configuration parameters:

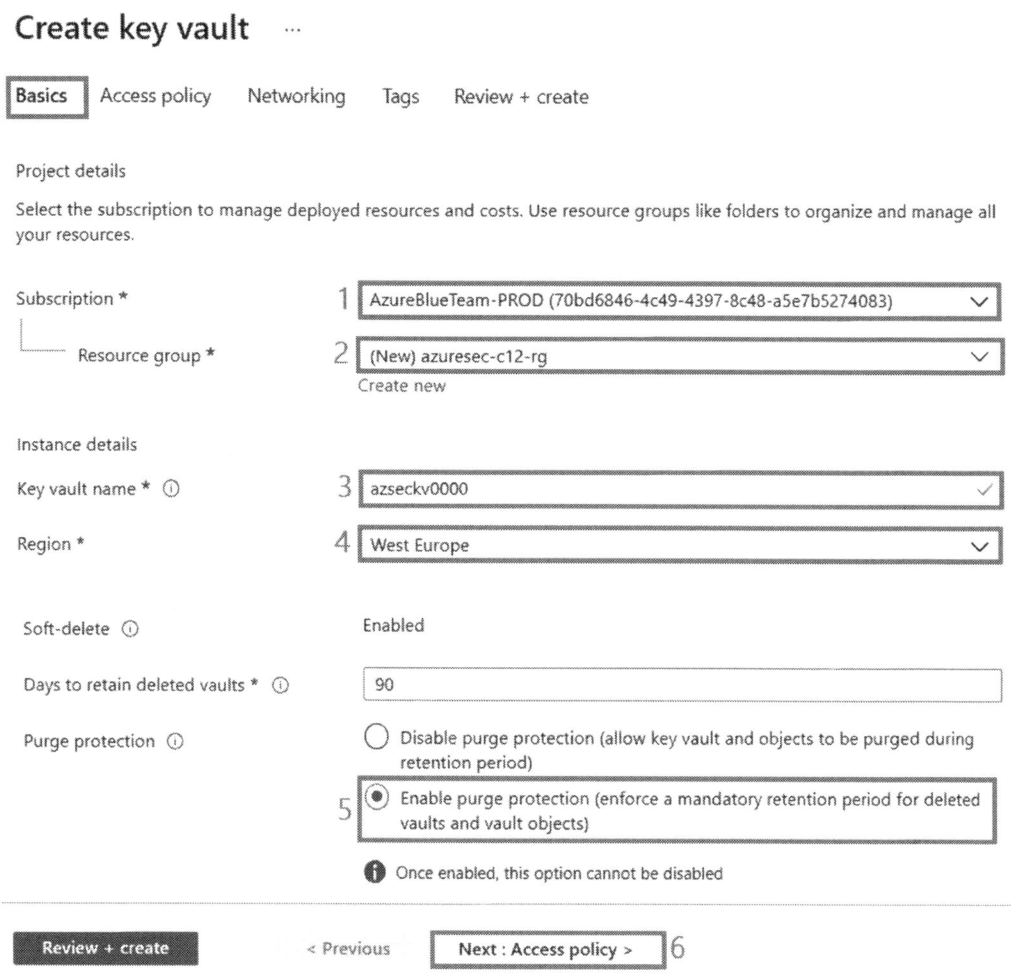

Create key vault ...

Basics | Access policy | Networking | Tags | Review + create

Project details

Select the subscription to manage deployed resources and costs. Use resource groups like folders to organize and manage all your resources.

Subscription * — 1 AzureBlueTeam-PROD (70bd6846-4c49-4397-8c48-a5e7b5274083)

Resource group * — 2 (New) azuresec-c12-rg

Create new

Instance details

Key vault name * — 3 azseckv0000

Region * — 4 West Europe

Soft-delete — Enabled

Days to retain deleted vaults * — 90

Purge protection — Disable purge protection (allow key vault and objects to be purged during retention period)

5 Enable purge protection (enforce a mandatory retention period for deleted vaults and vault objects)

Once enabled, this option cannot be disabled

Review + create | < Previous | Next : Access policy > 6

Figure 12.9 – Configure key vault basic parameters

10. In the **Access policy** tab, review and configure the following settings:

    Permission model: **Azure role-based access control**. This will allow us to use RBAC for vault object permissions.

Leave the other settings as their default values and click on **Review + create** to proceed to the **Review + create** tab:

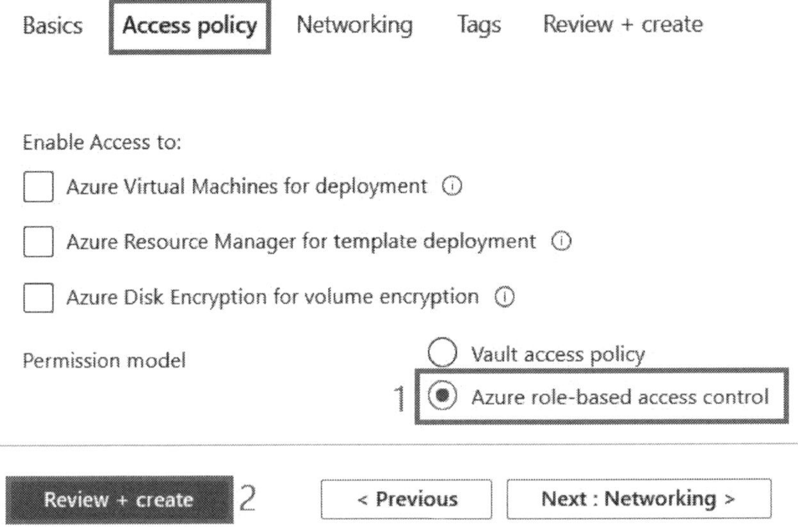

Figure 12.10 – Configure key vault access policy settings

11. Click on **Create** to begin the creation of the vault with the configured settings. Wait for the deployment to complete. Once it has completed, click on **Go to resource**:

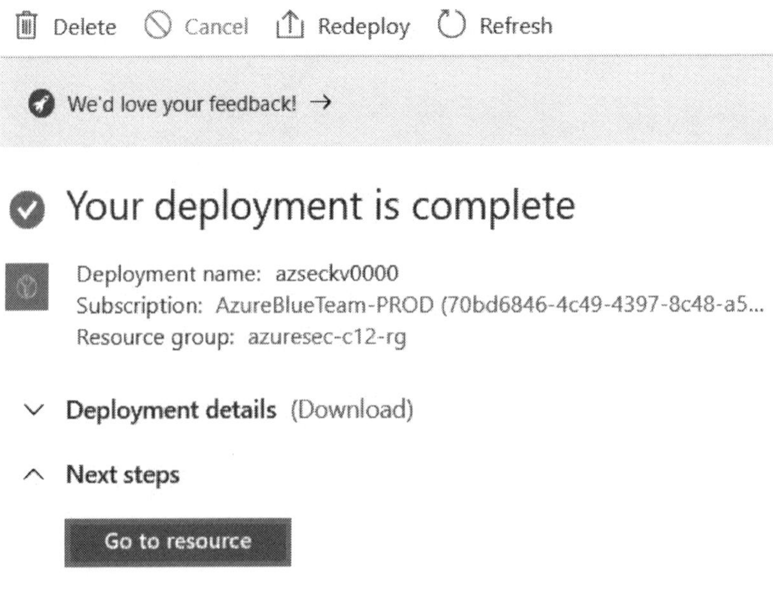

Figure 12.11 – Configure key vault access policy settings

12. In the resource blade of the key vault that was just created, verify that your administrator account does not have default access to the data plane of the vault by clicking on **Secrets** in the **Settings** section. You will receive a warning about not being authorized:

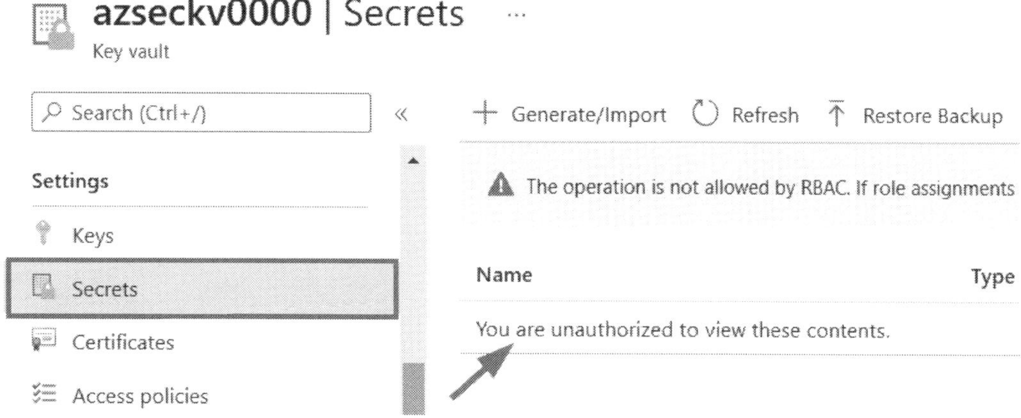

Figure 12.12 – Verify data plane access

13. To grant permissions to the data plane, we will need to use RBAC as that was the model that we configured when we created the vault. To do this, click on **Access control (IAM)** →**+ Add** →**Add role assignment**:

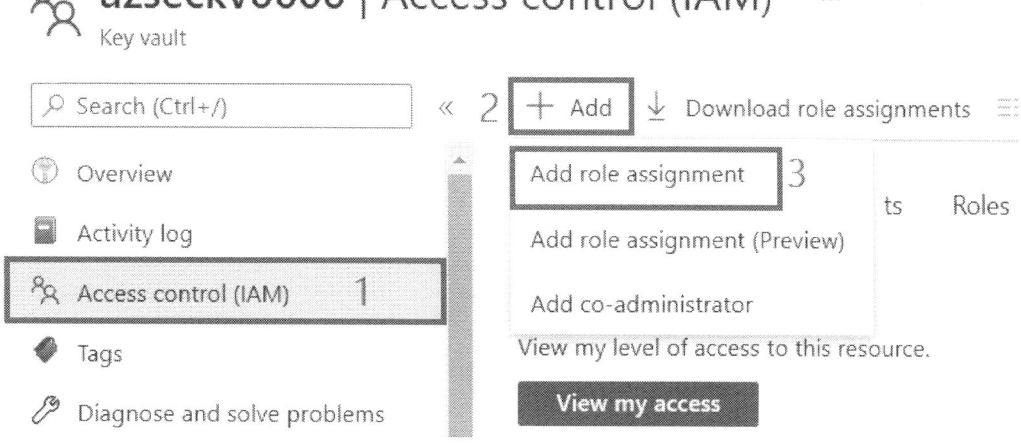

Figure 12.13 – Add role assignment to key vault

14. In the **Add role assignment** blade, configure the following to grant access to your current admin account:

    Role: **Key Vault Administrator**. This role grants full data plane access to the Key Vault resource.

    Assign access to: **User, group, or service principal**.

    Select: Select the administrator account that you are currently using.

    Click on **Save** to apply the role assignment.

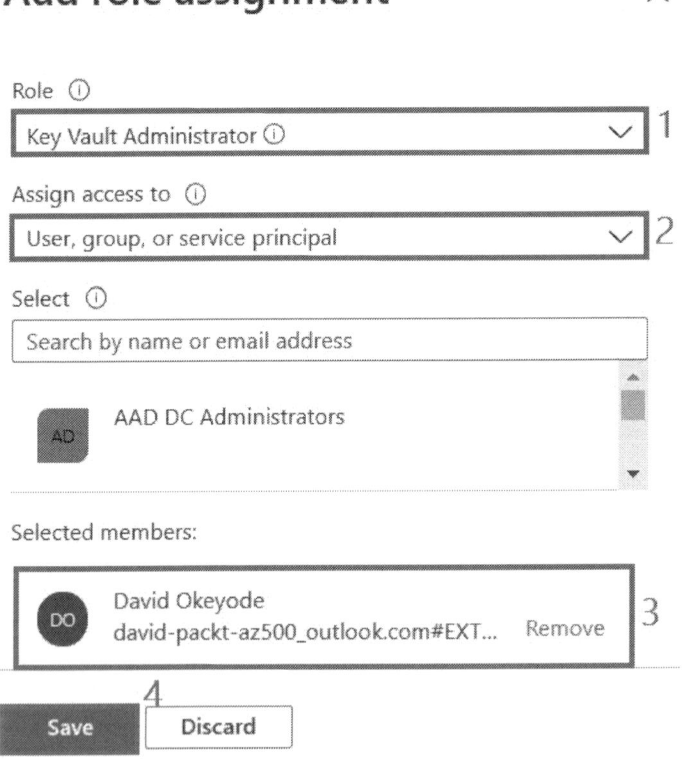

Figure 12.14 – Configure and apply the role assignment to the key vault

15. To add a new secret into the vault, click on **Secrets** (notice that the warning message is now gone). Click on **+ Generate/Import** and configure the following:

    Name: `Api-Key`

    Value: `123456789`

    Leave other settings as their default values, then click on **Create**:

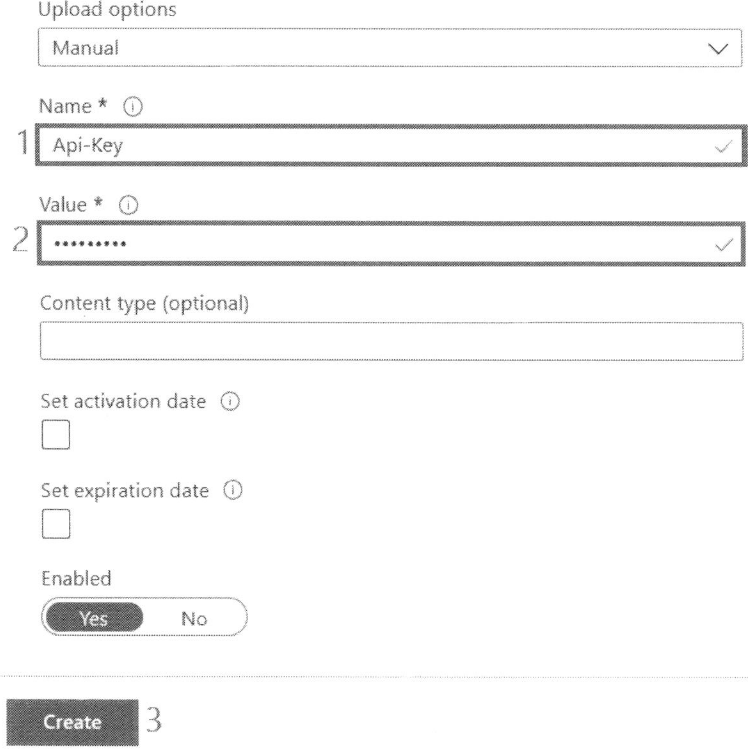

Figure 12.15 – Add a secret into the key vault

16. To allow the test service principal that we created earlier to read the value of this new secret, click on the **Api-Key** secret, then click on **Access control (IAM) →+ Add →Add role assignment**.

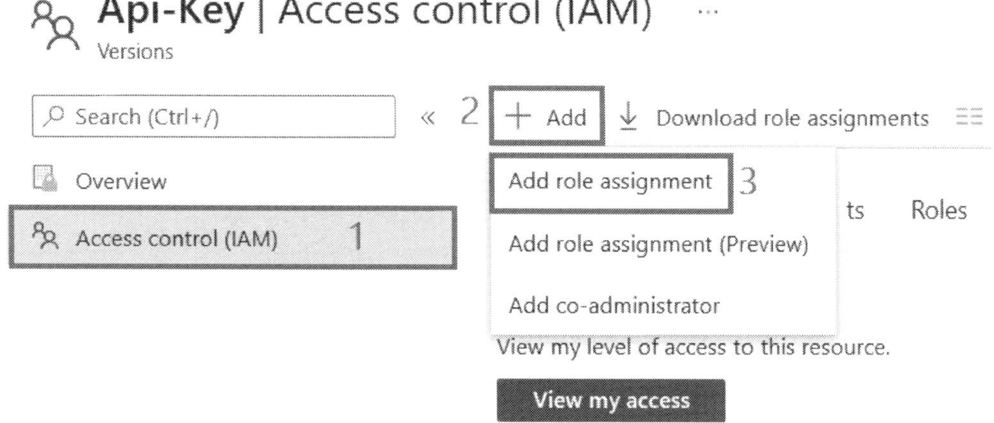

Figure 12.16 – Configure permission for a single secret

17. In the **Add role assignment** blade, configure the following to grant access to your current admin account:

    Role: **Key Vault Secrets User**. This role grants permission to read the content of secrets. In this scenario, we are granting permission to read a single secret.

    Assign access to: **User, group, or service principal**.

    Select: `app-kv-test`

    Click on **Save** to apply the role assignment:

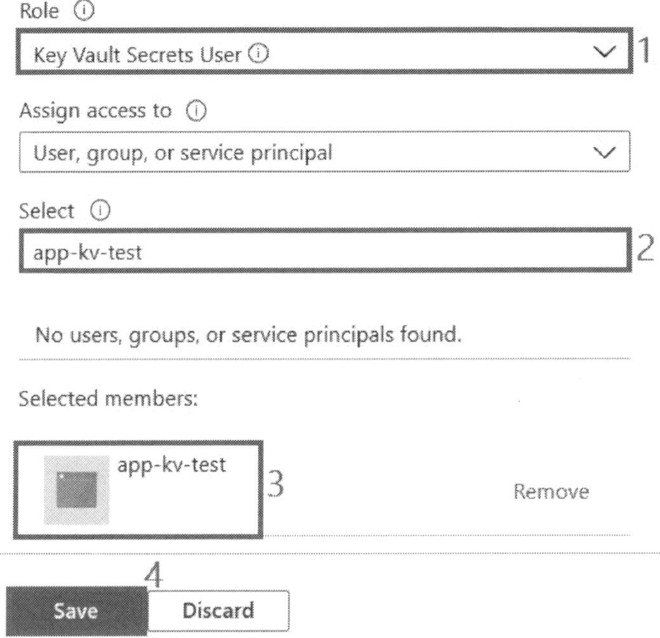

Figure 12.17 – Configure and apply the role assignment to the key vault secret

Before we can test, we will need the URL of the secret, so let's obtain it.

18. Still in the **Api-Key** secret blade, click on **Overview**, then click on the version number:

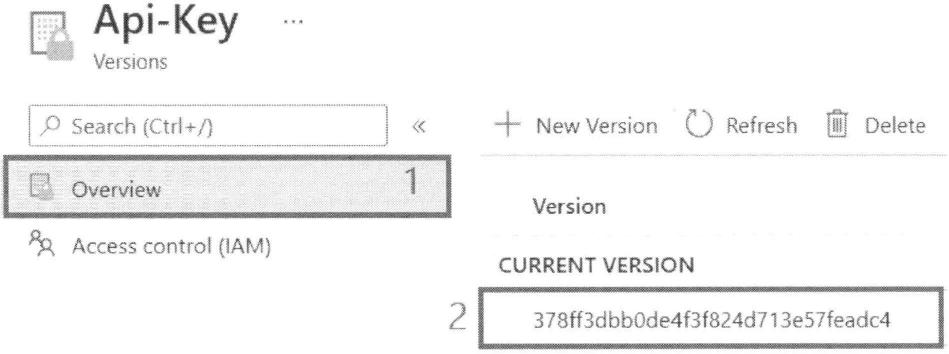

Figure 12.18 – Configure and apply role assignment to a key vault secret

19. In the **Secret Version** blade, copy the **Secret Identifier** URL and make a note of it. We will use this in a later step.

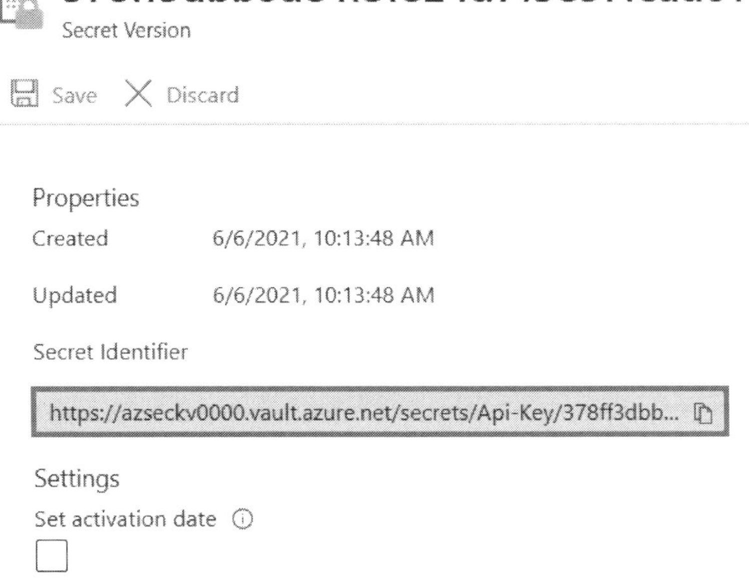

Figure 12.19 – Obtain the secret URL

To test this, we will authenticate using the test service principal in Cloud Shell and attempt to retrieve the value of the secret.

20. In the Azure portal, click on the **Cloud Shell** icon in the top-right corner. Select **Bash**.

21. In the **Bash** session within the **Cloud Shell** pane, run the following command to authenticate as the service principal that we created earlier. Replace `<APP_ID>` with the `appID` value from *Step 4*. Replace `<APP_PASSWORD>` with the password value from *Step 4*. Replace `<TENANT_ID>` with the tenant value from *Step 4*:

```
az login --service-principal --username <APP_ID>
--password <APP_PASSWORD> --tenant <TENANT_ID>
```

Here is a screenshot of the command and its output:

```
Bash
david@Azure:~$
david@Azure:~$ az login --service-principal --username "ba79b485-8065-49fc-ab45-0740e
85bcc4d" --password "cX-RO5AecZ1.ToSuq6Fx5a2M-8z0-~kOJQ" --tenant "7f3
"
Cloud Shell is automatically authenticated under the initial account signed-in with.
Run 'az login' only if you need to use a different account
[
  {
    "cloudName": "AzureCloud",
    "homeTenantId": "7f3",
    "id": "70bd6846-4c49-4397-8c48-a5e7b5274083",
    "isDefault": true,
    "managedByTenants": [],
    "name": "AzureBlueTeam-PROD",
```

Figure 12.20 – Authenticate with the service principal

22. Obtain an access token for Key Vault using the following command. The command will authenticate to Azure AD, obtain an access token for Key Vault, and store that token as a variable:

```
token=$(az account get-access-token --resource https://
vault.azure.net --query accessToken --output tsv)
```

23. Access the value of the secret using the access token obtained for the service principal. Replace `<SECRET_URI>` with the **Secret Identifier** URL that you made a note of in *Step 19*. You should be able to see the value of the secret in the vault!

```
curl <SECRET_URI>?api-version=2016-10-01 -H
"Authorization: Bearer $token" | jq
```

Here is a screenshot of the command and its output:

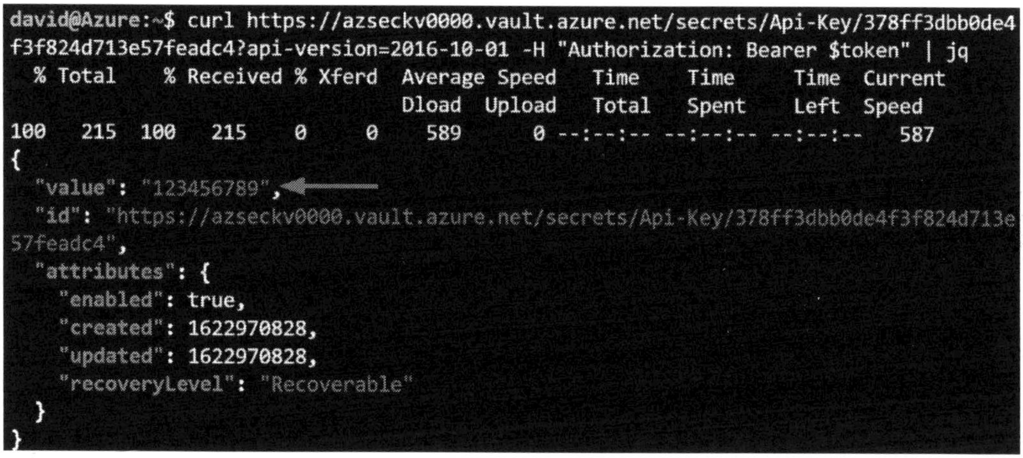

```
david@Azure:~$ curl https://azseckv0000.vault.azure.net/secrets/Api-Key/378ff3dbb0de4
f3f824d713e57feadc4?api-version=2016-10-01 -H "Authorization: Bearer $token" | jq
  % Total    % Received % Xferd  Average Speed   Time    Time     Time  Current
                                 Dload  Upload   Total   Spent    Left  Speed
100   215  100   215    0     0    589      0 --:--:-- --:--:-- --:--:--   587
{
  "value": "123456789",
  "id": "https://azseckv0000.vault.azure.net/secrets/Api-Key/378ff3dbb0de4f3f824d713e
57feadc4",
  "attributes": {
    "enabled": true,
    "created": 1622970828,
    "updated": 1622970828,
    "recoveryLevel": "Recoverable"
  }
}
```

Figure 12.21 – Retrieve the secret value from the key vault

Congratulations! You have now configured access to Key Vault resources using RBAC. In the next section, we will cover how to protect the resources in a vault.

Protecting Key Vault resources

Azure Key Vault has capabilities to protect us against accidental or malicious vault or vault object deletion and disasters. There are three main capabilities that we will cover in this section: **Soft-Delete**, **Purge Protection**, **Backup and Restore**. Let's start with the soft-delete feature.

Key Vault soft-delete allows us to recover both deleted vaults and deleted vault objects within a configurable retention period (*Figure 12.23*). This is similar to the recycle bin capability of the Windows operating system. With soft-delete enabled, a deleted secret, key, certificate, or vault will remain recoverable for a period of 7 to 90 calendar days (depending on what the administrator configures). Deleted vaults will remain in our subscription as hidden vaults. This feature is now enabled by default for all newly created vaults (you will see this when you do the hands-on exercise for this chapter).

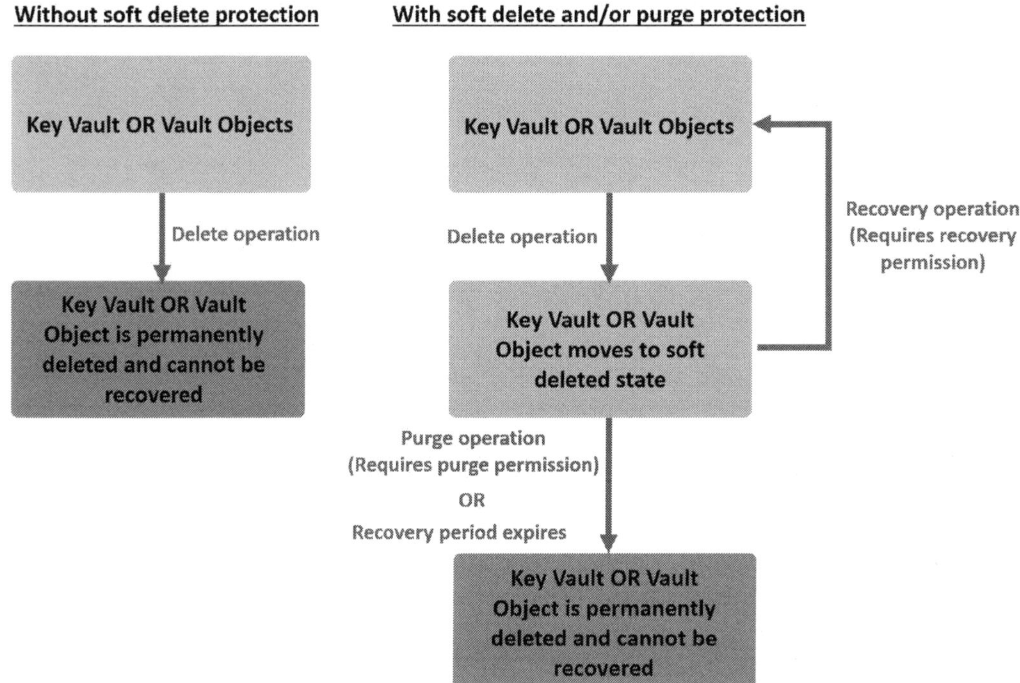

Figure 12.22 – Key Vault soft-delete and purge protection

Purge protection, on the other hand, is used to protect deleted vaults and objects during the retention period. When purge protection is enabled, vaults or vault objects in the deleted state cannot be purged (permanently deleted) until the retention period has expired. This allows us to enforce the retention policy of our organization even after a delete operation. *Figure 12.23* shows how soft-delete and purge protection work together to protect vaults and objects stored in them.

The third feature is the ability to back up and restore objects in the vault. This is a capability that is only used occasionally. The reason for this is Key Vault already has built-in capabilities to prevent data loss. For example, previous versions of objects in the vault cannot be deleted so this protects us even if someone maliciously corrupts a value in the vault – we can simply reference the previous version. Azure Key Vault content is also automatically replicated to another region within the same geography. This replication is transparent to the user and happens in the background. In the event of a region failure, Microsoft automatically fails over the service. This failover and even the failback happens automatically, and in the background, using DNS redirection.

So, in which scenario do we want to implement backup? The main reason is if we want to be able to recover objects that have been permanently deleted from the vault as, at the time of writing this book, backup can only be done on an object level. There is no Microsoft-provided way to back up an entire key vault in a single operation.

In the next hands-on exercise, you will implement protection for objects stored in a Key Vault resource.

Hands-on exercise – protecting Key Vault resources

Here are the tasks that we will complete in this exercise:

- **Task 1**: Verify soft-delete and purge protection.
- **Task 2**: Restore a deleted secret.
- **Task 3**: Configure backup and restore.

Here are the steps to complete the tasks:

1. Open a web browser and browse to the Azure portal.
2. In the **Search resources, services, and docs** box at the top of the portal, type `azseckv` and select the key vault that you created earlier, in the previous section of this chapter:

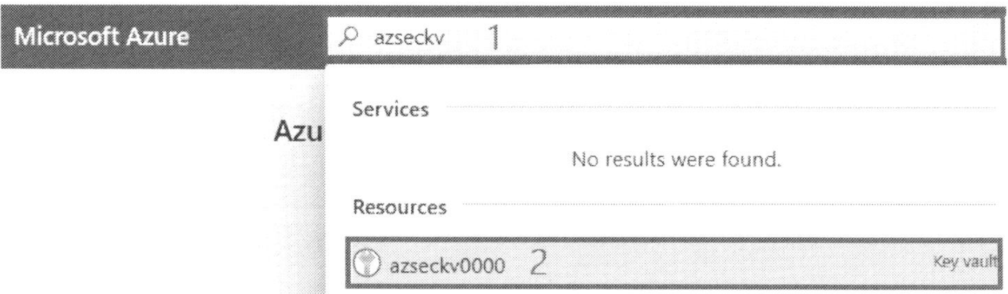

Figure 12.23 – Search and select the Key Vault resource

3. In the **azseckvXXXX | Secrets** blade, click on **Secrets** in the **Settings** section. Select the **Api-Key** secret that was created in the first exercise of this chapter:

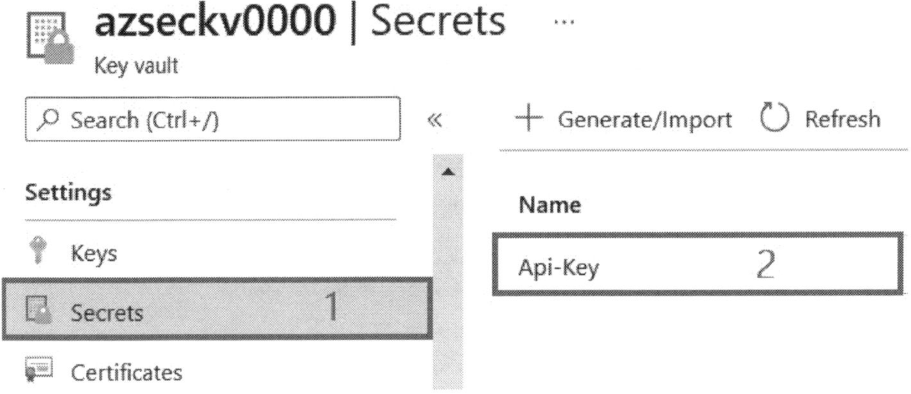

Figure 12.24 – Select the secret resource in Key Vault

4. In the **Api-Key** blade, click on **Delete**, then click on **Yes** to confirm the delete operation:

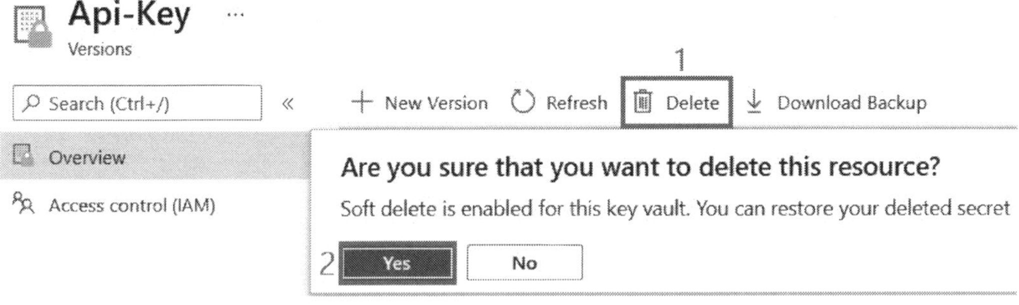

Figure 12.25 – Delete a secret from the vault

5. In the **azseckvXXXX | Secrets** blade, click on **Manage deleted secrets**:

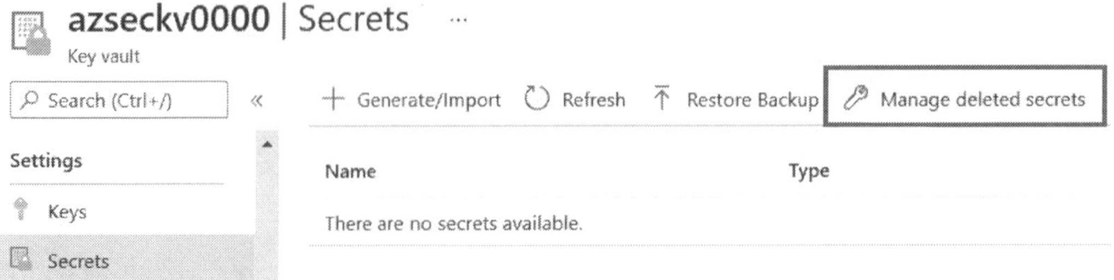

Figure 12.26 – Manage deleted secrets

6. In the **Manage deleted secrets** blade, select the **Api-Key** secret that was just deleted. Notice that the option to **Purge** is grayed out. This is because purge protection was enabled for this vault when we created it. Click on **Recover** to recover the deleted secret:

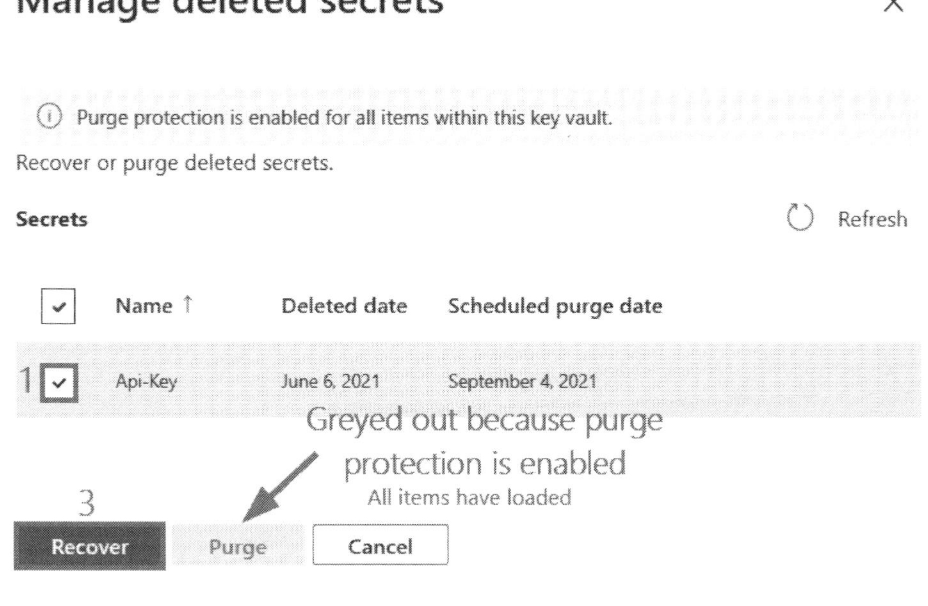

Figure 12.27 – Recover deleted secret

7. Click on **Refresh** and verify that the secret is recovered:

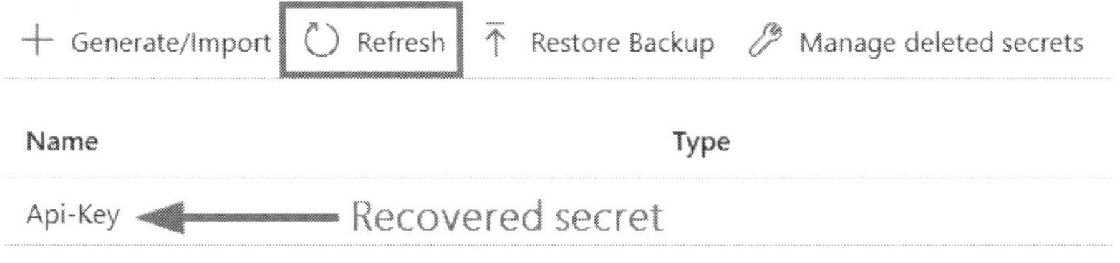

Figure 12.28 – Verify the recovered secret

8. Click on the recovered **Api-Key** secret, then click on **Download Backup**. Click on **Download** when prompted. This will download an encrypted backup copy of this secret to your system. You can use this backup to restore this secret even after it is permanently deleted.

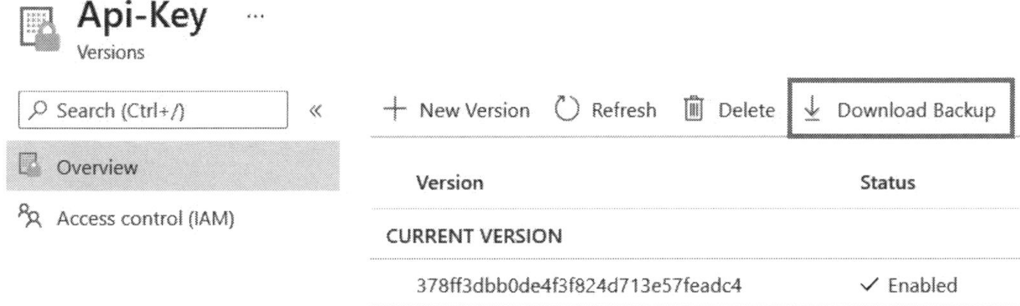

Figure 12.29 – Download the backup of a secret resource

Congratulations! You have implemented and verified protection for a Key Vault resource and its data. In the next section, we will clean up the resources that we created for the exercises.

Cleaning up resources

In the Azure portal, delete the `azuresec-c12-rg` resource group. This will remove all the Azure resources that we created for the exercises in this chapter.

In the Azure Cloud Shell, use the following command to delete the service principal that was created in this chapter:

```
az ad sp delete -id <APP_ID>
```

Replace `<APP_ID>` with the `appID` value that you noted in *Step 4* of the first exercise in this chapter.

Summary

In this chapter, we covered how to implement secret management using a Key Vault resource in Azure. The knowledge and skills that you have gained in this chapter have equipped you to mitigate the risk of exposing privileged credentials and sensitive application configurations in code by storing them securely in Key Vault.

In the next chapter, we will cover how to implement a good cloud governance strategy and how to manage security operations using Azure cloud-native tools. See you in the next chapter!

Question

As we conclude, here is a question for you to test your knowledge regarding this chapter's material. You will find the answer in the *Assessments* section of the *Appendix*:

1. You have an Azure subscription that contains an Azure key vault named `uksth-vault`. In the vault, you create a secret named `appsecret`. An application developer registers an application in **Azure Active Directory** (**Azure AD**). You need to ensure that the application can access `appsecret`. What should you do?

   a. In Azure AD, create a role.

   b. In Azure Key Vault, create a key.

   c. In Azure Key Vault, create an access policy.

   d. In Azure AD, enable Azure AD Application Proxy.

Further reading

To learn more on the subject, check out the following material:

- Azure Key Vault access control – `https://docs.microsoft.com/en-us/azure/key-vault/general/security-features`
- Azure Key Vault secrets, keys, and certificates – `https://docs.microsoft.com/en-us/azure/key-vault/general/about-keys-secrets-certificates`
- Azure Key Vault soft-delete – `https://docs.microsoft.com/en-us/azure/key-vault/general/soft-delete-overview`
- Azure Key Vault network security – `https://docs.microsoft.com/en-us/azure/key-vault/general/network-security`

13
Azure Cloud Governance and Security Operations

A good governance strategy helps us maintain control over the applications and resources that have been deployed in our Azure environments and reduces any risks that are introduced. Implementing security monitoring ensures that we can quickly identify, remediate, and investigate vulnerabilities and threats.

In this chapter, you will gain the knowledge and skills needed to implement governance using some of the native tools in Azure. You will also gain a solid understanding of how to monitor security operations in an Azure environment.

Here are the topics that we will cover in this chapter:

- Implementing Azure cloud governance
- Understanding logging and monitoring
- Addressing cloud security challenges with Security Center
- Managing security operations with Azure Sentinel

Let's get into this!

Technical requirements

To follow along with the instructions in this chapter, you will need the following:

- A PC with an internet connection.
- An Azure subscription. You can use the same subscription that you set up in the first chapter of this book.

Implementing Azure cloud governance

The traditional approach to enforcing organizational standards is to prevent teams from creating their own services, and instead to have the IT team define and deploy services on their behalf. This approach is often the solution in on-premises situations, but it reduces the agility of teams and slows down their ability to innovate.

A good *cloud* governance model should seek to enforce the security and compliance standards of the organization while allowing different teams to create and own their resources in the cloud. The Azure cloud provides several options that we can use to implement this model but for our objectives, we will cover management groups, Azure Policy, Azure RBAC, and Azure Blueprints. Let's start by understanding what management groups are and how we can make use of them to implement governance in Azure.

Understanding management groups

To keep things simple, a **management group** is a logical construct that allows us to group subscriptions. But why would we want to group subscriptions?

The first benefit is that it makes it much easier to manage multiple subscriptions as a single, logical group. This way, we can apply governance controls such as RBAC and Azure Policy *once* at the management group level and have them inherited by all the subscriptions in the group. This can be seen in the following diagram:

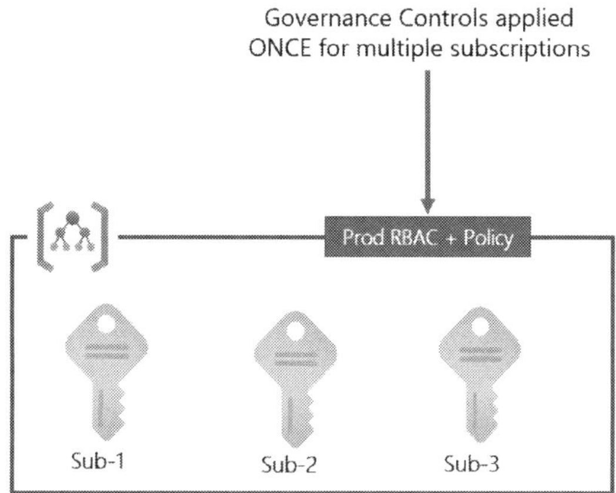

Figure 13.1 – Management group governance controls

The second benefit is visibility as we can aggregate reporting at a higher level. For example, instead of viewing billing for each subscription, we can group them and view billing for all the subscriptions in the group.

The next question is, how can we start using management groups? If an organization is new to Azure, then management groups are not enabled by default. There is an initial setup process to enable them. This can be done in the Azure portal by searching for the **Management groups** option and enabling it, as shown in the following screenshot:

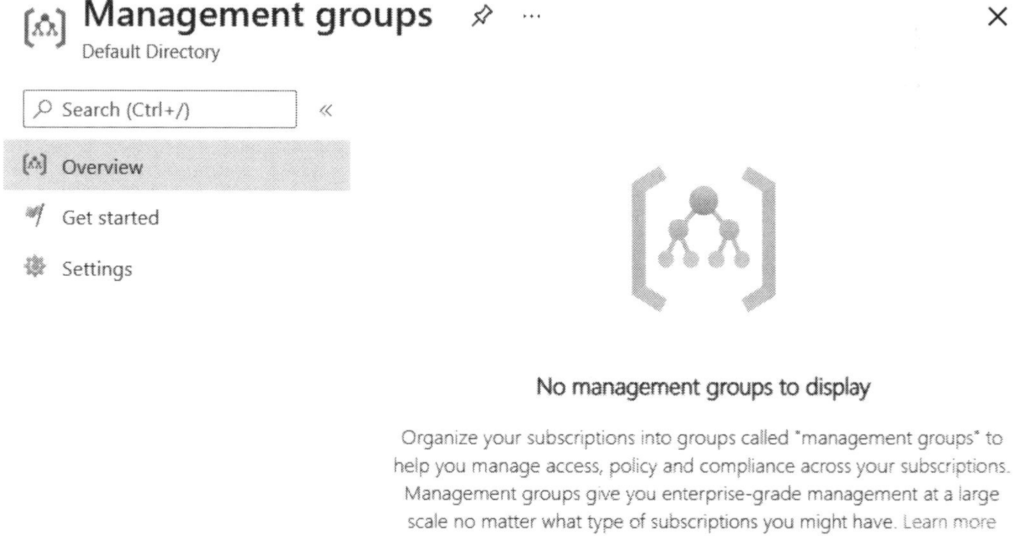

Figure 13.2 – Enabling management groups

Once the enabling process is completed, a **ROOT** management group will be created in the directory. At this point, all existing subscriptions in the directory are automatically made children of this root management group. There can only be one **ROOT** management group:

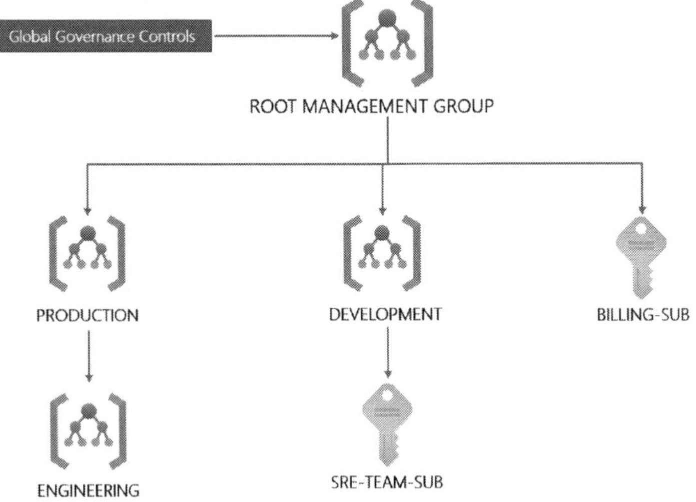

Figure 13.3 – Management group hierarchy

As shown in the preceding diagram, we can create child management groups under the root group and even nest groups within each other, up to six levels. This allows us to be flexible when we're designing a hierarchy that will fit our organization, *while still ensuring that we can apply security and governance policies globally at the root level* (*Figure 13.3*).

Once we have the root management group enabled, child management groups created, and our environment structured in the way that we want, it is time to start applying controls. Azure Policy is one of the main services that we can use to apply security and governance policies in Azure. We will cover this in the next section.

Understanding Azure Policy

Azure Policy is a configuration assessment and enforcement service. It can be used to *assess and enforce configuration* for both existing resources and new resources before they are deployed.

Let's look at how Azure Policy works for a moment. This will help us get a clearer understanding of this service. The first thing you must know is that the "policy engine" that does the assessment and enforcement configuration is embedded within Azure's control plane – **Resource Manager**. The significance of this is that any policy that we apply will be assessed, regardless of the management tool that users in our organizations use to provision resources – the Azure portal, Azure CLI, or Azure PowerShell.

Let's say that we have defined a policy that restricts the allowed VM sizes to only one size – the Standard_D2s_v3 with a deny effect (we will talk about effects later in this section), as shown in the following diagram:

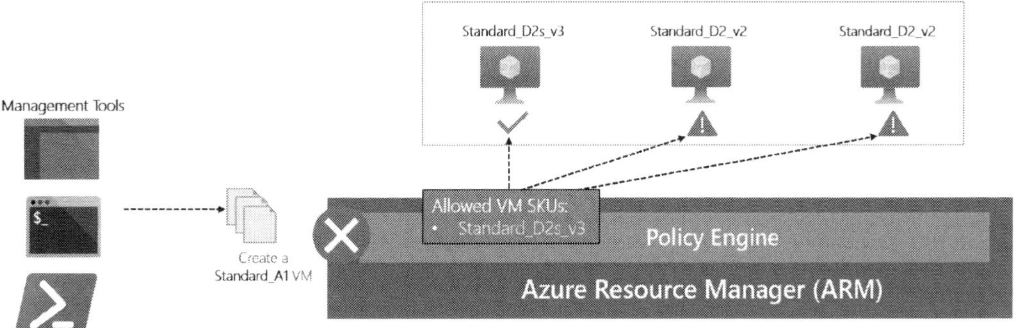

Figure 13.4 – Azure Policy example

Once applied, existing resources will be assessed against that policy, and they will be flagged for compliance or violation (existing resources will *not* be modified or stopped with a deny effect). However, new resource deployments that violate that policy will be blocked, regardless of the tool that is used, due to the deny effect.

To implement Azure Policy, there are three aspects to understand:

- The first aspect is the **policy definition**, where we define the configuration that we want to assess/enforce.
- The second aspect is the **policy assignment**, where we assign the defined policy at a resource hierarchy scope.
- And finally, we have the **policy evaluation**, where the definition will be assessed or enforced based on the effect that we configured.

Let's look at these three aspects in more detail.

Policy definition

An Azure Policy definition is a JSON template that defines the configuration that we want to check for and the effect to apply if there is a match. The structure of this template is in a classic `IF THIS, THEN THAT` format. In other words, if this configuration exists or does not exist, then apply this effect.

The following is the JSON structure of an Azure Policy definition:

```
{
    "if": {
        <condition> | <logical operator>
    },
    "then": {
        "effect": "deny | audit | append | auditIfNotExists |
deployIfNotExists | disabled | Modify"
    }
}
```

> **Note**
>
> Seven effects can be applied for a policy definition. They are briefly described here:
>
> `Deny`: Denies the configuration change from being applied.
>
> `Audit` and `AuditIfNotExists`: Does not stop the configuration change. It just logs a warning in the activity log.
>
> `Append` and `Modify`: Adds a configuration or alters the resource configuration before applying it.
>
> `DeployIfNotExists`: Deploys a template if the configuration does not exist.
>
> `Disabled`: Disables the policy definition.

In the example that we mentioned earlier, if the VM size is not `Standard_D2s_v3`, then apply a deny effect, the policy definition template will look like this:

```
{
  "if": {
    "allOf": [
      {
        "field": "type",
        "equals": "Microsoft.Compute/virtualMachines"
      },
      {
        "not": {
```

```
            "field": "Microsoft.Compute/virtualMachines/sku.
name",
            "in": "Standard_D2s_v3"
        }
      ]
    },
    "then": {
      "effect": "Deny"
    }
}
```

The good thing is that we do not need to start writing our own policy definitions from scratch: there are hundreds of built-in policy definitions already in Azure that we can start with. However, we can also write our own custom policy definitions.

After defining our policies, we can group them for easier assignment later. A grouping of policy definitions is called an **initiative**. The main use case of an initiative is to simplify policy assignments. Instead of assigning 100 individual policy definitions, we can group them as one initiative and assign them once:

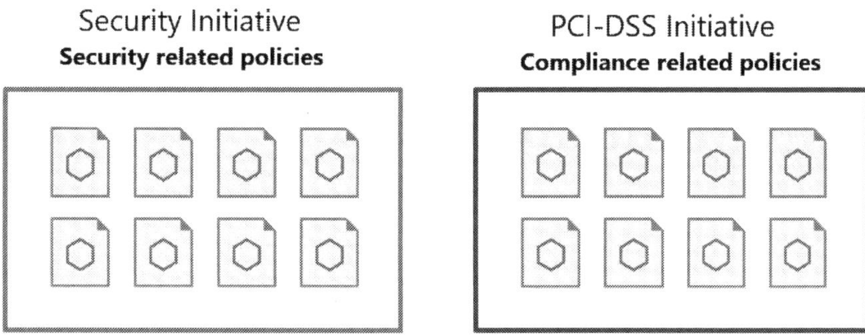

Figure 13.5 – Grouping policy definitions as initiatives

It is common for organizations to create initiatives that are in line with specific goals or purposes. For example, security-related policy definitions can be grouped as a security initiative, while policy definitions related to the PCI-DSS compliance framework can be grouped as a PCI-DSS initiative (*Figure 13.5*).

Policy assignment

Once we have our policy definition or initiative, we can assign it at different scopes in our resource hierarchy. We can assign policy definitions or initiatives at the management group level (both the root management group and child management group levels). This is useful if we want to apply consistent governance controls to multiple subscriptions in a group (*Figure 13.6*). We can also assign policy definitions/initiatives at the subscription and resource group levels (*Figure 13.6*), but *not* at the resource level:

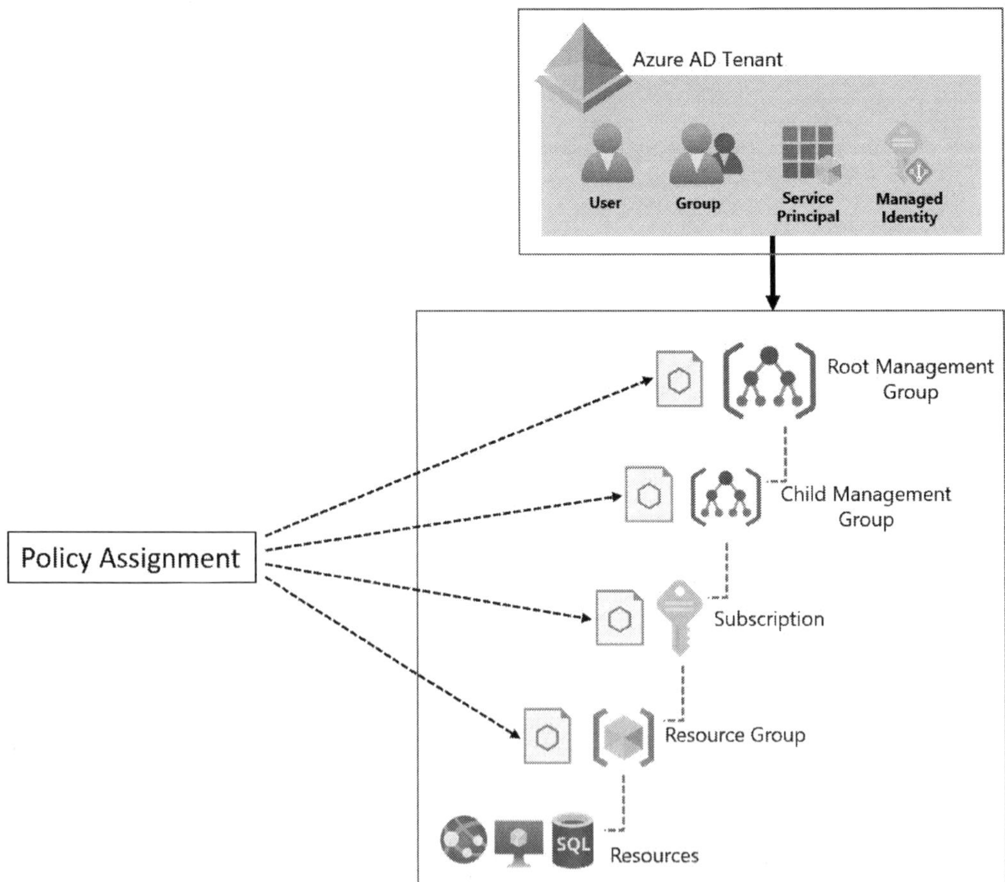

Figure 13.6 – Policy assignment at different scopes

Policy assignments are automatically inherited by all child resources. A definition or initiative that's applied to a subscription level will apply to all resource groups and resources in that subscription.

Exclusions can be added to policy assignments. For example, if we assign a definition at the subscription scope to prevent any network resources from being created, we can further exclude a resource group that has been designated to contain networking resources. We can then use RBAC to grant access to this networking resource group to administrators that have the responsibility of creating networking resources.

Another use case for exclusion is if we want a more permissive policy at a lower level of the hierarchy. For example, let's say we assign a policy at the root management group level that restricts resource creation to only the UK West and UK South regions. However, we want one subscription to be allowed to create resources in West Europe as well. What we can do here is exclude the subscription from the higher-level policy assignment and assign its own policy directly.

Policy evaluation

Once the policy has been defined and assigned, the evaluation process begins to assess both existing and new resource deployments. The effects that have been defined will then be applied.

Note that it could take around 30 minutes for the evaluation of existing resources to start when a policy definition is applied, or when an applied policy definition is updated.

While policies are great for applying guardrails to our cloud environments, we also want to control the access that users and applications have in our environment.

Understanding Azure RBAC

Access management for cloud resources is a critical security function for any organization that is using the cloud. Azure **Role-Based Access Control** (**RBAC**) is an authorization system that we can use to control who has access to Azure resources, and what they can do with those resources. We introduced this in *Chapter 2, Understanding Azure AD*, but we will discuss this further here.

At a high level, you can think of RBAC as granting security principals (users, groups, and applications) access to Azure resources by assigning roles to them. For example, RBAC can be used to grant a user access to manage all virtual machines in a subscription, while another user is granted access to manage all storage accounts across multiple subscriptions in a management group.

Azure RBAC is made up of the following components: security principals, role definitions, and role assignment. Security principals are the Azure AD objects that we can assign permissions to. They can be users, groups, service principals, or managed identities. We covered security principals in *Chapter 2*, *Understanding Azure AD*, so we will review the other components here.

Role definition

Role definition (sometimes referred to as role) describes a collection of permissions. A permission describes an action that can be performed on a resource, such as read, write, and delete. The actual content of a role definition defines different actions that are allowed or excluded, as well as the scope that a role can be applied to. For example, here are the permissions for the *Contributor* role in Azure:

```
{
  "assignableScopes": [
    "/"
  ],
  "description": "Grants full access to manage all resources, but does not allow you to assign roles in Azure RBAC, manage assignments in Azure Blueprints, or share image galleries.",
  "id": "/subscriptions/{subscriptionId}/providers/Microsoft.Authorization/roleDefinitions/b24988ac-6180-42a0-ab88-20f7382dd24c",
  "name": "b24988ac-6180-42a0-ab88-20f7382dd24c",
  "permissions": [
    {
      "actions": [
        "*"
      ],
      "notActions": [
        "Microsoft.Authorization/*/Delete",
```

```
            "Microsoft.Authorization/*/Write",
            "Microsoft.Authorization/elevateAccess/Action",
            "Microsoft.Blueprint/blueprintAssignments/write",
            "Microsoft.Blueprint/blueprintAssignments/delete",
            "Microsoft.Compute/galleries/share/action"
        ],
        "dataActions": [],
        "notDataActions": []
    }
  ],
  "roleName": "Contributor",
  "roleType": "BuiltInRole",
  "type": "Microsoft.Authorization/roleDefinitions"
}
```

Here, we can see that a role definition supports two types of operations:

- Control plane operations, which describe the management actions that the role can perform. These are defined in the `"actions": [ ]` section. An example of a management action is being permitted to create a storage account.
- Data plane operations, which describe the data actions (within a resource) that the role can perform. These are defined in the `"dataActions": [ ]` section. An example of a data action is being permitted to read the data that is stored in a storage account.

In the preceding permissions, we can also see that certain operations can be excluded for a role. The `"notActions": [ ]` section defines management actions that a role is restricted from performing, while the `"notDataActions": [ ]` section defines data actions that a role is restricted from performing.

In the example of the *Contributor* role, the role has permission to perform all management actions (`*`), but it is restricted (by the not actions definition) from performing authorization-related management actions, which means that the role cannot be used to assign permissions.

Scope

Scope is the level that we want permissions on. We can apply RBAC to any scope in the Azure resource hierarchy – the root management group, child management group, subscription, resource group, and even the resource itself, as shown here:

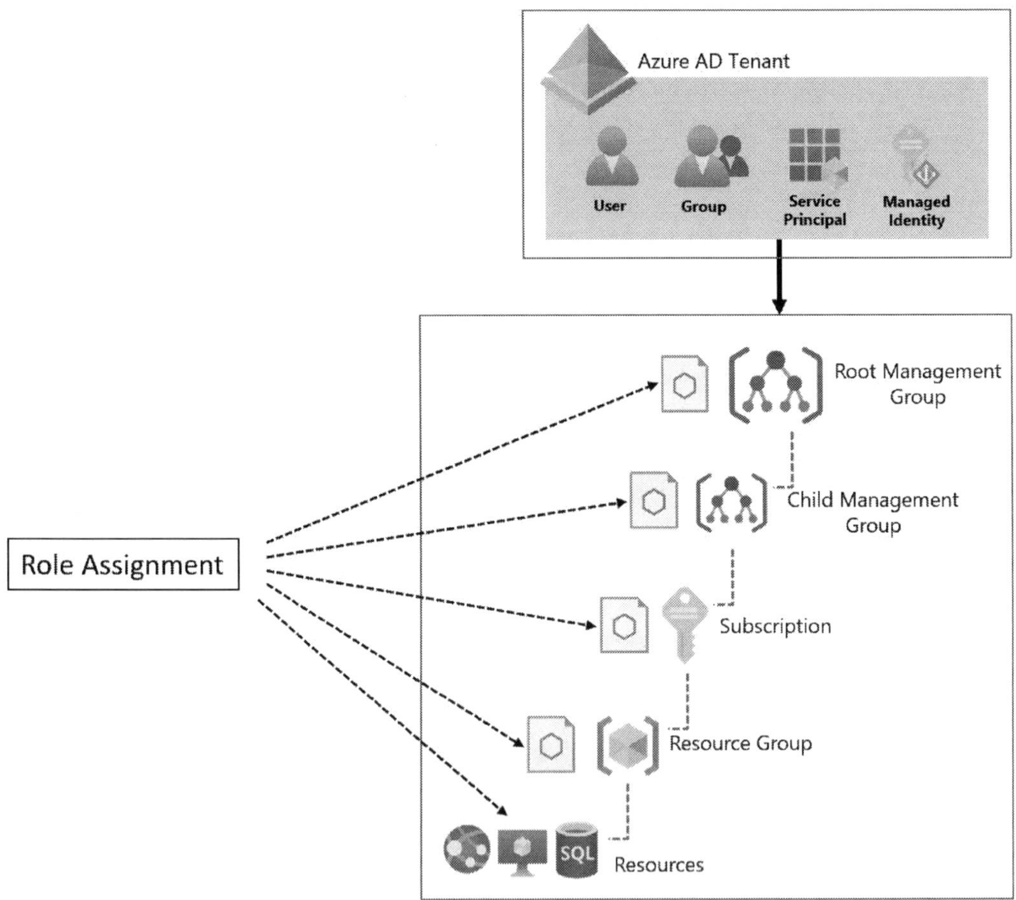

Figure 13.7 – Role assignment scopes

Scopes are structured in a parent-child relationship. When we grant access to a parent scope, those permissions are inherited by the child scopes:

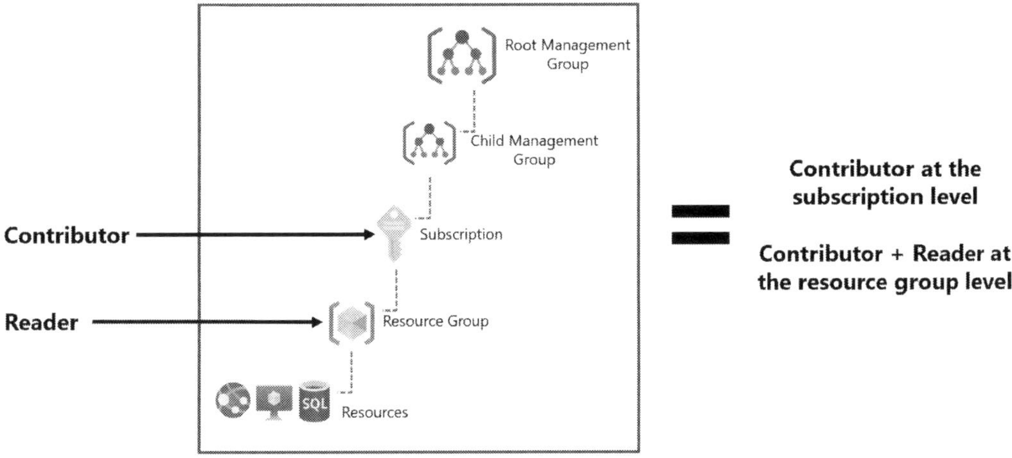

Figure 13.8 – Multiple role assignments

The result of assigning multiple roles at different scopes is a culmination of all the permissions (*Figure 13.8*).

Role assignment

Once we have determined the who, what, and where, we can combine those elements to grant the access that we want. Role assignment is the process of attaching a role definition to a user, group, service principal, or managed identity at a scope to grant access:

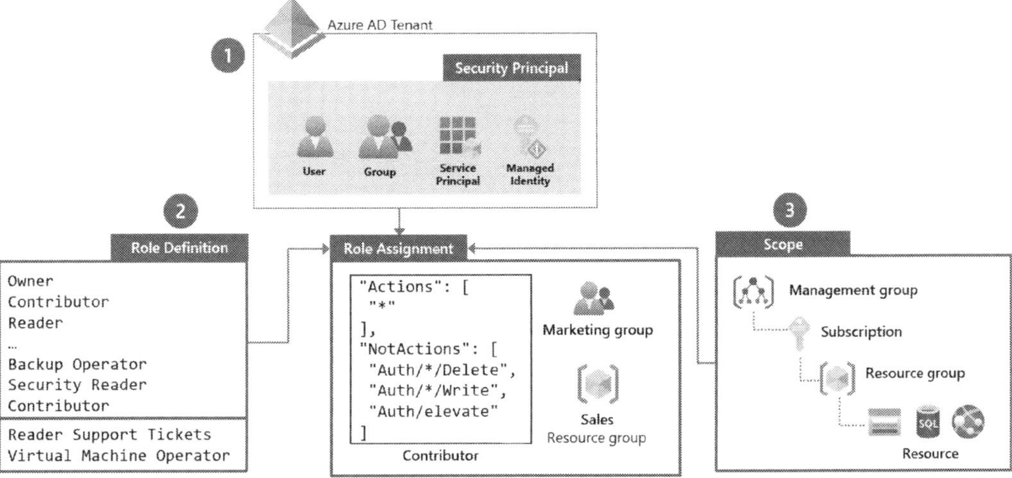

Figure 13.9 – Role assignment

The preceding diagram shows the Marketing group (security principal) being assigned the Contributor role (role definition) at the Sales resource group level (scope). In the following hands-on exercise, you will implement management groups and Azure Policy to establish governance for an Azure subscription.

Hands-on exercise – implementing management groups and Azure Policy

Here are the tasks that we will complete in this exercise:

- **Task 1**: Implement management groups
- **Task 2**: Implement Azure Policy
- **Task 3**: Test Azure Policy

Follow these steps to complete these tasks:

1. Sign in to the Azure portal at `https://portal.azure.com/`.
2. In the **Search resources, services, and docs** box at the top of the portal, type *Management groups* and select **Management groups** to navigate to the **Management groups** blade.
3. Review the messages at the top of the **Management groups** blade. If you have not created management groups previously, select **Start using management groups**.
4. Create a management group with the following settings:

   Management group ID: `azsec-first-MG`

   Management group display name: **First Child Management Group**
5. From the list of management groups, click the entry representing the newly created management group.
6. On the **azsec-first-MG** blade, click **Subscriptions**.
7. On the **azsec-first-MG | Subscriptions** blade, click **+ Add**. Then, on the **Add subscription** blade, from the **Subscription** drop-down list, select the subscription you are using in this lab and click **Save**. The following diagram shows the current state of our configuration based on what we have done in this exercise:

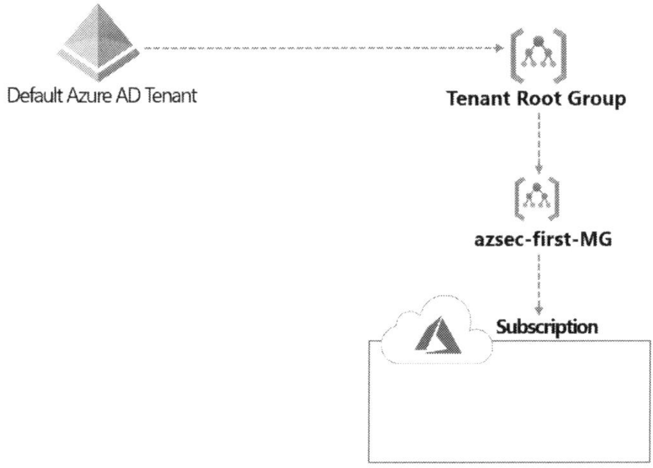

Figure 13.10 – Root management group and child management group

8. In the Azure portal, in the **Search resources, services, and docs** text box at the top of the Azure portal home page, type *Policy* and press *Enter*.
9. On the **Policy** blade, in the **Authoring** section, select **Definitions**. Review the built-in definitions. You can use the **Category** drop-down to filter the list of policies. Review the policies marked under the **Security** category.
10. In the **Search** text box, type *Allowed locations*.

> Note
>
> The **Allowed locations** policy allows you to restrict the location of your resources, not resource groups. To restrict the locations of resource groups, you can use the **Allowed locations for resource groups** policy.

11. Click the **Allowed locations** policy definition to display its details.
12. On the **Allowed locations** blade, click **Assign**.
13. On the **Basics** tab of the **Allowed locations** blade, click the ellipsis (**...**) button next to the **Scope** text box and, on the **Scope** blade, specify the following settings:

    Subscription: Select your Azure subscription.

    Resource group: Leave as the default.
14. Click **Select**.

15. On the **Allowed locations** blade, on the **Basics** tab, specify the following settings (leave the others with their default values):

    Assignment name: Data residency governance – East US

    Description: Allow resources to be created in East US Only for Subscription

    Policy enforcement: Enabled

    Click **Next**.

16. On the **Parameters** tab of the **Allowed locations** blade, from the **Allowed locations** drop-down list, select **East US** as the only allowed location.

> Note
>
> You can select more than one location. If the policy required a different set of parameters, this tab would provide those selections.

17. Click **Review + create**, followed by **Create**, to create the policy assignment. The following diagram shows the current state of the configuration based on the steps that we have completed already:

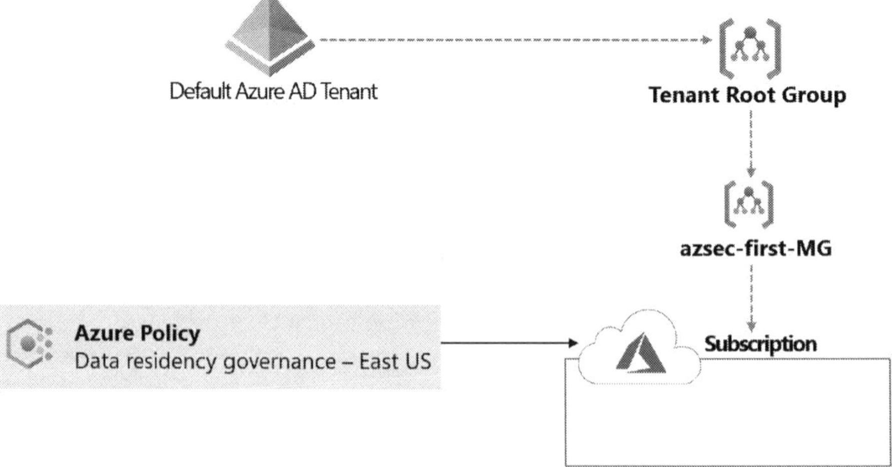

Figure 13.11 – Data residency governance policy assigned at the subscription scope

> **Note**
>
> You will see a notification stating that the assignment was successful and that the assignment might take around 30 minutes to complete.
>
> The reason the Azure Policy assignment might take up to 30 minutes to take effect is that it must replicate globally. Typically, this only takes a few minutes. If the next task fails, simply wait a few minutes and attempt its steps again.

Now, let's test the data residency governance policy that we just applied.

18. In the Azure portal, in the **Search resources, services, and docs** text box at the top of the Azure portal home page, type *Virtual networks* and press *Enter*.
19. On the **Virtual Networks** blade, click **+ New**.

> **Note**
>
> First, you must try to create a virtual network in UK South. Since this is not an allowed location, the request should be blocked.

20. On the **Basics** tab of the **Create virtual network** blade, specify the following settings (leave the others with their default values):

    Resource group: **Create new → azsec-c13-rg → OK**

    Name: `uksth-vnet`

    Region: **UK South**

    Click **Review + create**.
21. On the **Review + create** tab of the **Create virtual network** blade, take note of the **Validation failed** message.

> **Note**
>
> If the **Validation Failed** warning does not appear, click **Previous** and wait a few more minutes.

22. Click the error message to open the **Errors** blade. You will see a detailed error message stating that the deployment of the resource was disallowed by Azure Policy.
23. Close the **Errors** blade. Then, on the **Create virtual network** blade, click the **Basics** tab, and, from the **Region** drop-down list, select **East US**.

24. Click **Review + create** and verify that the validation passed. Then, click **Create** and verify that the virtual network was created successfully.
25. Go back to the **Subscription** blade and delete the policy assignment that we created to avoid future restrictions in our lab environment.

Congratulations! You have successfully implemented management groups and Azure Policy. In the next section, we will start to look at logging and monitoring. The knowledge that you will gain will give you a strong understanding of different types of logging data in Azure and some of the core monitoring services. Let's get into it!

Understanding logging and monitoring

When we talk about logging and monitoring, it is very easy to jump right into what we should be doing, but that is not where we should start in Azure. Security is a shared responsibility, as we emphasized in *Chapter 1, Introduction to Azure Security*, and this extends to security operations. The first place we should start with monitoring is getting visibility into what we are not responsible for but could impact us. For example, we do not manage the underlying storage infrastructure in Azure, yet something could be happening at that level that impacts the workload that we are running. In this section, we will cover three main services:

- Azure Service Health
- Azure Monitor
- Log Analytics

Let's look at each in detail.

Azure Service Health

Azure Service Health is a personalized Azure status monitoring service (personalized meaning it gives us information in the context of the resources and regions that we are using or that we have defined). It tracks four types of health events and highlights these to us:

Service issues: Problems with Azure services that a customer is using.

Planned maintenance: Upcoming maintenance tasks that may impact service availability and stability.

Health advisories: Upcoming changes in Azure services that may impact a customer; for example, Azure service features that will soon be deprecated or a resource usage quota that may soon be exceeded.

Security advisories: Security notifications related to services that an organization is using.

The great thing is that we can configure proactive notifications for this so that we are made aware when an issue is detected, or when there is an advisory that we need to act upon.

Azure Monitor

In terms of our responsibility for monitoring our services, Azure Monitor is critical for this. Azure Monitor is the central service for collecting and analyzing telemetry in Azure. It collects two fundamental types of data: metrics and logs.

The following diagram provides a high-level view of Azure Monitor. On the left are the sources for monitoring data; that is, Azure, operating systems, and custom sources. At the center of the diagram are the data stores for metrics and logs. Finally, on the right, we have the functions that Azure Monitor performs with this data, such as analysis, alerting, and streaming to external systems. You can see that this is a very comprehensive service!

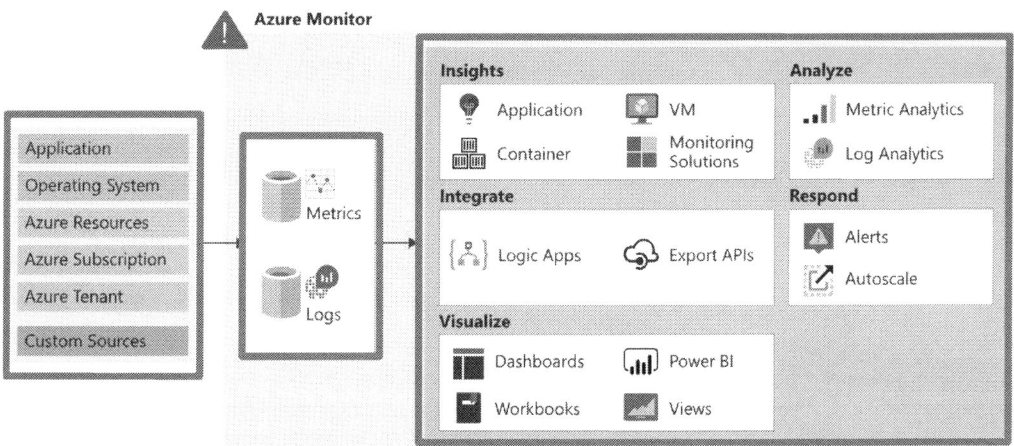

Figure 13.12 – Azure Monitor overview

Before we proceed, let's take a moment to review three of the core pieces of data for monitoring in Azure: Metrics, Activity Logs, and Resource Logs.

Understanding Metrics, Activity Logs, and Resource Logs

There is no security monitoring without data. Without raw information that we can collect from services, systems, and applications, there is nothing to analyze for insights and issues. Core monitoring in Azure consists of some key data: **Metrics**, **Activity logs**, and **Resource logs**. Let's begin with Metrics.

Metrics

Metrics are numerical values that describe some aspect of a system at a point in time. What does this mean? We primarily mean regular health and performance data from Azure resources that's emitted by the Azure platform into Azure Monitor. This is the equivalent of Resource Monitor information about CPU, memory, and network utilization, if you are familiar with the Windows OS. Data collected from here can be analyzed to uncover anomalies in resource behavior that could expose incidents such as crypto mining (due to unusual CPU utilization spikes) or data exfiltration (due to unusual network egress traffic):

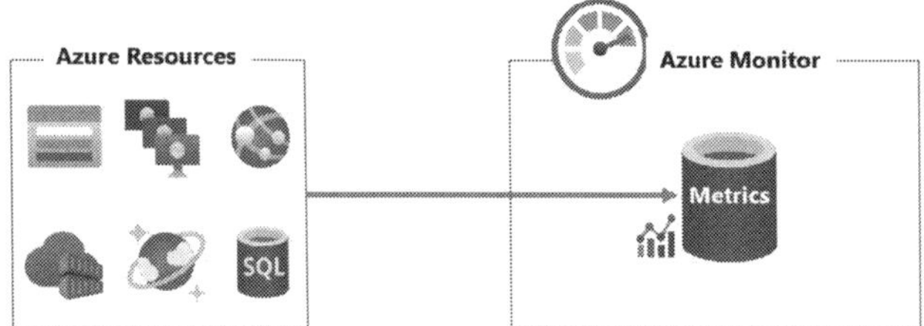

Figure 13.13 – Azure Metrics

How do we enable metrics collection? The good thing is that we do not need to do anything to enable metrics. They are enabled and collected by default. Once we have created an Azure resource that supports metrics, this data is collected by the Azure platform and sent into the Azure Monitor metrics data store.

How often is the data sent? Metrics are emitted every minute for most Azure resources. But there are a few metrics that are emitted every 5 minutes. More information can be found in this document: `https://docs.microsoft.com/en-us/azure/azure-monitor/essentials/metrics-supported`.

Where are they stored and how long are they retained? Metrics are stored in the metrics data store of Azure Monitor and retained for 93 days for free. We can export to a third-party service for longer retention.

What can we do with this data, once collected?

- We can analyze and visualize the data using a free tool called Metrics Explorer.
- We can visualize the data using Azure Monitor Workbooks, which is also free.
- We can configure Alerts using a metrics alert rule. There is a cost associated with alerts.
- We can use this data as a trigger for automated events such as autoscaling. For example, if the CPU metrics of an App service exceed the 80% threshold, automatically scale out.

Activity Logs

Activity Logs is a platform log in Azure that provides insights into subscription-level events. What does this mean? For example, when the configuration of an Azure resource is modified or when a virtual machine is started, this will be logged in Activity Logs. So, these are management plane events that have significant security benefits, such as being able to perform forensics in the event of a breach:

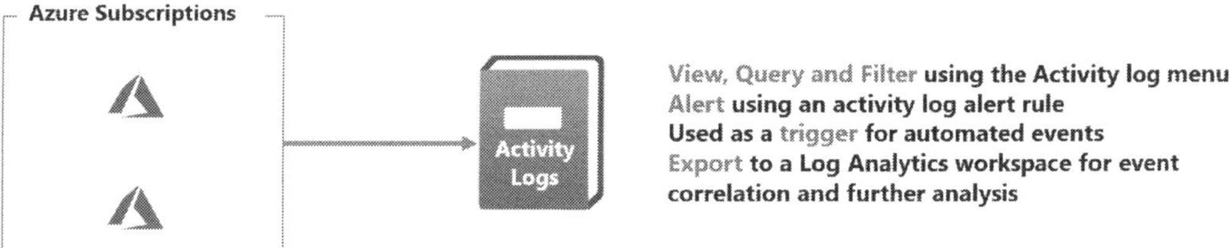

Figure 13.14 – Azure Activity Logs

How do we enable it? Similar to metrics, this is enabled by default! Whenever an administrative-level event or operation occurs in an Azure subscription, it is logged.

How long are they retained? Data is retained for 90 days in Azure, which means we can only review them as far back as the last three months.

Resource Logs

Resource Logs are logs that are generated by Azure resources, which is why they are referred to as resource logs. They used to be called diagnostic logs.

Are they collected by default as well? Unlike metrics and activity logs, resource logs are not collected by default. And the method of collection varies depending on the resource's type. For platform services that are managed by Microsoft, we can configure the diagnostic settings to collect resource logs, as shown here:

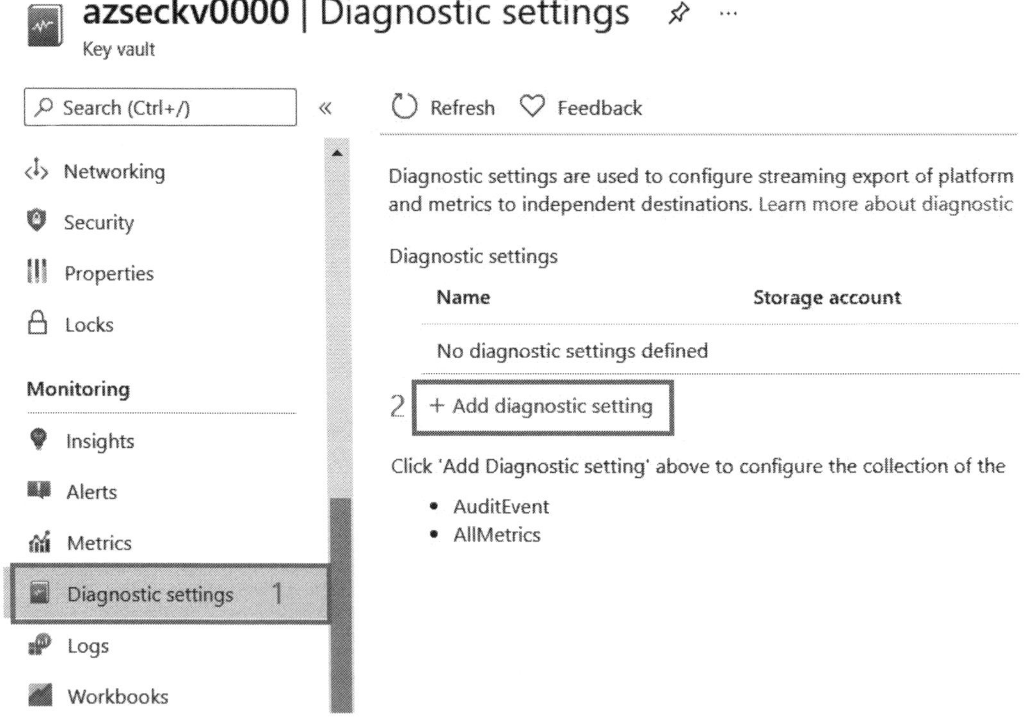

Figure 13.15 – Enabling Diagnostic settings for PaaS to collect resource logs

For IaaS services such as virtual machines and virtual machine scale sets, we can install an agent to collect the resource logs, as shown here:

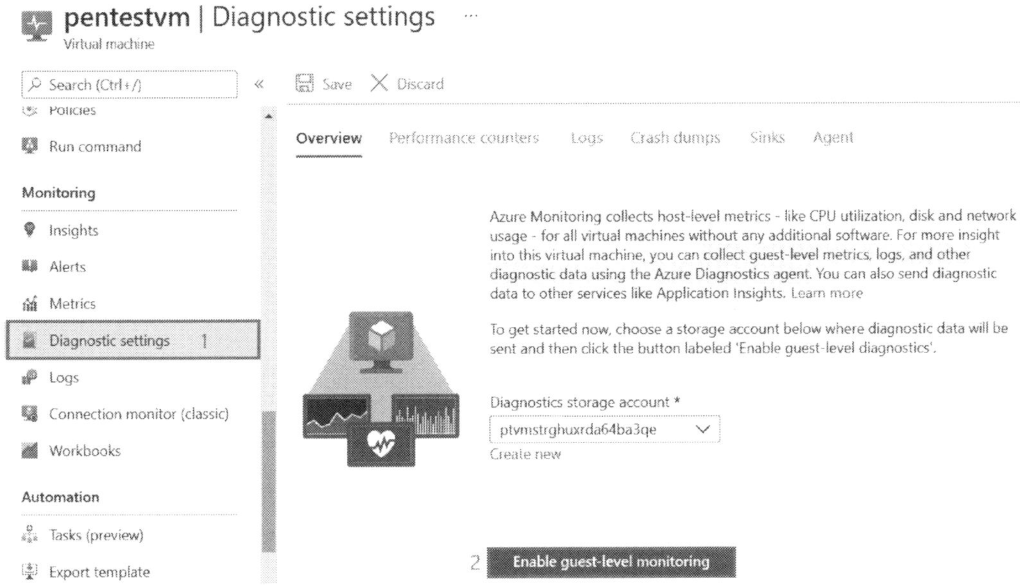

Figure 13.16 – Enabling Diagnostic settings for IaaS to collect resource logs

Where can we store the logs? We can select one of three options when we enable collection. We can send the logs to a Log Analytics workspace for event correlation and analysis, we can send the logs to an Azure Event Hub to forward outside of Azure to, for example, a third-party SIEM, or we can send the logs to Azure Storage for archiving or to be collected by another service. The following diagram highlights this:

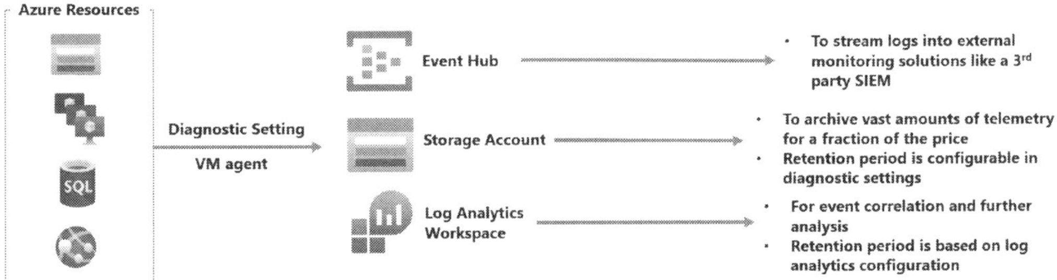

Figure 13.17 – Diagnostic setting options

Next, we'll look at Log Analytics.

Log Analytics

What is Log Analytics? At its core, it is a log aggregation and correlation tool. It collects and stores data from multiple log sources and allows us to query across the different logs using a custom query language. For example, if we have thousands of services implemented in Azure and we want to analyze their logs to identify the top 10 errors across different resource types, we can simply write a query in Log Analytics to obtain this information, so long as the data from all these sources is collected. Log Analytics replaced a previous service in Azure called **Operations Management Suite** (**OMS**).

The starting point for using Log Analytics is to create a Log Analytics workspace in our preferred Azure region. This is the resource that stores and organizes the data that we will be collecting. Once we have our workspace, we can start collecting data from different sources.

What sources can we collect data from? We can collect data from multiple sources, including metrics, activity logs, and resource logs, which we covered earlier. We can also collect data from VMs hosted anywhere (on-premises, Azure, or third-party cloud providers) using an agent, and also from custom sources using the REST API:

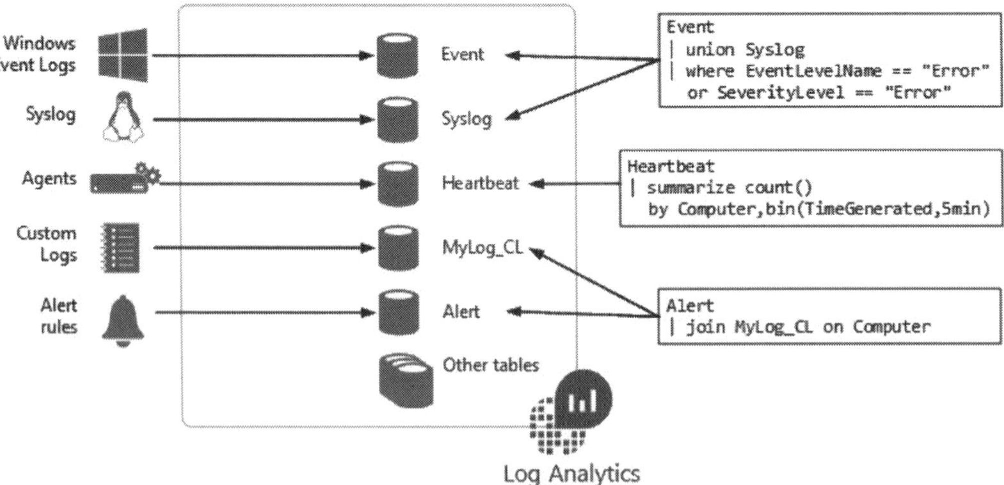

Figure 13.18 – Log Analytics workspace

Before data is stored in the Log Analytics workspace, it is organized into *tables* that store data from a particular source (*Figure 13.18*). For example, the Event table stores data collected from Windows event logs, the Syslog table stores data collected from Linux syslogs, the AzureActivity table stores Azure Activity log data, the AzureMetrics table stores Azure metrics data, and so on.

To retrieve, consolidate, and analyze data in the workspace, we use a query language called **Kusto Query Language** (**KQL**). A query syntax usually starts with the name of the table in the workspace that we are pulling data from, followed by the pipe symbol and a set of commands and operators to filter and process that data (see the examples shown in the preceding diagram).

For more complex analysis, you might use the `join` or `union` command to retrieve data from multiple tables to analyze the results together, as shown in the preceding diagram. Apart from searching for and analyzing workspace data using KQL, we can also save our search queries and visualize them, as well as configure alerts.

When it comes to analyzing data in our workspace, we can do the analysis ourselves using KQL, as mentioned earlier, *but* we can also use monitoring solutions to make things easier. Monitoring solutions include pre-defined analytics logic for gathering insights. So, the predefined logic will process data in our workspace without exposing us to the underlying queries.

Now that you have some understanding of monitoring and analysis in Azure, let's turn our attention to managing security operations for Azure environments, starting with the central service for managing security posture: Security Center!

Addressing cloud security challenges with Security Center

The main cause of breaches in the public cloud is the *misconfiguration of cloud services*. This is where Azure customers have configured resources and services in an insecure way. This misconfiguration is then exploited by attackers to breach their environment.

This challenge is compounded by the fact that *workloads in the cloud are dynamic and constantly changing*. This characteristic is both a strength and a challenge. On one hand, end users are empowered to do more. On the other hand, it is challenging to ensure that the ever-changing services and workloads are configured up to our security and compliance standards.

Attackers are also not relenting in their efforts. *Attacks are increasingly getting more sophisticated*, and they could be from anywhere – there are both internal threats and external threats.

The other challenge is that *security skills are in short supply*. We can see this just by looking at the logs that we covered earlier in this chapter alone. There is a wealth of security insights that can be obtained from activity logs and resource logs, but there's just not enough people or even expertise to identify every threat chain out there and deduce the right queries to detect them.

Azure Security Center (**ASC**) can help address some of these challenges. At its core, it provides three main functionalities:

- Cloud Security Posture Management
- Cloud Compliance Posture Management
- Threat protection

Let's look at these functionalities in detail.

Cloud Security Posture Management

First, let's talk about Cloud Security Posture Management. This is where Security Center uses Azure Policy (the same Azure Policy that we covered earlier) to monitor the configuration of our services in Azure and raises a flag if an insecure configuration is detected.

The way this works is that when we enable Security Center, a built-in, security-focused policy initiative is automatically assigned to all Security Center registered subscriptions. This policy initiative will continually discover new services that we are deploying in Azure and assess if they are configured according to security best practices. If they are not, they are flagged, and we get a prioritized list of recommendations for what we need to fix to harden our security posture. This built-in policy initiative is under the Security Center category and contains only Audit policies:

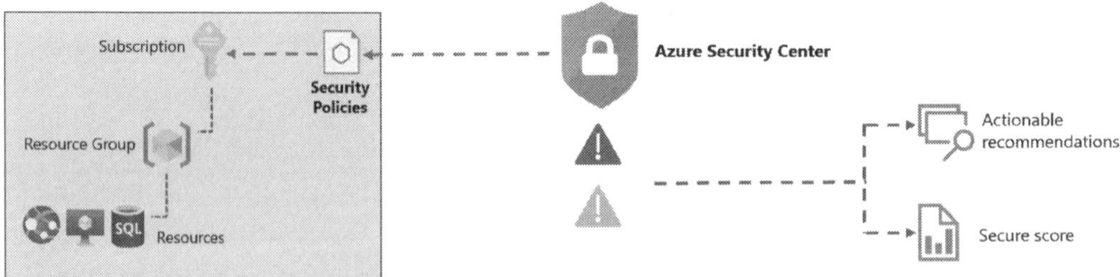

Figure 13.19 – ASC Security Posture Management

The main benefit of this functionality is that it can improve our security hygiene and reduce the attack surface. The output of this capability is a security score for your environment, along with actionable recommendations of what we can do to improve this score.

Cloud Compliance Posture Management

This functionality extends the posture management capability of Security Center to regulatory compliance frameworks.

When we register a subscription in Security Center, it automatically assigns policy initiatives that align with the Azure CIS, PCI DSS 3.2, ISO 27001, and SOC TSP regulatory standards. It will then flag services that have been configured in a way that is not compliant with the requirements of these frameworks. We can also download compliance reports in PDF format:

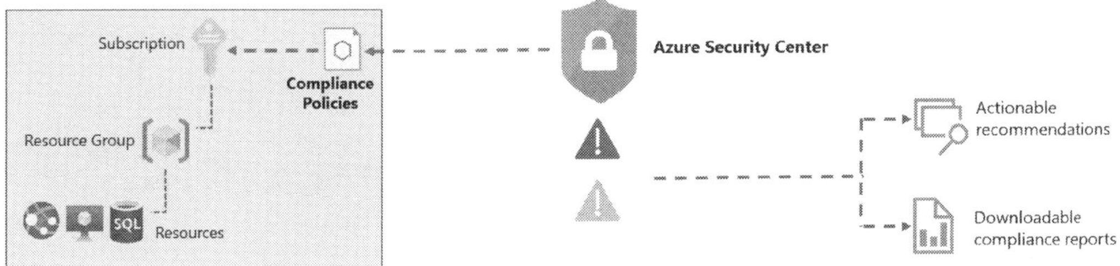

Figure 13.20 – ASC Compliance Posture Management

The main benefit of this functionality is that we can streamline the process to meet regulatory compliance requirements.

For both Security and Compliance Posture Management, organizations with multiple subscriptions that use management groups to structure their subscription hierarchy could configure Security Center policies at a central level, as shown in the following diagram:

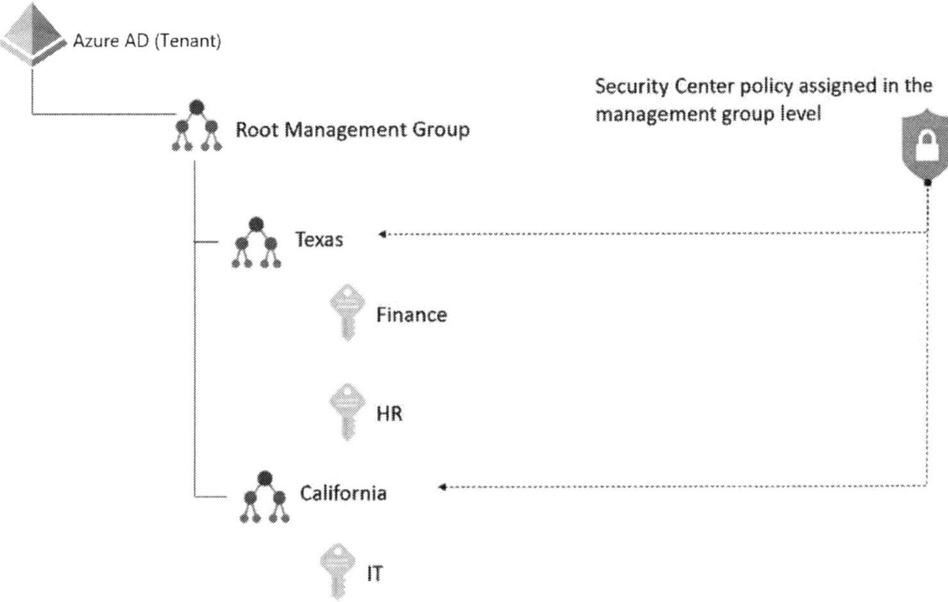

Figure 13.21 – ASC Centralized Policy Management

In the preceding diagram, Security Center policies have been assigned at a management group level instead of using individual subscriptions. We can do this from the Azure portal.

Threat protection

Following the recommendations of *both* Cloud Security Posture Management and Cloud Compliance Posture Management will help reduce the attack surface area of our Azure subscriptions and tenants!

However, Security Center extends its use case beyond the public cloud with its threat protection capabilities. You will also hear this capability being referred to as the Azure Defender module. And yes – this is the same Azure Defender that we have covered for other services in this book. This capability is powered by and managed in Security Center:

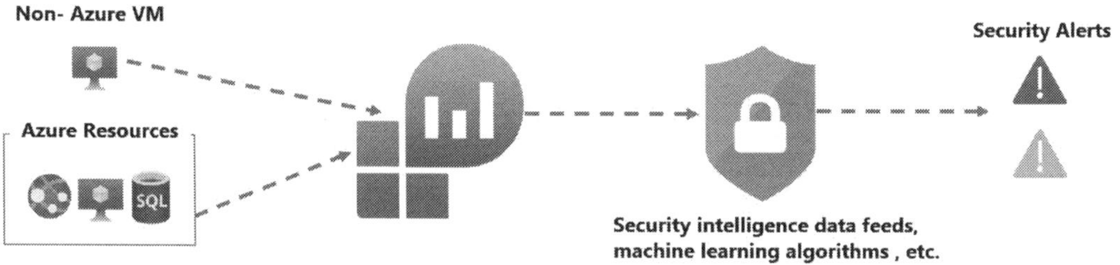

Figure 13.22 – Security center threat protection (Azure Defender)

The threat protection capabilities of Security Center allow us to address threats without requiring us to be security experts. It extends to both IaaS and PaaS services and covers three main areas:

- **Threat protection for Azure compute resources**: This covers Windows and Linux systems anywhere, not just in Azure. It also covers platform compute services in Azure such as App Service and Azure containers.
- **Threat protection for Azure data resources**: This covers platform storage and databases in Azure. This includes SQL Database and SQL Data Warehouse, Azure Storage, and Azure Cosmos DB.
- **Threat protection for Azure service layers**: This covers Azure DNS, Azure Resource Manager, and Azure Key Vault.

Events from all these different sources are collected in a Log Analytics workspace that is used by Security Center (*Figure 13.22*). Different methods are then used to identify and detect threats. This includes using information from security intelligence data feeds, machine learning algorithms, and reputation assessments (*Figure 13.22*).

Now that you understand what Security Center is about, let's turn our attention to another important Azure service for managing the overall security operations of both Azure and non-Azure environments: Azure Sentinel.

Managing security operations with Azure Sentinel

Azure Sentinel is a scalable, SIEM, and SOAR solution that's hosted on the Azure platform. What do we mean by this? Let's review what SIEM and SOAR are.

SIEM stands for **Security Information Event Management**. It works by collecting log and event data generated from multiple sources, collating the data on a centralized platform, and performing automated analysis of that data to detect threats. This is not a full description of what a SIEM is but a short review. Many SIEMs, including Azure Sentinel, have capabilities beyond these.

SOAR stands for **Security Orchestration, Automation, and Response**. SOAR allows companies to collect threat-related data from a range of sources and automate responses to those threats:

Figure 13.23 – SIEM and SOAR

Looking at the descriptions, it makes sense for these solutions to work together. SIEM collects logs and events from data sources and detects threats, while SOAR acts on detected threats and automates responses to them (*Figure 13.23*).

Azure Sentinel, being a cloud-native SIEM and SOAR solution, has four main aspects that we will cover:

- First, we *collect log and event data* from multiple sources, both inside Azure and outside Azure.
- Sentinel then *detects threats* using different methods.
- We can then investigate threats that have been detected in Sentinel.

- Finally, we can *automate responses to incidents* using something called playbooks:

Figure 13.24 – Four main aspects of Azure Sentinel

Let's look into these four aspects in more detail.

Data collection

To start using Azure Sentinel, we need to create a centralized place to store the data that we will be collecting. That centralized place is a Log Analytics workspace. This is the same workspace that we have discussed previously. In this scenario, **Azure Sentinel** is the frontend application, while a **Log Analytics Workspace** acts as the backend data store:

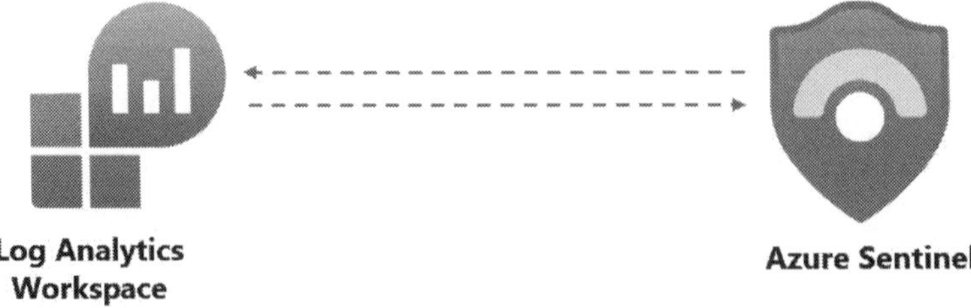

Figure 13.25 – Azure Sentinel workspace

Once we have our workspace, we need to collect log and event data for analysis and investigation:

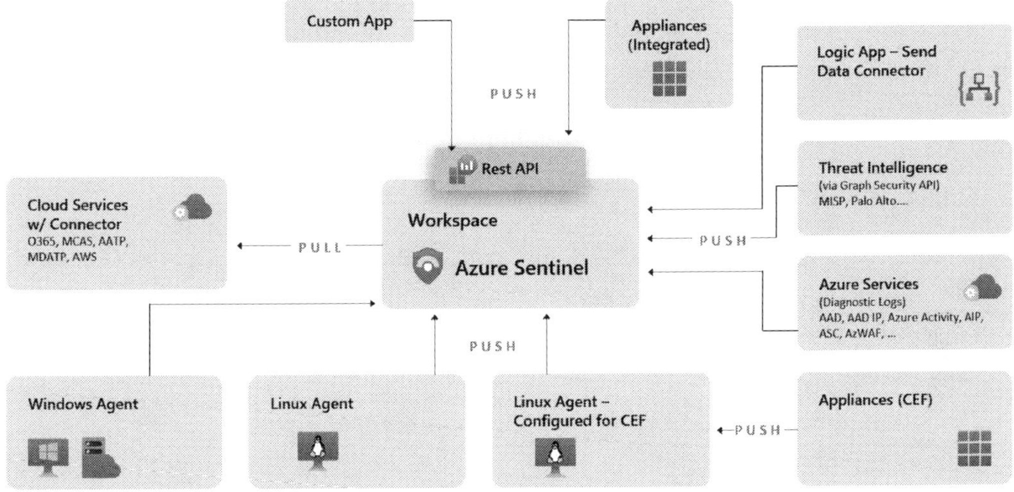

Figure 13.26 – Collecting data in the Sentinel workspace

Here are the different options that we have when it comes to collecting data in our Azure Sentinel workspace:

- We can collect data from Azure and other cloud services such as Office 365. We can even collect data from other cloud providers, such as the AWS platform.
- We can collect data from Windows and Linux operating systems using an agent.
- We can collect data from different applications, including custom ones, using the REST API.
- Some data can be collected in `PUSH` mode, where the sources push the data to Sentinel, while other data can be collected in `PULL` mode, where Sentinel reaches out to collect the data, usually on a schedule.
- Some sources require us to install an agent such as an operating system if others, especially those using the API, are agentless.
- Some data that's collected is `RAW LOGS`, while some are security events from other solutions, such as Security Center or even third-party security solutions.

So, as you can see, there is quite a range of options when it comes to collecting data.

Detecting threats

Having data is not enough – we also need insights from the data, which is why, after we have data in Azure Sentinel, we want to be proactive about analyzing that data to detect threats. To do this, Azure Sentinel provides out-of-the-box, built-in templates. These templates are called **Analytics Rule Templates**. They are designed by the Microsoft team, and they are based on known threats and common attack vectors. We can create **Analytics Rules** to analyze our data based on these built-in templates, but we can also create our own custom rules.

While analytics rules allow us to analyze our data to gain insights, **Workbooks** allow us to visualize and monitor data by creating dashboards. Similar to analytics, Sentinel also has built-in workbook templates that we can use to quickly create standard workbooks. We can also create our own custom workbooks from custom queries that we write using the KQL.

Investigating incidents

When a threat is detected by Sentinel using an Analytics rule, an incident is raised. An incident represents a detected threat and all the relevant evidence for investigating it. Sentinel allows us to group multiple related alerts under an incident to reduce alert fatigue.

Responding to incidents

For the response part of Sentinel, **playbooks** are used. A security playbook is a collection of procedures that can be triggered in response to an incident. Security playbooks in Azure Sentinel are based on Azure Logic Apps, which means that we get all the power, customization, and integration capabilities of Logic Apps.

The good thing is that we do not need to build everything from scratch. There are multiple playbooks that we can start with, all of which can be found in this GitHub repository: `https://github.com/Azure/Azure-Sentinel/tree/master/Playbooks`.

In the next hands-on exercise, you will implement Azure Sentinel to manage the security operations of an Azure subscription.

Hands-on exercise – implementing Azure Sentinel

Here are the tasks that we will complete in this exercise:

- **Task 1**: Create a Log Analytics workspace.
- **Task 2**: Onboard Azure Sentinel.
- **Task 3**: Connect Azure Activity to Sentinel.

- **Task 4**: Create a rule that uses the Azure Activity data connector.
- **Task 5**: Create a playbook.
- **Task 6**: Create a custom alert and configure the playbook as an automated response.
- **Task 7**: Invoke an incident and review the associated actions.

Follow these steps to complete these tasks:

1. Sign in to the Azure portal at `https://portal.azure.com/` using your administrator credentials.
2. In the Azure portal, in the **Search resources, services, and docs** text box at the top of the Azure portal home page, type **Log Analytics workspaces** and press *Enter*.
3. On the **Log Analytics workspaces** blade, click **+ New**.
4. On the **Basics** tab of the **Create Log Analytics workspace** blade, specify the following settings (leave the others with their default values):

   Subscription: Select your Azure subscription.

   Resource group: **azsec-c13-rg**.

   Name: `azsec-workspace-XXXX` (where XXXX is a random number).

   Region: Select a region close to you.
5. Click **Next: Pricing tier** >. On the **Pricing tier** tab of the **Create Log Analytics workspace** blade, accept the default **Pay-as-you-go (Per GB 2018)** pricing tier and click **Review + create**.
6. On the **Review + create** tab of the **Create Log Analytics workspace** blade, click **Create**.
7. In the Azure portal, in the **Search resources, services, and docs** text box at the top of the Azure portal home page, type **Azure Sentinel** and press *Enter*.
8. On the **Azure Sentinel** blade, click **+ New**.
9. On the **Add Azure Sentinel to a workspace** blade, select the Log Analytics workspace you created earlier and click **Add**.

> **Note**
>
> Azure Sentinel has very specific requirements for workspaces. For example, workspaces created by Azure Security Center cannot be used. You can find more information about this here: `https://docs.microsoft.com/en-us/azure/sentinel/quickstart-onboard`.

Next, we will configure Azure Sentinel to use the Azure Activity data connector.

10. In the Azure portal, on the **Azure Sentinel | Overview** blade, in the **Configuration** section, click **Data connectors**.
11. On the **Azure Sentinel | Data connectors** blade, review the list of available connectors, click the entry representing the **Azure Activity** connector (scroll to the right if needed), review its description, and then click **Open connector page**.
12. On the **Azure Activity** blade, click the **Configure Azure Activity logs** link.
13. On the **Azure Activity log** blade, click the entry representing the Azure subscription you are using in this lab and then click **Connect**.
14. Navigate back to the **Azure Sentinel | Data connectors** blade and click **Refresh**.
15. On the **Azure Sentinel | Data connectors** blade, click **Azure Activity**.
16. Verify that the **Azure Activity** pane displays the **Data received** graph (you might have to refresh your browser's page). The following diagram shows the current configuration that we have, based on the steps that we have completed:

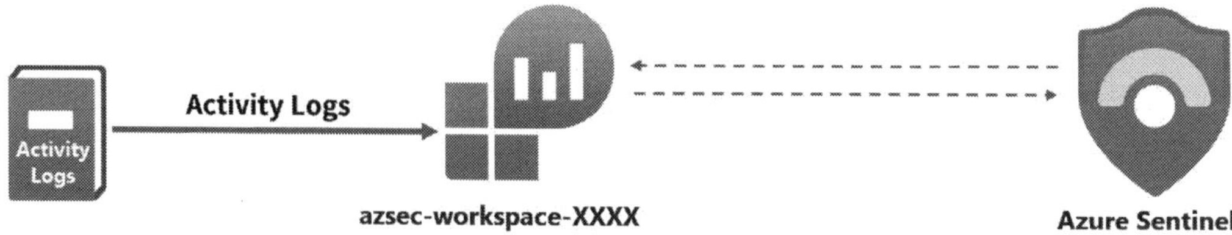

Figure 13.27 – Activity Logs connected to Azure Sentinel

> **Note**
> It may take over 5 minutes before the graph reflects any events included in the Azure Activity logs.

Next, we will create a rule that uses the Azure Activity data connector.

17. On the **Azure Sentinel | Configuration** blade, click **Analytics**.
18. On the **Azure Sentinel | Analytics** blade, click the **Rule templates** tab. Review the types of rules that you can create. Each rule is associated with a specific Data Source.

    In the listing of rule templates, type **Suspicious** into the search bar form and click the **Suspicious number of resource creation or deployment** entry associated with the **Azure Activity** data source. Then, in the pane displaying the rule template properties, click **Create rule** (scroll to the right of the page if needed). This rule has a medium severity.

19. On the **General** tab of the **Analytic rule wizard – Create new rule from template** blade, accept the default settings and click **Next: Set rule logic** >.
20. On the **Set rule logic** tab of the **Analytic rule wizard – Create new rule from template** blade, accept the default settings and click **Next: Incident settings** >.

    On the **Incident settings** tab of the **Analytic rule wizard – Create new rule from template** blade, accept the default settings and click **Next: Automated response** >. This is where you can add a playbook, implemented as a Logic App, to a rule to automate the process of remediating an issue.
21. On the **Automated response** tab of the **Analytic rule wizard – Create new rule from template** blade, accept the default settings and click **Next: Review** >.
22. On the **Review and create** tab of the **Analytic rule wizard – Create new rule from template** blade, click **Create**. You now have an active rule.

    Next, we will create a playbook. A security playbook is a collection of tasks that can be invoked by Azure Sentinel in response to an alert.
23. Download the following template file, which will be used later in this exercise: `https://raw.githubusercontent.com/PacktPublishing/Implementing-Microsoft-Azure-Security-Technologies/main/chapter-13/changeincidentseverity.json`.
24. In the Azure portal, in the **Search resources, services, and docs** text box at the top of the Azure portal home page, type *Deploy a custom template* and press *Enter*.
25. On the **Custom deployment** blade, click the **Build your own template in the editor** option.
26. On the **Edit template** blade, click **Load file**, locate the `changeincidentseverity.json` file that you downloaded in *Step 23*, and click **Open**.
27. On the **Edit template** blade, click **Save**.
28. On the **Custom deployment** blade, ensure that the following settings are configured (leave any others as their default values):

    Subscription: Select your Azure subscription.

    Resource group: **azsec-c13-rg**.

    Location: Select the same location that you have been using in this chapter.

    Playbook Name: **Change-Incident-Severity**.

    Username: Enter your email address.

    Click **Review + create** and then click **Create**.

Wait for the deployment to complete. The following diagram shows the configuration that we have implemented already:

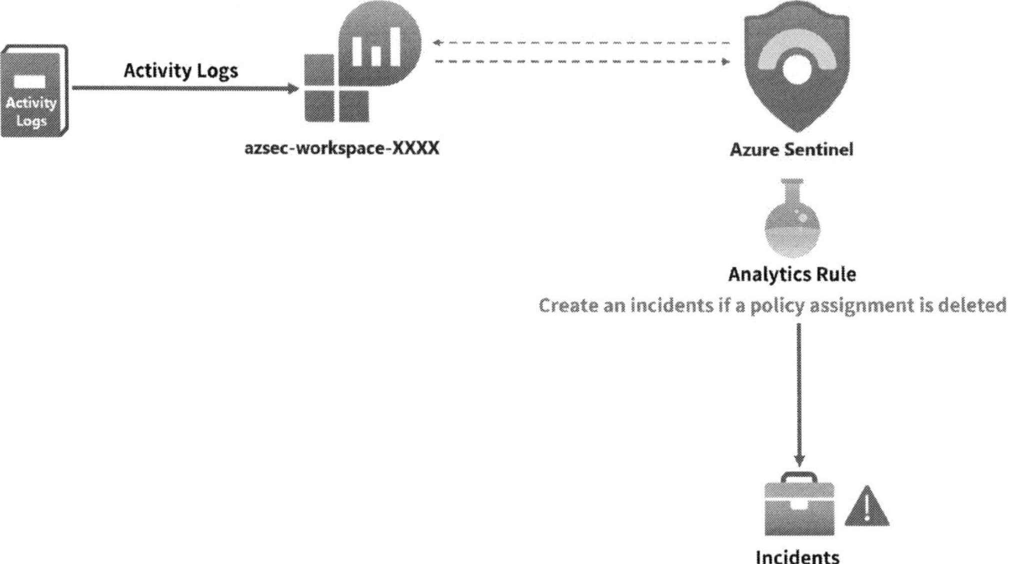

Figure 13.28 – Analytics rule in Sentinel

29. In the Azure portal, in the **Search resources, services, and docs** text box at the top of the Azure portal home page, type *Resource groups* and press *Enter* .
30. On the **Resource groups** blade, from the list of resource groups, click the **azsec-c13-rg** entry.
31. On the **azsec-c13-rg** resource group blade, in the list of resources, click the entry representing the newly created **Change-Incident-Severity** logic app.
32. On the **Change-Incident-Severity** blade, click **Edit**.

> Note
>
> On the **Logic Apps Designer** blade, each of the four connections displays a warning. This means that each needs to be reviewed and configured.

33. On the **Logic Apps Designer** blade, click the first **Connections** step.
34. Click **Add new**, ensure that the entry in the **Tenant** drop-down list contains your Azure AD tenant's name, and click **Sign-in**.
35. When prompted, sign in with your Azure administrator account.

36. Click the second **Connection** step and, from the list of connections, select the second entry, which represents the connection you created in the previous step.
37. Repeat the previous steps for the remaining two **Connection** steps.

> Note
>
> Ensure no warnings are displayed on any of the steps.

38. On the **Logic Apps Designer** blade, click **Save** to save your changes.

    Next, we will create a custom alert and configure a playbook as an automated response.

39. In the Azure portal, navigate back to the **Azure Sentinel | Overview** blade.
40. On the **Azure Sentinel | Overview** blade, in the **Configuration** section, click **Analytics**.
41. On the **Azure Sentinel | Analytics** blade, click **+ Create** and, from the drop-down menu, click **Scheduled query rule**.
42. On the **General** tab of the **Analytic rule wizard – Create new rule** blade, specify the following settings (leave the others with their default values):

    Name: **Response-Playbook**

    Tactics: **Initial Access**

43. Click **Next: Set rule logic** >.
44. On the **Set rule logic** tab of the **Analytic rule wizard – Create new rule** blade, in the **Rule query** text box, paste the following rule query:

```
AzureActivity
   | where ResourceProviderValue == "Microsoft.
Authorization"
   | where OperationNameValue == "Microsoft.Authorization/
policyAssignments/delete"
```

> Note
>
> This rule identifies the removal of the Azure Policy assignment. If you receive a parse error, IntelliSense may have added values to your query. Ensure the query matches; otherwise, paste the query into Notepad and then from Notepad to the rule query.

45. On the **Set rule logic** tab of the **Analytic rule wizard – Create new rule** blade, in the **Query scheduling** section, set **Run query every** to **5 Minutes**.
46. On the **Set rule logic** tab of the **Analytic rule wizard – Create new rule** blade, accept the default values of the remaining settings and click **Next: Incident settings** >.
47. On the **Incident settings** tab of the **Analytic rule wizard – Create new rule** blade, accept the default settings and click **Next: Automated response** >.
48. On the **Automated response** tab of the **Analytic rule wizard – Create new rule** blade, in the **Alert automation** dropdown list, select the checkbox next to the **Change-Incident-Severity** entry and click **Next: Review** >.
49. On the **Review and create** tab of the **Analytic rule wizard – Create new rule** blade, click **Create**.

> Note
>
> You now have a new active rule called **Response-Playbook**. If an event is identified by the rule logic, it will result in a medium severity alert, which will generate a corresponding incident.

Next, we will invoke an incident and review the associated actions.

50. In the Azure portal, navigate to the **Azure policy** blade and click on **Assignments**.

    Check your secure score. By now, it should have been updated.

51. In the **Policy | Assignments** blade, click the **ellipsis** button in front of **the Data residency governance – East US** policy assignment. Click **Delete assignment**, then click **Yes** to confirm the operation.
52. In the Azure portal, in the **Search resources, services, and docs** text box at the top of the Azure portal home page, type *Activity log* and press *Enter* .
53. Navigate to the **Activity log** blade and note that there's a **Delete policy assignment** entry. This may take a minute to appear.
54. In the Azure portal, navigate back to the **Azure Sentinel | Overview** blade.
55. On the **Azure Sentinel | Overview** blade, review the dashboard and verify that it displays an alert corresponding to the deletion of the just-in-time VM access policy.

> Note
>
> It can take up to 5 minutes for alerts to appear in the **Azure Sentinel | Overview** blade.

56. On the **Azure Sentinel | Overview** blade, in the **Threat Management** section, click **Incidents**.
57. Verify that the blade displays an incident with either a medium or high severity level.

> **Note**
>
> It can take up to 5 minutes for the incident to appear in the **Azure Sentinel | Incidents** blade.
>
> Review the **Azure Sentinel | Playbooks** blade. You will find a count of successful and failed runs. You have the option to assign a different severity level and status to an incident.

58. With that, you have created an Azure Sentinel workspace, connected it to Azure Activity logs, created a playbook and custom alerts that are triggered in response to the removal of just-in-time VM access policies, and verified that the configuration is valid.

In the next section, we will clean up the resources that we created for this chapter's exercises.

Cleaning up resources

In the Azure portal, delete the `azuresec-c13-rg` resource group. This will remove all the resources that we created for the exercises in this chapter.

Summary

Congratulations! You have come to the end of this chapter! In this chapter, we covered services that we can use to implement a solid cloud governance strategy in Azure. We also covered services that we can use to monitor the health, performance, and security operations of Azure services.

The skills that you have gained in this chapter have helped you learn how to reduce the risk of vulnerabilities being introduced into your Azure environments, as well as how to effectively identify and resolve threats that are detected.

Questions

As we conclude, here is a list of questions for you to test your knowledge regarding this chapter's material. You will find the answers in the *Assessments* section of the *Appendix*:

1. You need to ensure that when Azure Sentinel identifies a threat, an incident is automatically created. Which component of Sentinel should you implement?

   a. Analytics

   b. Data connectors

   c. Playbooks

   d. Workbooks

2. You need to ensure that when Azure Sentinel identifies a threat, a ticket is logged in a service management platform. Which component of Sentinel should you implement?

   a. Analytics

   b. Data connectors

   c. Playbooks

   d. Workbooks

Further reading

To learn more on the topics covered in this chapter, you can refer to the following links:

- Security Center Tiers: `https://azure.microsoft.com/en-gb/pricing/details/azure-defender/`
- Cloud Security Posture Management: `https://docs.microsoft.com/en-us/azure/security-center/tutorial-security-policy`
- Cloud Security Compliance Management: `https://docs.microsoft.com/en-us/azure/security-center/security-center-compliance-dashboard`
- Security Center Threat Protection: `https://docs.microsoft.com/en-us/azure/security-center/azure-defender`
- Onboard Azure Sentinel: `https://docs.microsoft.com/en-us/azure/sentinel/quickstart-onboard`

- Azure Sentinel Built-In Analytic Templates: `https://docs.microsoft.com/en-us/azure/sentinel/tutorial-detect-threats-built-in`
- Azure Sentinel Custom Analytic Rules: `https://docs.microsoft.com/en-us/azure/sentinel/tutorial-detect-threats-custom`
- Azure Sentinel Automated Threat Response: `https://docs.microsoft.com/en-us/azure/sentinel/tutorial-respond-threats-playbook`

Assessments

In the following pages, we will review all of the practice questions from each of the chapters in this book and provide the correct answers.

Chapter 1 – Introduction to Azure Security

1. **False** – Cloud security is a responsibility that both the Cloud provider (Microsoft) and the Cloud customers (us) share.
2. **a. Infrastructure as a Service (IaaS)**. If we are using an IaaS service such as a virtual machine, we have more security responsibilities to take care of.
3. **True** – The principles of digital security are the same whether our workload sits in a traditional on-premises data center or in a cloud environment such as Microsoft Azure. The way we apply those principles is what differs.
4. **c. Physical security**. The cloud provider is solely responsible for physical security.

Chapter 2 – Understanding Azure AD

1. **False** – Azure AD is Microsoft's cloud-based identity and access management service that supports modern authentication/authorization protocols.
2. **d. Internal user imported from ADFS**. Users cannot be imported from ADFS. It is a federation service. Other answer options are valid.
3. **c. Basic**. The basic edition of Azure AD has been deprecated.
4. **c. Change the membership type of "London-Group" to Assigned. Create two new groups that have dynamic memberships. Add the new groups to "London-Group"**. A dynamic group assignment can be either for devices or users, but not for both. The membership type will need to be modified and two dynamic groups added to it.

Chapter 3 – Azure AD Hybrid Identity

1. **d. Instant authentication**. There is no hybrid authentication method called instant authentication. Other answer options are valid.
2. **d. Pass-through authentication with seamless single sign-on**. With pass through authentication, authentication requests are fulfilled on-premises and it does not have the server management overhead of ADFS.
3. **c. The Synchronization Rules Editor** - The Synchronization Rules Editor can be used to configure complex synchronization rules like preventing users with certain attributes from being synchronized to Azure AD.
4. **False**. Passwords stores in Azure AD are NOT stored with a reversible encryption algorithm.
5. **c and d**. The Global administrator role in Azure AD and the Enterprise Admins group in Active Directory.

Chapter 4 – Azure AD Identity Security

1. **b. Applying policies to "all users" and "all cloud apps"**. This is not a best practice. As a minimum, break-glass accounts should be excluded from policies that have block access control.

Chapter 5 – Azure AD Identity Governance

1. **b. The user's access will be revoked and removed**. The option to "Take recommendation" is based on usage (whether a user has signed in recently within the past month). If the user has not signed in within the past month, the recommendation will be to revoke access.
2. **b. It means that the user can request to be assigned the role by PIM whenever they need it to perform a task**. Eligible assignment type means that the user has to go through a request process in PIM.

Chapter 6 – Implementing Perimeter Security

1. **a. Create a new subnet in the virtual network**. We need to create a subnet called `AzureFirewallSubnet`.
2. **a. Deploy Azure Front Door**. Azure Front Door is one of the services in Azure with WAF integration.

3. **a. A user-defined route**. A user-defined route is used to send traffic to a customer specified route path in Azure.

Chapter 7 – Implementing Network Security

1. **b. No, it will not be allowed** as the rule with the lowest priority will be the first to be matched.

Chapter 8 – Implementing Host Security

1. **a. Win-VM1 only**. Win-VM2 cannot be protected with Azure Disk Encryption as it is an A-Series VM.
2. **b. Add an extension to each VM using an automation script**. The Microsoft anti-malware agent can be deployed to Azure virtual machines using a VM extension.

Chapter 9 – Implementing Container Security

1. **b. The Linux image only**. Azure Defender currently only supports Linux image scans in the registry.
2. **a. Update the settings of AKS1 to enable Azure AD integration**. In order for users to authenticate using their Azure AD credentials, Azure AD integration will need to be enabled.
3. **a. From the Azure portal, modify the pricing tier settings of Security Center**. Azure Defender for Container Registry is an option that can be enabled in the Azure Defender plan of Security Center.

Chapter 10 – Implementing Storage Security

1. **a. Regenerate the storage account keys**. Regenerating the storage account keys will invalidate any token that has been signed with the keys.

Chapter 11 – Implementing Database Security

1. **c. Implement column-level encryption with Always Encrypted**.

Chapter 12 - Implement Secrets, Keys, and Certificate Management with Key Vault

1. **c. In Azure Key Vault, create an access policy**. There are two options to grant access to objects in a Key Vault resource. Using an access policy or applying a role assignment using RBAC

Chapter 13 - Azure Cloud Governance and Security Operations

1. **a. Analytics**. Using an Analytics rule, Sentinel can automatically create an incident when a threat is detected.
2. **c. Playbooks**. Using a playbook, we can trigger a response to an incident including raising a ticket in a service management platform.

Other Books You May Enjoy

If you enjoyed this book, you may be interested in these other books by Packt:

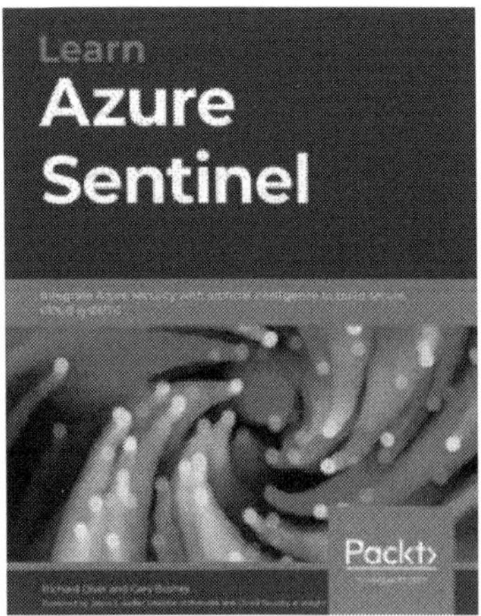

Learn Azure Sentinel

Richard Diver, Gary Bushey

ISBN: 978-1-83898-092-4

- Understand how to design and build a security operations center
- Discover the key components of a cloud security architecture
- Manage and investigate Azure Sentinel incidents
- Use playbooks to automate incident responses
- Understand how to set up Azure Monitor Log Analytics and Azure Sentinel
- Ingest data into Azure Sentinel from the cloud and on-premises devices
- Perform threat hunting in Azure Sentinel

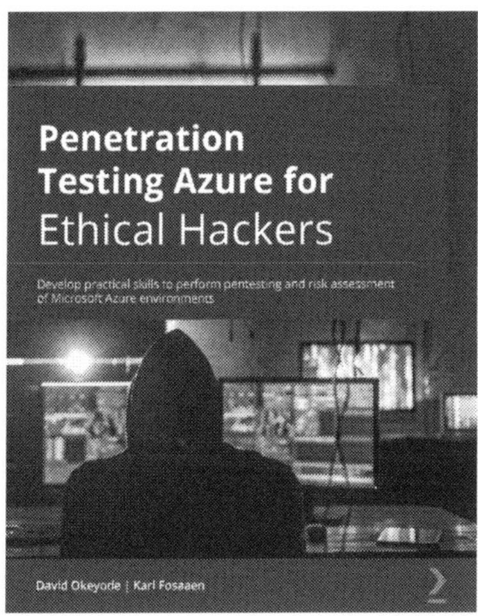

Penetration Testing Azure for Ethical Hackers

David Okeyode, Karl Fosaaen

ISBN: 978-1-83921-293-2

- Identify how administrators misconfigure Azure services, leaving them open to exploitation
- Understand how to detect cloud infrastructure, service, and application misconfigurations
- Explore processes and techniques for exploiting common Azure security issues
- Use on-premises networks to pivot and escalate access within Azure
- Diagnose gaps and weaknesses in Azure security implementations
- Understand how attackers can escalate privileges in Azure AD

Packt is searching for authors like you

If you're interested in becoming an author for Packt, please visit `authors.packtpub.com` and apply today. We have worked with thousands of developers and tech professionals, just like you, to help them share their insight with the global tech community. You can make a general application, apply for a specific hot topic that we are recruiting an author for, or submit your own idea.

Share Your Thoughts

Now you've finished *Microsoft Azure Security Technologies Certification and Beyond*, we'd love to hear your thoughts! Scan the QR code below to go straight to the Amazon review page for this book and share your feedback or leave a review on the site that you purchased it from.

`https://packt.link/r/1-800-56265-9`

Your review is important to us and the tech community and will help us make sure we're delivering excellent quality content.

Index

A

B

C

D

E

F

G

H

I

J

K

L

M

R

S

T

U

V

W

Made in the USA
Columbia, SC
30 April 2022